NON-GAUSSIAN
MERTON-BLACK-SCHOLES
THEORY

**ADVANCED SERIES ON STATISTICAL SCIENCE &
APPLIED PROBABILITY**

Editor: Ole E. Barndorff-Nielsen

Advanced Series on

Statistical Science &

Applied Probability

Vol. 9

NON-GAUSSIAN MERTON-BLACK-SCHOLES THEORY

Svetlana I. Boyarchenko
University of Texas at Austin, USA

Sergei Z. Levendorskiǐ
Rostov State University of Economics, Russia

World Scientific
New Jersey • London • Singapore • Hong Kong

Published by

World Scientific Publishing Co. Pte. Ltd.

P O Box 128, Farrer Road, Singapore 912805

USA office: Suite 1B, 1060 Main Street, River Edge, NJ 07661

UK office: 57 Shelton Street, Covent Garden, London WC2H 9HE

British Library Cataloguing-in-Publication Data
A catalogue record for this book is available from the British Library.

ISBN 981-02-4944-6

Printed in Singapore by Uto-Print

to our parents

Preface

By now, the drawbacks of the Gaussian modelling in Financial Markets and Investment under Uncertainty are well-known. In particular, Gaussian models cannot produce so-called fat tails of observed probability densities, which leads to under-pricing of financial risks. One can hardly make a mistake by saying that the under-pricing of the risk was the main reason for the Long Term Capital Management disaster or recent failures of rating agencies to warn investors of a series of the defaults of the investment-graded firms.

The purpose of the book is to introduce an analytically tractable and computationally effective class of non-Gaussian models for shocks (Regular Lévy Processes of Exponential type (RLPE)), and related analytical methods similar to the initial Merton-Black-Scholes approach, which we call the Merton-Black-Scholes theory (MBS-theory). The potential range of applications of the non-Gaussian variant of the MBS-theory is huge, and the list of results we have obtained so far does not exhaust all the possibilities.

As applications to Financial Mathematics, we solve pricing problems for several types of perpetual American options, barrier options, touch-and-out options and some other options, provide analogues of several approximate methods for pricing of American options in the finite horizon case, and deduce explicit analytical formulas for the locally risk-minimizing hedging. We suggest fast computational procedures for pricing of European options; they can be used for hedging and pricing of American and barrier options as well.

As applications to Corporate Governance, we consider problems of endogenous default, pricing of bonds of corporations, yield spreads of junk bonds, optimal leverage, optimal timing of investment under uncertainty and optimal choice of the installed capital, and the capital accumulation under non-Gaussian uncertainty. In particular, the correct form of the Marshallian law is suggested, and numerical results are produced to show how large the difference between prescriptions of Gaussian models and non-Gaussian ones can be. We also consider discrete time analogues of perpetual American options and the problem of the optimal choice of capital, and outline several possible directions in which the methods of the book can be developed further.

We tried to choose applications interesting for Financial engineers, specialists in Financial Economics, Real Options, and Partial Differential Equations (PDE) (especially in Pseudodifferential Operators (PDO)), and we hope that specialists in Stochastic Processes will benefit from the usage of PDO-technique in non-Gaussian situations. We also tried to make the book accessible for graduate students in relevant areas and mathematicians without prior knowledge of Finance and Economics.

As in the MBS-theory, we reduce problems of pricing of options, other derivative securities and corporate bonds, optimal timing of investment etc. to boundary value problems for the (generalized) Black-Scholes equation. In the MBS-theory, when stochastic processes are assumed Gaussian, the Black-Scholes equation is a differential one, while in the non-Gaussian case, it is a non-local pseudodifferential (or integro-differential) equation, the difference of properties being the same as the one between the infinitesimal generators of Gaussian Feller processes and non-Gaussian ones. We use Dynkin's formula, and basic results from the potential theory for the Markov processes, which is simpler than the modern sophisticated approach based on the theory of semimartingales. We hope that the reader will find refreshing a book on Mathematical Finance and Investment under Uncertainty, which makes no use of the Itô formula at all.

After a boundary value problem for the generalized Black-Scholes equation is developed, we use the PDO-technique to find the solution. The analytical part is unavoidably more difficult than the PDE-part in the Gaussian MBS-theory but we manage to use the most simple part of the theory of PDO by restricting ourselves to the case of RLPE: the generators of RLPE are PDO with constant symbols having fairly favourable properties. This is the reason why we solve the boundary value problems for the generalized Black-Scholes equation in the case when the shocks are modelled as RLPE but not as more general Feller processes. We may say that RLPE is the simplest class of processes with stationary independent increments if the Brownian motion (BM) is not available. The PDO-technique used in the book can be applied for a wide class of strong Feller processes generalizing the class RLPE in the same spirit as Gaussian diffusions generalize BM. To illustrate this point, we construct a class of Lévy-like Feller processes, and show how to price European options under these processes.

Certainly, it was difficult to aim simultaneously at economists and mathematicians from different fields: almost each part of the book may seem trivial to one of the groups of readers whereas the other groups may find this very part illuminating. Probably, it would be better to write a separate book for each group of readers, and in fact, we had already started to write a book on Pseudodifferential Operators with Applications to Finance and Economics, when during a discussion with Ole E. Barndorff-Nielsen it was decided that a book aimed at a wider audience should be written first.

Having in mind a diverse audience, we tried to write a book so that it was simple in the beginning and more technical in further chapters. The main part of the book, especially chapters on Investment under Uncertainty and Endogenous Default, are written (almost) as an economic publication though economists may find some parts of the exposition too terse. We wrote a detailed Introduction in order to explain informally the main ingredients of our approach, so that the reader can read any part of the book she is interested in conjunction with the Introduction and Chapter 3 only; for the reader who is interested in all technical details, in Chapter 2 we list main definitions and results of the theory of Lévy processes, which we use in the book, and provide a scheme for the reduction of the pricing problem to a boundary value problem for the generalized Black-Scholes equation; and we finish the book with rigorous proofs of the most technical statements and with a systematic list of the results of the theory of PDO, which are used in the book.

During our work on various topics covered in the book, we benefited from illuminating comments and suggestions by I. Bouchouev, J. Cvitanić, A. Dixit, D. Duffie, J. M. Harrison, I. Karatzas, G. Peskir, A. N. Shiryaev, and Ken-Iti Sato; long discussions with E. Eberlein and O. E. Barndorff-Nielsen were especially useful.

We are thankful to our son, Dmitriy Boyarchenko, who read the manuscript, finding errors, suggesting improvements in exposition, and correcting our grammar.

0.0.1 *General notation*

We denote the real (complex) n-dimensional space by $\mathbf{R}^n$ ($\mathbf{C}^n$); $\mathbf{R}^n_+$ denotes the cone of real vectors with non-negative components, and $\mathbf{R}^n_{++}$ stands for the cone of vectors with positive components. For $x, y \in \mathbf{R}^n$, $x \geq y$ means $x - y \in \mathbf{R}^n_+$, and $x > y$ means $x - y \in \mathbf{R}^n_{++}$. $\mathbf{Z}_+$ stands for the set of non-negative integers.

Unless otherwise stated, $\langle x, y \rangle$ denotes the standard scalar product of vectors $x, y \in \mathbf{R}^n$, and $|\cdot|$ denotes the standard norm in $\mathbf{R}^n$ (or in $\mathbf{C}^n$, depending on the context). The Lebesgue measure on $\mathbf{R}^n$ is denoted by dx, and the notation for partial derivatives used in the book is $\partial_j = \frac{\partial}{\partial x_j}$, $D_j = -i\partial_j$, where $i = \sqrt{-1}$.

For $x \in \mathbf{R}^n$ and a *multi-index* $\alpha = (\alpha_1, \ldots, \alpha_n) \in (\mathbf{Z}_+)^n$, set $|\alpha| = \alpha_1 + \ldots + \alpha_n$,

$$x^\alpha = x_1^{\alpha_1} \cdots x_n^{\alpha_n}, \ \partial^\alpha = \partial_1^{\alpha_1} \cdots \partial_n^{\alpha_n}, \ D^\alpha = D_1^{\alpha_1} \cdots D_n^{\alpha_n}.$$

If a is a function on $\mathbf{R}^n$, and α is a multi-index, then $a^{(\alpha)} = \partial^\alpha a$; and if a is a function on $\mathbf{R}^n_x \times \mathbf{R}^n_\xi$, then $a^{(\alpha)}_{(\beta)}(x, \xi) = \partial^\alpha_\xi D^\beta_x a(x, \xi)$.

For $U \subset \mathbf{R}^n$, $\mathbf{1}_U$ denotes the indicator function of U: $\mathbf{1}_U(x) = 1$ if $x \in U$ and 0 otherwise.

For real a, b, set $a \wedge b := \min\{a, b\}$, $a \vee b := \max\{a, b\}$, and $a_+ = a \vee 0$, $a_- = a - a_+$.

If B is viewed as a subset of a set U, then $B^c := U \setminus B$ denotes the complement of B in U.

For a subset B of a topological space, $\bar{B}$ denotes the closure of B, and B^o the interior.

$\mathcal{S}(\mathbf{R}^n)$ denotes the space of infinitely smooth functions vanishing at the infinity faster any power of $|x|$, together with all derivatives, and $C_0(\mathbf{R}^n)$ is the space of continuous functions vanishing at the infinity.

If B_1, B_2 are normed spaces, and $A : B_1 \rightarrow B_2$ is a bounded linear operator then $\|A\|_{B_1 \rightarrow B_2}$ denotes the operator norm of A.

For a positive integer m, $C_0^m(\mathbf{R}^n)$ (resp., $C^m(\mathbf{R}^n)$) denotes the space of m times continuously differentiable functions vanishing at infinity (resp., with each derivative up to order m uniformly bounded); the notation $L_p(\mathbf{R}^n)$, $p \in [1, +\infty]$, is also standard.

Depending on the context, $\mathcal{F}$ denotes the Fourier transform or a filtration on the filtered probability space Ω. The Fourier transform of a function f is denoted by $\hat{f}$.

Contents

Chapter 1

Introduction

In this chapter, we list both strong and weak points of the Gaussian MBS-theory, explain why it needs modification, describe informally the technique used in the book and present briefly the main results of the book.

1.1 The Gaussian Merton-Black-Scholes theory

1.1.1 *Strong points*

Ideally, an applied mathematical theory in Finance and Economics should possess the following merits:

(i) the theory has a wide range of applications;

(ii) in many situations of interest, the theory provides analytical answers in the form suitable for the analysis of the dependence of the endogenous variables on the exogenous parameters (comparative statics);

(iii) Mathematics used in the theory is accessible for the wide audience, in simplest situations at least;

(iv) moreover, it is strongly advisable that models of the theory can be explained and applied at the level of "the rule of the thumb";

(v) when the analytical solution is not known, effective numerical methods are available;

(vi) the basic principles of the theory and the answers it provides are in good agreement with the reality.

(If a model satisfies (ii), or better, (ii)–(iv), economists call it "tractable").

The Merton-Black-Scholes theory is so popular among practitioners and researches in Finance and Economics just because it satisfies criteria (i)–(v) almost to perfection. It has been successfully applied to most of the problems in Mathematical Finance, Financial Economics, theory of Real Options and in many other fields of Economics, essentially to any problem where the uncertainty matters, and in model situations the answers have been obtained in the form of fairly simple analytical expressions convenient for further analysis. Mathematics used in the MBS-theory is the theory of Partial Differential Equations (PDE), and in many cases of interest, only the knowledge of Ordinary Differential Equations (ODE) suffices. Being at the undergraduate level, ODE–technique is widely known, and its usage in the MBS-theory can be explained informally, as Dixit and Pindyck (1994) demonstrated. Finally, for PDE and ODE, a host of effective numerical methods is available.

1.1.2   *Drawbacks*

In the case of the MBS-theory, the motto: "Our vices are continuation of our virtues" [1] should be rephrased in the reverse order: "Our virtues are continuation of our vices". Both the simplicity and success of the MBS-theory stem from the possibility of reduction to boundary value problems for PDE or ODE, and this reduction becomes possible due to the choice of the simplest class of stochastic processes – Gaussian processes – to model the evolution of prices in financial and other markets. (The rival modern martingale approach, which tries to remain in the realm of Probability theory and avoid the usage of PDE and PDO whenever it can help it, also capitalizes on the extraordinary nice properties of Gaussian processes). In the basic Black-Scholes model, the price of a stock (or index, like the Standard & Poor 500 Index) follows the Geometric Brownian motion: $S_t = \exp X_t$, where X_t is the Brownian motion. Then the *probability density* $p_{\Delta t}(x)$ of the increments $X_{t+\Delta t} - X_t$ is given by

$$p_{\Delta t}(x) = \frac{1}{\sqrt{2\pi\sigma^2\Delta t}} \exp\left(-\frac{(x - \mu\Delta t)^2}{2\sigma^2\Delta t}\right), \qquad (1.1)$$

where μ and σ^2 are called the *drift* and *volatility*. As Eq. (1.1) shows, the tails of the probability density decay faster than an exponenial function as

---

[1] Translated from Russian

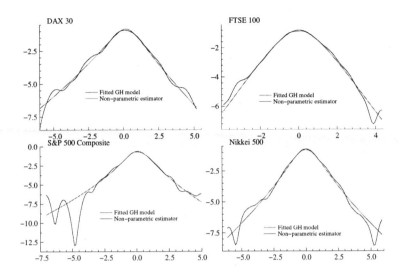

Fig. 1.1 Log-densities for major indices

$x \to \pm\infty$.

1.1.2.1 *Fat tails and anomalous skewness and kurtosis*

Unfortunately for the MBS-theory, empirical studies strongly reject the Gaussian model. Figure 1.1, kindly provided by Ole E. Barndorff-Nielsen and Neil Shephard, shows non-parametric estimators and fitted non-Gaussian Generalized Hyperbolic model for several major world indices. It is clearly seen that the tails of the log-densities decay approximately linearly; if the Gaussian model fitted well, the empirical log-densities would have been parabolas. Thus, BM fits poorly. In particular, the tails decay much slower than the BM model suggests: "the tails are fat". One may also notice that the central part is fitted well by the Lévy stable distribution (we will comment on the last observation in the next subsections).

The deviation from the Gaussianity can also be easily inferred from anomalous values of skewness and kurtosis of empirical $p_{\Delta t}$. Recall that the *mean*, m; *variance*, σ^2; *skewness*, λ_3; and *kurtosis*, $\kappa = \lambda_4$, of a probability distribution $p(x)dx$ are defined as follows:

$$m := \langle x \rangle := \int_{-\infty}^{+\infty} x p(x)dx; \quad \sigma^2 := \langle (x-m)^2 \rangle;$$

$$\lambda_3 := \frac{\langle (x-m)^3 \rangle}{\sigma^3}; \quad \kappa := \frac{\langle (x-m)^4 \rangle}{\sigma^4}.$$

For a Gaussian p, $\lambda_3 = 0$ and $\kappa = 3$, whereas for empirical $p(x)dx = p_{\Delta t}(x)dx$, the skewness $\lambda_{\Delta t,3}$ is non-zero, and the kurtosis $\kappa_{\Delta t}$ can be much larger than 3, especially for small Δt.

There exists another important feature of the financial markets which is not captured by the classical model of financial markets: the *quasi long range dependencies*. Whereas the estimated autocorrelation functions based on log price differences on stocks or currencies are generally closely consistent with an assumption of zero autocorrelation, the empirical autocorrelation functions of the absolute values or the squares of the returns may stay positive for many lags.

Thus, the model for the price process in the MBS-theory is unrealistic but it might not have been a very serious problem if the answers provided by the theory were in good agreement with reality. Much thinner tails of probability density of BM mean that under the Gaussian modelling, the extreme events such as large drops of a price are assigned negligible probabilities. This leads to under-pricing of financial risks with severe consequences like the Long Term Capital Management disaster. Even if one does not require that the theory takes the extreme events into account properly, one should expect that in relatively calm periods of the market activity the theory performs well, but the MBS-theory noticeably fails in this respect, too.

The most celebrated result of the theory, the Black-Scholes option pricing formula, seemed to produce fairly good approximations to observed option prices during the first several years after its invention, but later persistent deviations have been noticed. After October 1987 crash, the systematic errors increased, and in fact, for a long time practitioners have been using the Black-Scholes formula simply as a coding machine to re-express and interpret the observed option prices. To explain how the machine works, we describe briefly the Black-Scholes market and formula.

1.1.2.2   *The Black-Scholes market and formula*

Consider the market of a riskless bond yielding the constant rate of return $r > 0$, and an asset, whose price follows the Geometric Brownian motion: $S_t = \exp X_t$, where X_t is the Brownian motion with the *drift* and *diffusion coefficients* μ and σ^2; in Finance, σ^2 is called the *volatility*.

Consider a contract which gives to its holder the right, but not the obligation, to buy the underlying asset for the specified price (the *strike price*), K, at the specified *expiry date, T*. This contract is called the *European call option*. Denote its price at time $t < T$, conditioned on the current price (*spot price*), S_t, of the underlying asset by $F_{\text{call}}(S_t, t)$. The *Black-Scholes formula* reads

$$F_{\text{call}}(S_t, t) = S_t N(d_1) - K e^{-r\tau} N(d_2), \qquad (1.2)$$

where $\tau = T - t$ is the *time to expiry*,

$$d_1 = \frac{\ln(S_t/K) + (r + \sigma^2/2)\tau}{\sigma\sqrt{\tau}}, \quad d_2 = d_1 - \sigma\sqrt{\tau},$$

and

$$N(x) = \frac{1}{\sqrt{2\pi}} \int_{-\infty}^{x} e^{-t^2/2} dt$$

is the distribution function of the standard normal random variable. It is seen that for fixed r, T, t and S_t, Eq. (1.2) establishes a one-to-one correspondence between the option price and the volatility σ^2. Given the observed option price, we can use Eq. (1.2) to calculate the volatility which leads to this price. The volatility inferred in this way is called the *implied volatility*, as opposed to the *historic volatility* inferred from the observations of the dynamics of the price of the underlying asset. If the Black-Scholes formula were correct, the implied volatility, σ_{imp}, would have been independent of both the time to the expiry, τ, and the strike price, K, and equal to the historic volatility, σ. In reality, this is not the case.

1.1.2.3 *Volatility smile and volatility surface*

Figure 1.2 is a stylised graph of the implied volatility as a function of the moneyness S/K, τ being fixed. The reader can easily understand why it is called the *volatility smile*. If the Black-Scholes formula were correct, the graph would have been a straight line shown on the picture. Smiles of similar shapes were typically observed before October 1987 crash.

Later, the shape of the smile changed; sometimes, the smile is more pronounced, in other cases, it is downward sloping or upward sloping. It can even be a *frown*. In all cases, the shape of the smile depends on the time to the expiry, and becomes more pronounced for small τ. The graph of the implied volatility as a function of (K, τ) is called the *volatility surface*. The reader can find several examples of volatility surfaces in Chapter 4.

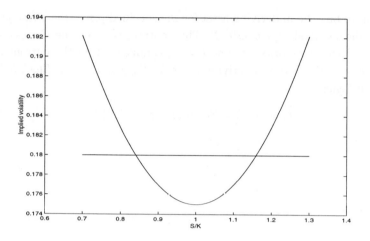

Fig. 1.2   Volatility smile

1.1.3   *Remedies for the MBS-theory*

1.1.3.1   *General remarks*

The volatility smile clearly demonstrates that the Black-Scholes model is not adequate. Some researches try to deduce the smile from various frictions and distortions in the market while keeping the Gaussian assumption intact, whereas others invent heuristic models to describe dynamics of the volatility surface. We believe that it is more reasonable to start with more realistic models for prices of the underlying securities rather than trying to mend the MBS-theory while remaining in the Gaussian world.

1.1.3.2   *Jump-diffusion models and stochastic volatility models*

The MBS-theory becomes more flexible if additional stochastic factors are introduced, as in the *jump-diffusion models*, where X_t is modelled as a mixture of independent BM and Poisson processes, or the diffusion coefficient itself is modelled as a stochastic process (stochastic volatility models). There is a good rationale in introducing jumps since jumps in prices are easy to notice, but jump-diffusion models either do not fit well to data, if the number of jumps is small, or they are not very tractable, if many jumps are allowed. *Stochastic volatility models (SV-models)* have the advantage of using an additional observable, the volatility, which increases the accuracy of the pricing, and they provide a modelling of the important quasi long range dependence typically observed in the financial markets, which is impossible with Lévy processes, but there is a price to pay: the usage of SV-models leads to PDE in the space of higher dimensions, and these PDE have variable coefficients. As a result, analytical formulas are usually not available, though there are some exceptional tractable cases for European options - see the commentary in the end of the chapter; for contracts with early exercise features, analytical formulas are unknown, and one has to resort to numerical methods from the very beginning.

There is another objection to the usage of jump-diffusion models, of a more fundamental nature: the empirical studies of high-frequency data suggest that the processes typically observed in Financial markets do not have a diffusion component at all. Notice that there are important situations, when the pricing under processes with a Gaussian component differs from the one under purely discontinuous processes not only quantitatively but qualitatively as well, the typical example being the pricing of a barrier option or touch-and-out option near the barrier.

1.1.3.3 *Lévy processes*

As a process with the independent stationary increments, the Brownian motion is a member of a wide family of *Lévy processes*. As early as in 1963, Mandelbrot suggested to use the *Lévy stable distributions* to model the returns in the Financial markets. Mandelbrot's idea is corroborated to some extent by the shape of the observed probability densities in the central part, where they are fitted well by Lévy stable distributions, but the tails of the Lévy stable distributions are too fat: polynomially decaying, whereas many empirical studies suggest that the tails decay exponentially; even worse, non-Gaussian stable distributions have infinite second moments, which contradicts the observed convergence of empirical probability distributions to Gaussian ones over longer time scale[2]. Finally, if X is the stable Lévy process under the measure chosen by the market, then the expectation of the stock price $E[e^{X_t}] = \infty$, which makes the model unsuitable for consistent pricing.

From the beginning of the 90th, several families of Lévy processes with probability densities having semi-heavy, that is, exponentially decaying

---

[2] The last observation explains why the Gaussian MBS-theory performs much better for options far from the expiry

tails[3] have been used to model stock returns and price options: *Variance Gamma Processes* (*VGP*), used by D. Madan with co-authors; *Normal Inverse Gaussian Processes* (*NIG*), used by O.E. Barndorff-Nielsen's group; *Hyperbolic Processes* and *Generalized Hyperbolic Processes* (HP and GHP) used by E. Eberlein's group; *Truncated Lévy Processes* (*TLP*, constructed by Koponen [4], used by J.-P. Bouchaud and his group, and extended by Boyarchenko and Levendorskiĭ; and *Normal Tempered Stable Lévy Processes* (*NTS Lévy* processes); we delegate the detailed discussion and references to Chapter 3. As A.N. Shiryaev remarked, the name TLP was misleading, and so we replace it with the name "*KoBoL processes*".

Processes of all the families listed above have been shown to fit better to the dynamics of historic prices, and pricing formulas for European options, based on these processes, also perform better than earlier models. Until recently, almost no effective analytical formulas in more difficult situations than the pricing of the European options and even simpler forwards and futures have been known, though by now, there are many papers and a couple of books devoted to various aspects of the general theory of modelling, pricing and hedging under Lévy processes. The main goal of the book is to partially fill in this gap, while remaining as close as possible to the initial Merton-Black-Scholes framework.

1.2   Regular Lévy Processes of Exponential type

When working with an empirical set of data, one specifies the type of the process, that is, chooses a parameterized family of processes, and then fits the parameters of the process to data. For a general theory like a non-Gaussian analogue of the MBS-theory, too specific information is not needed; in fact, unnecessary specification of the process makes the theory harder to understand. There are two ways to describe the properties of the process, which are sufficient but by no means necessary for our approach to work, and the classes of Lévy processes with exponentially decaying tails used in empirical studies of Financial markets and described in Subsection 1.1.3 enjoy these properties. From the point of view of Probability

---

[3]By semi-heavy or exponentially decaying tails we mean that the probability density behaves, for $x \to \pm\infty$, as $const \cdot |x|^{\rho\pm} \exp(-\sigma_\pm|x|)$, for some $\rho_\pm \in \mathbf{R}$ and $\sigma_\pm > 0$.

[4]Non-infinitely divisible *truncated Lévy distributions* had been constructed earlier by R.N. Mantegna

Theory, the most natural description comes in terms of the Lévy density, which can be visualized as the density of jumps of the process, but from the point of view of PDO-theory and Analysis in general, it is more convenient to work with the characteristic exponent of the Lévy process.

1.2.1 Characteristic function and exponent, Lévy measure and Lévy-Khintchine formula

Let $X = \{X_t\}_{t\geq 0}$ be a one-dimensional Lévy process on a probability triple $(\Omega, \mathcal{F}, \mathbf{P})$, and let $E = E^{\mathbf{P}}$ be the expectation operator under $\mathbf{P}$[5]. The reader can view Ω as a set of all trajectories of the process, and the σ-algebra $\mathcal{F}$ of subsets of Ω as a collection of all possible events. $(\Omega, \mathcal{F}, \mathbf{P})$ is a *filtered space*, in the sense that $\mathcal{F} = \cup_{t\geq 0}\mathcal{F}_t$, $\mathcal{F}_s \subset \mathcal{F}_t$ for $s \leq t$, and all $\mathcal{F}_t$ are σ-subalgebras of $\mathcal{F}$. Each $\mathcal{F}_t$ is generated by X_s, $0 \leq s \leq t$, that is, $\mathcal{F}_t$ is the smallest σ-subalgebra such that for any $0 \leq s \leq t$ and $-\infty \leq a < b \leq +\infty$, the preimage $X_s^{-1}((a,b))$ is in $\mathcal{F}_t$. Thus, $\mathcal{F}_t$ can be viewed as the information revealed at time t (we know the values, which the process X assumed up to the moment t).

Let X be a Lévy process on $\mathbf{R}$. Then the characteristic function of the distribution of the random variable X_t can be represented in the form $E[e^{i\xi X_t}] = \exp(-t\psi(\xi))$. The function ψ is called the *characteristic exponent* of X. By the *Lévy-Khintchine formula*, ψ admits the representation

$$\psi(\xi) = \frac{\sigma^2}{2}\xi^2 - i\gamma\xi + \int_{-\infty}^{+\infty}(1 - e^{i\xi x} + i\xi x \mathbf{1}_{[-1,1]}(x))\Pi(dx), \qquad (1.3)$$

where $\sigma \geq 0$ and $\gamma \in \mathbf{R}$ are constants, and Π is a measure on $\mathbf{R} \setminus \{0\}$ with $\int_{-\infty}^{+\infty}\min\{1, x^2\}\Pi(dx) < +\infty$. The parameters σ^2 and Π, appearing in Eq. (1.3), are called the *Gaussian coefficient*, and the *Lévy measure*, and the triple (σ^2, γ, Π) is called the *generating triplet*. The density of Π is called the *Lévy density*. If $\Pi = 0$, the process is Gaussian, and if $\sigma^2 = 0$, the Lévy process is a pure non-Gaussian process, without the diffusion component.

Example 1.1   Let $\nu \in (0, 2)$, and $\psi(\xi) = c|\xi|^\nu$. This is the characteristic exponent of the *stable Lévy process* of order ν, and the Lévy measure is

$$\Pi(dx) = c\Gamma(-\nu)^{-1}|x|^{-\nu-1}dx.$$

---

[5]For the list of basic definitions of Probability Theory, see Chapter 2

For $\nu = 2$, $\psi(\xi) = |\xi|^{\nu}$ is the characteristic exponent of the standard Brownian motion, and $\Pi = 0$.

1.2.2 *Definition of RLPE in 1D*

Loosely speaking, a Lévy process X is called a *Regular Lévy Process of Exponential type* (RLPE) if its Lévy density has a polynomial singularity at the origin and decays exponentially at the infinity. An almost equivalent loose definition is: the characteristic exponent is holomorphic in a strip $\Im \xi \in (\lambda_-, \lambda_+)$, continuous up to the boundary of the strip, and admits the representation

$$\psi(\xi) = -i\mu\xi + \phi(\xi),$$

where $\phi(\xi)$ stabilizes to a positively homogeneous function at the infinity:

$$\phi(\xi) \sim c|\xi|^{\nu}, \quad \text{as } \xi \to \infty, \quad \text{in the strip } \Im \xi \in (\lambda_-, \lambda_+). \qquad (1.4)$$

"Almost" means that though processes of BM, NIG, HP, GHP, KoBoL and NTS Lévy families satisfy conditions of both definitions, VGP satisfies the conditions of the first definition but not the second one, since the characteristic exponent behaves like $const \cdot \ln |\xi|$, as $\xi \to \infty$. For pricing of contingent claims of European type, the additional property Eq. (1.4) is not essential, but it is needed to obtain effective explicit formulas for the factors in the Wiener-Hopf factorization formula, which we need in the study of perpetual American options and barrier options. This is the reason why we will mainly use the second definition. The adjective "exponential" needs no explanation, and "regular" indicates that from the analytical point of view, RLPE is the most tractable subclass of Lévy processes, if the Brownian motion is not available (notice that BM is an RLPE). We will call ν the *order of the process*, λ_- and λ_+ the *steepness parameters*, and c the *intensity parameter* of the process. The λ_- (resp., λ_+) characterizes the rate of the exponential decay of the right (resp., left) tail of the probability densities, and c plays the part similar to the variance of the Brownian motion.

Example 1.2   For $\nu \in (0, 2]$, $\delta > 0$, $\alpha > |\beta|$, and $\mu \in \mathbf{R}$,

$$\psi(\xi) = -i\mu\xi + \delta[(\alpha^2 - (\beta + i\xi)^2)^{\nu/2} - (\alpha^2 - \beta^2)^{\nu/2}], \qquad (1.5)$$

is the characteristic exponent of an RLPE of order ν, with the steepness parameters $\lambda_- = -\alpha + \beta$ and $\lambda_+ = \alpha + \beta$. With $\nu = 2$, we obtain the characteristic exponent of the Brownian motion, and with $\nu = 1$, the characteristic exponent of the model NIG. When $\nu \neq 1, 2$, Eq. (1.5) gives the characteristic exponent of an NTS Lévy process.

Notice that if $\mu = 0$, then in the limit $\alpha \to 0$, Eq. (1.5) defines the characteristic exponent of the stable Lévy process.

1.2.3 *Infinitesimal generators of RLPE as PDO*

Let f belong to the space $C_0^2(\mathbf{R})$ of twice continuously differentiable functions vanishing at the infinity. Then for each $x \in \mathbf{R}$, there exists a limit

$$(Lf)(x) := \lim_{t \downarrow 0} \frac{E[f(x + X_t)] - f(x)}{t}, \tag{1.6}$$

and Lf is in $C_0(\mathbf{R})$, the space of continuous functions vanishing at the infinity. The map $f \mapsto Lf$ is called the *infinitesimal generator* of the process X. The infinitesimal generator admits an explicit representation in terms of the generating triplet:

$$Lf(x) = \frac{\sigma^2}{2} f''(x) + \gamma f'(x) + \int_{-\infty}^{+\infty} (f(x+y) - f(x) - \mathbf{1}_{\{|y| \leq 1\}}(y) f'(x)) \Pi(dy). \tag{1.7}$$

By using the Lévy-Khintchine formula, we derive from Eq. (1.7) the following formula for the action of L on oscillating exponents: for $\xi \in \mathbf{R}$,

$$Le^{ix\xi} = -\psi(\xi)e^{ix\xi}. \tag{1.8}$$

If f is sufficiently regular, for instance, f belongs to $\mathcal{S}(\mathbf{R})$, the space of functions of the class $C^\infty(\mathbf{R})$, rapidly decreasing at the infinity with all their derivatives, then we can decompose f into the Fourier integral

$$f(x) = (2\pi)^{-1} \int_{-\infty}^{+\infty} e^{ix\xi} \hat{f}(\xi) d\xi, \tag{1.9}$$

where $\hat{f}$ is the *Fourier transform* of f:

$$\hat{f}(\xi) = \int_{-\infty}^{+\infty} e^{-ix\xi} f(x) dx.$$

By applying Eq. (1.8) to Eq. (1.9), we obtain

$$Lf(x) = (2\pi)^{-1} \int_{-\infty}^{+\infty} e^{ix\xi} (-\psi(\xi)) \hat{f}(\xi) d\xi. \tag{1.10}$$

An operator of the form

$$Af(x) = (2\pi)^{-1} \int_{-\infty}^{+\infty} e^{ix\xi} a(x, \xi) \hat{f}(\xi) d\xi \qquad (1.11)$$

is called a *pseudodifferential operator (PDO)* with the *symbol a*. Thus, L is a PDO with the symbol $-\psi$, and therefore one can use the well-developed machinery of the theory of PDO[6].

In the theory of PDO, the properties of symbols of operators are crucial: the more regular symbols are, the more explicit results can be obtained, and here is the list of important properties, which characteristic exponents of RLPE enjoy.

- From the point of view of the theory of PDO, Lévy processes are convenient since the symbols of the infinitesimal generators are independent of the state variable, x (in the PDO-language, these are *constant* symbols), and therefore, many results can be obtained by using the simplest tools of Complex Analysis.
- To study boundary value problems, explicit formulas for the factors in the Wiener-Hopf factorization are needed, and Eq. (1.4) allows one to derive relatively simple formulas. This explains why the regularity condition in the definition of RLPE is important [7].
- The derivatives of characteristic exponents of processes of model classes of RLPE grow at the infinity slower than the characteristic exponents themselves (cf. Eq. (1.5)); this property allows one to generalize the class RLPE and construct a general class of Lévy-like Feller processes with good properties (see Chapter 14).
- Moreover, in empirical studies of Financial markets, the characteristic exponents are characterized by a large parameter, like the parameter α in Eq. (1.5), and so it is possible to develop approximate effective formulas. We will pursue this possibility in Chapters 7-8 and 10-11, where we study first-touch digital options, barrier options, investment under uncertainty and endogenous default.

So, the characteristic exponents of RLPE's enjoy almost all desirable properties but one: the so-called *transmission property*, which ensures that a solution of a regular boundary value problem, e.g., the Dirichlet problem,

---

[6]Of course, all these definitions and constructions generalize to the n-dimensional case

[7]Eq. (1.4) can be relaxed: see Chapter 15

with smooth data is smooth up to the boundary; elliptic differential boundary value problems satisfy the transmission property, the stationary Black-Scholes equation being an example. If RLPE is not a Brownian motion, the transmission property fails, and typically, a solution behaves near the boundary point x_0 like $\sim const|x - x_0|^\kappa$, where $\kappa \in (0,1)$ is determined by properties of the symbol. This observation indicates that near the boundary (e.g., near the barrier, for a barrier option), the difference between the answer the Gaussian model provides and the one, which an RLPE-model gives, can be very large indeed. It also allows us to obtain asymptotic formulas for a solution near the boundary. We use this possibility in Chapters 7-8 and 11, where we study the behaviour of prices of first-touch digitals and barrier options near the barrier, and junk bonds.

1.3 Pricing of contingent claims

The aim of this section is to introduce the basic notions of Mathematical Finance, namely, no-arbitrage assumption, equivalent martingale measure, complete and incomplete markets, redundant securities and replication, and hedging. First, we explain these notions in simple discrete-time models with a discrete space of states, next describe briefly the situation in the continuous time Gaussian Black-Scholes model, and after that discuss the pricing and hedging in the Lévy market.

1.3.1 *Discrete time models with a discrete space of states: No-arbitrage and equivalent martingale measures*

Consider a two-period model of a financial market with n securities. Let M be the number of possible states of the market tomorrow labelled by $\omega_1, \ldots, \omega_m$, and the probability of the state ω_j is anticipated to be p_j. Thus, $\sum_{j=1}^m p_j = 1, 0 < p_j < 1$. The n securities are given by $n \times m$ matrix D, with D_{jk} denoting the number of units of account paid by security j in state k. Thus, j-row D_j is the vector of *payoffs* of security j. Let S_j be the price of security j. Consider a *portfolio* $\theta = (\theta_1, \ldots, \theta_n) \in \mathbf{R}^n$, where θ_j denoted the number of shares of security j. If $\theta_j > 0$ (resp., $\theta_j < 0$), the investor is said to have a *long position* (resp., *short position*) in security j; both types of positions are allowed. Notice that $\theta_j < 0$ means that the investor must deliver θ_j shares of security j tomorrow. The portfolio θ

has the market value $S \cdot \theta = \sum_{j=1}^{n} S_j \theta_j$ and payoff $D^T \theta$. We say that a portfolio θ is an *arbitrage portfolio* if $S \cdot \theta \leq 0$ and $D^T \theta > 0$, or $S \cdot \theta < 0$ and $D^T \theta \geq 0$. If an arbitrage portfolio exists, there exists an opportunity of free lunches. In real financial markets, arbitrage opportunities may appear but they are promptly eliminated due to the activity of *arbitrageurs*, who make money by looking for those opportunities. Thus, the assumption of no free lunches is sufficiently realistic, and as we will see, it can be used as a cornerstone of the pricing theory.

Introduce an augmented payoff matrix

$$\mathcal{R} = \begin{bmatrix} -S \\ D^T \end{bmatrix}.$$

The *no-arbitrage* assumption implies that there does not exist a portfolio θ such that $\mathcal{R}\theta \geq 0$ and one of the components of $\mathcal{R}\theta$ is positive. By the separating hyperplane theorem, there exists a row vector $\tilde{\lambda} \in \mathbf{R}_{++}^{m+1}$ such that

$$\tilde{\lambda}\mathcal{R} = 0. \tag{1.12}$$

Since $\tilde{\lambda}$ is defined up to a positive scalar multiple, we may normalize to one its first component. Define by $\lambda \in \mathbf{R}_{++}^{m}$ the vector of the last m components of $\tilde{\lambda}$. Then the definition of $\mathcal{R}$ and Eq. (1.12) imply together that

$$S = \lambda D^T. \tag{1.13}$$

The λ is called the vector of state prices. Notice that Eq. (1.13) determines prices but makes no use of the probabilities p_j of the states of the market tomorrow. In other words, for the no-arbitrage pricing, only the information about possible future events but not their probabilities matter. Another interpretation is: if investors agree on the set of future events (possible values of securities prices tomorrow) and there are no arbitrage opportunities, they may disagree on probabilities of those events.

Suppose that our two-state model describes an investor who buys a portfolio of securities at time 0, and liquidates (that is, sells) it at time 1, with no dividends paid in between. Then D_{jk} admits a natural interpretation as the price of the security S_j in state k, at time 1. Denote $S_j(0) = S_j$, and define a random variable $S_j(1, \cdot)$ on the probability space $\Omega = \{\omega_k \mid k = 1, \ldots, m\}$ by $S_j(1, \omega_k) = D_{kj}$. Assume further that one of the securities, say, S_n, is the riskless bond (usually denoted by B) yielding a riskless return r; thus, $B(1, \omega) = (1 + r)B(0)$. In this case, the last of the equations in the system Eq. (1.13) is

$$B(0) = \sum_{k=1}^{m} \lambda_k (1 + r) B(0)$$

(notice that S in Eq. (1.13) is a row vector, so the equations are written in a row), and therefore, vector $q = (1 + r)\lambda$ satisfies the following two conditions:

$$0 < q_k < 1, \text{ all } k; \quad \sum_{k=1}^{m} q_k = 1. \qquad (1.14)$$

Thus, $\{q_k\}_{k=1}^{m}$ can be viewed as new probabilities of the states $\{\omega_k\}$; let $\mathbf{Q}$ denote the new probability measure on Ω, and $E^{\mathbf{Q}}$ the expectation operator under $\mathbf{Q}$. Introduce the discounted prices $S_j^*(1, \omega) = (1 + r)^{-1} S_j(1, \omega)$, and rewrite Eq. (1.13) as the expectation under the new measure:

$$S(0) = \sum_{k=1}^{m} q_k S^*(1, \omega_k) := E^{\mathbf{Q}}[S^*(1)]. \qquad (1.15)$$

The measure $\mathbf{Q}$ is called an *equivalent martingale measure (EMM)*. In examples below, the n-th security is the riskless bond, and hence, $D_n = [1 + r \cdots 1 + r]$.

Example 1.3   Let $n = m = 2$. If the first security is risky, then $d_{11} \neq d_{12}$, hence D_1 and D_2 are linearly independent, and the system Eq. (1.13) has the unique solution: the EMM exists and it is unique.

Example 1.4   Let $n = 2, m = 3$. If the first security is risky, then D_1 and D_2 are linearly independent, therefore solutions to Eq. (1.13) exist; since $m > n$, there are infinitely many of them. In this example, there are infinitely many EMM.

Example 1.5   Let $n = 3, m = 3$. Suppose that $D_1 = \alpha D_2$ ($\alpha \in \mathbf{R} \setminus \{0\}$). Then generically, Eq. (1.13) has no solutions. In this example, there is no EMM generically, and hence, it is possible to construct an arbitrage portfolio. We leave the construction as an exercise for the reader.

In the case of a similar $(T + 1)$-period model of n stocks paying no dividends, the probability space Ω consists of all trajectories of the n-dimensional process $S = \{S(t)\}_{0 \leq t \leq T}$. For a fixed t, and a collection of subsets $\{R(s)\}_{0 \leq s \leq t}$,

$R(s) \in \mathbf{R}^n_{++}$, denote by $A = A(R(0), \ldots, R(t))$ the set of trajectories, which pass via $R(s)$ at time $s = 0, \ldots, t$. Let $\mathcal{F}_t$ denote the subalgebra of the algebra of subsets of Ω generated by these sets of trajectories. $\mathcal{F}_t$ can be interpreted as the algebra of events corresponding to the information available at time t. We have $\mathcal{F}_s \subset \mathcal{F}_t$, $s \leq t$; the collection $\mathcal{F} := \{\mathcal{F}_t\}$ is called the *filtration*, and Ω is called a *filtered space*. Suppose that a probability measure $\mathbf{P}$ is introduced on the measure space $(\Omega, \mathcal{F}_T)$. We assume that any set in $\mathcal{F}_0$ has the probability 0 or 1, that is, the prices today are known for sure.

An investor chooses an initial portfolio $\theta(0)$, and adjusts the portfolio $\theta(t)$ at each moment $t = 1, \ldots, T-1$ so that $\theta(t-1) \cdot S(t) = \theta(t) \cdot S(t)$ (we assume that she has no additional source of income). In making her decisions, the investor takes into account the information available at time t; hence, $\theta(t)$ is an $(\Omega, \mathcal{F}_t)$-random variable; one says that a *trading strategy* $\theta = \{\theta(t)\}_{0 \leq t \leq T-1}$ is *adapted* to the filtration $\mathcal{F}$.

An adapted trading strategy θ provides an *arbitrage opportunity* if and only if one of the following two conditions is satisfied:

1) $S(0) \cdot \theta(0) \leq 0$, and $S(T) \cdot \theta(T-1) \geq 0$ always, and
   $E^{\mathbf{P}}[S(T) \cdot \theta(T-1)] > 0$;

2) $S(0) \cdot \theta(0) < 0$ and $E^{\mathbf{P}}[S(T) \cdot \theta(T-1)] \geq 0$.

Assume that one of the securities is a riskless bond with the dynamics $B(t) = (1+r)^t B(0)$. Introduce the discounted price process

$$S^*(t) = (1+r)^{-t} S(t).$$

The same sort of argument as in the two-period model above shows that if there is no arbitrage opportunity, then there exists a new probability measure $\mathbf{Q}$ on the same measure space $(\Omega, \mathcal{F}_T)$ such that for all $0 \leq s < t \leq T$,

$$S^*(s) = E^{\mathbf{Q}}[S^*(t) \mid \mathcal{F}_s], \tag{1.16}$$

where $E^{\mathbf{Q}}[S \mid \mathcal{F}_s]$ denotes the conditional expectation of a random variable S given $\mathcal{F}_s$. Since the set of events has not changed, the measures $\mathbf{P}$ and $\mathbf{Q}$ are equivalent, and Eq. (1.16) means that the discounted price processes are martingales under $\mathbf{Q}$. We see that if there is no arbitrage, there exists an EMM. It can be shown that the converse is also true: if there exists an EMM, there is no arbitrage.

Example 1.6 In the multi-period setting, analogues of Examples 1.3-

1.4 are binomial model and trinomial model, respectively. In the binomial model, at each time step, $S(t+1)/S(t)$ assumes the value u with probability $p \in (0,1)$, and the value d with probability $1 - p$; in the trinomial model, $S(t+1)/S(t)$ can assume three values, with probabilities $p_j \in (0,1)$, $j = 1, 2, 3$.

In the binomial model, the EMM is unique, and in the trinomial, there are infinitely many EMM. Clearly, the latter is more flexible in the sense that it is much easier to adjust its parameters to data.

1.3.2 *Discrete time models with a discrete space of states: Completeness of the market, and pricing of derivative securities*

For simplicity, consider the two-period model. A *contingent claim* is a contract with the specified payoff $F(\omega)$ for each state of the market tomorrow. The market is called *complete* if any contingent claim can be *replicated*, that is, if $\mathrm{Im}D^T = \mathbf{R}^m$. In other words, for any contingent claim, one can construct a portfolio (*replicating portfolio*) θ such that $F^T = D^T\theta$. An equivalent condition is: the payoff vectors of basic securities (that is, the rows of the payoff matrix D) span $\mathbf{R}^m$, which implies $n \geq m$. In other words, the number of spanning securities is not less than the number of future states of the world. In a complete market, Eq. (1.13) has a unique solution, and hence, there exists a unique EMM. It is clear that EMM is unique if and only if $n \geq m$ and $\mathrm{rank}D = m$ is maximal. If the market is complete, and $n > m$, we can choose a basis of $\mathbf{R}^m$ from the rows of the payoff matrix D. Suppose that the first m rows constitute a basis. Then the first m securities can be used to span the others; thus, the latter are *redundant*.

Example 1.7 In the two securities-two states model, suppose that the payoff on the risky security in the first state of the world tomorrow is greater than the one in the second state, that is, $d_{11} > d_{12}$. Introduce a call option on the risky security, with the strike price K, $d_{12} < K < d_{11}$. An option owner will exercise the option and buy 1-security tomorrow if the first of the possible states of the world materializes, and will not otherwise. Hence, the payoff row $F(1)$ is $[d_{11} - K \ 0]$, and the price $F(0)$ of the call option today is

$$F(0) = \lambda \cdot F(1)^T = \lambda_1(d_{11} - K) + \lambda_2 0 = \lambda_1(d_{11} - K), \qquad (1.17)$$

where λ are determined from Eq. (1.13).

In a complete financial market, it is possible to perfectly *hedge*. To hedge means to reduce risk against market fluctuations by making appropriate transactions. In a complete market, the risk can be completely eliminated: let F be a contingent claim, and θ a replicating portfolio. Then the portfolio $(F, -\theta)$ is riskless: in each possible state of the world tomorrow, the payoff of this portfolio is 0, and $-\theta$ is the perfect hedge for F.

If the market is incomplete, then rank$D < n$, and one can introduce additional securities in order to obtain a complete market. The creation of *derivative securities*, e.g., options of different kind, in real financial markets may be seen as attempts to make the market more complete and increase the possibility to hedge.

Example 1.8   Consider the two securities-three states model, which is incomplete, and hence it is impossible to hedge against some financial risks in the market: if $F^T \notin \mathrm{Im} D^T$, then there is no hedge for F. Suppose that $d_{11} \geq d_{12} > d_{13}$, and introduce the call option on the risky security, with the strike price K, $d_{13} < K < d_{12}$. Now we have the market with three securities and the payoff matrix

$$
D = \begin{bmatrix}
d_{11} & d_{12} & d_{13} \\
d_{11} - K & d_{12} - K & 0 \\
1 + r & 1 + r & 1 + r
\end{bmatrix}
$$

The reader can easily verify that rank$D = 3$ if and only if $d_{11} \neq d_{12}$. Thus, in the case $d_{11} = d_{12}$ the option is redundant, and in the case $d_{11} > d_{12}$ its introduction makes the market complete.

Had the real financial markets been complete, there would have been no need in the creation of derivative securities. This observation implies that models of incomplete financial markets are more realistic than models of complete markets.

In multi-period models, the situation is similar, only the role of a portfolio is played by a trading strategy (another name: dynamic portfolio). For details, see references in the review of literature at the end of the chapter.

1.3.3 *Absence of arbitrage, EMM and completeness in the Gaussian Black-Scholes model market*

Under certain regularity assumptions, all of the properties listed above—the no-arbitrage, completeness, in particular, possibility of replication of options and perfect hedge of options, and the existence of the unique EMM—hold in the Black-Scholes market. The no-arbitrage is equivalent to the existence of EMM. Moreover, it is possible to derive the formula for EMM by looking for the perfect hedging strategy. So, the Black-Scholes model has all the nice features one can imagine but it implies that there is no need to introduce options at all: all of them are redundant.

The reader can learn the Gaussian theory of financial markets from many excellent books - see the review of literature.

1.3.4 *Sufficient condition for no-arbitrage in a Lévy market and incompleteness of a Lévy market. The pricing formula for contingent claims of European type and the problem of a choice of EMM*

Consider a continuous-time model market of a riskless bond, the riskless rate of return being $r > 0$, and a risky stock. Suppose that the price of the stock evolves as $S(t) = \exp X(t)$, where X is a Lévy process under the *historic measure*[8] **P**. From general results due to Delbaen and Schachermayer (1994), it follows that the existence of EMM **Q**, which is absolutely continuous with respect to the historic measure, is equivalent to the no-arbitrage condition. So, as in the situations above, we can calculate prices by using an EMM, but if X is neither the Brownian motion nor the Poisson process, an EMM is not unique, and the market is incomplete. Moreover, typically there are infinitely many different EMM; we discuss the restrictions on the choice of EMM from a given class in Chapter 4. The first restriction is quite universal; we will refer to it as the *EMM-condition.*

In the continuous-time models, the discounted price process is given by $S^*(t) = e^{-rt}S(t)$, therefore, by applying Eq. (1.16) with $s = 0$ to the riskless bond and to the stock with the price dynamics $B(t) = B(0)e^{rt}$ and $S(t) = S(0) \exp X(t)$, respectively, and using the definition of the characteristic

---

[8]That is, the measure inferred from the observations of returns

exponent, we obtain, for each $t \geq 0$:

$$B(0) = B(0)e^{-t\psi^{\mathbf{Q}}(0)}, \quad \text{and} \quad S(0) = S(0)e^{-t(r+\psi^{\mathbf{Q}}(-i))},$$

hence $\psi^{\mathbf{Q}}(0) = 0$, which is satisfied for any process without killing, and

$$r + \psi^{\mathbf{Q}}(-i) = 0. \tag{1.18}$$

We call Eq. (1.18) the EMM-condition. There are more subtle restrictions; in particular, parameters c and ν in Eq. (1.4) must be the same for the historic measure and an EMM. Still, for any model class of RLPE, free parameters remain, and one can introduce additional degrees of freedom by considering mixtures of models processes. In Section 4, we produce numerical results to show how one can change the price of an option and the shape of the smile by playing with parameters of KoBoL.

Notice that if X is assumed to be Gaussian both under the historic measure and an EMM, then the condition: c in Eq. (1.4) is fixed means that the variance of the process does not change under the change of the measure, and the EMM-requirement Eq. (1.18) fixes the drift μ of an EMM:

$$r - \mu - \frac{\sigma^2}{2} = 0,$$

that is,

$$\psi^{\mathbf{Q}}(\xi) = \frac{\sigma^2}{2}\xi^2 - i(r - \frac{\sigma^2}{2})\xi. \tag{1.19}$$

The oldest variant of EMM is the *Esscher transform*, which have been used in Actuarial Science for several decades, and in Financial Mathematics, from the beginning of the last decade: in terms of the characteristic exponent, one looks for $\psi^{\mathbf{Q}}$ in the form

$$\psi^{\mathbf{Q}}(\xi) = \psi^{\mathbf{P}}(\xi - i\theta) - \psi^{\mathbf{P}}(-i\theta), \tag{1.20}$$

where θ is real, and the EMM-requirement Eq. (1.18) leads to the equation for θ

$$r + \psi^{\mathbf{P}}(-i(\theta + 1)) - \psi^{\mathbf{P}}(-i\theta) = 0. \tag{1.21}$$

For a chosen EMM $\mathbf{Q}$ and an European option with the expiry date T and the *terminal payoff* $g(X_T)$, the pricing formula Eq. (1.16) can be written as

$$F(S_t, t) = (2\pi)^{-1} \int \exp[ix\xi - \tau(r + \psi^{\mathbf{Q}}(\xi))]\hat{g}(\xi)d\xi, \tag{1.22}$$

where $x = \ln S_t$, $\tau = T - t$, with the integration over an appropriate line $\Im\xi = \sigma$; $\sigma \in (\lambda_-, \lambda_+)$ is determined by the type of the growth of the payoff g at the infinity. To deduce Eq. (1.22), it suffices to decompose g into the Fourier integral

$$\hat{g}(\xi) = \int_{-\infty}^{+\infty} e^{-ix\xi} g(x) dx, \qquad (1.23)$$

substitute into Eq. (1.16) and use the definition of the characteristic exponent.

Example 1.9 Consider a European call option with the strike price K and the expiry date T. The terminal payoff is $g(X(T)) = (e^{X(T)} - K)_+$, and the integral in Eq. (1.23) is well-defined for ξ in the half-plane $\Im\xi < -1$. Take any $\sigma < -1$, and calculate, for $\Im\xi = \sigma$:

$$
\begin{aligned}
\hat{g}(\xi) &= \int_{\ln K}^{+\infty} (e^{(-i\xi+1)x} - Ke^{-i\xi x}) dx \qquad (1.24) \\
&= \frac{Ke^{-i\xi \ln K}}{i\xi - 1} - \frac{Ke^{-i\xi \ln K}}{i\xi} \\
&= \frac{Ke^{-i\xi \ln K}}{(i\xi - 1)i\xi} \\
&= -\frac{Ke^{-i\xi \ln K}}{(\xi + i)\xi}.
\end{aligned}
$$

By substituting into Eq. (1.22), we obtain

$$F(S_t, t) = -\frac{K}{2\pi} \int_{-\infty+i\sigma}^{+\infty+i\sigma} \frac{\exp[ix\xi - \tau(r + \psi^Q(\xi))]}{(\xi + i)\xi} d\xi. \qquad (1.25)$$

The reader may be tempted to decompose the integral in the RHS of Eq. (1.22), as one does in the Gaussian case but she should not do that: it makes any numerical integration procedure to perform worse, since the integrand vanishes at infinity more slowly after the decomposition has been made.

The integral in Eq. (1.22), Eq. (1.25) being an example, can be calculated by using the Fast Fourier Transform (FFT) or its modifications; there are cases when FFT performs poorly, and other methods must be used. In some cases, the probability densities of probability distributions of a process can be calculated explicitly, and then the pricing formula can be written essentially in the same spirit as in the Gaussian case: only instead of the tabulated normal distribution another distribution is used.

When fitting the model to real data, the observed prices of the option are compared with the ones calculated from Eq. (1.22). There are many papers devoted to the derivation of the formula for EMM from the formula for the historic measure by using different heuristic and economic arguments (see a discussion in Chapter 4). We believe that the parameters of EMM should be inferred from data on both the stock and options, and not derived by some formal reasoning.

The perfect hedging in the Lévy market is impossible, and an investor can only try to minimize the risk, after some measure of the risk is chosen.

1.3.5   *On pricing based on the utility maximization*

The reader acquainted with Mathematical Finance has noticed that we never mentioned the utility maximization of an investor. Apart from the desire to make the book as short as possible, there is a more serious reason for this omission. Though the concept of the utility of an economic agent is very important for Economics and can be used to obtain many important *qualitative* conclusions, it is hardly suitable for the realistic *quantitative* analysis. In Economic literature, there is a host of utility functions with very different properties, some criticism of the concept of utility optimization per se,· and the disagreement about time horizon of economic agents, but even if we assume that the class of the utility functions for the investor is known and the investor optimizes her life-time utility as it is usually assumed (because it greatly simplifies the problem, not that it is very realistic), one may notice that the utility is not directly observable, and it is impossible to fit the parameters of the utility function to the data with any reasonable degree of accuracy. The no-arbitrage assumption and parameter fitting for EMM from a chosen class seems to be a much more reasonable procedure, and traders are known to dislike the utility optimization approach as well. On the other hand, one needs utility optimization in models of financial markets with frictions, for instance, for option pricing under transaction costs. The study of such situations goes beyond the scope of this book, anyway.

1.4 The Generalized Black-Scholes equation

1.4.1 *The informal derivation*

Let **Q** be an EMM chosen by the market. Consider a contingent claim whose life span is a deterministic time interval $[0, T]$, with terminal payoff g. Let Δt be small, and $t < T$, $t + \Delta t < T$. We can apply Eq. (1.22) with $t + \Delta t$ instead of T and $f(X(t + \Delta t), t + \Delta t)$ instead of $g(X_T)$:

$$f(x,t) = \int_{-\infty}^{+\infty} \exp[ix\xi - \Delta t(r + \psi^{\mathbf{Q}}(\xi))]\hat{f}(\xi, t + \Delta t)d\xi, \qquad (1.26)$$

where $\hat{f}$ is the Fourier transform of f w.r.t. the first argument. By expanding in the power series in Δt, dividing by Δt and passing to the limit as $\Delta t \to +0$, we obtain

$$\int_{-\infty}^{+\infty} e^{ix\xi}(-(r + \psi^{\mathbf{Q}}(\xi)) + \partial_t)\hat{f}(\xi, t)d\xi = 0. \qquad (1.27)$$

By using the definition of PDO, we can write Eq. (1.27) as

$$\partial_t f(x,t) - (r + \psi^{\mathbf{Q}}(D_x))f(x,t) = 0, \quad t < T. \qquad (1.28)$$

The same result can be obtained in a more transparent form, by writing Eq. (1.26) as

$$f(x,t) = \exp[-\Delta t(r + \psi^{\mathbf{Q}}(D))]f(x, t + \Delta t), \qquad (1.29)$$

and expanding into the power series in Eq. (1.29) rather than in Eq. (1.26).

If we add to Eq. (1.28) the terminal condition

$$f(x,T) = g(x), \quad x \in \mathbf{R}, \qquad (1.30)$$

and specify the type of the behaviour at the infinity (say, the price $f(x,t)$ of the call option is bounded by e^x, due to the evident no-arbitrage argument), we obtain the well-posed problem Eq. (1.28), Eq. (1.30). By solving it, we can recover Eq. (1.22) we started with. Certainly, there is not much sense in this procedure, but for more complicated contingent claims, no explicit pricing formula is known in advance, and so the reduction to an appropriate boundary problem with subsequent solution by analytical methods is reasonable.

Of course, to justify the formal derivation of Eq. (1.28), some regularity conditions must be imposed. We will not discuss them here, because the analytical derivation, which we have outlined, is inferior to the derivation based on Dynkin's formula or potential theory for Lévy processes: the latter can be applied to complex situations, where the life-time of a contingent claim is stochastic, whereas the naive derivation is applicable only in the case of the deterministic life-time.

Eq. (1.28) is the natural generalization of the Black-Scholes equation. To see this, recall that $D_x = -i\partial_x$, and substitute the characteristic exponent Eq. (1.19) into Eq. (1.28):

$$\partial_t f(x,t) - \left(r - (r - \frac{\sigma^2}{2})\partial_x - \frac{\sigma^2}{2}\partial_x^2\right) f(x,t) = 0,$$

or

$$\partial_t f + \frac{\sigma^2}{2}\partial_x^2 f + \left(r - \frac{\sigma^2}{2}\right) \partial_x f - rf = 0. \tag{1.31}$$

This is the Black-Scholes equation. In terms of the variable $S = e^x$, Eq. (1.31) assumes the standard form

$$\partial_t f + \frac{\sigma^2}{2}S^2\partial_S^2 f + rS\partial_S f - rf = 0. \tag{1.32}$$

1.4.2 An outline of the reduction of the pricing of contingent claims to boundary value problems for the generalized Black-Scholes equation: barrier options

For the first illustration, consider the *down-and-out call* option; this is an example of a *barrier option*. Unlike a European option, the life-time of a barrier option is random: should the price of the stock fall below the specified value H (the *barrier*) before the expiry date T, the option expires worthless or the option owner is entitled to some *rebate* $g^r(X_t, t)$. In the Gaussian case, the trajectories of the process are continuous, and hence the rebate must be specified at the barrier only but in the case of a Lévy process with discontinuous trajectories, the rebate must be specified for all values of $X_t = \ln S_t$ below the barrier $h := \ln H$. We conclude that the price of the down-and-out call option is the solution to the following boundary value problem:

$$\partial_t f(x,t) - (r + \psi^Q(D_x))f(x,t) = 0, \quad t < T, \tag{1.33}$$
$$f(x,T) = (e^x - K)_+, \quad x > h; \tag{1.34}$$

$$f(x,t) = g^r(x,t), \quad x \le h, t \le T; \quad (1.35)$$
$$f(x,t) = e^x + O(1), \quad x \to +\infty. \quad (1.36)$$

The last condition is justified as follows: if there is no barrier, we have the call option, for which Eq. (1.36) holds. The influence of the barrier decreases as the distance from it grows, hence the introduction of the barrier can change only by the $O(1)$ term in Eq. (1.36).

So far, the derivation of the problem Eq. (1.33)–Eq. (1.36) was formal. The rigorous derivation is based on one of the fundamental results of the general theory of Markov processes: Dynkin's formula. First, we introduce the early expiration region $B := \{(x,t) \mid x \le h\}$, next, we denote by $\tau(B)$ the hitting time of B by the two-dimensional process $\hat{X}_t = (X_t, t)$ (for the definitions, see Chapter 2), and then we express the price of the option as the sum of two expectations, the first one corresponding to the payoff in the case of the early expiration, and the second one to the case when the price of the underlying stock never crosses the barrier till the expiry date:

$$f(x,0) = E\left[e^{-r\tau(B)}g^r(X(\tau(B))) \mid X(0) = x, \ \tau(B) \le T\right] \quad (1.37)$$
$$+ \ E\left[e^{-rT}(e^{X(T)} - K)_+ \mid X(0) = x, \ \tau(B) > T\right].$$

Let $\hat{L} = \partial_t + L = \partial_t - \psi^Q(D_x)$ be the infinitesimal generator of the two-dimensional process $\hat{X}$. Dynkin's formula reads, for any stopping time τ:

$$f(x,0) = E\left[\int_0^\tau e^{-rs}(r - \hat{L})f(X(s), s)ds \mid X(0) = x\right] \quad (1.38)$$
$$+ \ E\left[e^{-r\tau}f(X(\tau), \tau) \mid X(0) = x\right].$$

Apply Eq. (1.38) with $\tau = \tau(B) \wedge T$, and compare with Eq. (1.37). In view of Eq. (1.34) and Eq. (1.35), we conclude that Eq. (1.33) must hold (this requires justification: see Chapter 2). Thus, the naive way of writing the boundary value problem for the price of an option is correct.

In many cases, for RLPE in particular, the justification is simplified significantly by using the potential theory of Lévy processes.

1.4.3 The case of interest bearing securities

Now suppose that during the life-time prior to expiry date τ (random or non-random), the owner of the security is entitled to a stream of revenues

with the density $g^o(X(t),t)$. The typical examples are bonds of corporations: a typical bond pays some interest during its life-time; when the bond
matures, it pays the principal, and in the (random) event of the default,
the bond expires worthless or some amount is paid. In this case, the price
of the security is the sum of the stochastic integral which expressed the
present value of the stream of revenues, and the expectation of the payoff
$g^e(X(\tau),\tau)$ on the expiration date:

$$
\begin{aligned}
f(x,0) \;=\; & E\left[\int_0^\tau e^{-rs}g^o(X(s),s)ds \mid X(0)=x\right] \qquad (1.39)\\
+\; & E\left[e^{-r\tau}g^e(X(\tau),\tau) \mid X(0)=x\right].
\end{aligned}
$$

If τ is the hitting time of a closed region $B \subset \mathbf{R} \times [0,+\infty)$, then by comparing Eq. (1.39) with Eq. (1.38), we obtain the boundary problem

$$
\begin{aligned}
\partial_t f(x,t) - (r + \psi^{\mathbf{Q}}(D_x))f(x,t) \;&=\; g^o(x,t),\ (x,t)\in B^c; \qquad (1.40)\\
f(x,t) \;&=\; g^e(x,t),\ (x,t)\in B. \qquad (1.41)
\end{aligned}
$$

1.4.4   *The generalized Merton-Black-Scholes theory*

The problem Eq. (1.40)-Eq. (1.41) is the general form of most of the problems which will be considered in this book, be they option pricing problems,
investment problems in Real Options theory (the problem of the capital accumulation is similar but more complicated) or pricing of defaultable bonds.
In each case, we know what the stream of revenues during the life-time is,
and what is the payoff at the expiry. The revenue density appears in the
RHS of the generalized Black-Scholes equation, and the payoff at the expiry
– in the RHS of the boundary condition. This procedure can be applied
formally though the rigorous treatment requires an additional justification.
As in the case of the barrier option below, usually the second expectation
in Eq. (1.39) admits a natural representation as a sum of two (or more)
expectations, and then the boundary condition Eq. (1.41) can be naturally
written as a system of boundary conditions. Usually, the first one comes
from the terminal condition (the payoff at the deterministic moment T),
and the second one represents the early exercise (or expiration) payoff.

Additional complications arise when the owner of the security can choose
the exercise time, that is, the region B (usually subject to some restrictions), the typical example being American options, but in such cases, we
also write down a problem of the form Eq. (1.40)-Eq. (1.41) and solve it

by analytical means. This is what we call the generalized Merton-Black-Scholes theory.

1.4.5 *Optimal stopping problems and the smooth pasting condition*

Consider the *American put option*, with the strike price K and the expiry date T. If exercised, it gives the option owner the payoff $g(x) = K - e^x$. Options of the European type can be exercised only at the expiry date, but the owner of an option of the American type has the right to exercise the option at any time $t \in [0, T]$. In other words, she chooses the optimal *early exercise boundary* $x = h(t)$ so that the option is exercised if and only if at time t, $X_t = \ln S_t$ reaches $h(t)$ or falls below $h(t)$, and in this case, she receives $K - e^x$. Introduce the exercise region $B := \{(x, t) \mid x \le h(t), t \le T\}$. Thus, we have a free boundary value problem, when both the exercise region B and the solution to the problem Eq. (1.40)–Eq. (1.41) must be found so that the solution $f(x, t) = f(B; x, t)$ be maximal. In the Gaussian theory, one usually finds the candidate for the boundary of B by the so-called *smooth pasting condition* (another name: the *smooth fit principle*). In the case of processes with jumps, this principle may fail, and so we solve the problem Eq. (1.40)–Eq. (1.41) for any candidate for the optimal exercise boundary, and choose the right one by using the explicit formula for $f(x, t)$. Since the explicit formula is available only in relatively simple cases, we manage to realize this program for *perpetual American options*, when the time horizon is infinite, and for some approximate discretization procedures for American options with the finite time horizon. Notice, however, that even in the Gaussian case the explicit solution for American options with the finite time horizon is not available.

1.4.6 *The case of a dividend-paying stock*

Suppose that the stock pays dividends at the constant rate $\lambda > 0$. Then the no-arbitrage argument shows that the process $\{e^{-(r+\lambda)t}S_t\}$ must be a martingale under the measure chosen by the market. In this case, we prefer to use the name a *risk-free measure* instead of EMM. The treatment of all the problems remains essentially the same, although in some cases, the results change. In particular, in the no-dividend case, it is non-optimal to exercise the American call option prior to expiry whereas in the case of a dividend-paying stock, there exists the early exercise boundary $S = H^*(t)$ such that the exercise is optimal when the spot price S_t reaches the level $H^*(t)$ or crosses it.

1.5   Analytical methods used in the book

1.5.1   *The Fourier transform, and Complex Analysis*

The Fourier transform is needed to write an analytic expression for the price of contingent claims of European type, in the form of the oscillating integrals; to calculate these integrals explicitly, simplify them or obtain approximate formulas, standard tools from Complex Analysis—the Cauchy theorem and the Residue theorem—are needed. All these tools are used in more complex situations as well.

1.5.2   *The Wiener-Hopf factorization and the Wiener-Hopf equation*

If the price of a claim is independent of time, the examples being perpetual American options and infinitely lived bonds, the generalized Black-Scholes equation becomes the stationary Black-Scholes equation, and we have to solve the boundary-value problems of the type:

$$(r + \psi^{\mathbf{Q}}(D))f(x) \;=\; g^o(x), \quad x > h; \tag{1.42}$$
$$f(x) \;=\; g^r(x), \quad x \leq h. \tag{1.43}$$

By introducing a new unknown $u = f - g^r$, we reduce to the problem

$$(r + \psi^{\mathbf{Q}}(D))u(x) \;=\; G(x), \quad x > h; \tag{1.44}$$
$$u(x) \;=\; 0, \quad x \leq h. \tag{1.45}$$

The problem Eq. (1.44)–Eq. (1.45) is called the *Wiener-Hopf equation*, and it can be solved by the *Wiener-Hopf factorization method*. The following scheme can be realized under fairly weak regularity assumptions on the data and the symbol $a(\xi) := r + \psi^{\mathbf{Q}}(\xi)$; in the case of an RLPE, the latter is sufficiently regular.

Step 1. Factorize $a(\xi)$, that is, represent it in the form

$$a(\xi) = a_+(\xi)a_-(\xi), \quad \xi \in \mathbf{R}, \tag{1.46}$$

where a_+ (resp., a_-) admits the analytic continuation into the half-plane $\Im\xi > 0$ (resp., $\Im\xi < 0$), and does not vanish there. If $a_\pm$ and $1/a_\pm$ are polynomially bounded in the corresponding half-plane, the factors are uniquely defined up to scalar multiples, due to the Liouville theorem, so in some cases, they can be guessed.

The factorization problem can be solved for fairly wide classes of symbols, by using analytical methods, and these constructions admit generalizations for the multidimensional case, when one considers the Wiener-Hopf equation in the half-space $x_n > 0$, and the analytic continuation is made with respect to the dual variable ξ_n.

When $\psi^{\mathbf{Q}}$ is the characteristic exponent of a one-dimensional Lévy process, the Wiener-Hopf factorization has an important probabilistic interpretation in terms of the *supremum* and *infimum* processes $M_t = \sup_{0\leq s\leq t} X_s$ and $N_t = \inf_{0\leq s\leq t} X_s$:

$$r(r + \psi^{\mathbf{Q}}(\xi))^{-1} = \phi_r^+(\xi)\phi_r^-(\xi), \tag{1.47}$$

where

$$\phi_r^+(\xi) = rE\left[\int_0^{+\infty} e^{-rt}e^{i\xi M_t}\,dt\right], \tag{1.48}$$

$$\phi_r^-(\xi) = rE\left[\int_0^{+\infty} e^{-rt}e^{i\xi N_t}\,dt\right]. \tag{1.49}$$

Certainly, Eq. (1.48)–Eq. (1.49) are not explicit, and some additional efforts are to be made to produce analytical formulas.

Step 2. The solution to the problem Eq. (1.44)–Eq. (1.45) in a natural function class exists (for instance, this is the case if the data are smooth and of compact support, and the solution is sought in the class of continuous bounded functions); the solution is unique and given by

$$u = \phi_r^-(D)\mathbf{1}_{(h,+\infty)}\phi_r^+(D)r^{-1}lG, \tag{1.50}$$

where lG is any sufficiently regular continuation of G from $(h,+\infty)$ on $\mathbf{R}$.

Step 3. Write down the RHS in Eq. (1.50) explicitly, by using the definition of PDO, and calculate it by using tools of Complex Analysis.

We would like to make several general comments.

(1) Though the Wiener-Hopf equation is not widely known in Economics and Finance, Steps 1–2 are easy to memorize and apply.

(2) The third step requires the knowledge of some technique of the reader, and in the end the final answer has to be computed numerically by using some integration procedure.

(3) Fortunately, for wide classes of processes and parameters values observed in real financial markets, effective approximate formulas are available, which we demonstrate in the main part of the book.

(4) The very form of Eq. (1.50) allows us to derive an algebraic equation for the optimal exercise price of the American perpetual options for fairly general class of payoffs, and for the investment threshold in Real Option theory; this equation is new even in the Gaussian case.

(5) The same form allows us to formulate the correct form of the Marshallian Law and naturally separate the two factors which influence the capital accumulation. These results are important for Economics, and are new in the Gaussian case as well.

(6) Finally, if the reader is willing to work with non-Gaussian Lévy processes, there is no hope to use differential equations as in the Black-Scholes theory anyway: Steps 1-3 are the simplest general scheme available.

In the case of American options with the finite time horizon, the explicit analytical methods are not available, but after the discretization of time, the Wiener-Hopf method can be applied as well.

1.5.3   *The case of the non-stationary Black-Scholes equation and the constant barrier*

Here the model example is the problem Eq. (1.33)–Eq. (1.36), with the possible inclusion of a non-zero term in the RHS of Eq. (1.33). If the data are independent of t, one can make the Fourier transform w.r.t. t (or the Laplace transform, depending on the taste of the reader) and reduce the problem to the family of problems on the line, which can be solved by the Wiener-Hopf method. By making the inverse transform, we obtain the result. In the case of more general payoffs, we introduce a new unknown satisfying the homogeneous boundary condition, and consider the resulting problem as the Cauchy problem on $(-\infty, T)$ with the data at $t = T$, for the ordinary differential operator of the first order, with the operator-valued coefficient. Once again, the problem can be solved by inverting a family of the Wiener-Hopf problems and two integration procedures.

1.5.4 The case of the non-constant barrier and multi-asset contracts

In this book, we consider only some special cases, when the reduction to one-dimensional problems on the line is possible. In the theory of PDO, there exists a well-developed machinery for handling multi-dimensional problems of this sort, approximate and numerical methods including.

1.5.5 Pseudodifferential operators

In all parts of the book but one, only PDO with constant symbols arise, and the corresponding part of the theory of PDO is, essentially, a part of Complex Analysis. However, in the study of NIG-like Feller processes, whose infinitesimal generators are PDO with non-constant symbols, all the main ingredients of the theory of PDO are needed.

1.6 An overview of the results covered in the book

1.6.1 Elements of the theory of Lévy processes

In Chapter 2, we list necessary definitions and results from the general theory of Lévy processes, and discuss in more detail the reduction of pricing problems to boundary value problems for the generalized Black-Scholes equation. In Chapter 3, RLPE are introduced, their main properties are derived, and model classes of RLPE are compared. The properties of the infinitesimal generators are discussed, and it is explained how one naturally comes to the definition of the class RLPE by using "naive" PDO-considerations. Explicit formulas for the factors in the Wiener-Hopf factorization formula are obtained.

1.6.2 Option pricing

In Chapter 4, we consider contingent claims of European type. We discuss the properties of the generalized Black-Scholes and the dependence of the properties on the choice of EMM. We calculate prices of several types of options, and produce numerical examples to show how the prices and volatility smiles depend on the choices of parameters of the model for the process and EMM. We derive an explicit formula for the locally risk-minimizing hedging ratio, which can be viewed as an analytical realization of M. Schweizer's idea of locally risk minimizing hedging. We show that for RLPE of order less than 2, the hedging ratio is Hölder continuous until expiry, even at the strike, whereas the Gaussian delta-hedge is discontinuous at the strike, at the expiry. This makes non-Gaussian RLPE-hedging much more stable than the Gaussian one. We produce numerical examples and compare the hedging ratio for different processes.

In Chapter 5, we consider perpetual American options. We formulate the optimal stopping problem, and the corresponding free boundary problem. We explicitly solve the problem for a fairly general payoff g, and show that in the case of the put options and similar more general options, the optimal exercise price $H = e^h$ is determined from the equation

$$(\phi_q^-(D)^{-1}g)(h) = 0,$$

where ϕ_q^- is determined from Eq. (1.49) with $q = r + \lambda$, where $\lambda \geq 0$ is the dividend rate. In particular, for the put, the equation reduces to

$$H = K\phi_q^-(-i) = KqE\left[\int_0^{+\infty} e^{-qt+N_t}dt\right],$$

where N_t is the infimum process.

In the case of calls, the exercise is optimal only if $\lambda > 0$ (which is the well-known fact), and then the optimal exercise price is determined by

$$H = K\phi_q^+(-i) = KqE\left[\int_0^{+\infty} e^{-qt+M_t}dt\right],$$

where M_t is the supremum process. For more general call-like options, the optimal exercise price is determined from the equation

$$(\phi_q^+(D)^{-1}g)(h) = 0.$$

By using these explicit formulas, we show that in some cases, the smooth pasting principle fails, and discuss its generalizations.

In Chapter 6, we consider the American options with the finite time horizon. The explicit formulas being non-available even in the Gaussian model, we consider RLPE-analogues of several approximate methods used in the Gaussian case. It is shown that the behaviour of the RLPE- price of the American put near expiry drastically differs from the one in the Gaussian case.

In Chapters 7 and 8, we derive explicit pricing formulas for touch-and-out options and barrier options, respectively. We consider the asymptotics of the price near the barrier, and explain why this is the place, where the Gaussian model differs most from non-Gaussian ones.

In Chapter 9, we consider simplest of the multi-asset contracts, and multi-asset hedging. We show that in the case of highly correlated assets in the portfolio, the difference between the Gaussian (seemingly) riskless portfolio and the RLPE-locally risk-minimizing one can be quite substantial. Notice that the main cause for the Long Term Capital Management disaster was the mispricing of risks, and the hedging model we suggest is not much more difficult to implement than the Gaussian hedging.

1.6.3 *Investment under uncertainty and capital accumulation*

In Chapter 10, we consider a risk-neutral, competitive, and value maximizing firm under demand uncertainty. The firm chooses optimal investment strategies; the investment is irreversible. This is a typical problem of Real Options theory (for the Gaussian variant of the theory, see Dixit and Pindyck (1996)). The problems of irreversible entry (resp., exit) from the market are quite similar to the option pricing problem for perpetual calls (resp., puts), if the possibility of the further expansion is ruled out. In the model of sequential capital accumulation, additional subtle points arise.

About a century ago, Marshall suggested a rule that a firm should *invest as long as the present value of expected marginal revenue is not less than the marginal cost of investment.* However, as Dixit and Pindyck (1996) pointed out, this rule did not take into consideration option-like characteristics of investment opportunities. The methods we introduce allow us to restate the *Marshallian law* as follows. Starting with the original price process, define a new process, called the infimum process for the price of the firm's output: $N_t = \inf_{0 \le s \le t} P_t$. Then the correct investment rule is: *in the formula for the profit function, replace the price process with the infimum process started at the current level of the price and invest as long as the present value of expected marginal revenue is not less than the marginal cost of investment.* This rule is applicable when the price can move in both directions.

We also write down an analytic formula for the expected level of the capital stock in terms of the infimum and supremum processes.

1.6.4 *Endogenous default and pricing of the corporate debt*

In Chapter 11, we extend the structural approach to credit risk modelling for the case of non-Gaussian processes. The central feature of this approach is an attempt to model explicitly the evolution of the assets of the firm. We focus on the choice of optimal capital structure and bankruptcy level by a firm which keeps a constant profile of debt, but we model the evolution of the assets of the firm as a Lévy process. Notice that models of credit risk relying on diffusion process for dynamics of the firms' assets cannot capture the basic features of credit risk observed in practice. In particular, empirical studies show that the credit spreads on corporate bonds are too high to be matched by diffusion approach. Also, under a diffusion process, firms never default by surprise because a sudden drop in the firm's value is impossible. Therefore, if a firm is not currently in financial distress, the probability of its default on very short-term debt is zero. This fact implies that the credit spreads tend to zero as the maturity of debt tends to zero, which contradicts empirical evidence.

We suggest using RLPE for problems of credit risk modelling and endogenous default as more realistic than diffusion processes and almost as tractable analytically as the latter. For a benchmark model, where the debt has infinite maturity, we present analytical solutions for the endogenous variables. In more complicated situations, an asymptotic solution may be possible.

We study the firm near the bankruptcy and suggest two types of approximate formulas for all endogenous variables. The first set of approximate formulas can be used very close to the default level, and the second set of approximate formulas is valid for Lévy processes with large truncation parameters, i.e., for the processes with not very fat tails, and the firm not very close to the bankruptcy level. These approximations do not neglect the effects of non-Gaussianity on one hand, and on the other hand, they allow to perform comparative statics analysis. Using the approximate solutions, we derive the optimal leverage for the firm. We produce several series of numerical examples which show that if the firm's value is not very far from the default level, the difference between the Gaussian and non-Gaussian models can be sizable, and very close to the bankruptcy level – very large indeed.

1.6.5 *Numerical methods*

In the literature on the non-Gaussian option pricing, one sees the statements like: "The Fast Fourier Transform (FFT) can be used". In Chapter 12, we discuss the limitations of FFT and suggest a very fast method for calculation of prices of European options under model classes of RLPE of order $\nu \in (0,1]$, that is, NIG, and KoBoL and NTS Lévy processes of order $\nu \in (0,1)$. We have not studied the new method for HP and GHP different from NIG. For calculation of individual option prices, the method is several hundred times (for options out of the money or deep in the money) faster than FFT. For parameter fitting purposes, it is necessary to calculate the prices of options for many values of the stock price, and here FFT with its ability to calculate the prices at many points at once may have some advantage. However, if one is satisfied with fitting of option prices for a hundred values of the stock prices or so, which is usually the case, then the new method is faster than FFT for processes of order less than one. For options near expiry, it is several times faster; the relative advantage of IAC decreases as the time to the expiry increases, and increases as the order of the process $\nu \downarrow 0$. For KoBoL of order 0.2, say, IAC can be 10-20 times faster than FFT, and by using additional devices, it is possible to enhance IAC further. For NIG, IAC is faster for options near expiry, and slower for options 3-5 days to maturity or more. The IAC-method can be applied for option pricing under Variance Gamma Processes as well, and in this situation, IAC is especially effective.

IAC has the following additional advantage: it allows for a fairly effective error estimates, which is impossible with FFT.

1.6.6 *Extensions*

In Chapter 13, we consider a discrete-time model, corresponding to perpetual American options, that is, Bermudan options. From the analytic point of view, there is not much difference with the corresponding continuous time models, but the model becomes (infinitely) more flexible.

In Chapter 14, we consider the simplest extension to the case of Feller processes: NIG-like Feller processes constructed by Ole E. Barndorff-Nielsen and Levendorskiĭ (2001). This is the first step for developing non-Gaussian analogues of interest rate models.

1.6.7 *Basics of PDO theory*

In the last two chapters, we provide the essentials of the theory of PDO used in the book. This is useful for a reader interested in the systematic exposition of technical tools used throughout the book, though we tried to explain the most essential things in the main body of the book. There is another aim of the chapter: a specialist with the PDE-background tends to regard the Black-Scholes equation as a primitive object of Mathematical Finance, and the exposition in Wilmott *et al.* (1993) is a model example of this approach. The basic theory presented in Chapter 15 allows the reader to calculate prices of contingent claims formally, without mentioning stochastic integrals, thereby providing the background for PDE-approach in non-Gaussian situations.

1.7 Commentary

The systematic exposition of the Gaussian theory of Mathematical Finance, at different levels, can be found in many monographs. Duffie (1996) is a very good book on the level intermediate between Economics and Mathematics; Hull (2000) is, probably, the best professional book on derivatives; Karatzas and Shreve (1997) and Shiryaev (1999) are excellent rigorous mathematical texts (in addition, Shiryaev (1999) discusses various fundamental aspects of non-Gaussian Mathematical Finance and empirical facts). The last two books and Musiela and Rutkowski (1997), which reviews hundreds of papers and results, focus mainly on martingale methods, whereas Wilmott *et al.* (1993, 1995) and Kwok (1998) use the PDE-approach and discuss relevant numerical methods. The monograph Dixit and Pindyck (1996) is an excellent exposition of the Gaussian Real Options theory for Economists, in the PDE-framework (mainly, 1D-case).

Non-Gaussian models (stable Lévy processes) have been introduced to Finance by Mandelbrot (1963); see also Fama (1965) and the collection of papers Mandelbrot (1997). On truncated Lévy distributions and their application to empirical studies of Financial markets, see Mantegna and Stanley (2000) and Bouchaud and Potters (2000). The last book contains theoretical results on non-Gaussian pricing and hedging of European options (under processes of Koponen's family as well), futures and forwards, and heuristic approximate methods for portfolio optimization and some other problems.

For stochastic volatility models see Zhu (2000), Barndorff-Nielsen and Shephard (2001c, 2001c, 2002), review paper Barndorff-Nielsen *et al.* (2001) and the bibliography there. Notice that there is an overlap of classes of SV-nodels and Lévy models; see the discussion in Barndorff-Nielsen and Shephard (2001a, 2001b, 2002) and Barndorff-Nielsen *et al.* (2001). It is remarkable that in op. cit. (see also the bibliography there), the volatility is driven by a Lévy process of Ornstein-Uhlenbeck type, and nevertheless, in some cases explicit pricing formulas for European options have been obtained (which is not typical for SV-models even in the Gaussian case; see however Heston (1993) and Duffie *et al.* (2000)). SV-model based on the hyperbolic motion, was constructed in Eberlein *et al.* (2001). For modelling of the evolution of the volatility surface, see Cont and da Fonséca (2001).

Chapter 2

Lévy processes

In the first three sections of this chapter, we basically follow Bertoin (1996) and Sato (1999) ([B] and [S]). The account is by no means complete, and the chapter is not meant to substitute for any standard text on Lévy processes. We only aim to provide the list of basic definitions and results, which are necessary should the reader want to go into the details of our constructions.

In Section 2.4, we consider the stochastic integral of a Lévy process stopped at the exterior of an open set, and deduce a boundary value problem for the generalized Black-Scholes equation, which the integral solves. This reduction is the cornerstone of the modified MBS-theory, and the main tool in Chapters 4-11 and 14. The reduction is based on the Dynkin formula and the representation of the q-order harmonic measure of a set relative to a point in terms of the q-potential measure. It admits a generalization to the case of a strong Markov process with absolutely continuous q-potential measure.

2.1 Basic notation and definitions

2.1.1 *Random variables*

Let Ω be a set. A collection $\mathcal{F}$ of subsets of Ω is called a *σ-algebra* if the following three conditions are satisfied:

(1) $\Omega \in \mathcal{F}$, $\emptyset \in \mathcal{F}$ ($\emptyset$ is the empty set);
(2) If $A_n \in \mathcal{F}$ for $n = 1, 2, \ldots$, then $\cup_{n=1}^{\infty} A_n$ and $\cap_{n=1}^{\infty} A_n$ are in $\mathcal{F}$;
(3) If $A \in \mathcal{F}$, then $A^c \in \mathcal{F}$.

A pair $(\Omega, \mathcal{F})$ is called a *measurable space*. A map $\mu : \mathcal{F} \to \mathbf{R}_+ = [0, +\infty)$ is called a *σ-additive measure* if

1) $\mu[\emptyset] = 0$, and
2) if $A_n \in \mathcal{F}, n = 1, 2, \ldots$, and $A_i \cap A_j = \emptyset$ for $i \neq j$, then

$$\mu[\cup A_j] = \sum \mu[A_n].$$

The triple $(\Omega, \mathcal{F}, \mu)$ is called a *measure space*. A measure space $(\Omega, \mathcal{F}, \mu)$ and the σ-algebra $\mathcal{F}$ are said to be *μ-complete* if $\mathcal{F}$ contains any $B \subset \Omega$ of outer measure 0: $\inf \mu[\{A \in \mathcal{F}| \ A \supset B\}] = 0$. If $\mathcal{F}$ is not complete, the *completion* of $\mathcal{F}$ is the smallest σ-algebra containing all subsets of Ω of outer measure 0.

The measure μ is called *finite* if $\mu(\Omega) < \infty$, and *σ-finite* if there is a sequence A_n of elements of $\mathcal{F}$ such that $\mu(A_n) < \infty$, and $\cup A_n = \Omega$.

Let $(\Omega, \mathcal{F}, \mathbf{P})$ and $(\Omega', \mathcal{F}', \mathbf{P}')$ be measure spaces. We say that $f : \Omega \to \Omega'$ is a *$(\mathcal{F}/\mathcal{F}')$-measurable function* or measurable function for short if for any $A' \in \mathcal{F}'$, $f^{-1}(A') \in \mathcal{F}$.

Theorem 2.1 *(The Radon-Nikodým Theorem) Let μ and ν be two σ-finite measures on the same measurable space $(\Omega, \mathcal{F})$.*

Then the following two statements are equivalent

(i) for $A \in \mathcal{F}$, $\nu(A) = 0$ implies $\mu(A) = 0$;

(ii) $\mu = f\nu$, for some non-negative measurable function f.

If either of conditions (i)-(ii) holds, then the measure μ is called *absolutely continuous* w.r.t. ν. One writes $f = \frac{d\mu}{d\nu}$ and calls f a version of the Radon-Nikodým density of μ relative to ν. If ν is absolutely continuous w.r.t. μ as well, μ and ν are called *equivalent measures*.

If $\mathbf{P}[\Omega] = 1$, the triple $(\Omega, \mathcal{F}, \mathbf{P})$ is called a *probability space* and $\mathbf{P}$ is called the *probability measure*. Any set $A \in \mathcal{F}$ is called an *event*, and $\mathbf{P}[A]$ is called the *probability* of the event A.

The σ-algebra generated by the open sets in $\mathbf{R}^n$, that is, the smallest σ-algebra that contains all open sets in $\mathbf{R}^n$, is denoted by $\mathcal{B}(\mathbf{R}^n)$ and called the *Borel σ-algebra*. A real-valued function on $\mathbf{R}^n$ is called measurable if it is $(\mathcal{B}(\mathbf{R}^n)/\mathcal{B}(\mathbf{R}))$-measurable. If $\mathbf{P}$ is absolutely continuous w.r.t. the Lebesgue measure dx, then $p = \frac{d\mathbf{P}}{dx}$ is called the *density* of the measure $\mathbf{P}$.

A mapping X from Ω into $\mathbf{R}^n$ is an *$\mathbf{R}^n$-valued random variable* (or random variable on $\mathbf{R}^n$) if it is $(\mathcal{F}/\mathcal{B}(\mathbf{R}))$-measurable. We write $\mathbf{P}[X \in B]$

for $\mathbf{P}[\{\omega \mid X(\omega) \in B\}]$. The map

$$\mathcal{B}(\mathbf{R}^n) \ni B \mapsto \mathbf{P}[X \in B] \in [0, +\infty)$$

defines a probability measure on $\mathcal{B}(\mathbf{R}^n)$, which is denoted by $\mathbf{P}_X(B)$ and called the *distribution* (or *law*) of X. Probability measures on $\mathcal{B}(\mathbf{R}^n)$ are called distributions on $\mathbf{R}^n$.

Let X be a real-valued random variable. If the integral $\int_\Omega X(\omega)\mathbf{P}(d\omega)$ exists, then it is called the *expectation* of X and denoted by $E[X]$. If $U \in \mathcal{F}$, we write

$$E[X; U] := E[X\mathbf{1}_U] := \int_U X(\omega)\mathbf{P}(d\omega).$$

If g is a measurable function and the integral

$$E[g(X)] = \int_{\mathbf{R}^n} g(x)\mathbf{P}_X(dx)$$

exists, then it is called the *expectation* of $g(X)$.

If X is a function on a measure space, and $X(\omega)$ satisfies a property A outside a set of 0 measure, then X is said to satisfy the property A *almost everywhere* (a. e.); if the measure space is a probability space, one says *almost surely* (a. s.) instead of almost everywhere.

Unless otherwise stated, a probability space is fixed, and random variables are defined on it.

Let T be a set, and $\{X_t\}_{t \in T}$ be a family of random variables. Then $\sigma(X_t : t \in T)$ denotes the smallest σ-subalgebra such that all X_t are $\sigma(X_t : t \in T)$-measurable. It is called the σ-algebra generated by $\{X_t\}_{t \in T}$.

Let $(\Omega, \mathcal{F}, \mathbf{P})$ be a probability space. Sub-σ-algebras $\mathcal{F}_1, \mathcal{F}_2, \ldots$ of $\mathcal{F}$ are called independent if, whenever $A_{j_k} \in \mathcal{F}_{j_k}$, and all j_k are distinct,

$$\mathbf{P}[A_{j_1} \cap \cdots \cap A_{j_n}] = \mathbf{P}[A_{j_1}] \cdots \mathbf{P}[A_{j_n}].$$

Let X_j be a $\mathbf{R}^{n_j}$-random variable, $j = 1, \ldots$ The family $\{X_j\}$ is called independent if σ-algebras $\sigma(X_1), \ldots$ are independent.

2.1.2 *Conditional expectation*

Let $\mathcal{F}'$ be a σ-subalgebra of $\mathcal{F}$, and let X be a random variable with $E[\|X\|] < \infty$. Then there exists a random variable Y such that
  (i) Y is $\mathcal{F}'$-measurable;

(ii) $E[\|Y\|] < \infty$;

(iii) for any $U \in \mathcal{F}'$, we have $E[Y;U] = E[X;U]$.

Moreover, if $\tilde{Y}$ is another random variable with these properties then $\tilde{Y} = Y$, a. s., that is, $\mathbf{P}[Y = \tilde{Y}] = 1$ (for the proof of these statements, see, e.g., Rogers and Williams (1994), II.39).

A random variable Y with properties (i)–(iii) is called a version of the conditional expectation $E[X|\mathcal{F}']$ of X given $\mathcal{F}'$, and we write $Y = E[X|\mathcal{F}']$, a. s.

2.1.3   *The Fourier transform and the Laplace transform.* *Characteristic functions*

We use the following definition of the *Fourier transform*, $\hat{f} = \mathcal{F}f$, of a function f:

$$\hat{f}(\xi) = \int_{\mathbf{R}^n} e^{-i\langle \xi, x\rangle} f(x) dx, \tag{2.1}$$

which is standard in the literature on PDO. The corresponding definition of the Fourier transform of a measure μ on $\mathbf{R}^n$ is

$$\hat{\mu}(\xi) = \int_{\mathbf{R}^n} e^{-i\langle \xi, x\rangle} \mu(dx). \tag{2.2}$$

The integral in Eq. (2.1) is well-defined if $f \in L_1(\mathbf{R}^n)$, and the integral in Eq. (2.2) is if the measure μ is finite: $\mu(\mathbf{R}^n) < \infty$. In particular, the Fourier transform is defined for a probability measure. If $\mathbf{P}_Y$ is absolutely continuous w.r.t. the Lebesgue measure, and p is the density of $\mathbf{P}_Y$, then $\hat{\mathbf{P}}_Y(\xi) = \hat{p}(\xi)$.

The definition of the Fourier transform of a measure μ, which is common in the probabilistic literature, coincides with the RHS in Eq. (2.2) modulo sign and is called the *characteristic function*. We denote it by $\check{\mu}$ to distinguish it from the Fourier transform. Thus,

$$\check{\mu}(\xi) = \hat{\mu}(-\xi).$$

The function

$$E[e^{i\langle \xi, Y\rangle}] = \int_{\mathbf{R}^n} e^{i\langle \xi, Y\rangle} \mathbf{P}_Y(dx) \tag{2.3}$$

is called the *characteristic function* of the distribution of a random variable Y, and denoted by $\check{\mathbf{P}}_Y$. We have $\check{\mathbf{P}}_Y(\xi) = \hat{\mathbf{P}}_Y(-\xi)$.

The *inverse Fourier transform* $\mathcal{F}^{-1}$ is defined by

$$f(x) = (2\pi)^{-n} \int_{\mathbf{R}^n} e^{i\langle \xi, x \rangle} \hat{f}(\xi) d\xi. \tag{2.4}$$

$\mathcal{F}$ and $\mathcal{F}^{-1}$ are mutual inverses on the space $\mathcal{S}(\mathbf{R}^n)$ of infinitely differentiable functions vanishing faster than any rational function at the infinity, together with all derivatives, and extend by continuity to bounded mutual inverses on $L_2(\mathbf{R}^n)$. By duality, the action of $\mathcal{F}$ and that of $\mathcal{F}^{-1}$ extend on the space $\mathcal{S}'(\mathbf{R}^n)$ of continuous linear functionals on $\mathcal{S}(\mathbf{R}^n)$; its elements are called distributions or *generalized functions*.

Certainly, one may change the definitions of the Fourier transform and its inverse and share the factor $(2\pi)^{-n}$ between $\mathcal{F}$ and $\mathcal{F}^{-1}$ differently. If we move $(2\pi)^{-n}$ into the RHS of Eq. (2.1), then Eq. (2.4), our definition of the inverse Fourier transform, becomes the definition of the Fourier transform common in the probabilistic literature. This discrepancy in the definition of the Fourier transform in these two fields of Mathematics will haunt us in many places below.

The *convolution* of two distributions μ_1 and μ_2 on $\mathbf{R}^n$ is the distribution $\mu = \mu_1 * \mu_2$ defined by

$$\mu(B) = \int \int_{\mathbf{R}^n \times \mathbf{R}^n} 1_B(x + y) \mu_1(dx) \mu_2(dy). \tag{2.5}$$

The *dual* measure to μ, denoted $\tilde{\mu}$, is defined by $\tilde{\mu}(B) = \mu(-B)$, where $-B = \{x \mid -x \in B\}$.

The next theorem lists several properties of the characteristic functions, or equivalently, the Fourier transform of measures. For the proofs and additional properties, see Section 2 in [S].

Theorem 2.2   *Let μ, μ_1, μ_2 be distributions on $\mathbf{R}^n$.*

(1) For any $\xi \in \mathbf{R}^n$, $\overline{\hat{\mu}(\xi)} = \hat{\mu}(-\xi)$.

(2) The characteristic function of $\tilde{\mu}$ is $\hat{\mu}(\xi)$.

(3) (Bochner's theorem) We have $\hat{\mu}(0) = 1$, $|\hat{\mu}(\xi)| \leq 1$ for any $\xi \in \mathbf{R}^n$, and $\hat{\mu}$ is uniformly continuous and nonnegative-definite in the sense that, for each $n = 1, 2, \ldots$, and $\xi_j, \xi_k \in \mathbf{R}^n$, $\eta_j, \eta_k \in \mathbf{C}^n$,

$$\sum_{j=1}^{n} \sum_{k=1}^{n} \hat{\mu}(\xi_k - \xi_j) \eta_j \bar{\eta}_k \geq 0. \tag{2.6}$$

Conversely, if $\phi : \mathbf{R}^n \to \mathbf{C}$ is continuous at 0, nonnegative-definite, and $\phi(0) = 1$, then $\phi(\xi)$ is the characteristic function of a distribution on $\mathbf{R}^n$.

(4) If $\hat{\mu}_1(\xi) = \hat{\mu}_2(\xi)$ for all $\xi \in \mathbf{R}^n$, then $\mu_1 = \mu_2$.

(5) If $\mu = \mu_1 * \mu_2$, then $\hat{\mu}(\xi) = \hat{\mu}_1(\xi)\hat{\mu}_2(\xi)$.

(6) If X_1 and X_2 are independent random variables *on $\mathbf{R}^n$, then*

$$\hat{P}_{X_1+X_2}(\xi) = \hat{P}_{X_1}(\xi)\hat{P}_{X_2}(\xi).$$

(7) Let X_j be $\mathbf{R}^{n_j}$-random variable, $j = 1, 2, \ldots, m$, and $X = \{X_j\}$. Then $X_1, \ldots, X_m$ are independent if and only if

$$\hat{P}_X(\xi) = \hat{P}_{X_1}(\xi_1) \cdots \hat{P}_{X_m}(\xi_m),$$

for $\xi = (\xi_1, \ldots, \xi_m) \in \mathbf{R}^n$, where $n = n_1 + \cdots + n_m$.

(8) If μ has a finite absolute moment of order $m \in \mathbf{N}$, that is,

$$\int_{\mathbf{R}^n} |x|^m \mu(dx) < \infty,$$

then $\hat{\mu}$ is a function of the class C^m, and for any $\alpha \in (\mathbf{Z}_+)^n$, satisfying $|\alpha| \leq m$, the moment

$$\langle \mu \rangle_\alpha := \int_{\mathbf{R}^n} x^\alpha \mu(dx) \tag{2.7}$$

can be found as

$$\langle \mu \rangle_\alpha = (-1)^{|\alpha|}(D^\alpha \hat{\mu})(0). \tag{2.8}$$

(9) If $\hat{\mu}$ is of the class C^m in the neighbourhood of the origin, where m is a positive even integer, then μ has the finite absolute moment of order m. In particular, if $\hat{\mu} \in C^\infty$, then μ has finite moments of any order, and they can be calculated from Eq. (2.8).

(10) If $\hat{\mu} \in L_1(\mathbf{R}^n)$, then μ is absolutely continuous w.r.t. the Lebesgue measure, and its density, call it g, is given by

$$g(x) = (2\pi)^{-n} \int_{\mathbf{R}^n} e^{i\langle x, \xi \rangle} \hat{\mu}(\xi) d\xi.$$

The *convolution* of two functions f and g, denoted $f * g$, is defined by

$$(f * g)(x) = \int_{\mathbf{R}^n} f(x - y)g(y)dy. \tag{2.9}$$

It is well-defined if, for instance, both f and g belong to $L_1(\mathbf{R}^n)$, and a straightforward calculation shows that

$$\widehat{f * g}(\xi) = \hat{f}(\xi)\hat{g}(\xi). \tag{2.10}$$

If μ_1 and μ_2 are absolutely continuous w.r.t. the Lebesgue measure dx, and their densities $p_1, p_2 \in L_1(\mathbf{R}^n)$, then μ is absolutely continuous as well, and its density p is the convolution of the densities p_1 and p_2.

The *Laplace transform* of a distribution on $[0, +\infty)$ is defined by

$$L_\mu(u) = \int_{[0,+\infty)} e^{-ux}\mu(dx), \quad \forall\, \Re u \geq 0. \tag{2.11}$$

Theorem 2.3   *Let μ_1, μ_2 and μ be distributions on $[0, +\infty)$. Then*

(i) If $L_{\mu_1}(u) = L_{\mu_2}(u)$, for all $u \geq 0$, then $\mu_1 = \mu_2$.
(ii) If $\mu = \mu_1 * \mu_2$, then $L_\mu(u) = L_{\mu_1}(u)L_{\mu_2}(u)$, for all $\Re u \geq 0$.
(iii) If $L_\mu(u)$ admits the analytic continuation into a wider half-plane, and for some $\sigma < 0$,

$$(2\pi i)^{-1} \int_{\sigma-i\infty}^{\sigma+i\infty} |L_\mu(u)|du < +\infty, \tag{2.12}$$

then μ is absolutely continuous w.r.t. the Lebesgue measure on $[0, +\infty)$, and its density is given by

$$g(x) = (2\pi i)^{-1} \int_{\sigma-i\infty}^{\sigma+i\infty} e^{xu} L_\mu(u)du < +\infty. \tag{2.13}$$

2.2   Lévy processes: general definitions

2.2.1   *Lévy processes and infinitely divisible distributions*

A family $X = \{X_t\}_{t\geq 0}$ of random variables on $\mathbf{R}^n$ with parameter $t \in [0, \infty)$ defined on a common probability space $(\Omega, \mathcal{F}, \mathbf{P})$ is called a *stochastic process*. X_t and $X_t(\omega)$ are sometimes denoted by $X(t)$ and $X(t, \omega)$, respectively. For $\omega \in \Omega$, a map $\mathbf{R}_+ \ni t \mapsto X_t(\omega) \in \mathbf{R}^n$ is called the *trajectory* (or *sample path*) of the process X. The index t is usually (and in this book) taken for time.

For $0 \leq t_0 < t_1 < \cdots < t_m$, the map

$$\mathcal{B}((\mathbf{R}^n)^m) \ni \times_{j=1}^m B_j \mapsto \mathbf{P}[X(t_1) \in B_1, \ldots, X(t_m) \in B_m] \in \mathbf{R}_+$$

defines a probability measure on $\mathcal{B}((\mathbf{R}^n)^m)$. The family of all such measures over all choices of m and $0 \le t_0 < t_1 < \cdots < t_m$ is called the *system of finite-dimensional distributions* of X. A stochastic process Y is called a *modification* of a stochastic process X if

$$\mathbf{P}[X_t = Y_t] = 1 \quad \text{for } t \in [0, +\infty).$$

Two stochastic processes X and Y (not necessarily defined on a common probability space) are *identical in law* if the system of finite-dimensional distributions are identical.

Definition 2.1   An $\mathbf{R}^n$-valued process $\{X_t\}_{t \ge 0}$ is called a *Lévy process* (or process with stationary independent increments) if it has the properties

(1) a trajectory of the process is right-continuous on $[0, \infty)$, with left limits at all $t > 0$, a.s.;
(2) for $0 \le t_0 < t_1 < \cdots < t_m$, the random variables $X_{t_0}, X_{t_1} - X_{t_0}, \ldots,$
$X_{t_m} - X_{t_{m-1}}$ are independent;
(3) $X_0 = 0$ a. s.;
(4) the distribution of $X_{t+s} - X_t$ does not depend on s;
(5) it is stochastically continuous, that is, for every $t \ge 0$ and $\epsilon > 0$,

$$\lim_{s \to t} \mathbf{P}[|X_s - X_t| > \epsilon] = 0.$$

A Lévy process on $\mathbf{R}^n$ is called an n-dimensional Lévy process. If the first condition is not required, X is called a *Lévy process in law*.

Denote by μ^m the m-fold convolution of a probability measure with itself:

$$\mu^m = \mu * \cdots * \mu \quad (m \text{ times}).$$

Definition 2.2   A probability measure μ on $\mathbf{R}^n$ is called *infinitely divisible* if, for any positive integer m, there is a probability measure μ_m on $\mathbf{R}^n$ such that $\mu = \mu_m^m$.

The collection of all infinitely divisible distributions is in one-to-one correspondence with the collection of all Lévy processes, when two processes identical in law are regarded as the same.

Theorem 2.4   *([S], Lemmas 7.6 and 7.9, and Theorems 7.10 and 11.5)*
    (i) If μ is infinitely divisible, then there exists a unique continuous function $\phi : \mathbf{R}^n \to \mathbf{C}$ such that $\phi(0) = 0$ and $\exp[\phi(\xi)] = \hat{\mu}(\xi)$; for every $t \ge 0$,

$\mu^t = \mathcal{F}^{-1}\exp[t\phi]$ *is well-defined and infinitely divisible, and there is a Lévy process in law, X, such that $\mathbf{P}_{X_t} = \mu^t$.*

(ii) If $\{X_t\}_{t\geq 0}$ is a Lévy process in law on $\mathbf{R}^n$, then for any $t \geq 0$, $\mathbf{P}_{X_t}$ is infinitely divisible and $\mathbf{P}_{X_t} = \mu^t$, where $\mu = \mathbf{P}_{X_1}$.

(iii) If X and Y are Lévy processes in law on $\mathbf{R}^n$ such that $\mathbf{P}_{X_1} = \mathbf{P}_{Y_1}$, then X and Y are identical in law.

(iv) Let X be a Lévy process in law on $\mathbf{R}^n$. Then it has a modification which is a Lévy process.

2.2.2 The Lévy-Khintchine formula and generating triplet

From the last theorem, it follows that if X is an n-dimensional Lévy process, the characteristic function of the distribution of X_t admits the representation

$$E[e^{i\langle \xi, X_t\rangle}] = e^{-t\psi(\xi)}, \quad \xi \in \mathbf{R}^n, \ t \geq 0. \qquad (2.14)$$

The function ψ is called the *characteristic exponent* of X. It characterizes the law of X in the sense that two Lévy processes with the same characteristic exponent have the same law.

The Lévy-Khintchine formula below describes all possible characteristic exponents, hence all Lévy processes.

Denote $D = \{x \mid |x| \leq 1\}$.

Theorem 2.5 *(i) Let X be a Lévy process on $\mathbf{R}^n$. Then its characteristic exponent admits the representation*

$$\psi(\xi) = \frac{1}{2}\langle A\xi, \xi\rangle - i\langle \gamma, \xi\rangle - \int_{\mathbf{R}^n}(e^{i\langle x,\xi\rangle} - 1 - i\langle x,\xi\rangle \mathbf{1}_D(x))\Pi(dx), \quad (2.15)$$

where A is a symmetric nonnegative-definite $n \times n$ matrix, $\gamma \in \mathbf{R}^n$, and Π is a measure on $\mathbf{R}^n$ satisfying

$$\Pi(\{0\}) = 0, \quad \int_{\mathbf{R}^n}(|x|^2 \wedge 1)\Pi(dx) < \infty. \qquad (2.16)$$

(ii) The representation Eq. (2.15) is unique.

(iii) Conversely, if A is a symmetric nonnegative-definite $n \times n$ matrix, $\gamma \in \mathbf{R}^n$, and Π is a measure on $\mathbf{R}^n$ satisfying Eq. (2.16), then there exists a Lévy process X defined by Eq. (2.14) and Eq. (2.15).

The triple (A, Π, γ) is called the *generating triplet* of X. The A and Π are called the *Gaussian covariance matrix* and *Lévy measure* of X. When $\Pi = 0$, X is Gaussian, and if $A = 0$, X is called purely non-Gaussian.

Notice that, essentially, the term $-i\langle x, \xi \rangle \mathbf{1}_D(x)$ in Eq. (2.15) is needed in order to ensure the convergence of the integral, and hence other functions can be (and are) used instead of $c(x) := \mathbf{1}_D(x)$, for instance, $c(x) = 1/(1 + |x|^2)$; the A and Π are independent of the choice of c. If Π satisfies the condition

$$\Pi(\{0\}) = 0, \quad \int_{\mathbf{R}^n} (|x| \wedge 1)\Pi(dx) < \infty, \tag{2.17}$$

which is stronger than Eq. (2.16), then Eq. (2.15) can be simplified

$$\psi(\xi) = \frac{1}{2}\langle A\xi, \xi \rangle - i\langle \gamma_0, \xi \rangle - \int_{\mathbf{R}^n} (e^{i\langle x, \xi \rangle} - 1)\Pi(dx), \tag{2.18}$$

where

$$\gamma_0 = \gamma - \int_{\mathbf{R}^n} x\mathbf{1}_D(x)\Pi(dx).$$

γ_0 is called the *drift* of X.

If the sample paths of a Lévy process have bounded variation on every compact time interval a. s., we say that the Lévy process has *bounded variation*. A Lévy process has bounded variation if and only if $A = 0$ and Eq. (2.17) holds (see, e.g., [B], p.15).

2.2.3 *Constructions of Lévy processes*

2.2.3.1 *Explicit constructions*

Some important classes of Lévy processes, e.g. Hyperbolic processes, are obtained by constructing a probability distribution and showing that it is infinitely divisible. In Chapter 3, we will construct extended Koponen's family and its analogue on a half-line by taking appropriate Lévy measures and making explicit calculations in Eq. (2.15). Once characteristic exponents of some Lévy processes are constructed, one can extend the list by using the following two general devices. The subordination is the way Variance Gamma Processes, Normal Inverse Gaussian processes and Normal Tempered Stable Lévy processes are constructed, and the linear transformation of Lévy processes can be used as an easy tool of construction of new processes from given ones.

2.2.3.2   *Subordinators and subordinated processes*

([B], Chapter 3; [S], Chapter 6)

A *subordinator* is a Lévy process taking values in $[0, +\infty)$, which implies that its trajectories are increasing. It allows interpreting a subordinator as a *"random time"*. *Subordination* is a transformation of a stochastic process through random time change by a subordinator independent of the original process. The resulting process is called subordinate to the original one. The idea of subordination is due to Bochner (1949); the subordination can be used to transform Markov processes into Markov processes, and Lévy processes into Lévy processes.

Since the non-decreasing paths have bounded variation, the Gaussian covariance of a subordinator is zero, and the Lévy measure satisfies Eq. (2.17). Hence, the characteristic exponent of a subordinator is of the form

$$\psi(\xi) = -i\gamma_0\xi + \int_0^{+\infty} (1 - e^{ix\xi})\Pi(dx). \tag{2.19}$$

The Laplace transform of the law of a subordinator Z can be expressed as

$$E[\exp(-\lambda Z_t)] = \exp(-t\Phi(\lambda)), \tag{2.20}$$

where $\Phi : \mathbf{R}_+ \to \mathbf{R}_+$ is called the *Laplace exponent* of Z. Thus,

$$\Phi(\lambda) = \psi(i\lambda) = \gamma_0\lambda + \int_0^{+\infty} (1 - e^{-\lambda x})\Pi(dx). \tag{2.21}$$

Clearly, $\Phi(\lambda)$ can be analytically extended into the upper half-plane $\Re\lambda > 0$.

Example 2.1   Let $\alpha \in (0, 1)$, and

$$\Phi(\lambda) = \lambda^\alpha = -\Gamma(-\alpha)^{-1} \int_0^{+\infty} (1 - e^{-\lambda x})x^{-1-\alpha}dx. \tag{2.22}$$

Then Z is called a stable subordinator with index α.

Theorem 2.6   *Let Z be a subordinator with the Laplace exponent Φ, let Y be a Lévy process with the characteristic exponent κ, and suppose that Z and Y are independent.*

Define $X_t(\omega) = Y_{Z_t(\omega)}(\omega)$, $t \geq 0$. Then X is a Lévy process with the characteristic exponent $\psi(\xi) = \Phi(\kappa(\xi))$.

For the proof and formulas for the generating triplet of ψ in terms of the drift and Lévy measure of Z and the generating triplet of Y, see [S], Theorem 30.1.

Example 2.2   By applying the stable subordinator with index α to the Brownian motion with zero drift, we obtain the stable process on $\mathbf{R}^n$, of index 2α, with the characteristic exponent of the form $c|\xi|^{2\alpha}$.

2.2.3.3   Linear transformations of Lévy processes

Theorem 2.7   *([S], Proposition 11.10) Let X be a Lévy process on $\mathbf{R}^n$ with generating triplet (A, Π, γ), and let U be $m \times n$ matrix. Then $\{UX_t\}$ is a Lévy process on $\mathbf{R}^n$ with generating triplet (A_U, Π_U, γ_U) given by*

$$A_U = UAU', \quad \Pi_U = \Pi U^{-1},$$

$$\gamma_U = U\gamma + \int_{\mathbf{R}^n} Ux(\mathbf{1}_{D_m}(Ux) - \mathbf{1}_{D_n}(x))\Pi(dx),$$

where ΠU^{-1} is the measure on $\mathbf{R}^m \setminus \{0\}$ defined by $(\Pi U^{-1})(B) = \Pi(\{x \mid Ux \in B\})$, and D_n is the unit ball in $\mathbf{R}^n$.

2.2.4   The Wiener-Hopf factorization

Let $(\Omega, \mathcal{F}, \mathbf{P})$ be a probability space, on which a one-dimensional Lévy process X is defined, and let Ω_0 be a subset of Ω such that for each $\omega \in \Omega_0$, the trajectory $X.(\omega)$ is right-continuous with left limits. Define, on Ω_0, $M_t = \sup_{0 \le s \le t} X_s$ and $N_t = \inf_{0 \le s \le t} X_s$. On $\Omega \setminus \Omega_0$, both M_t and N_t are set to be 0. $M = \{M_t\}$ and $N = \{N_t\}$ are called the *supremum* process and the *infimum* process, respectively.

The Laplace transform (in t) of the distribution of X_t or to be more precise, the function

$$q(q + \psi(\xi))^{-1} = q \int_0^{+\infty} e^{-qt} E[e^{i\xi X_t}] dt,$$

can be factorized by using the Laplace transforms (in t) of the distributions of the supremum and infimum processes. Among many factorization identities, we will use only the simplest one (Rogers and Williams (1994), p.81; [S], Theorems 45.2 and 45.5; for more detailed exposition, see [S], Section 45).

Theorem 2.8 (i) *Let $q > 0$. There exists a unique pair of infinitely divisible distributions p_q^+ and p_q^- having drift 0 supported on $(-\infty, 0]$ and $[0, +\infty)$, respectively, such that their Fourier transforms ϕ_q^+ and ϕ_q^- satisfy*

$$q(q + \psi(\xi))^{-1} = \phi_q^+(\xi)\phi_q^-(\xi), \quad \xi \in \mathbf{R}. \tag{2.23}$$

(ii) *The functions ϕ_q^+ and ϕ_q^- admit the following representations*

$$\phi_q^+(\xi) = q\int_0^{+\infty} e^{-qt}E[e^{i\xi M_t}]dt = q\int_0^{+\infty} e^{-qt}E[e^{i\xi(X_t - N_t)}]dt, \tag{2.24}$$

$$\phi_q^-(\xi) = q\int_0^{+\infty} e^{-qt}E[e^{i\xi N_t}]dt = q\int_0^{+\infty} e^{-qt}E[e^{i\xi(X_t - M_t)}]dt, \tag{2.25}$$

and

$$\phi_q^+(\xi) = \exp\left[\int_0^{+\infty} t^{-1}e^{-qt}dt \int_0^{+\infty} (e^{ix\xi} - 1)\mu^t(dx)\right], \tag{2.26}$$

$$\phi_q^-(\xi) = \exp\left[\int_0^{+\infty} t^{-1}e^{-qt}dt \int_{-\infty}^0 (e^{ix\xi} - 1)\mu^t(dx)\right]. \tag{2.27}$$

Notice that $\phi_q^+(\xi)$ (resp., $\phi_q^-(\xi)$) admits the analytic continuation into the upper half-plane $\Im\xi > 0$ (resp., lower half-plane $\Im\xi < 0$) and does not vanish there. Thus, Eq. (2.23) is a special case of the *Wiener-Hopf factorization* introduced in solving integral equations by Wiener and Hopf (1931), and widely used in the theory of boundary value problems for PDE and PDO.

The formulas Eq. (2.24)–Eq. (2.25) are by no means explicit though very convenient for theoretical considerations, and Eq. (2.26)–Eq. (2.27) are not effective, either. Simple analytical formulas can be obtained for special cases only.

Example 2.3 Let X be a Brownian motion with the drift γ and variance σ^2. Then the characteristic exponent is

$$\psi(\xi) = \frac{\sigma^2}{2}\xi^2 - i\gamma\xi.$$

It is clear that for $q > 0$, the equation $q + \psi(\xi) = 0$ has two roots $-i\beta_-$ and $-i\beta_+$ in the upper and lower half-planes, respectively, and therefore,

$q(q + \psi(\xi))^{-1}$ admits the factorization Eq. (2.23) with

$$\phi_q^+(\xi) = \frac{\beta_+}{\beta_+ - i\xi}, \quad \phi_q^-(\xi) = \frac{-\beta_-}{-\beta_- + i\xi}. \qquad (2.28)$$

Clearly, ϕ_q^- is the Fourier transform of the exponential distribution with parameter $-\beta_-$, and ϕ_q^+ is the Fourier transform of the dual to the exponential distribution with parameter β_+.

Example 2.4 Let X be a *spectrally negative* Lévy process, i.e., a Lévy process having no upward jumps. Then the law of $\{M_t\}$ is exponential (see, e.g., [B]), and therefore, for some $\beta = \beta(q) > 0$,

$$\phi_q^+(\xi) = \beta/(\beta - i\xi). \qquad (2.29)$$

Since $\phi_q^-(\xi)$ has no zeroes in the lower half-plane $\Im\xi < 0$, Eq. (2.23) implies that $-i\beta$ is the root of $q + \psi(\xi)$. After this root is found, which is a simple numerical procedure, we can calculate ϕ_q^+ from Eq. (2.29), and after that ϕ_q^- from Eq. (2.23).

The reader can consider spectrally positive Lévy processes by using the symmetry argument.

In Chapter 5, we will obtain fairly simple analytic expressions for the factors in Eq. (2.23), for Lévy processes of exponential type, and additional representation for regular Lévy processes of exponential type. For model processes, we will also derive approximate formulas with the leading terms of the form Eq. (2.28).

2.3 Lévy processes as Markov processes

2.3.1 *Markov property and Feller property*

Informally, a Markov process models the memoryless evolution of the price bundle $X(t) = (X_1(t), \dots, X_n(t))$ of n stocks in the market, with the future behaviour of the bundle depending on the past only through its current value. The property of spatial homogeneity of Lévy processes yields significant simplification of the theory.

To give a rigorous definition for the past at a given time, it is convenient to introduce the *filtration* $\{\mathcal{F}_t\}_{t \in [0,\infty]}$ in the σ-algebra $\mathcal{F}$, that is, for $t < +\infty$, $\mathcal{F}_t$ is the **P**-completed σ-subalgebra of $\mathcal{F}$ generated by $(X_s, 0 \le s \le t)$, and $\mathcal{F}_\infty$ stands for the **P**-completion of $\mathcal{F}$. Thus, $\mathcal{F}_s \subset \mathcal{F}_t$ if $s < t$. The σ-subalgebra $\mathcal{F}_t$ models the information available at time t.

From the definition of a Lévy process, it follows that for every $s \geq 0$, the process X' defined by $X'_t = X_{t+s} - X_s$ is independent of $\mathcal{F}_s$. Moreover, the finite-dimensional representations of X' are the same as that of X. These two statements taken together are referred to as the *simple Markov property* of Lévy processes. From this property, one deduces that the filtration $\{\mathcal{F}_t\}$ is right-continuous, that is $\mathcal{F}_t = \cap_{s>t}\mathcal{F}_s$, and the *Blumenthal zero-one law* holds: for any $\Lambda \in \mathcal{F}_0$, $\mathbf{P}[\Lambda] = 0$ or 1.

For every $x \in \mathbf{R}^n$, denote by $\mathbf{P}^x$ the law of $X + x$ under $\mathbf{P}$, that is, the law of the Lévy process started at x:

$$\mathbf{P}^x[X_{t_1} \in B_1, \ldots, X_{t_m} \in B_m] = \mathbf{P}[x + X_{t_1} \in B_1, \ldots, x + X_{t_m} \in B_m],$$

for $0 \leq t_1 < \cdots < t_m$ and $B_1, \ldots, B_m \in \mathcal{B}(\mathbf{R}^n)$. Thus, $\mathbf{P}^0 = \mathbf{P}$. Set $E^x[f(X_t)] := E[f(X_t)|X_0 = x]$, and introduce the family of convolution operators on $L_\infty(\mathbf{R}^n)$, indexed by $t \geq 0$:

$$P_t f(x) := E^x[f(X_t)] = \int_{\mathbf{R}^n} f(x + y)\mathbf{P}_{X_t}(dy).$$

We will use this notation in the case of any measurable non-negative f as well; in this case, $P_t f(x) = +\infty$ is possible and admissible.

The family $\{P_t\}_{t \in [0,+\infty)}$ is a *Markov semigroup*, in the sense that $P_0 = I$ (the identity operator), $P_s P_t = P_{t+s}$ for every $t, s \geq 0$, and $0 \leq P_t f \leq 1$ whenever $0 \leq f \leq 1$.

Denote by $C_0(\mathbf{R}^n)$ the space of continuous functions on $\mathbf{R}^n$ vanishing at the infinity. The semigroup $\{P_t\}_{t \in [0,+\infty)}$ of a Lévy process has the *Feller property*, that is, for every $f \in C_0(\mathbf{R}^n)$,

(i) $P_t f \in C_0(\mathbf{R}^n)$, for any $t \geq 0$;

(ii) $\lim_{t \to 0} P_t f = f$ (uniformly).

([S], Theorem 31.5). The same two statements hold if, instead of $C_0(\mathbf{R}^n)$, we use $\mathcal{C}_0(\mathbf{R}^n)$, the subspace of $L_\infty(\mathbf{R}^n)$ consisting of functions vanishing at the infinity ([B], Proposition I.1).

2.3.2 *Stopping times and the strong Markov property*

The simple Markov property can be reinforced by allowing for certain random times, that is, random variables with values in $[0, +\infty]$ instead of the deterministic time t.

A random time T is called a *stopping time* if for every $t \geq 0$, the event $\{T \leq t\}$ belongs to the σ-algebra $\mathcal{F}_t$. Since the filtration is right-continuous, we have that T is a stopping time if and only if $\{T < t\} \in \mathcal{F}_t$ for all $t \geq 0$. For an arbitrary random time T, we denote by $\mathcal{F}_T$ the **P**-completion of the σ-algebra generated by the process X killed at time T, $X \circ k_T$,[1] and the variable $\mathbf{1}_{\{T < +\infty\}} X_T$.

It can be checked that when T is a stopping time, $\mathcal{F}_T$ consists of events Λ such that $\{T \leq t\} \cap \Lambda \in \mathcal{F}_t$ for all $t \geq 0$. (Intuitively, a random variable T is a stopping time if one can decide whether $T \leq t$ or not by making observations of the evolution of X up to the moment t; $\Lambda \in \mathcal{F}_T$ if Λ is an event expressible by observations up to time T).

Theorem 2.9 *(The Strong Markov property). Let T be a stopping ime with $\mathbf{P}[T < +\infty] > 0$. Then conditionally on $\{T < +\infty\}$, the process $\{X_{T+t} - X_T\}_{t \geq 0}$ is independent of $\mathcal{F}_T$ and has the law* **P**.

By definition, a sample path of a Lévy process has left limits at all times, a. s. From the Feller property of the semigroup, one deduces a much stronger property called *quasi-left-continuity*.

Theorem 2.10 *Let $\{T_n\}_{n \in \mathbf{N}}$ be an increasing sequence of stopping times with $\lim_{n \to \infty} T_n = T$ a.s. Then $\lim_{n \to \infty} X_{T_n} = X_T$ a.s. on $\{T < \infty\}$. In particular, if $T_n < T$ a.s., then X is continuous at time T a.s. on $\{T < \infty\}$.*

Two important classes of examples of stopping times are provided by the first entrance time into a set $B \subset \mathbf{R}^n$, $T_B := \inf\{t \geq 0 \mid X_t \in B\}$, and the first hitting time of B, $T'_B := \inf\{t > 0 \mid X_t \in B\}$.

Lemma 2.1 *([B], p.22)*
a) Let B be open or closed. Then
    (i) both T_B and T'_B are stopping times;
    (ii) $X_{T_B} \in \bar{B}$ a.s. on $\{T_B < \infty\}$, and $X_{T'_B} \in \bar{B}$ a.s. on $\{T'_B < \infty\}$;
b) $T_B = T'_B$ $\mathbf{P}^x$-a.s. for every $x \in B^c \cup B^\circ$; in particular, $\mathbf{P}^x[T_B = T'_B] = 1$ for every x, if B is open.

Note that if B is closed, the last equality may fail for some x on the boundary of B.

---

[1] k_t denotes the *killing operator*: $k_t \omega(s) = \omega(s)$ if $s < t$, and ∂ otherwise, where ∂ denotes the cemetery point of the extended probability space $\Omega \cup \partial$ (for details, see [B], Section 0)

2.3.3 Resolvent operator and infinitesimal generator

Let $q > 0$. The *resolvent operator*, or *q-potential operator U^q*, is defined for every measurable non-negative function f by

$$U^q f(x) = \int_0^\infty e^{-qt} P_t f(x) dt = E^x \left[\int_0^\infty e^{-qt} f(X_t) dt \right].$$

The probabilistic interpretation is as follows: if $\tau = \tau(q)$ is the random time having an exponential law with parameter $q > 0$, and τ is independent of X, then $E[f(x + X_\tau)] = qU^q f(x)$, for all x.

The family of finite measures $(U^q(x, dy), \ x \in \mathbf{R}^n)$ associated to the resolvent operator by

$$U^q f(x) = \int_{\mathbf{R}^n} f(y) U^q(x, dy)$$

is called the *resolvent kernel*, or *q-potential kernel*. Clearly, for $B \in \mathcal{B}(\mathbf{R}^n)$, $U^q(x, B) = V^q(B - x)$, where $V^q(B)$, the *q-potential measure*, is given by

$$V^q(B) = E \left[\int_0^\infty e^{-qt} 1_B(X_t) dt \right] = (U^q 1_B)(0).$$

Hence, U^q is the convolution operator:

$$U^q f = V^q * f. \tag{2.30}$$

From the semigroup property of $\{P_t\}_{t\geq 0}$, the *resolvent equation* follows:

$$U^q - U^r + (q - r)U^q U^r = 0, \quad \forall \ q, r > 0,$$

and the resolvent equation implies that the image of $\mathcal{C}_0 := \mathcal{C}_0(\mathbf{R}^n)$ under U^q does not depend on q. We denote it by $\mathcal{D}$. The Feller property implies that for every function $f \in \mathcal{C}_0$, $\lim_{q\to+\infty} qU^q f = f$ in the uniform topology. Thus, $\mathcal{D}$ is dense in $\mathcal{C}_0$. By using the last observation and the resolvent equation once again, one deduces that the map $U^q : \mathcal{C}_0 \to \mathcal{D}$ is a bijection. We define the *infinitesimal generator $L : \mathcal{D} \to \mathcal{C}_0$* as the inverse to $U^q : \mathcal{C}_0 \to \mathcal{D}$. Thus,

$$U^q(q - L)f = f, \ \forall \ f \in \mathcal{C}_0, \tag{2.31}$$

and

$$(q - L)U^q f = f, \ \forall \ f \in \mathcal{D}. \tag{2.32}$$

We have, for every $t \geq 0, f \in L_1(\mathbf{R}^n) \cap L_\infty(\mathbf{R}^n)$ and $\xi \in \mathbf{R}^n$,

$$
\begin{aligned}
\mathcal{F}(P_t f)(\xi) &= E\left[\int_{\mathbf{R}^n} e^{-i\langle x,\xi\rangle} f(X_t + x) dx\right] \\
&= E\left[\int_{\mathbf{R}^n} e^{i\langle (X_t - y),\xi\rangle} f(y) dy\right] \\
&= E\left[e^{i\langle X_t,\xi\rangle}\right] \int_{\mathbf{R}^n} e^{-i\langle y,\xi\rangle} f(y) dy.
\end{aligned}
$$

Hence, by using the definition of the characteristic exponent, we conclude that

$$\mathcal{F}(P_t f)(\xi) = e^{-t\psi(\xi)} \mathcal{F}f(\xi), \ t \geq 0, \tag{2.33}$$

and therefore,

$$\mathcal{F}(U^q f)(\xi) = (q + \psi(\xi))^{-1} \mathcal{F}f(\xi), \tag{2.34}$$

which means that U^q is a PDO with the symbol $(q + \psi(\xi))^{-1}$:

$$U^q f = (q + \psi(D))^{-1} f. \tag{2.35}$$

We have shown that Eq. (2.35) holds for $f \in L_1(\mathbf{R}^n) \cap L_\infty(\mathbf{R}^n)$. In some situations of interest, f is unbounded, but the following condition holds:

$$(q + \Re\psi)^{-1} \hat{f} \in L_1. \tag{2.36}$$

Lemma 2.2 *If $f \in L_1$ and Eq. (2.36) holds, then Eq. (2.35) is valid.*

Proof. Since $f \in L_1$, we have

$$
\begin{aligned}
(U^q f)(x) &= \int_0^{+\infty} e^{-qt} (P_t f)(x) dt \\
&= \int_0^{+\infty} e^{-qt} (2\pi)^{-n} \int_{\mathbf{R}^n} e^{-i\langle x,\xi\rangle - t\psi(\xi)} \hat{f}(\xi) d\xi dt.
\end{aligned}
$$

Due to Eq. (2.36), the last integral computed in the reverse order $dt d\xi$ converges absolutely, and hence we can apply the Fubini theorem and obtain Eq. (2.35). □

Finally, for $f \in \mathcal{D}$ satisfying $Lf \in L_1(\mathbf{R}^n)$, we deduce

$$\mathcal{F}(Lf)(\xi) = -\psi(\xi) \mathcal{F}f(\xi), \tag{2.37}$$

and then

$$
\begin{aligned}
Lf(x) &= (\mathcal{F}^{-1}(-\psi(\cdot))\mathcal{F}f)(x) &\quad (2.38)\\
&= (2\pi)^{-n}\int_{\mathbf{R}^n}e^{i\langle x,\xi\rangle}(-\psi(\xi))\hat{f}(\xi)dx,
\end{aligned}
$$

which means that $L=-\psi(D_x)$ is a PDO with the symbol $-\psi$.

By using the same argument as in the one-dimensional case in Introduction, one can show that for $f\in\mathcal{S}(\mathbf{R}^n)$, the definition Eq. (2.38) coincides with the classical definition

$$
\begin{aligned}
Lf(x) &= \frac{1}{2}\sum_{j,k=1}^{n}a_{jk}\frac{\partial^2 f}{\partial x_j\partial x_k}+\langle\gamma,f'(x)\rangle &\quad (2.39)\\
&\quad +\int_{\mathbf{R}^n}(f(x+y)-f(x)-\mathbf{1}_D(y)\langle y,f'(x)\rangle)\Pi(dy).
\end{aligned}
$$

2.3.4 Dynkin's formula

Let T be a stopping time. From the strong Markov property, one deduces *Dynkin's formula*: for $g\in C_0:=C_0(\mathbf{R}^n)$, $q>0$ and $x\in\mathbf{R}^n$,

$$
U^q g(x)=E^x\left[\int_0^T e^{-qt}g(X_t)dt\right]+E^x\left[e^{-qT}U^q g(X_T)\right]. \quad (2.40)
$$

The stochastic integral in Eq. (2.40) is understood as

$$
E^x\left[\int_0^{+\infty}e^{-qt}\mathbf{1}_{\{t<T\}}(t)g(X_t)dt\right].
$$

Eq. (2.40) is also valid for any non-negative *universally measurable* function f– see [S], Eq. (41.3).[2] It follows that Eq. (2.40) holds for $g\in L_1+C_0$.

Lemma 2.3 *Let $(q-L)f:=(q+\psi(D))f$ belong to the class L_1+C_0 and satisfy Eq. (2.36). Then*

$$
f(x)=E^x\left[\int_0^T e^{-qt}(q-L)f(X_t)dt\right]+E^x\left[e^{-qT}f(X_T)\right]. \quad (2.41)
$$

Proof. Apply Eq. (2.40) to $g=(q-L)f$. Due to Eq. (2.36), Eq. (2.35) holds, and hence, $U^q(q-L)f=f$. Thus, Eq. (2.40) becomes Eq. (2.41).$\square$

---

[2]In situations which we consider in this book, only Borel functions will arise, so there is no need to give the definition of a universally measurable function here.

2.3.5   *Duality*

The process $\tilde{X} = -X$ is called the *dual process* of X; it is a Lévy process for the same triple $(\Omega, \mathcal{F}, \mathbf{P})$. The sign $\tilde{\;}$ is used to denote the q-resolvent $\tilde{U}^q$ and the infinitesimal generator $\tilde{L}$ of $\tilde{X}$, etc. For $x \in \mathbf{R}^n$, $\tilde{\mathbf{P}}^x$ denotes the law of $x + X$ under $\tilde{\mathbf{P}}$, that is, the law $\tilde{X}$ under $\mathbf{P}^{-x}$. It is clear that $\tilde{\psi}$ is the complex adjoint to ψ: $\tilde{\psi}(\xi) = \psi(-\xi), \xi \in \mathbf{R}^n$, and hence, $\tilde{L} = -\psi(-D)$.

The name "dual" stems from the following proposition.

Proposition 2.1   *Let f and g be non-negative measurable functions. We have for every $t \geq 0$*

$$\int_{\mathbf{R}^n} P_t f(x)g(x)dx = \int_{\mathbf{R}^n} f(x)\tilde{P}_t g(x)dx,$$

and for every $q > 0$,

$$\int_{\mathbf{R}^n} U^q f(x)g(x)dx = \int_{\mathbf{R}^n} f(x)\tilde{U}^q g(x)dx.$$

If f is in the domain of L, and g is in the domain of $\tilde{L}$, then

$$\int_{\mathbf{R}^n} Lf(x)g(x)dx = \int_{\mathbf{R}^n} f(x)\tilde{L}g(x)dx.$$

Proof.   The first statements is obtained by a change of variables, see [B], Proposition II.1.1 and [S], Proposition 41.7, and the last two follow.   □

2.3.6   *Absolutely continuous resolvents*

We start with a modification of the statements on p.25 in [B] and on p.p.288-289 in [S].

Theorem 2.11   *The following statements are equivalent:*

(i) *For some $q > 0$, the measure V^q is absolutely continuous w.r.t. the Lebesgue measure;*

(ii) *For any $q > 0$, the measure V^q is absolutely continuous w.r.t. the Lebesgue measure;*

(iii) *For some $q > 0$, and some $x \in \mathbf{R}^n$, the measure $U^q(x, dx)$ is absolutely continuous w.r.t. the Lebesgue measure;*

(iv) *For every $q > 0$, and every $x \in \mathbf{R}^n$, the measure $U^q(x, dx)$ is absolutely continuous w.r.t. the Lebesgue measure;*

(v) *The resolvent operators have the strong Feller property, that is, for every $q > 0$ and $f \in L_\infty(\mathbf{R}^n)$, the function $U^q f$ is continuous.*

When the assertions of Theorem 2.11 hold, we say that the resolvent kernel is absolutely continuous, or that the (ACP)-condition holds. The following Lemma gives convenient sufficient conditions which are satisfied by Regular Lévy Processes of Exponential type.

Lemma 2.4 *Let an n-dimensional Lévy process X satisfy (ACT)-condition, that is, the transition measures $\mathbf{P}_{X_t}$ are absolutely continuous for all $t > 0$. Then (ACP)-condition holds for X and for $(n+1)$-dimensional process $\{(X_t, t)\}$.*

Proof. Let p_t be the density of $\mathbf{P}_{X_t}$, and $B \times [a, b) \in \mathcal{B}(\mathbf{R}^n \times \mathbf{R}_+)$. Then

$$V^q(B \times [a, b)) = \int \int_{B \times [a,b)} e^{-qt} p_t(x) dx dt,$$

which proves (ACP)-condition for $\{(X_t, t)\}$. The proof for X is similar. $\square$

Let (ACP)-condition hold. Then Eq. (2.30) can be written as

$$U^q f(x) = \int_{\mathbf{R}^n} v^q(y - x) f(y) dy = (\tilde{v}^q * f)(x), \qquad (2.42)$$

where v^q is the density of V^q, and $\tilde{v}^q(x) = v^q(-x)$ is the density of $\tilde{V}^q$.

2.3.7 Operators P_B^q

Let $B \subset \mathbf{R}^n$ be an F_σ-set (for the general definition, see [S], p.279; for our purposes, it suffices to notice that Borel sets are F_σ-sets), and let T_B' be the hitting time of B by X. For $g \in L_\infty(B)$, define

$$P_B^q g(x) := E^x \left[e^{-qT_B'} g(X_{T_B'}) \right]. \qquad (2.43)$$

The map $g \mapsto P_B^q g(x)$ defines the measure which is called the q-order harmonic measure of B relative to x. By gathering Proposition 42.13, Theorem 42.5 and Definition 42.6 from [S], we obtain

Lemma 2.5 *Let B be an F_σ-set. There exists a σ-finite measure $d\mu_B$ supported on $\bar{B}$ such that*

$$P_B^q 1(x) = \int_{\mathbf{R}^n} v^q(y - x) d\mu_B(y).$$

From Lemma 2.5, we deduce for a closed B:

$$\langle P_B^q 1, (q - \tilde{L})w \rangle_{L_2} = 0, \quad \forall \, w \in C_0^\infty(B^c), \qquad (2.44)$$

where $B^c := \mathbf{R}^n \setminus B$, $\tilde{L} = -\bar{\psi}(D) = -\psi(-D)$ is the generator of the dual process, and $L_2 = L_2(\mathbf{R}^n; \mathbf{R})$ is the real space.

We need a more general result:

Lemma 2.6   *Let $B \subset \mathbf{R}^n$ be closed, and g be a bounded measurable function. Then*

$$\langle P_B^q g, (q - \tilde{L})w \rangle_{L_2} = 0, \quad \forall \, w \in C_0^\infty(B^c). \qquad (2.45)$$

Proof.   We derive Eq. (2.45) from Eq. (2.44) by using an additional assumption which holds for RLPE's: the characteristic exponent ψ of X admits the analytic continuation into a tube domain $\mathbf{R}^n + iU$, where U is an open subset of $\mathbf{R}^n$, containing 0.

For $\gamma \in \mathbf{R}^n$, define a function u_γ by $u_\gamma(x) = e^{\langle \gamma, x \rangle}$. As the first step of the proof, we show that Eq. (2.45) holds with $g = u_\gamma$ provided $q + \psi(-i\gamma) > 0$. Change the probability measure: $\mathbf{P}_\gamma = e^{\langle \gamma, x \rangle + t\psi(-i\gamma)}\mathbf{P}$. Under the new measure, X is the Lévy process with the characteristic exponent $\psi_\gamma(\xi) = \psi(\xi - i\gamma) - \psi(-i\gamma)$ since

$$E^{\mathbf{P}_\gamma}\left[e^{i\xi X_t}\right] = E^{\mathbf{P}}\left[e^{t\psi(-i\gamma)+i\langle \xi - i\gamma, X_t \rangle}\right] = \exp[-t(\psi(\xi - i\gamma) - \psi(-i\gamma))].$$

Let E_γ, $\{P_{\gamma,t}\}_{t\geq 0}$ and L_γ be the corresponding expectation operator, semigroup and infinitesimal generator. We have

$$
\begin{aligned}
e^{-\langle \gamma, x \rangle}(P_t u_\gamma g)(x) &= \int_{\mathbf{R}^n} e^{-\langle \gamma, x \rangle} e^{\langle \gamma, x+y \rangle} g(x+y) \mathbf{P}(X_t \in dy) \\
&= e^{-t\psi(-i\gamma)} \int_{\mathbf{R}^n} g(x+y) e^{\langle \gamma, y \rangle + t\psi(-i\gamma)} \mathbf{P}(X_t \in dy) \\
&= e^{-t\psi(-i\gamma)}(P_{\gamma,t} g)(x),
\end{aligned}
$$

therefore

$$e^{-\langle \gamma, x \rangle} P_B^q u_\gamma(x) = E_\gamma^x\left[e^{-(q+\psi(-i\gamma))T_B'}\right] =: P_{\gamma,B}^{q+\psi(-i\gamma)} 1(x).$$

Since $q + \psi(-i\gamma) > 0$, Eq. (2.44) applies to $P_{\gamma,B}^{q+\psi(-i\gamma)} 1$ and $\tilde{L}_\gamma$:

$$(P_{\gamma,B}^{q+\psi(-i\gamma)} 1, (q + \psi(-i\gamma) - \tilde{L}_\gamma)w) = 0, \quad \forall \, w \in C_0^\infty(B^c),$$

or equivalently,

$$(u_\gamma^{-1} P_B^q u_\gamma, (q + \psi(-i\gamma) - \tilde{L}_\gamma) u_\gamma w') = 0, \quad \forall\, w' \in C_0^\infty(B^c),$$

and finally,

$$(P_B^q u_\gamma, (q - u_\gamma^{-1}(\tilde{L}_\gamma - \psi(-i\gamma)) u_\gamma) w') = 0, \quad \forall\, w' \in C_0^\infty(B^c).$$

We have $L_\gamma = -\psi(D - i\gamma) + \psi(-i\gamma)$, therefore

$$\begin{aligned}
u_\gamma(L_\gamma - \psi(-i\gamma)) u_\gamma^{-1} &= -u_\gamma \psi(D - i\gamma) u_\gamma^{-1} \\
&= -e^{\langle \gamma, x \rangle} \psi(D - i\gamma) e^{-\langle \gamma, x \rangle} \\
&= -\psi(D) \\
&= L,
\end{aligned}$$

and hence $u_\gamma^{-1}(\tilde{L}_\gamma - \psi(-i\gamma)) u_\gamma = \tilde{L}$. Eq. (2.45) with $g = u_\gamma$ has been proved.

For the next step, consider a compact B and an arbitrary bounded measurable g. We can approximate g in the L^∞-norm by continuous functions, and each continuous function by polynomials (the Stone-Weierstrass theorem). Fix $\epsilon > 0$ such that the ball $V(\epsilon) := \{\gamma \mid \|\gamma\| \le \epsilon\} \subset U$. Since for any multi-index α,

$$\lim_{\gamma \to 0} \prod_{j=1}^n \gamma_j^{-\alpha_j} (e^{\gamma_j x_j} - 1)^{\alpha_j} \to \prod_{j=1}^n x_j^{\alpha_j},$$

uniformly in $x \in B$, we can approximate g in the L^∞-norm by a sequence of functions of the form

$$g_N(x) = \sum_{-\gamma \in \Gamma_N} c_{N,\gamma} e^{\langle \gamma, x \rangle},$$

where $\Gamma_N \subset V(\epsilon)$ is finite. Since Eq. (2.45) is valid for $g = u_\gamma$, provided $-\gamma \in U$ and $q + \psi(-i\gamma) > 0$, it holds for $g = g_N$ provided $\epsilon > 0$ is sufficiently small. By passing to the limit $\epsilon \to 0, N \to +\infty$, we conclude that Eq. (2.45) holds for any bounded measurable g and compact B.

It remains to drop the assumption that B is bounded. Notice that it suffices to consider non-negative g. For $R > 0$, set $B(R) = B \cap V(R)$. We have

$$E^x \left[e^{-q T'_{B(R)}} g(X(T'_{B(R)})) \right] \le E^x \left[e^{-q T'_B} g(X(T'_B)) \right] + \|g\|_\infty E^x \left[e^{-q T'_{B \setminus B(R)}} \right],$$

and

$$E^x \left[e^{-qT_B'} g(X(T_B')) \right] \le E^x \left[e^{-qT_{B(R)}'} g(X(T_{B(R)}')) \right] + ||g||_\infty E^x \left[e^{-qT_{B \setminus B(R)}'} \right].$$

For a Lévy process, $T'(B \setminus B(R)) \to +\infty$ as $R \to +\infty$, a.s., hence

$$E^x \left[e^{-qT_{B \setminus B(R)}'} \right] \to 0 \quad \text{as } R \to +\infty,$$

and we conclude that for any x,

$$P_{B(R)}^q g(x) \to P_B^q g(x), \quad \text{as } R \to +\infty.$$

Eq. (2.45) holds with $B(R)$ instead of B, hence

$$\int_{\mathbf{R}^n} P_{B(R)}^q g(x)(q - \tilde{L})w(x)dx = 0, \quad \forall \, w \in C_0^\infty(B^c).$$

The integrand converges pointwise to $P_B^q g(x)(q - \tilde{L})w(x)$ as $R \to +\infty$, and it is bounded by a function of the class $L_1(\mathbf{R}^n)$, uniformly in R, since $(q - \tilde{L})w \in L_1(\mathbf{R}^n)$, and $P_{B(R)}^q g(x)$ is bounded uniformly in R and x. By passing to the limit, we finish the proof of Eq. (2.45). $\qquad \square$

2.4   Boundary value problems for the Black-Scholes-type equation

This section is the focal point, where Probability and Analysis meet to produce in the end analytical formulas for prices of contingent claims and value functions of firms in Real Options theory. By definition, each of those prices and value functions is a sum of the stochastic integral which represent the expected discounted stream of payments (or revenues) during the lifetime of the contingent claim or the firm, and the expected terminal payoff in the end. By using Dynkin's formula and the potential theory, we deduce the pseudo-differential equation for the price in the region, where the contingent claim remains alive, and the terminal payoff translates into the boundary condition. Unlike in the Gaussian case, the boundary condition is non-local: the unknown function must be specified not only at the boundary but the other side of the boundary as well. On solving the boundary problem in an appropriate function class and obtaining a formula for the unique solution in this class, we obtain the price we have been looking for. In the last step, we use standard technical tools from elements of the theory of generalized functions, the theory of PDO and Complex Analysis.

2.4.1   Boundary problems for the stationary Black-Scholes type equation

Let X be an n-dimensional Lévy process satisfying (ACP)-condition, let $B \subset \mathbf{R}^n$ be a closed set, let T_B' be the hitting time of B by X, let $g^o \in L_\infty(B)$ and $g^c \in L_\infty(B^c)$ be non-negative functions, and consider

$$f(x) = E^x \left[\int_0^{T_B'} e^{-qt} g^c(X_t) dt \right] + E^x \left[e^{-q T_B'} g^o(X_{T_B'}) \right]. \qquad (2.46)$$

We have already mentioned in Introduction (and will see in Chapters IV-IX) that prices of various derivative securities in the financial market are naturally defined by expressions like Eq. (2.46).

Theorem 2.12   *Let X be an n-dimensional Lévy process satisfying (ACP)-condition. Then the stochastic expression Eq. (2.46) is a bounded solution to the following boundary value problem*

$$
\begin{align}
(q - L)f(x) &= g^c(x), \quad x \in B^c, & (2.47) \\
f(x) &= g^o(x), \quad x \in B, & (2.48)
\end{align}
$$

where Eq. (2.47) is understood in the sense of generalized functions:

$$\langle f, (q - \tilde{L})w \rangle_{L_2} = \langle g^c, w \rangle_{L_2}, \qquad (2.49)$$

for all $w \in C_0^\infty(B^c)$.

Proof.   Set $f^c = U^q g^c$. Then $(q - L)f^c = g^c$, therefore

$$\langle f^c, (q - \tilde{L})w \rangle_{L_2} = \langle g^c, w \rangle_{L_2}, \quad \forall w \in C_0^\infty(B^c),$$

and it remains to show that $f^o := f - f^c$ satisfies Eq. (2.49) with $g^c = 0$. In view of Eq. (2.45), it suffices to show that $f^o = P_B^q h$ for some bounded measurable h. But

$$
\begin{align}
f^o(x) &= -E^x \left[\int_{T_B'}^{+\infty} e^{-qt} g^c(X_t) dt \right] + P_B^q g^o(x) \\
&= -E^x \left[e^{-q T_B'} E^{X(T_B')} \left[\int_0^{+\infty} e^{-qt} g^c(X_t) dt \right] \right] + P_B^q g^o(x) \\
&= -E^x \left[e^{-q T_B'} U^q g^c(X_{T_B'}) \right] + P_B^q g^o(x) \\
&= P_B^q h(x),
\end{align}
$$

where $h = -U^q g^c + g^o$ is measurable and bounded.   □

Remark 2.1 a) In each concrete case, we find bounded solutions of the problem Eq. (2.47)-Eq. (2.48) by using tools from Analysis; in many cases, the bounded solution is unique, and in other cases, assuming that g^c and g^o are continuous and bounded, we single out the solution we need as the unique continuous bounded solution.

b) In many applications, the data g^o and g^c may be unbounded. Suppose that g^o and g^c are non-negative, measurable and finite a.e. Then we use the following scheme:

   (i) construct a sequence of non-negative bounded measurable g_n^o (resp., g_n^c) with compact support, which converge pointwise to g^o (resp., g^c), a.e.: $g_n^o(x) \uparrow g^o(x)$ and $g_n^c(x) \uparrow g^c(x)$;
   (ii) find the unique bounded solution u^n of the problem Eq. (2.47)-Eq. (2.48) with the data g_n^o and g_n^c (or the unique continuous bounded solution);
   (iii) calculate the limit $u := \lim_{n \to +\infty} u^n$; by the Monotone Convergence Theorem, this is the price of the derivative security or the value of the firm.

c) If g^o (and/or g^c) changes sign, we represent it as the difference of the non-negative function, and calculate separately the stochastic integrals for the non-negative data.

d) If the process does not satisfy (ACP)-condition, we can solve the problem Eq. (2.47)-Eq. (2.48), and after that check that Dynkin's formula is applicable to u^n, that is, $(q - L)u^n$ is non-negative and universally measurable. Luckily, RLPE's do satisfy (ACP)-condition, as we will see in Chapter 3.

2.4.2 *Boundary problems for the non-stationary Black-Scholes type equation*

Let $T > 0$ be the deterministic time, let D be a closed subset of $\mathbf{R}_x^n \times (-\infty, T]$, and set $D^T = \{x \mid (x, T) \notin D\}$, $B^c = \{(x, t) \notin D \mid t \in (-\infty, T)\}$. Let $g^r \in L_\infty(D)$, $g^T \in L_\infty(D^T)$ and $g^c \in L_\infty(B^c)$ be non-negative. Let T_D' be the hitting time of D by an $(n + 1)$-dimensional process $\{(X_t, t)\}$, and for $(x, t) \in \mathbf{R}^n \times [0, T]$ consider

$$f(x,t) \;=\; E^{x,t}\left[\int_0^{T_D' \wedge T} e^{-qs} g^c(X_s, s) ds\right] \tag{2.50}$$

$$+ E^{x,t}[e^{-qT_D'} g^r(X_{T_D'}, T_D') \mathbf{1}_{\{T_D' \leq T\}}]$$

$$+ E^{x,t}[e^{-qT} g^T(X_T) \mathbf{1}_{\{T_D' > T\}}].$$

We will see that the prices of contingent claims with finite time horizon, e.g., barrier options, can be expressed in this form.

Theorem 2.13 *Let X be an n-dimensional Lévy process satisfying (ACP)-condition. Then the stochastic integral Eq. (2.50) is a bounded solution to the following boundary value problem*

$$(q - \partial_t - L)f(x,t) \;=\; g^c(x,t), \quad \forall\; (x,t) \in B^c; \tag{2.51}$$

$$f(x, T) \;=\; g^T(x), \quad \forall\; x \in D^T; \tag{2.52}$$

$$f(x, t) \;=\; g^r(x, t), \quad \forall\; (x, t) \in D, \tag{2.53}$$

where Eq. (2.51) is understood in the sense of generalized functions:

$$\langle f, (q + \partial_t - \tilde{L})w\rangle_{L_2} = \langle g^c, w\rangle_{L_2}, \tag{2.54}$$

for all $w \in \mathcal{S}(\mathbf{R}^n \times \mathbf{R})$ s.t. supp $w \subset B^c$.

Proof. Introduce an $(n+1)$-dimensional Lévy process $\{\hat{X}_t\} := \{(X_t, t)\}$, denote its infinitesimal generator by $\hat{L}$, and define the function g^o on $B :=$ $\mathbf{R}^n \times \mathbf{R} \setminus B^c$ by

$$g^o(x,t) = \begin{cases} g^T(x), & t = T \text{ and } x \in D^T \\ g^r(x,t), & t \leq T \text{ and } (x,t) \in D \\ 0, & t > T \text{ and } x \in \mathbf{R}^n. \end{cases}$$

We can write Eq. (2.50) as Eq. (2.46), with (x,t) and $\hat{X}$ in place of x and X:

$$f(x,t) = E^{x,t}\left[\int_0^{T_B'} e^{-qs} g^c(\hat{X}_s) ds\right] + E^{x,t}[e^{-qT_B'} g^o(\hat{X}_{T_B'})] \tag{2.55}$$

From Lemma 2.4, $\hat{X}$ satisfies (ACP)-condition, therefore we can apply Theorem 2.12 to Eq. (2.55), and obtain Eq. (2.51)–Eq. (2.53), with $\hat{L}$ in Eq. (2.51) in place of $\partial_t + L$. It remains to note that the two operators are equal. $\square$

Remark 2.2 More general payoffs, and processes which do not satisfy (ACP)-condition, can also be considered.

Remark 2.3 Since the proof of Theorem 2.12 is based on the results from the theory of Markov processes having absolutely continuous potential measures, the main results of this section admit the straightforward generalizations for Markov processes.

2.5 Commentary

For the systematic treatment of the general theory of Lévy processes, see [B], [S], and for a shorter exposition, Rogers and Williams (1994); for the general theory of Markov processes, see Blumenthal and Getoor (1968), Rogers and Williams (1994), Sharpe (1989) and the bibliography there.

Chapter 3

Regular Lévy Processes of Exponential type in 1D

In this Chapter, we introduce families of RLPE which are used in empirical studies of financial markets not only by researchers, but by some practitioners as well. Then we give two general definitions of RLPE and study basic properties of characteristic exponents of RLPE.

3.1 Model Classes

3.1.1 *An overview*

D.B. Madan with corroborators were the first to use Lévy processes different from the stable ones, namely, *Variance Gamma Processes* (VGP)—see Madan and Seneta (1990), Madan, Carr and Chung (1998)—in financial modelling. A host of processes has been introduced, starting from the family of Generalized Hyperbolic distributions constructed by Barndorff-Nielsen (1977): *Hyperbolic Processes* (HP) and *Normal Inverse Gaussian* (NIG) processes were constructed in Eberlein and Keller (1995) and Barndorff-Nielsen (1998), respectively, and their generalizations: *Generalized Hyperbolic Processes* (GHP), and *Normal Tempered Stable Lévy Processes* (NTS Lévy) - in Eberlein and Prause (2001), Prause (1998), Raible (2000), and Barndorff-Nielsen and Levendorskiĭ (2001), Barndorff-Nielsen and Shephard (2001c), respectively. By now the list of papers, where processes of this cluster have been used for modelling behaviour of asset prices and term structure of interest rates, pricing of derivative securities, and risk management, is fairly long: Barndorff-Nielsen and Jiang (1998), Eberlein, Keller and Prause (1998), Prause(1998), Eberlein and Raible (1999), Eberlein *et al.* (2000a, 2000b), Eberlein (2001a, 2000b), Eberlein and Prause (2001), Barndorff-Nielsen and Prause (2001), Barndorff-Nielsen and Shephard (2001c). In Barndorff-Nielsen and Shephard (2001c), *Normal Modified Stable laws* were constructed, thereby generalizing the class of Generalized Hyperbolic distributions. For extensions to Feller processes and stochastic volatility models, see Chapter 14 and Commentary to Chapter 1, respectively.

(Non-infinitely divisible) *Truncated Lévy distributions* were constructed and used for financial modelling purposes by Mantegna and Stanley (1994, 1997); see also the monograph Mantegna and Stanley (2000). Novikov (1994) and Koponen (1995) introduced infinitely divisible analogues of truncated Lévy distributions. The extension of Koponen's family was constructed in Boyarchenko and Levendorskiĭ (1999a, 1999b, 2000); we will call it *KoBoL* family. Later this family was used by Carr *et al.* (2001) under the name CGMY-model. It was shown that processes of the KoBoL family provide good fit for many equities.

Below, we provide technical details of the derivation of necessary formulas mainly for KoBoL processes, since for these processes, all proofs can be made in full by using very simple analytical tools, and Variance Gamma Processes can be regarded as members of KoBoL family. The reader can find technical details concerning processes of the other families in op. cit.

3.1.2 *KoBoL family: direct construction via the Lévy-Khintchine formula*

3.1.2.1 *Definition in terms of the Lévy measure*

For $\nu < 2$ and $\lambda > 0$, set

$$\Pi^+(\nu, \lambda; dx) = x_+^{-\nu-1} e^{-\lambda x} dx, \quad \Pi^-(\nu, \lambda; dx) = x_-^{-\nu-1} e^{\lambda x} dx,$$

where $x_+ = \max\{x, 0\}$, $x_- = x_+ - x$.

Definition 3.1 A Lévy process X is called a *KoBoL process* of *order* $\nu < 2$ if it is a purely discontinuous Lévy process with the Lévy measure of the form

$$\Pi(dx) = c_+ \Pi^+(\nu, -\lambda_-; dx) + c_- \Pi^-(\nu, \lambda_+; dx), \tag{3.1}$$

where $c_\pm > 0$, and $\lambda_- < 0 < \lambda_+$.

λ_+ and λ_- are called the *steepness parameters* of the process.

Clearly,

$$\int_{-\infty}^{+\infty} \min\{1, x^2\} \Pi^{\pm}(\nu, \lambda; dx) < +\infty,$$

therefore Eq. (3.1) defines a Lévy measure. Since the condition

$$\int_{-\infty}^{+\infty} \min\{1, |x|\} \Pi^{\pm}(\nu, \lambda; dx) < +\infty$$

is satisfied if and only if $\nu < 1$, we conclude that a KoBoL process is a finite variation process if and only if $\nu < 1$.

3.1.2.2 *The characteristic exponent*

To compute the characteristic exponent of a KoBoL process, define $\psi^{\pm}(\nu, \lambda; \xi)$ by the Lévy-Khintchine formula Eq. (1.3) with $\sigma = \gamma = 0$ and $\Pi(dx) = \Pi^{\pm}(\nu, \lambda; dx)$. The following lemma will be proved at the end of this subsection.

Lemma 3.1 *For $\nu < 2$ and $\lambda > 0$, there exists $C(\nu, \lambda)$ such that*

$$\psi^{\pm}(\nu, \lambda; \xi) = \pm i\xi C(\nu, \lambda) + \phi(\nu, \lambda; \pm \xi), \qquad (3.2)$$

where
   a) if $\nu < 2, \nu \neq 0, 1$, then

$$\phi(\nu, \lambda; \xi) = \Gamma(-\nu)[\lambda^{\nu} - (\lambda - i\xi)^{\nu}]; \qquad (3.3)$$

   b) if $\nu = 0$, then

$$\phi(0, \lambda; \xi) = \ln(\lambda - i\xi) - \ln \lambda; \qquad (3.4)$$

   c) if $\nu = 1$, then

$$\phi(1, \lambda; \xi) = \lambda \ln \lambda - (\lambda - i\xi) \ln(\lambda - i\xi). \qquad (3.5)$$

From Lemma 3.1, we deduce

Lemma 3.2 *The characteristic exponent of a KoBoL process of order ν is of one of the following forms:*

(i) if $\nu < 2$, $\nu \neq 0,1$, then

$$\psi(\xi) = -i\mu\xi + c_+\Gamma(-\nu)[(-\lambda_-)^\nu - (-\lambda_- - i\xi)^\nu] + c_-\Gamma(-\nu)[\lambda_+^\nu - (\lambda_+ + i\xi)^\nu]; \tag{3.6}$$

(ii) if $\nu = 0$, then

$$\psi(\xi) = -i\mu\xi + c_+[\ln(-\lambda_- - i\xi) - \ln(-\lambda_-)] + c_-[\ln(\lambda_+ + i\xi) - \ln\lambda_+]; \tag{3.7}$$

(iii) if $\nu = 1$, then

$$\begin{aligned}\psi(\xi) &= -i\mu\xi + c_+[(-\lambda_-)\ln(-\lambda_-) - (-\lambda_- - i\xi)\ln(-\lambda_- - i\xi)] \\ &\quad + c_-[\lambda_+\ln\lambda_+ - (\lambda_+ + i\xi)\ln(\lambda_+ + i\xi)], \end{aligned} \tag{3.8}$$

where $\mu \in \mathbf{R}$, $c_\pm > 0$, and $\lambda_- < 0 < \lambda_+$.

Notice that we can (and will) use Eq. (3.6)–Eq. (3.8) to define KoBoL processes, without referring to the initial definition in terms of the Lévy measure.

The triple (ν, c_+, c_-) essentially determines the shape of the probability density in a neighbourhood of the origin. The smaller the ν and the larger the $c_\pm$, the higher the peak in the centre of the probability distribution, and in the case $c_+ \neq c_-$, the fall-off from the peak is asymmetric. The order of the process coincides with the order (in the sense of the theory of PDO) of the real part of the symbol $-\psi(\xi)$ of the generator $L = -\psi(D)$ of the process unless $\nu = 0$ or $\nu = 1$, when the standard definition of the order of a PDO does not apply. The steepness parameters determine the rate of exponential decay in far parts of the tails of the probability density: the smaller the λ_+ (resp., $-\lambda_-$), the heavier the left (resp., right) tail. Typically, $-\lambda_- > \lambda_+$, that is, the left tail is heavier.

Usually, a good fit to observed data can be achieved with the choice $c_+ = c_-$. We call this constant the *intensity* of the process, and denote it by c. The c plays the part similar to that of the variance of a Brownian motion. To simplify the formulas, in the sequel we restrict ourselves to the case $c_\pm = c$. The formulas Eq. (3.6)–Eq. (3.8) simplify as follows:

if $\nu < 2$, $\nu \neq 0,1$, then

$$\psi(\xi) = -i\mu\xi + c\Gamma(-\nu)[(-\lambda_-)^\nu - (-\lambda_- - i\xi)^\nu + \lambda_+^\nu - (\lambda_+ + i\xi)^\nu]; \tag{3.9}$$

if $\nu = 0$, then

$$\psi(\xi) = -i\mu\xi + c[\ln(-\lambda_- - i\xi) - \ln(-\lambda_-) + \ln(\lambda_+ + i\xi) - \ln\lambda_+]; \tag{3.10}$$

if $\nu = 1$, then

$$\psi(\xi) = -i\mu\xi + c[(-\lambda_-)\ln(-\lambda_-) - (-\lambda_- - i\xi)\ln(-\lambda_- - i\xi)] \\ + \lambda_+ \ln\lambda_+ - (\lambda_+ + i\xi)\ln(\lambda_+ + i\xi)]. \tag{3.11}$$

From Eq. (3.9)–Eq. (3.11), it is clearly seen that a mixture of KoBoL-processes of the same order ν and steepness parameters λ_- and λ_+ but different μ and c is a KoBoL process with the same ν, λ_- and λ_+. In other words, a subclass of KoBoL distributions with fixed ν, λ_- and λ_+ is closed under convolution, as the class of normal distributions is.

3.1.2.3 *Moments of a KoBoL process*

Lemma 3.3 *For the first four central moments, we have*

$$m_1 : = m_{1,\tau}/\tau = i\psi'(0); \tag{3.12}$$

$$m_2 : = m_{2,\tau}/\tau = \psi''(0); \tag{3.13}$$

$$m_3 : = \lim_{\tau \to 0} m_{3,\tau}/\tau = -i\psi^{(3)}(0); \tag{3.14}$$

$$m_4 : = \lim_{\tau \to 0} m_{4,\tau}/\tau = -\psi^{(4)}(0). \tag{3.15}$$

The proof will be given at the end of the subsection. Of course, Lemma 3.3 is valid not only for KoBoL processes, but we will use it mainly for them. For a KoBoL process of order $\nu \neq 1$, by using the property $\Gamma(1+x) = x\Gamma(x)$ of the Gamma function, we deduce from Eq. (3.9)–Eq. (3.10) and Eq. (3.12)–Eq. (3.15)

$$m_1 = \mu + c\Gamma(1-\nu)[(-\lambda_-)^{\nu-1} - \lambda_+^{\nu-1}]; \tag{3.16}$$

$$m_k = c\Gamma(k-\nu)[(-\lambda_-)^{\nu-k} + (-1)^k \lambda_+^{\nu-k}], \ k \geq 2. \tag{3.17}$$

We leave to the reader the computation of the derivatives of the characteristic exponents of KoBoL processes, and their evaluation at 0, for KoBoL processes of order 1.

Consider the typical case of the fatter left tail, that is, $\lambda_+ < -\lambda_-$. Since $\Gamma(x) > 0$ for $x > 0$, we conclude that $m_3 < 0$, hence, the probability distribution is negatively skewed. Due to $\nu < 2$, m_2 and m_4 increase as λ_+ and/or $-\lambda_-$ decrease, and for small τ, the skewness

$$\lambda_{3,\tau} = \frac{m_{3,\tau}}{m_{2,\tau}^{3/2}} \sim \tau^{-1/2} \frac{m_3}{m_2^{3/2}} \tag{3.18}$$

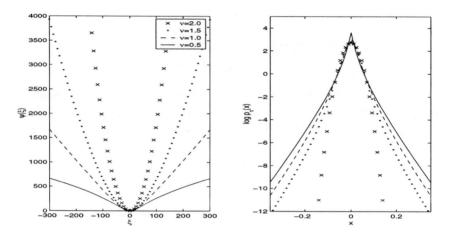

Fig. 3.1   The characteristic exponent and log-density of a KoBoL process: dependence on the order of the process. Parameters: $\mu = 0, \lambda_+ = -\lambda_- = 24, m_2 = 0.18, \tau = 1$ day, $\nu \in \{0.5; 1.0; 1.5; 2\}$

and the kurtosis

$$\kappa = \frac{m_{4,\tau}}{m_{2,\tau}^2} \sim \tau^{-1} \frac{m_4}{m_2^2} \tag{3.19}$$

grow unboundedly as $\tau \to +0$, which agrees with empirical observations in real financial markets. Notice that Eq. (3.18)- Eq. (3.19) hold for all RLPE (and any Lévy process with the sufficiently regular characteristic exponent).

3.1.2.4   *Graphs of characteristic exponents and probability densities of different KoBoL processes*

To compare Gaussian and non-Gaussian processes, we choose the parameters so that the first and second central moments, $m_{1,\tau}$ and $m_{2,\tau}$, of probability densities of different processes coincide. It allows us to illustrate the errors which arise when a non-Gaussian process is modelled as a Gaussian one, the drift and variance being inferred from the first two moments of the observed probability densities.

In Fig. 3.1, we take $\mu = 0, \lambda_+ = -\lambda_- = 24$; then $m_1 = 0$. For each $\nu \in \{0.5; 1; 1.5\}$, c is chosen so that $m_2 = 0.18$ is independent of ν. $\nu = 2$ denotes the case of the Brownian motion with zero drift and variance $\sigma^2 = 0.18$.

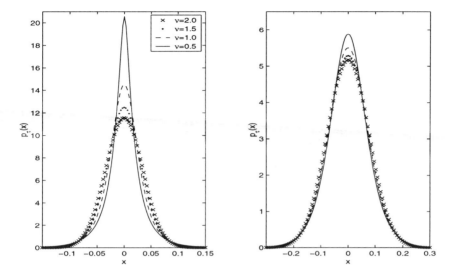

Fig. 3.2 Probability density of a KoBoL process: dependence on time and the order of the process. Parameters: $\mu = 0, \lambda_+ = -\lambda_- = 24, m_2 = 0.3, \nu \in \{0.5; 1.0; 1.5; 2\}$. Left panel: $\tau = 1$ day, right panel: $\tau = 5$ days.

In Fig. 3.2, we illustrate how the probability density of a KoBoL process evolves in time, and in Fig. 3.3, how it depends on the asymmetry parameter $\beta = (\lambda_+ + \lambda_-)/2$.

In Fig. 3.4, we fix $\nu = 1.4$, $m_2 = 0.18$, and see how the skewness and kurtosis depend on λ_+ and λ_-.

3.1.2.5 *Proofs of technical lemmas*

Proof of Lemma 3.1 The case of "-" sign easily reduces to the case of "+" sign by a change of variables $x \mapsto -x$, $\xi \mapsto -\xi$, therefore it suffices to prove Eq. (3.2)- Eq. (3.5) for "+" sign only.

a) If $\nu < 0$, we may write

$$\psi^+(\nu, \lambda; \xi) = \int_0^{+\infty} x^{-\nu-1} e^{-\lambda x} dx - \int_0^{+\infty} x^{-\nu-1} e^{-(\lambda - i\xi)x} dx + C(\nu, \lambda),$$

where

$$C(\nu, \lambda) = i\xi \int_0^1 x^{-\nu} e^{-\lambda x} dx.$$

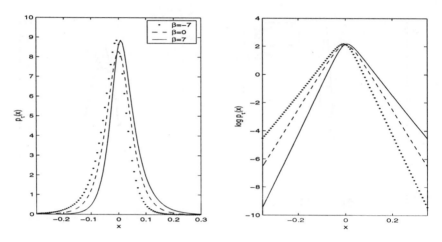

Fig. 3.3   Probability density and log-density of a KoBoL process: dependence on $\beta = (\lambda_+ + \lambda_-)/2$. Parameters: $\mu = 0, \nu = 0.5, \lambda_\pm = 24 \pm \beta$, $m_2 = 0.3$, $\tau = 3$ days.

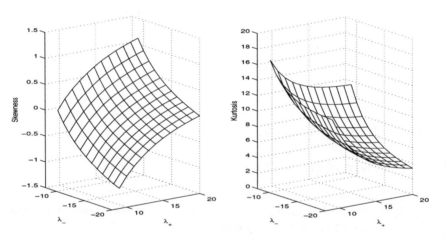

Fig. 3.4   Skewness and kurtosis of the probability density of a KoBoL process: dependence on the steepness parameters. Parameters: $\mu = 0, \nu = 1.4$, $m_2 = 0.18$, $\tau = 1$ day.

By making changes of variables $x = y/\lambda$ in the first integral, and $x = y/(\lambda - i\xi)$ in the second one, we obtain Eq. (3.2) with $\phi(\nu, \lambda; \xi)$ given by Eq. (3.3).

In the case $\nu \in (0,1)$, we integrate by part:

$$
\begin{aligned}
\psi^+(\nu,\lambda;\xi) &= -\frac{1}{\nu}\left\{\int_1^{+\infty}\left(e^{-\lambda x}-e^{-(\lambda-i\xi)x}\right)dx^{-\nu}\right.\\
&\quad \left.+\int_0^1\left(e^{-\lambda x}-e^{-(\lambda-i\xi)x}+i\xi x e^{-\lambda x}\right)dx^{-\nu}\right\}\\
&= -\frac{1}{\nu}\left\{\left(e^{-\lambda x}-e^{-(\lambda-i\xi)x}\right)x^{-\nu}\Big|_1^{+\infty}\right.\\
&\quad +\int_1^{+\infty}\left(\lambda e^{-\lambda x}-(\lambda-i\xi)e^{-(\lambda-i\xi)x}\right)x^{-\nu}dx\\
&\quad +\left(e^{-\lambda x}-e^{-(\lambda-i\xi)x}+i\xi x e^{-\lambda x}\right)x^{-\nu}\Big|_0^1\\
&\quad \left.+\int_0^1\left(\lambda e^{-\lambda x}-(\lambda-i\xi)e^{-(\lambda-i\xi)x}+i\xi(\lambda x-1)e^{-\lambda x}\right)x^{-\nu}dx\right\}\\
&= -\frac{1}{\nu}\left\{\int_0^{+\infty}\left(e^{-\lambda x}-e^{-(\lambda-i\xi)x}\right)x^{-\nu}dx\right.\\
&\quad \left.+i\xi[e^{-\lambda}+\int_0^1(\lambda x-1)e^{-\lambda x}x^{-\nu}dx]\right\}\\
&= -\frac{\Gamma(1-\nu)}{\nu}[\lambda^\nu-(\lambda-i\xi)^\nu]+i\xi C(\nu,\lambda),
\end{aligned}
$$

where

$$
C(\nu,\lambda)=[-e^{-\lambda}+\int_0^1(1-\lambda x)e^{-\lambda x}x^{-\nu}dx]/\nu=\int_0^1 x^{-\nu}e^{-\lambda x}dx.
$$

Since $-\nu\Gamma(-\nu)=\Gamma(1-\nu)$, Eq. (3.2)–Eq. (3.3) have been proved.

Finally, if $\nu \in (1,2)$, we integrate by part twice, and arrive at the same formulas Eq. (3.2)–Eq. (3.3), with

$$
C(\nu,\lambda)=-(\nu-1)^{-1}[e^{-\lambda}+\lambda C(\nu-1,\lambda)].
$$

b) If $\nu=0$, we differentiate $\psi^+(0,\lambda,\xi)$ w.r.t. $\mu=-i\xi$ and get

$$
\begin{aligned}
\frac{\partial\psi^+(0,\lambda,\xi)}{\partial\mu} &= \int_1^{+\infty}e^{-(\mu+\lambda)x}dx+\int_0^1\left(e^{-(\mu+\lambda)x}-e^{-\lambda x}\right)dx\\
&= \frac{1}{\mu+\lambda}-\frac{1-e^{-\lambda}}{\lambda}.
\end{aligned}
$$

Since $\psi^+(0,\lambda,0) = 0$, we can obtain $\psi^+(0,\lambda,\xi)$ by integration:

$$
\begin{aligned}
\psi^+(0,\lambda,\xi) &= \int_0^{-i\xi} \left(\frac{1}{\mu+\lambda} - \frac{1-e^{-\lambda}}{\lambda} \right) d\mu \\
&= \ln \frac{\lambda - i\xi}{\lambda} + i\xi \frac{1-e^{-\lambda}}{\lambda}.
\end{aligned}
$$

c) If $\nu = 1$, we differentiate $\psi^+(1,\lambda,\xi)$ with respect to λ and get $-\psi^+(0,\lambda,\xi)$. Clearly, $\lim_{\lambda\to+\infty} \psi^+(1,\lambda,\xi) = 0$, therefore we can find $\psi^+(1,\lambda,\xi)$ by integration:

$$
\begin{aligned}
\psi^+(1,\lambda,\xi) &= \int_\lambda^{+\infty} \psi^+(0,\mu,\xi)d\mu \\
&= \int_\lambda^{+\infty} \left(\ln(\mu - i\xi) - \ln\mu - i\xi \frac{e^{-\mu}-1}{\mu} \right) d\mu \\
&= ((\mu - i\xi)\ln(\mu - i\xi) - \mu + i\xi - \mu\ln\mu + \mu + i\xi\ln\mu)|_\lambda^{+\infty} \\
&\quad - i\xi \int_\lambda^{+\infty} \frac{e^{-\mu}}{\mu} d\mu \\
&= \lambda\ln\lambda - (\lambda - i\xi)\ln(\lambda - i\xi) - i\xi \left[1 + \ln\lambda + \int_\lambda^{+\infty} \frac{e^{-\mu}}{\mu} d\mu \right]
\end{aligned}
$$

(here we have used $\lim_{\mu\to+\infty}[(\mu - i\xi)\ln(\mu - i\xi) - \mu\ln\mu - ik(1+\ln\mu)] = 0$), and Eq. (3.2) and Eq. (3.5) follow.

Proof of Lemma 3.3. Since

$$
p_\tau(x) = (2\pi)^{-1} \int_{-\infty}^{+\infty} e^{-ix\xi - \tau\psi(\xi)} d\xi, \tag{3.20}
$$

we have

$$
\begin{aligned}
m_{1,\tau} &= \int_{-\infty}^{+\infty} x p_\tau(x) dx \\
&= (2\pi)^{-1} \int_{-\infty}^{+\infty} \int_{-\infty}^{+\infty} x e^{-ix\xi - \tau\psi(\xi)} d\xi dx \\
&= i(2\pi)^{-1} \int_{-\infty}^{+\infty} \int_{-\infty}^{+\infty} e^{-\tau\psi(\xi)} de^{-ix\xi} dx \\
&= i\tau(2\pi)^{-1} \int_{-\infty}^{+\infty} \int_{-\infty}^{+\infty} e^{-ix\xi} \psi'(\xi) e^{-\tau\psi(\xi)} d\xi dx.
\end{aligned}
$$

Since for $f \in \mathcal{S}(\mathbf{R})$,

$$f(0) = (\mathcal{F}^{-1}\hat{f})(0) = (2\pi)^{-1} \int_{-\infty}^{+\infty} \int_{-\infty}^{+\infty} e^{-ix\xi} f(\xi) d\xi dx, \qquad (3.21)$$

we conclude that Eq. (3.12) holds.

Further,

$$
\begin{aligned}
m_{2,\tau} &= \int_{-\infty}^{+\infty} (x - m_{1,\tau})^2 p_\tau(x) dx \\
&= \int_{-\infty}^{+\infty} x^2 p_\tau(x) dx - m_{1,\tau}^2 \\
&= (2\pi)^{-1} \int_{-\infty}^{+\infty} \int_{-\infty}^{+\infty} x^2 e^{-ix\xi - \tau\psi(\xi)} d\xi dx - m_{1,\tau}^2,
\end{aligned}
$$

and integrating by part twice and using Eq. (3.21) and Eq. (3.12), we obtain Eq. (3.13). Eq. (3.14) and Eq. (3.15) are derived similarly.

3.1.3 *Normal Inverse Gaussian processes and Normal Tempered Stable Lévy Processes: construction via subordination*

As early as in 1973, Clark modelled financial processes by subordination of Brownian motion, in the discrete time model, and Madan and Seneta (1990) were the first who introduced a model (Variance Gamma) which used a Lévy process as a subordinator. We start with a family of processes which are the most convenient from the analytical point of view.

Let $\nu \in (0,2)$, $\delta > 0$, and let $p(x; \nu, \delta)$ denote the probability density function of the positive $\nu/2$-stable law $S(\nu, \delta)$ on $\mathbf{R}_+$ with the Laplace exponent $\delta(2\theta)^{\nu/2}$. For $\gamma > 0$, define the exponentially tempered version of $p(x; \nu, \delta)$ by

$$p(x; \nu, \delta, \gamma) = e^{\delta\gamma^\nu} p(x; \nu, \delta) e^{-\frac{1}{2}\gamma^2 x}. \qquad (3.22)$$

The distribution with density Eq. (3.22) ($\nu \in (0,2), \delta > 0, \gamma > 0$) is referred to as a *tempered stable law*, and we denote it by $TS(\nu, \delta, \gamma)$. $TS(\nu, \delta, \gamma)$ is infinitely divisible, and its Lévy density and characteristic exponent are given by

$$u(x) = \delta \frac{\nu 2^{\nu/2-1}}{\Gamma(1 - \nu/2)} x^{-1-\nu/2} e^{-\frac{1}{2}\gamma^2 x},$$

$$\Phi(\theta) = \delta[(\gamma^2 + 2\theta)^{\nu/2} - \gamma^\nu]. \tag{3.23}$$

Let $Y(\beta)$ be the Brownian motion with drift β, and let X be the subordination of $Y(\beta)$ by $TS(\nu, \delta, \gamma)$. Then the characteristic exponent of X, denote it ϕ, is of the form

$$\phi(\xi) = \Phi\left(\frac{1}{2}\xi^2 - i\beta\xi\right),$$

and by using Eq. (3.23), we obtain

$$\phi(\xi) = \delta[(\alpha^2 - (\beta + i\xi)^2)^{\nu/2} - (\alpha^2 - \beta^2)^{\nu/2}],$$

where $\alpha > |\beta|$ is found from $\gamma = (\alpha^2 - \beta^2)^{1/2}$. By adding the drift, we obtain the characteristic exponent of a *Normal Tempered Stable (NTS)* Lévy process

$$\psi(\xi) = -i\mu\xi + \delta[(\alpha^2 - (\beta + i\xi)^2)^{\nu/2} - (\alpha^2 - \beta^2)^{\nu/2}]. \tag{3.24}$$

The $\alpha - \beta$ (resp., $\alpha + \beta$) describe the rate of decay of the right (resp., left) tail, and δ plays the part of the variance of a Brownian motion.

In the case $\nu = 1$, the characteristic exponents of *Normal Inverse Gaussian Processes (NIG)* obtain:

$$\psi(\xi) = -i\mu\xi + \delta[(\alpha^2 - (\beta + i\xi)^2)^{1/2} - (\alpha^2 - \beta^2)^{1/2}]. \tag{3.25}$$

From Eq. (3.25), it is clearly seen that a mixture of NIG-processes with the same α and β but different μ and δ is a NIG process with the same α and β. In other words, a subclass of normal inverse gaussian distributions with fixed α and β is closed under convolution, as the class of normal distributions is. From Eq. (3.24), the same conclusions hold for NTS Lévy processes of a fixed order.

NIG have another important property: for any $t > 0$, the following explicit analytical formula for the probability density is available:

$$p_t(x) = \frac{\alpha}{\pi} \exp[t(\delta\sqrt{\alpha^2 - \beta^2} - \beta\mu) + \beta x]\frac{K_1(\alpha\delta\langle(x/t - \mu)/\delta\rangle)}{\langle(x/t - \mu)/\delta\rangle}, \tag{3.26}$$

where $\langle y \rangle = (1 + |y|^2)^{1/2}$, and K_1 denotes the modified Bessel function of the third kind with index 1.

By using Eq. (3.12)–Eq. (3.15) and Eq. (3.24)–Eq. (3.25), one can easily calculate moments of probability distributions of NTS Lévy and NIG processes.

It can be shown that an NTS Lévy process is a finite variation process if and only if $\nu < 1$. In particular, NIG are not finite variation processes.

3.1.4 *Variance Gamma Processes*

As it was mentioned in Section 3.1.1, *Variance Gamma Processes (VGP)* can be defined as purely discontinuous Lévy processes with the Lévy density of the form $c(x_+^{-1} e^{\lambda - x} + x_-^{-1} e^{\lambda + x})$. Then the characteristic exponents are given by Eq. (3.10), but a more common form of the characteristic exponent of a VGP is

$$\psi(\xi) = -i\mu\xi + c[\ln(\alpha^2 - (\beta + i\xi)^2) - \ln(\alpha^2 - \beta^2)], \qquad (3.27)$$

where $\alpha > |\beta| \geq 0$, $c > 0$ and $\mu \in \mathbf{R}$. Similarly to NIG, a VGP without the drift is a subordination of a Brownian motion; this time, the subordinator is a Gamma process with the Laplace exponent of the form

$$\Phi(\theta) = c[\ln(\lambda + 2\theta) - \ln \lambda],$$

where $\lambda > 0$. Similarly to KoBoL and NIG processes, a mixture of VGPs with the same α and β but different μ and c is a VGP with the same α and β.

3.1.5 *Hyperbolic Processes and Generalized Hyperbolic Processes*

Generalized hyperbolic distributions were introduced by Barndorff-Nielsen (1977) as variance-mean mixtures of normal distributions. The Lebesgue density of a generalized hyperbolic distribution depends on five parameters:

$$d(x; \lambda, \alpha, \beta, \delta, \mu) = \frac{(\alpha^2 - \beta^2)^{\lambda/2}(\delta^2 + (x - \mu)^2)^{(\lambda - 1/2)/2}}{\sqrt{2\pi}\alpha^{\lambda - 1/2}\delta^\lambda K_\lambda(\delta\sqrt{\alpha^2 - \beta^2})} \qquad (3.28)$$
$$\times K_{\lambda - 1/2}(\alpha\sqrt{\delta^2 + (x - \mu^2)2})\exp[\beta(x - \mu)],$$

where K_γ denotes the modified Bessel function of the third kind with index λ. An integral representation of K_γ is given by

$$K_\gamma(z) = \frac{1}{2}\int_0^\infty y^{\gamma - 1}\exp[-0.5z(y + y^{-1})]dy. \qquad (3.29)$$

The α, β, μ and δ play the same parts as in the case of *normal inverse gaussian distributions*, which obtain as a subclass of the class of generalized hyperbolic distributions with $\lambda = -1/2$. By changing λ, one changes the heaviness of the tails of the distribution. With $\lambda = 1$, one obtains the subclass of *hyperbolic distributions*, with heavier tails. The densities of the hyperbolic distributions are expressed by the following simple formula

$$d(x) = \frac{\sqrt{\alpha^2 - \beta^2}}{2\alpha\delta K_1(\delta\sqrt{\alpha^2 - \beta^2})} \exp[-\alpha\sqrt{\delta^2 + (x - \mu)^2} + \beta(x - \mu)], \quad (3.30)$$

which explains the name "hyperbolic": the graph of $\ln d(x)$ is a hyperbola, whereas in the case of normal distribution, we get a parabola.

The characteristic function of a generalized hyperbolic distribution is given by

$$\phi(\xi) = e^{i\mu\xi} \left(\frac{\alpha^2 - \beta^2}{\alpha^2 - (\beta + i\xi)^2} \right)^{\lambda/2} \frac{K_\lambda(\delta\sqrt{\alpha^2 - (\beta + i\xi)^2})}{K_\lambda(\delta\sqrt{\alpha^2 - \beta^2})} \quad (3.31)$$

for $|\beta + i\xi| < \alpha$. A generalized hyperbolic distribution is infinitely divisible, and the density of the Lévy measure is: if $\lambda \geq 0$, then

$$g(x) = \frac{e^{\beta x}}{\pi^2 |x|} \left(\int_0^\infty \frac{\exp\left(-\sqrt{2y + \alpha^2}|x|\right)}{y \left(J_\lambda^2(\delta\sqrt{2y}) + Y_\lambda^2(\delta\sqrt{2y})\right)} dy + \lambda e^{-\alpha|x|} \right), \quad (3.32)$$

and if $\lambda < 0$, then

$$g(x) = \frac{e^{\beta x}}{\pi^2 |x|} \int_0^\infty \frac{\exp\left(-\sqrt{2y + \alpha^2}|x|\right)}{y \left(J_{-\lambda}^2(\delta\sqrt{2y}) + Y_{-\lambda}^2(\delta\sqrt{2y})\right)} dy. \quad (3.33)$$

Here J_λ and Y_λ are the Bessel functions of the first and second order, respectively.

By using the correspondence between infinitely divisible distributions and Lévy processes, one can define a *Generalized Hyperbolic Process (GHP)* as the Lévy process $\{X_t\}$ with $E[e^{i\xi X_1}]$ given by the RHS in Eq. (3.31).

We will need the asymptotics of $g(x)$ as $x \to +0$.

Lemma 3.4   *As $x \to 0$,*

$$g(x) = \frac{\delta}{\pi}|x|^{-2} + O(|x|^{-1}). \quad (3.34)$$

Proof.   From the well-known asymptotic formulas for Bessel functions it follows that the denominators of the integrands in Eq. (3.32) and Eq. (3.33) stabilize to positive constants as $y \to +0$, and have the following asymptotics, as $y \to +\infty$:

$$y\left(\frac{2}{\pi\delta\sqrt{2y}} + O(y^{-1})\right) = \frac{\sqrt{2y}}{\pi\delta}(1 + O(y^{-1/2})). \qquad (3.35)$$

Hence, by making the change of variable $y = |x|^{-2}z^2/2$ in Eq. (3.32) and Eq. (3.33) and using Eq. (3.35), we obtain Eq. (3.34). $\qquad\qquad\square$

From Eq. (3.34), we conclude that all Generalized Hyperbolic Processes are of infinite variation; in particular, NIG and HP are.

3.1.6 Comparison of the tail behaviour of probability densities for different model classes of processes

For GHP and NTS Lévy processes, NIG in particular, and for VGP, set $\lambda_- = -\alpha + \beta, \lambda_+ = \alpha + \beta$. Then for all model classes, λ_- is characterized by the behaviour of any probability density $p_\tau(x)$ as $x \to +\infty$:

$$\forall\, \omega > \lambda_-, \quad \limsup_{x \to +\infty} e^{-\omega x}p_\tau(x) < +\infty, \qquad (3.36)$$

and

$$\forall\, \omega < \lambda_-, \quad \lim_{x \to +\infty} e^{-\omega x}p_\tau(x) = +\infty. \qquad (3.37)$$

For KoBoL, NTS Lévy processes and VGP, Eq. (3.36)-Eq. (3.37) easily follow from the formulas for the characteristic exponents; for GHP, the verification of Eq. (3.36)–Eq. (3.37) requires more effort. It follows from Eq. (3.36)–Eq. (3.37) that if two model processes are characterized by different $\lambda_-(1) < \lambda_-(2)$, then the right tails of probability densities of the second process are fatter, independently of the classes the processes belong to, and of the orders of the processes.

If $\lambda_-(1) = \lambda_-(2)$, then the behaviour may differ: for instance, Eq. (3.36) holds with $\omega = \lambda_-$ for KoBoL processes of order $\nu > 0$ and NTS Lévy processes of any order $\nu \in (0,2)$, whereas Eq. (3.37) holds with the same $\omega = \lambda_-$ for VGP and HP. Thus, the right tails of probability densities of the latter group of processes are fatter than those of the former group, but this observation has hardly any practical significance: it is very difficult to infer λ_- from any empirical data set, and hence an error in λ_- will dominate an additional subtle difference in the tail behaviour.

It can be shown that of two KoBoL processes with the same λ_-, the one of the lower order has the fatter right tail, and the same is true of NTS Lévy processes.

In the same manner, λ_+ is characterized by the behaviour of the left tail.

3.2 Two definitions of Regular Lévy Processes of Exponential type

3.2.1 *Definition in terms of the Lévy measure*

Definition 3.2 Let $\lambda_- < 0 < \lambda_+$. We call X a *Lévy process of exponential type* $[\lambda_-, \lambda_+]$ if its Lévy measure satisfies

$$\int_{-\infty}^{-1} e^{-\lambda_+ x} \Pi(dx) + \int_{1}^{+\infty} e^{-\lambda_- x} \Pi(dx) < \infty. \tag{3.38}$$

Lemma 3.5 *Let X be a Lévy process of exponential type $[\lambda_-, \lambda_+]$. Then*

(i) *the characteristic exponent ψ is holomorphic in the strip $\Im \xi \in (\lambda_-, \lambda_+)$, and continuous up to the boundary of the strip;*

(ii) *there exist C and $\nu > 0$ such that for all ξ in the strip $\Im \xi \in [\lambda_-, \lambda_+]$,*

$$|\psi(\xi)| \le C(1 + |\xi|)^\nu; \tag{3.39}$$

(iii) *for any $q > 0$, there exist $\delta > 0$ and $\sigma_- < 0 < \sigma_+$ such that for any $[\omega_-, \omega_+] \subset (\sigma_-, \sigma_+)$ and all ξ in the strip $\Im \xi \in [\omega_-, \omega_+]$,*

$$q + \Re \psi(\xi) \ge \delta, \tag{3.40}$$

where $\delta = \delta(q, \omega_-, \omega_+) > 0$;

(iv) *if $\sigma_\pm$ satisfy*

$$q + \psi(i(\sigma_- + 0)) \ge 0, \quad \text{and} \quad q + \psi(i(\sigma_+ - 0)) \ge 0, \tag{3.41}$$

then Eq. (3.40) holds;

(v) *for any $q > 0$, the equation*

$$q + \psi(\xi) = 0 \tag{3.42}$$

has at most one purely imaginary root in the lower (resp., upper) half-plane, call it $-i\beta_+$ (resp., $-i\beta_-$);

(vi) the root $-i\beta_{\mp}$ exists if and only if

$$q + \psi(i(\lambda_{\pm} \mp 0)) < 0, \tag{3.43}$$

and if it exists, it is a simple root.

Proof. (i) is immediate from Eq. (3.38), and (ii) can be easily deduced from the Lévy-Khintchine formula, by considering separately the integrals over $|x| \leq |\xi|^{-1}$ and $|x| \geq |\xi|^{-1}$.

(iii)-(iv) Set $M_1(\sigma) = \int_{-\infty}^{+\infty} e^{-\sigma x} \mu^1(dx)$, where $\mu^1(dx)$ is the probability distribution of X_1. By differentiating twice, we conclude that M_1 is convex, and clearly, $M_1(0) = 1 < e^q$. Hence, there exist $\omega_- < 0 < \omega_+$ and $\delta > 0$ such that for all $\sigma \in [\omega_-, \omega_+]$, $M_1(\sigma) \leq e^{q-\delta}$.

Now, for any $\xi \in \mathbf{R}$, and these σ,

$$\exp(-\Re\psi(\xi + i\sigma)) = |\exp(-\psi(\xi + i\sigma))| =$$

$$= \left| \int_{-\infty}^{+\infty} e^{i\xi x - \sigma x} \mu^1(dx) \right| \leq \int_{-\infty}^{+\infty} e^{-\sigma x} \mu^1(dx),$$

therefore Eq. (3.40) holds with $\sigma_- = \inf \omega_-, \sigma_+ = \sup \omega_+$, and Eq. (3.41) implies Eq. (3.40).

(v)-(vi) Notice that by the proof of (iii), $\sigma \mapsto q + \psi(i\sigma)$ is concave and equals to $q > 0$ at 0. $\square$

For the sake of brevity, from now on we consider processes with Lévy measures (almost) symmetric in a neighbourhood of the origin.

Definition 3.3 Let $\lambda_- < 0 < \lambda_+$ and $\nu \in [0,2)$. A purely non-Gaussian Lévy process is called a *Regular Lévy Process of Exponential type* $[\lambda_-, \lambda_+]$ and order ν if its Lévy measure satisfies Eq. (3.38) and, in a neighbourhood of zero, admits a representation $\Pi(dx) = f(x)dx$, where f satisfies the following condition:

there exist $\nu' < \nu, c > 0$, and $C > 0$ such that

$$\left| f(x) - c|x|^{-\nu-1} \right| \leq C|x|^{-\nu'-1}, \quad \forall |x| \leq 1. \tag{3.44}$$

Notice that a regular Lévy process of exponential type has bounded variation if and only if $\nu < 1$, since this is equivalent to $\int_{-\infty}^{+\infty} (|x| \wedge 1)\Pi(dx) < +\infty$.

All model classes in Section 3.1 are RLPE in the sense of Definition 3.3:

- KoBoL processes with $c_+ = c_-$, of order $\nu > 0, \nu \neq 1$, are RLPE of order ν and exponential type $[\lambda_-, \lambda_+]$;

- KoBoL processes with $c_+ = c_-$, of order 1, are RLPE of order 1 and any exponential type $[\lambda'_-, \lambda'_+] \subset (\lambda_-, \lambda_+)$;
- VGP are RLPE of order 0 and any exponential type $[\lambda'_-, \lambda'_+] \subset (\lambda_-, \lambda_+)$;
- NTS Lévy processes of order ν are RLPE of order ν and exponential type $[-\alpha + \beta, \alpha + \beta]$; in particular,
- NIG processes are RLPE of order 1 and exponential type $[-\alpha + \beta, \alpha + \beta]$;
- all GHP are RLPE of order 1 and any exponential type $[\lambda_-, \lambda_+] \subset (-\alpha + \beta, \alpha + \beta)$.

3.2.2 *Definition in terms of the characteristic exponent*

The same calculations as in the proof of Lemma 3.1 prove that an RLPE of order $\nu > 0$ in the sense of Definition 3.3 is an RLPE in the sense of the following definition.

Definition 3.4   Let $\lambda_- < 0 < \lambda_+$ and $\nu \in (0, 2]$. A Lévy process is called a *Regular Lévy Process of Exponential type* $[\lambda_-, \lambda_+]$ and *order* $\nu > 0$ if the following two conditions are satisfied:

(i) the characteristic exponent admits a representation

$$\psi(\xi) = -i\mu\xi + \phi(\xi), \qquad (3.45)$$

where ϕ is holomorphic in the strip $\Im\xi \in (\lambda_-, \lambda_+)$, is continuous up to the boundary of the strip, and admits a representation

$$\phi(\xi) = c|\xi|^\nu + O(|\xi|^{\nu_1}), \qquad (3.46)$$

as $\xi \to \infty$ in the strip $\Im\xi \in [\lambda_-, \lambda_+]$, where $\nu_1 < \nu$;

(ii) there exist $\nu_2 < \nu$ and C such that the derivative of ϕ in Eq. (3.45) admits a bound

$$|\phi'(\xi)| \leq C(1 + |\xi|)^{\nu_2}, \quad \Im\xi \in [\lambda_-, \lambda_+]. \qquad (3.47)$$

One can easily generalize both definitions by using $c_\pm \geq 0$ in Eq. (3.44) on the half-axis $\pm x > 0$, and in Eq. (3.46), as $\Re\xi \to \pm\infty$.

From now on, we exclude RLPE of order 0, VGP in particular, from our consideration, since the logarithmic behaviour of the characteristic exponent as $\xi \to +\infty$ leads to technical complications at many places; in fact, only for pricing of options of the European type, VGP are as convenient as the other RLPE's. Each time one has to consider barriers or early exercise boundaries, one has to use the Wiener-Hopf factorization, which can be done much simpler when the characteristic exponent grows polynomially at the infinity. At the same time, we include Brownian motions: according to Definition 3.4, they are RLPE of order 2 and any exponential type. Notice that a mixture of independent RLPE is an RLPE, the order being the largest one of the orders of the components, and the exponential type being the intersection of the exponential types of the components. In particular, any RLPE with a non-trivial Gaussian component is of order 2.

3.3   Properties of the characteristic exponents and probability densities of RLPE

Clearly, an RLPE is a Lévy process of exponential type, therefore the properties listed in Lemma 3.5 hold for any RLPE. In addition, from Eq. (3.40) and Eq. (3.45)–Eq. (3.46), we deduce the following lemma.

Lemma 3.6   *Let X be an RLPE of order $\nu > 0$ and exponential type $[\lambda_-, \lambda_+]$. Then*

(i) There exist $\delta > 0$ and C such that for all ξ in the strip $\Im \xi \in [\lambda_-, \lambda_+]$,

$$q + \Re \psi(\xi) \geq c(1 + |\xi|)^{\nu} - C. \qquad (3.48)$$

(ii) For any $q > 0$, there exist $\delta > 0$ and $\sigma_- < 0 < \sigma_+$ such that for any $[\omega_-, \omega_+] \subset (\sigma_-, \sigma_+)$ and all ξ in the strip $\Im \xi \in [\omega_-, \omega_+]$,

$$q + \Re \psi(\xi) \geq \delta(1 + |\xi|)^{\nu}, \qquad (3.49)$$

where $\delta = \delta(q, \omega_-, \omega_+) > 0$.

Theorem 3.1   *For any $\tau > 0$, the probability density p_τ of an RLPE is infinitely smooth and exponentially decay at the infinity together with all its derivatives.*

   In particular, an RLPE satisfies the (ACT)-condition.

Proof.   Take $\omega \in (\lambda_-, \lambda_+)$. Then from Eq. (3.20) and Eq. (3.45)–Eq. (3.46),

$$e^{-\omega x} p_\tau(x) \ = \ (2\pi)^{-1} \int_{-\infty}^{+\infty} e^{-ix(\xi - i\omega) - \tau \psi(\xi)} d\xi$$

$$= (2\pi)^{-1} \int_{-\infty-i\omega}^{+\infty-i\omega} e^{-ix\xi-\tau\psi(\xi+i\omega)} d\xi$$

$$= (2\pi)^{-1} \int_{-\infty}^{+\infty} e^{-ix\xi-\tau\psi(\xi+i\omega)} d\xi. \qquad (3.50)$$

The last equality obtains when we shift the line of integration. To justify the shift, we use the Cauchy theorem and Eq. (3.48). Differentiate w.r.t. x under the integral sign in Eq. (3.50) $s = 0, 1, \ldots$ times; from Eq. (3.48), we conclude that the resulting integrand admits the estimate via

$$C_s (1 + |\xi|)^s \exp[-\delta|\xi|^\nu],$$

and therefore the integral converges absolutely and uniformly in x. Hence, $e^{-\omega x} p_\tau(x)$ and any of its derivatives are uniformly bounded w.r.t. x. □

We leave to the reader the formulation and proof of a similar statement about $p_\tau(x)$ as a function of two variables, defined on the open half-plane $\tau > 0$.

The characteristic exponents from model classes enjoy additional important properties. The following lemma will be needed to derive simple approximate formulas for the factors in the Wiener-Hopf factorization formula. We managed to prove this lemma only for model classes of RLPE, on the case-by-case basis. We conjecture that this lemma holds for a much wider variety of RLPE if not for all RLPE.

Lemma 3.7   *Let X be one of the model processes, of order $\nu > 0$ and exponential type $[\lambda_-, \lambda_+]$.*
   Then

   (i) the ϕ in Eq. (3.45) admits the analytic continuation into the complex plane with two cuts: $(-i\infty, i\lambda_-]$ and $[i\lambda_+, +i\infty)$, and outside any neighbourhood of $i\lambda_-$ and $i\lambda_+$ satisfies the following estimate:

$$|\phi(\xi)| \le C(1 + |\xi|)^\nu; \qquad (3.51)$$

   (ii) all the roots in the plane with the cuts are purely imaginary.

Proof.   See Boyarchenko and Levendorskiĭ (2002a).   □

3.4 Properties of the infinitesimal generators

Let either $\nu \geq 1$ or $\mu = 0$. Then from Eq. (3.45)–Eq. (3.46), we conclude that there exists $C > 0$ such that for all ξ in the strip $\Im\xi \in [\lambda_-, \lambda_+]$,

$$|\psi(\xi)| \leq C(1 + |\xi|)^\nu. \tag{3.52}$$

The bound Eq. (3.52) means that the infinitesimal generator $L = -\psi(D)$ is a PDO of order ν, and Eq. (3.49) means that $q - L$ is a strongly elliptic PDO of order ν. Moreover, since both estimates are valid on any line $\Im\xi = \omega \in [\omega_-, \omega_+]$, $q - L$ is a strongly elliptic operator in spaces with exponential weights (see Chapter 15). Thus, $q - L$ enjoys very favourable properties from the point of view of the general theory of operators on the line (in the multi-dimensional case, in the whole space), but if a boundary is present as it is the case with barrier options and options of the American type, then for RLPE, which are not Brownian motion, the following important property of elliptic differential operators fails: *a solution to a sufficiently regular boundary problem, e.g., the Dirichlet problem, with smooth data, is smooth up to the boundary.* This failure leads to the most significant differences between the behaviour of prices of contingent claims near the boundary in the Gaussian model, and the behaviour of the same prices in non-Gaussian models.

The final remark is: if $\nu \in (0, 1)$ and $\mu \neq 0$, then $q - L$ is no longer strongly elliptic since the upper bound for the symbol $q + \psi(\xi)$:

$$|q + \psi(\xi)| \leq C(1 + |\xi|)$$

is of a greater order than the lower bound Eq. (3.49). This leads to additional problems with solutions near the boundary, in particular, to the failure of the smooth pasting principle for optimal stopping problems.

3.5 A "naive approach" to the construction of RLPE or why they are natural from the point of view of the theory of PDO

If one wants to construct a non-Gaussian process with exponentially decaying tails of the density functions, whose generator looks as simple as possible and possesses the most tractable properties from the point of view of the theory of pseudo-differential operators, then one naturally guesses the formula for the infinitesimal operator of the NIG Lévy process. Here is a list of observations which naturally lead to NIG Lévy:

(i) the generator of the Brownian motion is $\frac{\sigma^2}{2}\Delta$, but the tails of a Gaussian distribution decay faster than an exponential function;

(ii) stable non-Gaussian Lévy processes have generators of the form $L = -\delta| - \Delta|^{\nu/2}$, where $\delta > 0$ and $\nu \in (0,2)$, and their symbols are non-smooth at the origin: $-\delta|\xi|^\nu$, which leads to polynomial decay of the tails of the density functions;

(iii) the tails of the density functions observed in financial markets, in turbulence and in many other fields of study usually have exponential decay; this means that the symbols of generators must be not only smooth but holomorphic in a strip of the form $\Im\xi \in (\lambda_-, \lambda_+)$, where $\lambda_- < 0 < \lambda_+$ (in the multi-dimensional case, in a tube domain $\Im\xi \in U$, where $U \in \mathbf{R}^n$ is an open set containing 0).

The natural candidate for a generator with the property (iii) is

$$L = -\delta[(\alpha^2 - \Delta)^{\nu/2} - \alpha^\nu], \qquad (3.53)$$

where $\alpha > 0$, $\delta > 0$, and if we want an asymmetric version, we simply shift the strip:

$$L = -\delta[(\alpha^2 - (\beta + iD)^2)^{\nu/2} - (\alpha^2 - \beta^2)^{\nu/2}], \qquad (3.54)$$

where $\alpha > 0$, $\delta > 0$, $\alpha > |\beta|$, and $D = -i\partial$ is the standard notation in the theory of PDO; it has the symbol ξ (The last terms in Eq. (3.53) and Eq. (3.54) are needed to ensure that $L \cdot 1 = 0$, which is necessary for a process without killing). Eq. (3.54) gives the infinitesimal generator of a (multi-dimensional) NTS Lévy process, and in the simplest case of the square root, of a (multi-dimensional) NIG.

3.5.1 *Modified Stable Processes and RLPE*

NIG, HP and GHP have been constructed as follows. By using Generalized Inverse Gaussian (GIG) distributions to mix normal laws, one constructs the corresponding NIG, Hyperbolic and Generalized Hyperbolic distributions; since GIG are infinitely divisible, the resulting distributions also are, and we can use the latter to construct Lévy processes. Barndorff-Nielsen and Shephard (2001c) introduced an extension of the family of GIG to a class of distributions on $\mathbf{R}_{++}$, the *Modified Stable* or *MS* laws. As GIG laws, MS Laws are obtained from one of the positive κ $(\kappa \in (0,1))$ laws by exponential and power tempering (or tilting). By using MS distributions as mixing distributions for normal variance-mean mixtures, Barndorff-Nielsen and Shephard (2001c) introduced and study *Normal Modified Stable* laws. They surmise (but have not proved) that MS laws are infinitely divisible, and so this construction may lead to a new important class of Lévy processes. Our guess is that this class will be a subclass of RLPE, as NIG, HP and GHP are.

3.6 The Wiener-Hopf factorization

We derive two representations for the factors in the *Wiener-Hopf factorization* formula Eq. (2.23), and approximate formulas for the factors.

3.6.1 *The case of Lévy processes of exponential type*

We fix a branch of ln by the requirement $\ln a \in \mathbf{R}$ for $a > 0$. We also fix $\omega_- < 0 < \omega_+$, for which Eq. (3.40) hold.

Theorem 3.2 *Let X be a Lévy process of exponential type, let there exist $c, \nu > 0$ such that*

$$q + \Re\psi(\xi) \geq c(1 + |\xi|)^\nu, \quad \Im\xi \in [\omega_-, \omega_+], \tag{3.55}$$

and let for $\omega = \omega_\pm$,

$$\int_{-\infty+i\omega}^{+\infty+i\omega} \frac{|\psi'(\eta)|}{(1+|\eta|)(q + \Re\psi(\eta))} d\eta < +\infty. \tag{3.56}$$

Then

a) $\phi_q^+(\xi)$ admits the analytic continuation into a half-plane $\Im\xi > \omega_-$ and can be calculated as follows:

$$\phi_q^+(\xi) = \exp\left[(2\pi i)^{-1}\int_{-\infty+i\omega_-}^{+\infty+i\omega_-} \frac{\psi'(\eta)}{q + \psi(\eta)} \ln\frac{\eta - \xi}{\eta} d\eta\right] \tag{3.57}$$

$$= \exp\left[(2\pi i)^{-1}\int_{-\infty+i\omega_-}^{+\infty+i\omega_-} \frac{\xi\ln(q + \psi(\eta))}{\eta(\xi - \eta)} d\eta\right]; \tag{3.58}$$

b) $\phi_q^-(\xi)$ admits the analytic continuation into a half-plane $\Im\xi < \omega_+$ and can be calculated as follows:

$$\phi_q^-(\xi) \;=\; \exp\left[-(2\pi i)^{-1}\int_{-\infty+i\omega_+}^{+\infty+i\omega_+} \frac{\psi'(\eta)}{q+\psi(\eta)}\ln\frac{\eta-\xi}{\eta}d\eta\right] \quad (3.59)$$

$$=\; \exp\left[-(2\pi i)^{-1}\int_{-\infty+i\omega_+}^{+\infty+i\omega_+} \frac{\xi\ln(q+\psi(\eta))}{\eta(\xi-\eta)}d\eta\right]; \quad (3.60)$$

c) $\phi_q^+(\xi)^{-1}$ (resp., $\phi_q^-(\xi)^{-1}$) admits the analytic continuation into a wider half-plane $\Im\xi > \lambda_-$ (resp., $\Im\xi < \lambda_+$) by

$$\phi_q^+(\xi)^{-1} = q^{-1}(q+\psi(\xi))\phi_q^-(\xi), \quad \Im\xi \in (\lambda_-, \omega_-]; \quad (3.61)$$

$$\phi_q^-(\xi)^{-1} = q^{-1}(q+\psi(\xi))\phi_q^+(\xi), \quad \Im\xi \in [\omega_+, \lambda_+). \quad (3.62)$$

Proof.   a) Consider the expression under the exponent sign in Eq. (2.26):

$$f(\xi): \;=\; \int_0^{+\infty} \frac{e^{-qt}}{t}\int_0^{+\infty} (e^{ix\xi}-1)\mu^t(dx)dt$$

$$=\; \int_0^{+\infty} \frac{e^{-qt}}{t}\int_0^{+\infty} (e^{ix\xi}-1)(2\pi)^{-1}\int_{-\infty}^{+\infty} e^{-ix\eta-t\psi(\eta)}d\eta dx dt.$$

On the strength of Eq. (3.55), we may apply the Cauchy theorem and shift the line of integration:

$$f(\xi) = \int_0^{+\infty} \frac{e^{-qt}}{t}\int_0^{+\infty} (e^{ix\xi}-1)(2\pi)^{-1}\int_{-\infty+i\omega_-}^{+\infty+i\omega_-} e^{-ix\eta-t\psi(\eta)}d\eta dx dt.$$

Now the inner double integral converges absolutely, hence we can apply the Fubini theorem and integrate w.r.t. x first:

$$=\int_0^{+\infty} \frac{e^{-qt}}{t}(2\pi i)^{-1}\int_{-\infty+i\omega_-}^{+\infty+i\omega_-} e^{-t\psi(\eta)}((\eta-\xi)^{-1}-\eta^{-1})d\eta dt.$$

Integrate by part:

$$=\int_0^{+\infty} \frac{e^{-qt}}{t}(2\pi i)^{-1}\int_{-\infty+i\omega_-}^{+\infty+i\omega_-} \ln\frac{\eta-\xi}{\eta}t\psi'(\eta)e^{-t\psi(\eta)}d\eta dt$$

$$=(2\pi i)^{-1}\int_0^{+\infty}\int_{-\infty+i\omega_-}^{+\infty+i\omega_-} \ln\frac{\eta-\xi}{\eta}\psi'(\eta)e^{-t(q+\psi(\eta))}d\eta dt.$$

From Eq. (3.56), the integral above calculated in the reverse order $dt d\eta$ converges absolutely. Hence we can apply the Fubini theorem once again and obtain Eq. (3.57); integrating in Eq. (3.57) by part, we arrive at Eq. (3.58).

b) The dual process $\tilde{X}$ is of exponential type $[-\lambda_+, -\lambda_-]$, its characteristic exponent is $\bar{\psi}$, and $[-\omega_+, -\omega_-]$ plays the part of $[\omega_-, \omega_+]$ in Lemma 3.5. Write down the Wiener-Hopf factorization for $\tilde{X}$ and apply the complex conjugation; then the "+"-factor for $\tilde{X}$ becomes the "-"-factor for X, and Eq. (3.57) for $\tilde{X}$ becomes Eq. (3.59) for X.

c) follows from Eq. (2.23) and Lemma 3.5, (i). $\qquad\square$

Remark 5.1 If X is an RLPE in the sense of Definition 3.4, then Eq. (3.56) and Eq. (3.55) hold; hence, Theorem 3.2 holds as well.

Lemma 3.8 *Let ω_- and ω_+ be as in Theorem 3.2.*

Then there exists $C > 0$ such that in the half-plane $\pm\Im\xi \geq \pm\omega_\mp$, $\phi_q^\pm$ admits estimates

$$(1 + |\xi|)^{-C} \leq |\phi_q^\pm(\xi)| \leq (1 + |\xi|)^C. \tag{3.63}$$

Proof.   In Eq. (3.57) and Eq. (3.59), make change of variables $\eta \mapsto |\xi|\eta$ and use Eq. (3.39) to notice that the expressions under the exponential sign admit an estimate via $C \ln(2 + |\xi|)$. $\qquad\square$

Eq. (3.63) is insufficient for the proofs below. More information about properties of the factors is obtained in the next subsection.

3.6.2   *The Wiener-Hopf factorization for RLPE*

Let $\sigma_- < 0 < \sigma_+$ be from Eq. (3.40). Fix $\lambda > \max\{-\sigma_-, \sigma_+\}$, and set $\Lambda_\pm(\xi)^s = (\lambda \mp i\xi)^s = \exp[s \ln(\lambda \mp i\xi)]$. Next, choose $d > 0$ and $\kappa_-, \kappa_+ \in \mathbf{R}$ so that

$$B(\xi) := d^{-1}\Lambda_+(\xi)^{-\kappa_+}\Lambda_-(\xi)^{-\kappa_-}(q + \psi(\xi)) \tag{3.64}$$

satisfies

$$\lim_{\xi \to \pm\infty} B(\xi) = 1. \tag{3.65}$$

Choices of d, κ_+ and κ_- depending on properties of ψ, hence on ν, μ and c in Eq. (3.45)–Eq. (3.46), we have to consider four cases.

(1) If $\nu \in (1, 2)$ or $\nu \in (0, 1]$ and $\mu = 0$, we set $d = c, \kappa_+ = \kappa_- = \nu/2$.

(2) If $\nu \in (0,1)$ and $\mu > 0$, we set $d = \mu$, $\kappa_+ = 1, \kappa_- = 0$.

(3) If $\nu \in (0,1)$ and $\mu < 0$, we set $d = |\mu|$, $\kappa_+ = 0, \kappa_- = 1$.

(4) If $\nu = 1$, we set $d = (c^2 + \mu^2)^{1/2}$, $\kappa_\pm = 1/2 \pm \pi^{-1}\arctan(\mu/c)$.

In all cases, Eq. (3.65) follows from Eq. (3.45)–Eq. (3.46). In the first three cases, Eq. (3.65) is immediate, and in the last case, the simplest way is to check that $\ln B(\xi) \to 0$ as $\xi \to \pm\infty$:

$$\lim_{\xi \to \pm\infty} \ln B(\xi) = \pm\frac{\pi i}{2}\kappa_+ \mp \frac{\pi i}{2}\kappa_- + \ln \frac{c \mp i\mu}{(c^2 + \mu^2)^{1/2}}$$
$$+ \lim_{\xi \to \pm\infty}(-\kappa_+ - \kappa_- + 1)\ln|\xi|$$
$$= \pm(\kappa_+ - \kappa_-)\frac{\pi i}{2} \mp i\arctan\frac{\mu}{c} = 0$$

by our choice of κ_+ and κ_-.

The last factor in Eq. (3.64) assumes values in a half-plane $\Re z > 0$ by Eq. (3.40), and the same is true of the product of the first three factors, since the first one is positive, $\Lambda_-(\xi)$ and $\Lambda_+(\xi)$ assume values in the half-plane but in different quadrants, and $0 \leq \kappa_\pm \leq 1$. Hence, for all $\xi \in \mathbf{R}$, $-\pi < \arg B(\xi) < \pi$, and therefore, $b = \ln B$ is well-defined on $\mathbf{R}$. Fix $\omega_- < 0 < \omega_+$ such that $\sigma_- < \omega_-, \omega_+ < \sigma_+$, where $\sigma_\pm$ are from Eq. (3.40), and notice that all the arguments above are valid on any line $\Im\xi = \sigma \in [\omega_-, \omega_+]$. Next, for $\tau > \omega_-$, $\tau_1 \in [\omega_-, \tau)$ and real ξ, set

$$b_+(\xi + i\tau) = \frac{i}{2\pi}\int_{-\infty+i\tau_1}^{+\infty+i\tau_1}\frac{b(\eta)}{\xi + i\tau - \eta}d\eta \qquad (3.66)$$

(by the Cauchy theorem, $b_+(\eta + i\tau)$ is independent of a choice of τ_1), and for $\tau < \omega_+$, $\tau_2 \in (\tau, \omega_+]$ and real ξ, set

$$b_-(\xi + i\tau) = -\frac{i}{2\pi}\int_{-\infty+i\tau_2}^{+\infty+i\tau_2}\frac{b(\eta)}{\xi + i\tau - \eta}d\eta. \qquad (3.67)$$

It follows from Eq. (3.45), Eq. (3.46), Eq. (3.64) and Eq. (3.65) that there exist $C, C_1, \rho > 0$ such that for any η in a strip $\Im\eta \in [\omega_-, \omega_+]$,

$$|B(\eta) - 1| \leq C(1 + |\eta|)^{-\rho},$$

and therefore,

$$|b(\eta)| \leq C_1(1 + |\eta|)^{-\rho}. \qquad (3.68)$$

Hence, the integrals in Eq. (3.66)–Eq. (3.67) converge, and $b_+(\xi)$ (resp., $b_-(\xi)$) is well-defined in a half-plane $\Im\xi > \omega_-$ (resp., $\Im\xi < \omega_+$).

We set

$$a_\pm(\xi) = \Lambda_\pm(\xi)^{\kappa_\pm} \exp b_\pm(\xi).$$

Theorem 3.3

a) a_+ (resp., a_-) is holomorphic in a half-plane $\Im\xi > \omega_-$ (resp., $\Im\xi < \omega_+$). It admits the analytic continuation into a wider half-plane $\Im\xi > \lambda_-$ (resp., $\Im\xi < \lambda_+$), and the continuous extension up to the boundary, by

$$\begin{align}
a_+(\xi) &= d^{-1}(q + \psi(\xi))/a_-(\xi), \quad \Im\xi \in [\lambda_-, \omega_-], \tag{3.69}\\
a_-(\xi) &= d^{-1}(q + \psi(\xi))/a_+(\xi), \quad \Im\xi \in [\omega_+, \lambda_+]; \tag{3.70}
\end{align}$$

b) on a strip $\Im\xi \in [\lambda_-, \lambda_+]$,

$$q + \psi(\xi) = da_+(\xi)a_-(\xi); \tag{3.71}$$

c) there exist $C, c > 0$ and $\rho_1 > 0$ such that in a half-plane $\Im\xi \geq \omega_-$,

$$c(1 + |\xi|)^{\kappa_+} \leq |a_+(\xi)| \leq C(1 + |\xi|)^{\kappa_+}; \tag{3.72}$$

$$|a_+(\xi)^{\pm 1} - \Lambda_+(\xi)^{\pm\kappa_+}| \leq C(1 + |\xi|)^{\pm\kappa_+ - \rho_1}; \tag{3.73}$$

and in a half-plane $\Im\xi \leq \omega_+$,

$$c(1 + |\xi|)^{\kappa_-} \leq |a_-(\xi)| \leq C(1 + |\xi|)^{\kappa_-}, \tag{3.74}$$

$$|a_-(\xi)^{\pm 1} - \Lambda_-(\xi)^{\pm\kappa_-}| \leq C(1 + |\xi|)^{\pm\kappa_- - \rho_1}; \tag{3.75}$$

d) factors in Eq. (2.23) and Eq. (3.71) are related by

$$\phi_q^\pm(\xi)^{-1} = a_\pm(\xi)/a_\pm(0). \tag{3.76}$$

Proof. a) The first statement is straightforward by Eq. (3.68), and once c) is proved, the second one follows since $d^{-1}(q + \psi(\xi))$ is holomorphic on a strip $\Im\xi \in (\lambda_-, \lambda_+)$, and admits the continuous extension up to the boundary of the strip.

b) By the residue theorem, we have for $\tau_1 \in (\omega_-, \Im\xi)$ and $\tau_2 \in (\Im\xi, \omega_+)$

$$
\begin{aligned}
b_+(\xi) &= \frac{i}{2\pi} \left(\int_{-\infty+i\tau_1}^{+\infty+i\tau_1} - \int_{-\infty+i\tau_2}^{+\infty+i\tau_2} \right) \frac{b(\eta)}{\xi - \eta} d\eta \\
&\quad + \frac{i}{2\pi} \int_{-\infty+i\tau_2}^{+\infty+i\tau_2} \frac{b(\eta)}{\xi - \eta} d\eta \\
&= b(\xi) - b_-(\xi).
\end{aligned}
$$

Hence, $\exp b_+(\xi) \exp b_-(\xi) = B(\xi)$, and Eq. (3.71) is immediate on a narrow strip $\omega_- < \Im\xi < \omega_+$; on a wider strip $\Im\xi \in [\lambda_-, \lambda_+]$, it holds by construction: see Eq. (3.69) and Eq. (3.70).

c) By using Eq. (3.68), we obtain

$$
|(\xi + i\tau - \eta)^{-1} b(\eta)| \le C(1 + |\xi - \eta|)^{-1}(1 + |\eta|)^{-\rho}.
$$

By considering separately a region, where $|\xi - \eta| \ge |\xi|/2$, and its complement, it is easy to show that the RHS admits an upper bound via

$$
C_1(1 + |\xi|)^{-\rho_1}(1 + |\eta|)^{-1-\rho_1} + C_1(1 + |\xi|)^{-\rho_1}(1 + |\xi - \eta|)^{-1-\rho_1},
$$

where $\rho_1 = \min\{1, \rho\}/2 > 0$. By integrating, we obtain for ξ in a half-plane $\Im\xi \ge \omega_-$ (see Eq. (3.66)–Eq. (3.67))

$$
|b_\pm(\xi)| \le C_3(1 + |\xi|)^{-\rho_1}, \tag{3.77}
$$

and Eq. (3.72)–Eq. (3.75) follow from Eq. (3.77) and the definition of $a_\pm$.

d) Notice that $a_\pm$, $1/a_\pm$, $\phi_q^\pm$ and $1/\phi_q^\pm$ are bounded by a polynomial in the half-plane $\pm\Im\xi \ge \pm\omega_\mp$, therefore, by comparing Eq. (2.23) and Eq. (3.71), we conclude that $a_\pm\phi_q^\pm$ is holomorphic, polynomially bounded and non-vanishing on the complex plane. By the Liouville theorem, this is constant, and taking into account that $\phi_q^\pm(0) = 1$, we obtain Eq. (3.76). □

3.6.3   *Approximate formulas for the factors in the case of NIG, HP, KoBoL and NTS Lévy processes*

We can write these formulas down for both representations (in Eq. (2.23) and Eq. (3.71)). In the case of the former, the argument and formulas are shorter. We use Eq. (3.57) and Lemma 3.7 to transform the line of integration into the contour along the banks of the cut $(-i\infty, i\lambda_-]$. In empirical studies of financial markets, λ_+ and $-\lambda_-$ are usually large, of order 20-50, and then for typical values of other parameters, both roots

$-i\beta_{\pm}$ in Lemma 3.5 exist. Therefore, in the process of transformation, the contour crosses the simple pole at $\eta = -i\beta_+$. By the residue theorem, we obtain, for ξ in the upper half-plane,

$$\phi_q^+(\xi) = \exp\left[\ln\frac{-i\beta_+}{-i\beta_+ - \xi} + \Phi_q^+(\xi)\right],$$

where

$$\Phi_q^+(\xi) = (2\pi)^{-1}\int_{-\infty}^{\lambda_-}\left[\frac{\psi'(iz-0)}{q+\psi(iz-0)} - \frac{\psi'(iz+0)}{q+\psi(iz+0)}\right]\ln\frac{-z-i\xi}{-z}dz. \tag{3.78}$$

Thus,

$$\phi_q^+(\xi) = \frac{\beta_+}{\beta_+ - i\xi}\exp\Phi_q^+(\xi). \tag{3.79}$$

Similarly, from Eq. (3.59), we deduce, for ξ in the lower half-plane,

$$\phi_q^-(\xi) = \frac{-\beta_-}{-\beta_- + i\xi}\exp\Phi_q^-(\xi), \tag{3.80}$$

where

$$\Phi_q^-(\xi) = (2\pi)^{-1}\int_{\lambda_+}^{+\infty}\left[\frac{\psi'(iz-0)}{q+\psi(iz-0)} - \frac{\psi'(iz+0)}{q+\psi(iz+0)}\right]\ln\frac{z+i\xi}{z}dz. \tag{3.81}$$

If $-\lambda_-$ (resp., λ_+) is large, $|\Phi_q^+(\xi)|$ (resp., $|\Phi_q^+(\xi)|$) is small uniformly in ξ in the upper (resp., lower) half-plane, which can be easily seen from the explicit formulas for the characteristic exponents and Eq. (3.78) (resp., Eq. (3.81)). Hence, we may calculate the integrals in Eq. (3.78) and Eq. (3.81) with a large relative error and still obtain $\phi_q^+(\xi)$ from Eq. (3.79) and $\phi_q^-(\xi)$ from Eq. (3.80) with good accuracy. This observation can be used to develop effective numerical procedures. In fact, even the simple approximations

$$\phi_q^+(\xi) \sim \frac{\beta_+}{\beta_+ - i\xi}, \quad \phi_q^-(\xi) \sim \frac{-\beta_-}{-\beta_- + i\xi} \tag{3.82}$$

produce errors of several percent only, for many typical parameters values. In Section 5.2, we demonstrate how Eq. (3.80)-Eq. (3.82) can be applied to obtain simple approximate formulas for the perpetual American put. Since the (approximate) factors in Eq. (3.82) look exactly as the factors in the Gaussian case, the comparison of Eq. (2.28) and Eq. (3.82) provides an analytical explanation why a simple adjustment of parameters of the Gaussian model can give fairly good fit even in an apparently non-Gaussian situation.

Chapter 4

Pricing and hedging of contingent claims of European type

We start with several constructions of an equivalent martingale measure (EMM). Then, assuming that an EMM is chosen, we derive the generalizations of the Black-Scholes pricing formula and the Black-Scholes equation (GBE). We discuss properties of GBE, and study the dependence of GBE on a choice of EMM. In the last section, we derive an explicit analytic formula for the weights of the locally risk-minimizing portfolio.

4.1 Equivalent Martingale Measures in a Lévy market

Consider a continuous-time model market of a riskless bond, the *riskless rate* of return being $r > 0$, and a risky stock. Suppose that the price of the stock evolves as $S(t) = \exp X(t)$, where X is a Lévy process under the historic measure $\mathbf{P}$. From general results due to Delbaen and Schachermayer (1994), it follows that no-arbitrage pricing is possible under any EMM $\mathbf{Q}$, which is absolutely continuous with respect to the historic measure. If X is a non-Gaussian process, then typically an EMM is not unique, and the market is incomplete. Moreover, often there are infinitely many different EMM, and the choice of an EMM is a non-trivial problem, especially because of the general result due to Eberlein and Jacod (1997), who showed for wide class of processes, that by choosing an appropriate EMM, one can obtain any price of a European contingent claim, which belongs to the evident no-arbitrage interval. For instance, they showed for a European call option with strike K, the expiry date T and the constant rate r, that the values of the option computed under different EMM, span the whole interval from $(S(0) - e^{-rT})_+$ to $S(0)$, which is the smallest interval in which all

97

prices must lie due to the no-arbitrage considerations.

Föllmer and Schweizer (1991) used a hedging argument to advocate a choice of the EMM which is closest to the historic measure in a relative entropy sense $\int \log(d\mathbf{Q}/d\mathbf{P})d\mathbf{Q}$. Another approach is to use the optimisation argument see e.g. Naik and Lee (1990), Keller (1997), Kallsen (1998, 2000), Goll and Kallsen (2000) Goll and Rüschendorf (2000). In particular, in Naik and Lee (1990) and Keller (1997), it is shown that the Esscher transform of the historic measure is optimal w.r.t. some optimisation criterion. The Esscher transform was introduced by F. Esscher in 1932 in Actuarial science; see the general discussion in Shiryaev (1999). Madan and Milne (1991) were the first to use it in Finance, it was also used in Eberlein *et al.* (1998) and many other empirical studies of financial markets.

We start with the Esscher transform of the historic measure $\mathbf{P}$, and then discuss more general constructions. The reader may safely skip the general case for the first reading, since all the results in the following sections and chapters are formulated for any EMM under assumption that the choice has already been made (by using observed prices on the stock and derivatives, say). All the numerical examples but one are produced for the Esscher transform.

4.1.1 *Esscher transform*

Let X be a Lévy process on a filtered probability space $(\Omega, \mathcal{F}, (\mathcal{F}_t), \mathbf{P})$. We look for an EMM $\mathbf{Q}$ satisfying

$$\frac{d\mathbf{Q}}{d\mathbf{P}}|_{\mathcal{F}_t} = \exp[\theta X(t) - d(\theta, t)], \qquad (4.1)$$

where $d(\theta, t)$ is a constant. Thus, the density process of the Esscher transform enjoys the following special property: it depends on the current value $X(\omega, t)$ but not on the whole prehistory of the process, that is, on $X(\omega, s), s \in [0, t]$; for a general density process, this property may fail. The discounted price process of the stock $S^*(t) = e^{-rt}S(t)$ must be a martingale under $\mathbf{Q}$, therefore for $t > 0$, we have

$$S(0) = E^{\mathbf{Q}}[S^*(t)] = S(0)E^{\mathbf{P}}[e^{(1+\theta)X(t) - d(\theta, t) - rt}],$$

where $E^{\mathbf{Q}}$ (resp., $E^{\mathbf{P}}$) is the expectation operator under $\mathbf{Q}$ (resp., $\mathbf{P}$). By using the definition of the characteristic exponent of a Lévy process, we conclude that for any $t > 0$

$$-t\psi^{\mathbf{P}}(-i(1+\theta)) - d(\theta, t) - rt = 0. \tag{4.2}$$

By applying the same consideration to the riskless bond with the dynamics $B(t) = B(0)e^{rt}$, we obtain

$$-t\psi^{\mathbf{P}}(-i\theta) - d(\theta, t) = 0. \tag{4.3}$$

From Eq. (4.3), we find $d(\theta, t) = -t\psi^{\mathbf{P}}(-i\theta)$, and by substituting into Eq. (4.2) and dividing by t, we obtain the equation for θ:

$$-r - \psi^{\mathbf{P}}(-i(1+\theta)) + \psi^{\mathbf{P}}(-i\theta) = 0. \tag{4.4}$$

Let a solution to Eq. (4.4) exist. Then the Esscher transform exists, and Eq. (4.1) can be written as

$$\frac{d\mathbf{Q}}{d\mathbf{P}}\big|_{\mathcal{F}_t} = \exp[\theta X(t) + t\psi^{\mathbf{P}}(-i\theta)].$$

We conclude that the characteristic exponent of X under $\mathbf{Q}$ is given by

$$\psi^{\mathbf{Q}}(\xi) = \psi^{\mathbf{P}}(\xi - i\theta) - \psi^{\mathbf{P}}(-i\theta). \tag{4.5}$$

Example 4.1   Let $W(t)$ be the standard Brownian Motion, and let $X(t) = \mu t + \sigma W(t)$ be a Brownian Motion with a drift.

Then $\psi^{\mathbf{P}}(\xi) = \frac{\sigma^2}{2}\xi^2 - i\mu\xi$, and Eq. (4.4) turns into

$$r = -(-i(1+\theta)\sigma)^2/2 + \mu(1+\theta) + (-i\theta\sigma)^2/2 - \mu\theta. \tag{4.6}$$

Eq. (4.6) has a unique solution $\theta = -(\mu + \sigma^2/2 - r)/\sigma^2$, and Eq. (4.5) gives the well-known formula for the characteristic exponent of a Brownian motion under the equivalent martingale measure:

$$\psi^{\mathbf{Q}}(\xi) = \frac{\sigma^2}{2}\xi^2 - i\xi\left(r - \frac{\sigma^2}{2}\right). \tag{4.7}$$

Eq. (4.7) can also be obtained from Girsanov's theorem.

For an arbitrary Lévy process, Eq. (4.4) may have no real solutions, and hence, the Esscher transform may not exist. The following lemma shows that if it exists, it is unique, and provides a necessary and sufficient condition for the existence of the Esscher transform.

Lemma 4.1   *Let X be of exponential type $[\lambda_-, \lambda_+]$ with $\lambda_+ - \lambda_- > 1$, under the historic measure $\mathbf{P}$.*

Then

(i) *the function* $f(\theta) = -\psi^{\mathbf{P}}(-i(\theta+1)) + \psi^{\mathbf{P}}(-i\theta)$ *is strictly increasing on* $[-\lambda_+, -\lambda_- - 1]$;

(ii) *Eq. (4.4) has at most one root on* $[-\lambda_+, -\lambda_- - 1]$;

(iii) *Eq. (4.4) has a root on* $(-\lambda_+, -\lambda_- - 1)$ *if and only if*

$$\lim_{\theta \to -\lambda_+ + 0} f(\theta) < r < \lim_{\theta \to -\lambda_- - 1 - 0} f(\theta). \tag{4.8}$$

Proof. Parts (ii) and (iii) follow from (i), and to prove (i), it suffices to show that $f'(\theta) > 0$, $\forall \, \theta \in (-\lambda_+, -\lambda_- - 1)$. Let $p_1(x)dx$ be the law of X_1. Set

$$I(b,a) = \int_{-\infty}^{+\infty} x^b e^{ax} p_1(x)dx,$$

$$F(a) = \ln I(0,a),$$

and represent f in a form $f(a) = F(a+1) - F(a)$. Clearly, it suffices to show that F' increases, or even simpler:

$$F''(\theta) > 0, \quad \forall \, \theta \in (-\lambda_+, -\lambda_- - 1). \tag{4.9}$$

We have

$$
\begin{aligned}
F''(\theta) &= \left[\int_{-\infty}^{+\infty} x^2 e^{\theta x} p_1(x)dx \int_{-\infty}^{+\infty} e^{\theta x} p_1(x)dx \right. \\
&\quad \left. - \left(\int_{-\infty}^{+\infty} x e^{\theta x} p_1(x)dx \right)^2 \right] \times \left[\int_{-\infty}^{+\infty} e^{\theta x} p_1(x)dx \right]^{-2} \\
&= (I(2,a)I(0,a) - I(1,a)^2)/I(0.a)^2,
\end{aligned}
$$

and by the Cauchy-Schwarz inequality, $I(2,a)I(0,a) \geq I(1,a)^2$. Since x and 1 are linearly independent, the last inequality is strict, and Eq. (4.9) and Lemma obtain. $\qquad \square$

Notice that condition Eq. (4.8) is easy to verify once an explicit formula for $\psi^{\mathbf{P}}$ is chosen. For processes in the empirical studies of financial markets, Eq. (4.8) is usually satisfied.

4.1.2 General case

We assume that X is a purely discontinuous Lévy process under **P**, with the generating triplet $(0, b, \Pi(dx))$. For a similar result for processes with the non-trivial Gaussian component, see Proposition 2.19 in Raible (2000).

Following Eberlein and Jacod (1997), we write $\mathcal{M}_r$ for the (possibly empty) class of measures locally equivalent to **P**, under which $e^{-rt}S(t)$ is a martingale, and $\mathcal{M}'_r$ for a subclass of $\mathcal{M}_r$ under which X is again a Lévy process; $\mathcal{Y}_{b,r}(\Pi(dx))$ denotes a class of functions $y : \mathbf{R} \to (0, +\infty)$ such that

$$\int_{-\infty}^{+\infty} (\sqrt{y(x)} - 1)^2 \Pi(dx) + \int_{\{x>1\}} (e^x - 1)y(x)\Pi(dx) < +\infty, \qquad (4.10)$$

and

$$b - r + \int_{-\infty}^{+\infty} ((e^x - 1)y(x) - x\mathbf{1}_{[-1,1]}(x))\Pi(dx). \qquad (4.11)$$

Theorem 4.1 *a) If $\mathcal{Y}_{b,r}(\Pi(dx)) = \emptyset$, then $\mathcal{M}_r = \mathcal{M}'_r = \emptyset$.*

b) If $\mathcal{Y}_{b,r}(\Pi(dx)) \neq \emptyset$, then both $\mathcal{M}_r$ and $\mathcal{M}'_r$ are non-empty, and for each $y \in \mathcal{Y}_{b,r}(\Pi(dx))$, there is a measure $\mathbf{Q} \in \mathcal{M}'_r$ under which X is again a Lévy process with the generating triplet $(0, b', \Pi'(dx))$, where

$$b' = b + \int_{-1}^{1} x(y(x) - 1)\Pi(dx), \qquad (4.12)$$

and

$$\Pi'(A) = \int_A y(x)\Pi(dx); \qquad (4.13)$$

conversely, if $\mathbf{Q} \in \mathcal{M}'_r$ is the measure under which X is a Lévy process, then its generating triplet is $(0, b', \Pi'(dx))$, where b' and $\Pi'(dx)$ are given by Eq. (4.12) and Eq. (4.13).

*c) Let y and $\mathbf{Q}$ be as in b). Then the characteristic exponents of X under **P** and **Q** are related by*

$$\psi^{\mathbf{Q}}(\xi) - \psi^{\mathbf{P}}(\xi) = \int_{-\infty}^{+\infty} (1 - e^{ix\xi})(y(x) - 1)\Pi(dx), \qquad (4.14)$$

and Eq. (4.12) can be written as

$$r + \psi^{\mathbf{Q}}(-i) = 0. \qquad (4.15)$$

Proof.   a) and the first part of b) are Proposition 1 in Eberlein and Jacod (1997); the converse part of b) is from Proposition 2.19 in Raible (2000). Notice that the integral in Eq. (4.12) converges due to the Cauchy-Schwarz inequality:

$$\left(\int_{-1}^{1} x(y(x)-1)\Pi(dx)\right)^2 \le \int_{-1}^{1}(\sqrt{y(x)}-1)^2\Pi(dx)\int_{-1}^{1}(\sqrt{y(x)}+1)^2 x^2\Pi(dx).$$

The first factor in the RHS is finite due to Eq. (4.10), and the second factor is bounded since both $\Pi(dx)$ and $y(x)\Pi(dx)$ are Lévy measures.

c) We use Eq. (4.12) and Eq. (4.13)

$$
\begin{aligned}
\psi^{\mathbf{Q}}(\xi) &= -ib'\xi + \int_{-\infty}^{+\infty}(1 - e^{ix\xi} + ix\xi\mathbf{1}_{[-1,1]}(x))y(x)\Pi(dx) \\
&= -ib\xi + \int_{-\infty}^{+\infty}(1 - e^{ix\xi} + ix\xi\mathbf{1}_{[-1,1]}(x))\Pi(dx) \\
&\quad + \int_{-\infty}^{+\infty}(1 - e^{ix\xi})(y(x) - 1)\Pi(dx) \\
&= \psi^{\mathbf{P}}(\xi) + \int_{-\infty}^{+\infty}(1 - e^{ix\xi})(y(x) - 1)\Pi(dx),
\end{aligned}
$$

and Eq. (4.14) follows. Eq. (4.15) is immediate.   □

It is straightforward to deduce from Theorem 4.1 the following description of a wide class of EMM for an RLPE.

Theorem 4.2   *Let X be an RLPE in the sense of the first definition, of order $\nu > 0$ and exponential type $[\lambda_-, \lambda_+]$, where $\lambda_- < -1 < 0 < \lambda_+$.*

Let $\gamma > \nu/2$, $\mu_- < -1 < 0 < \mu_+$, and let y be a positive measurable function which satisfies Eq. (4.11) and the following conditions:

$$
\begin{aligned}
|y(x) - 1| &\le C|x|^{\gamma}, & |x| &\le 1; & (4.16) \\
y(x) &\le Ce^{(-\lambda_+ + \mu_+)x}, & x &< -1; & (4.17) \\
y(x) &\le Ce^{(-\lambda_- + \mu_-)x}, & x &> 1. & (4.18)
\end{aligned}
$$

Then

(i) *there exists a measure $\mathbf{Q} \in \mathcal{M}'_r$ under which X is an RLPE of order ν and exponential type $[\mu_-, \mu_+]$, with the generating triplet $(0, b', \Pi'(dx))$;*

(ii) the characteristic exponent of X under $\mathbf{Q}$ is given by Eq. (4.14). It is holomorphic in the strip $\Im\xi \in (\mu_-, \mu_+)$ and continuous up to the boundary of the strip, and admits a representation

$$\psi^{\mathbf{Q}}(\xi) = -i\mu\xi + \phi^{\mathbf{Q}}(\xi), \tag{4.19}$$

where μ is the same as μ in Eq. (3.45) for $\psi^{\mathbf{P}}$, and $\phi^{\mathbf{Q}}$ enjoys the property Eq. (3.46):

(iii) there exists $\nu_2 < \nu$ such that as $\xi \to \infty$ in the strip $\Im\xi \in [\mu_-, \mu_+]$,

$$\phi^{\mathbf{Q}}(\xi) = c|\xi|^{\nu} + O(|\xi|^{\nu_2}), \tag{4.20}$$

where c is the same as c in Eq. (3.46) for $\psi^{\mathbf{P}}$.

Proof. From Eq. (4.16)–Eq. (4.18) and the conditions on the rate of the decay of the Lévy density $\Pi(dx)$, we see that Eq. (4.10) holds, and (i) follows from Theorem 4.1. In view of Eq. (3.45)–Eq. (3.46) and Eq. (4.14), it suffices to show that the RHS in Eq. (4.14) is holomorphic in the strip $\Im\xi \in [\mu_-, \mu_+]$, and satisfies an estimate

$$\left| \int_{-\infty}^{+\infty} (1 - e^{ix\xi})(y(x) - 1)\Pi(dx) \right| = O(|\xi|^{\nu_2}). \tag{4.21}$$

as $\xi \to \infty$ in the strip. The analyticity in the strip has been discusses already, and Eq. (4.21) is proved by using Eq. (4.16) in the same way as the conditions of the second definition of RLPE were deduced from the conditions of the first one. (See Chapter 3). $\qquad\square$

It is easy to construct many functions y which satisfy the conditions of Theorem 4.2, thereby constructing many examples of EMM.

Example 4.2 Let X be a KoBoL of order $\nu > 0$, with steepness parameters $\lambda_- < -1 < 0 < \lambda_+$. Take $a, d > 0$, $\gamma \in (\nu/2, \nu)$, and to give more weight to negative jumps, choose $\mu_+ \in (0, \lambda_+)$, and set

$$y(x) = e^{ax} + dx_-^{\gamma} e^{(\mu_+ - \lambda_+)x}.$$

(The second term makes the left tail of the Lévy density fatter). Then Eq. (4.10) holds, and direct computations (essentially the same as in the calculation of a KoBoL process in Section 3.1) show that

$$\psi^{\mathbf{Q}}(\xi) = \psi^{\mathbf{P}}(\xi - ia) - \psi^{\mathbf{P}}(-ia) + cd\Gamma(\gamma - \nu)(\mu_+^{\nu-\gamma} - (\mu_+ + i\xi)^{\nu-\gamma}). \tag{4.22}$$

If

$$r + \psi^{\mathbf{P}}(-i - ia) - \psi^{\mathbf{P}}(-ia) + cd\Gamma(\gamma - \nu)(\mu_+^{\nu-\gamma} - (\mu_+ + 1)^{\nu-\gamma}) = 0, \quad (4.23)$$

then Eq. (4.11) holds, and $\mathbf{Q}$ is an EMM.

If Eq. (4.23) has a solution, then generically, the manifold of solutions is two-dimensional, and hence, we obtain a two-parameter family of EMM. By taking more terms in the definition of y, we can obtain EMM depending on more parameters.

4.2 Pricing of European options and the generalized Black-Scholes formula

From now on, we assume that an EMM $\mathbf{Q}$ is chosen, and that X is an RLPE under EMM, of order $\nu > 0$ and exponential type $[\lambda_-, \lambda_+]$. We will assume that $\lambda_- < -1 < 0 < \lambda_+$, which is close to the necessary conditions: $\lambda_- \leq -1$ is necessary for the stock to be priced, and $\lambda_+ \geq 0$ holds for any exponential Lévy process. The case $\lambda_- = -1, \lambda_+ = 0$ can also be considered but at the expense of more technical and lengthy constructions.

To simplify the notation, we denote the expectation operator and characteristic exponent under $\mathbf{Q}$ by E and ψ, respectively, the only exception being the section on the locally risk-minimizing hedging, where we will use both the historic measure and an EMM.

4.2.1 *Pricing formulas: convolution with the pricing kernel and the Fourier-inversion formula*

Let $g(X_T)$ be the (non-negative) terminal payoff for a contingent claim with the expiry date T. Then at time $t < T$, the no-arbitrage price of the claim can be found from

$$e^{-rt}F(S_t, t) = E[e^{-rT}g(X_T) \mid X_t = x], \quad (4.24)$$

where $x = \ln S_t$. Let an explicit formula for the probability density of X under $\mathbf{Q}$ be known as it is the case with NIG. Then we deduce from Eq. (4.24)

$$F(S_t, t) = e^{-r\tau} \int_{-\infty}^{+\infty} p_\tau(y)g(x + y)dy,$$

where $\tau = T - t$ is the time to the expiry; by the change of variable $y \mapsto y - x$,

$$F(S_t, t) = e^{-r\tau} \int_{-\infty}^{+\infty} p_\tau(y - x)g(y)dy. \tag{4.25}$$

In the general case, p_τ can be expressed in terms of the characteristic exponent, by using the Fourier transform

$$p_\tau(x) = (2\pi)^{-1} \int_{-\infty}^{+\infty} e^{-ix\xi - \tau\psi(\xi)}d\xi, \tag{4.26}$$

and Eq. (4.25) assumes the form

$$F(S_t, t) = (2\pi)^{-1} \int_{-\infty}^{+\infty} \int_{-\infty}^{+\infty} e^{i(x-y)\xi - \tau(r+\psi(\xi))}g(y)d\xi dy. \tag{4.27}$$

Let g be measurable, and let there exist $\sigma \in (\lambda_-, \lambda_+)$ such that the function g_σ defined by $g_\sigma(x) := e^{\sigma x}g(x)$ belongs to the class $L_1(\mathbf{R})$. Then we can define

$$\hat{g}(\xi) = \int_{-\infty}^{+\infty} e^{-iy\xi}g(y)dy$$

on the line $\Im\xi = \sigma$. On the strength of Eq. (3.48), we can apply the Cauchy theorem and shift the line of the integration in the inner integral in Eq. (4.27):

$$F(S_t, t) = (2\pi)^{-1} \int_{-\infty}^{+\infty} \int_{-\infty+i\sigma}^{+\infty+i\sigma} e^{i(x-y)\xi - \tau(r+\psi(\xi))}g(y)d\xi dy.$$

Now the integral converges absolutely, and we can change the order of integration and obtain

$$F(S_t, t) = (2\pi)^{-1} \int_{-\infty+i\sigma}^{+\infty+i\sigma} e^{ix\xi - \tau(r+\psi(\xi))}\hat{g}(\xi)d\xi. \tag{4.28}$$

Set $f(x, t) = F(e^x, t)$. Then by using the notation of PDO, we can write Eq. (4.28) as

$$f(x, t) = \exp[-\tau(r + \psi(D_x))]g(x). \tag{4.29}$$

4.2.2   Call and put options

For the call option with the strike price K, the terminal payoff is $g(X_T) = (e^{X_T} - K)_+$, and hence $g_\sigma \in L_1(\mathbf{R})$ for any $\sigma < -1$. Since $\lambda_- < -1$, we can choose $\sigma \in (\lambda_-, -1)$, and apply Eq. (4.28). The direct calculation gives

$$
\begin{aligned}
\hat{g}(\xi) &= \int_{-\infty}^{+\infty} e^{-ix\xi}(e^x - K)_+ dx \\
&= \int_{\ln K}^{+\infty} (e^{x(1-i\xi)} - Ke^{-i\xi x}) dx \\
&= \frac{e^{(1-i\xi)\ln K}}{i(\xi+i)} - \frac{e^{(1-i\xi)\ln K}}{i\xi} \\
&= -\frac{Ke^{-i\xi\ln K}}{\xi(\xi+i)},
\end{aligned}
\tag{4.30}
$$

and by substituting into Eq. (4.28), we obtain the pricing formula for the European call option:

$$
F_{\mathrm{call}}(S_t, t) = -\frac{K}{2\pi} \int_{-\infty+i\sigma}^{+\infty+i\sigma} \frac{\exp[i\xi\ln(S_t/K) - \tau(r + \psi(\xi))]}{\xi(\xi+i)} d\xi,
\tag{4.31}
$$

where $\sigma \in (\lambda_-, -1)$ is arbitrary. This is the generalization of the Black-Scholes formula for calls.

Similarly, for the put option with the strike price K, the terminal payoff is $g(X_T) = (K - e^{X_T})_+$, and hence $g_\sigma \in L_1(\mathbf{R})$ for any $\sigma > 0$. Since $\lambda_+ > 0$, we can choose $\sigma \in (0, \lambda_+)$, and apply Eq. (4.28). The result is

$$
F_{\mathrm{put}}(S_t, t) = -\frac{K}{2\pi} \int_{-\infty+i\sigma_2}^{+\infty+i\sigma_2} \frac{\exp[i\xi\ln(S_t/K) - \tau(r + \psi(\xi))]}{\xi(\xi+i)} d\xi,
\tag{4.32}
$$

where $\sigma_2 \in (0, \lambda_+)$ is arbitrary.

The integrals in Eq. (4.31)–Eq. (4.32) can be calculated by using the Fast Fourier Transform (FFT), its modifications, and other methods. We consider these methods in Chapter 12.

Since the integrand in Eq. (4.31)–Eq. (4.32) is meromorphic in the strip $\Im\xi \in [\sigma, \sigma_2]$ with two poles at $\xi = -i$ and $\xi = 0$ and decays as $\xi \to \infty$ in the strip, we may shift the line of the integration in Eq. (4.31) up. The line of integration crosses the two poles, and the residue theorem gives

$$
F_{\mathrm{call}}(S_t, t) = -\frac{K}{2\pi}(2\pi i)\frac{\exp[i(-i)\ln(S_t/K) - \tau(r + \psi(-i))]}{-i}
$$

$$-\frac{K}{2\pi}(2\pi i)\frac{\exp[i0\ln(S_t/K) - \tau(r + \psi(0))]}{i}$$
$$+F_{\text{put}}(S_t, t).$$

By taking into account that $\psi(0) = 0$ and $r + \psi(-i) = 0$, since we price the options under an EMM, we obtain the so-called *put-call parity* relation

$$F_{\text{call}}(S_t, t) = S_t - Ke^{-r\tau} + F_{\text{put}}(S_t, t). \tag{4.33}$$

Of course, the put-call parity relation can be deduced in a much simpler way, and it is valid for no-arbitrage pricing under any process, for which the option prices are finite: it suffices to notice that the difference between the payoff of the call and the payoff of the put, with the same strike price, is equal to $S_T - K$, and apply Eq. (4.24).

4.2.3   *Numerical examples: the comparison with the Black-Scholes formula, and the shapes of the smile*

First, we give several series of examples for put pricing under KoBoL processes, when an EMM is the Esscher transform of the historic measure. The characteristic exponent of the process under the historic measure is of the form

$$\psi(\xi) = -i\mu\xi + c\Gamma(-\nu)[\lambda_+{}^\nu - (\lambda_+ + i\xi)^\nu + (-\lambda_-)^\nu - (-\lambda_- - i\xi)^\nu],$$

where $\mu \in \mathbf{R}, \nu \in (0, 2], \nu \neq 1, c > 0$, and $\lambda_+ > 0 > \lambda_-$ (in the case $\nu = 1$, the formula for the characteristic exponent is different: see Eq. (3.8)). When $\nu = 2$, we obtain a Brownian motion. Parameters are chosen so that the Esscher transform exists. In each series, we vary the strike-price ratio S/K, and one of the parameters, the remaining ones being fixed; the spot price of the stock is 100. To facilitate the comparison with the Black-Scholes formula, in each series we fix $m_1 = i\psi'(0)$ and $m_2 = \psi''(0)$. On the left panel, we plot the difference between the Black-Scholes price and the KoBoL price of the put, and on the right panel, we plot the implied volatility. Were the Black-Scholes model correct, the implied volatility would have been equal to m_2, and the implied volatility surface flat. The reader is advised to compare the pictures below with similar pictures in Eberlein *et al.* (1998) and Eberlein and Prause (2001) for option pricing under Hyperbolic Processes, Normal Inverse Gaussian processes and Generalized Hyperbolic processes.

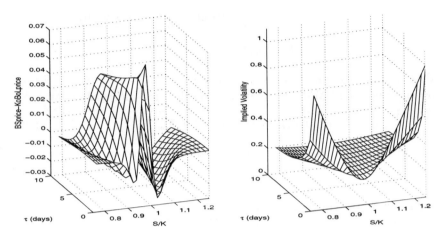

Fig. 4.1   Black-Scholes price vs. KoBoL price: dependence on the moneyness and time to expiry. Parameters: $r = 0.05, m_1 = 0.12, m_2 = 0.18, \nu = 1.4, \lambda_- = -24, \lambda_+ = 20$.

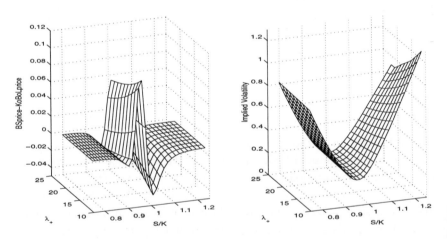

Fig. 4.2   Black-Scholes price vs. KoBoL price: dependence on the moneyness and the left steepness parameter, λ_+. Parameters: $r = 0.05, m_1 = 0.12, m_2 = 0.18, \nu = 1.4, \lambda_- = -24, \tau = 1$ (day).

In Fig. 4.1, it is easily seen that the volatility smile becomes more pronounced as $\tau \to 0$. Fig. 4.2 demonstrates that in the region where the steepness parameters are large, the dependence of the price on these parameters is weak. This is the good news since the steepness parameters

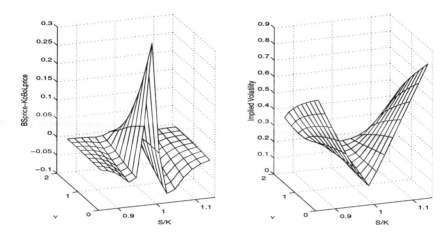

Fig. 4.3   Black-Scholes price vs. KoBoL price: dependence on the moneyness and the order of the process, ν. Parameters: $r = 0.05, m_1 = 0.12, m_2 = 0.18, \lambda_- = -24, \lambda_+ = 20, \tau = 1$ (day).

are especially difficult to infer from the data with a reasonable degree of accuracy. In the region where the steepness parameters are small, the dependence of the price on these parameters can be quite sizable. Since λ_+ and $-\lambda_-$ do not differ much, the smile is almost symmetric. By playing with steepness parameters, it is not difficult to obtain smiles of different shapes.

Fig. 4.3 shows that the order of the process, ν, is the most important parameter. As $\nu \to 2$ and/or $\min\{\lambda_+, -\lambda_-\} \to +\infty$ so that m_1 and m_2 remain fixed, the KoBoL price converges to the Black-Scholes price; the difference is especially large for small ν and/or λ_+ and $-\lambda_-$.

In the last series of numerical examples, we consider the process which is characterized by the same parameters as in Fig. 4.1 (in particular, $\nu = 1.4, \lambda_+ = 20, \lambda_- = -24$), but instead of the Esscher transform, we use the family of EMM constructed in Example 4.2, with $\mu_+ = 0.5, \gamma = 1$, and $a = \theta, \theta + 0.05, \ldots, \theta + 0.3$. For each value of a, we find d so that the EMM-condition $r + \psi^Q(-i) = 0$ holds. Thus, $a = \theta$ gives the Esscher transform. The larger the a, the more weight the EMM places on extreme events.

By comparing Fig. 4.1-4.3 with Fig. 4.4, we see that it is easier to obtain asymmetric smiles with EMM different from the Esscher transform.

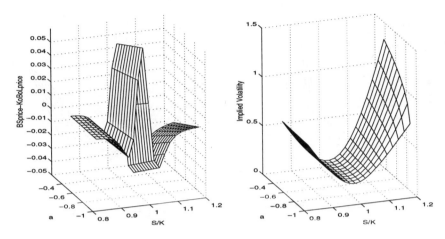

Fig. 4.4   Black-Scholes price vs. KoBoL price: EMM from Example 4.2. Parameters: $r = 0.05, m_1 = 0.12, m_2 = 0.18, \nu = 1.4, \lambda_- = -24, \lambda_+ = 20, \mu_+ = 0.5, \gamma = 1, \tau = 1$ (day).

4.2.4   *The problem of the model fitting and evaluation*

Once a model for the observed process (i.e., for the historic measure and for an EMM are chosen) one has to fit the parameters of the historic measure and EMM to data. Different methods can be used:

- all the parameters can be obtained by the maximum likelihood method or the method of least squares;
- some of the parameters can be determined separately by using other considerations, and the rest are determined by the maximum likelihood method, etc.

Clearly, it is easier to fit the parameters of the historic measure to data, and the parameters of the historic measure can be used to find some parameters of an EMM, due to Theorem 4.1, which implies some relationship between sets of the parameters of $\mathbf{P}$ and $\mathbf{Q}$. In particular, if X is an RLPE under $\mathbf{P}$, of order $\nu \in (0, 2)$, then it is an RLPE under $\mathbf{Q}$, of the same order, and with the same constant $c > 0$ in Eq. (3.46). Should one decide to look for $\mathbf{P}$ and $\mathbf{Q}$ in the same model class of RLPE, then after the parameters of $\mathbf{P}$ are fitted to the historic data and the EMM-condition $r + \psi^{\mathbf{Q}}(-i) = 0$ is taken into account, not many free parameters remain. For instance, in the case of KoBoL family, with c and ν fixed, the EMM condition determine the line of admissible points in the $(\mu, \lambda_-, \lambda_+)$-plane. In the case of GHP, not only the order 1 and the parameter $\delta(= c$ in the general definition of RLPE) are the same for **P** and **Q**, but the drift parameter μ as well (see Raible (2000), Proposition 2.20). Since the class GHP is a 5-parametric family, the EMM-condition leaves 2 free parameters. If one wishes to work with a subclass of NIG, only one free parameter remains.

Finally, we would like to notice that by using the asymptotic formulas for the prices of the up-and-out and down-and-out options near the barrier, which we obtain in Chapter 7 (or similar formulas for barrier options), and the observed prices of these options near the barrier, we can infer whether there is a diffusion component or not. Further, if there is none and hence, the process is of order $\nu \in (0, 2)$, then one can obtain the following information about the EMM chosen by the market without using the data on the stock itself: first, whether ν belongs to $(1, 2)$, $(0, 1)$ or $\{1\}$, and then

(i) if $\nu \in (1, 2)$, then to find ν;
(ii) if $\nu = 1$, then to obtain a simple relation between the parameters c and μ in Eq. (3.45)-Eq. (3.46);
(iii) if $\nu \in (0, 1)$, then decide whether the drift $\mu = 0$ or not, and

- if $\mu = 0$, then to find ν;
- if $\mu \neq 0$, then to find the sign of μ.

Thus, the data on the touch-and-out options and barrier options near the barrier can be used to decide whether the chosen class of processes is suitable for pricing of options on a given stock or not.

For more details, see the next section.

4.3 Generalized Black-Scholes equation and its properties for different RLPE and different choices of EMM, and implications for parameter fitting

Differentiate $f(x, t) = F(e^x, t)$ w.r.t. t by using Eq. (4.28) in the domain $t < T, x \in \mathbf{R}$; due to Eq. (3.48), we may differentiate under the integral sign and obtain, by using the definition of PDO:

$$
\begin{aligned}
\frac{\partial f}{\partial t}(x, t) &= (2\pi)^{-1} \int_{-\infty+i\sigma}^{+\infty+i\sigma} (r + \psi(\xi)) e^{ix\xi - \tau(r+\psi(\xi))} \hat{g}(\xi) d\xi \\
&= (r + \psi(D_x))(2\pi)^{-1} \int_{-\infty+i\sigma}^{+\infty+i\sigma} e^{ix\xi - \tau(r+\psi(\xi))} \hat{g}(\xi) d\xi
\end{aligned}
$$

$$= (r + \psi(D_x))f(x,t).$$

We conclude that the price f of a contingent claim of the European type satisfies the following equation

$$(\partial_t - (r + \psi^{\mathbf{Q}}(D_x)))f(x,t) = 0, \quad t < T,\ x \in \mathbf{R}. \qquad (4.34)$$

This is the generalization of the Black-Scholes equation. It can be deduced formally, by differentiating Eq. (4.29).

In the Introduction, we have demonstrated that if X is a Brownian motion then Eq. (4.34) becomes the Black-Scholes equation. Notice that we can write Eq. (4.34) in the form

$$(r - \tilde{L}^{\mathbf{Q}})f(x,t) = 0, \quad t < T,\ x \in \mathbf{R}, \qquad (4.35)$$

where $\tilde{L}^{\mathbf{Q}} = \partial_t + L^{\mathbf{Q}}$, and $L^{\mathbf{Q}} = -\psi^{\mathbf{Q}}(D_x)$ is the infinitesimal generator of X under $\mathbf{Q}$.

In Eq. (4.34), we have explicitly indicated an EMM $\mathbf{Q}$ in order to discuss the dependence of properties of the operator in the generalized Black-Scholes equation on a choice of an EMM $\mathbf{Q}$. From Eq. (4.19)–Eq. (4.20) and Eq. (3.45)–Eq. (3.46), we conclude that the difference $\psi^{\mathbf{Q}}(\xi) - \psi^{\mathbf{P}}(\xi)$ grows slower than $\Re\psi^{\mathbf{P}}(\xi)$, as $\xi \to \infty$ in the common strip of the analyticity. In the language of the theory of PDO, this means that the replacement of $\psi^{\mathbf{P}}$ with $\psi^{\mathbf{Q}}$ is a weak perturbation, and the local properties of the operator remain essentially the same. In particular, we will see that the orders of the factors in the Wiener-Hopf factorization formula are independent of the choice of EMM, and derive from this observation that the leading term of the price of a barrier option (or a touch-and-out option) near the barrier is independent of a choice of EMM. This property can be used to infer some relations for parameters (ν, c) (and in the case $\nu \le 1$, for μ as well) of an RLPE from observed prices of barrier options and touch-and-out options.

General properties of the Generalized Black-Scholes equation depend on the order of the process as follows: if $\nu \ge 1$ or $\nu < 1$ but the drift $\mu = 0$, then the stationary part of $\psi^{\mathbf{Q}}$ is strongly elliptic, and it is not if $\nu < 1$ and $\mu \ne 0$. In the latter case, the price of a barrier option (and a touch-and-out option) may be discontinuous at the barrier, whereas in the former case, these prices are always continuous up to the boundary. Thus, by using the empirical data, it is possible to decide whether processes of order $\nu < 1$ with the non-zero drift are suitable for modelling purposes at all. From the point of view of the theory of PDO, strongly elliptic operators enjoy much more favourable properties than non-strongly-elliptic ones, and so it is advisable to use processes of order $\nu \geq 1$ or processes of order $\nu < 1$ with zero drift.

4.4 Other European options

We consider several examples; the reader can easily calculate the prices of other options.

4.4.1 *Power options*

Consider a call-like option with the payoff $(S_T^\beta - K)_+$, where $\beta > 0$ is typically equal to 2. In order that the price be finite, we need to assume that $\beta \leq -\lambda_-$. Assume for simplicity that the inequality is strict; then the calculations are essentially the same as for the call option above, and the result is

$$F(S_t, t) = -\frac{K}{2\pi} \int_{-\infty+i\sigma}^{+\infty+i\sigma} \frac{\beta \exp[i\xi \ln(S_t/K^{1/\beta}) - \tau(r + \psi(\xi))]}{\xi(\xi + i\beta)} d\xi, \quad (4.36)$$

for any $\sigma \in (\lambda_-, -\beta)$.

4.4.2 *Digital options*

For the *digital call option* with the strike price K, the terminal payoff is 1, if $S_T \geq K$, and 0 otherwise. Hence, $g(x) = \mathbf{1}_{[K,+\infty)}(x)$, and for any $\sigma < 0$, and $\Im \xi = \sigma$,

$$
\begin{aligned}
\hat{g}(\xi) &= \int_{-\infty}^{+\infty} e^{-ix\xi} g(x) dx \\
&= \int_{\ln K}^{+\infty} e^{-ix\xi} dx \\
&= \frac{\exp[-i\xi \ln K]}{i\xi}.
\end{aligned}
$$

We choose $\sigma \in (\lambda_-, 0)$, and substitute into Eq. (4.28):

$$F(S_t, t) = (2\pi)^{-1} \int_{-\infty+i\sigma}^{+\infty+i\sigma} e^{i\xi \ln(S_T/K)} (i\xi)^{-1} d\xi. \quad (4.37)$$

Similarly, for the *digital put option* with the strike price K, the terminal payoff is 1, if $S_T \leq K$, and 0 otherwise, and we obtain

$$F(S_t, t) = (2\pi)^{-1} \int_{-\infty+i\sigma_2}^{+\infty+i\sigma_2} e^{i\xi \ln(S_T/K)} (i\xi)^{-1} d\xi, \qquad (4.38)$$

for any $\sigma_2 \in (0, \lambda_+)$.

4.4.3 *Combinations*

There are several types of options whose payoffs are linear combinations of various calls, puts, and constants. For instance, a *straddle* is the option with the payoff of the form

$$g(S_T) = |S_T - K| - C = (K - S_T)_+ + (S_T - K)_+ - C,$$

therefore the price of the straddle is

$$F_{\text{straddle}}(S_t, t) = F_{\text{call}}(S_t, t) + F_{\text{put}}(S_t, t) - e^{-r\tau}C, \qquad (4.39)$$

and an explicit expression can be obtained by substituting Eq. (4.31)–Eq. (4.32) into Eq. (4.39).

Similarly, the reader can calculate prices of other combinations. Typically, the payoffs are piece-wise linear in S, though power analogues can also be considered.

4.4.4 *General case: the condition on the rate of growth of the payoff at the infinity and the origin*

Generically, the payoff may be non-zero in neighbourhoods of both $S_T = 0$ and $S_T = +\infty$, and there may be no $\sigma \in (\lambda_-, \lambda_+)$ such that $g_\sigma(\cdot) = e^\sigma \cdot g(\cdot)$ is of the class $L_1(\mathbf{R})$. In this case, we assume that g is measurable (one is tempted to say "continuous" but there are options with discontinuous payoffs), and that there exist $\omega_-, \omega_+ \in (\lambda_-, \lambda_+)$ such that

$$e^{\omega_\pm \cdot} \mathbf{1}_{\mathbf{R}_\pm}(\cdot)g(\cdot) \in L_1(\mathbf{R}).$$

For any x_0, decompose the terminal payoff g in the sum of the following two functions

$$g^+(x_0; x) = \mathbf{1}_{[x_0, +\infty)}(x)g(x), \quad g^-(x_0; x) = \mathbf{1}_{(-\infty, x_0]}(x)g(x),$$

and calculate the option price

$$
\begin{aligned}
F(g; S_t, t) &= F(g^+; S_t, t) + F(g^-; S_t, t) \qquad (4.40)\\
&= (2\pi)^{-1} \int_{-\infty+i\omega_-}^{+\infty+i\omega_-} e^{ix\xi - \tau\psi(\xi)} \widehat{g^-}(\xi) d\xi \\
&\quad + (2\pi)^{-1} \int_{-\infty+i\omega_+}^{+\infty+i\omega_+} e^{ix\xi - \tau\psi(\xi)} \widehat{g^+}(\xi) d\xi.
\end{aligned}
$$

In order that the integrals converge better, it is advisable to choose x_0 to be one of the zeroes of g, if g is continuous; if it is not, a point of the discontinuity is a reasonable choice.

4.5 Hedging

4.5.1 *General discussion*

In the Black-Scholes model of the complete market, without frictions and constraints, the hedging problem is solved easily, and the risk can be completely hedged away. If the market is incomplete then the problem of the risk minimization, hence, the problem of the choice of an appropriate measure of risk arise. We derive the explicit formula for the *weights* of the *locally risk-minimizing* portfolio, and we do not require that the portfolio be self-financed; the idea of the locally risk-minimization is due to M. Schweizer (see Föllmer and Schweizer (1991)). This type of hedging is by no means the only one. The mean-variance approach to hedging is due to Föllmer and Sondermann (1986). They considered the optimisation problem

$$
\min E[(H - V_T^{x,\theta})^2]
$$

where the contingent claim H is an $\mathcal{F}_T$-measurable square integrable random variable, $V_T^{x,\theta}$ is the terminal value of a self-financed portfolio of the riskless bond and a risky asset with initial capital x and quantity θ invested in the risky asset. Föllmer and Sondermann (1986) solved the mean-variance problem in the martingale case, by the direct application of the Galtchouk-Kunita-Watanabe projection theorem. In the semimartingale case, this quadratic optimisation problem is solved by Gouriéroux *et al.* (1996). For further references and the extensive discussion of the *mean-variance hedging*, see Musiela and Rutkowski (1997) and Pham *et al.* (1998), and many other approaches to hedging, with variations, can be found in the references at the end of the chapter. For hedging under processes of Koponen's family, see Bouchaud and Potters (2000) and Matacz (2000).

We have chosen the *locally-risk minimizing hedging* in order to demonstrate in the simplest situation how the PDO-technique allows one to obtain analytical results.

4.5.2   *Locally risk-minimizing hedging ratio*

Suppose that an investor can go short in the money account, and consider the following problem: given the investor's wealth $W(t)$ at time $t < T$, where T is the expiration date of an option, construct a portfolio short one option, and long $\theta(t)$ shares of the stock, with the minimal expected variance the next infinitesimal moment $t + \Delta t < T$; the residual

$$w_0(t) := W(t) + F(S(t), t) - \theta(t)S(t) \tag{4.41}$$

is invested into the money account.

The price of the portfolio at time $t + \Delta t$ is

$$W(t + \Delta t) = -F(S(t + \Delta t), t + \Delta t) + \theta(t)S(t + \Delta t) + e^{rt}w_0(t);$$

we calculate the variance of wealth under **P** conditioned on the information available at the date t. Let $E_t^{\mathbf{P}}$ be the corresponding expectation operator. Then

$$
\begin{aligned}
& E_t^{\mathbf{P}}[(W(t + \Delta t) - E_t^{\mathbf{P}}[W(t + \Delta t)])^2] \\
= \; & E_t^{\mathbf{P}}[(F(S(t + \Delta t), t + \Delta t) - E_t^{\mathbf{P}}[F(S(t + \Delta t), t + \Delta t)])^2] \\
& - 2\theta(t)E_t^{\mathbf{P}}[(F(S(t + \Delta t), t + \Delta t) - E_t^{\mathbf{P}}[F(S(t + \Delta t), t + \Delta t)]) \\
& \qquad \times (S(t + \Delta t) - E_t^{\mathbf{P}}[S(t + \Delta t)])] \\
& + \theta(t)^2 E_t^{\mathbf{P}}[(S(t + \Delta t) - E_t^{\mathbf{P}}[S(t + \Delta t)])^2].
\end{aligned}
$$

Minimizing w.r.t. $\theta(t)$, we obtain the following first order condition:

$$\theta(t) = \theta(t, x; \Delta t) = \frac{FS(t, \Delta t)}{SS(t, \Delta t)}, \tag{4.42}$$

where

$$SS(t, \Delta t) = E_t^{\mathbf{P}}[S(t + \Delta t)^2] - E_t^{\mathbf{P}}[S(t + \Delta t)]^2,$$

and

$$
\begin{aligned}
FS(t, \Delta t) \;=\; & E_t^{\mathbf{P}}[F(S(t + \Delta t), t + \Delta t)S(t + \Delta t)] \\
& - E_t^{\mathbf{P}}[F(S(t + \Delta t), t + \Delta t)]E_t^{\mathbf{P}}[S(t + \Delta t)].
\end{aligned}
$$

Suppose that under $\mathbf{P}$, X is of exponential type $[\lambda_-, \lambda_+]$ with $\lambda_- \leq -2$; then $SS(t, \Delta t) < +\infty$, and an explicit formula for $SS(t, \Delta t)$ is immediate from the definition of the characteristic exponent

$$
SS(t, \Delta t) = \left(e^{-\Delta t \psi^{\mathbf{P}}(-2i)} - e^{-2\Delta t \psi^{\mathbf{P}}(-i)} \right) S(t)^2.
$$

By expanding into the Taylor series around $\Delta t = 0$, we obtain

$$
SS(t, \Delta t) = (-\psi^{\mathbf{P}}(-2i) + 2\psi^{\mathbf{P}}(-i))S(t)^2 \Delta t + O(\Delta t^2). \tag{4.43}
$$

To obtain a similar representation for $FS(t, \Delta t)$, we need an additional restriction on $[\lambda_-, \lambda_+]$, the exponential type of X under $\mathbf{P}$, and a similar restriction on $[\mu_-, \mu_+]$, the exponential type of X under $\mathbf{Q}$. Both depend on the rate of growth of the terminal payoff $g(X_T)$ of the option at the infinity. We assume that for some $\sigma \in (\mu_-, \mu_+)$, $g_\sigma \in L_1(\mathbf{R})$, and $\lambda_- < \sigma - 1 < \lambda_+$; then the justification of the following calculations is an easy exercise.

First, notice an evident formula for the infinitesimal generator $\hat{L}$ of the two-dimensional process $\{\hat{H}_t\} = \{(X_t, t)\}$, where X is regarded as a Lévy process under $\mathbf{P}$:

$$
\hat{L} = \partial_t + L^{\mathbf{P}} = \partial_t - \psi^{\mathbf{P}}(D_x). \tag{4.44}
$$

By using Eq. (4.44), we obtain

$$
E_t^{\mathbf{P}}[F(S(t + \Delta t), t + \Delta t)S(t + \Delta t)] - F(S(t), t)S(t) \tag{4.45}
$$

$$
= (\partial_t - \psi^{\mathbf{P}}(D_x))f(x, t)e^x \Delta t + o(\Delta t),
$$

and

$$
E_t^{\mathbf{P}}[F(S(t + \Delta t), t + \Delta t)] - F(S(t), t) \tag{4.46}
$$

$$
= (\partial_t - \psi^{\mathbf{P}}(D_x))f(x, t)\Delta t + o(\Delta t).
$$

Since

$$
\psi^{\mathbf{P}}(D_x)e^x v(x) = e^x \psi^{\mathbf{P}}(D_x - i)v(x),
$$

and

$$
\begin{aligned}
E_t^{\mathbf{P}}[S(t+\Delta t)] - S(t) &= (\exp[-\Delta t \psi^{\mathbf{P}}(-i)] - 1)S(t) \\
&= \Delta t \psi^{\mathbf{P}}(-i)e^x + o(\Delta t),
\end{aligned}
$$

we derive from Eq. (4.45)-Eq. (4.46) the representation

$$
\begin{aligned}
FS(t, \Delta t) &= e^x \Delta t [-\psi^{\mathbf{P}}(D_x - i) + \psi^{\mathbf{P}}(D_x) \qquad (4.47) \\
&\quad + \psi^{\mathbf{P}}(-i)] F(e^x, t) + o(\Delta t).
\end{aligned}
$$

Now we can substitute the result and Eq. (4.43) into Eq. (4.42), and obtain

$$
\theta(t, x; \Delta t) = e^{-x} B^{\mathbf{P}}(D_x) F(e^x, t) + O(\Delta t),
$$

where $x = \ln S(t)$, and

$$
B^{\mathbf{P}}(\xi) = \frac{-\psi^{\mathbf{P}}(\xi - i) + \psi^{\mathbf{P}}(\xi) + \psi^{\mathbf{P}}(-i)}{-\psi^{\mathbf{P}}(-2i) + 2\psi^{\mathbf{P}}(-i)}. \qquad (4.48)
$$

In the limit $\Delta t \to +0$, we obtain

$$
\theta(t, x) = e^{-x} B^{\mathbf{P}}(D_x) F(e^x, t). \qquad (4.49)
$$

Example 4.3   Let X_t be a Brownian motion. Then

$$
\psi(\xi) = -i\mu\xi + \sigma^2 \xi^2 / 2,
$$

and therefore,

$$
B^{\mathbf{P}}(\xi) = \frac{-(\xi - i)^2 + (\xi)^2 + (-i)^2}{-(-2i)^2 + 2(-i)^2} = \frac{2i\xi}{2} = i\xi.
$$

Hence,

$$
B^{\mathbf{P}}(D_x) = i(-i\partial_x) = \partial_x,
$$

and

$$
\theta(t, x) = (\partial_x f) \cdot e^{-x} = \partial_S F(S(t), t).
$$

Thus, we recover the standard Black-Scholes *delta-hedging* result.

4.5.3 *Continuity of the locally risk-minimizing hedging ratio till the expiry*

In the Black-Scholes model, for calls and puts, $\theta(t,x)$ is discontinuous for options at the money, near expiry, i.e., at $(t,x) = (T,q)$, where $x = \ln S$, $q = \ln K$, and S and K are the spot and strike prices, respectively.

Let X be a mixture of independent RLPE of order $\nu < 2$, each satisfying Eq. (3.45)–Eq. (3.46) with $\nu_1 < 1$. Then from Eq. (3.45)–Eq. (3.46), it follows that

$$|B^{\mathbf{P}}(\xi)| \le C(1 + |\xi|)^\rho, \tag{4.50}$$

where $\rho = \min\{\nu - 1, \nu_1\} < 1$. By using Eq. (4.31), we conclude that in the case of a European call option, say, $\theta = \theta(t,x)$ is defined for all $(t,x) \in [0,T) \times \mathbf{R}$ by

$$\theta(t,x) = -\frac{K}{2\pi S} \int_{-\infty+i\sigma}^{+\infty+i\sigma} \frac{\exp[i\xi \ln(S/K) - \tau(r + \psi^{\mathbf{Q}}(\xi))]B^{\mathbf{P}}(\xi)}{\xi(\xi+i)} d\xi,$$

where $\sigma \in (\min\{\mu_-, \lambda_- - 1\}, -1)$. From Eq. (4.50), it follows that the integrand is bounded (in modulus) by

$$C_1(1 + |\xi|)^{-1-\epsilon},$$

where $\epsilon > 0$, and C_1 can be chosen the same for each $t < T$ and S/K on any compact. Since the integrand depends on t continuously, we conclude that $\theta(t,x)$ is continuous (in fact, Hölder continuous) on $(-\infty, +\infty) \times (-\infty, T]$.

This makes the hedging under purely discontinuous RLPE models more stable than the Gaussian hedging, near expiry; and at the strike, much more stable indeed.

4.5.4 *Numerical Examples*

In Fig. 4.5, we plot the KoBoL θ and the difference between θ's in the Gaussian and KoBoL models. We assume that the EMM is the Esscher transform of the historic measure, and we vary the time to expiry, τ, from 6 hours to 1 hour. We see that the KoBoL θ remains essentially stable whereas the difference with the Black-Scholes θ tangibly increases.

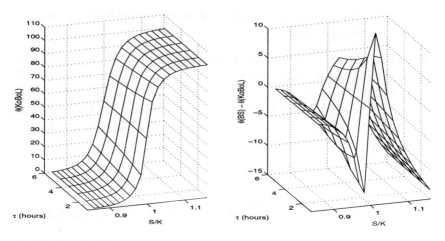

Fig. 4.5 Black-Scholes θ vs. KoBoL θ: dependence on the moneyness and time to expiry. Parameters: $r = 0.05, m_1 = 0.12, m_2 = 0.18, \nu = 1.4, \lambda_- = -24, \lambda_+ = 20, K = 100$.

4.6 Commentary

The results of this chapter are obtained in Boyarchenko and Levendorskii (1999a, 2000, 2001a). For the detailed study and empirical results on option pricing under Hyperbolic Processes and Generalized Hyperbolic Processes, see Eberlein *et al.* (1998), Keller (1997), Prause (1998), Raible (2000), Eberlein and Prause (2001). For different analytical formulas for option pricing and hedging under non-Gaussian processes, see Bouchaud and Potters (2000) and Matacz (2000).

Chapter 5

Perpetual American options

In this chapter, we consider several types of perpetual American options.
We start with the American puts and calls, and then consider more general
payoffs. We show that in some cases, the smooth pasting principle fails,
and discuss generalizations of this principle

5.1 The reduction to a free boundary problem for the stationary generalized Black-Scholes equation

5.1.1 General discussion

Options of the European type can be exercised only at the expiry date, T,
but the owner of the option of the *American* type has the right to exercise
the option at any time $t \in [0, T]$. If the expiry date is far away, one can use
the idealization $T = \infty$. An American option with the infinite time horizon
is called a *perpetual* option.

Let the riskless rate $r > 0$ and the dividend rate $q_0 \geq 0$ of the stock
be fixed, let $S_t = \exp X_t$ be the price process of the stock under a chosen
EMM; we assume that X is an RLPE. Let $g(X_t)$ be the payoff function
of a perpetual American option on the stock. For instance, for a put,
$g(x) = K - e^x$, and for a call, $g(x) = e^x - K$, where K is the strike price;
for the formulation of our results, it is more convenient to use $g(x)$ rather
than $\max\{g(x), 0\}$. Clearly, this departure from the conventional notation
is quite admissible since it is non-optimal to exercise the option in the
region $g(x) < 0$. The option owner chooses the optimal strategy, that is,
the stopping time τ, in order to maximize the expected discounted payoff

121

$E^x[e^{-q\tau}g(X_\tau)]$, where $x = \ln S$ is the logarithm of the spot price, $q = r + q_0$, and the expectation is taken under the EMM (see Shiryaev (1999), XVIII, 2). We consider stopping times satisfying $0 \leq \tau = \tau(\omega) < \infty$, $\omega \in \Omega$; the class of such stopping times will be denoted $\mathcal{M}$. Thus, $V_*(x)$, the *rational price* of the perpetual American option, is given by

$$V_*(x) = \sup_{\mathcal{M}} E^x[e^{-q\tau}g(X_\tau)]. \tag{5.1}$$

5.1.2   *Free boundary value problem for the price of the perpetual American option*

Suppose that the optimal stopping time is the *hitting time* of the exterior of an open set $\mathcal{C} \subset \mathbf{R}$:

$$\tau_* = \inf\{t \geq 0 \mid X_t \notin \mathcal{C}\}. \tag{5.2}$$

On the strength of Theorem 3.1 and Lemma 2.4, an RLPE satisfies (ACP)-condition, hence, in the case of $g \in L_\infty(B)$, where $B = \mathbf{R} \setminus \mathcal{C}$, we can apply Theorem 2.12 and conclude that V_* is a bounded solution to the following boundary value problem:

$$(q - L)u(x) \;=\; 0, \qquad x \in \mathcal{C}, \tag{5.3}$$

$$u(x) \;=\; g(x), \quad x \notin \mathcal{C}. \tag{5.4}$$

where $L = -\psi(D)$ is the infinitesimal generator of X (In the case of a non-bounded g, the approximation of g by bounded functions and the limiting procedure are needed to justify Eq. (5.3)-Eq. (5.4) - see Remark 2.1.) Notice that not only the function u is unknown but the boundary $\partial\mathcal{C}$ as well. Thus, we have a *free boundary value problem*. In the pure diffusion case, one finds a candidate for the optimal stopping time Eq. (5.2) or equivalently a boundary of $\mathcal{C}$ by using the smooth fit principle, which says that the optimal choice of the boundary ensures that $u \in C^1$, whereas with an non-optimal choice, u' is discontinuous at the boundary. Notice that this heuristic principle requires certain regularity of g, and after the boundary and solution are found, one has to verify that the solution is indeed optimal.

We will see that in the case of RLPE, the smooth pasting principle may fail, and so we will use other heuristic considerations to find the boundary. In cases when $\mathcal{C}$ is a semi-bounded interval with the boundary h (we denote the corresponding class of stopping times by $\mathcal{M}_0$), we obtain an explicit formula for $u = u(h, x)$, and by analysing the properties of the latter, find the unique candidate for the optimal h. The verification of the sufficient optimality conditions in the class $\mathcal{M}_0$ is relatively simple: we will be able to directly compare $V = V(h, x)$ for different h, and check that the candidate for the optimal boundary is indeed optimal.

5.1.3 Main Lemma

The verification of the optimality in the class $\mathcal{M}$ is much more tricky. Consider the following free boundary value problem.

Given a non-negative continuous function g, find an open set C and a function V such that Eq. (5.3)-Eq. (5.4) hold, and

$$V(x) \geq g(x), \quad x \in C; \tag{5.5}$$

$$(q - L)V(x) \geq 0, \quad x \notin \bar{C}. \tag{5.6}$$

Lemma 5.1 *Let* $(\tilde{C}, \tilde{V})$ *be a solution to Eq. (5.3)–Eq. (5.6) such that* $\tilde{V}$ *is continuous, let* τ_* *be the hitting time of* $\tilde{C}$, *and let*

$$\tilde{W} := (q - L)\tilde{V} \quad be\ universally\ measurable; \tag{5.7}$$

$$U^q \tilde{W} = \tilde{V}. \tag{5.8}$$

Then τ_* *and* $V_* = \tilde{V}$ *solve the optimization problem Eq. (5.1).*

In all applications in this book, $\tilde{W}$ will be Borel, so there is no need to give the definition of a universally measurable function here.

Proof. Due to Eq. (5.3) and Eq. (5.6), $\tilde{W}$ is non-negative, and by Eq. (5.7), it is universally measurable, therefore for any stopping time τ, Eq. (2.40) holds:

$$U^q \tilde{W}(x) = E^x \left[\int_0^\tau e^{-qt} \tilde{W}(X_t) dt \right] + E^x \left[e^{-q\tau} U^q \tilde{W}(X_\tau) \right]. \tag{5.9}$$

By substituting Eq. (5.8) into Eq. (5.9), we obtain

$$\tilde{V}(x) = E^x \left[\int_0^\tau e^{-qt}(q - L)\tilde{V}(X_t) dt \right] + E^x \left[e^{-q\tau} \tilde{V}(X_\tau) \right]. \tag{5.10}$$

From Eq. (5.10), Eq. (5.6) and Eq. (5.3), we conclude that for any stopping time τ,

$$\tilde{V}(x) \geq E^x \left[e^{-q\tau} \tilde{V}(X_\tau) \right], \tag{5.11}$$

a.e. (Eq. (5.6) and Eq. (5.3) say nothing about $\tilde{W}$ at ∂C but this is unnecessary: ∂C has the Lebesgue measure 0, and therefore for a.e. x, $U^q(x, \partial C) = 0$ - see [S], Proposition 41.9). From Eq. (5.10) and Eq. (5.3), for a chosen stopping time τ_*,

$$\tilde{V}(x) = E^x \left[e^{-q\tau_*} \tilde{V}(X_{\tau_*}) \right]. \tag{5.12}$$

By using Eq. (5.5) and Eq. (5.4), we deduce from Eq. (5.11) and Eq. (5.12)

$$\tilde{V}(x) \geq E^x [e^{-q\tau} g(X_\tau)],$$
$$\tilde{V}(x) = E^x [e^{-q\tau_*} g(X_{\tau_*})],$$

a. e. Set $V_* = \tilde{V}$. Since $\tilde{V}$ is continuous, we can omit "a.e." and conclude that a pair (τ_*, V_*) is the optimal stopping time and the rational price. $\square$

5.2   Perpetual American put: the optimal exercise price and the rational put price

5.2.1   *Main Theorem*

In this section, we consider the perpetual American put with the strike price K and the payoff $g(x) = K - e^x$. The riskless interest rate is $r > 0$, and $q_0 \geq 0$ is the *dividend rate*. We set $q = r + q_0$, and we assume that X is an RLPE of exponential type $[\lambda_-, \lambda_+]$, where $\lambda_- < -1 < 0 < \lambda_+$, under the EMM **Q** chosen by the market. In the statement of the next theorem, we use $\sigma_+ > 0$ introduced in Lemma 3.5.

Theorem 5.1   *The optimal exercise region for the perpetual American put is $S \leq H_*$ or equivalently $x \leq h_*$, where*

$$H_* = e^{h_*} = K\phi_q^-(-i), \tag{5.13}$$

and the rational put price is given by

$$V_*(x) = -\frac{K}{2\pi} \int_{-\infty+i\omega_+}^{+\infty+i\omega_+} \frac{\exp[i(x - h_*)\xi]\phi_q^-(\xi)}{\xi(\xi + i)} d\xi, \tag{5.14}$$

for any $\omega_+ \in (0, \sigma_+)$.

Example 5.1   Let X be a Brownian motion, let the volatility be σ^2, and let there be no dividends, that is, $q = r$. Let $\beta_- = -2r/\sigma^2$ be the negative root of the characteristic equation

$$\frac{\sigma^2}{2}\beta^2 + (r - \frac{\sigma^2}{2})\beta - r = 0$$

of the stationary Black-Scholes equation

$$\frac{\sigma^2}{2}V'' + (r - \frac{\sigma^2}{2})V' - rV = 0.$$

Then from Eq. (2.28), $\phi_q^-(\xi) = (-\beta_-)/(-\beta_- + i\xi)$, and Eq. (5.13) and Eq. (5.14) assume the form

$$H_* = e^{h_*} = K\beta_-/(\beta_- - 1),\tag{5.15}$$

and

$$V_*(x) = -\frac{K}{2\pi i}\int_{-\infty+i\omega_+}^{+\infty+i\omega_+} \frac{\exp[i(x - h_*)\xi](-\beta_-)}{(\xi + i\beta_-)\xi(\xi + i)}d\xi,\tag{5.16}$$

respectively. The condition $\omega_+ \in (0, \sigma_+)$ implies that the line $\Im\xi = \omega_+$ lies below the pole $\xi = -i\beta_-$ of the integrand, therefore by pushing the line of the integration up to the infinity, we cross this only pole in the upper half-plane. By applying the residue theorem, we derive from Eq. (5.16)

$$V_*(x) = \frac{K\exp[\beta_-(x - h_*)]}{1 - \beta_-},$$

or

$$V_*(x) = \left(\frac{K}{1-\beta_-}\right)^{1-\beta_-}(-\beta_-)^{-\beta_-}e^{\beta_- x}.\tag{5.17}$$

Eq. (5.15) and Eq. (5.17) are due to Merton (1973), who derived them by using the ODE technique and smooth pasting principle.

Remark 5.2 On comparing Eq. (5.13) and Eq. (2.26), one is tempted to write Eq. (5.13) in the form

$$H_* = e^{h_*} = KE[e^{N_T}],\tag{5.18}$$

where $\{N_t\}$ is the infimum process, and T is an exponential random variable of mean q^{-1}, independent of X. In fact, this interpretation is a bit misleading: from the proof, which is valid for more general payoffs, it follows that the right interpretation of Eq. (5.13) is:

the optimal h_* is the solution to the equation

$$(U_M^q(q-L)g)(x) = 0, \qquad (5.19)$$

where U_M^q is the resolvent of the supremum process.

We will also see that the general form for Eq. (5.14) is

$$V_*(x) = qU_N^q \mathbf{1}_{(-\infty,h_*]}U_M^q(q-L)g. \qquad (5.20)$$

In the following subsections, we

(1) show how to guess the unique candidate for the optimal stopping time in the class $\mathcal{M}_0$ of hitting times $\tau(a)$ of segments $(-\infty, a]$,
(2) show how to prove, relatively simply, for any RLPE, that this is indeed the optimal stopping time in the class $\mathcal{M}_0$, and then
(3) produce more involved proof of optimality in the class $\mathcal{M}$, for any mixture of independent model RLPE,
(4) discuss the smooth pasting condition, and
(5) obtain simple approximate formulas.

After Theorem 5.1 was obtained, Mordecki (2000) proved it (in the form Eq. (5.18)) for any Lévy process by using the different technique. Notice that in Section 5.5 we manage to prove the optimality of Eq. (5.19) in the class $\mathcal{M}_0$ for wider class of payoffs, and the more practically oriented reader may be satisfied with a straightforward proof of the optimality in the intuitively natural class $\mathcal{M}_0$.

5.2.2 Proof of optimality in the class $\mathcal{M}_0$

For h and $x \in \mathbf{R}$, set

$$V(h,x) := E^x[e^{-q\tau(h)}g(X_{\tau(h)})]. \qquad (5.21)$$

Lemma 5.2 Let there exist h_* with the following properties:

a) if $h < h_*$, then there exists x such that

$$V(h,x) < g(x); \qquad (5.22)$$

b) for any $x \geq h_*$,

$$V(h_*,x) \geq g(x); \qquad (5.23)$$

c) if $h > h_*$, then for any $x \geq h$,

$$V(h_*, x) \geq V(h, x). \tag{5.24}$$

Then $\tau(h_*)$ is an optimal stopping time in the class $\mathcal{M}_0$.

Proof. Clearly, the rational price of the option must satisfy Eq. (5.23), hence Eq. (5.22) excludes $h < h_*$. Due to Eq. (5.23), h_* is an admissible choice, and Eq. (5.23)–Eq. (5.24) ensure that a choice $h > h_*$ is no better than h_*. □

To apply Lemma 5.2, we need an explicit formula for $V(h, x)$. We derive it by applying the Wiener-Hopf method to the problem Eq. (5.3)-Eq. (5.4), which now assumes the form

$$(q - L)V(x) = 0, \qquad x > h, \tag{5.25}$$
$$V(x) = g(x), \qquad x \leq h. \tag{5.26}$$

Set

$$w(x) = (\phi_q^-(D)^{-1}g)(x).$$

Theorem 5.2 *For any $h \in \mathbf{R}$, a solution to the problem Eq. (5.3)-Eq. (5.4) in the class of measurable functions bounded on $[h, +\infty)$ exists, and*

(i) *if $\kappa_- = 1$, then a continuous bounded solution is unique. It is given by*

$$V = \phi_q^-(D)\mathbf{1}_{(-\infty, h)}\phi_q^-(D)^{-1}g; \tag{5.27}$$

(ii) *if $\kappa_- \in (0, 1)$, then a bounded solution is unique. It is given by Eq. (5.27), and it is continuous;*

(iii) *if $\kappa_- = 0$, then a bounded solution is unique. It is given by Eq. (5.27), and it is continuous if and only if $w(h) = 0$;*

(iv) *if $\kappa_- \in (0, 1]$, then $V'(h - 0) = V'(h + 0)$ if and only if $w(h) = 0$.*

We postpone the proof till Subsection 5.3.6.

To guess the unique candidate h_* for the boundary of the optimal exercise region, first, notice that for $\beta < \sigma_+$,

$$\phi_q^-(D)^{\pm 1}e^{\beta x} = \phi_q^-(-i\beta)^{\pm 1}e^{\beta x} \tag{5.28}$$

(for the sign "+", it is immediate from the definition of ϕ_q^-, and the formula for the sign "-" follows), and $\phi_q^-(0) = 1$. Second, write Eq. (5.27) for $x > h$, as

$$V(h, x) = \int_{-\infty}^{h} p_q^-(x - y)w(y)dy, \qquad (5.29)$$

and then as

$$V(h, x) = g(x) - \int_{h}^{+\infty} p_q^-(x - y)w(y)dy. \qquad (5.30)$$

Recall that $p_q^- = \mathcal{F}^{-1}\phi_q^-$ is the probability density supported on $[0, +\infty)$, and suppose that $w(h) > 0$; then $w(x) > 0$ in a right neighbourhood of h, and from Eq. (5.30), we conclude that there exists x s.t. $V(h, x) < g(x)$. Hence, such an h is non-optimal. Define $\tilde{h}$ as the solution to the equation $w(x) = 0$, that is,

$$\tilde{h} = \ln(K\phi_q^-(-i)). \qquad (5.31)$$

If $w(h) < 0$, then $w(x) \leq w(h) < 0$ for each $x \geq h$, and therefore from Eq. (5.30), we conclude that for each $x > h$,

$$V(h, x) \geq g(x) - w(h).$$

Since for $x \leq h$, $V(h, x) = g(x)$, we see that $V(h, x)$ is discontinuous at h; moreover, it jumps down as x crosses h from above. One cannot expect such strange behaviour of the rational put price, therefore we guess that the optimal h_* must be $\tilde{h}$. Note that Eq. (5.31) is another form of Eq. (5.13), and that with this choice of h, Eq. (5.27) assumes the form Eq. (5.14). To see this, set $v(h, x) = \mathbf{1}_{(-\infty,h)}(x)w(x)$, calculate, for $\Im\xi = \omega_+ > 0$,

$$
\begin{aligned}
\hat{v}(\tilde{h}, \xi) &= \int_{-\infty}^{\tilde{h}} e^{-ix\xi}(K - e^x\phi_q^-(-i))dx \\
&= Ke^{-i\tilde{h}\xi}(-i\xi)^{-1} - e^{\tilde{h}}\phi_q^-(-i)(1 - i\xi)^{-1} \\
&= Ke^{-i\tilde{h}\xi}[(-i\xi)^{-1} - (1 - i\xi)^{-1}]
\end{aligned}
$$

(the last equality follows from Eq. (5.31)), and then apply the definition of PDO to

$$V(\tilde{h}, x) = \phi_q^-(D)v(\tilde{h}, x).$$

To verify that $\tilde{h}$ is the optimal solution in the class $\mathcal{M}_0$, it suffices to show that for each $h > \tilde{h}$ and $x > h$,

$$V(h, x) \leq V(\tilde{h}, x). \tag{5.32}$$

But for $y > \tilde{h}$, $w(y) < 0$, and therefore from Eq. (5.29), we conclude that

$$V(h, x) - V(\tilde{h}, x) = \int_{\tilde{h}}^{h} p_q^-(x - y)w(y)dy \leq 0.$$

5.2.3   *Proof of optimality in the class* $\mathcal{M}$

Set $h = \tilde{h}, \mathcal{C} = (h, +\infty)$, define $\tilde{V}$ by Eq. (5.27), and verify conditions of Lemma 5.1. Eq. (5.3)-Eq. (5.4) hold by construction, and Eq. (5.5) follows from Eq. (5.30) and the inequality $w(y) \leq 0$ for $y \geq \tilde{h}$. To check Eq. (5.6)-Eq. (5.8), we set $v(\tilde{h}, \cdot) = \mathbf{1}_{(-\infty, \tilde{h})}(\cdot)w(\cdot)$, and calculate

$$\begin{aligned} \tilde{W} : & = (q - L)\tilde{V} \\ & = q(q^{-1}(q + \psi(D)))\phi_q^-(D)v(\tilde{h}, \cdot) \\ & = q\phi_q^+(D)^{-1}v(\tilde{h}, \cdot). \end{aligned}$$

Under the choice Eq. (5.31), $\hat{v}(\tilde{h}, \xi)$ decays as $|\xi|^{-2}$, as $\xi \to \infty$, therefore in the case $\kappa_+ < 1$, the Fourier transform of $\tilde{W}$ admits a bound via $C(1 + |\xi|)^{-1-\epsilon}$, where $\epsilon > 0$. Hence, $\tilde{W} \in C_0(\mathbf{R})$, and Eq. (5.7)-Eq. (5.8) hold.

If $\kappa_+ = 1$, then from Eq. (3.73)-Eq. (3.76), we deduce the representation

$$\phi_q^+(D)^{-1} = a_+(0)^{-1}(1 - iD) + f(D),$$

where $f(\xi)$ admits a bound via $C(1+|\xi|)^\rho$ with some $\rho < 1$, in the half-plane $\Im\xi > \omega_-$, where $\omega_- < 0$. The argument above shows that $f(D)v(\tilde{h}, \cdot) \in C_0(\mathbf{R})$, and evidently, $(1 - iD)v(\tilde{h}, \cdot)$ is bounded, decays at the infinity and is smooth except for the point $\tilde{h}$, where it jumps. Hence, Eq. (5.7)-Eq. (5.8) hold in the case $\kappa_+ = 1$ as well.

It remains to verify Eq. (5.6). Since

$$\phi_q^+(\xi)^{-1} = q^{-1}(q + \phi_q^+(\xi))\phi_q^-(\xi),$$

we have $\tilde{W}(x + \tilde{h}) = KW(x)$, where

$$W(x) = (2\pi)^{-1} \int_{-\infty+i\omega_+}^{+\infty+i\omega_+} \frac{\exp[ix\xi](q + \psi(\xi))\phi_q^-(\xi)}{-i\xi(1 - i\xi)} d\xi. \qquad (5.33)$$

Thus, we need to show that

$$W(x) \geq 0, \quad x < 0. \qquad (5.34)$$

We formulate sufficient conditions for Eq. (5.34) to hold; they are satisfied by any model RLPE, and any mixture of independent model RLPE. Of the process, we require

(i) the function ϕ in Eq. (3.46) admits the analytic continuation into the lower half-plane with the cut $(-i\infty, i\lambda_-]$, and admits the bound Eq. (3.51) in this half-plane, outside a neighbourhood of $i\lambda_-$; and if $\nu = 2$, there exist c and $\nu_1 < 2$ such that $\phi(\xi) - c\xi^2$ satisfy Eq. (3.51) with ν_1 instead of ν;

(ii) in a neighbourhood of $i\lambda_-$, ϕ may have a weak singularity:

$$|\phi(\xi)| \leq C|\xi - i\lambda_-|^{-\alpha}, \qquad (5.35)$$

for some $\alpha < 1$;

(iii) for any $z \in (-\infty, \lambda_-)$, the limit

$$\Psi_-(z) = i[\psi(iz-0) - \psi(iz+0)] \quad \text{exists and is non-positive.} \qquad (5.36)$$

Lemma 5.3 *Let X be a mixture of independent BM, HP, NIG, NTS Lévy and KoBoL. Then (i)-(iii) hold.*

Proof. Notice that if (i)-(iii) hold for two independent Lévy processes, then (i)-(iii) hold for the mixture of these processes, and therefore, it suffices to verify (i)-(iii) for each model class separately. The verification of (i) for NIG (and more generally, NTS Lévy) and KoBoL is trivial due to the simplicity of the analytic expressions in Eq. (3.23) and Eq. (3.6). In both cases, the characteristic exponents are continuous at the ends of the cuts, and there is no singularity mentioned in (ii).

Verification of (iii) for NTS Lévy processes: here $\lambda_- = -\alpha + \beta$, and for $z < -\alpha + \beta$,

$$\begin{aligned}
\Psi_-(z) &= i\delta[(\alpha^2 - (\beta + i(iz - 0))^2)^{\nu/2} - (\alpha^2 - (\beta + i(iz + 0))^2)^{\nu/2}] \\
&= i\delta[(\alpha^2 - (\beta - z - i0)^2)^{\nu/2} - (\alpha^2 - (\beta - z + i0)^2)^{\nu/2}]
\end{aligned}$$

$$
\begin{aligned}
&= i\delta[(\alpha^2 - (\beta - z)^2 + i0)^{\nu/2} - (\alpha^2 - (\beta - z)^2 - i0)^{\nu/2}] \\
&= i\delta((z - \beta)^2 - \alpha^2)^{\nu/2}[e^{i\pi\nu/2} - e^{-i\pi\nu/2}] \\
&= -\delta((z - \beta)^2 - \alpha^2)^{\nu/2} 2\sin[\pi\nu/2] < 0.
\end{aligned}
$$

Verification for KoBoL: for $z < \lambda_-$,

$$
\begin{aligned}
\Psi_-(z) &= ic\Gamma(-\nu)[-(-\lambda_- - i(iz - 0))^{\nu} + (-\lambda_- - i(iz + 0))^{\nu}] \\
&= -ic\Gamma(-\nu)[(-\lambda_- + z + i0)^{\nu} - (-\lambda_- + z - i0)^{\nu}] \\
&= -ic\Gamma(-\nu)(-z + \lambda_-)^{\nu}[e^{i\pi\nu} - e^{-i\pi\nu}] \\
&= c\Gamma(-\nu)(-z + \lambda_-)^{\nu} 2\sin(\pi\nu) < 0,
\end{aligned}
$$

since $\Gamma(-\nu)\sin(\pi\nu) < 0$.

The formula for the characteristic exponent of HP being more involved, the verification of (i)-(iii) for HP is rather long, and we omit it here.   □

The verification of optimality for model classes RLPE is finished with the next lemma.

Lemma 5.4   *Let X be an RLPE satisfying (i)-(iii). Then Eq. (5.34) hold.*

Proof.   By using (i)-(iii), we can transform the contour of integration in Eq. (5.33), and reduce to the integral over the banks of the cut $(-i\infty, i\lambda_-]$. In the process of the transformation, the contour crosses two simple poles at $\xi = 0$ and $\xi = -i$ (if $-i$ is a root of $q + \psi(\xi)$, as it is in the case of puts on a non-dividend paying stock, there is no second pole, but there is no need to consider this case separately: the corresponding term below will be automatically 0), which gives the first two terms; in the integral over the banks of the cut, we make the change of the variable $\xi = iz$. The result is

$$
\begin{aligned}
W(x) &= q - (q + \psi(-i))\phi_q^-(-i)e^x \\
&\quad + (2\pi)^{-1} \int_{-\infty}^{\lambda_-} \frac{\Psi_-(z)\phi_q^-(iz)\exp[-zx]}{z(z+1)} dz.
\end{aligned}
\tag{5.37}
$$

For $z \le 0$, $\phi_q^-(iz) > 0$, and since $\lambda_- < -1$, the denominator of the integrand is positive (the integral is over the interval $z < \lambda_-(< -1)$, hence both factors in the denominator are negative, and the product positive). From Eq. (5.36), the integrand is negative, and for any $-z > 0$, the function $\exp[-zx]$ is an increasing function of x. Hence, the integrand is a decreasing function of x on $(-\infty, 0)$. By definition of σ_-, $(q + \psi(-i\sigma)) > 0$ on $(\sigma_-, 0)$, and since $0 < 1 \leq -\sigma_-$, $(q + \psi(-i))\phi_q^-(-i) \geq 0$. It follows that W decreases on $(-\infty, 0)$, and hence it suffices to show that $W(+0) \geq 0$. If $\kappa_+ < 1$, the integrand is absolutely integrable uniformly in $x \in (-\infty, 0]$, and therefore

$$
\begin{aligned}
W(+0) &= W(0) \\
&= q - (q + \psi(-i))\phi_q^-(-i) + (2\pi)^{-1} \int_{-\infty}^{\lambda_-} \frac{\Psi_-(z)\phi_q^-(iz)}{z(z+1)} dz.
\end{aligned}
$$

By transforming the contour of integration back, and taking into account that $(q + \psi(\xi))\phi_q^-(\xi) = q\phi_q^+(\xi)^{-1}$, we arrive at

$$
W(+0) = W(0) = q(2\pi)^{-1} \int_{-\infty+i\sigma}^{+\infty+i\sigma} \frac{d\xi}{\phi_q^+(\xi)(-i\xi)(1-i\xi)}.
$$

The integrand is holomorphic in the upper half-plane $\Im \xi > 0$ and admits an estimate via $C(1 + |\xi|)^{-2+\kappa_+}$, for $\Im \xi \geq \sigma > 0$. Hence, we can push the line of integration up, and in the limit $\sigma \to +\infty$ obtain zero. This finishes the proof in the case $\kappa_+ < 1$.

If $\kappa_+ = 1$, we can represent $(q + \psi(\xi))\phi_q^-(\xi) = q\phi_q^+(\xi)^{-1}$ in the form

$$
(q + \psi(\xi))\phi_q^-(\xi) = qa_+(0)^{-1}(-i\xi) + \chi(\xi),
$$

where $a_+(0) > 0$, and χ enjoys all the properties of $(q + \psi(\xi))\phi_q^-(\xi)$ in the case $\kappa_+ < 1$, which have been used above. Hence, if we use χ instead of $(q + \psi(\xi))\phi_q^-(\xi)$ in the constructions above, we obtain a non-negative function. To finish the proof, it remains to notice that

$$
\begin{aligned}
W_1(x) &:= (2\pi)^{-1} \int_{-\infty+i\sigma}^{+\infty+i\sigma} \frac{\exp[ix\xi]qa_+(0)^{-1}(-i\xi)}{(-i\xi)(1-i\xi)} d\xi \\
&= qa_+(0)^{-1}\mathbf{1}_{(-\infty,0]}(x)e^x \geq 0.
\end{aligned}
$$

$\square$

5.2.4 Failure of the smooth pasting principle for some RLPE's and its substitute

Theorem 5.3 *Let ϕ_q^- satisfy*

$$
\int_{-\infty+i\sigma}^{+\infty+i\sigma} |\phi_q^-(\xi)(1-i\xi)^{-1}| d\xi < +\infty, \tag{5.38}
$$

for some $\sigma \in (0, \sigma_+)$. Then the price of the perpetual American put satisfies the smooth pasting principle.

Proof. By differentiating under the integral sign in Eq. (5.14), we obtain $V'_* = v$, where

$$v(x) := -\frac{K}{2\pi} \int_{-\infty+i\sigma}^{+\infty+i\sigma} e^{i(x-h_*)\xi} \phi_q^-(\xi)(1-i\xi)^{-1}d\xi < +\infty.$$

Hence, V_* is smooth if and only if v is continuous. Under condition Eq. (5.38), the Fourier transform of v is of the class $L_1(\mathbf{R})$, therefore v is continuous, and the smooth pasting principle holds. □

Theorem 5.4 *Let ϕ_q^- admit a representation $\phi_q^-(\xi) = c + \chi(\xi)$, where $c \neq 0$, and χ satisfies*

$$\int_{-\infty+i\sigma}^{+\infty+i\sigma} |\chi(\xi)(1-i\xi)^{-1}|d\xi < +\infty.$$

Then the smooth pasting principle fails.

Proof. This time we obtain that $v = v_1 + v_2$, where v_1 is continuous, and

$$v_2(x) = -\frac{cK}{2\pi} \int_{-\infty+i\sigma}^{+\infty+i\sigma} \frac{\exp[i(x-h_*)\xi]d\xi}{1-i\xi} = -cK\mathbf{1}_{(-\infty,h_*)}(x)e^{x-h_*},$$

which is discontinuous. □

Notice that for an RLPE, Eq. (5.38) fails if and only if $\mu > 0$ and $\nu \in (0,1)$; this is the case of a process of bounded variation, with positive drift.

As we already saw, the natural candidate for the optimal exercise price is determined from the equation

$$w(x) := \phi_q^-(D)^{-1}g(x) = 0,$$

and this candidate can be singled out formally in one of the following forms:

I. If there is a unique h such that $V(h; \cdot)$ is continuous, this h is the candidate; if $V(h; \cdot)$ is continuous for all h, the candidate is chosen by the standard smooth pasting principle.

II. If there is h such that $V'_x(h; h \pm 0)$ are finite, then h is the optimal boundary.

The second principle works for purely non-Gaussian RLPE, i.e., for RLPE of order $\nu < 2$.

In all cases, one may say that the optimal choice of h makes $V(h, \cdot)$ "more regular" at h than generically.

5.2.5 *Approximate formulas for the case of model RLPE*

Let the steepness parameter λ_+ be large, and let $-i\beta_-$ be the root of the "characteristic equation" $q + \psi(\xi) = 0$ in the upper half-plane. By using the crude approximation Eq. (3.82), we deduce from Eq. (5.13) and Eq. (5.14) the approximations

$$H_{\mathrm{ap}} = e^{h_{\mathrm{ap}}} = K\beta_-/(\beta_- - 1),$$

and

$$V_{\mathrm{ap}}(x) = -\frac{K}{2\pi i} \int_{-\infty + i\omega_+}^{+\infty + i\omega_+} \frac{\exp[i(x - h_{\mathrm{ap}})\xi](-\beta_-)}{(\xi + i\beta_-)\xi(\xi + i)} d\xi,$$

respectively, which look exactly like Eq. (5.15)-Eq. (5.16) in the Brownian motion case. However, if one fits an RLPE by a Brownian motion, one obtains the different β_-, and the different optimal exercise price and rational put price. Generically, the larger the λ_+, the smaller the differences between the exact solution (h_*, V_*) and the approximation $(h_{\mathrm{ap}}, V_{\mathrm{ap}})$, and between (h_*, V_*) and the Gaussian result.

5.2.6 *Proof of Theorem 5.2*

By the change of the variable $x \mapsto h + x$, we reduce the proof of Theorem 5.2 to the case $h = 0$. Next, take any $\gamma \in (0, \sigma_+)$, and for a function f, introduce the notation $f_\gamma(x) = e^{\gamma x} f(x)$. Denote

$$a(D) := q + \psi(D) = q - L,$$

substitute $V(x) = e^{-\gamma x} V_\gamma(x)$ into Eq. (5.25), after that multiply Eq. (5.25) and Eq. (5.26) by $e^{\gamma x}$, and use the equality

$$e^{\gamma x} a(D) e^{-\gamma x} = a(D + i\gamma). \tag{5.39}$$

We obtain

$$a(D + i\gamma) V_\gamma(x) = 0, \qquad x > 0; \tag{5.40}$$

$$V_\gamma(x) \;=\; g_\gamma(x), \quad x \leq 0. \tag{5.41}$$

Notice that g_γ decays exponentially as $x \to -\infty$ together with all derivatives: on $(-\infty, 0]$,

$$|g_\gamma^{(s)}(x)| \leq C_s e^{-\gamma|x|}, \tag{5.42}$$

for each $s = 0, 1, 2, \ldots$ (for the next steps of the proof, Eq. (5.42) for $s \leq 2$ suffices). Construct G_γ which coincides with g_γ on $\mathbf{R}_-$ and admits a bound Eq. (5.42) on $\mathbf{R}$, for $s \leq 2$, and set $u_\gamma = V_\gamma - G_\gamma$, $F_\gamma = -a(D + i\gamma)G_\gamma$. Then u_γ solves the problem

$$a(D + i\gamma)u_\gamma(x) \;=\; F_\gamma(x), \quad x > 0; \tag{5.43}$$
$$u_\gamma(x) \;=\; 0, \qquad x \leq 0. \tag{5.44}$$

Eq. (5.42) implies that $G_\gamma \in H^2(\mathbf{R})$, and from Eq. (3.45)–Eq. (3.46) we conclude that $F_\gamma \in H^{2-\bar\nu}(\mathbf{R})$, where $\bar\nu = \nu$, if $\nu \geq 1$ or $\mu = 0$, and $\bar\nu = \max\{\nu, 1\}$ otherwise. Recall that we are looking for V which is measurable and bounded on $(0, +\infty)$. Hence, we are looking for u_γ which is measurable and admits a bound via $Ce^{\gamma x}$. We want to reduce the problem to the case of an unknown function of the class $L_2(\mathbf{R}_+)$. Since $\sigma_- < 0$, we can choose $\gamma' \in (\sigma_- - \gamma, -\gamma)$. Set

$$u_{\gamma,\gamma'}(x) = e^{\gamma' x}u_\gamma(x), \quad F_{\gamma,\gamma'}(x) = e^{\gamma' x}F_\gamma(x),$$

substitute $u_\gamma(x) = e^{-\gamma' x}u_{\gamma,\gamma'}(x)$ into Eq. (5.43) and Eq. (5.44), and after that multiply Eq. (5.43) by $e^{\gamma' x}$. By using Eq. (5.39), we obtain

$$a(D + i(\gamma + \gamma'))u_{\gamma,\gamma'}(x) \;=\; F_{\gamma,\gamma'}(x), \quad x > 0; \tag{5.45}$$
$$u_{\gamma,\gamma'}(x) \;=\; 0, \qquad x \leq 0. \tag{5.46}$$

Now $u_{\gamma,\gamma'} \in L_2(\mathbf{R}_+)$, and on the strength of Eq. (3.45)–Eq. (3.46), Theorem 15.4 gives

$$a(D + i(\gamma + \gamma'))u_{\gamma,\gamma'} \in H^{-\bar\nu}(\mathbf{R}).$$

Hence, the expressions on both sides of Eq. (5.45) belong to $H^{-\bar\nu}(\mathbf{R})$, and the support of their difference, call it F_-, is a subset of $(-\infty, 0]$. This means that $F_- \in \overset{\circ}{H}{}^{-\bar\nu}(\mathbf{R}_-)$, and we can write the Wiener-Hopf equation Eq. (5.45) in the form

$$a(D + i(\gamma + \gamma'))u_{\gamma,\gamma'} = F_{\gamma,\gamma'} + F_-. \tag{5.47}$$

Multiply by q^{-1}, and then apply $\phi_q^+(D + i(\gamma + \gamma'))$. Since in the strip $\Im\xi \in (\lambda_-, \lambda_+)(\supset (\sigma_-, \sigma_+) \supset (\sigma_-, 0))$

$$q^{-1}a(\xi) = \phi_q^+(\xi)^{-1}\phi_q^-(\xi)^{-1}$$

and by our choice, $\gamma + \gamma' \in (\sigma_-, 0)$, we obtain

$$\phi_q^-(D + i(\gamma + \gamma'))^{-1}u_{\gamma,\gamma'} = K + K_-, \qquad (5.48)$$

where

$$
\begin{aligned}
K : &= q^{-1}\phi_q^+(D + i(\gamma + \gamma'))F_{\gamma,\gamma'} \\
&= q^{-1}\phi_q^+(D + i(\gamma + \gamma'))e^{\gamma'x}(-a(D + i\gamma))G_\gamma \\
&= -\phi_q^-(D + i(\gamma + \gamma'))^{-1}e^{\gamma'x}G_\gamma,
\end{aligned}
$$

and

$$K_- := q^{-1}\phi_q^+(D + i(\gamma + \gamma'))F_-.$$

By construction, $G_\gamma \in H^2(\mathbf{R})$, and

$$u_{\gamma,\gamma'} \in L_2(\mathbf{R}_+) = \overset{o}{H}{}^0(\mathbf{R}_+), \quad F_- \in \overset{o}{H}{}^{-\bar\nu}(\mathbf{R}_-).$$

From Theorem 3.3, we know that for any $\sigma \in (\sigma_-, \sigma_+)$,

$$c(1 + |\xi|)^{\kappa_\pm} \leq |\phi_q^\pm(\xi)| \leq C(1 + |\xi|)^{\kappa_\pm}, \quad \pm\Im\xi \geq \sigma,$$

where $C, c > 0$ depend on σ, therefore

$$\phi_q^-(D + i(\gamma + \gamma'))^{-1}u_{\gamma,\gamma'} \in \overset{o}{H}{}^{-\kappa_-}(\mathbf{R}_+), \quad K_- \in \overset{o}{H}{}^{-\kappa_-}(\mathbf{R}_-), \quad K \in H^{-\kappa_-}(\mathbf{R}_+).$$

Notice that $\kappa_- \in [0, 1]$, and consider two cases: a) $\kappa_- \in [0, 0.5)$; b) $\kappa_- \in [0.5, 1]$.

In case a), $H^{-\kappa_-}(\mathbf{R})$ is the direct sum of the subspaces $\overset{o}{H}{}^{-\kappa_-}(\mathbf{R}_\pm)$, the projections being $\theta_\pm$, the closures of the-multiplication-by-$1_{\mathbf{R}_\pm}$-operators defined on a dense subset $L_2(\mathbf{R}) \subset H^{-\kappa_-}(\mathbf{R})$. Hence, we deduce from Eq. (5.48):

$$\phi_q^-(D + i(\gamma + \gamma'))^{-1}u_{\gamma,\gamma'} = -\theta_+\phi_q^-(D + i(\gamma + \gamma'))^{-1}e^{\gamma'x}G_\gamma. \qquad (5.49)$$

Next, we multiply Eq. (5.49) by $\phi_q^-(D + i(\gamma + \gamma'))$, which establishes an isomorphism between $\overset{o}{H}{}^{-\kappa_-}(\mathbf{R}_+)$ and $L_2(\mathbf{R}_+)$:

$$u_{\gamma,\gamma'} = -\phi_q^-(D + i(\gamma + \gamma'))\theta_+\phi_q^-(D + i(\gamma + \gamma'))^{-1}e^{\gamma'x}G_\gamma. \qquad (5.50)$$

Then we multiply Eq. (5.50) by $e^{-\gamma' x}$ and use Eq. (5.39):

$$u_\gamma = -\phi_q^-(D+i\gamma)\theta_+ \phi_q^-(D+i\gamma)^{-1}G_\gamma.$$

After that, we return to

$$
\begin{aligned}
V_\gamma &= G_\gamma + u_\gamma \\
&= G_\gamma - \phi_q^-(D+i\gamma)\theta_+ \phi_q^-(D+i\gamma)^{-1}G_\gamma \\
&= \phi_q^-(D+i\gamma)\theta_- \phi_q^-(D+i\gamma)^{-1}G_\gamma.
\end{aligned}
$$

Since G_γ coincides with g_γ on $\mathbf{R}_-$, Eq. (3.74) and Eq. (3.76) ensure that $\operatorname{supp} \phi_q^-(D+i\gamma)^{-1}(G_\gamma - g_\gamma) \subset [0, +\infty)$. Thus,

$$\theta_- \phi_q^-(D+i\gamma)^{-1}G_\gamma = \theta_- \phi_q^-(D+i\gamma)^{-1}g_\gamma,$$

and in the formula for V_γ, we may replace G_γ with g_γ. By using Eq. (5.39), we finally arrive at

$$V = \phi_q^-(D)\theta_- \phi_q^-(D)^{-1}g, \tag{5.51}$$

which is Eq. (5.27). This proves the first two statements in (ii)-(iii), in case a). To study the continuity of V, consider $w := \phi_q^-(D)^{-1}g$. Clearly, $w \in H^{2-\kappa_-}(\mathbf{R})$, and since $2 - \kappa_- > 1/2$, we can apply Theorem 15.15, and obtain

$$\theta_- \phi_q^-(D)^{-1}g = w(0)(1-iD)^{-1}\delta + (1-iD)^{-1}\theta_-(1-iD)\phi_q^-(D)^{-1}g, \tag{5.52}$$

where δ is the Dirac delta-function. From Eq. (5.51)-Eq. (5.52),

$$V = w(0)V_1 + V_2, \tag{5.53}$$

where

$$V_1 = \phi_q^-(D)(1-iD)^{-1}\delta,$$

and

$$V_2 = \phi_q^-(D)(1-iD)^{-1}\theta_-(1-iD)\phi_q^-(D)^{-1}g.$$

Notice that for any $\epsilon > 0$, $\delta \in H^{-1/2-\epsilon}(\mathbf{R})$, and $\theta_-(1-iD)\phi_q^-(D)^{-1}g \in H^0(\mathbf{R})$. Hence, $V_2 \in H^1(\mathbf{R})$. If $\kappa_- > 0$, we obtain $V_1 \in H^{1/2+\rho}(\mathbf{R})$, for any $\rho \in (0, \kappa_-)$, and therefore, the same is true of V. But for $s > 1/2$, $H^s(\mathbf{R}) \subset C_0(\mathbf{R})$, and therefore, V is continuous. This finishes the proof of (ii) for the case $\kappa_- \in (0, 0.5)$.

If $\kappa_- = 0$, we have from Eq. (3.75) and Eq. (3.76)

$$\phi_q^-(D) = a_-(0) + T(D), \qquad (5.54)$$

where $T(\xi)$ admits an estimate

$$|T(\xi)| \leq C(1 + |\xi|)^{-m}, \quad \Im\xi \leq \omega_+,$$

with $m < 0$, therefore from Eq. (5.53), we conclude that

$$V = a_-(0)w(0)(1 - iD)^{-1}\delta + V_3, \qquad (5.55)$$

where $V_3 \in C_0(\mathbf{R})$. It is straightforward to check that the Fourier transform of $\mathbf{1}_{(-\infty,0]}(x)e^x$ is $(1 - i\xi)^{-1}$, therefore $(1 - iD)^{-1}\delta = \mathbf{1}_{(-\infty,0]}e^x$, and we conclude from Eq. (5.55), that V is continuous if and only if $w(0) = 0$. Part (iii) has been proved.

Now we prove part (ii) in the case $\kappa_- \in [0.5, 1)$ and part (i). We notice that for $s \in (-3/2, -1/2)$, the decomposition of $H^s(\mathbf{R})$ into the sum of the subspaces $\overset{o}{H}{}^s(\mathbf{R}_\pm)$ is not direct, the intersection of the latter couple being an 1D-subspace $\mathbf{C} \cdot \delta$, where δ is the Dirac delta-function. It follows that in Eq. (5.49), an additional term $C\delta$ may appear, and in Eq. (5.51), the term $C\phi_q^-(D)\delta$, where C is a constant. If $\kappa_- \in (0,1)$, we can show with the help of Eq. (3.75) and Eq. (3.76), that

$$\phi_q^-(D)\delta(x) = (2\pi)^{-1}\int_{-\infty}^{+\infty} e^{ix\xi}\phi_q^-(\xi)d\xi$$

is unbounded as $x \to +0$. Further, for $\kappa_- > 0$, V in Eq. (5.51) belongs to $H^s(\mathbf{R})$ for some $s > 1/2$, and hence, is continuous. We conclude that $C\phi_q^-(D)\delta + V$ is bounded only in the case $C = 0$, and so we are left with the same Eq. (5.51). This finishes the proof of (ii)-(iii).

If $\kappa_- = 1$, then the argument above shows that V in Eq. (5.51) is continuous, and the same argument shows that $\phi_q^-(D)\delta(x)$ is discontinuous at 0. Hence, in order to get a continuous solution, we need $C = 0$. This finishes the proof of part (i).

The last part (iv) can be proved by the same argument, after differentiating in Eq. (5.51). Theorem 5.2 has been proved.

5.3 Perpetual American call

5.3.1 *Main results*

The terminal payoff for the call is unbounded: $g(x) = e^x - K$, which leads to some complications. The standard general argument, due to Merton (1973), which can be found in many books (see, e.g., Shiryaev (1999)), shows that if the stock pays no dividends, then in the case of the finite time horizon, it is optimal to exercise the American call only at the expiration date; for the limiting case of the perpetual call, this translates into the theorem that for any stopping rule there is a better one. Hence, we consider the case of a dividend-paying stock, when $q = r + q_0 > r$. Notice that under condition $q > r$, $q + \psi^Q(-i) > 0$, therefore the proof of Eq. (3.40) shows that there exist $\sigma_- < -1 < 0 < \sigma_+$ such that Eq. (3.40) holds for any $[\omega_-, \omega_+] \subset (\sigma_-, \sigma_+)$.

Theorem 5.5 *Let the dividend rate be positive, and let X be a regular Lévy process of exponential type $[\lambda_-, \lambda_+]$, where $\lambda_- < -1 < 0 < \lambda_+$. Then the optimal stopping time is the hitting time of the interval $[h^*(K), +\infty)$, where*

$$e^{h^*(K)} := H^*(K) := K\phi_q^+(-i), \qquad (5.56)$$

and the rational call price is given by

$$V^*(x) = -\frac{K}{2\pi} \int_{-\infty+i\omega_-}^{+\infty+i\omega_-} \frac{\exp[i(x - h^*)\xi]\phi_q^+(\xi)}{\xi(\xi + i)} d\xi, \qquad (5.57)$$

where $\omega_- \in (\sigma_-, -1)$ is arbitrary.

Remark 5.3 a) As in the case of the put, our method proves the optimality in the class $\mathcal{M}_0$, for any RLPE, and in the class $\mathcal{M}$, for any mixture of independent model RLPE.

b) After Theorem 5.5 was obtained, Mordecki (2000) proved that it holds for any Lévy process satisfying $E[e^{X_t}] < +\infty$, in the form

$$H^*(K) = e^{h^*(K)} = KE[e^{M_T}], \qquad (5.58)$$

where M is the supremum process, and T is an exponential random variable with the mean q^{-1}.

c) Our proof shows that the natural general form for Eq. (5.56) is

$$E[((q - L)g)(N_T)] = 0, \qquad (5.59)$$

where $g(x) = e^x - K$, and N is the infimum process, and for Eq. (5.57), the general form is

$$V^*(x) = \phi^+(D)\mathbf{1}_{[h^*,+\infty)}\phi^+(D)^{-1}g. \qquad (5.60)$$

In the next Section, we will obtain Eq. (5.59)-Eq. (5.60) for more general payoffs.

d) From the point of view of the analytical technique, which we use, the principal difference between the case $q > r$ and the case $q = r$ is that in the former case, the condition Eq. (3.40) holds with $\omega_- < -1 < 0 < \omega_+$, and in the latter case, due to the EMM-condition $r + \psi^Q(-i) = 0$, it holds with $\omega_- > -1$ only. [1] A less important issue is the unboundedness of the payoff, which forces one to approximate the payoff by a sequence of bounded payoffs $\{g_n\}$ in order that Theorem 2.12 be applicable (cf. Remark 2.1). Modulo this approximation, the proofs and statements for the put can easily be transformed into their analogs for the call by changing the direction on the real axis and the reflection of the complex plane w.r.t. the origin. In particular, the essentially new elements appear only in the proof of the analog of Eq. (5.27).

5.3.2 *Proof of optimality in the case of unbounded payoffs*

Let $h, x \in \mathbf{R}$. Denote by $\tau(h)$ the hitting time of the segment $[h, +\infty)$, and define $V(h, x)$ by Eq. (5.21):

$$V(h, x) := V(g; h, x) := E^x[e^{-q\tau(h)}g(X_{\tau(h)})].$$

Similarly to Lemma 5.2, we have

Lemma 5.5 *Let there exist h^* with the following properties:*

a) if $h > h^*$, then there exists x such that

$$V(h, x) < g(x); \qquad (5.61)$$

---

[1] To be more specific, in the former case, the real part of the operator $q - L = q + \psi^Q(D)$ is positive-definite on the L_2-space of function which grow as e^x as $x \to +\infty$, whereas in the latter case, e^x is an eigenfunction of $q - L$.

b) *for any* $x \leq h^*$,

$$V(h^*, x) \geq g(x); \tag{5.62}$$

c) *if* $h < h^*$, *then for any* $x \leq h$,

$$V(h^*, x) \geq V(h, x). \tag{5.63}$$

Then $\tau(h^*)$ *is an optimal stopping time in the class* $\mathcal{M}_0$.

To derive an explicit formula for $V(h, x) = V(g; h, x)$, we use Theorem 2.12 but unlike in the case of puts, we cannot do it directly since this time g in unbounded. Construct a pointwise increasing sequence $\{\chi_n\} \subset C^\infty(\mathbf{R})$ converging pointwise to 1, s.t. for each n, $\chi_n(x)$ is non-negative, equals 1 on $(-\infty, h]$ and vanishes for sufficiently large x. Then set $g_n = g\chi_n$. Clearly, we may consider only h such that $g(h) \geq 0$, and then on $[h, +\infty)$ $g_n(x) \uparrow g(x)$ pointwise. Hence, by the dominant convergence theorem, for any x,

$$V(g_n; h, x) \uparrow V(g; h, x), \quad n \to \infty. \tag{5.64}$$

Since g_n is bounded, we can apply Theorem 2.12 and conclude that $V(g_n; h, \cdot)$ is a bounded solution to the following problem

$$(q - L)V(x) = 0, \qquad x < h, \tag{5.65}$$
$$V(x) = g_n(x), \qquad x \geq h. \tag{5.66}$$

Further, by replacing all the signs in the statement and the proof of Theorem 5.2, we find that the unique bounded measurable solution (and in the case $\kappa_+ = 1$, the unique continuous bounded solution) is given by

$$V(g_n; h, \cdot) = \phi_q^+(D)\mathbf{1}_{(h,+\infty)}\phi_q^+(D)^{-1}g_n. \tag{5.67}$$

By using Eq. (3.72) and Eq. (3.76), it is easy to obtain

$$\mathbf{1}_{(h,+\infty)}\phi_q^+(D)^{-1}(g_n - \mathbf{1}_{(h,+\infty)}g_n) = 0.$$

Hence, we can write Eq. (5.67) as

$$V(g_n; h, \cdot) = \phi_q^+(D)\mathbf{1}_{(h,+\infty)}\phi_q^+(D)^{-1}g_n(h; \cdot), \tag{5.68}$$

where $g_n(h; \cdot) := \mathbf{1}_{(h,+\infty)}g_n$. Take $\gamma \in (\sigma_-, -1)$, set $g_{n,\gamma}(h; x) = e^{\gamma x}g_n(h; x)$, multiply Eq. (5.68) by $e^{\gamma x}$, and use the equality

$$e^{\gamma x}\phi_q^+(D)^{\pm 1}e^{-\gamma x} = \phi_q^+(D + i\gamma)^{\pm 1}. \tag{5.69}$$

The result is

$$V(g_n; h, \cdot) = e^{-\gamma x} \phi_q^+(D + i\gamma) \mathbf{1}_{(h, +\infty)} \phi_q^+(D + i\gamma)^{-1} g_{n,\gamma}(h; \cdot). \quad (5.70)$$

Due to the choice of γ, a sequence $\{g_{n,\gamma}(h; \cdot)\}$ consists of bounded functions exponentially decaying at the infinity, and for each $x \geq h$, $g_{n,\gamma}(h; x) \uparrow g_{\gamma}(h; x)$ (which is also bounded and exponentially decays at infinity). Hence, $g_{n,\gamma}(h; \cdot) \to g_{\gamma}(h; \cdot)$ in $L_2(\mathbf{R})$, and therefore, in the sense of generalized functions,

$$V(g_n; h, \cdot) \to W(g; h, \cdot), \quad (5.71)$$

where

$$W(g; h, \cdot) = e^{-\gamma x} \phi_q^+(D + i\gamma) \mathbf{1}_{(h, +\infty)} \phi_q^+(D + i\gamma)^{-1} g_{\gamma}(h; \cdot).$$

By using Eq. (3.72) and Eq. (3.76), we can show that

$$W(g; h, \cdot) = e^{-\gamma x} \phi_q^+(D + i\gamma) \mathbf{1}_{(h, +\infty)} \phi_q^+(D + i\gamma)^{-1} g_{\gamma},$$

and by using Eq. (5.69), we obtain

$$W(g; h, \cdot) = \phi_q^+(D) \mathbf{1}_{(h, +\infty)} \phi_q^+(D)^{-1} g.$$

Compare Eq. (5.64) with Eq. (5.71). Since the limit in the sense of generalized functions is unique, we have $W(g; h, \cdot) = V(g; h, \cdot)$ in the sense of the generalized functions. By explicitly computing $W(g; h, \cdot)$:

$$W(g; h, x) = (2\pi)^{-1} \int_{-\infty + i\gamma}^{+\infty + i\gamma} e^{ix\xi} \phi_q^+(\xi) \left[-\frac{\phi_q^+(-i)^{-1} e^{(1-i\xi)h}}{1 - i\xi} + \frac{K e^{-i\xi h}}{-i\xi} \right] d\xi,$$

where $\gamma \in (\sigma_-, -1)$, it is easy to check that $W(g; h, \cdot)$ is continuous on $(h, +\infty)$ but if two continuous functions define the same generalized function, they coincide.

To sum up, we have shown that

$$V(g; h, \cdot) = \phi_q^+(D) \mathbf{1}_{[h, +\infty)} \phi_q^+(D)^{-1} g. \quad (5.72)$$

We set $w(x) = \phi_q^+(D)^{-1} g(x)$, and prove that the optimal h^* in Lemma 5.5 is the solution to the equation $w(x) = 0$, that is, $\phi_q^+(-i)^{-1} e^{h^*} - K = 0$. This and the rest of the proof can be done in essentially the same manner as in the case of puts.

5.4 Put-like and call-like options: the case of more general payoffs

5.4.1 *Put-like options*

In the set up of Subsection 5.3, we consider payoff functions $g(x)$ more general than $K - e^x$. Let $\sigma_+ > 0$ be from Lemma 3.5, let $h \in \mathbf{R}$, and consider the problem Eq. (5.25)-Eq. (5.26).

Theorem 5.6 *Let g and its derivatives $g^{(s)} = D^s g$, $s = 0, 1, 2$, be measurable, and satisfy the following estimates*

$$|g^{(s)}(x)| \leq Ce^{-\omega'_+ x}, \quad x \leq h, \tag{5.73}$$

$$|g^{(s)}(x)| \leq Ce^{-\omega'_- x}, \quad x \geq h, \tag{5.74}$$

where $\omega'_- < \omega'_+ < \sigma_+$. Then all the statements of Theorem 5.2 hold.

Proof. Eq. (5.73)-Eq. (5.74) are the very conditions we used in the proof of Theorem 5.2, with only one exception: if $\omega'_+ > 0$, then in the proof, we must take $\gamma \in (\omega'_+, \sigma_+)$. ☐

Remark 5.4 Notice that Eq. (5.74) is not a real restriction: if g fails to satisfy this condition, we can replace g with any lg, which coincides with g on $(-\infty, h]$ and satisfies Eq. (5.74). In particular, for any such lg,

$$V = \phi_q^-(D)\mathbf{1}_{(-\infty,h]}\phi_q^-(D)^{-1}lg, \tag{5.75}$$

which is understood as

$$V(x) = (2\pi)^{-1} \int_{-\infty+i\omega_+}^{+\infty+i\omega_+} e^{ix\xi}\phi_q^-(\xi)\hat{v}(\xi)d\xi, \tag{5.76}$$

where $v = \mathbf{1}_{(-\infty,h]}\phi_q^-(D)^{-1}lg$, and $\omega_+ \in (\omega'_+, \sigma_+)$ is arbitrary.
Set $w(x) = (\phi_q^-(D)^{-1}g)(x)$.

Theorem 5.7 *Let Eq. (5.73)–Eq. (5.74) hold with $\omega'_- < \omega'_+ < \sigma_+$ and some h, and let there exist $\tilde{h}_1 \leq \tilde{h}_2$ such that the following conditions are satisfied:*

$$w(x) > 0, \quad \forall x < \tilde{h}_1; \tag{5.77}$$

$$w(x) = 0, \quad \forall \tilde{h}_1 \leq x \leq \tilde{h}_2; \tag{5.78}$$

$$w(x) < 0, \quad \forall x > \tilde{h}_2. \tag{5.79}$$

Then for any $\tilde{h} \in [\tilde{h}_1, \tilde{h}_2]$, $\tau(\tilde{h})$ is an optimal stopping time in the class $\mathcal{M}_0$, and the rational option price is given by

$$V_*(x) = (2\pi)^{-1} \int_{-\infty+i\omega_+}^{+\infty+i\omega_+} e^{ix\xi} \phi_q^-(\xi)\hat{v}(\xi)d\xi, \qquad (5.80)$$

where $\omega_+ \in (\omega_+', \lambda_+)$, and $v = \mathbf{1}_{(-\infty, \tilde{h}]}w$.

Proof. We repeat the proof of optimality in the class $\mathcal{M}_0$ for the put, by making use of Lemma 5.2 and Theorem 5.6 instead of Theorem 5.2. □

Notice that Eq. (5.78) can be written in the form Eq. (5.19).

Consider payoffs of the form

$$g(x) = \sum_{j=1}^{m} c_j \exp(\gamma_j x), \qquad (5.81)$$

where $-\sigma_+ < \gamma_1 \leq \gamma_2 \leq \cdots$. Then Eq. (5.74) and Eq. (5.73) hold, and in concrete cases, conditions Eq. (5.77)-Eq. (5.79) are easy to verify since

$$w(x) = \sum_{j=1}^{l} c_j \phi_q^-(-i\gamma_j)^{-1} e^{\gamma_j x}. \qquad (5.82)$$

In particular, if they are satisfied then $\tilde{h}_1 = \tilde{h}_2$; call it h_*. Notice that the necessary condition for Eq. (5.77) and Eq. (5.79) is $c_1 > 0$ and $c_l < 0$, respectively.

Example 5.2 Suppose, the option owner has the right to sell a share of the stock for $K + a\sqrt{S}$, where S is the spot price. Then

$$\begin{aligned} g(x) &= K + ae^{x/2} - e^x, \\ w(x) &= K + a\phi_q^-(-i/2)^{-1}e^{x/2} - \phi_q^-(-i)^{-1}e^x, \end{aligned}$$

and the optimal exercise boundary is $h_* = \sqrt{Y}$, where Y is the unique positive root of the equation

$$K + a\phi_q^-(-i/2)^{-1}Y - \phi_q^-(-i)^{-1}Y^2 = 0.$$

When h_* is found, one can easily calculate $v = \mathbf{1}_{(-\infty, h_*]}w$ and $\hat{v}(\xi)$, for any ξ in the strip $\Im\xi \in (0, \sigma_+)$:

$$\hat{v}(\xi) = \int_{-\infty}^{h^*} e^{-ix\xi}[K + a\phi_q^-(-i/2)^{-1}e^{x/2} - \phi_q^-(-i)^{-1}e^x]dx$$

$$= \frac{Ke^{-ih_*\xi}}{-i\xi} + a\phi_q^-(-i/2)^{-1}\frac{e^{(0.5-i\xi)h_*}}{0.5-i\xi} - \phi_q^-(-i)^{-1}\frac{e^{(1-i\xi)h_*}}{1-i\xi},$$

and after substituting into Eq. (5.80), obtain the rational option price:

$$
\begin{aligned}
V_*(x) &= (2\pi)^{-1}\int_{-\infty+i\omega_+}^{+\infty+i\omega_+} e^{i(x-h_*)\xi}\phi_q^-(\xi) \\
&\quad \times \left[\frac{K}{-i\xi} + \frac{ae^{0.5h_*}}{\phi_q^-(-i/2)(0.5-i\xi)} - \frac{e^{h_*}}{\phi_q^-(-i)(1-i\xi)}\right]d\xi,
\end{aligned}
$$

where $\omega_+ \in (0,\sigma_+)$ is arbitrary. By using the approximation Eq. (3.82) for $\phi_q^-(\xi)$, we obtain the approximation to the rational option price:

$$
\begin{aligned}
V_{\mathrm{ap}}(x) &= (2\pi)^{-1}\int_{-\infty+i\omega_+}^{+\infty+i\omega_+} e^{i(x-h_*)\xi}\frac{-\beta_-}{-\beta_-+i\xi} \\
&\quad \times \left[\frac{K}{-i\xi} + \frac{ae^{0.5h_*}}{\phi_q^-(-i/2)(0.5-i\xi)} - \frac{e^{h_*}}{\phi_q^-(-i)(1-i\xi)}\right]d\xi.
\end{aligned}
$$

The integrand has the only pole $\xi = -i\beta_-$ hanging above the line of integration, and this pole is simple. By pushing the line of integration up and using the residue theorem, we obtain the following approximation:

$$V_{\mathrm{ap}}(x) = De^{\beta_-(x-h_*)}, \quad x > h_*,$$

where

$$D = K + \frac{-\beta_- ae^{0.5h_*}}{\phi_q^-(-i/2)(0.5-\beta_-)} - \frac{-\beta_- e^{h_*}}{\phi_q^-(-i)(1-\beta_-)}.$$

The next theorem shows that for model RLPE, the stopping time obtained in Example 5.2 is optimal not only in the class $\mathcal{M}_0$ but in the class $\mathcal{M}$ as well.

Theorem 5.8 *Assume the following conditions:*

a) X is a mixture of independent model RLPE;
b) g can be represented in the form

$$g(x) = \sum_{k=1}^{l} c_k^+ \exp[\gamma_k^+ x] - \sum_{k=1}^{l} c_k^- \exp[\gamma_k^- x], \qquad (5.83)$$

where $c_k^{\pm}$ are positive, $\gamma_k^+ > -\sigma_+$, $k = 1, \ldots, l$, are not necessarily different, as well as $\gamma_k^- > -\sigma_+$, $k = 1, \ldots, l$, and satisfy

$$\gamma_k^+ < \gamma_k^-, \quad \forall\, k; \tag{5.84}$$

c) for all k, the solution to the equation

$$c_k^+ \phi_q^- (-i\gamma_k^+)^{-1} e^{\gamma_k^+ h} = c_k^- \phi_q^- (-i\gamma_k^-)^{-1} e^{\gamma_k^- h} \tag{5.85}$$

is the same; call it h_*.

Then $\tau(h_*)$ is the optimal stopping time in the class $\mathcal{M}$, and the rational option price is given by Eq. (5.80) with any $\omega_+ \in (\max_j(-\gamma_j), \sigma_+)$, $\tilde{h} = h_*$, and

$$\hat{v}(\xi) = \sum_{j=1}^{l} c_j^+ \phi_q^- (-i\gamma_j^+)^{-1} e^{(\gamma_j^+ - i\xi)h_*} \frac{\gamma_j^- - \gamma_j^+}{(\gamma_j^+ - i\xi)(\gamma_j^- - i\xi)}. \tag{5.86}$$

Proof. Recall that in the case of the put option, we managed to check all the conditions of optimality but Eq. (5.6) for any RLPE, and the same argument is valid here, even for much more general payoffs than Eq. (5.81). Thus, the additional conditions b) and c) are needed to verify Eq. (5.6).

Eq. (5.83) allows us to represent g as a sum of payoffs of the form

$$g_j(x) = c_j^+ e^{\gamma_j^+ x} - c_j^- e^{\gamma_j^- x}; \tag{5.87}$$

and Eq. (5.85) implies that $h_* = h_*(g_j)$ is the same for all j. But when h_* is the same for all payoffs g_j, Eq. (5.6) is evidently "additive" w.r.t. g in the sense that if it holds for all $V_*(g_j, x)$ defined by g_j, then it holds for $V_*(g, x)$. Thus, it remains to consider the payoff Eq. (5.87), and we can repeat the proof of Eq. (5.6) for the put with the straightforward changes. $\qquad \square$

5.4.2 *Call-like options*

In the set up of Subsection 5.4, we consider payoff functions $g(x)$ more general than $e^x - K$. The statements and the proofs are obtained from the ones by reflection of the real axis w.r.t. the origin, with the corresponding changes of signs and signs of inequalities. We start with an auxiliary result about the Wiener-Hopf equation on $(-\infty, h)$.

Let $\sigma_- < 0$ be from Lemma 3.5, and consider the problem

$$(q - L)V(x) = 0, \qquad x < h, \tag{5.88}$$

$$V(x) = g(x), \qquad x \geq h. \tag{5.89}$$

Theorem 5.9 *Let g and its derivatives $g^{(s)} = D^s g$, $s = 0, 1, 2$, be measurable, and satisfy the estimates Eq. (5.73)-Eq. (5.74) with $\sigma_- < \omega'_- < \omega'_+$. Then for any $h \in \mathbf{R}$, a solution to the problem Eq. (5.88)-Eq. (5.89) in the class of functions bounded on $(-\infty, h]$ exists, and*

(i) *if $\kappa_+ = 1$, then a continuous bounded solution is unique. It is given by*

$$V = \phi_q^+(D)\mathbf{1}_{[h,+\infty)}\phi_q^+(D)^{-1}g; \tag{5.90}$$

(ii) *if $\kappa_+ \in (0,1)$, then a bounded solution is unique. It is given by Eq. (5.90), and it is continuous;*
(iii) *if $\kappa_+ = 0$, then a bounded solution is unique. It is given by Eq. (5.90), and it is continuous if and only if $(\phi_q^+(D)^{-1}g)(h) = 0$;*
(iv) *if $\kappa_+ \in (0,1]$, then $V'(h-0) = V'(h+0)$ if and only if $(\phi_q^+(D)^{-1}g)(h) = 0$.*

Remark 5.5 Notice that Eq. (5.73) is not a real restriction: if g fails to satisfy this condition, we can replace g with any lg which coincides with g on $[h, +\infty)$ and satisfies Eq. (5.73). In particular, for any such lg,

$$V(x) = \phi_q^+(D)\mathbf{1}_{[h,+\infty)}\phi_q^+(D)^{-1}lg, \tag{5.91}$$

which is understood as

$$V(x) = (2\pi)^{-1}\int_{-\infty+i\omega_-}^{+\infty+i\omega_-} e^{ix\xi}\phi_q^+(\xi)\hat{v}(\xi)d\xi, \tag{5.92}$$

where $v = \mathbf{1}_{[h,+\infty)}\phi_q^+(D)^{-1}lg$, and $\omega_- \in (\sigma_-, \omega'_-)$ is arbitrary.
Set

$$w(x) = (\phi_q^+(D)^{-1}g)(x).$$

Theorem 5.10 *Let Eq. (5.73)-Eq. (5.74) hold with $\sigma_- < \omega'_- < \omega'_+$ and some h, and let there exist $\tilde{h}_1 \leq \tilde{h}_2$ such that the following conditions are satisfied:*

$$w(x) < 0, \qquad \forall\, x < \tilde{h}_1; \tag{5.93}$$

$$w(x) = 0, \quad \forall \, \tilde{h}_1 \leq x \leq \tilde{h}_2; \qquad (5.94)$$

$$w(x) > 0, \quad \forall \, x > \tilde{h}_2. \qquad (5.95)$$

Then for any $\tilde{h} \in [\tilde{h}_1, \tilde{h}_2]$, $\tau(\tilde{h})$ *is an optimal stopping time in the class* $\mathcal{M}_0$, *and the rational option price is given by*

$$V^*(x) = (2\pi)^{-1} \int_{-\infty+i\omega_-}^{+\infty+i\omega_-} e^{i(x-\tilde{h})\xi} \phi_q^+(\xi)\hat{v}(\xi)d\xi, \qquad (5.96)$$

where $\omega_- \in (\sigma_-, \omega'_-)$, *and* $v = \mathbf{1}_{[\tilde{h},+\infty)}w$.

Notice that Eq. (5.94) can be written in the form Eq. (5.59).

Consider payoffs of the form Eq. (5.81), where $\gamma_1 \leq \gamma_2 \leq \cdots < -\sigma_-$. Then Eq. (5.74) and Eq. (5.73) hold, and in concrete cases, conditions Eq. (5.93)-Eq. (5.95) are easy to verify since

$$w(x) = \sum_{j=1}^{l} c_j \phi_q^+(-i\gamma_j)^{-1} e^{\gamma_j x}. \qquad (5.97)$$

In particular, if they are satisfied then $\tilde{h}_1 = \tilde{h}_2$; call it h^*. Notice that the necessary condition for Eq. (5.93) and Eq. (5.95) is $c_1 < 0$ and $c_l > 0$, respectively.

Theorem 5.11   *Assume the following conditions:*

a) X is a mixture of independent model RLPE;
b) g can be represented in the form

$$g(x) = -\sum_{k=1}^{l} c_k^+ \exp[\gamma_k^+ x] + \sum_{k=1}^{l} c_k^- \exp[\gamma_k^- x], \qquad (5.98)$$

where $c_k^{\pm}$ are positive, $\gamma_k^+ < -\sigma_-$, $k = 1, \ldots, l$, are not necessarily different, as well as $\gamma_k^- < -\sigma_-$, $k = 1, \ldots, l$, and satisfy

$$\gamma_k^+ < \gamma_k^-, \quad \forall \, k; \qquad (5.99)$$

c) for all k, the solution to the equation

$$c_k^+ \phi_q^+(-i\gamma_k^+)^{-1} e^{\gamma_k^+ h} = c_k^- \phi_q^+(-i\gamma_k^-)^{-1} e^{\gamma_k^- h} \qquad (5.100)$$

is the same; call it h^*.

Then $\tau(h^*)$ *is the optimal stopping time in the class* $\mathcal{M}$, *and the rational option price is given by Eq. (5.96) with any* $\omega_+ \in (\sigma_-, \min_j(-\gamma_j))$, $\tilde{h} = h^*$, *and*

$$\hat{v}(\xi) = -\sum_{j=1}^{l} c_j^+ \phi_q^+ (-i\gamma_j^+)^{-1} e^{(\gamma_j^+ - i\xi)h^*} \frac{\gamma_j^- - \gamma_j^+}{(\gamma_j^+ - i\xi)(\gamma_j^- - i\xi)}. \qquad (5.101)$$

5.5 Commentary

The results of this chapter are obtained in Boyarchenko and Levendorskiĭ (2002a) but several of key points of the proofs in op. cit. are essentially simplified here, and the exposition is somewhat different. In the Brownian motion case, the price of the perpetual call (under the historic measure) was calculated by McKean (1965); the pricing problem for the perpetual put was solved by Merton (1973). For diffusions with jumps, the prices of the perpetual puts and calls were computed in Mordecki (1998, 1999). For RLPE, the price of perpetual American put was calculated in Boyarchenko and Levendorskiĭ (1998, 1999b, 2000), in terms of the factors in the Wiener-Hopf factorization formula, and in the earlier version of Boyarchenko and Levendorskiĭ (2002a), which was circulated in (2000), the calls were considered, too. In op. cit., it was surmised that the results in terms of the factors in the Wiener-Hopf factorization formula should hold for any Lévy process. Later, Mordecki (2000) announced the pricing formulas for puts and calls in terms of the infimum and supremum processes, respectively, for any Lévy process. Mordecki used the reduction to the similar result in Darling et al.(1972) for puts, in the discrete time (for the formulation, see Chapter 13), and a variant of this result for calls which he derived.

For applications of the Wiener-Hopf method to the Queuing theory and Insurance, see Borovkov (1972) and Prabhu (1980).

Chapter 6

American options: finite time horizon

In the finite horizon case, there are no explicit analytical pricing formulas
even in the Brownian motion case. We formulate the free boundary value
problem for the price of an American option, and consider several analogues
of approximate methods used in the Gaussian option pricing theory. We
also derive an approximate formula for the early exercise boundary near the
maturity and show that its behaviour in the RLPE-case drastically differs
from the behaviour in the Gaussian case.

6.1 General discussion

6.1.1 The free boundary problem

Consider an American option with the expiry date T and the payoff function
$g(X_t, t)$; since the option owner has the right to exercise the option any
instant t before or on the expiry date, g may depend not only on the log-
spot price X_t but on t as well. We assume that the riskless rate $r > 0$ is
constant, and X is an RLPE under the risk-neutral measure $\mathbf{Q}$ chosen by
the market. The option owner chooses her optimal exercise policy in order
to maximize the expected discounted payoff

$$V_*(x, t) = \sup_\tau E^{\mathbf{Q}}[e^{-r\tau} g(X_\tau, \tau) \mid X_0 = x],$$

where supremum is taken over the set of stopping times satisfying $\tau(\omega) \leq T$, $\forall\, \omega \in \Omega$.

Let $L = L^{\mathbf{Q}}$ be the infinitesimal generator of X under $\mathbf{Q}$. Assume that
the optimal stopping time is of the form $\tau'_B \wedge T$, where τ'_B is the hitting time

151

152 American options: finite time horizon

of a closed set $B \subset \mathbf{R} \times (-\infty, T]$ by a two-dimensional process $\hat{X}_t = (X_t, t)$. Set $\mathcal{C} = \mathbf{R} \times [0, T) \setminus B$ (this is the region where the option remains alive), and consider the following boundary value problem

$$(\partial_t + L - r)V(x,t) = 0, \qquad (x,t) \in \mathcal{C}; \qquad (6.1)$$
$$V(x,t) = g(x,t), \quad (x,t) \in B \text{ or } t = T; \qquad (6.2)$$
$$V(x,t) \geq g(x,t), \quad t \leq T, \ x \in \mathbf{R}; \qquad (6.3)$$
$$(\partial_t + L - r)V(x,t) \leq 0, \qquad t < T, \ (x,t) \notin \bar{\mathcal{C}}. \qquad (6.4)$$

Denote by $\hat{L} = \partial_t + L$ the infinitesimal generator of the two-dimensional process $\hat{X}$, and by $\hat{U}^r$ its resolvent.

Theorem 6.1 *Let the following conditions hold:*

a) the r-potential measure of ∂B is zero: $\hat{U}^r 1_{\partial B} = 0$, a. e.;
b) V_* is a continuous solution to the problem Eq. (6.1)-Eq. (6.4);
c) $W_* := (r - \hat{L})V_*$ is universally measurable, and
d) $\hat{U}^r W_* = V_*$.

Then B is the optimal early exercise region, and V_* is the rational option price.

Proof. Repeat the proof of Lemma 5.1 with the process $\hat{X}$ instead of X, taking into account that a sample path of $\hat{X}$ cannot cross the line $t = T$ by a jump. □

For the detailed study of the free boundary problem for the American put in the Gaussian case, see monographs Musiela and Rutkowski (1997), Karatzas and Shreve (1998), Shiryaev (1999) and the bibliography in op. cit.

6.1.2 *The role of dividends and non-zero interest rate*

In the case of a non-dividend paying stock, the process $\{e^{-rt}S_t\}$ is a martingale under $\mathbf{Q}$, which translates into the EMM condition

$$r + \psi^{\mathbf{Q}}(-i) = 0 \qquad (6.5)$$

for the characteristic exponent $\psi^{\mathbf{Q}}$ of the process X, under $\mathbf{Q}$. If the stock pays dividends at the constant rate $\lambda > 0$, then $\{e^{-(r-\lambda)t}S_t\}$ is a martingale under $\mathbf{Q}$, and the EMM condition assumes the form

$$r - \lambda + \psi^{\mathbf{Q}}(-i) = 0. \tag{6.6}$$

Eq. (6.6) implies that

$$r + \psi^{\mathbf{Q}}(-i) > 0; \tag{6.7}$$

and from the technical point of view, this is the difference between Eq. (6.5) and Eq. (6.7) which leads to Merton's (1973) result on the *no-early-exercise* of the American call on a non-dividend-paying stock. Merton's no-arbitrage argument is universal; in particular, it is valid not only in the Gaussian case, but also for any Lévy process.

Similarly, if the interest rate is zero: $r = 0$, then it is non-optimal to exercise the American put before maturity.

6.2 Approximations of the American put price

We consider RLPE-analogues of three methods of approximate pricing of the American put, popular in Gaussian Mathematical Finance; the American call on a dividend-paying stock and other types of American options can be treated similarly. The problem of pricing of American contingent claims being of great practical interest, there exist a host of other methods (see, e.g., Hull (2000), Kwok (1998), Musiela and Rutkowski (1997), Wilmott *et al.* (1993), and the bibliography there).

6.2.1 *Geske-Johnson approximation*

The approximation proposed by Geske and Johnson (1984) uses the discretization of the time parameter and the backward induction, as in any other standard discrete time approach. Assume that the option can be exercised only on the deterministic dates $t_1 < t_2 < \cdots < t_n = T$. An option which can be exercised before expiry but only on dates $t_1 < t_2 < \cdots < t_n$ fixed in advance is called a Bermudan option; thus, the *Geske-Johnson approximation* is an approximation of an American option by the corresponding Bermudan option. In the Gaussian case, the explicit analytical formula for the joint distribution of the stock prices $(S_{t_1}, \ldots, S_{t_n})$ is known, and so the application of the following procedure is straightforward.

Let $v_j(x) = V(e^x, t_j)$ be the value of the option at time $t = t_j$. For $j = n$, when $t_n = T$, v_n is the terminal payoff: $v_n(x) = \max\{K - e^x, 0\}$. At time t_j, $j = n - 1, n - 2, \ldots, 1$, the option owner chooses the optimal exercise boundary h_j as the solution to the equation

$$K - e^x = e^{-r\tau_j} E^x[v_{j+1}(X_{t_j})], \qquad (6.8)$$

where $\tau_j = t_{j+1} - t_j$. In Eq. (6.8), the LHS is the payoff at the current level of the log-price, x, and the RHS is the discounted expected value of keeping the option alive. If an analytical formula for the probability density p_t of the process X_t under $\mathbf{Q}$ is known, as is the case with NIG, or tabulated, which can be done for any model RLPE, then Eq. (6.8) can be solved numerically, and after the optimal exercise boundary h_j is found, v_j is calculated as

$$v_j(x) = \begin{cases} e^{-r\tau_j} \int_{-\infty}^{+\infty} p_{\tau_j}(y) v_{j+1}(x + y) dy, & x > h_j, \\ K - e^x, & x \leq h_j. \end{cases}$$

In the Brownian motion case, it is known that Eq. (6.8) has a unique solution, and the sequence $\{v_j\}$ converges to the option exact price when $\Delta := \max \tau_j \to 0$; one should expect that the same holds in the RLPE-case as well. To estimate the limit, one may use Richardson's approximation scheme (see, e.g., Musiela and Rutkowski (1997)).

6.2.2 *Analytic method of lines*

Carr and Faguet (1994) suggested to use the *time discretization* in the Black-Scholes equation. They studied the Brownian motion case; in our non-Gaussian situation, we discretize the derivative ∂_t in the generalized Black-Scholes equation Eq. (6.1). In the Gaussian case, it is possible to use the smooth pasting principle to replace the optimality conditions Eq. (6.3)-Eq. (6.4). Since we have shown in the case of perpetual American put that the smooth pasting principle may fail in the non-Gaussian case, we have to find the optimal discretized boundary by other means similar to the ones used in the perpetual option case.

Divide $[0, T]$ into n subperiods by points $t_j = j\Delta, j = 0, 1, \ldots, n$, where $\Delta = T/n$, and denote by $v_j(x)$ the approximation to $V(x, t_j)$. Then $v_n(x) = \max\{K - e^x, 0\}$, and by discretizing the derivative ∂_t in Eq. (6.1), we obtain, for $j = n - 1, n - 2, \ldots, 0$,

$$\Delta^{-1}(v_{j+1} - v_j) - (r + \psi(D_x))v_j(x) = 0, \quad x > h_j,$$

or

$$(1 + \Delta(r + \psi(D_x)))v_j(x) = v_{j+1}(x), \quad x > h_j. \tag{6.9}$$

Eq. (6.2) assumes the form

$$v_j(x) = g(x), \quad x \leq h_j, \tag{6.10}$$

where $g(x) = K - e^x$. Set $q = \Delta^{-1} + r$,

$$a_\Delta(\xi) = 1 + \Delta(r + \psi(\xi)) = \Delta(q + \psi(\xi)),$$

factorize a_Δ:

$$a_\Delta(\xi) = (1 + r\Delta)\phi_q^+(\xi)^{-1}\phi_q^-(\xi)^{-1},$$

where $\phi_q^\pm$ is the Fourier transform of a probability distribution $P_q^\pm(dx)$ supported on $\mathbf{R}_\mp$ (see Chapter 5), and solve the problem Eq. (6.9)-Eq. (6.10) by using the Wiener-Hopf factorization method.

Denote by v_{j1} the solution to the problem Eq. (6.9)-Eq. (6.10) with $v_{j+1} = 0$. Theorem 5.2 gives

$$v_{j1} = \phi_q^-(D)\mathbf{1}_{(-\infty,h_j]}\phi_q^-(D)^{-1}g,$$

and reasoning the same way as in the proof of Theorem 5.2, we can show that the solution to the problem Eq. (6.9)-Eq. (6.10) with $g = 0$, call it v_{j2}, is given by

$$v_{j2} = (1 + r\Delta)^{-1}\phi_q^-(D)\mathbf{1}_{[h_j,+\infty)}\phi_q^+(D)v_{j+1}.$$

Clearly, $v_j = v_{j1} + v_{j2}$, hence

$$
\begin{aligned}
v_j &= \phi_q^-(D)\mathbf{1}_{(-\infty,h_j]}\phi_q^-(D)^{-1}g \\
&\quad + (1 + r\Delta)^{-1}\phi_q^-(D)\mathbf{1}_{[h_j,+\infty)}\phi_q^+(D)v_{j+1} \\
&= g - \phi_q^-(D)\mathbf{1}_{[h_j,+\infty)}\phi_q^-(D)^{-1}g \\
&\quad + (1 + r\Delta)^{-1}\phi_q^-(D)\mathbf{1}_{[h_j,+\infty)}\phi_q^+(D)v_{j+1} \\
&= (K - e^x) + (1 + r\Delta)^{-1}\phi_q^-(D)\mathbf{1}_{[h_j,+\infty)}w_j,
\end{aligned}
$$

where

$$
\begin{aligned}
w_j &= \phi_q^+(D)v_{j+1} - (1 + r\Delta)\phi_q^-(D)^{-1}(K - e^x) \\
&= \phi_q^+(D)v_{j+1} - (1 + r\Delta)(K - \phi_q^-(-i)^{-1}e^x) \\
&= \phi_q^+(D)[v_{j+1} + e^x - (1 + r\Delta)K].
\end{aligned}
$$

To derive the last equality, we have used the EMM-condition $r + \psi(-i) = 0$, and the Wiener-Hopf factorization at $\xi = -i$:

$$
\phi_q^-(-i)^{-1}\phi_q^+(-i)^{-1} = \frac{1 + \Delta(r + \psi(-i))}{1 + r\Delta} = (1 + r\Delta)^{-1}.
$$

Hence,

$$
v_j = (K - e^x) + (1 + r\Delta)^{-1}\phi_q^-(D)\mathbf{1}_{[h_j, +\infty)}\phi_q^+(D)z_j, \qquad (6.11)
$$

where

$$
z_j(x) = v_{j+1}(x) + e^x - (1 + r\Delta)K.
$$

Lemma 6.1 *For $j = n - 1, \dots, 0$, the function $w_j = \phi_q^+(D)z_j$ is increasing, and it changes the sign.*

Proof. We have $v_n = (K - e^x)_+$, whence $z_{n-1}(x) = (e^x - K)_+ - r\Delta K$ is increasing, and hence so is

$$
\begin{aligned}
w_{n-1}(x) &= (\phi_q^+(D)z_{n-1})(x) \\
&= \int_{-\infty}^{+\infty} z_{n-1}(x + y)P_q^+(dy).
\end{aligned}
$$

Now, by a similar argument, from Eq. (6.11) we deduce that

$$
\begin{aligned}
z_{n-2} &= e^x - K + v_{n-1} - rK\Delta \\
&= (1 + r\Delta)^{-1}\phi_q^-(D)\mathbf{1}_{[h_{n-1}, +\infty)}\phi_q^+(D)z_{n-1} - rK\Delta
\end{aligned}
$$

is increasing, and so is w_{n-2}. By iterating, we deduce that w_j is increasing for all j.

To show that w_j changes sign, notice that

$$
0 \leq v_j(x) < K, \quad \forall x \qquad (6.12)
$$

(Eq. (6.12) will be proved at the end of the proof of Lemma). By using Eq. (6.12), we derive

$$\limsup_{x \to -\infty} w_j(x) = \limsup_{x \to -\infty} [\phi_q^+(D)v_{j+1} + \phi_q^+(-i)e^x - (1+r\Delta)K]$$
$$< \phi_q^+(D)K - K \le K - K = 0,$$

and

$$\lim_{x \to +\infty} w_j(x) = \lim_{x \to +\infty} [\phi_q^+(D)v_{j+1} + \phi_q^+(-i)e^x - (1+r\Delta)K] = +\infty;$$

therefore, w_j changes sign.

It remains to prove Eq. (6.12). By Theorem 5.2, for $j < n$, v_j is the unique bounded (or unique bounded continuous) solution to the problem Eq. (6.9)-Eq. (6.10), hence from Theorem 2.12 we conclude that v_j can be represented in the form of the stochastic integral

$$v_j(x) = E^x \left[\int_0^{\tau_j} e^{-qt} \Delta^{-1} v_{j+1}(X_t) dt \right] + E^x \left[e^{-q\tau_j} (K - e^{X_{\tau_j}}) \right],$$

where τ_j is the hitting time of $(-\infty, h_j]$. Since $v_n(x) = \max\{K - e^x, 0\} \in [0, K)$, we find that v_{n-1} is non-negative, and it admits an upper bound via

$$E^x[K(\Delta^{-1} q^{-1}(1 - e^{-q\tau_j}) + e^{-q\tau_j})] < K,$$

that is, v_{n-1} satisfies Eq. (6.12). By iterating, we derive Eq. (6.12) for $j = n - 2, \ldots, 0$. □

From Lemma 6.1, w_j has the only zero, call it $h_{j,*}$.

Theorem 6.2 *The optimal exercise boundary at time t_j is $h_{j,*}$, $j = n - 1, n - 2, \ldots, 0$.*

Proof. To stress the dependence on the exercise boundary h_j, we write $v_j(h_j; x)$ instead of $v_j(x)$. Clearly, w_j is negative to the left of $h_{j,*}$, and positive to the right of it. Hence, with a choice $h_j < h_{j,*}$, $\mathbf{1}_{[h_j, +\infty)} w_j$ is negative in a right neighbourhood of h_j, and since $\phi_q^-(D)$ is the convolution operator with the kernel supported on the positive axis, we conclude that

$$v_j(h_j, x) = K - e^x + \phi_q^-(D)\mathbf{1}_{[h_j, +\infty)} w_j(x)$$
$$< K - e^x$$

at some points, which is impossible if the choice of h_j is optimal. If $h_j > h_{j,*}$, then

$$\mathbf{1}_{[h_j,+\infty)}w_j(x) < \mathbf{1}_{[h_{j,*},+\infty)}w_j(x)$$

on $[h_{j,*}, h_j)$, and both sides coincide on the complement to this interval. We conclude that

$$v_j(h_j, x) \le v_j(h_{j,*}, x), \quad \forall\, x$$

(and for some x, the inequality is strict), which finishes the proof of Theorem. □

To sum up: the algorithm for the discrete time approximation to the optimal exercise boundary and the rational put price is as follows:
1. Set $h_{n,*} = \ln K, \quad v_n(x) = \max\{K - e^x, 0\}$;
2. For $j = n - 1, n - 2, \ldots$, define

$$w_j = \phi_q^+(D)[v_{j+1} + e^x - (1 + r\Delta)K],$$

next find $h_{j,*}$ as the unique solution to the equation

$$w_j(x) = 0,$$

and set

$$v_j(x) = K - e^x + (1 + r\Delta)^{-1}\phi_q^-(D)\mathbf{1}_{[h_{j,*},+\infty)}w_j(x).$$

6.2.3   *Carr's randomization*

Carr (1998) suggested the following procedure in the Gaussian case. The first step of the procedure remains the same in the non-Gaussian case, and we end up with the same algorithm as in the analytical method of lines. First, we divide the period $[0, T]$ into n sub-periods of the length $\Delta = T/n$, next, set $t_j = j\Delta$, and find approximations h_j and v_j to the optimal exercise boundary by using the backwards induction. We have $v_n(x) = \max\{g(x), 0\}$, where $g(x) = K - e^x$; for $j = n-1, n-2, \ldots, 0$, the approximation v_j is defined as

$$v_j(x) = \max_{h_j} V(v_{j+1}, h_j; x),$$

where $V(v, h; x)$ is the value of a barrier option with the terminal payoff v, the down-and-out barrier h, and the rebate g (we may assume that only barriers h s.t. $g(x) \geq 0$ for all $x \leq h$ are considered); the maturity date, τ, is a random variable which is exponentially distributed with scale parameter $\lambda = 1/\Delta$. Hence,

$$v_j(x) = \max_{h_j} \lambda \int_0^{+\infty} e^{-\lambda t} U(v_{j+1}, h_j; x, t) dt,$$

where $U(v_{j+1}, h_j; x, t)$ is the value (at time 0) of a barrier option with the maturity date t, the terminal payoff v_{j+1}, down-and-out barrier h_j, and rebate g. From Theorem 2.13, we conclude that $U(v_{j+1}, h_j; x, t)$ is equal to $W(x, 0)$ (the arguments v_{j+1}, h_j, t are suppressed), where $W(x, s)$ is a bounded solution to to the following boundary value problem

$$\begin{aligned}
\partial_s W(x, s) - (r + \psi(D_x))W(x, s) &= 0, & x > h_j, \ s < t; \\
W(x, t) &= v_{j+1}(x), & x > h_j; \\
W(x, s) &= K - e^x, & x \leq h_j, \ s \leq t.
\end{aligned}$$

By making the change of variable $s = t - \tau$, and applying the Laplace-Carson transform[1] w.r.t. τ, we obtain the family of problems

$$\begin{aligned}
\lambda v_j(x) + (r + \psi(D_x))v_j(x) &= \lambda v_{j+1}(x), & x > h_j, & \qquad (6.13) \\
v_j(x) &= K - e^x, & x \leq h_j. & \qquad (6.14)
\end{aligned}$$

Divide Eq. (6.13) by λ, and take into account that $\lambda^{-1} = \Delta$; we see that the problem Eq. (6.13)-Eq. (6.14) turns into the problem Eq. (6.9)-Eq. (6.10), and as in the preceding subsection, the free boundary h_j must to be chosen so as to ensure that the solution is optimal. The result is the procedure described at the end of Subsection 6.2.2

6.3 American put near expiry

6.3.1 *Behaviour of the early exercise boundary near the maturity date*

To simplify the formulas, we normalize the strike price K to 1. In the Brownian motion case, the following asymptotics of the optimal exercise

---

[1]The Laplace-Carson transform differs from the standard Laplace transform by an additional λ-factor.

boundary $x = h(T - t)$ is known

$$h(T - t) \sim -\sigma\sqrt{(t - T)\ln(T - t)}, \qquad (6.15)$$

as $t \to T - 0$ (see, e.g., Barles *et al.* (1995) and Lamberton (1995)). We have been unable to study the behaviour of the optimal early exercise boundary near the expiry in the proper continuous time setting; instead, we study the asymptotics of the boundary point $h_{n-1} = h(\Delta)$ at the last moment before expiry, as $\Delta \to 0$, in the discretization of the continuous time model. We believe that the asymptotics of $h(\Delta)$ can be used as a good proxy for the asymptotics of the boundary near expiry.

We study NTS Lévy processes, NIG in particular; similarly, KoBoL and Hyperbolic processes can be treated. The main result is that in many cases, in particular, for processes of order $\nu \in [1, 2)$, the limit of $h(\Delta)$ is negative, and not zero, as in the Gaussian case. Notice the opposite effect for the boundary far from expiry: the numerical results for the optimal exercise price h_* of the perpetual American put show that typically, the Gaussian model gives smaller h_*, and we may conclude that in the non-Gaussian case, the optimal exercise boundary is more flat than in the Gaussian case. This observation shows that there is some compensation for the apparent difficulties with the design of appropriate numerical procedures for pricing of the American put in the non-Gaussian case.

For processes of order between 0 and 1, the behaviour of $h(\Delta)$ of various types is possible, depending on all the parameters of the process; we will not list the corresponding formulas here.

6.3.2 *A general equation for $h(\Delta)$ in the case of NTS processes*

Consider the equation for $h_{n-1} = h(\Delta)$:

$$\phi_q^+(D)[(1 - e^x)_+ + e^x - 1 - r\Delta] = 0.$$

Rewrite it as

$$\phi_q^+(D)[(e^x - 1)_+ - r\Delta] = 0,$$

and then, by using the equality

$$\phi_q^+(D) \cdot 1 = \phi_q^+(0) \cdot 1 = 1,$$

and the definition of PDO, as

$$(2\pi)^{-1}\int_{-\infty+i\omega_-}^{+\infty+i\omega_-}\frac{e^{ix\xi}\phi_q^+(\xi)}{-i\xi(1-i\xi)}d\xi=r\Delta, \tag{6.16}$$

where $\omega_-\in(\lambda_-,-1)$ is arbitrary. Since

$$\phi_q^+(\xi)=\frac{q}{(q+\psi(\xi))\phi_q^-(\xi)},$$

we continue the transformation of the equation for $x=h(\Delta)$:

$$(2\pi)^{-1}\int_{-\infty+i\omega_-}^{+\infty+i\omega_-}\frac{e^{ix\xi}q\,d\xi}{(q+\psi(\xi))\phi_q^-(\xi)(-i\xi)(1-i\xi)}=r\Delta. \tag{6.17}$$

In the NTS Lévy case, $\lambda_\pm=\pm\alpha+\beta$, and the formula for the characteristic exponent of an NTS Lévy process is

$$\psi(\xi)=-i\mu\xi+\delta[(\alpha^2-(\beta+i\xi)^2)^{\nu/2}-(\alpha^2-\beta^2)^{\nu/2}].$$

By transforming the line of the integration in Eq. (6.17) into the integral over the cut in the lower half-plane, and multiplying both sides by q, we obtain

$$(2\pi)^{-1}\int_{-\infty}^{-\alpha+\beta}\frac{e^{-xz}q^2[\psi(iz+0)-\psi(iz-0)]i\,dz}{\phi_q^-(iz)z(1+z)(q+\psi(iz+0))(q+\psi(iz-0))}=rq\Delta. \tag{6.18}$$

Notice that

$$rq\Delta=r(\Delta^{-1}+r)\Delta\to r\quad\text{as }\Delta\to0, \tag{6.19}$$

and

$$\begin{aligned}\psi(iz\pm0)&=\mu z-\delta(\alpha^2-\beta^2)^{\nu/2}+\delta(\alpha^2-(\beta-z\pm i0)^2)^{\nu/2}\\&=\mu z-\delta(\alpha^2-\beta^2)^{\nu/2}+\delta((\beta-z)^2-\alpha^2)^{\nu/2}e^{\mp i\pi\nu/2}.\end{aligned}$$

We conclude that

$$\begin{aligned}[\psi(iz+0)-\psi(iz-0)]i&=\delta((\beta-z)^2-\alpha^2)^{\nu/2}(e^{-i\pi\nu/2}-e^{i\pi\nu/2})i\\&=2\delta\sin\frac{\pi\nu}{2}((\beta-z)^2-\alpha^2)^{\nu/2},\end{aligned} \tag{6.20}$$

and

$$\begin{aligned}(q+\psi(iz+0))(q+\psi(iz-0))&=(q+\mu z-\delta(\alpha^2-\beta^2)^{\nu/2})^2 \tag{6.21}\\&+\delta^2((\beta-z)^2-\alpha^2)^\nu\end{aligned}$$

$$+2\delta \cos \frac{\pi \nu}{2}((\beta - z)^2 - \alpha^2)^{\nu/2}$$
$$\cdot (q + \mu z - \delta(\alpha^2 - \beta^2)^{\nu/2}).$$

Lemma 6.2   *a) On the half-axis $z < 0$, $\phi_q^-(iz)$ admits a bound*

$$c_1(1 - zq^{-1/\nu})^{\kappa_-} \leq \phi_q^-(iz) \leq c_2(1 - zq^{-1/\nu})^{\kappa_-}, \qquad (6.22)$$

where $c_1, c_2 > 0$ are independent of $q \geq 1$ and $z < 0$.
   b) If $0 < -zq^{-1/\nu}$ and $-zq^{-1/\nu} \to 0$, as $q \to +\infty$, then

$$\phi_q^-(iz) \sim 1. \qquad (6.23)$$

Proof.   a) Set $\lambda = -iq$, and let $a_-(\lambda, \xi)$ be the factor defined in Chapter 7. Then $\phi_q^-(\xi) = a_-(\lambda, 0)/a_-(\lambda, \xi)$, and Eq. (6.22) follows from Eq. (7.37).
   b) In Eq. (3.60), make the change of variable $\eta = i\omega_+ + q^{1/\nu}\eta'$ and use Eq. (3.45)-Eq. (3.47) to show that the integral under the exponential sign vanishes as $q \to +\infty$. $\square$

Now we are ready to study Eq. (6.18). It is convenient to consider separately the following cases:

a) $\nu \in (1, 2)$;
b) $\nu = 1$;
c) $\nu \in (0, 1)$ and $\mu = 0$;
d) $\nu \in (0, 1)$ and $\mu < 0$;
e) $\nu \in (0, 1)$ and $\mu > 0$.

6.3.3   *The case of processes of order $\nu \in [1, 2)$*

We confine ourselves to this case; the processes of order less than 1 can be considered in the similar fashion but possible types of behaviour of $h(\Delta)$ are numerous.

Theorem 6.3   *Let $\nu \in [1, 2)$. Then for sufficiently small $\Delta > 0$, the solution $x = h(\Delta)$ to Eq. (6.18) exists; it is unique, and as $\Delta \to 0$, $h(\Delta) \to \bar{h}$, where $\bar{h}$ is the unique negative solution to the equation*

$$\int_{-\infty}^{-\alpha+\beta} e^{-xz} \frac{((\beta - z)^2 - \alpha^2)^{\nu/2}}{z(z+1)} dz = \frac{r\pi}{\delta \sin \frac{\pi \nu}{2}}. \qquad (6.24)$$

Before proving Theorem 6.3, we make two remarks. First, the solution to Eq. (6.24) exists, and it is unique since the LHS decreases monotonically from $+\infty$ to 0 as x goes from 0 down (when $x = 0$, the integral diverges due to the condition $\nu \geq 1$).

Second, as $r \to 0$, we have $\bar{h} \to -\infty$, which makes the RLPE model much more reasonable than its Gaussian counterpart. Recall that the early exercise in non-optimal in the case $r = 0$ (see, e.g., Musiela and Rutkowski (1997)) but nevertheless, in the Gaussian model, for arbitrary small $r > 0$, the early exercise boundary satisfies $h(\Delta) \to 1(= K)$ as $\Delta \to 0$.

Proof. First we consider the case $\nu \in (1,2)$. Suppose that the following two assumptions hold:

   a) $h = h(\Delta) \to 0$ as $q = \Delta^{-1} + r \to +\infty$;

   b) $-h(\Delta) \geq Aq^{-1/\nu}$, where $A > 0$ is independent of q.

Then on $(2h^{-1}, h^{-1})$, we have $e^{-xz} \leq e^{-2}$, $q+\psi(iz\pm0) \asymp q$, and $\phi_q^-(iz) \asymp 1$ due to Eq. (6.22)[2] Therefore, the LHS in Eq. (6.18) is bounded away from zero by

$$c \int_{2/h}^{1/h} (-h)^{2-\nu} dz = c_1(-h)^{1-\nu},$$

where $c, c_1 > 0$ are independent of q. Since $1 - \nu < 0$, we conclude that the LHS in Eq. (6.18) is unbounded as $q \to +\infty$ whereas the RHS stabilizes to r. Hence, the solution with properties a) and b) does not exist.

Now assume that a) holds but instead of b), $-hq^{1/\nu} = O(1)$. Then on $(-2q^{1/\nu}, -q^{1/\nu})$, we have $e^{-xz} = O(1)$, $q + \psi(iz \pm 0) \asymp q$, and $\phi_q^-(iz) \asymp 1$. Hence, the LHS in Eq. (6.18) is bounded away from zero by $c_2 q^{(\nu-1)/\nu} \to +\infty$ as $q \to \infty$, and hence for large q, Eq. (6.18) is impossible.

We are left with the only possibility: $h = h(\Delta) < 0$ is bounded away from zero uniformly in $q \geq C$, for sufficiently large C. But when $x = h$ satisfies this property, the leading term of the asymptotics of the integral in the LHS of Eq. (6.18) is determined by the integral over any interval of the form $(-q^\epsilon, -\alpha + \beta)$, where $\epsilon > 0$ is an arbitrary constant. By using Eq. (6.23), we see that the leading term of the LHS in Eq. (6.18) is equal to the LHS in Eq. (6.24). This finishes the proof of Theorem 6.3 in the case $\nu \in (1,2)$.

[2]For two functions f and g we write $f \asymp g$ if $f = O(g)$ and vice versa.

Now, let $\nu = 1$. Then the LHS in Eq. (6.18) admits a bound from below via

$$c_3 \int_{-q}^{-1} e^{-xz}(-z)^{-1}dz = c_3 \int_{1}^{q} e^{xz}z^{-1}dz.$$

If $x \to 0$ and $-xq$ is bounded, then the last integral is unbounded as a function of q, and hence, Eq. (6.18) is impossible. Suppose that $-x = A/q$, where A is bounded away from zero as $q \to \infty$, and change the variable $z = (-x)^{-1}z'$; we obtain

$$\int_{1}^{q} e^{xz}z^{-1}dz = \int_{-x}^{A} \frac{dz}{e^{z'}z'} \to +\infty \quad \text{as } x \to -0,$$

and the proof finishes as in the case $\nu \in (1, 2)$. $\qquad\square$

Chapter 7

First-touch digitals

In this chapter, we consider simplest options, which are reducible to boundary value problems with both the terminal condition and a fixed early exercise boundary. This makes the problem analytically tractable in contrast to free boundary value problems for American options with the finite time horizon. For first-touch digitals, the terminal payoff is zero, which makes the problem technically simpler than similar problems for barrier options. We also show that in a neighbourhood of the barrier, the non-Gaussian RLPE-prices differ significantly from the Gaussian prices, not only quantitatively but qualitatively as well.

7.1 An overview

A *first-touch digital* is a digital contract which pays \$ 1 when and if a specific event occurs. Consider the first-touch digital (another name is a *touch-and-out option*) which pays \$ 1 the first time the stock price S hits or crosses the level H from above. Possibly, it would be better say "hits $(0, H]$". For simplicity, in the sequel we say "crosses the level H". If the stock price never crosses the level H before time T, the claim expires worthless. Denote by $V_d(H, T; S, t)$ the no-arbitrage price of such a contract. It can be interpreted as an American put-like option with the digital payoff. Since the payoff is the same for all levels of the stock price below the barrier, it is optimal to exercise the option the first time the level H is crossed. The formulas for the value $V_u(H, T; S, t)$ of the similar contract, which pays \$ 1 the first time the stock price crosses the level H from below, easily follow by the reflection of the real axis w.r.t. the origin. For explicit pricing formulas for

165

the case when the dynamics of the stock price is modelled as the geometric Brownian motion, see, e.g., Ingersoll (2000); general formulas for the RLPE-case were obtained in Boyarchenko and Levendorskiĭ (2001a, 2002b), where more general rebates than here were considered, namely, first-touch power options, which pay not \$ 1 but S^β; and first-touch contracts which pay a non-zero amount iff the first barrier has been crossed but the second one (situated farther) has not. Notice that the contracts of this sort do not make sense in the Gaussian theory since a continuous trajectory stops at the barrier.

In addition to exact albeit complicated formulas, we obtain several simpler approximate formulas. The first formula is valid near the boundary H, and the next two are valid for options far from the terminal date. From the asymptotic formula for the price of the first-touch digital as the price of the underlying approaches the barrier we conclude that if there is no Gaussian component and the process is purely discontinuous then the difference between the option prices in the Gaussian model and in the RLPE model is especially large near the boundary. Moreover, different RLPE models usually produce essentially different types of behaviour, which can be used to decide, which type of processes fits the data better.

7.2 Exact pricing formulas for first-touch digitals

The riskless rate $r > 0$ is constant, and an EMM $\mathbf{Q}$ is chosen so that under $\mathbf{Q}$, $\{X_t\} = \{\ln S_t\}$ is an RLPE of order $\nu \in (0,2]$ and exponential type $[\lambda_-, \lambda_+]$, where $\lambda_- < -1 < 0 < \lambda_+$; ψ denotes the characteristic exponent of X under the risk-neutral measure chosen by the market.

Set $x = \ln(S/H)$, $u(x,t) = V_{\mathrm{d}}(H,T;S,t)$. Then for $t < T$ and $x \in \mathbf{R}$,

$$u(x,t) = E[e^{-rT'}\mathbf{1}_{T' \leq T} \mid X_t = x], \qquad (7.1)$$

where T' is the hitting time of $(-\infty, 0]$ by X. By using Theorem 2.13, we obtain

Theorem 7.1   *The u is a solution to the following problem:*

$$(\partial_t - (r + \psi(D_x)))u(x,t) = 0, \quad x > 0,\ t < T, \qquad (7.2)$$
$$u(x,t) = 1, \quad x \leq 0,\ t \leq T, \qquad (7.3)$$
$$u(x,T) = 0, \quad x > 0, \qquad (7.4)$$

in the class of bounded measurable functions.

Set $\tau = T - t, v(x, \tau) = u(x, T - \tau)$, and rewrite Eq. (7.2)-Eq. (7.4) as follows:

$$(\partial_\tau + r + \psi(D_x))v(x, \tau) = 0, \quad x > 0, \ \tau > 0, \tag{7.5}$$
$$v(x, \tau) = 1, \quad x \leq 0, \ \tau \geq 0, \tag{7.6}$$
$$v(x, 0) = 0, \quad x > 0. \tag{7.7}$$

To solve the problem Eq. (7.5)-Eq. (7.7), make the Fourier transform w.r.t. τ; since the terminal condition Eq. (7.7) is homogeneous, we obtain the following family of the problems on $\mathbf{R}$, parameterised by λ with $\Im\lambda < 0$:

$$(i\lambda + r + \psi(D_x))\hat{v}(x, \lambda) = 0, \quad x > 0, \tag{7.8}$$
$$\hat{v}(x, \lambda) = (i\lambda)^{-1}, \quad x \leq 0. \tag{7.9}$$

Denote by $\theta_\pm$ the indicator function of $\mathbf{R}_\pm$. We are going to apply the Wiener-Hopf method in the form Theorem 5.6, to the problem Eq. (7.8)-Eq. (7.9).

When $i\lambda$ is real, and $q := i\lambda + r > 0$, we can use the formulas obtained in Chapter 3. To stress the dependence on λ, we change the notation of Chapters 2 and 3, and write $a(\lambda, \xi) = i\lambda + r + \psi(\xi)$, $\phi_\pm(\lambda, \xi)$ and $a_\pm(\lambda, \xi)$ instead of $a(\xi)$, $\phi_q^\pm(\xi)$ and $a_\pm(\xi)$. Notice that $\kappa_\pm$, the orders of the factors $a_\pm(\lambda, \cdot)$, are independent of λ.

The following consideration shows that we can use the factorization identities obtained in Chapter 3, for λ in the half-plane $\Im\lambda \leq \sigma_0$ provided $\sigma_0 > 0$ is sufficiently small. Formulas for $\phi^\pm$ remain the same but in order to get convenient estimates for $a_\pm$, uniformly in λ in an appropriate subset of the complex plane, the construction has to be adjusted.

Recall that in the case of an RLPE, $a(\lambda, \xi)$ admits the analytic continuation w.r.t. ξ into a strip containing the real axis, and moreover, for each $q = i\lambda + r > 0$, there exist $\sigma_- < 0 < \sigma_+$ such that

$$\Re a(\lambda, \xi) > c_0, \quad \forall \ \Im\xi \in (\sigma_-, \sigma_+). \tag{7.10}$$

(In Chapters 3 and 5, we used Eq. (7.10) with $c_0 = 0$; clearly, we can choose $-\sigma_- > 0$ and $\sigma_+ > 0$ so that Eq. (7.10) holds with $c_0 > 0$). It follows that if $\sigma_0 > 0$ is sufficiently small, then Eq. (7.10) holds uniformly in λ in the half-space $\Im\lambda \le \sigma_0$, and therefore we can repeat the constructions of Chapter 5 for these λ.

By applying Theorem 5.6, we find

$$\hat{v}(\cdot,\lambda) = \phi_-(\lambda,D)(i\lambda)^{-1}\theta_-. \tag{7.11}$$

(Cf. Eq. (5.27)). If $\kappa_- < 1$, the solution is unique in the class of bounded functions, and if $\kappa_- = 1$, it is unique in the class of bounded continuous functions. Notice that the condition $\kappa_- = 1$ holds (or fails) for all λ simultaneously. The equality $\kappa_- = 1$ implies that either the process is of order 2 and hence has a diffusion component, or it is a process of order $\nu \in (0,1)$ and $\mu < 0$, that is, a process of bounded variation, with negative drift. In both cases, by using Eq. (7.1), we obtain that u is continuous. Explicitly, Eq. (7.11) is

$$\hat{v}(x,\lambda) = (2\pi)^{-1}\int_{-\infty+i\omega_+}^{+\infty+i\omega_+} e^{ix\xi}\phi_-(\lambda,\xi)(\lambda\xi)^{-1}d\xi,$$

where $\omega_+ \in (0,\sigma_+)$ is arbitrary, and v is obtained by the Fourier inversion

$$v(x,\tau) = (2\pi)^{-2}\int_{-\infty+i\sigma}^{+\infty+i\sigma}\int_{-\infty+i\omega_+}^{+\infty+i\omega_+} e^{i(\tau\lambda+x\xi)}\phi_-(\lambda,\xi)(\lambda\xi)^{-1}d\xi d\lambda, \tag{7.12}$$

where $\sigma < 0$. We integrate by part w.r.t. ξ and λ in the open quadrant $(0,+\infty)^2$, and by using the explicit formula for ϕ_-, obtain the integrand, which (locally w.r.t. x and τ) admits a bound via

$$C(1+|\xi|)^{-1-\epsilon}(1+|\lambda|)^{-1-\epsilon},$$

for some $C,\epsilon > 0$. We conclude that v is continuous on $(0,+\infty)^2$, therefore Eq. (7.12) gives the price we are looking for. By returning to the initial variables, we obtain

Theorem 7.2 *For $S > H$ and $t < T$,*

$$V_d(H,T;S,t) = (2\pi)^{-2}\int_{-\infty+i\sigma}^{+\infty+i\sigma}\int_{-\infty+i\omega_+}^{+\infty+i\omega_+} \tag{7.13}$$
$$\cdot e^{i((T-t)\lambda+\ln(S/H)\xi)}\phi_-(\lambda,\xi)(\lambda\xi)^{-1}d\xi d\lambda,$$

for $\sigma < 0$ and $\omega_+ \in (0,\sigma_+)$ sufficiently close to 0.

By making the inversion of the x-axis w.r.t. the origin, which leads to the change $X \mapsto \tilde{X}$, $S \mapsto -S$, $H \mapsto -H$, $\xi \mapsto -\xi$, and $\phi_-(\lambda,\xi) \mapsto \phi_+(\lambda,-\xi)$, and then making the change of variable $\xi \mapsto -\xi$ in the integral, we obtain the following theorem.

Theorem 7.3 *For $S < H$ and $t < T$,*

$$V_u(H,T;S,t) \;=\; -(2\pi)^{-2} \int_{-\infty+i\sigma}^{+\infty+i\sigma} \int_{-\infty+iw_-}^{+\infty+iw_-} \tag{7.14}$$
$$\cdot e^{i((T-t)\lambda + \ln(S/H)\xi)} \phi_+(\lambda,\xi)(\lambda\xi)^{-1} d\xi d\lambda,$$

for $\sigma < 0$ and $w_- \in (\sigma_-, 0)$.

The reader may notice that Eq. (7.13) and Eq. (7.14) are not computationally effective, though relatively short. Below, we derive fairly effective formulas; some of them are long, however.

7.3 The Wiener-Hopf factorization with a parameter

The reader interested in the main formulas but not in the technical details of the proofs can skip the next section, where we study the analytic continuation of the factors in the Wiener-Hopf factorization formula w.r.t. an additional parameter λ, and obtain necessary estimates.

7.3.1 *Formulas for the factors revisited*

To derive asymptotic formulas, we need both Eq. (2.23) and Eq. (3.71), but we need them for λ in a domain of the complex plane, which contains a set of the form

$$\Sigma(\epsilon,\theta) = i\epsilon + \Sigma(\theta),$$

where

$$\Sigma(\theta) = \{\lambda \mid \arg\lambda \in (-\pi/2 - \theta, -\pi/2 + \theta)\},$$

with $\epsilon, \theta > 0$, and the best situation is when a choice $\theta > \pi/2$ is possible. Moreover, we need to have certain uniform estimates for the factors not only w.r.t. ξ in appropriate half-planes, but w.r.t. $\lambda \in \Sigma(\epsilon,\theta)$ as well. In such situations, the standard terminology in the theory of PDO is *"the factorization with a parameter"*.

For the convenience of the reader, we rewrite Eq. (3.71) and Eq. (3.57)-Eq. (3.60):

$$\frac{r + i\lambda}{r + i\lambda + \psi(\xi)} = \phi_+(\lambda, \xi)\phi_-(\lambda, \xi); \qquad (7.15)$$

the formulas for $\phi_+(\lambda, \xi)$, $\Im\xi > \sigma_-$, are

$$\phi_+(\lambda, \xi) = \exp\left[\frac{1}{2\pi i}\int_{-\infty + i\rho_-}^{+\infty + i\rho_-}\frac{\xi\ln(i\lambda + r + \psi(\eta))}{\eta(\xi - \eta)}d\eta\right] \qquad (7.16)$$

$$= \exp\left[\frac{1}{2\pi i}\int_{-\infty + i\rho_-}^{+\infty + i\rho_-}\frac{\psi'(\eta)}{i\lambda + r + \psi(\eta)}\ln\frac{\eta - \xi}{\eta}d\eta\right]; \qquad (7.17)$$

where $\rho_- \in (\sigma_-, \Im\xi)$, and the formulas for $\phi_-(\lambda, \xi)$, $\Im\xi < \sigma_+$, are

$$\phi_-(\lambda, \xi) = \exp\left[-\frac{1}{2\pi i}\int_{-\infty + i\rho_+}^{+\infty + i\rho_+}\frac{\xi\ln(i\lambda + r + \psi(\eta))}{\eta(\xi - \eta)}d\eta\right] \qquad (7.18)$$

$$= \exp\left[-\frac{1}{2\pi i}\int_{-\infty + i\rho_+}^{+\infty + i\rho_+}\frac{\psi'(\eta)}{i\lambda + r + \psi(\eta)}\ln\frac{\eta - \xi}{\eta}d\eta\right], \qquad (7.19)$$

where $\rho_+ \in (\Im\xi, \sigma_+)$. Recall that in Chapter 3, the formulas have been proved for $i\lambda + r > 0$. Clearly, each of the expressions in Eq. (7.15) and Eq. (7.16)-Eq. (7.19) admits the analytic continuation w.r.t. λ into some domain, but to study the estimates for the factors in the Wiener-Hopf factorization formula, the second representation of the factors is more appropriate.

Eq. (3.71) assumes the form

$$a(\lambda, \xi) = da_+(\lambda, \xi)a_-(\lambda, \xi), \qquad (7.20)$$

and what is important, to obtain the answer in a simple form, we have to modify the constructions in Chapter 3 in order that $a_\pm(\lambda, \xi)$ be holomorphic w.r.t. λ in a neighbourhood of some set $\Sigma(\epsilon, \theta)$ and satisfy uniform estimates there. To this end, we need an additional restriction on the order of an RLPE. We have to consider separately two cases. The first case is $\nu \in (1, 2]$. Under this assumption, it possible to obtain good uniform estimates for $\lambda \in \Sigma(\epsilon, \theta)$ with $\theta > \pi/2$. The second case is $\nu \leq 1$, and here we impose the additional condition:

$$\text{if } \nu \in (0, 1) \quad \text{then } \mu = 0. \qquad (7.21)$$

In the second case, a good estimate for the factors $a_\pm$ can be obtained on $\lambda \in \Sigma(\epsilon, \theta)$ with $\theta < \pi/2$, which is not sufficient for certain purposes. The choice $\theta > \pi/2$ is still possible but only when $a_\pm(\lambda, \xi)$ are constructed as functions which are not holomorphic w.r.t. λ (see Chapter 8).

Let c, μ, ν be as in Eq. (3.45)-Eq. (3.46). If $\nu \in (1, 2]$ or $\nu \in (0, 1)$ and $\mu = 0$, set $d = c$, $\kappa_\pm = \nu/2$; if $\nu = 1$, set $d = (\mu^2 + c^2)^{1/2}$, $\kappa_\pm = 0.5 \pm \pi^{-1} \arctan(\mu/c)$. Thus, d and $\kappa_\pm$ are the same as in Chapters 3 and 5. For $s \in \mathbf{R}$, set

$$\Lambda_\pm(\lambda, \xi)^s = \left((i\lambda + r)^{1/\nu} \mp i\xi \right)^s,$$

and fix $\theta \in (0, \pi\nu/2)$. If $\nu > 1$, we can (and will) choose $\theta > \pi/2$.

If $\rho_- < 0$, and $\epsilon > 0$, are sufficiently small, then $\Lambda_+(\lambda, \xi)^s$ is well-defined in the region $\lambda \in \Sigma(\epsilon, \theta), \Im\xi > \rho_-$, and satisfies there an estimate

$$|\Lambda_+(\lambda, \xi)^s| \geq c(1 + |\lambda|^{1/\nu} + |\xi|)^s, \tag{7.22}$$

where $c > 0$. Similarly, if $\rho_+ > 0$, and $\epsilon > 0$ are sufficiently small, then $\Lambda_-(\lambda, \xi)^s$ is well-defined in the region $\lambda \in \Sigma(\epsilon, \theta), \Im\xi < \rho_+$, and satisfies there an estimate

$$|\Lambda_-(\lambda, \xi)^s| \geq c(1 + |\lambda|^{1/\nu} + |\xi|)^s, \tag{7.23}$$

where $c > 0$. Further, define

$$B(\lambda, \xi) = \frac{i\lambda + r + \psi(\xi)}{d\Lambda_+(\lambda, \xi)^{\kappa_+} \Lambda_-(\lambda, \xi)^{\kappa_-}}. \tag{7.24}$$

Due to Eq. (7.10), $b(\lambda, \xi) := \ln B(\lambda, \xi)$ is well-defined for ξ in a sufficiently narrow strip $\Im\xi \in [\rho_-, \rho_+]$, where $\rho_- < 0 < \rho_+$, and $\lambda \in \Sigma(\epsilon, \theta)$, provided $\epsilon > 0$ is sufficiently small. For ξ in the half-plane $\Im\xi > \rho_-$ and $\lambda \in \Sigma(\epsilon, \theta)$, set

$$b_+(\lambda, \xi) = \frac{1}{2\pi i} \int_{-\infty + i\rho_-}^{+\infty + i\rho_-} \frac{b(\lambda, \eta)}{\eta - \xi} d\eta, \tag{7.25}$$

$$a_+(\lambda, \xi) = d\Lambda_+(\lambda, \xi)^{\kappa_+} \exp[b_+(\lambda, \xi)], \tag{7.26}$$

and for ξ in the half-plane $\Im\xi < \rho_+$ and $\lambda \in \Sigma(\epsilon, \theta)$, set

$$b_-(\lambda, \xi) = -\frac{1}{2\pi i} \int_{-\infty + i\rho_+}^{+\infty + i\rho_+} \frac{b(\lambda, \eta)}{\eta - \xi} d\eta, \tag{7.27}$$

$$a_-(\lambda,\xi) = \Lambda_-(\lambda,\xi)^{\kappa_-}\exp[b_-(\lambda,\xi)]. \qquad (7.28)$$

The functions Eq. (7.26), Eq. (7.28) satisfy Eq. (7.20), and the factors in Eq. (7.20)-Eq. (7.15) are related by

$$\phi_+(\lambda,\xi) = \frac{a_+(\lambda,0)}{a_+(\lambda,\xi)}, \qquad (7.29)$$

$$\phi_-(\lambda,\xi) = \frac{a_-(\lambda,0)}{a_-(\lambda,\xi)}. \qquad (7.30)$$

7.3.2 Analytic continuation of the factors w.r.t. λ

If $\nu > 1$, fix $\theta \in (\pi/2, \pi\nu/2)$; if $\nu \in (0,1]$, fix $\theta \in (0,\pi\nu/2)$, and assume that Eq. (7.21) holds.

Lemma 7.1 *Let X be an RLPE. Then there exist $C, c_1 > 0$, $\rho_- < 0 < \rho_+$ and $\epsilon > 0$ such that for all ξ in the strip $\Im\xi \in [\rho_-,\rho_+]$ and all $\lambda \in \Sigma(\epsilon,\theta)$ the following three estimates hold:*

$$|i\lambda + r + \psi(\xi)| \geq c_1(1 + |\lambda| + |\xi|^\nu); \qquad (7.31)$$

$$-\pi < \arg B(\lambda,\xi) < \pi; \qquad (7.32)$$

and

$$C^{-1} \leq |B(\lambda,\eta)| \leq C. \qquad (7.33)$$

Proof. It follows from Eq. (3.45)-Eq. (3.46) and Eq. (7.21), that as $\lambda \to \infty$, and $\xi \to \infty$ in the strip $\Im\xi \in [\lambda_-,\lambda_+]$,

$$i\lambda + r + \psi(\xi) \sim \begin{cases} i\lambda + c|\xi|^\nu, & \nu \neq 1 \\ i\lambda - i\mu\xi + c|\xi|, & \nu = 1. \end{cases}$$

Now, if $C, R > 0$ are large enough, then Eq. (7.31)–Eq. (7.33) hold for all (ξ,λ) outside the ball $|\lambda|^2 + |\xi|^2 \leq R^2$, which satisfy $\Im\xi \in [\lambda_-,\lambda_+]$, $\arg\lambda \in [-\pi/2 - \theta, -\pi/2 + \theta]$. This can be shown as follows. If $\nu \leq 1$, the estimates are evident due to the assumption $0 < \theta < \pi\nu/2 \leq \pi/2$, and if $\nu > 1$, then it suffices to notice that

$$|i\lambda + c|\xi|^\nu|^2 = |\Re\lambda|^2 + |-\Im\lambda + c|\xi|^\nu|^2$$

dominates the RHS in Eq. (7.31).

Fix these R and C. It remains to find $C, c_1 > 0$, $\rho_- < 0 < \rho_+$ and $\epsilon > 0$ such that Eq. (7.31)–Eq. (7.33) hold for all (ξ, λ) inside the ball of radius R, such that $\Im\xi \in [\rho_-, \rho_+]$ and $\lambda \in \Sigma(\epsilon, \theta)$. On the strength of Eq. (3.45)-Eq. (3.46), there exist $c_0 > 0$, $-\rho_- > 0$ and $\rho_+ > 0$ such that $r + \Re\psi(\xi) \geq 2c_0$. Set $\epsilon = c_0/R$. Then for $\lambda \in \Sigma(\epsilon, \theta)$ satisfying $|\lambda| \leq R$, we have $\Re(i\lambda) \geq -c_0$, and Eq. (7.31)-Eq. (7.33) follow. □

From now on, we assume that the conditions of Lemma 7.1 hold, and use ϵ, ρ_-, ρ_+ constructed in this lemma. We also fix arbitrary $\omega_- \in (\rho_-, 0)$ and $\omega_+ \in (0, \rho_+)$.

Lemma 7.2   *a) There exist $C, C_1, c_1 > 0$ such that for all ξ in the half-plane $\Im\xi \geq \omega_-$ and all $\lambda \in \Sigma(\epsilon, \theta)$,*

$$|b_+(\lambda, \xi)| \leq C, \tag{7.34}$$

and

$$c_1(1 + |\lambda|^{1/\nu} + |\xi|)^{\kappa_+} \leq |a_+(\lambda, \xi)| \leq C_1(1 + |\lambda|^{1/\nu} + |\xi|)^{\kappa_+}; \tag{7.35}$$

b) There exists $C, C_1, c_1 > 0$ such that for all ξ in the half-plane $\Im\xi \leq \omega_+$ and all $\lambda \in \Sigma(\epsilon, \theta)$,

$$|b_-(\lambda, \xi)| \leq C, \tag{7.36}$$

and

$$c_1(1 + |\lambda|^{1/\nu} + |\xi|)^{\kappa_-} \leq |a_-(\lambda, \xi)| \leq C_1(1 + |\lambda|^{1/\nu} + |\xi|)^{\kappa_-}. \tag{7.37}$$

Proof.   We prove Eq. (7.34)-Eq. (7.35); Eq. (7.36)-Eq. (7.37) are proved similarly. It suffices to prove Eq. (7.34); Eq. (7.35) is an evident corollary.

By using Eq. (3.45)-Eq. (3.47) and Eq. (7.33), we easily obtain the following estimates

$$|B(\lambda, \eta) - 1| \leq C_1(1 + |\lambda| + |\eta|^{\nu'})/(1 + |\lambda| + |\eta|^{\nu}); \tag{7.38}$$

$$|\partial_\eta B(\lambda, \eta)/B(\lambda, \eta)| \leq C_2(1 + |\lambda|^{1/\nu} + |\eta|)^{\nu'-\nu}, \tag{7.39}$$

where C_1 and C_2 are independent of $\lambda \in \Sigma(\epsilon, \theta)$ and η in a strip $\Im\eta \in [\rho_-, \rho_+]$, as well as all constants below, and $\nu' < \nu$.

By making the shift in the ξ-space, we may assume that in Eq. (7.25), $\eta \in \mathbf{R}$, and $\sigma := \Im\xi > 0$. Change the variable $\xi \to \xi + i\sigma$, set $K =$

$(|\lambda| + 1)^{1/\nu}$, and for each pair (λ, ξ), introduce intervals $J_j \subset \mathbf{R}$:

$$
\begin{aligned}
J_1 &= \{\eta \mid |\eta - \xi| \le K\}, \\
J_2 &= \{\eta \mid |\eta - \xi| > K, |\eta| \le K\}, \\
J_3 &= \{\eta \mid |\eta - \xi| \ge |\eta|, |\eta| > K\}, \\
J_4 &= \{\eta \mid K < |\eta - \xi| < |\eta|, |\eta| > K\}.
\end{aligned}
$$

By using the mean value theorem and Eq. (7.39), we obtain

$$
\frac{b(\lambda, \eta)}{\xi + i\sigma - \eta} = \frac{b(\lambda, \xi)}{\xi + i\sigma - \eta} + R(\lambda, \xi, \eta, \sigma), \tag{7.40}
$$

where

$$
|R(\lambda, \xi, \eta, \sigma)| \le C_3 (1 + |\lambda|)^{(\nu' - \nu)/\nu}. \tag{7.41}
$$

Since

$$
\left| \int_{-K}^{K} \frac{d\eta}{i\sigma - \eta} \right| = \left| \ln \frac{-K - i\sigma}{K - i\sigma} \right| \le 2\pi,
$$

we deduce from Eq. (7.40)-Eq. (7.41) and Eq. (7.33)

$$
\left| \int_{J_1} \frac{b(\lambda, \eta) d\eta}{\xi + i\sigma - \eta} \right| \le 2\pi \ln C + C_3 \int_{|\eta - \xi| \le K} (1 + |\lambda|)^{(\nu' - \nu)/\nu} d\eta = C_4. \tag{7.42}
$$

To prove the following estimate, only Eq. (7.33) is needed:

$$
\left| \int_{J_2} \frac{b(\lambda, \eta) d\eta}{\xi + i\sigma - \eta} \right| \le C_5 \int_{|\eta| \le K} (1 + |\lambda|)^{-1/\nu} d\eta = C_6. \tag{7.43}
$$

Further, we infer from Eq. (7.38) that b admits an estimate of the same form as $B - 1$, and using this estimate on J_3, we obtain

$$
\left| \int_{J_3} \frac{b(\lambda, \eta) d\eta}{\xi + i\sigma - \eta} \right| \le C_7 \int_{|\eta| \ge K} \frac{1 + |\lambda| + |\eta|^{\nu'}}{|\eta|(1 + |\lambda| + |\eta|^{\nu})} d\eta. \tag{7.44}
$$

By changing the variable $\eta = K\eta'$, we see that the RHS in Eq. (7.44) is bounded uniformly in $\lambda \in \Sigma(\epsilon, \theta), \xi \in \mathbf{R}, \sigma > 0$. Since $\nu' \in [0, \nu)$, a function

$$
f(s) = (1 + |\lambda| + s^{\nu'})/(1 + |\lambda| + s^{\nu})
$$

is decreasing on $[0, +\infty)$, and therefore, we deduce from Eq. (7.38) an estimate, for $\eta \in J_4$,

$$|b(\lambda, \eta)| \leq C_8 (1 + |\lambda| + |\xi - \eta|^{\nu'})/(1 + |\lambda| + |\xi - \eta|^{\nu}). \qquad (7.45)$$

From Eq. (7.45),

$$\left| \int_{J_4} \frac{b(\lambda, \eta) d\eta}{\xi + i\sigma - \eta} \right| \leq C_8 \int_{|\xi-\eta| \geq K} \frac{1 + |\lambda| + |\xi - \eta|^{\nu'}}{|\xi - \eta|(1 + |\lambda| + |\xi - \eta|^{\nu})} d\eta, \qquad (7.46)$$

and the change of variable $\eta = \xi + K\eta'$ shows that the RHS in Eq. (7.46) is bounded uniformly in $\lambda \in \Sigma(\epsilon, \theta)$.

By gathering bounds Eq. (7.42)-Eq. (7.44) and Eq. (7.46), we obtain Eq. (7.34). $\qquad \square$

Lemma 7.3 *a) For any N, there exist $C, \rho > 0$ such that if $\Im\xi \geq \omega_-$, $\lambda \in \Sigma(\epsilon, \theta)$, and $|\lambda| \leq N \ln(|\xi| + 1)$, then*

$$|b_+(\lambda, \xi)| \leq C(1 + |\xi|)^{-\rho}, \qquad (7.47)$$

and

$$|a_+(\lambda, \xi) - d\Lambda_+(\lambda, \xi)^{\kappa_+}| \leq C(1 + |\xi|)^{\kappa_+ - \rho}; \qquad (7.48)$$

b) For any N, there exist $C, \rho > 0$ such that if $\Im\xi \leq \omega_+$, $\lambda \in \Sigma(\epsilon, \theta)$, and $|\lambda| \leq N \ln(|\xi| + 1)$, then

$$|b_-(\lambda, \xi)| \leq C(1 + |\xi|)^{-\rho}, \qquad (7.49)$$

and

$$|a_-(\lambda, \xi) - \Lambda_-(\lambda, \xi)^{\kappa_-}| \leq C(1 + |\xi|)^{\kappa_- - \rho}. \qquad (7.50)$$

Proof. a) and b) are proved similarly, and Eq. (7.48) is immediate from Eq. (7.47). To prove the latter, take $\epsilon \in (0, 1)$, and consider the integrand in Eq. (7.25) in the regions $|\eta| \leq \langle\xi\rangle^\epsilon$, and $|\eta| \geq \langle\xi\rangle^\epsilon$, where $\langle\xi\rangle = (1 + |\xi|^2)^{1/2}$.

For $|\eta| \leq \langle\xi\rangle^\epsilon$, we have

$$|\xi - \eta|^{-1} \leq C\langle\xi\rangle^{-1},$$

and for any $\sigma > 0$,

$$\left| \ln \frac{i\lambda + r + \psi(\eta)}{d\Lambda_+(\lambda, \eta)^{\kappa_+}\Lambda_-(\lambda, \eta)^{\kappa_-}} \right| \leq C_\sigma \langle\eta\rangle^\sigma.$$

Hence, for a positive c_2 and $\Im\xi \geq c_2 + \rho_-$, we obtain an estimate

$$\left| \int_{-\infty+i\rho_-}^{+\infty+i\rho_-} \frac{b(\lambda,\eta)}{\xi - \eta} 1_{|\eta| \leq \langle\xi\rangle^\epsilon}(\eta) d\eta \right| \leq C\langle\xi\rangle^{-1+\epsilon(1+\sigma)}.$$

If $|\eta| \geq \langle\xi\rangle^\epsilon$, we use Eq. (3.45)-Eq. (3.46) to obtain that

$$\frac{i\lambda + r + \psi(\eta)}{d\Lambda_+(\lambda,\eta)^{\kappa_+}\Lambda_-(\lambda,\eta)^{\kappa_-}} = 1 + O(\langle\eta\rangle^{-\rho_1}),$$

where $\rho_1 = \nu - \nu_1 > 0$, therefore

$$b(\lambda,\eta) = O(\langle\eta\rangle^{-\rho_1}).$$

Now, to finish the proof of Eq. (7.47), it remains to notice that

$$\int_{-\infty}^{+\infty} \frac{d\eta}{\langle\eta\rangle^{\rho_1}\langle\xi - \eta\rangle} \leq C\langle\xi\rangle^{-\rho_1/2}.$$

$\square$

Lemma 7.4   *a) There exist $C, \rho > 0$ such that for all ξ in the half-plane $\Im\xi \geq \omega_-$ and all $\lambda \in \Sigma(\epsilon,\theta)$,*

$$|\partial_\lambda b_+(\lambda,\xi)| \leq C(1 + |\lambda|^{1/\nu} + |\xi|)^{-\rho}, \qquad (7.51)$$

and

$$|\partial_\lambda(a_+(\lambda,\xi)^{\pm 1})| \leq C(1 + |\lambda|^{1/\nu} + |\xi|)^{\pm\kappa_+ - \rho}; \qquad (7.52)$$

b) There exists $C, \rho > 0$ such that for all ξ in the half-plane $\Im\xi \leq \omega_+$ and all $\lambda \in \Sigma(\epsilon,\theta)$,

$$|\partial_\lambda b_-(\lambda,\xi)| \leq C(1 + |\lambda|^{1/\nu} + |\xi|)^{-\rho}, \qquad (7.53)$$

and

$$|\partial_\lambda(a_-(\lambda,\xi)^{\pm 1})| \leq C(1 + |\lambda|^{1/\nu} + |\xi|)^{\pm\kappa_- - \rho}. \qquad (7.54)$$

Proof.   It suffices to prove Eq. (7.51). We have, with some $C_1, C_2, \rho_1 > 0$,

$$\begin{aligned} |\partial_\lambda B(\lambda,\eta)| &\leq C_1(1 + |\lambda| + |\eta|)^{-\rho_1}, \\ |B(\lambda,\eta)| &\leq C_2, \end{aligned}$$

and therefore,

$$|\partial_\lambda b(\lambda,\eta)| \leq C_3(1 + |\lambda|)^{-\rho_1/2}(1 + |\eta|)^{-\rho_1/2}. \qquad (7.55)$$

From Eq. (7.55), we see that to finish the proof, it suffices to apply the estimate

$$\int_{-\infty}^{+\infty} \frac{d\eta}{\langle\lambda\rangle^{\rho_1/2}\langle\eta\rangle^{\rho_1/2}\langle\xi-\eta\rangle} \leq C\langle\lambda\rangle^{-\rho_1/2}\langle\xi\rangle^{-\rho_1/4}.$$

□

7.4 Price near the barrier

We consider $v(x,\tau) = V_d(H,T;S,t)$, the reader can easily reformulate the results for $V_d(H,T;S,t)$.

7.4.1 *Asymptotics as $x \to +0$, and $\tau > 0$ is fixed*

In this Subsection, we fix $\tau > 0$, and compute the leading term of the asymptotics of $v(x,\tau)$ as $x \to +0$.

7.4.1.1 *Main Theorem*

We start with the case $\nu > 1$. Let $\theta \in (\pi/2, \pi\nu/2)$ and $\epsilon > 0$ be sufficiently small so that all the estimates of the Section 7.3 are valid on the set $\Sigma(\epsilon,\theta)$ defined at the beginning of Section 7.3. Choose a symmetric contour $\mathcal{L} \subset \Sigma(\epsilon,\theta)$, which passes below the origin and coincides with the line of the form $\lambda(s) = -C_0 + i\sigma_- + (1 - i\epsilon)s$ in the neighbourhood of $s = -\infty$, where $\epsilon > 0$. Of course, the symmetry condition is imposed to simplify the formulation only.

Set

$$\mathcal{D}(\tau) = (2\pi i)^{-1} \int_{\mathcal{L}} e^{i\lambda\tau} a_-(\lambda,0)\lambda^{-1} d\lambda. \tag{7.56}$$

(Here the normalization

$$a_-(\lambda,\xi)/(1+i\xi)^{\kappa_-} \to 1 \quad \text{as } \xi \to \pm\infty$$

is important).

Theorem 7.4 *Let $\nu > 1$. Then there exists $\delta > 0$ such that as $x \to +0$,*

$$v(x,\tau) = 1 - \Gamma(\kappa_- + 1)^{-1}\mathcal{D}(\tau)x^{\kappa_-} + O(x^{\kappa_-+\delta}). \tag{7.57}$$

Remark 7.1

a) The asymptotics Eq. (7.57) holds not only for processes of order $\nu > 1$ but for processes of order 1, and for processes of order $\nu \in (0,1)$, if $\mu = 0$, as well; only the factors in the Wiener-Hopf factorization formula have to be defined differently, as in Chapter 8. The proof remains the same.

b) The asymptotics Eq. (7.57) is uniform on each segment $[\tau_0, +\infty)$ of the positive half-axis in the sense that for each $\tau_0 > 0$, the constant in the O-term can be chosen the same for all $\tau \geq \tau_0$.

c) If there is a Gaussian component, then $\kappa_- = 1$, and from Eq. (7.57) we conclude that the solution is of the class C^1 up to the boundary. If there is no Gaussian component and Eq. (7.21) holds, then $\kappa_- \in (0,1)$, and the price of the option behaves not as in the Gaussian case.

d) Still, the relative error of the Gaussian approximation is not large here since the leading term is 1 in the both models. Similar effect is more pronounced for barrier options without a rebate and junk bonds, since in these cases, the ratio of the RLPE-price to the Gaussian price may be very large indeed.

7.4.1.2 *Numerical example*

We take the riskless rate $r = 0.05$, and assume that under the EMM chosen by the market, X is a NIG with parameters $\delta = 7.2$, $\alpha = 40$, $\beta = 8$, and μ, fixed by the EMM requirement $r + \psi^Q(-i) = 0$. Then $\kappa_- = 0.5682$, and therefore, near the barrier, for $\tau > 0$ fixed (and not too small) the difference $1 - v(x, \tau)$ behaves approximately like $const \cdot \sqrt{x}$. The numerical calculations show that this is really the case (see Fig. 7.1). Recall that in the Gaussian model, the price is smooth up to the boundary, and therefore, the difference $1 - v(x, \tau)$ is approximately linear as a function of x, near the barrier. Thus, one should expect the significant difference between NIG and Gaussian prices, the latter being calculated for the volatility $\sigma^2 = (\psi^Q)''(0)$; this difference is apparent on Fig. 7.2.

Further, from Eq. (7.57), we conclude that for a fixed $\tau > 0$, the function

$$W(x, \tau) := (1 - v(x, \tau))/x^{\kappa_-}$$

is approximately constant near the barrier, and Fig. 7.3 demonstrates this effect.

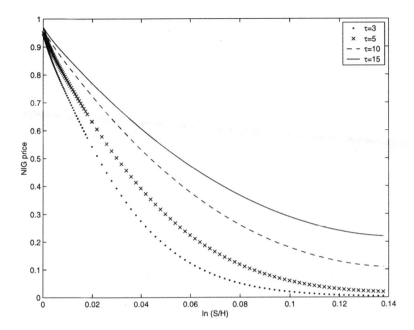

Fig. 7.1 The NIG-price of the down-and-out option, at $\tau = 3, 5, 10$ and 15 days to expiry. Parameters: $r = 0.05, \delta = 7.2, \alpha = 40, \beta = 8$.

7.4.1.3 *Proof of Theorem 7.4*

Proof. By shifting the line of the inner integration in Eq. (7.12) and using the residue theorem, we obtain in the region $x > 0, \tau > 0$:

$$v = 1 + f,$$

where $f(x, \tau)$ is given by

$$f(x, \tau) = (2\pi)^{-2} \int_{-\infty+i\sigma}^{+\infty+i\sigma} \int_{-\infty+i\omega_-}^{+\infty+i\omega_-} e^{i(\tau\lambda + x\xi)} \phi_-(\lambda, \xi)(\lambda\xi)^{-1} d\xi d\lambda, \quad (7.58)$$

$\sigma < 0$ and $\omega_- \in (\sigma_-, 0)$.

Integrate by part w.r.t. λ in Eq. (7.58). In view of Eq. (7.54), we obtain absolutely converging integral. Moreover, we can justify the deformation of the line $\Im\lambda = \sigma$ into the contour $\mathcal{L}$. After that we integrate by part once

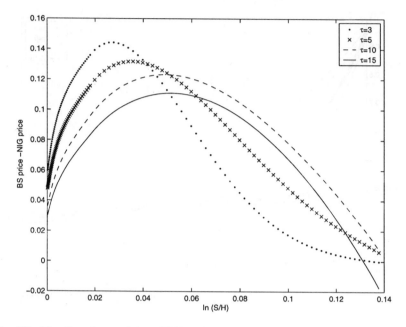

Fig. 7.2   The Gaussian model vs. NIG model: the price of the down-and-out option, at
$\tau = 3, 5, 10$ and 15 days to expiry. Parameters: $r = 0.05, \delta = 7.2, \alpha = 40, \beta = 8$.

again and obtain

$$f(x,\tau) = (2\pi)^{-2} \int_{\mathcal{L}} \int_{-\infty+i\omega_-}^{+\infty+i\omega_-} e^{i(\tau\lambda+x\xi)} \frac{a_-(\lambda,0)}{a_-(\lambda,\xi)\lambda\xi} d\xi d\lambda. \qquad (7.59)$$

(Here we have used Eq. (7.30)). Notice that there exist $C, c_0 > 0$ such that

$$\Im\lambda \geq c_0|\lambda|, \quad \forall\, \lambda \in \mathcal{L}: \ |\lambda| \geq C.$$

Hence, the integrand in Eq. (7.59) admits an estimate via

$$Ce^{-c_0\tau|\lambda|}(1+|\lambda|)^{\kappa_-/\nu}(1+|\lambda|^{1/\nu}+|\xi|)^{-\kappa_-}|\xi|^{-1}|\lambda|^{-1},$$

and therefore the Fubini theorem applies:

$$f(x,\tau) = (2\pi)^{-2} \int_{-\infty+i\omega_-}^{+\infty+i\omega_-} \int_{\mathcal{L}} e^{i(\tau\lambda+x\xi)} \frac{a_-(\lambda,0)}{a_-(\lambda,\xi)\xi\lambda} d\lambda d\xi. \qquad (7.60)$$

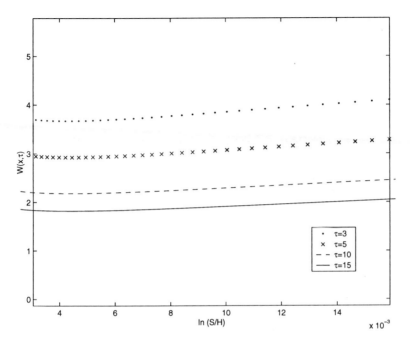

Fig. 7.3   Graph of $W(x,\tau)$ near the barrier. Parameters: $r = 0.05, \delta = 7.2, \alpha = 40, \beta = 8$, at $\tau = 3, 5, 10$ and 15 days to expiry.

In addition, there exist N, C such that if $|\lambda| \geq N \ln(|\xi| + 1)$, then

$$\left| e^{i\lambda\tau} \frac{a_-(\lambda, 0)}{a_-(\lambda, \xi)\xi\lambda} \right| \leq C \exp[-\tau|\lambda|c_0/2]\langle\xi\rangle^{-\kappa_- - 2}, \quad \forall \, \Im\xi \leq \omega_-,$$

and the same estimate holds for

$$e^{i\lambda\tau} \frac{a_-(\lambda, 0)}{(1 + i\xi)^{\kappa_- + 1}\lambda}.$$

From Eq. (7.50), on the set $|\lambda| \leq N \ln(|\xi| + 1)$, $\Im\xi \leq \omega_-$ we have the estimate

$$\left| e^{i\lambda\tau} \left(\frac{a_-(\lambda, 0)}{a_-(\lambda, \xi)i\xi\lambda} - \frac{a_-(\lambda, 0)}{(1 + i\xi)^{\kappa_- + 1}\lambda} \right) \right| \leq C_2 \exp[-c_0\tau|\lambda|]|\lambda|^{-1}\langle\xi\rangle^{-\kappa_- - 1 - \rho},$$

for some $\rho > 0, C_2 > 0$. By taking the last three estimates together, we derive the representation

$$\int_{\mathcal{L}} e^{i\lambda\tau} \frac{a_-(\lambda,0)}{a_-(\lambda,\xi)i\xi\lambda}d\lambda = (1+i\xi)^{-\kappa_--1}\int_{\mathcal{L}} e^{i\lambda\tau}\frac{a_-(\lambda,0)}{\lambda}d\lambda + \hat{w}(\xi), \quad (7.61)$$

where $\hat{w}(\xi)$ is holomorphic in the half-plane $\Im\xi \leq \omega_-$ and admits an estimate

$$|\hat{w}(\xi)| \leq C\langle\xi\rangle^{-\kappa_--1-\rho}, \quad \Im\xi \leq \omega_-, \qquad (7.62)$$

with some $\rho > 0$. It follows from Eq. (7.62), that for any $\epsilon > 0$, w belongs to the Sobolev space $H^{\kappa_-+1/2+\rho-\epsilon}(\mathbf{R})$ and vanishes on $(-\infty, 0]$. But for any $s > 1/2$ and $\epsilon \in (0, s-1/2)$, $H^s(\mathbf{R})$ is embedded into the Hölder space $C^{s-1/2-\epsilon}(\mathbf{R})$, therefore $w \in C^{\kappa_-+\rho-\epsilon}(\mathbf{R})$, $\forall\, \epsilon > 0$. Since w vanishes on $(-\infty, 0]$, we conclude that

$$w(x) = O(x^{\kappa_-+\rho-\epsilon}), \quad \forall\, \epsilon > 0. \qquad (7.63)$$

Further,

$$(2\pi)^{-1}\int_{-\infty+i\omega_-}^{+\infty+i\omega_-} e^{ix\xi}(1+i\xi)^{-\kappa_--1}d\xi = \Gamma(\kappa_-+1)^{-1}x_+^{\kappa_-}e^{-x}, \qquad (7.64)$$

and by combining Eq. (7.61), Eq. (7.63) and Eq. (7.64), we arrive at

$$f(x,\tau) = -\Gamma(\kappa_-+1)^{-1}\mathcal{D}(\tau)x_+^{\kappa_-} + O(x^{\kappa_-+\rho-\epsilon}). \qquad (7.65)$$

Since $v = 1 + f$, Eq. (7.57) follows from Eq. (7.65). $\qquad\qquad\square$

7.4.2 Asymptotics as $x \to +0$ and $\tau \to +\infty$

Transform the contour $\mathcal{L}$ into a contour $\mathcal{L}_1$ lying above the line $\Im\lambda = \sigma_+ > 0$; if σ_+ is not large, we remain in the domain of the analyticity of $a_-(\lambda, 0)$. By using the residue theorem, we obtain

$$\mathcal{D}(\tau) = a_-(0,0) + (2\pi i)^{-1}\int_{\mathcal{L}_1} e^{i\lambda\tau}a_-(\lambda,0)\lambda^{-1}d\lambda. \qquad (7.66)$$

The second term in Eq. (7.66) exponentially vanishes as $\tau \to +\infty$, and we obtain from Eq. (7.57):

Theorem 7.5 *There exist $\delta > 0$ and $\sigma_+ > 0$ such that as $x \to +0$ and $\tau \to +\infty$,*

$$v(x,\tau) = 1 - \frac{a_-(0,0)}{\Gamma(\kappa_- + 1)}x_+^{\kappa_-} + O(x^{\kappa_- + \delta}) + O(e^{-\sigma_+\tau}). \qquad (7.67)$$

7.5 Asymptotics as $\tau \to +\infty$

The result of this section is intuitively clear: when the terminal date is far away, the price is essentially independent of time, the generalized Black-Scholes equation reduces to the stationary one, and therefore, the price is approximately equal to the solution of the stationary boundary value problem on the half-axis. The formal proof is as follows.

In Eq. (7.58), transform the line of the integration $\Im\lambda = \sigma$ into the contour $\mathcal{L}$, next change the order of the integration as in the beginning of the proof of Theorem 7.4, and then transform $\mathcal{L}$ into $\mathcal{L}_1$. Then, similarly to Theorem 7.5, we obtain

Theorem 7.6 *There exists $\sigma_+ > 0$ such as $\tau \to +\infty$, uniformly in $x \in [0, +\infty)$,*

$$v(x,\tau) = (2\pi)^{-1} \int_{-\infty+i\omega_+}^{+\infty+i\omega_+} e^{ix\xi}\phi_-(0,\xi)(-i\xi)^{-1}d\xi + O(e^{-\sigma_+\tau}), \qquad (7.68)$$

where $\omega_+ > 0$ is sufficiently small.

Note that in the proofs of Theorem 7.5 and Theorem 7.6, an additional assumption on ν is used but they can be proved for any ν, in the same way as the pricing formula for the perpetual American options was derived in Chapter 5.

Chapter 8

Barrier options

Barrier options are reducible to boundary value problems with a non-trivial terminal condition and a fixed early expiration boundary. In the event of early expiration, the option owner may be entitled to a rebate, that is, the boundary condition can be both homogeneous and inhomogeneous. In contrast to the Gaussian case, a rebate (if any) must be specified not at the barrier only but everywhere on the other side of the barrier as well.

8.1 Types of barrier options

8.1.1 *Standard barrier options*

Consider a contract which pays the specified amount at the terminal date, provided during the life-time of the contract, the price of the underlying asset does not cross a specified *barrier* $S = H(t)$ from above (*down-and-out barrier options*) or from below (*up-and-out barrier options*). When the barrier is crossed, the option expires worthless or the option owner is entitled to some *rebate*. For simplicity, we study constant barriers only, though non-constant barriers can also be examined.

Consider barrier options on a stock, without a rebate. The standard variety of these options comprises four types of down-and-out and up-and-out options, and four types of down-and-in and up-and-in options. The "out" options with the barrier H are

(1) the down-and-out call option with the terminal payoff $(S_T - K)_+$; we denote by $V_{\text{do;call}}(K, H, T; S, t)$ the price of this contract at the

time t and spot-price S;

(2) the down-and-out put option;

(3) the up-and-out put option;

(4) the up-and-out call option.

An "in" option becomes the European option when the specified barrier is crossed (before or on the terminal date); otherwise it expires worthless. For instance, the up-and-in call option becomes the European call option when the barrier is crossed from below; we denote its price by $V_{\mathrm{ui;call}}(K, H, T; S, t)$. Similarly, one defines the up-and-in put option, and down-and-in puts and calls. In all states of nature, a European option pays the same amount as the portfolio of the down-and-out option and up-and-in option with the same barrier (of course, this is pertinent to a portfolio of the up-and-out option and down-and-in option with the same barrier as well), therefore the standard no-arbitrage consideration shows that the pricing problem for an "in" option reduces to the pricing problem of the corresponding "out" option and a European option, for instance,

$$V_{\mathrm{di,call}}(K, H, T; S, t) = V_{\mathrm{call}}(K, T; S, t) - V_{\mathrm{uo,call}}(K, H, T; S, t), \qquad (8.1)$$

where $V_{\mathrm{call}}(K, T; S, t)$ is the price of the European call with the same strike K and expiry date T. The equalities similar to Eq. (8.1) hold for other pairs of barrier options, therefore it suffices to write the explicit formulas for "out" options only.

8.1.2   *Options with a rebate*

Suppose that when the barrier is crossed from above, a European option expires but the option owner is entitled to some rebate. If the rebate is a constant equal to R, then the standard no-arbitrage consideration shows that the price of the barrier option with a rebate is equal to the price of the portfolio, which consists of the same type of the barrier option but without a rebate, and the first-touch digital with the payoff R. The same observation holds for "up" options, and similarly, options with more general rebates can be considered.

The first-touch digitals having been studied in Chapter 7, we conclude that it suffices to consider barrier options without a rebate. In this case, from the mathematical point of view, the pricing problem is a backward parabolic equation on the half-line, and so the answer can be deduced from the general theory of Chapter 15. We illustrate the usage of the general theory by explicitly solving the pricing problem for the European down-and-out call $V_{\text{do;call}}(K, H, T; S, t)$ in the case $K < H$. Similarly, other barrier options can be considered. For the pricing formulas of other barrier options, more general payoffs and rebates including, see Boyarchenko and Levendorskii (2002b), where simpler and more direct approach is used. Notice, however, that the general theory of Chapter 15 admit a straightforward generalization for the case of option pricing under Lévy-like Feller processes, when only approximate analytical formulas can be obtained (see the end of Chapter 16), whereas the approach in Boyarchenko and Levendorskii (2002b) relies on the explicit analytical representation of the solution, and therefore, it is more difficult to generalize the latter approach.

8.2 Down-and-out call option without a rebate

8.2.1 *Reduction to the boundary problem for the Generalized Black-Scholes equation*

We assume that the riskless rate $r > 0$ is constant, and under a risk-neutral measure chosen by the market, X is an RLPE, of order ν and exponential type $[\lambda_-, \lambda_+]$, where $\lambda_- < -1 < 0 < \lambda_+$.

Set $x = \ln S$, denote by $g(x) = (e^x - K)\mathbf{1}_{[0,+\infty)}(x)$ the terminal payoff of a down-and-out call option with the barrier $H = 1$, without a rebate. Let $v(x, t) = V_{\text{do}}(g; 1, T; S, t)$ be the price of the option at the time $t < T$ and spot price $S > 1$. Then

$$v(x, t) = E^{(x,t)}\left[e^{(t-T)r}g(X_T)\mathbf{1}_{\tau_0 > T}\right],$$

where τ_0 is the hitting time of $(-\infty, 0]$ by the process X. According to the general scheme described in Section 2.4, we approximate g by a sequence of non-negative functions g_n with compact support, which converges to g pointwise: $g_n(x) \uparrow g(x)$ for any $x \geq 0$. The standard construction of such a sequence is as follows: take a non-increasing function $\chi \in C^\infty(\mathbf{R})$ such that $\chi(x) = 1$ for $x < 1$, $\chi(x) = 0$ for $x > 2$, and $0 \leq \chi(x) \leq 1$ for $x \in [1, 2]$, and set $g_n(x) = g(x)\chi(x/n)$. Set

$$v_n(x, t) = E^{(x,t)}\left[e^{(t-T)r}g_n(X_T)\mathbf{1}_{\tau_0 > T}\right].$$

On the strength of the dominated convergence theorem, we conclude that for any $(x, t) \in (0, +\infty) \times [0, T)$,

$$v_n(x, t) \uparrow v(x, t). \qquad (8.2)$$

By applying Theorem 2.13 to $v_n(x, t)$, we find that v_n is a bounded measurable solution to the following problem

$$(\partial_t - (r + \psi(D_x)))v_n(x, t) = 0, \qquad x > 0, \ t < T; \qquad (8.3)$$
$$v_n(x, T) = g_n(x), \qquad x > 0. \qquad (8.4)$$
$$v_n(x, t) = 0, \qquad x \leq 0, \ t \leq T. \qquad (8.5)$$

Set $\tau = T - t$, and $w_n(x, \tau) = v_n(x, t)$; we obtain the Cauchy problem for a pseudodifferential parabolic operator on $\mathbf{R}_+$, with the zero boundary condition:

$$(\partial_\tau + (r + \psi(D_x)))w_n(x, t) = 0, \qquad x > 0, \ \tau > 0; \qquad (8.6)$$
$$w_n(x, 0) = g_n(x), \qquad x > 0. \qquad (8.7)$$
$$w_n(x, \tau) = 0, \qquad x \leq 0, \ \tau \geq 0. \qquad (8.8)$$

Here the initial data $g_n \in \overset{o}{H}{}^{s'}(\mathbf{R}_+)$, for any $s' < 1/2$, since g_n is smooth up to the boundary $x = 0$, and has the compact support, and the unknown w_n is bounded and measurable. Take $\gamma \in (\lambda_-, -1)$, and define $w_{n,\gamma}(x) = e^{\gamma x} w_n(x)$. Similarly, define $g_{n,\gamma}, g_\gamma$, and w_γ. The choice of γ is explained as follows: $g_\gamma(x)$ must decay as $x \to +\infty$ so that $g_\gamma \in L_2(\mathbf{R}_+)$. Thus, if we consider a payoff with the different rate of growth at the infinity, another choice of γ may be needed; and for up-and-out put option, say, when the problem on $\mathbf{R}_-$ is to be considered, and the payoff stabilizes to a constant as $x \to -\infty$, one should choose $\gamma \in (0, \lambda_+)$.

Substitute $w_n(x) = e^{-\gamma x} w_{n,\gamma}$ and $g_n(x) = e^{-\gamma x} g_{n,\gamma}$ into Eq. (8.6)-Eq. (8.8), next multiply by $e^{\gamma x}$, and use the equality

$$e^{\gamma x} \psi(D_x) e^{-\gamma x} = \psi(D_x + i\gamma);$$

the result is

$$(\partial_\tau + (r + \psi(D_x + i\gamma)))w_{n,\gamma}(x, t) = 0, \qquad x > 0, \ \tau > 0; \quad (8.9)$$
$$w_{n,\gamma}(x, 0) = g_{n,\gamma}(x), \quad x > 0, \qquad (8.10)$$
$$w_{n,\gamma}(x, \tau) = 0, \qquad x \leq 0, \ \tau \geq 0. \ (8.11)$$

Recall that we understand the problem Eq. (8.9)-Eq. (8.11) in the sense of generalized functions, and we look for a solution which is bounded and measurable on the strip $[0, +\infty) \times [0, T]$. The standard argument shows that such a solution is unique, and we will explicitly construct it by using the representation theorem for analytical semigroups.

8.2.2 *Reduction to the Cauchy problem for an ordinary differential operator with the operator-valued coefficient*

Set $a(\xi) = r + \psi(\xi)$, $\tilde{w}_{n,\gamma}(\tau) := w_{n,\gamma}(\cdot, \tau)$. Let p_+ be the restriction-to-$\mathbf{R}_+$ operator; consider

- $p_+ a(D_x + i\gamma)$ as an unbounded operator A_γ in $L_2(\mathbf{R}_+)$ with the domain $\mathcal{D}(A_\gamma) = \{u = (A_\gamma + CI)^{-1}v \mid v \in L_2(\mathbf{R})\}$, and
- the problem Eq. (8.9)–Eq. (8.11) as the Cauchy problem for an ordinary differential equation with the operator coefficient:

$$\tilde{w}'_{n,\gamma}(\tau) + A_\gamma \tilde{w}_{n,\gamma}(\tau) = 0, \quad \tau > 0, \qquad (8.12)$$
$$\tilde{w}_{n,\gamma}(0) = g_{n,\gamma}, \qquad (8.13)$$

and the unknown $\tilde{w}_{n,\gamma}$ is regarded as a continuous (vector)-function on $[0, +\infty)$, assuming values in $\mathcal{D}(A_\gamma)$.

Here I denotes the identity operator, and C is large enough so that on the line $\Im\xi = \gamma$,

$$\Re a(\xi + i\gamma) + C \geq c_0(1 + |\xi|)^\nu, \qquad (8.14)$$

with some $c_0 > 0$; the existence of such C and c_0 follows from Eq. (3.45)-Eq. (3.46).

The inverse $(A_\gamma + CI)^{-1}$ is constructed as follows. Under condition Eq. (8.14), the symbol $a(\xi + i\gamma) + C$ admits a factorization

$$a(\xi + i\gamma) + C = a_{\gamma,C;+}(\xi) a_{\gamma,C;-}(\xi),$$

and we define

$$(A_\gamma + CI)^{-1}v = a_{\gamma,C;-}(D)^{-1}\theta_+ a_{\gamma,C;+}(D)^{-1}lv,$$

where $lv \in L_2(\mathbf{R})$ is an arbitrary extension of $v \in L_2(\mathbf{R}_+)$. Since $a_{\gamma,C;\pm}(\xi)^{-1}$ are bounded in the upper and lower half-planes, respectively, we have:

1) on the strength of Theorem 15.13, $\theta_+ a_{\gamma,C;+}(D)^{-1} lv$ is independent of the choice of $lv \in L_2(\mathbf{R})$, and the map

$$L_2(\mathbf{R}_+) \ni v \mapsto \theta_+ a_{\gamma,C;+}(D)^{-1} lv \in L_2(\mathbf{R}_+)$$

is bounded;

2) on the strength of Theorem 15.12, the map

$$L_2(\mathbf{R}_+) \ni f \mapsto a_{\gamma,C;-}(D)^{-1} f \in L_2(\mathbf{R}_+)$$

is bounded.

Hence, $(A_\gamma + CI)^{-1}$ is a bounded operator in $L_2(\mathbf{R}_+)$, and a direct calculation shows that it is the inverse to

$$A_\gamma + CI : \mathcal{D}(A_\gamma) \to L_2(\mathbf{R}_+).$$

(see Theorem 15.22). On the formal level, the system Eq. (8.12)-Eq. (8.13) is easy to solve:

$$\tilde{w}_{n,\gamma}(\tau) = \exp[-\tau A_\gamma] g_{n,\gamma}, \tag{8.15}$$

but in order to justify the answer, and to ensure the calculation of the limit Eq. (8.2), some additional efforts are to be made. In order that the representation theorem for analytical semigroups (Theorem 15.18) be applicable, we have to impose an additional restriction on the order ν and μ in Eq. (3.45):

$$\text{if } \nu \in (0,1), \quad \text{then } \mu = 0. \tag{8.16}$$

Under this condition, the elliptic part of the Generalized Black-Scholes equation is strongly elliptic, which makes the study of the corresponding (backward) parabolic equation especially simple, and allows one to obtain an answer in the form of the absolutely converging integral, which is important for numerical implementation. The advantage of the general approach outlined in Chapter 15 for PDO with constant symbols, and at the end of Chapter 16, for PDO with variable symbols, is that the perturbation arguments can be used relatively easily; and these arguments are necessary for any approximate solution to be validated, hence, for any generalization to the case of Lévy-like Feller processes to be made (cf. Chapter 14, where the approximate pricing under Lévy-like Feller processes is studied).

The rigorous sense can be assigned to Eq. (8.15) as follows. Suppose, we have shown that the *resolvent* $(\lambda + A_\gamma)^{-1}$ satisfies an estimate

$$||(1 + |\lambda|)(\lambda + A_\gamma)^{-1}|| \leq C_1, \tag{8.17}$$

where C_1 is independent of λ on the contour of the form $\Sigma_{\theta,C} := \{\lambda \mid |\lambda| \geq C, \ \arg \lambda \in (-\theta, \theta)\}$, where $C \geq 0$ and $\theta \in (\pi/2, \pi)$. Then we can apply Theorem 15.18, and obtain

$$\tilde{w}_{n,\gamma}(\tau) = (2\pi i)^{-1} \int_{\mathcal{L}_{\theta,C}} e^{\tau\lambda}(\lambda + A_\gamma)^{-1} g_{n,\gamma} d\lambda, \tag{8.18}$$

where $\mathcal{L}_{\theta,C}$ is the boundary of $\Sigma_{\theta,C}$. Moreover, for any $\tau > 0$, the RHS defines an operator, which is bounded in $L_2(\mathbf{R}_+)$. From our construction of the sequence $\{g_{n,\gamma}\}_{n\geq 1}$, it follows that it converges in $L_2(\mathbf{R}_+)$ to g_γ; hence, by passing to the limit in Eq. (8.18), and multiplying by $e^{-\gamma x}$, we obtain

$$\lim_{n \to \infty} w_n(\cdot, \tau) = (2\pi i)^{-1} \int_{\mathcal{L}_{\theta,C}} e^{\tau\lambda} e^{-\gamma \cdot}(\lambda + A_\gamma)^{-1} e^{\gamma \cdot} g d\lambda. \tag{8.19}$$

When we construct the resolvent, we will be able to show that the RHS in Eq. (8.19) is a continuous function; hence, the limit on the LHS is the price of the down-and-out call option we have been looking for:

$$w(\cdot, \tau) = (2\pi i)^{-1} \int_{\mathcal{L}_{\theta,C}} e^{\tau\lambda} e^{-\gamma \cdot}(\lambda + A_\gamma)^{-1} e^{\gamma \cdot} g d\lambda. \tag{8.20}$$

As it is to be expected, the resolvent will appear to be of the form

$$(\lambda + A_\gamma)^{-1} = a_-(\lambda, D + i\gamma)^{-1}\theta_+ a_+(\lambda, D + i\gamma)^{-1}, \tag{8.21}$$

where $a_\pm(\lambda, \xi)$ are properly constructed factors in the Wiener-Hopf factorization formula. In the case $\nu > 1$, we can use the factors $a_\pm$ constructed in Chapter 7 (notice that the "λ" here corresponds to "$i\lambda$" in Chapter 7), but in the case $\nu \leq 1$, this construction fails. An appropriate construction will be given in the next subsection, and now we finish the calculation of the price.

By using Eq. (8.21) and the equality

$$e^{-\gamma x} a_\pm(\lambda, D + i\gamma)^{-1} e^{\gamma x} = a_\pm(\lambda, D)^{-1},$$

we can rewrite Eq. (8.20):

$$w(\cdot,\tau) = (2\pi i)^{-1} \int_{\mathcal{L}_{\theta,C}} e^{\tau\lambda} a_-(\lambda,D)^{-1} \theta_+ a_+(\lambda,D)^{-1} g d\lambda. \qquad (8.22)$$

In the simplest case $g(x) = (e^x - K)\mathbf{1}_{[0,+\infty)}(x)$, which we consider here,

$$\begin{aligned}
\theta_+ a_+(\lambda,D)^{-1}g &= \theta_+ a_+(\lambda,D)^{-1}(e^x - K) \\
&= \theta_+(a_+(\lambda,-i)^{-1}e^x - Ka_+(\lambda,0)^{-1}),
\end{aligned}$$

and since the Fourier transform of the function on the RHS is equal to

$$a_+(\lambda,-i)^{-1}(i\xi - 1)^{-1} - Ka_+(\lambda,0)^{-1}(i\xi)^{-1},$$

we arrive at the pricing formula

$$\begin{aligned}
w(x,\tau) &= (2\pi i)^{-1} \int_{\mathcal{L}_{\theta,C}} \int_{-\infty+i\sigma}^{+\infty+i\sigma} e^{\tau\lambda+ix\xi} a_-(\lambda,\xi)^{-1} \qquad (8.23) \\
&\quad \cdot [a_+(\lambda,-i)^{-1}(i\xi-1)^{-1} - Ka_+(\lambda,0)^{-1}(i\xi)^{-1}]d\xi d\lambda.
\end{aligned}$$

We have proved

Theorem 8.1 *The rational price of the down-and-out call option with the barrier $H = 1$ and the strike $K < H$ is given by*

$$\begin{aligned}
V_{do;call}(K,1,T;S,t) &= \frac{1}{2\pi i} \int_{\mathcal{L}_{\theta,C}} \int_{-\infty+i\sigma}^{+\infty+i\sigma} e^{(T-t)\lambda+i\xi \ln S} a_-(\lambda,\xi)^{-1} \quad (8.24) \\
&\quad \cdot [a_+(\lambda,-i)^{-1}(i\xi-1)^{-1} - Ka_+(\lambda,0)^{-1}(i\xi)^{-1}]d\xi d\lambda.
\end{aligned}$$

8.2.3 Construction of the resolvent, and the Wiener-Hopf factorization with a parameter

Parameters θ and C can be found as follows.

Lemma 8.1 *Let Eq. (8.16) hold. Then there exist $\theta \in (\pi/2,\pi)$, $C \geq 0$ and $c_0 > 0$ such that for any $\lambda \in \Sigma_{\theta,C}$ and ξ in the strip $\Im\xi \in [\lambda_-,\lambda_+]$,*

$$|\lambda + a(\xi)| \geq c_0(1 + |\lambda| + |\xi|^\nu). \qquad (8.25)$$

Proof. From Eq. (3.45)-Eq. (3.46), we conclude that there exist $R, c_1 > 0$ such that for all ξ in the strip $\Im\xi \in [\lambda_-,\lambda_+]$, outside the ball of radius R, centered at 0,

$$\Re a(\xi) \geq 2c_1(1 + |\xi|)^\nu. \qquad (8.26)$$

Consider the subset

$$U(C, c_1) := \{(\lambda, \xi) \mid \lambda \in \mathbf{C}, \Im\xi \in [\lambda_-, \lambda_+], \ C \leq |\lambda| \leq c_1(1 + |\xi|)^\nu\}.$$

If C is sufficiently large then on $U(C, c_1)$, we have $|\xi| \geq R$, hence Eq. (8.26) holds, and therefore, Eq. (8.25) holds as well, with some $c_0 > 0$. If $C_1 > 0$ is sufficiently large, and $|\lambda| \geq C_1(1+|\xi|)^\nu$, then from Eq. (3.45)-Eq. (3.46), we conclude that Eq. (8.25) holds, with possibly another $c_0 > 0$. Finally, let c_1 and C_1 be chosen as above. Then on a set $V(c_1, C_1, C)$, defined by

$$c_1(1 + |\xi|)^\nu \leq |\lambda| \leq C_1(1 + |\xi|)^\nu, \quad |\lambda| \geq C,$$

we have, as $C \to +\infty$:

$$\lambda + a(\xi) \sim \lambda + c|\xi|^\nu, \quad \text{if } \nu \neq 1, \tag{8.27}$$

and

$$\lambda + a(\xi) \sim \lambda - i\mu\xi + c|\xi|, \quad \text{if } \nu = 1. \tag{8.28}$$

Define $W(c_1, C_1, C, \theta)$ as a subset of $V(c_1, C_1, C)$, where $\arg\lambda \in [-\theta, \theta]$. It is evident from Eq. (8.27)-Eq. (8.28) that if $\theta - \pi/2$ is small, and C is large, then on $W(c_1, C_1, C, \theta)$, Eq. (8.25) hold.

This finishes the proof of Lemma. □

Notice the importance of the condition Eq. (8.16): if $\nu \in (0,1)$ and $\mu \neq 1$, then it is impossible to obtain the estimate Eq. (8.25).

Now, by using Eq. (8.25), we will construct the Wiener-Hopf factorization of $a(\lambda, \xi) := \lambda + a(\xi)$. The reader may notice that we have changed the notation of Chapter 7 in order to use the standard form of Eq. (8.18). If $\nu > 1$, then we can use the factorization constructed in Chapter 7, with the factors analytic w.r.t. $\lambda \in \Sigma_{\theta,C}$. In other cases, this nice factorization is impossible, and the construction must be changed.

Fix a branch of $\ln$ by the requirement that $\ln y$ is real for $y > 0$, set $\Lambda_\pm(\lambda, \xi)^s = (1 + |\lambda|^{1/\nu} \mp i\xi)^s = \exp[s\ln(1 + |\lambda|^{1/\nu} \mp i\xi)]$, and choose $d > 0$ and $\kappa_-, \kappa_+ \in \mathbf{R}$ as in the case $\lambda = 0$ in Chapter 3:

1) if $\nu \in (0,2], \nu \neq 1$, we set $d = c, \kappa_- = \kappa_+ = \nu/2$;
2) if $\nu = 1$, we set $d = (c^2 + \mu^2)^{1/2}, \kappa_\pm = 1/2 \pm \pi^{-1}\arctan(\mu/c)$.

The next steps are analogues of the corresponding steps in the constructions of the factors in the Wiener-Hopf factorization formula in Chapter 3, but two additional subtle points are to be taken into account:

(i) for each $\lambda \in \Sigma_{\theta,C}$, the Wiener-Hopf factorization formula must be proved for ξ not only in a sufficiently narrow strip containing the real axis, as in Chapter 3, but for all ξ in the strip (λ_-, λ_+), and

(ii) the estimates must be uniform w.r.t. $\lambda \in \Sigma_{\theta,C}$, and ξ from any strip of the form $\Im\xi \in [\rho_-, \rho_+]$, where $\lambda_- < \rho_- < \rho_+ < \lambda_+$.

These two conditions allow us to derive the pricing formula for any continuous payoff which grows as S^β as $S \to +\infty$, for any $\beta \in (-\lambda_+, -\lambda_-)$ [1] Notice that due to the EMM-condition $r + \psi(-i) = 0$, (ii) fails if $C = 0$ and $\rho_- = -1$. This observation highlights the importance of the flexibility of the contour $\Sigma_{\theta,C}$. In particular, with the choice $C = 0$, it is impossible to use the pricing formula for the down-and-out call.

With our choice of $\kappa_\pm$, function

$$B(\lambda, \xi) := d^{-1}\Lambda_+(\lambda, \xi)^{-\kappa_+}\Lambda_-(\lambda, \xi)^{-\kappa_-}(\lambda + a(\xi)) \qquad (8.29)$$

satisfies for all $\lambda \in \Sigma_{\theta,C}$, $\xi \in \mathbf{R}$ and $\sigma \in [\lambda_-, \lambda_+]$

$$\lim_{\xi \to \pm\infty} B(\lambda, \xi + i\sigma) = 1, \qquad (8.30)$$

and $b(\lambda, \xi + i\sigma) = \ln B(\lambda, \xi + i\sigma)$ is well-defined for these λ, ξ, σ; the proof is the same as in Chapter 3.

Lemma 8.2 *For any $\lambda \in \Sigma_{\theta,C}$ and $\sigma \in [\lambda_-, \lambda_+]$, the winding number around the origin of the curve $\{B(\lambda, \xi + i\sigma) \mid -\infty < \xi < +\infty\}$ is zero:*

$$(2\pi)^{-1}\int_{\xi=-\infty}^{\xi=+\infty} d\arg B(\lambda, \xi + i\sigma) = 0. \qquad (8.31)$$

Proof. From Eq. (8.25), $B(\lambda, \xi) \neq 0 \; \forall \; \lambda \in \Sigma_{\theta,C}$ and ξ in the strip $\Im\xi \in [\lambda_-, \lambda_+]$. Taking Eq. (8.30) into account, we conclude that the LHS in Eq. (8.31) is an integer. Moreover, this integer is independent of $\lambda \in \Sigma_{\theta,C}$ and $\sigma \in [\lambda_-, \lambda_+]$. If $C > 0$ is large enough, and $\lambda = C$, then from Eq. (3.45)-Eq. (3.46), the last factor in Eq. (8.29) assumes values in a half-plane $\Re z > 0$. The same holds for the product of the first three factors, since the first one is positive, $\Lambda_-(\lambda, \xi)$ and $\Lambda_+(\lambda, \xi)$ assume values in the same half-plane but in different quadrants, and $0 < \kappa_\pm \leq 1$. Hence, for all ξ in the strip $\Im\xi \in [\lambda_-, \lambda_+]$, we have $-\pi < \arg B(C, \xi) < \pi$, and therefore, Eq. (8.31) holds. $\qquad \square$

---

[1] In fact, at the expense of more technical argument, (i)-(ii) can be established for all ξ in the strip $\Im\xi \in [\lambda_-, \lambda_+]$, and then $\beta = -\lambda_-$ can be allowed as well.

Under condition Eq. (8.31), $b(\lambda, \xi) := \ln B(\lambda, \xi)$ is well-defined on $\Sigma_{\theta,C} \times \{\xi \mid \Im\xi \in [\lambda_-, \lambda_+]\}$. Next, for real ξ, $\sigma > \lambda_-$ and $\sigma_1 \in (\lambda_-, \sigma)$, we set

$$b_+(\lambda, \xi + i\sigma) = -(2\pi i)^{-1} \int_{-\infty+i\sigma_1}^{+\infty+i\sigma_1} \frac{b(\lambda, \eta)}{\xi + i\sigma - \eta} d\eta, \qquad (8.32)$$

and for real ξ, $\sigma < \lambda_+$ and $\sigma_2 \in (\sigma, \lambda_+)$, we set

$$b_-(\lambda, \xi + i\sigma) = (2\pi i)^{-1} \int_{-\infty+i\sigma_2}^{+\infty+i\sigma_2} \frac{b(\lambda, \eta)}{\xi + i\sigma - \eta} d\eta. \qquad (8.33)$$

By the Cauchy theorem, $b_\pm(\lambda, \xi + i\sigma)$ are independent of choices of σ_1 and σ_2.

It follows from Eq. (3.45), Eq. (3.46), Eq. (8.30) and Eq. (8.31), that there exist $C, \rho > 0$ such that for all η in the strip $\Im\eta \in [\lambda_-, \lambda_+]$,

$$|b(\lambda, \eta)| \leq C(1 + |\eta|)^{-\rho},$$

where C depends on λ but not on η (and $\rho > 0$ is independent of both λ and η). Hence, the integrals in Eq. (8.32) and Eq. (8.33) converge, and $b_\pm(\lambda, \xi)$ are well-defined and holomorphic in a half-plane $\pm\Im\xi > \pm\lambda_\mp$.

The next lemma can be proved as the similar statement in Chapter 7.

Lemma 8.3 *For any $[\omega'_-, \omega'_+] \subset (\lambda_-, \lambda_+)$, there exists $C_1 > 0$ such that*

$$|b_+(\lambda, \xi)| \leq C_1, \quad \forall \lambda \in \Sigma_{\theta,C}, \quad \Im\xi \geq \omega'_-, \qquad (8.34)$$

and

$$|b_-(\lambda, \xi)| \leq C_1, \quad \forall \lambda \in \Sigma_{\theta,C}, \quad \Im\xi \leq \omega'_+. \qquad (8.35)$$

By the residue theorem, for $\lambda_- < \sigma_1 < \sigma < \sigma_2 < \lambda_+$,

$$\begin{aligned}
b_+(\lambda, \xi + i\sigma) + b_-(\lambda, \xi + i\sigma) &= -(2\pi i)^{-1} \left(\int_{-\infty+i\sigma_1}^{+\infty+i\sigma_1} - \int_{-\infty+i\sigma_2}^{+\infty+i\sigma_2} \right) \\
&\quad \cdot \frac{b(\lambda, \eta)}{\xi + i\sigma - \eta} d\eta \\
&= b(\lambda, \xi + i\sigma).
\end{aligned}$$

Hence, $B_\pm = \exp b_\pm$ satisfy $B = B_+ B_-$ on $\Sigma_{\theta,C} \times \{\xi \mid \Im\xi \in (\omega_-, \omega_+)\}$, and if we set

$$\begin{aligned}
a_-(\lambda, \xi) &= \Lambda_-(\lambda, \xi)^{\kappa_-} B_-(\lambda, \xi), \\
a_+(\lambda, \xi) &= d\Lambda_+(\lambda, \xi)^{\kappa_+} B_+(\lambda, \xi),
\end{aligned}$$

then for $\lambda \in \Sigma_{\theta,C}$, $\Im\xi \in (\omega_-, \omega_+)$,

$$\lambda + a(\xi) = a_+(\lambda, \xi)a_-(\lambda, \xi). \qquad (8.36)$$

Lemma 8.4

a) *For any $\lambda \in \Sigma_{\theta,C}$, $a_+(\lambda, \xi)$ is holomorphic in the half-plane $\Im\xi > \lambda_-$, and satisfies an estimate*

$$c(1 + |\lambda|^{1/\nu} + |\xi|)^{\kappa_+} \le |a_+(\lambda, \xi)| \le C(1 + |\lambda|^{1/\nu} + |\xi|)^{\kappa_+}, \qquad (8.37)$$

where $C, c > 0$ are independent of $\lambda \in \Sigma_{\theta,C}$ and ξ in the half-plane $\Im\xi \ge \omega_-$ (but may depend on $\omega_- > \lambda_-$);

b) *For any $\lambda \in \Sigma_{\theta,C}$, $a_-(\lambda, \xi)$ is holomorphic in the half-plane $\Im\xi < \lambda_+$, and satisfies an estimate*

$$c(1 + |\lambda|^{1/\nu} + |\xi|)^{\kappa_-} \le |a_-(\lambda, \xi)| \le C(1 + |\lambda|^{1/\nu} + |\xi|)^{\kappa_-}, \qquad (8.38)$$

where $C, c > 0$ are independent of $\lambda \in \Sigma_{\theta,C}$ and ξ in the half-plane $\Im\xi \le \omega_+$ (but may depend on $\omega_+ < \lambda_-$);

c) *for all $\lambda \in \Sigma_{\theta,C}$ and ξ in the strip $\lambda_- \le \Im\xi \le \lambda_+$, Eq. (8.36) holds;*

d) *factors in Eq. (8.36) are uniquely defined by properties a) and b), up to scalar multiples, depending on λ.*

Proof. Clearly, $\Lambda_\pm(\lambda, \xi)^{\kappa_\pm}$ satisfy a) and b), and since $b_\pm$ are holomorphic and bounded on the same sets due to Eq. (8.34)–Eq. (8.35), a) and b) are proved; Eq. (8.36) has already been proved.

To prove d), fix λ, and suppose, $\lambda + a(\xi) = a'_+(\lambda, \xi)a'_-(\lambda, \xi)$ is another factorization with the same properties. Then $a'_+(\lambda, \xi)/a_+(\lambda, \xi)$ (resp., $a'_-(\lambda, \xi)/a_-(\lambda, \xi)$) is holomorphic in the upper half-plane $\Im\xi > \lambda_-$ (resp., the lower half-plane $\Im\xi < \lambda_+$). Both functions are bounded and non-zero, and coincide on $\mathbf{R}$. Hence, the analytic continuation of any of them is a bounded holomorphic function on $\mathbf{C}$. By the Liouville theorem, it must be constant. $\square$

8.2.4 *Proof of Eq. (8.17) and continuity of the RHS in Eq. (8.19)*

The resolvent is defined by

$$(A_\gamma + \lambda)^{-1}g = a_-(\lambda, D + i\gamma)^{-1}\theta_+ a_+(\lambda, D + i\gamma)^{-1}lg, \qquad (8.39)$$

where lg is an arbitrary extension of g. Represent the operator on the LHS of the estimate Eq. (8.17) in the form

$$(1 + |\lambda|)(A_\gamma + \lambda)^{-1}g = A'_{\gamma,-} A'_{\gamma,+}g,$$

where

$$A'_{\gamma,-} = (1 + |\lambda|)^{\kappa_-} a_-(\lambda, D + i\gamma)^{-1},$$

and

$$A'_{\gamma,+} = \theta_+ (1 + |\lambda|)^{\kappa_+} a_+(\lambda, D + i\gamma)^{-1} l.$$

From Eq. (8.37) and Eq. (8.38), we conclude that both operators are bounded in $L_2(\mathbf{R}_+)$ (see Theorem 15.12 and Theorem 15.13), uniformly in λ, and hence, Eq. (8.17) has been proved.

To prove the continuity, we notice that $g_\gamma \in \overset{o}{H}{}^s(\mathbf{R}_+)$, for any $s < 0.5$ since g is the restriction to $[0, +\infty)$ of a smooth function, which exponentially decays at the infinity together with its derivative. Take $s < 0.5$ such that $s + \kappa_- > 0.5$. By using Eq. (8.37) and Eq. (8.38) once again, we can show that the resolvent is bounded as an operator from $\overset{o}{H}{}^s(\mathbf{R}_+)$ to $\overset{o}{H}{}^{s+\kappa_-}(\mathbf{R}_+)$, uniformly in $\lambda \in \Sigma_{\theta,C}$. Hence, $(A_\gamma + \lambda)^{-1}g_\gamma \in \overset{o}{H}{}^{s+\kappa_-}(\mathbf{R}_+)$, uniformly in $\lambda \in \Sigma_{\theta,C}$, and therefore, for each τ, $w_\gamma(\cdot, \tau) \in \overset{o}{H}{}^{s+\kappa_-}(\mathbf{R}_+)$. It remains to notice that if $s + \kappa_- > 0.5$, then $\overset{o}{H}{}^{s+\kappa_-}(\mathbf{R}_+) \subset C_0([0, +\infty))$.

The continuity of the RHS in Eq. (8.19) has thus been proved.

8.3   Asymptotics of the option price near the barrier

Consider the price of a barrier option without a rebate near the barrier. It can be shown that if the time to the expiry is fixed then its behavior is qualitatively the same as of $W(x, \tau) := 1 - V(x, \tau)$, where $V(x, \tau)$ is the price of the corresponding first-touch digital. See Fig.7.1-7.3, which clearly demonstrate how significant the difference from the Gaussian case can be.

8.4   Commentary

Various aspects of pricing of barrier options have been considered in a number of papers and books, see e.g. Rubinstein and Reiner (1991), Wilmott *et al.* (1995), Musiela and Rutkowski (1997), Hull (2000) and the bibliography there, but to the best of our knowledge only Gaussian processes have been allowed.

For the double barrier options with both upper and lower barriers (also in the Gaussian case) see Geman and Yor (1996), Pelsser (2000), and the bibliography there.

The results of this chapter, in a more general set-up, and by using a bit different technique, are obtained in Boyarchenko and Levendorskiĭ (2002b).

Chapter 9

Multi-asset contracts

The variety of derivative products on several assets is huge - see the references at the end of the chapter, where fairly comprehensive overviews for the Gaussian case can be found; in many cases, it is possible to obtain RLPE-analogues of the results of the Gaussian theory.

We construct multi-dimensional analogues of RLPE, and calculate prices of (power) forwards and several types of European options in the RLPE market of several assets. We calculate weights of a locally risk-minimizing portfolio of several underlying assets and a contingent claim of the European type, and the prices of the Asian options of the simplest type.

9.1 Multi-dimensional Regular Lévy Processes of Exponential type

In the Gaussian case, the evolution of the tuple of several assets can be modelled as

$$\ln S_j(t) = b_j t + \sum_{l=1}^{n} \sigma_{lj} W_l(t),$$

where $b_j, j = 1, \ldots, n$, are constants, $\Sigma := [\sigma_{lj}]$ is a symmetric matrix, and $W(t) = (W_1(t), \ldots, W_n(t))$ is an $\mathbf{R}^n$-valued standard Brownian motion process. In other words, each component of a multi-dimensional Brownian motion is represented as a mixture of independent Brownian one-dimensional motions. For a generic non-Gaussian Lévy process, the similar reduction to finite mixtures of one-dimensional processes is impossible.

The definition of multi-dimensional KoBoL uses the decomposition into an integral of one-dimensional subordinators (Lévy processes on a ray; in 1D-case, two subordinators are mixed: on $\mathbf{R}_+$ and $\mathbf{R}_-$). Multi-dimensional VGP, NIG, HP, GHP and NTS Lévy processes are obtained via subordination of multi-dimensional Brownian motions, by using the same subordinators as in 1D-case.

9.1.1   *Multi-dimensional KoBoL family*

For the sake of brevity, we construct multi-dimensional KoBoL processes of order $\nu \in (0,2)$, $\nu \neq 1$, and leave to the reader the construction of the multi-dimensional analogue of the KoBoL process of order 1.

Denote by (ρ, ϕ) the polar coordinates in $\mathbf{R}^n$, and by $\langle \cdot, \cdot \rangle$ the standard scalar product in $\mathbf{R}^n$. Let $\Pi'(d\phi)$ and λ be a finite measure and positive continuous function, respectively, on the unit sphere S_{n-1}, and let $\mu \in \mathbf{R}^n$. Set

$$\Pi(dx) = \rho^{-\nu-1} \exp(-\lambda(\phi)\rho) d\rho \Pi'(d\phi).$$

By repeating the proof of Lemma 3.1, which treats the 1D-case, we conclude that there exists $\gamma \in \mathbf{R}^n$ such that the generating triplet $(0, \gamma, \Pi(dx))$ defines the characteristic exponent

$$\psi(\xi) = -i\langle \mu, \xi \rangle + \Gamma(-\nu) \int_{S_{n-1}} [\lambda(\phi)^\nu - (\lambda(\phi) - i\langle \xi, \phi \rangle)^\nu] \Pi'(d\phi).$$

By applying Theorem 2.7, we can obtain a more general class of characteristic exponents.

Lemma 9.1   *Let Σ be a positive-definite $n \times n$ matrix, let $\Pi'(d\phi)$ and λ be a finite measure and positive continuous function, respectively, on the unit sphere S_{n-1}, and let $\mu \in \mathbf{R}^n$. Then the following formula defines a characteristic exponent of a Lévy process:*

$$\psi(\xi) = -i\langle \mu, \xi \rangle + \Gamma(-\nu) \int_{S_{n-1}} [\lambda(\phi)^\nu - (\lambda(\phi) - i\langle \Sigma\xi, \phi \rangle)^\nu] \Pi'(d\phi). \quad (9.1)$$

Notice that if $\mu = 0$, then as $\max \lambda(\phi) \to 0$, the characteristic exponent Eq. (9.1) converges to the characteristic exponent of a stable Lévy process.

Definition 9.1   *Let $\nu \in (0,2)$, $\nu \neq 1$. The Lévy process with the characteristic exponent Eq. (9.1) is called a KoBoL process of order ν.*

The class of characteristic exponents Eq. (9.1) is too large for parameters fitting purposes since the function λ and the measure Π' belong to infinite-dimensional spaces. The following subclass of the KoBoL family depends on the finite number of parameters, and still seems to be sufficiently rich for practical applications. Another possibility is to use a measure $\Pi'(d\phi)$ supported on a finite subset of the unit sphere.

Example 9.1 Let $\Lambda > 0$ and $\beta \in \mathbf{R}^n$ satisfy $||\beta|| < \Lambda$; then $\lambda(\phi) := \Lambda + \langle \beta, \phi \rangle$ is positive on S_{n-1}. Let $c > 0$, $\mu \in \mathbf{R}^n$, and $\Pi'(d\phi) = cd\phi$, where $d\phi$ is the standard measure on S_{n-1}. Then the conditions of Definition 9.1 are satisfied, and Eq. (9.1) reduces to

$$\psi(\xi) = -i\langle \mu, \xi \rangle \tag{9.2}$$
$$+c\Gamma(-\nu) \int_{S_{n-1}} [(\Lambda + \langle \beta, \phi \rangle)^\nu - (\Lambda + \langle \beta, \phi \rangle - i\langle \Sigma\xi, \phi \rangle)^\nu]d\phi.$$

We call a Lévy process with the characteristic exponent Eq. (9.2) a KoBoL process of order ν, with the intensity parameter c, steepness parameter Λ, asymmetry parameter β, pseudo-covariance matrix Σ, and pseudo-drift μ.

Direct calculations show that

$$i\frac{\partial \psi}{\partial \xi_j}(0) = \mu_j + c\Gamma(1-\nu) \int_{S_{n-1}} (\Lambda + \langle \beta, \phi \rangle)^{\nu-1}(\Sigma\phi)_j d\phi, \tag{9.3}$$
$$\frac{\partial^2 \psi}{\phi_j \phi_k}(0) = c\Gamma(2-\nu) \int_{S_{n-1}} (\Lambda + \langle \beta, \phi \rangle)^{\nu-2}(\Sigma\phi)_j(\Sigma\phi)_k d\phi. \tag{9.4}$$

If a KoBoL with the characteristic exponent Eq. (9.1) fits well to empirical data, but one tries to fit the Gaussian process to the same data, the drift and covariance matrix of the Gaussian process will be given by the RHS in Eq. (9.3) and Eq. (9.4), respectively. This remark can be used when one compares results in KoBoL and Gaussian cases.

9.1.2 *Normal Inverse Gaussian processes and Normal Tempered Stable Lévy processes*

Let $\nu \in (0,2)$, $\delta > 0, \gamma > 0$, and let $TS(\nu, \delta, \gamma)$ be infinitely divisible distribution introduced in Subsection 3.1.3; its Laplace exponent is given by Eq. (3.23):

$$\Phi(\theta) = \delta[(\gamma^2 + 2\theta)^{\nu/2} - \gamma^\nu]. \tag{9.5}$$

Let $Y(\beta^0)$ be the n-dimensional Brownian motion with the drift $\beta^0 \in \mathbf{R}^n$ and (non-degenerate) variance-covariance matrix A, and let X be the subordination of $Y(\beta^0)$ by $TS(\nu, \delta, \gamma)$. Then the characteristic exponent of X, denote it ϕ, is of the form

$$\phi(\xi) = \Phi\left(\frac{1}{2}\langle A\xi, \xi\rangle - i\langle\beta^0, \xi\rangle\right),$$

and by using Eq. (9.5) and letting

$$\beta = A^{-1}\beta^0, \quad \alpha^2 = \gamma^2 + \langle A\beta, \beta\rangle,$$

we obtain

$$\phi(\xi) = \delta\{[\alpha^2 - \langle A(\beta + i\xi), \beta + i\xi\rangle]^{\nu/2} - [\alpha^2 - \langle A\beta, \beta\rangle]^{\nu/2}\}.$$

Here $\langle\cdot, \cdot\rangle$ denotes the standard scalar product both in $\mathbf{R}^n$ and in $\mathbf{C}^n$ regarded as $\mathbf{R}^{2n}$ with the basis $\{e_1, \cdots, e_n; ie_1, \cdots, ie_n\}$. With this identification, A acts in $\mathbf{R}^{2n}$ as a block-diagonal matrix, each of the diagonal blocks being equal to the $n \times n$ matrix A.

By adding the drift, we obtain the characteristic exponent of a *Normal Tempered Stable* (NTS) Lévy process

$$\begin{aligned}\psi(\xi) \quad &= \quad -i\langle\mu, \xi\rangle \\ &+ \delta\{[\alpha^2 - \langle A(\beta + i\xi), \beta + i\xi\rangle]^{\nu/2} - [\alpha^2 - \langle A\beta, \beta\rangle]^{\nu/2}\}. \end{aligned} \quad (9.6)$$

With $\nu = 1$, this is a characteristic exponent of a NIG process.

9.1.3 *Hyperbolic Processes, Generalized Hyperbolic Processes and Variance Gamma Processes*

These processes can be constructed as in 1D-case in Subsection 3.1.4 and Subsection 3.1.5, with the n-dimensional Brownian motion in place of the one-dimensional one. For instance, a multi-dimensional VGP is defined by

$$\psi(\xi) = -i\langle\mu, \xi\rangle + \delta\ln\frac{\alpha^2 - \langle A(\beta + i\xi), \beta + i\xi\rangle}{\alpha^2 - \langle A\beta, \beta\rangle}. \quad (9.7)$$

9.1.4 *Definition of multi-dimensional RLPE*

Consider the characteristic exponent of a KoBoL process. Since λ is continuous and positive, $\bar{\lambda} := \min\lambda(\phi) > 0$, and therefore, ψ satisfies the following conditions:

(a) there exists a bounded open set $U \in \mathbf{R}^n$ containing the origin such that ψ admits the analytic continuation into the tube domain $\mathbf{R}^n + iU \subset \mathbf{C}^n$, and the continuous extension up to the boundary of the tube domain;

(b)

$$\psi(\xi) = -i\langle \mu, \xi \rangle + \psi_1(\xi), \tag{9.8}$$

where ψ_1 has the following asymptotics, as $\xi = \eta + i\sigma \to \infty$ in the tube domain $\mathbf{R}^n + iU$:

$$\psi_1(\xi) = \psi_\infty(\eta/|\eta|)|\eta|^\nu + O(|\eta|^{\nu - \epsilon}), \tag{9.9}$$

where $\epsilon = 1$, and ψ_∞ is a positive positively homogeneous degree zero function:

$$\psi_\infty(s\eta) = \psi_\infty(\eta) > 0, \quad \forall\ s > 0, \eta \in \mathbf{R}^n \setminus 0. \tag{9.10}$$

Definition 9.2 We say that a Lévy process X is a Regular Lévy Process of Exponential type (RLPE), of order $\nu \in (0, 2]$, if its characteristic exponent satisfies conditions a) and b) with some $\epsilon > 0$.

KoBoL processes provide examples of RLPE of order $\nu \in (0, 2)$, HP and NIG are RLPE's of order 1, and Gaussian processes and its independent mixtures with other RLPE's are RLPE's of order 2. To incorporate VGP into the class of RLPE-processes, the condition Eq. (9.9) must be replaced with the following one:

$$\psi_1(\xi) = \psi_\infty(\eta/|\eta|) \ln |\eta| + O(|\eta|^{-\epsilon}), \tag{9.11}$$

where $\epsilon > 0$, and ψ_∞ is a positive positively homogeneous degree zero function. If Eq. (9.11) holds, we call X an RLPE of order 0.

9.2 European-style contracts

We consider *forward contracts*, European puts and calls, and *exchange* and *basket* options. The market consists of $n \geq 1$ stocks with the price processes $S_j(t) = \exp X_j(t)$, $j = 1, \ldots, n$, and a riskless bond yielding the constant rate of return $r > 0$. We assume that $X = (X_1, \ldots, X_n)$ is an RLPE under the historic measure $\mathbf{P}$.

9.2.1 *The Esscher transform*

In this subsection, we show that all the classes of processes described in Section 9.1 are closed under the Esscher transform, provided certain natural mild restrictions are met. We look for an EMM satisfying

$$dQ = e^{\langle \kappa, X_t \rangle - ct} dP,$$

where $\kappa \in \mathbf{R}^n$ and $c \in \mathbf{R}$ are to be found. Let $F(S(t), t) = f(X_t, t)$ be the underlying security in the market or contingent claims priced in the market; then its discounted price under the EMM $\mathbf{Q}$ is

$$E^{\mathbf{Q}, x}[e^{-rt} f(X_t, t)] = E^{\mathbf{P}, x}[e^{\langle \kappa, X_t \rangle - (c+r)t} f(X_t, t)]. \tag{9.12}$$

The EMM–condition means, in effect, that for the price of the riskless bond and the price for any of the underlying stocks, we must have

$$E^{\mathbf{Q}, x}[e^{-rt} f(X_t, t)] = f(x, 0), \quad t > 0. \tag{9.13}$$

By applying Eq. (9.12) and Eq. (9.13) to the riskless bond, whose price is deterministic: $f(X_t, t) = e^{rt}$, and using the definition of the characteristic exponent, we obtain the following equation

$$e^{-t(\psi^{\mathbf{P}}(-i\kappa) - c)} = 1,$$

whence

$$c = \psi^{\mathbf{P}}(-i\kappa); \tag{9.14}$$

and by applying Eq. (9.12) and Eq. (9.13) to any of the underlying stocks, that is, with $f(x, t) = e^{x_j}$, $j = 1, \ldots, n$, and taking Eq. (9.14) into account, we derive

$$e^{x_j - t(\psi^{\mathbf{P}}(-ie_j - i\kappa) - \psi^{\mathbf{P}}(-i\kappa) + r)} = e^{x_j}, \quad j = 1, \ldots, n.$$

Here $\{e_j\}_{j=1}^n$ is the standard basis in $\mathbf{R}^n$. Thus, we have the following system of equations to determine κ:

$$\psi^{\mathbf{P}}(-ie_j - i\kappa) - \psi^{\mathbf{P}}(-i\kappa) + r = 0, \quad j = 1, \ldots, n, \tag{9.15}$$

and if a solution exists, we can define the Esscher transform of the historic measure $\mathbf{P}$ by

$$dQ = e^{\langle \kappa, X_t \rangle - \psi^{\mathbf{P}}(-i\kappa)t} dP. \tag{9.16}$$

From Eq. (9.16), we derive the following formula for the characteristic exponent $\psi^{\mathbf{Q}}$ of the process X under $\mathbf{Q}$:

$$\psi^{\mathbf{Q}}(\xi) = \psi^{\mathbf{P}}(\xi - i\kappa) - \psi^{\mathbf{P}}(-i\kappa). \tag{9.17}$$

We will use Eq. (9.17) in numerical examples.

In the Brownian motion case, $\psi^{\mathbf{P}}$ is a second-order polynomial, hence Eq. (9.15) is a linear system of n equations with n unknowns, therefore if the Brownian motion is non-degenerate, the system has the only solution κ. Notice that for typical parameters' values, $\| \kappa \|$ is of order 1. In general, the system Eq. (9.15) may have no solutions, one or many, but if X is a KoBoL with the large $\alpha := \Lambda$ or NIG, NTS Lévy, HP, GHP and VGP with large α (large w.r.t. the other parameters of the process, which is usually the case as the empirical studies of the financial markets reveal), then the characteristic exponent $\psi^{\mathbf{P}}$ admits a representation

$$\psi^{\mathbf{P}}(\xi) = -i\langle b, \xi\rangle + \frac{1}{2}\langle \text{Hess } \xi, \xi\rangle + R(\alpha, \xi), \tag{9.18}$$

where $b = \partial\psi^{\mathbf{P}}(0)$, Hess is the Hessian of $\psi^{\mathbf{P}}$, evaluated at 0, and $R(\alpha, \xi)$ is small (together with its derivatives) in a region where $\| \xi \| \leq 2$, provided α is large enough. If the inverse of Hess is bounded uniformly w.r.t. the large parameter α, then by inserting Eq. (9.18) into Eq. (9.15) and using the standard perturbation argument, it can easily be shown that Eq. (9.15) has the unique solution in the ball $\| \kappa \| \leq 2$. This solution can be found both in the form of a series in negative powers of the large parameter α, and numerically, by using any standard iteration method with $\kappa_0 = 0$ as the initial approximation.

9.2.2 *Pricing of power forwards*

We assume that the parameters of the historic measure $\mathbf{P}$ and the EMM $\mathbf{Q}$ chosen by the market have been fitted to the data, and therefore, the analytical formulas for the characteristic exponents $\psi^{\mathbf{P}}(\xi)$ and $\psi^{\mathbf{Q}}(\xi)$ are known. Let $F(S(t), t) = f(X(t), t)$ be the no-arbitrage price of the contract with the expiry date T and the terminal payoff $G(S(T)) = g(X(T))$. Then for $\tau := T - t > 0$,

$$f(x, t) = \exp[-\tau(r + \psi^{\mathbf{Q}}(D_x))]g(x). \tag{9.19}$$

For $\alpha = (\alpha_1, \ldots, \alpha_n) \in -U$, set $S(T)^\alpha := S_1(T)^{\alpha_1} \cdots S_n(T)^{\alpha_n}$, and consider the power forward with the delivery price K, and the terminal payoff $G(S(T)) = S(T)^\alpha - K$. Due to the condition $-\alpha \in U$, this forward contract is priced in the market, and its price $F(S,t) = f(x,t)$ at time t is

$$f(x,t) = \exp[-\tau(r + \psi^{\mathbf{Q}}(D_x))](e^{\langle \alpha, x \rangle} - K).$$

From the equality

$$\psi^{\mathbf{Q}}(D)e^{\langle \alpha, x \rangle} = \psi^{\mathbf{Q}}(-i\alpha)e^{\langle \alpha, x \rangle}, \tag{9.20}$$

we obtain

$$F(S(t), t) = e^{(t-T)(r + \psi^{\mathbf{Q}}(-i\alpha))} S(t)^\alpha - e^{(t-T)r} K. \tag{9.21}$$

Notice that at the initiation, the price of the forward contract must be 0, and therefore, the delivery price is defined at time 0 by

$$K = e^{-T\psi^{\mathbf{Q}}(-i\alpha)} S(0)^\alpha.$$

9.2.3 *Pricing of European options on one asset*

Let $F_{\text{call};n}(S(t), t)$ be a European call on the last stock, S_n, with the expiry date T and the strike price K. Set $f(x,t) = F_{\text{call};n}(e^{x_1}, \ldots, e^{x_n}; t)$, and $g(x) := g_n(x_n) = (e^{x_n} - K)_+$. Further, divide the dual variables into two groups $\xi = (\xi', \xi_n)$, where $\xi' = (\xi_1, \ldots, \xi_{n-1})$, and notice that the Fourier transform of the identity is the Dirac delta function; hence, for $\tau = T - t > 0$ and any $\sigma < -1$ such that $\sigma e_n \in U$,

$$
\begin{aligned}
f(x,t) &= (2\pi)^{-n} \int_{\mathbf{R}^{n-1}} \int_{-\infty+i\sigma}^{+\infty+i\sigma} e^{i\langle x, \xi \rangle - \tau(r + \psi^{\mathbf{Q}}(\xi))} \hat{g}(\xi) d\xi \\
&= (2\pi)^{-n} \int_{\mathbf{R}^{n-1}} \int_{-\infty+i\sigma}^{+\infty+i\sigma} e^{i\langle x, \xi \rangle - \tau(r + \psi^{\mathbf{Q}}(\xi))} \delta_{\xi'=0} \hat{g}_n(\xi_n) d\xi \\
&= (2\pi)^{-n} \int_{\mathbf{R}^{n-1}} \int_{-\infty+i\sigma}^{+\infty+i\sigma} e^{i\langle x, \xi \rangle - \tau(r + \psi^{\mathbf{Q}}(0, \xi_n))} \delta_{\xi'=0} \hat{g}_n(\xi_n) d\xi \\
&= (2\pi)^{-1} \int_{-\infty+i\sigma}^{+\infty+i\sigma} e^{i x_n \xi_n - \tau(r + \psi^{\mathbf{Q}}(0, \xi_n))} \hat{g}_n(\xi_n) d\xi_n,
\end{aligned}
$$

or

$$F_{\text{call};n}(S, t) = (2\pi)^{-1} \int_{-\infty+i\sigma}^{+\infty+i\sigma} e^{i \xi_n \ln S_n - \tau(r + \psi^{\mathbf{Q}}(0, \xi_n))} \hat{g}_n(\xi_n) d\xi_n. \tag{9.22}$$

In other words, the pricing formula is the same as in the case of one stock $S(t) = \exp X(t)$, where X is an 1D Lévy process with the characteristic exponent $\psi^Q(0, \cdot)$. We leave to the reader the verification of the fact that $\psi^Q(0, \cdot)$ is the characteristic exponent of a Lévy process in 1D.

The other types of European options on one asset or on weighted geometric averages of several assets are priced in the same fashion.

9.2.4 *Pricing of exchange options and basket options*

For simplicity, we consider the market of two stocks. Let $F(S(t), t)$ be a European option which gives its owner the right to exchange the first asset S_1 for the second asset S_2 at the expiry date T, for the price $\$K$. The payoff function is $\max\{G(S(T)), 0\}$, where $G(e^x) = g(x) = e^{x_2} - e^{x_1} - K$, and its Fourier transform cannot be calculated in a simple closed from. This undermines the effectiveness of the direct application of the pricing formula Eq. (9.19). Instead, we suggest the following approximate procedure, which works reasonably well if the time to expiry is not too large, and the steepness parameter (Λ in the KoBoL model, and α in HP, NIG, and NTS Lévy model) is large. The same procedure applies to a basket option with the payoff $(e^{x_2} + e^{x_1} - K)_+$, and to other types of exchange and basket options.

Set $\mathcal{Z}_0 = \{x \mid g(x) = 0\}$, and $\mathcal{Z}_\pm = \{x \mid \pm g(x) > 0\}$, and let $X(0)$ be the vector of log-spot prices. Consider the following three cases:

a) $X(0) \in \mathcal{Z}_-$ is far from $\mathcal{Z}_0$;
b) $X(0) \in \mathcal{Z}_+$ is far from $\mathcal{Z}_0$;
c) $X(0)$ is near $\mathcal{Z}_0$.

Certainly, "far" and "near" do not have the exact meaning; presumably, "at the distance more than 0.25" and "at the distance less than 0.25" can be used, and if the results do not agree with the desired error at the boundary, where "far" becomes "near", one can change the definitions of "far" and "near".

In the case a), we set $f(X(0), t) = 0$.

In the case b), we expand $G(S)$ in the Taylor series around $S(0)$:

$$G(S) \sim \sum_\alpha c_\alpha(S(0))(S - S(0))^\alpha,$$

pick up terms up to a fixed order m (we believe that $m = 4$ suffices)

$$G(S) \sim \sum_{|\alpha| \leq m} c_\alpha(S(0))(S - S(0))^\alpha,$$

and after multiplying out, obtain an approximation for $g(x) = G(S)$ of the form

$$g(x) \sim \sum_{|\alpha| \leq m} d_\alpha(S(0))e^{\langle \alpha, x \rangle}. \tag{9.23}$$

Now, by substituting the approximation Eq. (9.23) into Eq. (9.19), and using Eq. (9.20), we obtain

$$F(S(0), 0) \sim \sum_{|\alpha| \leq m} d_\alpha(S(0))e^{-T(r + \psi^Q(-i\alpha))} S(0)^\alpha. \tag{9.24}$$

Notice that the construction in the case b) presupposes that $\mathcal{Z}_0$, where $\max\{g(x), 0\}$ loses smoothness, is sufficiently far so that the influence of $\mathcal{Z}_0$ can be neglected.

In the case c), we cannot neglect it, and the procedure becomes more complicated. Let $X_{00} \in \mathcal{Z}_0$ be the closest point to $X(0)$. In a neighbourhood U of X_{00}, which contains $X(0)$ but is not too large (probably, for typical parameters' values, the neighbourhood of radius 0.4-0.5 will do), we introduce the new coordinate system as follows. Let $x = x(x_1')$ be the parameterisation of $\mathcal{Z}_0$ in the neighbourhood of X_{00}, s.t. $X_{00} = x(0)$, and set $x_2' = \ln(g(x) + K_1)$, where $K_1 > 0$ is sufficiently large so that $g(x) + K_1$ is positive and bounded away from zero in the chosen neighbourhood U. Then in U, $g(x) = e^{x_2'} - K_1$, and the payoff becomes the payoff of a European call: $\max\{e^{x_2'} - K_1, 0\}$. By making the change of variables in the Cauchy problem for the generalized Black-Scholes equation

$$\begin{aligned}
(\partial_t - (r + \psi^Q(D_x)))f(x, t) &= 0, & t < T, \\
f(x, T) &= \max\{g(x), 0\},
\end{aligned}$$

we obtain

$$\begin{aligned}
(\partial_t - (r + \tilde{\psi}^Q(x', D_{x'})))f(x', t) &= 0, & t < T, & \quad (9.25) \\
f(x', T) &= \max\{e^{x_2'} - K_1, 0\}, & & \quad (9.26)
\end{aligned}$$

where $\tilde{\psi}^Q(x', D_{x'})$ is the PDO $\psi^Q(D_x)$ written in the new coordinate system. The calculus of PDO allows one to write down the asymptotic expansion of the symbol, and after that, obtain the approximate solution to the problem Eq. (9.25)-Eq. (9.26). For details, see Section 16.5.

9.3 Locally risk–minimizing hedging with a portfolio of several assets

9.3.1 *The set-up*

Assume that the investor can go short in the money account, and consider the following problem:

> given a basket of (derivative) securities F, which are priced in the market, and the investor's wealth at time t, $W(t)$, construct a portfolio
>
> $$(F(S(t), t); \ \theta_1(t)S_1(t), \ldots, \theta_n(t)S_n(t))$$
>
> with the minimal variance the next infinitesimally close moment $t + \Delta t$, assuming that the residual
>
> $$w_0(t) := W(t) - F(S(t), t) - \sum_{j=1}^{n} \theta_j(t)S_j(t) \qquad (9.27)$$
>
> is invested into the money account.

The problem and construction of the hedging portfolio can easily be modified for the case when F is a basket containing not only derivatives but some of the basic securities S_{j_l}, $l = 1, \ldots, m$; in this case, the corresponding $\theta_{j_l}(t)$ are assumed to be zero. The modification for the case of the restricted borrowing is also possible.

The locally risk-minimizing formulas for the weights of the hedging portfolio, constructed in the paper, admit a natural modification for the case of Lévy-like Feller processes constructed by Barndorff-Nielsen and Levendorskiĭ (see Chapter 14). This modification can be applied to portfolios containing bonds and stocks.

As in the one-asset-case in Chapter 4, we show that the weights of the hedging portfolio for a European option are continuous up to the expiry date even at the strike price, where they are discontinuous in the Gaussian case.

We derive simple formulas for "power forward" contracts, and then we use these formulas to obtain effective approximate hedging formulas for other claims, e.g., exchange options and basket options.

Numerical examples for locally risk-minimizing hedging under KoBoL processes show that even not near the expiry, the weights of the hedging portfolio in our model can significantly differ from the ones in the Gaussian model with the same covariance matrix. The effect of fat tails is especially strong in the case of highly correlated stocks.

9.3.2   *Weights of the hedging portfolio*

Let $E_t^{\mathbf{Q}}$ be the expectation operator under $\mathbf{Q}$ conditioned on the information available at time t. In order for the formulas which we derive below to make sense, it is necessary for the following two conditions to hold

(i) F and S_j, $j = 1, \ldots, n$, are priced under $\mathbf{Q}$, that is,

$$E_t^{\mathbf{Q}}[F(S(t + \Delta t), t + \Delta t)] < \infty,$$

and

$$E_t^{\mathbf{Q}}[S_j(t + \Delta t)] < \infty, \ \forall \, j = 1, \ldots, n;$$

(ii) F, S_j, FS_j, and $S_j S_k$, $j, k = 1, \ldots, n$, are priced under $\mathbf{P}$.

Let X be an RLPE both under the historic measure $\mathbf{P}$ and the EMM $\mathbf{Q}$ chosen by the market, and let $U^{\mathbf{P}}$ and $U^{\mathbf{Q}}$ be the corresponding open sets in Definition 9.2. Let $\{e_j\}_{j=1}^n$ be the standard basis in $\mathbf{R}^n$. We will use the identity

$$\psi^{\mathbf{Q}}(D)e^{x_j} = e^{x_j}\psi^{\mathbf{Q}}(D - ie_j), \tag{9.28}$$

which is valid if $-e_j$ is in $U^{\mathbf{Q}}$. It can easily be shown by using Eq. (9.20) and Eq. (9.28), that if F is the price of a European option with the terminal payoff $G(S(T)) = g(X(T))$ admitting the estimate

$$G(S_T) \leq C \max\{1, S_1(T), \ldots, S_n(T)\}, \tag{9.29}$$

and

$$-e_j \in U^{\mathbf{Q}}, \quad -e_j, \ -e_j - e_k \in U^{\mathbf{P}} \tag{9.30}$$

for all $j, k = 1, \ldots, n$, then conditions (i) and (ii) are satisfied. Notice that Eq. (9.29) holds for European calls and puts.

Fix t, and denote $x_j = \ln S_j(t)$, $f(x,t) = F(e^{x_1}, \ldots, e^{x_n}; t)$.
The price of the portfolio at time $t + \Delta t$ is

$$W(t + \Delta t) = F(S(t + \Delta), t + \Delta t) + \sum_{j=1}^{n} \theta_j(t) S_j(t + \Delta t) + e^{r\Delta t} w_0(t),$$

where $w_0(t)$ is the residual in Eq. (9.27), and we assume that the investor chooses $\theta(t)$ to minimize the variance of $W(t+\Delta t)$ under the historic measure **P**, conditioned on the information available at the date t. We calculate

$$E_t^{\mathbf{P}}[(W(t + \Delta t) - E_t^{\mathbf{P}}[W(t + \Delta t)])^2]$$
$$= E_t^{\mathbf{P}}[(F(S(t + \Delta t), t + \Delta t) - E_t^{\mathbf{P}}[F(S(t + \Delta t), t + \Delta t)])^2]$$
$$+ 2\sum_{j=1}^{n} \theta_j(t) E_t^{\mathbf{P}}[(F(S(t + \Delta t), t + \Delta t) - E_t^{\mathbf{P}}[F(S(t + \Delta t), t + \Delta t)])$$
$$\times (S_j(t + \Delta t) - E_t^{\mathbf{P}}[S_j(t + \Delta t)])]$$
$$+ \sum_{j,k=1}^{n} \theta_j(t)\theta_k(t) E_t^{\mathbf{P}}[(S_j(t + \Delta t) - E_t^{\mathbf{P}}[S_j(t + \Delta t)])$$
$$\times (S_k(t + \Delta t) - E_t^{\mathbf{P}}[S_k(t + \Delta t)])].$$

Minimizing w.r.t. $\theta(t)$, we obtain the following first order conditions: for $j = 1, \ldots, n$,

$$\sum_{k=1}^{n} \theta_k(t) E_t^{\mathbf{P}}[(S_j(t + \Delta t) - E_t^{\mathbf{P}}[S_j(t + \Delta t)])(S_k(t + \Delta t) - E_t^{\mathbf{P}}[S_k(t + \Delta t)])]$$
$$= -E_t^{\mathbf{P}}[(F(S(t + \Delta t), t + \Delta t) - E_t^{\mathbf{P}}[F(S(t + \Delta t), t + \Delta t)])(S_j(t + \Delta t)$$
$$- E_t^{\mathbf{P}}[S_j(t + \Delta t)])]$$

or, equivalently,

$$(9.31)$$

$$\sum_{k=1}^{n} \theta_k(t) \left(E_t^{\mathbf{P}}[S_j(t + \Delta t) S_k(t + \Delta t)] - E_t^{\mathbf{P}}[(S_k(t + \Delta t)] E_t^{\mathbf{P}}[S_k(t + \Delta t)]) \right)$$
$$= -E_t^{\mathbf{P}}[(F(S(t + \Delta t), t + \Delta t) S_j(t + \Delta t)] + E_t^{\mathbf{P}}[F(S(t + \Delta t), t + \Delta t)]$$
$$\times E_t^{\mathbf{P}}[S_j(t + \Delta t)].$$

The explicit formula for the terms on the LHS is immediate from the definition of the characteristic exponent (and from Eq. (9.20)):

$$E_t^{\mathbf{P}}[S_j(t+\Delta t)S_k(t+\Delta t)] = \exp(-\Delta t\psi^{\mathbf{P}}(-i(e_j+e_k)))S_j(t)S_k(t), \quad (9.32)$$

and

$$E_t^{\mathbf{P}}[S_j(t+\Delta t)]E_t^{\mathbf{P}}[S_k(t+\Delta t)] = \exp(-\Delta t(\psi^{\mathbf{P}}(-ie_j)+\psi^{\mathbf{P}}(-ie_k)))S_j(t)S_k(t). \quad (9.33)$$

By applying the Taylor formula to Eq. (9.32) and Eq. (9.33) around $\Delta t = 0$, we see that the LHS admits the representation

$$\sum_{k=1}^n \theta_k(t)S_j(t)S_k(t)\left[-\psi^{\mathbf{P}}(-i(e_j+e_k))+\psi^{\mathbf{P}}(-ie_j)+\psi^{\mathbf{P}}(-ie_k)\right]\Delta t+o(\Delta t).$$
$$(9.34)$$

Notice an evident formula for the infinitesimal generator $\hat{L}$ of the $(n+1)$-dimensional process $\{\hat{X}_t\} = \{(X_t,t)\}$, when X is regarded as a Lévy process under $\mathbf{P}$:

$$\hat{L} = \partial_t + L^{\mathbf{P}} = \partial_t - \psi^{\mathbf{P}}(D_x). \quad (9.35)$$

By using Eq. (9.35), we obtain for the terms in the RHS of Eq. (9.31)

$$E_t^{\mathbf{P}}[F(S(t+\Delta t),t+\Delta t)S_j(t+\Delta t)] - F(S(t),t)S_j(t) \quad (9.36)$$

$$= (\partial_t - \psi^{\mathbf{P}}(D_x))f(x,t)e^{x_j}\Delta t + o(\Delta t),$$

and

$$E_t^{\mathbf{P}}[F(S(t+\Delta t),t+\Delta t)] - F(S(t),t) \quad (9.37)$$

$$= (\partial_t - \psi^{\mathbf{P}}(D_x))f(x,t)\Delta t + o(\Delta t).$$

From Eq. (9.28), we can rewrite Eq. (9.36) as

$$E_t^{\mathbf{P}}[F(S(t+\Delta t),t+\Delta t)S_j(t+\Delta t)] - F(S(t),t)S_j(t) \quad (9.38)$$

$$= S_j(t)(\partial_t - \psi^{\mathbf{P}}(D_x - ie_j))f(x,t)\Delta t + o(\Delta t),$$

and by gathering Eq. (9.37)–Eq. (9.38) and using Eq. (9.33), we see that the RHS in Eq. (9.31) admits the representation

$$S_j(t)[\psi^{\mathbf{P}}(D_x - ie_j) - \psi^{\mathbf{P}}(D_x) - \psi^{\mathbf{P}}(-ie_j)]f(x,t)\Delta t + o(\Delta t). \quad (9.39)$$

By inserting Eq. (9.34) and Eq. (9.39) into Eq. (9.31), dividing by Δt and $S_j(t)$ and passing to the limit $\Delta t \to +0$, we obtain, for $j = 1, \ldots, n$:

$$\sum_{k=1}^{n} \theta_k(t) S_k(t) \left[-\psi^{\mathbf{P}}(-i(e_j + e_k)) + \psi^{\mathbf{P}}(-ie_j) + \psi^{\mathbf{P}}(-ie_k) \right] \qquad (9.40)$$

$$= -[-\psi^{\mathbf{P}}(D_x - ie_j) + \psi^{\mathbf{P}}(D_x) + \psi^{\mathbf{P}}(-ie_j)] f(x, t).$$

For $\alpha, \beta \in -U^{\mathbf{P}} + i\mathbf{R}^n$, such that $\alpha + \beta \in -U^{\mathbf{P}} + i\mathbf{R}^n$, set

$$
\begin{aligned}
A(\alpha, \beta) &= -\psi^{\mathbf{P}}(-i(\alpha + \beta)) + \psi^{\mathbf{P}}(-i\alpha) + \psi^{\mathbf{P}}(-i\beta), \\
A(iD, \beta) &= -\psi^{\mathbf{P}}(D - i\beta) + \psi^{\mathbf{P}}(D) + \psi^{\mathbf{P}}(-i\beta).
\end{aligned}
$$

Further, introduce a matrix

$$COV := COV(X) := [A(e_j, e_k)]_{j,k=1}^{n},$$

a row vector with operator-valued components

$$A(iD) := A(X; iD) := [A(iD, e_j)]_{j=1,\ldots,n},$$

and a row vector

$$w(t) := w(S(t), t) = [\theta_j(t) S_j(t)]_{j=1,\ldots,n}$$

of fractions of wealth invested in the underlying stocks. Then we can rewrite Eq. (9.40) as

$$COV\, w(t)^T = -A(iD)^T f(x, t). \qquad (9.41)$$

If

$$COV \neq 0, \qquad (9.42)$$

we can solve Eq. (9.41)

$$w(t)^T = -COV^{-1} A(iD)^T f(x, t). \qquad (9.43)$$

Notice that if X is a Brownian motion, then

$$\psi^{\mathbf{P}}(\xi) = -i\langle \beta, \xi \rangle + \frac{1}{2} \sum_{j,k=1}^{n} a_{jk} \xi_j \xi_k,$$

The direct calculation shows that $COV(X) = [a_{jk}]$ is the covariance matrix, and

$$A(iD, e_j) = \sum_{k=1}^{n} a_{jk}\partial_j.$$

Thus, in the Gaussian case, Eq. (9.41) reduces to the standard *delta-hedging* result, which gives the riskless portfolio. In the non-Gaussian case, the locally risk-minimizing formula Eq. (9.43) does not determine a riskless portfolio, the latter being non-existent.

If Eq. (9.42) holds, and an explicit formula for $F(S,t) = f(x,t)$ is available, Eq. (9.43) can be used to calculate $w = w(t)$. Notice that Eq. (9.43) gives locally risk-minimizing weights for any contingent claim, not necessarily of the European type.

9.3.3 Hedging of European claims

Let F be a European claim with the payoff $g(X(T))$ at the expiry date T, and $\tau = T - t$ is the time to the expiry, then

$$f(x,t) = (2\pi)^{-n} \int_{-\infty+i\sigma_1}^{+\infty+i\sigma_1} \cdots \int_{-\infty+i\sigma_n}^{+\infty+i\sigma_n} e^{i\langle x,\xi\rangle - \tau(r+\psi^Q(\xi))} \hat{g}(\xi)d\xi_1 \cdots d\xi_n,$$

(9.44)

where $\hat{g}(\xi)$ is the Fourier transform of g, and the choice of real σ_j, $j = 1, 2, \ldots, n$, is determined by the type of the contingent claim (for instance, for the put on the last stock, one takes $\sigma_n > 0$ such that $-\sigma_n e_n \in U^Q$, and $\sigma_1 = \cdots = \sigma_{n-1} = 0$). Therefore in Eq. (9.43),

$$A(iD, e_j)f(x,t) = (2\pi)^{-n} \int_{-\infty+i\sigma_1}^{+\infty+i\sigma_1} \cdots \int_{-\infty+i\sigma_n}^{+\infty+i\sigma_n}$$

(9.45)

$$\exp\left[i\langle x,\xi\rangle - \tau(r + \psi^Q(\xi))\right] A(i\xi, e_j)\hat{g}(\xi)d\xi_1 \cdots d\xi_n.$$

If the terminal payoff depends on the price of the last stock only: $g(X_T) = g_n(X_T(n))$, for instance, if F is the price of a European put on the last stock, then $\hat{g}(\xi) = \hat{g}_n(\xi_n) \otimes \delta_{\xi'=0}$, where $\xi' = (\xi_1, \ldots, \xi_{n-1})$, and hence Eq. (9.45) reduces to a much simpler expression

$$A(iD, e_j)f(x,t) = (2\pi)^{-1} \int_{-\infty+i\sigma_n}^{+\infty+i\sigma_n}$$

(9.46)

$$\cdot \exp\left[ix_n\eta - \tau(r + \psi^Q(0,\eta e_n))\right] A(i\eta e_n, e_j)\hat{g}_n(\eta)d\eta.$$

Theorem 9.1 *Let X be an RLPE of order $\nu \in (0, 2)$, satisfying*

$$\nu - \epsilon < 1, \tag{9.47}$$

where $\epsilon > 0$ is from Eq. (9.9), let Eq. (9.30) holds, and let $F(S(t), t)$ be the price of the European put or call.

Then the weights of the locally risk-minimizing hedging portfolio given by Eq. (9.43) and Eq. (9.46) are continuous up to the expiry date, for all strikes.

Proof. For European puts and calls, the Fourier transform of the terminal payoff decays as $|\eta|^{-2}$, as $\eta \to \infty$, and hence, under condition Eq. (9.47), the integrand in Eq. (9.46) is bounded (in modulus) by an integrable function $C(1 + |\eta|)^{-2+\nu-\epsilon}$. Since the integrand is a continuous function in $(x, \tau) \in \mathbf{R} \times [0, +\infty)$, we conclude that the integral is continuous on the same set, too. $\square$

As the proof shows, the result is valid for *straddles*, *strangles* and essentially any other European contingent claim used in real Financial markets, with the payoff, which is continuous, piecewise smooth, and satisfies (i) and (ii) of the previous section (but it fails for digitals, of course).

Since the Gaussian delta-hedge produces discontinuous weights at the strike and expiry, our result Eq. (9.43)–Eq. (9.46) in the non-Gaussian RLPE-case differs drastically from the Gaussian hedging, near expiry and strike. The difference can be substantial in other regions of (x, t)–space as well, especially in the market, where some of the assets are highly correlated stocks.

9.3.4 *Locally risk-minimizing hedging of "power forwards"*

Consider the power forward with the terminal payoff of the form $S(T)^\alpha :=$ $S_1(T)^{\alpha_1} \cdots S_n(T)^{\alpha_n} - K$ and the price

$$F(S, t) = e^{-\tau(r + \psi^Q(-i\alpha))} S^\alpha - K e^{-\tau r},$$

where $\tau = T - t$. By using an equality

$$A(iD, e_j) e^{\langle \beta, x \rangle} = A(\beta, e_j) e^{\langle \beta, x \rangle}, \tag{9.48}$$

and taking into account that $A(0, e_j) = 0$, we derive from Eq. (9.43)

$$w(t)^T = -e^{-\tau(r + \psi^Q(-i\alpha))} COV^{-1} A(\alpha)^T S^\alpha, \tag{9.49}$$

where $A(\alpha) = [A(\alpha, e_1) \ldots A(\alpha, e_n)]$.

9.3.5   *Approximate locally risk-minimizing hedging: general case*

Suppose that we know a reasonably good approximation for the price $F(S,t)$ in a neighbourhood of a fixed point (S^0, t_0), of the form

$$F(S,t) = \sum_{|\alpha| \leq m} d_\alpha(S^0, t_0; t)(S - S^0)^\alpha, \qquad (9.50)$$

where $|\alpha| = \alpha_1 + \cdots + \alpha_n$. (We believe that for practical purposes, $m = 4$ should suffice.) If the intensity of large shocks is small (in the KoBoL model, this means that Λ is large, and in the models with subordinated Gaussian processes, α is large), then for the locally risk-minimizing hedging purposes, these are the values in a relatively small neighbourhood of $(S(t_0), t_0)$, that matter most, and hence, the approximation Eq. (9.50) seems reasonable.

Multiply out in Eq. (9.50) and obtain a representation of the form

$$F(S,t) = \sum_{|\alpha| \leq m} p_\alpha(S^0, t_0; t)S^\alpha, \qquad (9.51)$$

and after that, use Eq. (9.48) with $\beta \in \{\alpha^1, \ldots, \alpha^N\} := \{\alpha \mid |\alpha| \leq m\}$. The result is

$$w(S(t_0), t_0)^T = -COV^{-1} \sum_{|\alpha| \leq m} p_\alpha(S^0, t_0; t_0)(S^0)^\alpha A(\alpha)^T.$$

9.4   Weighted discretely sampled geometric average

An *Asian* option is the name used to denote options whose terminal payoff depend on the average asset values during some period of the option life time. There are Asian options both of the European style and the American style; the averaging can be in continuous time, e.g., with the payoff of the form

$$G(S(T); A(T_0, T)) = (A(T_0, T) - K)_+,$$

where

$$A(T_0, T) = (T - T_0)^{-1} \int_{T_0}^{T} S(u)du,$$

or in the discrete time, when $A(T_0, T)$ is replaced with an average price $A^N(t_0, T)$ on sampling dates $0 < t_0 < \cdots < t_N = T$:

$$A^N(t_0, T) = (N+1)^{-1} \sum_{k=0}^{N} S(t_k).$$

The popular numerical approach to the valuation of Asian options is based on the approximation of the arithmetic average by the geometric average. This approximation is known to significantly underprice the option (see the discussion in Musiela and Rutkowski (1997)) but is computationally very simple. The averaging with different weights are also used, and the "basket" variant of the weighted discretely sampled geometric average is technically no more difficult.

Let $\delta^m \in \mathbf{R}_+^n$, $m = 0, \ldots, N$ be vector of weights for stocks at the sampling dates, and define the weighted discretely sampled geometric average as

$$J(t) = \sum_{t_m \leq t} \langle \delta^m, X(t_m) \rangle.$$

Consider an option with the terminal payoff depending on both $X(T)$ and $J(T)$: $g(X(T), J(T))$.

In addition to the observable vector of log-spot prices at time t, $X(t)$, we have the observable $J(t)$, and clearly, the price of the option at time t depends on the triple $(X(t), J(t), t)$; denote this price $f(X(t), J(t); t)$. At a sampling date t_m,

$$f(x, J; t_m - 0) = f(x, J + \langle \delta^m, x \rangle; t_m), \qquad (9.52)$$

and by using the Taylor formula:

$$\begin{aligned} F(J+x) &= \sum_{s \geq 0} (s!)^{-1} \partial_J^s F(J) x^s \qquad (9.53) \\ &= \exp[x \partial_J] F(J), \end{aligned}$$

we can rewrite Eq. (9.52) as

$$f(x, J; t_m - 0) = \exp\left[\langle \delta^m, x \rangle \partial_J\right] f(x, J; t_m). \qquad (9.54)$$

Set $t_{-1} = 0$. On each interval $[t_m, t_{m+1})$, $J(t)$ is constant, and therefore the price $f(x, J; t)$ can be calculated as the price of a European option with the terminal payoff $f(X(t_{m+1}), J; t_{m+1} - 0)$:

$$f(x, J; t) = \exp[(t - t_{m+1})(r + \psi^{\mathbf{Q}}(D_x))]f(x, J; t_{m+1} - 0). \qquad (9.55)$$

Let $t \in [t_m, t_{m+1})$. By using Eq. (9.54) and Eq. (9.55), we derive

$$f(x, J; t) = \exp[(t - t_{m+1})(r + \psi^{\mathbf{Q}}(D_x))] \exp\left[\langle \delta^{m+1}, x \rangle \partial_J\right]$$
$$\cdot \prod_{k=m+1}^{N-1} \exp[(t_k - t_{k+1})(r + \psi^{\mathbf{Q}}(D_x))] \exp\left[\langle \delta^{k+1}, x \rangle \partial_J\right] g(x, J).$$

Denote the Fourier transform of f and g w.r.t. J by $\hat{f}$ and $\hat{g}$, respectively, and let η be the variable dual to J. Then

$$\hat{f}(x, \eta; t) = \exp[(t - t_{m+1})(r + \psi^{\mathbf{Q}}(D_x))] \exp[\langle \delta^{m+1}, x \rangle i\eta]$$
$$\cdot \prod_{k=m+1}^{N-1} \exp[(t_k - t_{k+1})(r + \psi^{\mathbf{Q}}(D_x))] \exp[\langle \delta^{k+1}, x \rangle i\eta] \hat{g}(x, \eta).$$

Set $\gamma^k = \sum_{s=k}^{N} \delta^s$. By using the commutation relation

$$\exp[b(D_x)] \exp[i\langle \gamma, x \rangle] = \exp[i\langle \gamma, x \rangle] \exp[b(D_x + \gamma)],$$

we can move all the $\exp[\langle \delta^s, x \rangle i\eta]$- factors to the left, and obtain

$$\hat{f}(x, \eta; t) = \exp[\langle \gamma^{m+1}, x \rangle i\eta] \exp[(t - t_{m+1})(r + \psi^{\mathbf{Q}}(D_x + \gamma^{m+1}\eta))]$$
$$\cdot \exp\left[\sum_{k=m+1}^{N-1} (t_k - t_{k+1})(r + \psi^{\mathbf{Q}}(D_x + \gamma^{k+1}\eta))\right] \hat{g}(x, \eta)$$
$$= \exp[(t - T)r] \exp[\langle \gamma^{m+1}, x \rangle i\eta] \exp[\Phi(D_x, \eta; t)] \hat{g}(x, \eta),$$

where

$$\Phi(D_x, \eta; t) = (t - t_{m+1}) \psi^{\mathbf{Q}}(D_x + \gamma^{m+1}\eta) \qquad (9.56)$$
$$+ \sum_{k=m+1}^{N-1} (t_k - t_{k+1}) \psi^{\mathbf{Q}}(D_x + \gamma^{k+1}\eta).$$

By using the Fourier transform, one easily computes

$$\phi(x, J; t) = \exp[\Phi(D_x, D_J; t)] g(x, J), \qquad (9.57)$$

and then one finds

$$f(x, J; t) = e^{(t-T)r} \phi(x, J + \langle \gamma^{m+1}, x \rangle; t). \qquad (9.58)$$

Here we have used the equality

$$\mathcal{F}^{-1} \exp[\langle \gamma^{m+1}, x \rangle i\eta] \mathcal{F} = \exp[\langle \gamma^{m+1}, x \rangle \partial_J]$$

and Eq. (9.53).

If g is independent of x, which is the most popular case, the answer simplifies considerably:

$$\phi_0(J; t) = \exp[\Phi(0, D_J; t)] g(J), \qquad (9.59)$$

and

$$f(x, J; t) = e^{(t-T)r} \phi_0(J + \langle \gamma^{m+1}, x \rangle; t). \qquad (9.60)$$

We have proved the following theorem.

Theorem 9.2 *At time* $t \in [t_m, t_{m+1})$*, the price*

$$F(S(t), J(t); t) = f(X(t), J(t); t)$$

of the Asian option with the payoff function g *is given by Eq. (9.56)-Eq. (9.58). If* g *is independent of* x*, then the simpler formulas Eq. (9.59)-Eq. (9.60) hold.*

Chapter 10

Investment under uncertainty and capital accumulation

Here we consider a risk-neutral, price-taking, and value-maximizing firm under demand uncertainty. The firm chooses optimal investment strategies; the investment is irreversible. We suggest a Marshallian-like form for the investment rule. It is applicable when the price can move in both directions, and uses the infimum process of the price instead of the price process itself. We also present an explicit formula for the expected level of the capital stock in terms of the infimum and supremum processes. Both results are new even for the Gaussian case. We derive simple approximate formulas, which facilitate the comparative statics analysis. Other problems of Real Options theory can be treated in the same fashion.

10.1 Irreversible investment and uncertainty

Here we analyse a benchmark model of *irreversible investment* under uncertainty. The investor is a competitive, risk-neutral, and value-maximizing firm. The firm's *production function* satisfies conventional properties such as monotonicity, concavity, and the *Inada conditions*. The latter conditions at zero ensure that it is always optimal to enter the market therefore we are interested in the optimal *investment strategies* of a firm, which has been on the market for some time. Time is continuous. For simplicity, we assume that the only source of uncertainty is the unit price of the firm's output, which follows a stochastic process. Even though there is empirical evidence (see, for instance, Yang and Brorsen (1992) or Deaton and Laroque (1992)) that distributions of commodity prices exhibit significant skewness and fat tails, traditionally the price process $P = \{P_t\}_{t \geq 0}$ is modelled as a Gaussian process, for example, the geometric Brownian motion. We model the price, P_t, as $P_t = \exp(X_t)$, where $X = \{X_t\}_{t\geq 0}$ is an RLPE. We demonstrate that RLPE are not less tractable in models of investment under uncertainty than Gaussian processes, the former being more realistic than the latter.

At each moment of time, the firm's manager has to decide whether to increase or not the stock of capital given the current stock and the market price. If the firm suffered an adverse demand shock in the past, its capital stock may be too big for the current price level, but since investment is irreversible, the firm has to stay put. Should the price increase, it may become optimal to invest, and in this case, the manager needs to determine the optimal amount of new capital. We assume that it is optimal to invest when the price crosses a certain barrier, which is called the *investment threshold*. As soon as the investment threshold is determined, the optimal amount of investment follows automatically, as we will see later.

There are at least two different prescriptions how to choose the *trigger price* of investment. One of them is known for almost a century, and is called the *net present value* (NPV) rule, or the *Marshallian law*. This rule (in marginal terms) says that investment is optimal as long as the present value of the expected marginal revenue does not exceed the marginal cost of investment. The second rule was spelled out by Dixit and Pindyck (1996), and it is based on the option pricing approach to the problems of investment under uncertainty. Dixit and Pindyck (1996) pointed out that the NPV rule was incorrect since it did not take into consideration the option-like nature of investment decisions. To correct the Marshallian prescription, the marginal cost of investment has to be multiplied by a certain factor. This correction factor comes from a solution to a so-called fundamental quadratic equation and has no economic meaning.

We use the *Real Options* approach as well and solve the problem essentially by the method of Chapter 5, because the choice of the investment threshold is similar to the choice of the optimal exercise price of a perpetual American call option. Our approach not only allows deriving an analytical solution for the case of output price following an RLPE, but also yields several new insights. The most operational one from the standpoint of economic applications is a modified version of the Marshallian law.

We consider only such processes that the price can move both upwards and downwards with positive probability. If the price process is non-decreasing almost surely, the irreversibility does not matter, and the Marshallian law is correct. On the other hand, if the price process is non-increasing almost surely in t, then the firm will never increase the capital stock further, because the state of the market can only deteriorate. When the price can move in both directions with non-zero probability, starting with the original price process, it is possible to introduce a non-trivial *infimum* price process. $N = \{N_t = \inf_{0 \leq s \leq t} P_t\}_{t \geq 0}$. The solution to the problem under consideration allows us to resurrect the Marshallian law to a certain extent. We state that it is optimal to invest as long as the present value of expected marginal revenue, computed for the infimum price process instead of the original price process, does not exceed the marginal cost of investment. Notice that this investment rule reflects the "*bad news principle*", which was first formulated by Bernanke (1983). The critical price which triggers new investment depends on downward moves, because the ability to avoid the consequences of "bad news" leads us to postpone investment decisions. The main advantage of our investment rule is that it obviates the need to introduce the correction factor like in Dixit and Pindyck (1996). In other words, the firm's manager may remain in the Marshallian world as long as she keeps in mind infimum processes instead of real ones.

10.2 The investment threshold

Here we specify the objective of the firm and sketch the solution technique. Details can be found in Boyarchenko (2001).

The firm's objective is to maximize the total expected discounted profit:

$$\Pi(K, x) = \max_{\{K_t\}} E^x \left[\int_0^{+\infty} e^{-rt} (e^{X_t} G(K_t) - rK_t) dt \right], \qquad (10.1)$$

where the meaning of the stochastic integral above is explained in Boyarchenko (2001). Here we treat the spot log-price, x, and the level of accumulated capital, K, as state variables, and K_t as a control variable. Due to irreversibility of investment, in each state (K, x), $K_t \geq K$.

In order the stochastic integral in Eq. (10.1) were bounded, we impose the following conditions:

a) resource constraint: there exists $\bar{K} < \infty$, s.t. $K_t < \bar{K}$, $\forall t$;
b) $\bar{M} \equiv E \left[\int_0^{+\infty} e^{-rt+X_t} dt \right] < \infty$.

Following the tradition in the literature, we are going to view the space of state variables as a (disjoint) union of two regions: inaction and action ones. For all pairs (K, x) belonging to the *inaction region*, it is optimal to keep the capital stock unchanged. In the *action region*, investment becomes optimal. Let the inaction region be closed. Denote by Γ the boundary of the inaction region. Then the investment strategy defined by the choice of the inaction region can be viewed as follows:

(i) do not invest as long as $X_t \le h(K)$, where $h(K)$ is defined by $(K, h(K)) \in \Gamma$;

(ii) invest when $X_t > h(K)$, and increase the capital stock up to the level $\phi(X_t)$ defined by $(\phi(X_t), x) \in \Gamma$.

It follows from (i) and (ii), that h is non-decreasing and continuous a. e. with each point of discontinuity is of the first kind, and $h(K + 0) = h(K)$, $\forall K$. Denote the set of such h by $\mathcal{H}$ and notice that every $h \in \mathcal{H}$ uniquely defines the boundary of the inaction region. To argue this, we notice that $h \in \mathcal{H}$ defines the boundary of the inaction region by $(\phi(x), x) \in \Gamma \Leftrightarrow \exists K : x \in [h(K - 0), h(K)]$; and Γ together with the rules (i) and (ii) uniquely define the strategy. Thus, we can restate the original firm's problem in an equivalent way: find the investment threshold $x = h(K)$, $h \in \mathcal{H}$, which separates the inaction and action regions. Let $W(K, x; a)$ be the NPV of the firm when $a \in \mathcal{H}$ is chosen as the investment barrier, that is

$$W(K, a; h) = E^x \left[\int_0^{+\infty} e^{-rt} (e^{X_t} G(K_t) - rK_t) dt \right]. \tag{10.2}$$

In Boyarchenko (2001), it is shown that the stochastic integral in Eq. (10.2) is well-defined given conditions a) and b) and the properties of the production function. The (optimal) investment threshold, $h \in \mathcal{H}$, satisfies

$$W(K, x; h) \ge W(K, x; a), \ \forall \, a \in \mathcal{H}, \tag{10.3}$$

or equivalently, $W(K, x; h) = \Pi(K, x)$.

The conventional solution technique is to write the Bellman equation for Eq. (10.3) in the inaction region; and apply the Ito lemma to obtain a second order differential equation w.r.t. the value function $V(K, P) := \Pi(K, x) = W(K, x; h)$. To specify the solution to this equation and to find the investment threshold $P = H(K) = e^{h(K)}$, one uses boundedness of $V(K, P)$ as $P \to 0$; the value matching condition $V_K(K, H(K)) = 1$, and the smooth-pasting condition $V_{KP}(K, H(K)) = 0$. Evidently, this technique is not suitable for non-Gaussian modelling because the equations, which arise in such models, cannot be differential any more; they are pseudo-differential equations. Besides, as we have seen it in Chapter 5, the smooth-pasting condition does not always hold for non-Gaussian processes.

We solve the problem as follows. First, we show that the value function $W(K, x; h)$ is differentiable w.r.t. its first argument and formulate the sufficient conditions for the investment threshold in terms of this derivative. Next, we fix a prospective candidate for the investment threshold and show that the derivative satisfies the Wiener-Hopf equation. By using the Wiener-Hopf method, we derive an explicit formula for $W_K(K, x; h)$. From this formula, it is possible to conjecture the investment threshold. Finally, we check that the sufficient conditions hold for the obtained threshold. As a result, we arrive at the following equation for the current level of price, $H(K)$, which triggers the new investment for the firm:

$$E\left[\int_0^\infty e^{-rt} N_t G'(K) dt \mid N_0 = H(K)\right] = C'(K).$$

This is the Marshallian law but with the infimum process started at the current level of the price instead of the original price process. We would like to stress that our argument provides the revised Marshallian law for more general form of dependence on the stochastic factor of both the revenue and cost (cf. Chapter 5 for similar results for perpetual American options).

10.3 Capital accumulation under RLPE

The next important problem, which can be solved in the framework of our model is the accumulation of capital in the long run. As it was stressed by Hubbard (1994), the benchmark models of investment under uncertainty considered in Dixit and Pindyck (1996), do not suggest specific predictions about the level of investment. Since the investment rule itself is not observable, one has to use the data on investment and capital stock to evaluate investment models; this shows the importance of theoretical results on the long-run *capital accumulation*. Abel and Eberly (1999) examine the behaviour of the capital stock in the long run and calculate explicitly the impacts of irreversibility and uncertainty on the expected long-run capital stock. They assume that an exogenous demand shock follows a geometric Brownian motion. Two types of effect are revealed: the *user cost effect*, which tends to reduce the capital stock, and the *hangover effect*, which arises because the irreversibility prevents a firm from selling capital when its marginal revenue product is low. Neither of these effects dominates globally, so the effect of increased uncertainty cannot be determined unambiguously.

We address a similar problem in the case when the output price follows an RLPE. To this end, we specify the production function as a Cobb-Douglas one, i.e., $G(K) = dK^\theta$, $\theta \in (0, 1)$; the marginal cost is normalized to unity. We consider a new born firm with the price process P starting at $P_0 = 1$. As before, our reasoning is valid when prices move both upwards and downwards. We introduce a (non-trivial) *supremum* price process as $M = \{M_T = \sup_{0 \le s \le t} P_t\}_{t \ge 0}$ and derive the following formula for the expected value $E[K_t]$ of the capital, K_t, at time t:

$$E[K_t] = (\theta d W_-)^{1/(1-\theta)} W_+(t), \tag{10.4}$$

where W_- and $W_+(t)$ are determined by the infimum process and supremum one, respectively:

$$W_- = E\left[\int_0^{+\infty} e^{-rt} N_t dt \mid N_0 = 1\right],$$
$$W_+(t) = E[M_t^{1/(1-\theta)} \mid M_0 = 1].$$

The suggested form shows that in making investment decisions under uncertainty, the anticipation of future negative shocks mostly matters. In addition, it allows us to separate two effects of the increasing uncertainty on the capital accumulation, working in the opposite directions: the increase of the downward uncertainty, measured by the infimum process, increases the investment threshold thereby decreasing the optimal level of the capital stock, but the increase of the upward uncertainty, measured by an increasing function of the supremum process, increases the expected capital stock each instant the investment threshold is crossed. For a similar factorization formula, in different terms, in a model of a firm which chooses both capital and labour under the Gaussian process, see Abel and Eberly (1999). As in Abel and Eberly (1999), we obtain explicit formulas for W_- and $W_+(t)$; the formula for $W_+(t)$ is fairly complicated but we show that for large t a good approximate formula is valid

$$W_+(t) = HE(\infty)e^{at} + O(e^{\epsilon t}),$$

where $HE(\infty)$ is given by a much simpler expression than $W_+(t)$ itself,

$\epsilon > 0$ is arbitrary, and $a \equiv t^{-1} \ln E[P_t^{1/(1-\theta)} \mid P_0 = 1]$; a is assumed positive. If the last condition fails, then in the model of the completely reversible investment the expected level of the capital decreases with time. Following Abel and Eberly (1999), we compare Eq. (10.4) with the corresponding formula for the capital accumulation in the case of completely reversible investment

$$E[K_t^R] = (\theta dW_-^R)^{1/(1-\theta)} W_+^R(t),$$

where

$$W_-^R = E\left[\int_0^{+\infty} e^{-rt} P_t dt \mid P_0 = 1\right],$$
$$W_+^R(t) = E[P_t^{1/(1-\theta)} \mid P_0 = 1] = e^{at},$$

by considering the ratio of the expected levels of accumulated capital

$$\kappa(t) = \frac{E[K_t]}{E[K_t^R]} = UC \cdot HE(t),$$

where

$$UC = (W_-/W_-^R)^{1/(1-\theta)}$$

is the user-cost effect, and

$$HE(t) = \frac{E[M_t^{1/(1-\theta)} \mid M_0 = 1]}{E[P_t^{1/(1-\theta)} \mid P_0 = 1]}$$

– the hangover effect of the irreversibility, and study how both these effects and the ratio $\kappa(t)$ itself depend on parameters of the process. Clearly, $UC < 1$ (unless the process is non-decreasing), and $HE(t) > 1$ (unless the process is non-increasing), so that both effects work in the opposite directions, and the joint effect on the capital accumulation is ambiguous: $\kappa(t)$ can be larger or smaller than 1, depending on parameters of the process.

10.4 Computational results

Dixit and Pindyck (1996) show that the Marshallian law prescribes very low trigger price of investment. A natural question which arises in our model is how the investment threshold changes if one considers a regular Lévy process instead of a Gaussian process with the same first and second moments $\mu_{1,\Delta t}$ and $\mu_{2,\Delta t}$ of observed probability density $p_{\Delta t}(x)$ of the process X, for a chosen small time interval Δt; for small Δt, $\mu_{1,\Delta t}/\Delta t$ and $\mu_{2,\Delta t}/\Delta t$ are good proxies for the first two coefficients in the Taylor expansion of the characteristic exponent $\psi(k)$ at $k = 0$; they can be used to infer the parameters of a RLPE process (in the Gaussian modelling, they are the drift and variance).

To answer this question, we calculated the investment threshold for different regular Lévy processes of exponential type with the same "drift" and "variance"

$$\lim_{\Delta t \downarrow 0} \mu_{1,\Delta t}/\Delta t, \quad \text{and} \quad \lim_{\Delta t \downarrow 0} \mu_{2,\Delta t}/\Delta t, \tag{10.5}$$

and we found that usually the threshold decreases (insignificantly) as we replace the Gaussian process with a regular Lévy processes of exponential type with the same "drift" and "variance"; only for "very non-Gaussian" processes of order close to zero we found sets of parameters for which the threshold increased. This result can be explained as follows. When one fits the Gaussian curve to a real probability density, one is bound to disregard the extreme events, and so, in fact, the "drift" and "variance" for a Gaussian process inferred from the real data do not coincide with the ones in Eq. (10.5) which one obtains by using a larger portion of rare events than in the Gaussian modelling: Eq. (10.5) based on the larger data set, gives larger value of the variance and hence it is incorrect to compare Gaussian processes and non-Gaussian ones by using the first two moments – or even the first 3 or 4 moments, since all of them are suitable tools of describing the behaviour of probability density near zero, being the coefficients of the Taylor series at zero.

Hence, a much more natural question is: what can be an effect of taking into account more and more data on rare events. To answer this question, we consider a series of KoBoL processes with the characteristic exponent Eq. (3.6); we fix $r = 0.06, \mu = -0.06, c = c_- = c_+ = 0.09, \nu = 1.6$, and see how the moments $\lim_{\Delta t \downarrow 0} \mu_{j,\Delta t}/\Delta t$, $j = 2, 3, 4$ ("variance", "skewness" and "kurtosis") of the process and the investment threshold[1] change with steepness parameters λ_+ and λ_-, which describe the fatness of the left and the right tail, respectively.

The choice $\nu = 1.6$ means that near zero, the probability density does

[1]The latter depends on the production function, of course; we plot the factor $\phi_r^-(-i)$, which characterizes the process in the formula for the investment threshold.

not differ too much from a Gaussian one, and the decrease of λ_+ (respectively, $-\lambda_-$) can be interpreted as the taking into account the more and more of negative (respectively, positive) large jumps. We believe that the result of this computational experiment is instructive. We allow λ_- to vary from -30 to -22, and λ_+ from $-\lambda_-$ to $-\lambda_- - 8$, and we see that though the variance does not change much, the threshold changes four-fold. The other observation is that the threshold is much more sensitive to the increase in skewness than in variance and kurtosis. Consider two cases: 1) $\lambda_- = -30$ remains fixed and λ_+ decreases from 30 to 22, and 2) both λ_+ and $-\lambda_-$ decrease from 30 to 22. In the first case, the variance and kurtosis increase less than in the second case, and the threshold and modulus of skewness increased more in the first case. So even this insignificant increase of variance: by less than 7 % (and more significant increase of skewness and kurtosis), which can easily be disregarded in practice since they come mostly from the tails of the probability density, and hence, can be left over as too extreme events, can have a dramatic impact on the investment threshold.

The results of the numerical example highlight the importance of obtaining the correct estimates for the parameters of an RLPE governing the underlying stochastic variable. In principle, it is possible to infer these parameters from the moments (up to the fourth order) of the corresponding probability distribution. However, this will provide a good fit for the central part of the distribution only, but not for the tails of the distribution. To obtain parameter estimates fitting the whole distribution, more sophisticated methods should be used.

Now we consider the errors which may arise when one uses Gaussian models in non-Gaussian situations. both in non-Gaussian and Gaussian models. Consider the same firm and process as in the example for the investment threshold above, with $r = 0.06$, $\theta = 0.33$ and $d = r/\theta$ in the Cobb-Douglas function, $c = 0.5, \nu = 1.1$. We change λ_+ in a wider range from 2 to 30; λ_- changes in the range from -30 to -10. So, here we allow for much fatter left tail. Following Abel and Eberly (1999), we determine the last parameter, μ, from the requirement that the expected rate of growth of the price remains constant. For each set of parameters, which define a non-Gaussian KoBoL process $X_t = \ln P_t$, we take the Gaussian process with the same variance as that of X_t.

The numerical results show (see Boyarchenko (2001) for details) that the investment threshold in the non-Gaussian case decreases up to 15 percent, the capital accumulated during 10 years by 13 percent. This means that though the Gaussian model may be too pessimistic about the unobserved investment threshold, it certainly can be too optimistic about observed quantities such as capital accumulated.

The real-world processes may deviate from Gaussian ones even more (for instance, the left tail can be even fatter, and the figures clearly show that with the further decrease in λ_+, the capital accumulation will be depressed much more). This example illustrates that the capital accumulation is mainly depressed by the possibility of large downward jumps, which is not taken into account properly by Gaussian models.

10.5   Approximate formulas and the comparative statics

Let $-\lambda_-$ and λ_- be large, which means that the rate of the exponential decay of the tails of the probability density is large. Then for typical parameters' values for model classes of RLPE (Normal Inverse Gaussian processes, Hyperbolic processes and KoBoL family), the equation $r + \psi(\xi) = 0$ has exactly two solutions; both of them are purely imaginary: $-i\beta_\pm$, where $\beta_- < 0 < \beta_+$. In this respect, model classes of RLPE are similar to Brownian motion, but their characteristic exponents are not holomorphic in the whole complex plane. Further, the approximate formulas Eq. (3.82) are valid, which look like the exact formulas in the Brownian motion case. It can be shown that for typical parameters' values, the relative error of Eq. (3.82) is several percent or less. For details, see Chapter 5, where the next correction term is given. Hence, these formulas can be used for comparative statics purposes, and *in this approximate form, RLPE-modelling is not more difficult than in the Brownian motion case - and more realistic at the same time.*

Chapter 11

Endogenous default and pricing of the corporate debt

We explicitly solve the problem of optimal capital structure endogenous default in Leland (1994a) setting, for a firm which assets follow a regular Lévy process of exponential type. This setting is highly stylised but nevertheless highlights several important issues. We express the endogenous default boundary in terms of the infimum process for the process of the assets of the firm, and therefore, the result makes sense for any Lévy process. Formulas for the value of the firm and values of equity and debt are also suitable for any Lévy process. For model classes RLPE, we suggest simple approximate formulas, which are valid for the firm very close to the bankruptcy level, and show that in this region, the equity's value can be much less than the one given by the Gaussian model.

For RLPE with large steepness parameters we suggest simple approximations to solutions, which are valid not very close to the default boundary. This allows one to study relatively easily the dependence of endogenous variables on parameters of the process and other exogenous variables.

11.1 An overview

Two approaches to *credit risk* modelling can mainly be divided into two categories: *intensity based models*, where the primitive is a stochastic model for the default event (see the monograph Bielecki and Rutkowski (2001), and in the non-Gaussian setting, Eberlein *et al.* (2000a, 2000b), Eberlein and Özkan (2001), and the bibliography there), and the *structural approach*. In this Chapter, we apply the structural approach to credit risk modelling for the case of non-Gaussian processes. The central feature of this approach is an attempt to model explicitly the evolution of the assets of the firm. The structural approach was pioneered by Black and Scholes (1973) and Merton (1974) and extended by Black and Cox (1976), Longstaff and Schwartz (1995). In a series of papers, Leland (1994a, 1994b) and Leland and Toft (1996) focus on the choice of optimal capital structure and bankruptcy level by a firm which keeps a constant profile of debt.

All the aforementioned structural models of credit risk have relied on diffusion process to model the evolution of the firm's assets. While the diffusion approach is convenient, it cannot capture the basic features of credit risk observed in practice. In particular, Jones, Mason and Rosenfeld (1984) find that the *credit spreads* on corporate bonds are too high to be matched by diffusion approach. Also, under a diffusion process, firms never default by surprise because a sudden drop in the firm's value is impossible. Therefore, if a firm is not currently in financial distress, the probability of its default on very short-term debt is zero. This fact implies that the credit spreads tend to zero as the maturity of debt tends to zero, which contradicts empirical evidence (see, for example, Fons (1994) and Sarig and Warga (1989)).

The first thing that must be said about realistic models of the assets of the firm is that jumps of essentially any size have to be incorporated. Moreover, both negative and positive jumps have to be admitted to capture the evolution of assets in the information economy. One of the ways to divert from the diffusion approach is to model the underlying asset process as a jump-diffusion process. Zhou (1997) uses a jump-diffusion model in the framework of the structural approach to valuing default-risky securities. Under a jump-diffusion approach, a firm can default instantaneously because of a sudden drop in its value. The model allows for matching the size of credit spreads on corporate bond to empirical data. However, the bankruptcy level is given exogenously in Zhou's model, and the author does not study the optimal capital structure. It is also necessary to mention that in order that jump-diffusion models could be fitted well to empirical data, many jumps have to be incorporated, which makes the models not very efficient from both the analytical and computational points of view.

Here we study the optimal *capital structure* and *endogenous default* by modelling the evolution of the firm's assets as a Lévy process. One of the advantages of models based on Lévy processes is that such models admit any number of jumps (infinite number including). Realistic models can be obtained within a family of regular Lévy processes of exponential type. Our goal is to show that RLPE are analytically tractable for problems of credit risk modelling and endogenous default. Roughly speaking, we are going to demonstrate that RLPE are the "second-best" if the Brownian motion fails to produce realistic results.

We solve the endogenous default problem by using essentially the same approach as in Chapters 5 and 10. We take any candidate for the level of bankruptcy and calculate the corresponding candidate for the value of equity by applying the Wiener-Hopf method. After this, we show that there is only one candidate for the level of bankruptcy for which the found equity satisfies certain natural conditions. The optimality can be proved as in Chapter 5.

The plan of the Chapter is as follows. In Section 11.2, we specify and solve a simple endogenous default problem. In Sections 11.3 and 11.4, we study the firm near the *bankruptcy*, and a solvent firm, respectively. and suggest two types of approximate formulas for all endogenous variables. The first set of approximate formulas can be used very close to the default level, and the second set of approximate formulas is valid for Lévy processes with large truncation parameters, i.e., for the processes with not very fat tails, and the firm not very close to the bankruptcy level. These approximations do not neglect the effects of non-Gaussianity on one hand, and on the other hand, they allow to perform comparative statics analysis. In Section 11.5, using the approximate solutions, we derive the optimal *leverage* for the firm. We produce several series of numerical examples which show that for the firm not very far from the default level, the difference between the Gaussian and non-Gaussian models can be sizable, and very near the bankruptcy level – very large indeed. In Section 11.6 we discuss the results obtained in the Chapter and address the comparative statics issue. Technical results are proved in Section 11.7.

11.2 Endogenous default

Consider a firm whose assets evolve according to the law

$$V_t = \exp X_t, \tag{11.1}$$

where $X = \{X_t\}_{t \geq 0}$ is a Lévy process, started at $x = X_0$, under a given EMM Q. The stochastic process V is assumed to be unaffected by the financial structure of the firm. Following the tradition in the relevant literature (see, for example, Leland (1994a)) we assume that a riskless asset exists and pays a constant interest rate $r > 0$.

The firm issues *debt*, which attracts *coupon payment* $C dt$ when the firm is solvent. In the event of default at time t, a fraction $\alpha \in (0,1)$ of the firm's value is lost to *bankruptcy costs*, therefore the debt holders receive $(1 - \alpha)V_t = (1 - \alpha)\exp X_t$. Let $V_B = e^h$ be the *bankruptcy level*, i.e., the firm defaults should the value of its assets fall below V_B. Let $\tau(h)$ be the hitting time of $(-\infty, h]$ by X. For $D(X_t)$, the value of the debt, we have

$$D(x) = E^x \left[\int_0^{\tau(h)} e^{-rt} C dt \right] + E^x \left[e^{-r\tau(h)}(1 - \alpha)e^{X_{\tau(h)}} \right]. \qquad (11.2)$$

By applying Theorem 2.12, we obtain

$$(r - L)D(x) = C, \qquad x > h, \qquad (11.3)$$
$$D(x) = (1 - \alpha)e^x, \quad x \le h, \qquad (11.4)$$

where $L = -\psi(D)$ is the infinitesimal generator of X.

Eq. (11.3)–Eq. (11.4) are analogues of the stationary Black-Scholes equation (3) and (6i) in Leland (1994a); condition (6ii) in the above paper also holds but it suffices to assume that D is continuous and bounded.

Next, following the steps of Leland (1994a), we consider the value of the bankruptcy costs $BC(x)$. This time, we have no stream of payments, and hence $BC(x)$ satisfies the homogeneous generalized Black-Scholes equation:

$$(r - L)BC(x) = 0, \quad x > h, \qquad (11.5)$$

and the boundary condition is

$$BC(x) = \alpha e^x, \quad x \le h. \qquad (11.6)$$

Eq. (11.5) is the analogue of (8i) in Leland (1994a); the condition (8ii) in that paper is valid here as well. In fact, it suffices to require that BC is continuous and bounded; such a solution is unique.

Now we consider *tax benefits*, $TB(x)$, associated with debt financing. These benefits resemble a security that pays a constant coupon τC^1 as long as the firm is solvent, and pays nothing at the bankruptcy. Hence,

---

[1] τ here should not be confused with the stopping time $\tau(h)$ above; the latter will not appear any more

$TB(x)$ solves the problem

$$(r - L)TB(x) = \tau C, \quad x > h, \tag{11.7}$$
$$TB(x) = 0, \quad x \le h, \tag{11.8}$$

and it is also continuous and bounded.

The total value of the firm is the sum of its assets and tax benefits less the bankruptcy costs:

$$v(x) = e^x + TB(x) - BC(x). \tag{11.9}$$

The value of *equity* is the total value of the firm less the value of debt:

$$E(x) = v(x) - D(x); \tag{11.10}$$

it can be represented as

$$E(x) = e^x + f(x), \tag{11.11}$$

where $f(x) = TB(x) - BC(x) - D(x)$. Notice that problems Eq. (11.3)–Eq. (11.4), Eq. (11.5)–Eq. (11.6) and Eq. (11.7)–Eq. (11.8) are boundary problems for a linear operator on the same half-axis, each having a unique solution. This means that f is a unique bounded solution to the boundary problem of the same sort, only with the data being the sum of the data of the above problems, i.e.,

$$(r - L)f(x) = (\tau - 1)C, \quad x > h,$$
$$f(x) = -\alpha e^x - (1 - \alpha)e^x$$
$$= -e^x, \quad x \le h.$$

Now it is easy to see that $f(x)$, $D(x)$, $TB(x)$, $BC(x)$ are solutions to the following boundary problem:

$$(r - L)u(x) = A_0, \quad x > h, \tag{11.12}$$
$$u(x) = A_1 e^x, \quad x \le h, \tag{11.13}$$

where $h, A_0, A_1 \in \mathbf{R}$ are constants. Therefore we will first characterize the solution to Eq. (11.12)–Eq. (11.13), and then find $f(x)$, $D(x)$, $TB(x)$, $BC(x)$ substituting the corresponding values for A_0 and A_1. By the same argument, it suffices to consider separately Eq. (11.12)-Eq. (11.13) in the cases $A_0 = 0$ and $A_1 = 0$. In the first case, Theorem 5.2 is applicable, and the answer is

$$A_1 \phi_r^-(D) \mathbf{1}_{(-\infty, h]} \phi_r^-(D)^{-1} e^x = A_1 [e^x - e^h \phi_r^-(-i)^{-1} \Psi_1(x - h)],$$

where

$$\Psi_1(x) = \phi_r^-(D) \theta_+(x) e^x, \tag{11.14}$$

and $\theta_\pm$ is the indicator function of $\mathbf{R}_\pm$. In the second case, the modification of the part of the proof of Theorem 5.2 gives the unique bounded measurable solution $A_0 r^{-1} \Psi_0(\cdot - h)$, where

$$\Psi_0 = \phi_r^-(D) \theta_+. \tag{11.15}$$

We have proved

Lemma 11.1 *For any $h \in \mathbf{R}$ and $A_0, A_1 \in \mathbf{C}$, the problem Eq. (11.12)–Eq. (11.13) has the unique solution in the class of bounded measurable functions. For $x > h$, it is given by*

$$u(x) = A_0 r^{-1} \Psi_0(x - h) + A_1 [e^x - e^h \phi_r^-(-i)^{-1} \Psi_1(x - h)]. \tag{11.16}$$

Now we can calculate $E(x) - e^x$ by using Eq. (11.15)–Eq. (11.16) with $A_0 = C(\tau - 1)$ and $A_1 = -1$, and obtain for $x > h$,

$$
\begin{aligned}
E(x) &= e^x + \frac{C(\tau - 1)}{r} \Psi_0(x - h) - e^x + e^h \phi_r^-(-i)^{-1} \Psi_1(x - h) \\
&= \frac{C(\tau - 1)}{r} \Psi_0(x - h) + e^h \phi_r^-(-i)^{-1} \Psi_1(x - h) \\
&= \left[\frac{C(\tau - 1)}{r} + e^h \phi_r^-(-i)^{-1} \right] \Psi_0(x - h) \\
&\quad + e^h \phi_r^-(-i)^{-1} [\Psi_1(x - h) - \Psi_0(x - h)];
\end{aligned}
$$

simplifying, we obtain

$$E(x) = \phi_r^-(D) g_h(x), \tag{11.17}$$

where

$$g_h(x) = \theta_+(x - h) \left[\frac{C(\tau - 1)}{r} + e^x \phi_r^-(-i)^{-1} \right]. \tag{11.18}$$

Recall that ϕ_r^- is the Fourier image of the probability distribution p_r^-, supported at $[0, +\infty)$, hence, Eq. (11.17) can be written as the convolution

$$E(x) = (p_r^- * g_h)(x) = \int_h^x p_r^-(x-y)w(y)dy, \qquad (11.19)$$

where

$$w(y) = r^{-1}C(\tau - 1) + e^y \phi_r^-(-i)^{-1}.$$

The value of the firm's equity having being obtained, the next step should be to determine the level of bankruptcy for the case, when the firm can choose this level, i.e., in the absence of a covenant (for example, positive net-worth requirement). Leland (1994a) computes the endogenous level of bankruptcy by using a smooth pasting condition: $dE/dV|_{V=V_B} = 0$. However, as we already saw in Chapter 5, the smooth pasting fails for some non-Gaussian processes. Therefore, we are going to find the optimal bankruptcy level as in Chapter 5, without resorting to the smooth pasting principle.
Set

$$\begin{aligned} d(h) &= \lim_{x \to h+0} w(x) \qquad (11.20) \\ &= r^{-1}C(\tau - 1) + e^h \phi_r^-(-i)^{-1}. \end{aligned}$$

Notice that due to Eq. (11.20), $d(h) \geq 0$ iff $w(x) > 0 \; \forall \; x > h$. If $d(h) < 0$, we deduce from Eq. (11.19)–Eq. (11.20) that $E(x)$ is negative at some points $x > h$, which is impossible. Hence, $h \geq h_*$, where h_* solves $d(h) = 0$, or

$$V_B = e^{h_*} = \frac{C(1-\tau)}{r} \phi_r^-(-i), \qquad (11.21)$$

and it remains to show that with any choice $h > h_*$, the value of the equity

$$E(h; x) = e^h \phi_r^-(-i)^{-1} \Psi_1(x - h) - \frac{C(1-\tau)}{r} \Psi_0(x - h) \qquad (11.22)$$

is less than or equal to $E(h_*; x)$, for any $x > h$. By using Eq. (11.19), we obtain

$$E(h_*; x) - E(h; x) = \int_{h_*}^h p_r^-(x - y)w(y)dy. \qquad (11.23)$$

Since $w(y) \geq 0$ on $[h_*, +\infty)$, we conclude that $E(h_*; x) \geq E(h; x)$, and the optimality [2] has been verified.

Thus, we have proved the following theorem.

Theorem 11.1 *The optimal default level* $V_B = e^{h_*}$ *is given by Eq. (11.21).*

Rewrite Eq. (11.21) as

$$V_B = C(1-\tau)E\left[\int_0^\infty e^{-rt}e^{n_t}\,dt\right],\qquad(11.24)$$

where $\{n_t\}$ is the infimum process. It follows from Eq. (11.24), that the asset value, V_B, at which bankruptcy occurs is proportional to the coupon, C, independent of bankruptcy costs, α, and decreases as the corporate tax rate, τ, increases. Moreover, we can see that the bankruptcy level does not depend on the current asset value, V, but it depends on the parameters of the infimum process for the firm's assets.

In the case of the Brownian motion, the bankruptcy level Eq. (11.21) is exactly the same as determined by the smooth pasting condition in Leland (1994a); it can be shown exactly as in Chapter 5, where we have shown that our general optimal exercise price for the perpetual American put coincides with Merton's result if X is the Brownian motion.

Now we determine the values of the firm's equity, debt, tax benefits, bankruptcy costs and the value of the firm itself, given the value of the assets and the level of bankruptcy, the former being a linear function of the coupon C. By substituting Eq. (11.21) into Eq. (11.22), we obtain the value of equity under the optimal choice of the default level

$$E(x) = \frac{C(1-\tau)}{r}[\Psi_1(x-h_*) - \Psi_0(x-h_*)],\qquad(11.25)$$

and Eq. (11.16) assumes the form

$$u(x) = A_0 r^{-1}\Psi_0(x-h_*) + A_1[e^x - \frac{C(1-\tau)}{r}\Psi_1(x-h_*)].\qquad(11.26)$$

With $A_0 = C$ and $A_1 = 1-\alpha$, we derive from Eq. (11.26) the value of debt

$$D(x) = (1-\alpha)e^x + \frac{C}{r}\Psi_0(x-h_*) - \frac{C(1-\tau)(1-\alpha)}{r}\Psi_1(x-h_*),\qquad(11.27)$$

[2]In the restricted class of hitting times of semibounded segments $(-\infty, h]$; the verification of the optimality in the wider class $\mathcal{M}$ can be made exactly as in Chapter 5.

hence the value of the firm is

$$v(x) = (1 - \alpha)e^x + \frac{\tau C}{r}\Psi_0(x - h_*) + \frac{C(1 - \tau)\alpha}{r}\Psi_1(x - h_*), \quad (11.28)$$

the tax benefits obtain with $A_0 = \tau C$ and $A_1 = 0$,

$$TB(x) = \frac{\tau C}{r}\Psi_0(x - h_*), \quad (11.29)$$

and the bankruptcy costs are

$$BC(x) = \alpha[e^x - \frac{C(1 - \tau)}{r}\Psi_1(x - h_*)]. \quad (11.30)$$

By using formulas Eq. (11.27)–Eq. (11.30), we can compute the rate of return on the debt

$$R(x) = C/D(x), \quad (11.31)$$

the *yield spread*

$$YS(x) = R(x) - r, \quad (11.32)$$

and the leverage

$$L(x) = D(x)/v(x). \quad (11.33)$$

By using the explicit formulas for the factors $\phi_r^{\pm}$, first, h_* can be calculated from Eq. (11.21), then $\Psi_0(x - h_*)$ and $\Psi_1(x - h_*)$ from Eq. (11.15)–Eq. (11.14). Finally, the values in Eq. (11.25) and Eq. (11.27)–Eq. (11.33) can be computed. However, since the formulas for the factors involve integrals, it is difficult to use them for comparative statics purposes. Therefore, we are going to derive approximate formulas for all the relevant values.

11.3 Equity of a firm near bankruptcy level and the yield spread for junk bonds

Consider the firm near the bankruptcy, i.e., the case of V/V_B near 1, or equivalently, $x := \ln(V/V_B) > 0$ small. Clearly, this is the situation when the presence of jumps must be felt in the first place, and hence the Gaussian models can be expected to produce serious errors, and we show that the mistake in the valuation of the firm equity near the bankruptcy level may differ by hundreds percent – even a thousand percent – between Gaussian and non-Gaussian models.

We start with the following approximate formulas, which are valid as $x \to +0$; in these formulas, the exponent κ_- appears, which is opposite to the order of the factor $\phi_r^-(\xi)$ in the Wiener-Hopf factorization formula. To be more specific, from Eq. (3.75)-Eq. (3.76), as $\xi \to \pm\infty$,

$$\phi_r^-(\xi) = a_-(0)(1+i\xi)^{-\kappa_-} + O(|\xi|^{-\kappa_- -\rho}), \qquad (11.34)$$

where $\rho \in (0, \nu - \nu_1)$ is arbitrary. For RLPE of order $\nu \in (1,2]$ or of order $\nu \in (0,1]$ with the drift coefficient $\mu = 0$, $\kappa_- = \nu/2$; for processes of order 1, κ_- can assume any value from $(0,1)$, depending on μ, and for processes of order less than 1, $\kappa_- = 0$, if $\mu > 0$, and $\kappa_- = 1$, if $\mu < 0$. Finally, it is possible to show that for a more general class of processes than RLPE any $\kappa_- \in (-0.5, 1.5)$ can be realised, the model example being

$$\begin{aligned}\psi(\xi) &= -i\mu\xi \qquad (11.35)\\ &+c_+\Gamma(-\nu)[\lambda_+{}^\nu - (\lambda_+ + i\xi)^\nu] + c_-\Gamma(-\nu)[(-\lambda_-)^\nu - (-\lambda_- - i\xi)^\nu]\end{aligned}$$

with $c_+ \neq c_-$ (see Chapter 15).

In the last Section, we will derive from Eq. (11.34) the following approximate formulas, as $x \to +0$:

$$\Psi_0(x) = \frac{a_-(0)}{\Gamma(\kappa_-+1)}x^{\kappa_-} + O(x^{\kappa_-+\rho}), \qquad (11.36)$$

$$\Psi_1(x) = \frac{a_-(0)}{\Gamma(\kappa_-+1)}x^{\kappa_-} + O(x^{\kappa_-+\rho}), \qquad (11.37)$$

$$\Psi_1(x) - \Psi_0(x) = \frac{a_-(0)}{\Gamma(\kappa_-+2)}x^{\kappa_-+1} + O(x^{\kappa_-+1+\rho}), \qquad (11.38)$$

for any $\rho \in (0, \nu - \nu_1)$. Notice that the order of the leading terms in Eq. (11.34)–Eq. (11.38) depend only on κ_-, which can be regarded as a measure of the asymmetry of PDF in the central part; the O-terms in Eq. (11.36) and Eq. (11.37) differ as follows from Eq. (11.38). It is possible to write down the next terms in the asymptotic formulas Eq. (11.34)– Eq. (11.38), but they are more involved.

Notice that even the simple formula Eq. (11.38) allows one to deduce the following approximation for the equity value near the bankruptcy level:

$$E = \frac{C(1-\tau)a_-(0)}{r\Gamma(\kappa_-+2)}\left(\ln\frac{V}{V_B}\right)^{\kappa_-+1}. \qquad (11.39)$$

In the Gaussian case, $\kappa_- = 1$, and for processes of order less than one, $\kappa_- = \nu/2 + \kappa_{-,1}$, where $\kappa_{-,1} \in (-0.5, 0.5)$ is greater than 0, equal to 0 or less than 0 depending on the asymmetry of probability densities of the process (with the characteristic exponent Eq. (11.35), say): if the upward jumps prevail, $\kappa_{-,1} < 0$, and if the downward jumps do, then $\kappa_{-,1} > 0$. Clearly, for V close to the bankruptcy level V_B, when $h = \ln(V/V_B)$ is close to 0, the ratio of the equity in the non-Gaussian model to the one in the Gaussian model can be very large indeed: 10 or even more.

We may apply the approximate formulas Eq. (11.36)-Eq. (11.37) to the formulas Eq. (11.27)–Eq. (11.33) for other endogenous variables, and derive, for instance,

$$D = (1 - \alpha)V + \frac{C(1 - (1 - \tau)(1 - \alpha))a_-(0)}{r\Gamma(\kappa_- + 1)} \left(\ln \frac{V}{V_B} \right)^{\kappa_-}. \qquad (11.40)$$

Since the error of the approximation Eq. (11.40) is of the same order as the value of equity in Eq. (11.39) or even larger, the usage of these formulas for the calculation of the leverage makes no sense: the only result will be: the leverage is approximately one, which is evident. (With the next terms in Eq. (11.34)– Eq. (11.38), more information can be obtained).

For the return on the debt and the yield spread more informative formulas are available:

$$R = \frac{C}{D} \sim \frac{C}{(1 - \alpha)V_B} = \frac{r}{(1 - \alpha)(1 - \tau)\phi_r^-(-i)}, \qquad (11.41)$$

$$YS = \frac{C}{D} - r = \frac{r[1 - (1 - \alpha)(1 - \tau)\phi_r^-(-i)]}{(1 - \alpha)(1 - \tau)\phi_r^-(-i)}. \qquad (11.42)$$

They give the limit values of the return on the debt and the yield spread of the firm near the bankruptcy level. In Fig.11.1 we plot the default level V_B and the limit values of the yield spread in the KoBoL model, and the ratios of these quantities in the non-Gaussian model to the ones in the Gaussian model with the same volatility, for the interest rate $r = 0.06$, corporate tax level $\tau = 0.35$, and bankruptcy cost $\alpha = 0.5$; the characteristic exponent is given by Eq. (11.35) with $c_- = c_+ = c$, $\nu = 1.2$, and the steepness parameters λ_- and λ_+ varying from -30 to -8 and from 30 to 8, respectively. The volatility vol=0.35 is fixed, which defines c as a function of λ_- and λ_+, from

$$\text{vol} = c\Gamma(-\nu)\nu(\nu-1)[\lambda_+{}^{\nu-2} + (-\lambda_-)^{\nu-2}];$$

the drift coefficient μ is determined from the EMM requirement

$$r + \psi(-i) = 0 \qquad (11.43)$$

and Eq. (11.35), i.e.,

$$\mu = r + c\Gamma(-\nu)[\lambda_+{}^{\nu} - (\lambda_+ + 1)^{\nu} + (-\lambda_-)^{\nu} - (-\lambda_- - 1)^{\nu}]. \qquad (11.44)$$

We see that for the limit value of the yield spread, the difference between the non-Gaussian case and the Gaussian one is much smaller, only several percent.

11.4   The case of a solvent firm

If the firm is not near the bankruptcy level, i.e., $h = \ln(V/V_B)$ is not very small, the approximate formulas above are not good or even not applicable at all. Fortunately, there exists another set of approximate formulas, which give good approximations, if h is not very small – and if it is large, these approximations are very good indeed. Namely, as we noticed in Lemma 3.7 and used in Chapters 5 and 7, the models classes of RLPE: TLP, NIG, NTS Lévy and HP, have a very useful property, namely, $a(\xi) = r + \psi(\xi)$ admits the analytic continuation into the complex plane with cuts $(-i\infty, i\lambda_-]$ and $[i\lambda_+, +\infty)$, has no zeroes outside the imaginary axis, and at most 1 zero in $(0, i\lambda_+)$ and at most one zero in $(i\lambda_-, 0)$.

Moreover, for parameter values typically observed in Financial Markets, both zeroes exist, and the steepness parameters are large. Denote the zero in the upper half-plane by $i\beta$ (in Chapters 3, 5 and 7, it was denoted by $-i\beta_-$). In the last Section, we will show that under these conditions, the following approximate equalities hold:

$$\Psi_0(x) \quad \sim \quad 1 + \beta^{-1}K(\beta)e^{-\beta x}, \qquad (11.45)$$

$$\Psi_1(x) \quad \sim \quad e^x \phi_r^-(-i) + (1+\beta)^{-1}K(\beta)e^{-\beta x}, \qquad (11.46)$$

where

$$K(\beta) = \frac{r}{i\psi'(i\beta)\phi_r^+(i\beta)}. \qquad (11.47)$$

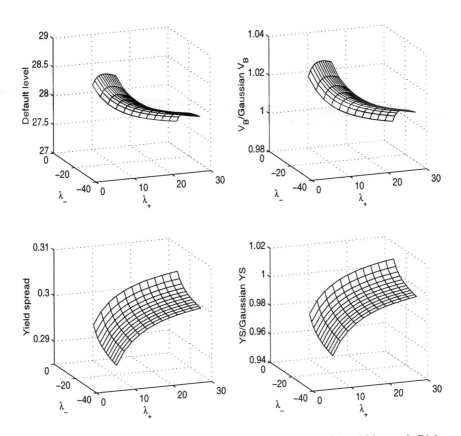

Fig. 11.1   Left panels: the default level V_B and the limit value of the yield spread. Right panels: KoBoL model vs. Gaussian model. Parameters: $r = 0.06$, $\tau = 0.35$, $\alpha = 0.5$; vol=0.35, $\nu = 1.2$

Below, we will see that in order to get the correct dependence (in terms of curvature) of the value of the firm and the value of equity on asset value, $K(\beta)$ should be negative, which is the case here. To see this, notice first that

$$\frac{\phi_r^+(i\beta)}{r} = E\left[\int_0^{+\infty} e^{-rt}e^{-\beta m_t} dt \mid m_t = 0\right]$$

where $\{m_t \equiv \sup_{0 \le s \le t} X_t\}$ is the supremum process for X_t (see Eq. (2.24)), and so it is positive. Hence, it suffices to prove that $i\psi'(i\beta)$ is negative.

But $\Psi(0) = r > 0$, $\Psi(\beta) = 0$, and Ψ is concave as it was shown in the proof of Lemma 3.5, and we conclude that the function $\Psi(z) := r + \psi(iz)$ is decreasing at $z = \beta$.

For a BM, the approximate equalities Eq. (11.45)–Eq. (11.46) are exact ones. Moreover, $K(\beta) = -\beta$ and

$$
\begin{aligned}
\Psi_0(x) &= 1 - e^{-\beta x}, \\
\Psi_1(x) &= \frac{\beta}{\beta + 1}(e^x - e^{-\beta x}).
\end{aligned}
$$

It is easy to verify that the following approximations for Eq. (11.27)–Eq. (11.33), which we derive by substituting Eq. (11.45)–Eq. (11.46), are similar to exact answers in Leland (1994a) (compare Eq. (7), (9) and (11)–(13) there (it may be not so easily seen since the formulas in op. cit. are written in different variables):

$$
\begin{aligned}
E &= \frac{C(1-\tau)}{r}\left[e^x\frac{r}{C(1-\tau)} - 1 - K(\beta)(\beta^{-1} - (1+\beta)^{-1})e^{-\beta(x-h)}\right] \\
&= V - \frac{C(1-\tau)}{r}\left[1 + \frac{K(\beta)}{\beta(\beta+1)}\left(\frac{V}{V_B}\right)^{-\beta}\right]; \quad\quad (11.48)
\end{aligned}
$$

$$
\begin{aligned}
D &= (1-\alpha)e^x + Cr^{-1}(1 + \beta^{-1}K(\beta)e^{-\beta(x-h)}) \\
&\quad - \frac{C(1-\tau)(1-\alpha)}{r}\left(e^x\frac{r}{C(1-\tau)} + (\beta+1)^{-1}K(\beta)e^{-\beta(x-h)}\right) \\
&= \frac{C}{r}\left[1 + K(\beta)\left[\frac{1}{\beta} - \frac{(1-\tau)(1-\alpha)}{\beta+1}\right]\left(\frac{V}{V_B}\right)^{-\beta}\right]; \quad\quad (11.49)
\end{aligned}
$$

$$
v = V + \frac{C\tau}{r}\left[1 + \frac{K(\beta)}{\beta(\beta+1)}\left(1 + \beta + \frac{(1-\tau)\alpha\beta}{\tau}\right)\left(\frac{V}{V_B}\right)^{-\beta}\right]; \quad (11.50)
$$

$$
TB = \frac{\tau C}{r}\left[1 + \frac{K(\beta)}{\beta}\left(\frac{V}{V_B}\right)^{-\beta}\right]; \quad\quad (11.51)
$$

$$
\begin{aligned}
BC &= \alpha\left[V - \frac{C(1-\tau)}{r}\left[\frac{Vr}{C(1-\tau)} + \frac{K(\beta)}{\beta+1}\left(\frac{V}{V_B}\right)^{-\beta}\right]\right] \\
&= -\frac{\alpha C(1-\tau)}{r}\frac{K(\beta)}{\beta+1}\left(\frac{V}{V_B}\right)^{-\beta}. \quad\quad (11.52)
\end{aligned}
$$

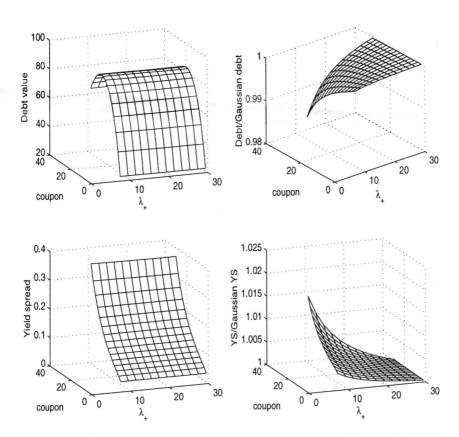

Fig. 11.2   Left panels: the value of the debt and the yield spread. Right panels: KoBoL model vs. Gaussian model. Parameters: $r = 0.06$, $\tau = 0.35$, $\alpha = 0.5$; vol=0.35, $\nu = 1.2$, $\lambda_- = -30$.

First, we apply these approximate formulas to study the dependence of the value of the debt and the yield spread on the coupon and the steepness parameter λ_+ describing the left tail (see Fig.11.2). We see that the dependence is of the same type as in the Gaussian model in Leland (1994a); in this series of examples, the difference between the Gaussian model and non-Gaussian one is relatively small, up to 3.5 percent.

The next series of numerical examples shows that the difference between non-Gaussian and Gaussian models can be significant not only very close

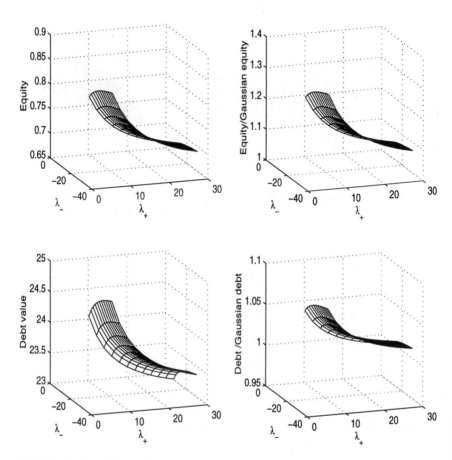

Fig. 11.3 Left panels: equity and debt value. Right panels: KoBoL model vs. Gaussian model. Parameters: $V/V_B = 1.2, C = 10, r = 0.06, \alpha = 0.5, \tau = 0.35$, vol$=0.35, \nu = 1.2$.

to the bankruptcy level (see Fig.11.3-11.4). We fix the ratio of the firm assets to the bankruptcy level $V/V_B = 1.2$, which makes the approximate formulas Eq. (11.48)–Eq. (11.51) applicable, with a small error, if λ_+ and $-\lambda_-$ are not small; and this is the case we consider here: both λ_+ and $-\lambda_-$ vary from 30 to 8. We see that the non-Gaussian equity value and the Gaussian one can differ by 23 percent. In this series of examples, the value of the debt in non-Gaussian model can be larger by 6 percent than in the Gaussian model, the same holds for the firm's value, and the yield spread; the leverage differs insignificantly.

11.5 Endogenous debt level and endogenous leverage

Now it is straightforward to verify that $E(V)$ is a convex function of the asset value V, which is due to the fact that $K(\beta) < 0$. This reflects the "option-like" nature of equity, even if debt has an infinite horizon. The value of the firm, v, is strictly concave in V for positive C and τ. Notice that v is also strictly concave in C, so it is possible to find the optimal coupon C^* as a solution to

$$1 + \frac{K(\beta)}{\beta} \left(1 + \beta + \frac{(1-\tau)\alpha\beta}{\tau} \right) \left(\frac{V}{V_B} \right)^{-\beta} = 0,$$

where V_B is given by Eq. (11.21). Whence we derive

$$C^* = \frac{Vr}{(1-\tau)\phi_{\bar{r}}^-(-i)} \left[-\frac{K(\beta)}{\beta} \left(1 + \beta + \frac{(1-\tau)\alpha\beta}{\tau} \right) \right]^{-1/\beta}. \qquad (11.53)$$

It is interesting to notice that the optimal value of the firm and the optimal value of debt are exactly the same functions of C^* as in Leland (1994a), i.e.,

$$v^* = V + \frac{C^*\tau}{r} \frac{\beta}{\beta+1}, \qquad (11.54)$$

$$D^* = \frac{mC^*}{r} \frac{\beta}{\beta+1}, \qquad (11.55)$$

where

$$m = 1 + \frac{1-\tau}{\beta+1+(1-\tau)\alpha\beta/\tau}.$$

The optimal return on debt is equal to

$$R^* = C^*/D^* = \frac{r(\beta+1)}{m\beta},$$

which is again the same expression as in the diffusion case, but for a different β.

Numerical examples show that as far as $-\lambda_-$ and λ_+ are not small, only the endogenous coupon and the default level can differ by 3 percent; the values of other endogenous variables change less when we replace the Gaussian model with the non-Gaussian one, of the same variance.

248

11.6 Conclusion

We applied the structural approach to modelling of the optimal capital structure and endogenous default, when the evolution of underlying assets follows a Lévy process. We started with a simple benchmark model of Leland (1994a) where the debt had infinite maturity. Formulas obtained for endogenous variables in the model, are suitable for any Lévy processes. However, we suggested using a wide family of regular Lévy processes of exponential type as the "second best" as compared to diffusion processes in terms of tractability. For these processes, analytical expressions for the endogenous variables are available, and in more complicated situations, an asymptotic solution can be possible.

We developed two types of approximate formulas; the first type is suitable for a firm very close to the bankruptcy level, and we used them to show that near the bankruptcy level, the value of the equity in the non-Gaussian model can differ several times from the Gaussian model; this striking difference is natural since the presence of jumps must be felt near the default boundary in the first place.

If the firm is not very close to the default level, the approximation above is not very good or not applicable at all, but in this region, another approximate formulas are suggested. We exploited the special structure of the characteristic exponent of RLPE with large steepness parameters (the case supported by empirical evidence), in order to obtain a relatively simple tractable approximations for the solutions of the non-Gaussian model. The tractability of these approximate solutions can even amount to comparative statics. The solutions look like those in the diffusion model, but this does not mean that some Gaussian model can produce the same result. There are many coefficients in the whole set of formulas, and it is impossible to fit all of them by using just one parameter - the variance; for complex models, even two-three parameters may be not enough. So, non-Gaussianity still tells in the values of the above coefficients.

The explanation of the fact that seemingly Gaussian-like type of formulas are capable of capturing non-Gaussian effects stems from the following observations. First, the approximation has small errors and for these errors, the explicit bounds are available. On the other hand, the coefficients in the formulas differ from the naive Gaussian ones by much larger margin.

These approximate formulas can be used for the comparative statics purposes by following the next steps.

First, it is possible to study the dependence of the root β on the parameters of the process. For instance, for a KoBoL process with $-\lambda_- = \lambda_+$, one can show that β is a decreasing function in ν, λ_+ and c^{-1}, and for a model class of NIG, the root β can be found as a positive solution to a certain quadratic equation, with coefficients explicitly determined by the characteristics of the process. In this case, the comparative statics for β is as simple as in the BM case.

Second, if the truncation parameters are not small, an approximate formula $\phi_r^-(-i) = \beta/(\beta + 1)$ is valid, and this formula can be used for comparative statics purposes. The error in this formula is larger than the errors in the approximate formulas for Ψ_0 and Ψ_1, and so for computations, it is better to calculate $\phi_r^-(-i)$ by using more accurate numerical procedures. Similarly, the approximation to $K(\beta)$ in terms of β can be obtained.

Third, by using approximations for endogenous variables, one can study comparative statics of those as functions of β, $\phi_r^-(-i)$, $K(\beta)$, and eventually, as functions of the parameters of the process.

Notice, however, that the numerical results above show that for relatively large values of the steepness parameters, the significant difference with the Gaussian models is observed for a firm near the bankruptcy level, hence the second set of approximate formulas can produce results essentially different from the Gaussian ones only when the firm is not far from the bankruptcy level.

The exact formulas can produce sizable difference with the Gaussian model for a firm far from bankruptcy, but only if one of the truncation parameters is small, i.e., the corresponding tail is fairly fat.

We believe that the most exciting effects of non-Gaussianity will be revealed in a model with finite maturity of debt, and in the more detailed study of junk bonds, which can be done by using the technique employed in Chapters 7 and 8 for the study of barrier options and first-touch digitals.

11.7 Auxiliary results

11.7.1 *Proof of Eq. (11.36)–Eq. (11.38)*

The Fourier transform of Ψ_j is well-defined in any half-plane of the form $\Im\xi < \sigma$, where $\sigma < -j$, and is given by

$$\hat{\Psi}_j(\xi) = \phi_r^-(\xi)(i\xi - j)^{-1}.$$

Notice that as $\xi \to \infty$ in the same half-plane,

$$(i\xi - j)^{-1} = (1 + i\xi)^{-1} + O(|\xi|^{-2}),$$

therefore it follows from Eq. (11.34) that for $j = 0, 1$,

$$\phi_r^-(\xi)(i\xi - j)^{-1} = a_-(0)(1 + i\xi)^{-\kappa_- - 1} + \hat{f}_j(\xi), \qquad (11.56)$$

where $\hat{f}(\xi) = O(|\xi|^{-\kappa_- - 1 - \rho})$, as $\xi \to \infty$ in the half-plane $\Im\xi \le \sigma$. Hence, for any $\epsilon > 0$, $F_j := e^{-jx}\mathcal{F}^{-1}\hat{f}_j$ belongs to the Sobolev space $H^{s-\epsilon}(\mathbf{R})$, where $s = \kappa_- + 1 + \rho - 1/2$; by the Sobolev embedding theorem, $H^{s-\epsilon}(\mathbf{R})$ is embedded into the Hölder space $C^{s-\epsilon-1/2-\epsilon_1}(\mathbf{R})$, for any $\epsilon_1 > 0$. Since $\rho \in (0, \nu - \nu_1)$ is arbitrary, we conclude that $F_j \in C^{\kappa_- + \rho_1}(\mathbf{R})$, for any $\rho_1 \in (0, \nu - \nu_1)$.

A direct calculation shows that for any $\kappa > 0$,

$$\mathcal{F}(x_+^{\kappa-1} e^{-x})(\xi) = \int_0^{+\infty} e^{-ix\xi} x^{\kappa-1} e^{-x} dx \qquad (11.57)$$
$$= \Gamma(\kappa)(1 + i\xi)^{-\kappa},$$

and from the definition of Ψ_j, $j = 0, 1$:

$$\Psi_j(x) = (2\pi)^{-1} \int_{-\infty+i\sigma}^{+\infty+i\sigma} e^{ix\xi} \phi_r^-(\xi)(i\xi - j)^{-1} d\xi,$$

for any $\sigma < -j$, and from Eq. (11.56)-Eq. (11.57) it follows that

$$\Psi_j(x) = a_-(0)\Gamma(\kappa_- + 1)^{-1} x_+^{\kappa_-} e^{-x} + e^{jx} F_j(x). \qquad (11.58)$$

We know that $\Psi_j(x) = 0$ for any $x \le 0$, hence from Eq. (11.58), F_j also vanishes on $(-\infty, 0]$. Since $F_j \in C^{\kappa_- + \rho}(\mathbf{R})$, for any $\rho \in (0, \nu - \nu_1)$, we conclude that as $x \to +0$,

$$F_j(x) = O(x^{\kappa_- + \rho}). \qquad (11.59)$$

Eq. (11.58)–Eq. (11.57) prove Eq. (11.36)-Eq. (11.37), and Eq. (11.38) is proved similarly, the equality

$$\Psi_1(x) - \Psi_0(x) = -(2\pi)^{-1} \int_{-\infty+i\sigma}^{+\infty+i\sigma} e^{ix\xi} \phi_r^-(\xi)(i\xi - 1)^{-1}(i\xi)^{-1} d\xi,$$

for any $\sigma < -1$, being used.

11.7.2 *Proof of Eq. (11.45)–Eq. (11.46)*

Take $\sigma < -1$. Then we can write

$$\Psi_0(x) = (2\pi)^{-1} \int_{-\infty+i\sigma}^{+\infty+i\sigma} e^{ix\xi} \phi_r^-(\xi)(i\xi)^{-1} d\xi.$$

$\psi(\xi)$ admits the analytic continuation into the complex plane with cuts $(-i\infty+i\lambda_-], [i\lambda_+, +i\infty)$, and it has only one zero $i\beta$ in the upper half-plane. Therefore we can use the Wiener-Hopf factorization formula Eq. (2.23) to define the meromorphic continuation of $\phi_r^-(\xi)$ into the complex plane with the cut $[i\lambda_+, +i\infty)$ and the only pole at $k = i\beta$. Notice that as $\xi \to i\beta$,

$$
\begin{aligned}
\phi_r^-(\xi) &= \frac{r}{(r + \psi(\xi))\phi_-^+(\xi)} \\
&= \frac{r}{(r + \psi(i\beta) + \psi'(i\beta)(\xi - i\beta))\phi_r^+(i\beta)} + O(1) \\
&= \frac{r}{\psi'(i\beta)(\xi - i\beta)\phi_r^+(i\beta)} + O(1) \\
&= K(\beta)(\xi - i\beta)^{-1} + O(1). \quad (11.60)
\end{aligned}
$$

Transform the contour of integration $\Im\xi = \sigma$ by pushing it up; first, it crosses the pole $\xi = 0$, and then $\xi = i\beta$, and in the end we obtain the contour

$$\mathcal{L} = (+i\infty - 0, i\lambda_+ - 0) \cup (i\lambda_+ + 0, +i\infty + 0).$$

On the strength of the residue theorem, and from Eq. (11.60), we obtain

$$\Psi_0(x) = 1 + K(\beta)\beta^{-1}e^{-\beta x} + (2\pi i)^{-1} \int_{\mathcal{L}} e^{ix\xi} \phi_r^-(\xi)\xi^{-1} dk, \quad (11.61)$$

and similarly,

$$\Psi_1(x) = \phi_r^-(-i)e^x + K(\beta)(\beta+1)^{-1}e^{-\beta x} + (2\pi i)^{-1} \int_{\mathcal{L}} e^{ix\xi} \phi_r^-(\xi)(\xi+i)^{-1} d\xi. \quad (11.62)$$

By comparing Eq. (11.61)–Eq. (11.62) to Eq. (11.45)–Eq. (11.46), we see that it remains to show that the integrals in Eq. (11.61)–Eq. (11.62) are small. To see this, make the change of the variable $\xi = iz$ on the contour $\mathcal{L}$; in the result, we obtain, for $\alpha = 0, 1$,

$$(2\pi i)^{-1} \int_{\mathcal{L}} e^{ix\xi} \phi_r^-(\xi)(\xi + i\alpha)^{-1} d\xi =$$

$$= (2\pi)^{-1} \int_{\lambda_+}^{+\infty} e^{-zx} \Phi(z)(z+\alpha)^{-1} dz,$$

where

$$\Phi(z) = i(\phi_r^-(iz-0) - \phi_r^-(iz+0)).$$

For model classes of RLPE, $\Phi(z)$ grows at the infinity not faster than Cz^ν – see, e.g., Eq. (11.35) – and hence, we conclude that the integrals in Eq. (11.61)–Eq. (11.62) admit a bound via

$$C \int_{\lambda_+}^{+\infty} e^{-zx} z^{\nu-1} dz = -Cx^{-1} \int_{\lambda_+}^{+\infty} z^{\nu-1} de^{-zx}$$

$$= Cx^{-1}\lambda_+{}^{\nu-1} e^{-\lambda_+ x} + Cx^{-1}(\nu-1) \int_{\lambda_+}^{+\infty} e^{-zx} z^{\nu-2} dz.$$

If λ_+ is large and $x > 0$ is not too small, then we conclude that the integrals in Eq. (11.61)–Eq. (11.62) are small. For instance, if $x = 0.2$ (that is, we are 20 percent from the default level), ν is close to 1 and $\lambda_+ = 40$, which is quite often the case in the real financial markets, then the upper bound for the integrals is less than 0.01.

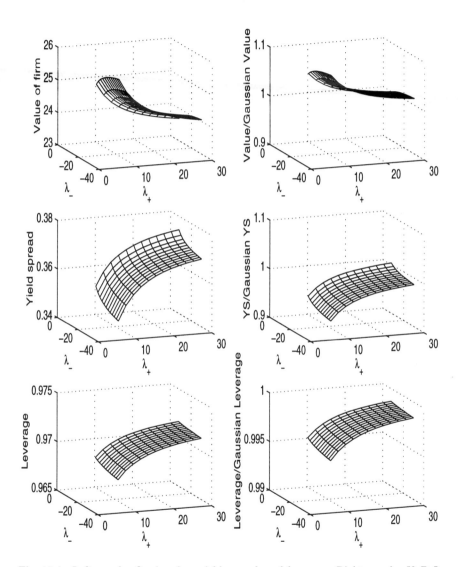

Fig. 11.4 Left panels: firm's value, yield spread, and leverage. Right panels: KoBoL model vs. Gaussian model. Parameters: $V/V_B = 1.2$, $C = 10$, $r = 0.06$, $\alpha = 0.5$, $\tau = 0.35$, vol=0.35, $\nu = 1.2$.

Chapter 12

Fast pricing of European options

We consider the Fast Fourier Transform (FFT), and a new method of option pricing based on the transformation of the line of integration into the integral over an appropriate cut in the complex plane (integration-along-cut method - IAC). The method is applicable for option pricing under VGP, NTS Lévy and KoBoL of order less than 1, and NIG.

12.1   Introduction

Option pricing under non-Gaussian Lévy processes has a serious disadvantage from the computational point of view since an explicit formula for the price kernel is usually not available, and even if the explicit formula is known as it is the case with Normal Inverse Gaussian processes, the computations are more time-consuming than in the Gaussian case. Madan and Carr (1998) suggested to use an explicit formula for the characteristic exponent of a Lévy process and the Fast Fourier Transform (FFT). However, FFT can produce significant errors for options not at the money, close to expiry, and in op. cit., for FFT, no general effective procedure for the choice of the line of the integration and sufficient number of points for a required upper bound of the computational error were suggested.

We consider a new method, which allows one to calculate option prices fast, and extremely fast just prices of options out of the money and deep in the money, even close to the expiry, with good accuracy. The method is applicable to option pricing under several families of Lévy processes used in empirical and theoretical studies of financial markets, and hopefully, for option pricing under some stochastic volatility models as well. The method is based on the transformation of the line of integration into the integral over the banks of an appropriate cut in the complex plane, which is related to the characteristic exponent of the process. As a short-hand notation, the name *IAC (integration along a cut)* method is suggested.

If one calculates the price of the European put or call for just one value of the stock price out of the money or deep in the money, then for a given upper bound of the computational error, IAC can be hundreds times faster (or even more) than FFT. For options at the money, the relative advantage of IAC as compared to FFT, is not that significant. Nevertheless, even if one calculates the prices of an option at a hundred points or so, which is needed for the parameter fitting purposes, then for many processes, IAC can be several times faster than FFT for options close to the expiry; for processes of order close to zero, 10-20 times faster. For some processes, there is a region in parameters' space where FFT with its ability to calculate the option prices for many spot prices at once performs better. Typically, the relative strength of IAC increases as the option approaches the maturity.

Notice that we can effectively control the computational error of IAC, which is not possible with FFT. By using this property, it is possible to show that FFT method with parameters' values used in Carr and Madan (1998) may provide significant error, and compare the speed of IAC and FFT for a given upper bound of the computational error (see Levendorskii and Zherder (2001)).

The basic idea of IAC – to change the contour of integration in order to obtain the integral with a better rate of convergence – is the same as that of the saddle point method (SPM) (see, e.g., Fedoryuk (1988)), and in principle, SPM is faster. However, the choice of the optimal contour for SPM can be rather tricky, and for IAC, the choice is quite straightforward. Another nice property of IAC is that the resulting integrand is a real-valued function; this property enhances the speed of calculations.

After reduction to the cut is made, we have to calculate an integral of the form

$$I(u,v) = \int_1^{+\infty} e^{-zu} f(v,z) dz, \qquad (12.1)$$

where $u \geq 0$ is proportional to, roughly speaking, a linear function of the distance between the log spot price and the log strike price, and $v > 0$ is proportional to the time to the expiry, τ. The upper bound for f can easily be obtained for model classes of RLPE. This allows one to estimate effectively the error of the replacement of the semi-infinite interval of the integration with a finite one. One can easily calculate the derivatives of f w.r.t. z, obtain a bound for an appropriate derivative, and then find the error of a chosen integration procedure. By using the upper bound for the error, we find the number of points necessary to achieve the required accuracy. If the option prices at many points are needed, and hence the values of $I(u, v)$ are to be calculated for $(u =)u_0 < u_1 < \cdots$, we find the number of points, which is necessary to calculate $I(u_0, v)$ with the desired computational error, calculate the array of values $f(v, z_j)$ at these points, and use the array to calculate $I(u_s, v)$ for all s.

Notice that there are many additional possibilities to enhance the speed of the calculations. For instance, one can find the asymptotics of the integrand as $z \to \infty$ and use this asymptotic expansion in the calculation of the integral in a suitably chosen neighbourhood of the infinity, with a desired error. In some cases, the whole contour lies in this neighbourhood of the infinity; in cases when a part of the contour remains outside the neighbourhood, one can use simple standard integration procedures to calculate the integral over the remaining part of the contour. In many cases, the numerical integration requires the calculation of values of the integrand in several dozen of points or just several points, which makes the calculation extremely fast.

Our starting point is the following observation made in Chapter 3 about properties of model classes of RLPE. Namely, VGP, together with the other model classes of RLPE listed above, enjoy the following property, which is crucial for IAC: the characteristic exponent of X is holomorphic in the complex plane with two cuts on the imaginary axis (one in the upper half-plane, and the other in the lower one), and the same holds for mixtures of independent processes of aforementioned types.

For payoffs of interest, like the ones for European calls and puts, and for many others, their Fourier images are meromorphic with poles outside the cuts, hence, one can fairly freely transform the contour of integration, by using the Cauchy theorem and the residue theorem.

Using these observations, we can transform the line of integration and obtain an integral with a better rate of convergence. The method suggested here, IAC, uses the contour, which passes along the banks of an appropriate cut in the complex plane. Notice that this reduction procedure can be justified for an RLPE of order less than or equal to 1: for VGP, NIG, and KoBoL and NTS Lévy processes of order $\nu \leq 1$; for processes of order $\nu > 1$, after reduction to the cut, the integrand grows at infinity, and hence, IAC is not applicable. We have not checked whether IAC is applicable for all GHP. Since the formula for the characteristic exponent of a GHP, which is not a NIG, is rather complicated, and the relative advantage of IAC is small for processes of order 1, we surmise that it is not rational to apply IAC to the other GHP's (though this question deserves a more careful study).

The implementation of the method requires the detailed calculations involving the characteristic exponent. We illustrate the usage of the method by calculating the price of the European put option under the KoBoL processes of order $(0,1)$.

12.2 Transformation of the pricing formula for the European put

Consider the model market of a riskless bond and a stock. Let $r > 0$ be a (constant) riskless rate, and let $S_t = \exp X_t$ be the price process of the stock. We assume that X is a Lévy process under an EMM $\mathbf{Q}$ chosen by the market; ψ is the characteristic exponent of X under $\mathbf{Q}$. We assume that the steepness parameters satisfy $\lambda_- < -1 < 0 < \lambda_+$.

Consider the European put with the strike price K and the terminal date T. The payoff at the expiry equals $\max\{K - S_T, 0\}$, and without loss of generality, we may assume that $K = 1$. Then

$$\hat{g}(\xi) = \int_{-\infty}^{+\infty} e^{-ix\xi}(1 - e^x)_+ dx$$

$$= \frac{1}{(-i\xi)(-i\xi + 1)}$$

is well-defined in the half-plane $\Im\xi > 0$ and admits the meromorphic extension into the complex plane with two poles at $\xi = 0$ and $\xi = -i$. Assume that X is a KoBoL, and denote by $f(x,t)$ the price of the American put at time t and spot price e^x. Take $\sigma \in (0, \lambda_+)$, and express $f(x,t)$ as (for details, see Levendorskiĭ and Zherder (2001))

$$f(x,t) = \frac{R_0}{2\pi} \int_{-\infty+i\sigma}^{+\infty+i\sigma} \frac{\exp[i\xi(x + \tau\mu) + \tau c_\nu((\lambda_+ + i\xi)^\nu + (-\lambda_- - i\xi)^\nu)]}{-i\xi(-i\xi + 1)} d\xi,$$

$$(12.2)$$

where $c_\nu = c\Gamma(-\nu)$, and

$$R_0 = \exp[-\tau r - \tau c_\nu(\lambda_+{}^\nu + (-\lambda_-)^\nu)]. \qquad (12.3)$$

Set

$$
\begin{aligned}
d_\nu &= \lambda_+{}^\nu + (-\lambda_-)^\nu, \\
\kappa &= \lambda_+ + (-\lambda_-), \\
\chi_+ &= \lambda_+/\kappa, \\
\chi_- &= -\lambda_-/\kappa,
\end{aligned}
$$

and notice that $\chi_+ + \chi_- = 1$. By changing the variable $\xi \to \kappa\xi$, we obtain

$$
\begin{aligned}
f(x,t) = \frac{R_0}{2\pi\kappa} \int_{-\infty+i\sigma/\kappa}^{+\infty+i\sigma/\kappa} & \frac{\exp[i\xi\kappa(x+\tau\mu)]}{-i\xi(-i\xi+1/\kappa)} \\
& \cdot \exp[\kappa^\nu \tau c_\nu((\chi_- - i\xi)^\nu + (\chi_+ + i\xi)^\nu)]d\xi.
\end{aligned}
$$

Introduce new parameters:

$$
\begin{aligned}
U &= \kappa(x+\tau\mu), \\
V &= -\kappa^\nu \tau c_\nu, \\
\rho &= 1/\kappa, \\
\sigma_1 &= \sigma/\kappa,
\end{aligned}
$$

and denote:

$$R_1 = \frac{R_0}{2\pi\kappa} = \frac{\exp(-\tau r + V(\chi_-^\nu + \chi_+^\nu))}{2\pi\kappa}. \qquad (12.4)$$

We have $U \in \mathbf{R}$, $V \in \mathbf{R}$, $\rho < 1$, $\sigma_1 \in (0, \chi_+)$, and

$$f(x,t) = R_1 \int_{-\infty+i\sigma_1}^{+\infty+i\sigma_1} \frac{\exp[iU\xi - V((\chi_- - i\xi)^\nu + (\chi_+ + i\xi)^\nu)]}{-i\xi(-i\xi+\rho)}d\xi. \qquad (12.5)$$

In the next section, we describe two methods of computation of Eq. (12.5): FFT and IAC.

12.3 FFT and IAC

12.3.1 *Fast Fourier Transform*

In this subsection we follow Carr and Madan (1998); for a detailed treatment of *FFT*, see Elliot and Rao (1982). The *Fast Fourier Transform* is an efficient algorithm which is used for computing sums of the following form:

$$\hat{X}(k) = \sum_{j=1}^{N-1} e^{-i\frac{2\pi}{N}(j-1)(k-1)} x(j), \quad k = 1, .., N, \tag{12.6}$$

where N is a power of 2. The analogous algorithm for computing the sum

$$x(j) = \sum_{k=1}^{N-1} e^{i\frac{2\pi}{N}(j-1)(k-1)} \hat{X}(k), \quad j = 1, .., N, \tag{12.7}$$

is called the inverse Fast Fourier Transform (iFFT).

Denote σ_1 by σ, and rewrite Eq. (12.5) as follows

$$\frac{f(x,t)}{R_1} = \int_{-\infty+i\sigma}^{+\infty+i\sigma} \frac{\exp\{iU\xi - V[(\chi_- - i\xi)^\nu + (\chi_+ + i\xi)^\nu]\}}{-i\xi(-i\xi + \rho)} d\xi$$

$$= A \int_{-\infty}^{+\infty} \frac{\exp\{ixz + iz\tau\mu - V[(\chi_- - iz + \sigma)^\nu + (\chi_+ + iz - \sigma)^\nu]\}}{-i(z + i\sigma)(-iz + \sigma + \rho)} dz,$$

where $A = e^{-\kappa\sigma(x+\tau\mu)}$. Introduce

$$R(x;\sigma) = R_1 e^{-\kappa\sigma(x+\tau\mu)},$$

and

$$\psi(z;\sigma) = \frac{\exp\{iz\tau\mu - V[(\chi_- - iz + \sigma)^\nu + (\chi_+ + iz - \sigma)^\nu]\}}{(-iz + \sigma)(-iz + \sigma + \rho)}$$

then

$$f(x,t) = R(x;\sigma) \int_{-\infty}^{+\infty} e^{ixz} \psi(z;\sigma) dz. \tag{12.8}$$

For a chosen step of numerical integration η, we use the trapezoidal rule for the integral Eq. (12.8) and obtain an approximation for $f(x,t)$:

$$f(x,t) \approx R(x;\sigma) \sum_{j=1}^{N} e^{ixz_j} \psi(z_j;\sigma)\eta, \tag{12.9}$$

where $z_j = \eta(j-1)$. FFT returns N values of x with a regular spacing of size λ, so that values for x are

$$x_k = -b + \lambda(k-1), \quad k = 1, 2, .., N,$$

where $b = \frac{N\lambda}{2}$. With $x = x_k$, equation Eq. (12.9) becomes

$$f(x_k, t) \approx R(x_k; \sigma) \sum_{j=1}^{N} e^{iz_j(-b+\lambda(k-1))} \psi(z_j; \sigma)\eta, \qquad (12.10)$$

and substituting $z_j = \eta(j-1)$ into Eq. (12.10) yields:

$$f(x_k, t) \approx R(x_k; \sigma) \sum_{j=1}^{N} e^{i\lambda\eta(k-1)(j-1)} e^{-ibz_j} \psi(z_j; \sigma)\eta. \qquad (12.11)$$

To apply the FFT, one couples λ and η by

$$\lambda\eta = \frac{2\pi}{N}. \qquad (12.12)$$

This restriction plays a role of some kind of "the uncertainty principle": if we choose η small in order to obtain a fine grid for the integration, then we obtain relatively large spacing λ on the "moneyness" line. To overcome this difficulty we should increase the number of points N and use more accurate method; for example, one can incorporate (as in Carr and Madan (1998)) Simpson's rule weightings in summation:

$$f(x_k, t) \approx R(x_k; \sigma) \sum_{j=1}^{N} e^{i\lambda\eta(k-1)(j-1)} e^{-ibz_j} \psi(z_j; \sigma) \frac{\eta}{3} [3 + (-1)^j - 1\delta_{j-1}],$$

$$(12.13)$$

where δ_n is the Kronecker symbol.

The sum in Eq. (12.13) is of the form Eq. (12.6), hence it can be computed by FFT. Notice that it is rather difficult to estimate the error of this computational scheme.

12.3.2 *Integration-along-cut method*

Let $\nu \in (0,1)$. We consider the integral Eq. (12.5) in the following two cases: a) $U \geq 0$; b) $U < 0$.

12.3.2.1 *Case a)*

If $U \geq 0$, we push the contour of integration to the cut in the upper half-plane, the choice of a cut being defined by a natural requirement: $iU\xi$ is negative at the cut. As a result, we obtain

$$f(x,t) = R_1 \int_{i\chi_+}^{+i\infty} \frac{\exp[iU\xi]}{-i\xi(-i\xi+\rho)} \left[e^{-V\phi(\xi+0)} - e^{-V\phi(\xi-0)} \right] d\xi,$$

where $\phi(\xi) = (\chi_- - i\xi)^\nu + (\chi_+ + i\xi)^\nu$.

By changing variables $\xi \to iz$, $z \in \mathbf{R}$, we obtain:

$$f(x,t) = R_1 \int_{\chi_+}^{+\infty} i\frac{\exp[-Uz]}{z(z+\rho)} \left[e^{-V\phi(iz+0)} - e^{-V\phi(iz-0)} \right] dz.$$

For $z > \chi_+$, we have

$$\begin{aligned}
\phi(iz \pm 0) &= (\chi_- + z \mp i0)^\nu + (\chi_+ - z \pm i0)^\nu \\
&= (\chi_- + z)^\nu + (z - \chi_+)^\nu e^{\pm i\nu\pi} \\
&= (\chi_- + z)^\nu + (z - \chi_+)^\nu (\cos(\nu\pi) \pm i\sin(\nu\pi)).
\end{aligned}$$

Set

$$a_\nu = \cos(\nu\pi), \quad b_\nu = \sin(\nu\pi), \qquad (12.14)$$

then

$$\exp[V\phi(iz+0)) - \exp(-V\phi(iz-0)]$$

$$\begin{aligned}
&= \exp(-V(\chi_- + z)^\nu - V(z-\chi_+)^\nu a_\nu) \left(e^{-iV(z-\chi_+)^\nu b_\nu} - e^{iV(z-\chi_+)^\nu b_\nu} \right) \\
&= -2i \exp(-V(\chi_- + z)^\nu - V(z-\chi_+)^\nu a_\nu) \sin(V(z-\chi_+)^\nu b_\nu),
\end{aligned}$$

and

$$\begin{aligned}
f(x,t) = \ &2R_1 \int_{\chi_+}^{+\infty} \frac{\exp[-Uz]\sin(Vb_\nu(z-\chi_+)^\nu)}{z(z+\rho)} \\
&\cdot \exp\left(-V[(\chi_- + z)^\nu + a_\nu(z-\chi_+)^\nu] \right) dz.
\end{aligned}$$

By changing the variable $z \to z + \chi_+$, we come to

$$f(x,t) \qquad\qquad\qquad\qquad\qquad\qquad\qquad\qquad (12.15)$$

$$= 2R_1 e^{-U\chi_+} \int_0^{+\infty} \frac{\exp[-Uz]\sin(Vb_\nu z^\nu)}{(z+\chi_+)(z+\chi_+ +\rho)} \exp\left(-V[(1+z)^\nu + a_\nu z^\nu] \right) dz.$$

Introduce the family of integrals

$$\mathcal{I}(\nu, u, v, \rho_1, \rho_2) = \int\limits_{0}^{+\infty} \frac{e^{-zu}\sin(vb_\nu z^\nu)}{(z+\rho_1)(z+\rho_2)} \exp\left(-v[(1+z)^\nu + a_\nu z^\nu]\right) dz,$$

(12.16)

where $u \geq 0$, $v > 0$, $\rho_1 > 0$, $\rho_2 > \rho_1$, $\nu \in (0,1)$. Thus, in the case $U \geq 0$, the computation of $f(x,t)$ reduces to the computation of the integrals in Eq. (12.16):

$$f(x,t) = 2R_1 e^{-U\chi_+} \mathcal{I}(\nu, U, V, \chi_+, \chi_+ + \rho).$$

(12.17)

12.3.2.2 Case b)

In the case $U < 0$, we push the contour of integration in Eq. (12.2) to the cut in the lower half-plane. In the process of the transformation, the contour crosses two simple poles $\xi = 0$ and $\xi = -i$. Using the residue theorem, we obtain

$$
\begin{aligned}
f(x,t) &= \exp(-\tau r) - \exp(x) \\
&\quad + R_1 \int_{-i\chi_-}^{-i\infty} \frac{\exp[iU\xi]}{-i\xi(-i\xi + \rho)} \left[e^{-V\phi(\xi-0)} - e^{-V\phi(\xi+0)}\right] d\xi.
\end{aligned}
$$

Making the change of variables $\xi = -iz$ yields

$$
\begin{aligned}
f(x,t) &= \exp(-\tau r) - \exp(x) \\
&\quad + R_1 \int_{\chi_-}^{\infty} (-i) \frac{\exp[Uz]}{-z(-z + \rho)} \left[e^{-V\phi(-iz-0)} - e^{-V\phi(-iz+0)}\right] dz.
\end{aligned}
$$

For $z > \chi_-$,

$$
\begin{aligned}
\phi(-iz \pm 0) &= (\chi_- - z \mp i0)^\nu + (\chi_+ + z \pm i0)^\nu \\
&= (\chi_+ + z)^\nu + (z - \chi_-)^\nu e^{\mp i\nu\pi} \\
&= (\chi_+ + z)^\nu + (z - \chi_-)^\nu (\cos(\nu\pi) \mp i\sin(\nu\pi));
\end{aligned}
$$

therefore, by using the notation of Eq. (12.14),

$$\exp(-V\phi(-iz - 0)) - \exp(-V\phi(-iz + 0)) =$$

$$
\begin{aligned}
&= \exp(-V(\chi_+ + z)^\nu - V(z - \chi_-)^\nu a_\nu)\left(e^{iV(z-\chi_-)^\nu b_\nu} - e^{-iV(z-\chi_-)^\nu b_\nu}\right) \\
&= 2i\exp(-V(\chi_+ + z)^\nu - V(z - \chi_-)^\nu a_\nu)\sin(V(z - \chi_-)^\nu b_\nu).
\end{aligned}
$$

Hence

$$f(x,t) = \exp(-\tau r) - \exp(x)$$
$$+2R_1 \int_{\chi_-}^{+\infty} \frac{\exp[Uz]\sin(Vb_\nu(z-\chi_-)^\nu)}{z(z-\rho)}$$
$$\cdot \exp\left(-V[(\chi_+ + z)^\nu + a_\nu(z-\chi_-)^\nu]\right) dz.$$

Change the variable $z \mapsto z + \chi_-$:

$$f(x,t) = \exp(-\tau r) - \exp(x) + \tag{12.18}$$
$$+2R_1 e^{U\chi_-} \int_0^{+\infty} \frac{\exp[Uz]\sin(Vb_\nu z^\nu)}{(z+\chi_-)(z+\chi_- - \rho)} \exp\left(-V[(1+z)^\nu + a_\nu z^\nu]\right) dz,$$

and use the notation of Eq. (12.16):

$$f(x,t) = \exp(-\tau r) - \exp(x) + 2R_1 e^{U\chi_-} \mathcal{I}(\nu, -U, V, \chi_-, \chi_- - \rho). \tag{12.19}$$

We conclude that any numerical procedure for the integral Eq. (12.16), together with Eq. (12.19), can be used to compute $f(x,t)$ in the case $U < 0$.

Example. In the case $\nu = 0.5$, we have $a_\nu = 0$, $b_\nu = 1$, and the integral becomes especially simple:

$$\mathcal{I}(0.5, u, v, \rho_1, \rho_2) = \int_0^{+\infty} \frac{e^{-zu}\sin(v\sqrt{z})}{(z+\rho_1)(z+\rho_2)} \exp\left(-v\sqrt{1+z}\right) dz. \tag{12.20}$$

12.4   Comparison of FFT and IAC

When applied to the computation of a discrete approximation of an integral, FFT produces an error, which depends on the value of the return parameter, and becomes significant at the end of the interval of integration. To reach the required accuracy, usually one should choose a large number of points of integration.

Applying IAC, first, we choose a finite interval so that the integral over the neighbourhood of the infinity is less than $\epsilon/2$, where $\epsilon > 0$ is the desired error, and in the numerical integration over a finite interval, we use the Simpson method, after an appropriate change of the variable has been made; the number of points should be chosen so that the error of the method is less than $\epsilon/2$, too.

Numerical experiments produced in Levendorskiĭ and Zherder (2001) show that this scheme works well for large λ_-, λ_+, and, if λ_-, λ_+ are fixed, for not large c_ν. The last property can be reformulated as follows: IAC works better for small τ, usually, less than 10 days to expiry. Also, IAC is preferable for $\nu \in (0, 0.5)$, or even for ν from a wider interval, in certain region of the space of other parameters. For instance, for $\nu \in (0.125, 0.5)$ and λ_+ and $-\lambda_-$ of order 40-50, IAC is 15 times faster than FFT, when one calculates the prices of the put options at 100 points in the moneyness interval (0.7, 1.05), 3 days to expiry.

On the contrary, FFT works better for c_ν large and ν of order 0.5 and larger.

Finally, the speed of IAC can be enhanced by using additional devices mentioned in the Introduction.

On the two figures below, we show results of numerical experiments, which supplement the numerical results in Levendorskiĭ and Zherder (2001). We fix r and all the parameters of KoBoL but one (μ), which is determined from the EMM-requirement $r + \psi(-i) = 0$.

We study the dependence of the ratio of the computational time (IAC vs. FFT) needed to calculate 100 option prices in the moneyness interval (0.75, 1.05), with the given upper bound for the error $\epsilon = 10^{-4}$. Notice that we were able to use relatively small number of points for FFT just because we knew the result with the error less than $\epsilon = 10^{-5}$ from the test calculation made with the help of IAC; hence, in practice, FFT would have required even more time.

In Fig. 12.1, the dependence on c and the order of the process is shown; $\tau = 3$ (day) is fixed, and in Fig. 12.2, we show the dependence on the order and the time to expiry.

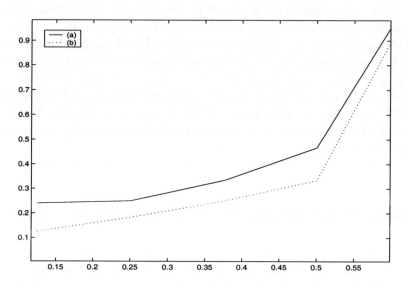

Fig. 12.1   The ratio $t(IAC)/t(FFT)$. Parameters: $\epsilon = 10^{-4}$, $r = 0.03$, $\tau = 3$; $\lambda_+ = 35$, $\lambda_- = -55$; a) $c = 5$; b) $c = 3$.

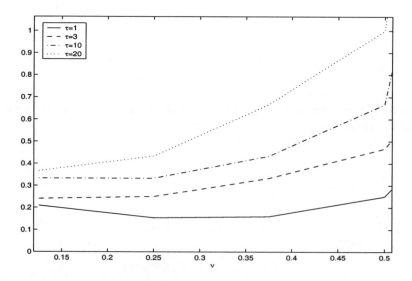

Fig. 12.2   The ratio $t(IAC)/t(FFT)$. Parameters: $\epsilon = 10^{-4}$, $r = 0.03$; $\lambda_+ = 35$, $\lambda_- = -55$, $c = 5$.

Chapter 13

Discrete time models

We consider perpetual Bermudan options and more general perpetual American options in discrete time. For wide classes of processes and pay-offs, we obtain exact analytical pricing formulas in terms of the factors in the Wiener-Hopf factorization formulas. Simple formulas are derived in the case when the original probability density is approximated by exponential polynomials.

13.1 Bermudan options and discrete time models

In discrete time, one can make very weak assumptions on the underlying stochastic process, and yet obtain analytical solutions; at the same time, the discrete time approach makes it possible to solve the pricing problem for non-standard American options known as Bermudan options. A *Bermudan option* can be exercised on specified dates only, during the life of the option. An example of a Bermudan option is a bond option whose exercise is restricted to coupon payment dates. Consider a Bermudan option which can be exercised at the prescribed dates $t_j = j\Delta t$ only, and the corresponding perpetual American option in discrete time: the answer for the latter option gives the optimal exercise price and the price of the Bermudan option on the prescribed dates, the price of the Bermudan option at time $t \in (t_j, t_{j+1})$ can be calculated as the price of the European option with the expiry date t_{j+1}, and the price of the Bermudan option at time t_{j+1} as the terminal payoff.

The state space in our model is $\mathbf{R}$, and not a discrete set as in multinomial models (for these models, see, for example, Duffie (1996) and Shiryaev

267

(1999)). We assume that the increments are identically distributed and independent but we do not suppose that the transition density is infinitely divisible so that it is possible to pass to the continuous time limit.

The optimal stopping problem for a perpetual American call option in discrete time was solved by Darling, Ligget, and Taylor (1972), and Mordecki (2000) has obtained the pricing formula for a perpetual American put by applying the technique of op. cit. The aforementioned results are obtained with the probabilistic technique, without explicit analytical formulas, and it is not clear how to apply this technique to other types of perpetual American options.

In this Chapter, we include the results obtained in Boyarchenko and Levendorskiǐ (2001b). They are the discrete-time analogue of the results of Chapter 5, and the technique is similar. After the general formula for the optimal exercise price for a Bermudan option is obtained, we consider an example, when the model for shocks makes it impossible to pass to the continuous time limit.

The approach developed in this chapter makes it possible to solve a discrete time version of the model examined in Chapter 10. From our point of view, discrete time models are more relevant for Economics in general, and Real options in particular. In the first place, such setting allows one to make only week assumptions on the underlying stochastic process X. Second, we believe this model to be especially useful in cases when the time interval between observations is not very small, as it is the case in the theory of Real Options. Notice that even though the Real Options literature to date has provided many insights into capital budgeting decision-making, theoretical models are not widely used by practitioners. Among one of the primary reasons for that, Lander and Pinches (1999) point out that many of the required modelling assumptions are often violated in practical real options applications. In particular, this concerns the choice of the stochastic process for the underlying variable. As we already mentioned it in Chapter 10, in spite of the fact that the normality of the process is rejected by empirical evidence, Gaussian processes are often used in the investment literature. The second reason for theoretical models being rarely used by practitioners is technical involvement of the models. The task of fitting the parameters of a model process to the data by no means makes life easier. In a discrete time model, the empirical probability density can be approximated by exponential polynomials with desired accuracy and simplicity (although there is certainly a tradeoff between these two). After that, to obtain the analytical expression for the investment threshold one has only to find roots of two polynomials - an easy task for any practitioner.

13.2 A perpetual American put in a discrete time model

13.2.1 *Process specification*

Time is discrete: we consider only dates t_k, $k = 0, 1, \ldots$, when the option can be exercised, and we assume them to be equally spaced: $\Delta := t_{j+1} - t_j$ is independent of j. We normalize $\Delta = 1$. Consider a market of a riskless bond and a stock. We assume that the stock pays no dividend. Let the riskless rate be fixed and let $S = \{S_n\}_{n \geq 0}$, $S_n = \exp X_n$, be the price process of the stock. Let $Y, Y_1, \ldots Y_n, \ldots$ be independent and identically distributed random variables on the probability space Ω, and let $P(dx)$ be the probability distribution of Y. We assume that under a chosen EMM, the log-price X_n admits a decomposition into a sum of n independent and identically distributed random variables $Y_1, \ldots Y_n$: $X_n = Y_1 + Y_2 + \cdots + Y_n$. Of $P(dx)$, we require

$$\int_{-\infty}^{+\infty} e^x P(dx) < \infty. \tag{13.1}$$

This condition is necessary in order that the stock be priced under the chosen EMM, and the requirement that $\{S_n\}$ is a martingale under the chosen EMM assumes the form

$$1 - e^{-r} \int_{-\infty}^{+\infty} e^x P(dx) = 0, \tag{13.2}$$

where $e^{-r} < 1$ is the discount factor per period.

The condition Eq. (13.1) implies that the Fourier transform of $P(dx)$, $\hat{p}$, is holomorphic in the strip $\Im \xi \in (0, 1)$ and continuous up to the boundary of the strip. To simplify the study of the pricing problem, we impose additional conditions on $\hat{p}$. We assume that $\hat{p}$ is holomorphic and bounded in a wider strip:

$$|\hat{p}(\xi)| \leq C, \quad \Im \xi \in (-\lambda_+, -\lambda_-), \tag{13.3}$$

where $\lambda_- < -1 < 0 < \lambda_+$, and there exist positive constants ϵ_0, C_0, and ρ

such that

$$|\hat{p}(\xi)| \leq C_0(1+|\xi|)^{-\rho}, \quad \Im\xi \in (-\epsilon_0, \epsilon_0). \tag{13.4}$$

Notice that Eq. (13.4) implies that $P(dx)$ is absolutely continuous: $P(dx) = p(x)dx$, and Eq. (13.4) is satisfied if p is continuous, differentiable a. e., and

$$\int_{-\infty}^{+\infty} e^{\epsilon_0|x|}|p'(x)|dx < +\infty.$$

Eq. (13.4) can be relaxed but we believe that this condition is weak enough for practical purposes.

13.2.2   The pricing problem for a perpetual American option as an optimal stopping problem

Consider a perpetual Bermudan option on the stock, i.e., a perpetual option that can be exercised on specified dates only. Let $g(X_t)$ be the payoff function for the option: for a put $g(x) = K - e^x$, and for a call $g(x) = e^x - K$, where K is the strike price. Denote by $V_*(x)$ the rational price of the perpetual Bermudan put; then (see e.g. Shiryaev (1999). XVIII, 2)

$$V_*(x) = \sup_{\tau \in \mathcal{M}} E^x[e^{-r\tau}g(X_\tau)], \tag{13.5}$$

where $\mathcal{M}$ denotes the set of all stopping times $\tau = \tau(\omega)$, satisfying $\tau(\omega) < \infty$, $\omega \in \Omega$.

As in Chapter 5, first we will find a solution to Eq. (13.5) in the class $\mathcal{M}_0$ of hitting times $\tau(a)$ of segments $(-\infty, a]$. To this end, we consider $V(h; x)$, given by Eq. (5.21), which is the price of the put, when h is chosen as the exercise boundary. The sufficient conditions for the optimal exercise boundary are given by Lemma 5.2. Since this lemma is stated in terms of the value function $V(h, x)$, we need an explicit formula for it. To obtain such a formula, one can proceed as follows.

Fix h, a prospective candidate for the optimal exercise boundary, then the option pricing problem can be written as

$$V(x) = e^{-r}E[V(x+Y)], \quad \text{if } x > h; \tag{13.6}$$

$$V(x) = g(x), \qquad\qquad \text{if } x \leq h; \tag{13.7}$$

here (with some abuse of notation) $V(x) := V(h;x)$. We can rewrite Eq. (13.6) as

$$V(x) = e^{-r} \int_{-\infty}^{+\infty} p(y)V(x+y)dy \qquad (13.8)$$

$$= e^{-r} \int_{-\infty}^{+\infty} p(y-x)V(y)dy, \quad x > h.$$

By introducing the symbol $a(\xi) = 1 - e^{-r}\hat{p}(-\xi)$, and using an equality

$$\int_{-\infty}^{+\infty} p(y-x)u(y)dy = (\mathcal{F}^{-1}\hat{p}(-\xi)\mathcal{F}(u))(x),$$

we may rewrite Eq. (13.8) as

$$(a(D)V)(x) = 0, \quad x > h, \qquad (13.9)$$

Introduce a function g_1, which coincides with g on $(-\infty, h]$; and it is continuous on $[h, +\infty)$ and vanishes faster than $e^{-\epsilon_0 x}$ as $x \to +\infty$. Set $u(x) = V(x+h) - g_1(x+h)$, then we obtain from Eq. (13.9) and Eq. (13.7) the following system of equations:

$$(a(D)u)(x) = -a(D)g_1(x+h), \quad x > 0; \qquad (13.10)$$
$$u(x) = 0, \qquad\qquad\qquad x \le 0. \qquad (13.11)$$

Thus, the original problem has been reduced to the Wiener-Hopf equation. As in the previous chapters, we can obtain the solution to Eq. (13.10)–Eq. (13.11) using the Wiener-Hopf method. After the solution is obtained, it is easy to guess the necessary condition for the exercise boundary. In fact, under our standing assumption on the process, the optimal exercise boundary is determined by the requirement: $V(h; \cdot)$ is continuous at h. We call this requirement the *continuous pasting* condition as opposed to the smooth pasting condition, which never holds in discrete time.

It can be shown (for details see Boyarchenko and Levendorskiĭ (1998)) that the necessary condition is similar to Eq. (5.31), so that an explicit formula for h obtains. After that, one has only to check that the sufficient conditions hold for this h. This is done exactly as in Subsection 5.2.2. Finally, by using the following sufficient condition from Darling *et al.* (1972), one can prove the optimality in the same fashion as it was done in op. cit. for calls.

Lemma 13.1   *Let $Y, Y_1, Y_2, \ldots$ be independent and identically distributed random variables, let $X_0 = 0$ and $X_n = Y_1 + \cdots + Y_n$ for $n \geq 1$. Let g and f be non-negative functions and z a constant satisfying $0 \leq z \leq 1$. If for all x,*

$$f(x) \geq g(x) \tag{13.12}$$

and

$$f(x) \geq E[zf(x+Y)], \tag{13.13}$$

then

$$f(x) \geq E[z^T g(x + X_T)] \tag{13.14}$$

for all x and all stopping times T.

Evidently, the last statement can be used to justify the solution in the same way as Main Lemma in Chapter 5 was used.

Thus, we solve the pricing problem for perpetual options in discrete time by essentially the same method as in continuous time. The only issue remains to be addressed is the Wiener-Hopf factorization in discrete time models. This is done in the next Section.

13.3   The Wiener-Hopf factorization

13.3.1   *General formulas*

Set $\bar{X}_n = \max_{0 \leq j \leq n} X_j$, and $\underline{X}_n = \min_{0 \leq j \leq n} X_j$; their analogues in continuous time are called the supremum and infimum processes, respectively. Let $z \in (0, 1)$, and let T be a random variable independent of $\{Y_j\}$ and taking values in $\{0, 1, \ldots\}$, with $P(T = n) = (1 - z)z^n$.

Theorem 13.1   *(Spitzer (1964))*

$$E\left[e^{i\xi X_T}\right] = (1 - z)/[1 - z\hat{p}(-\xi)] \tag{13.15}$$

$$= E\left[e^{i\xi \bar{X}_T}\right] E\left[e^{i\xi \underline{X}_T}\right]. \tag{13.16}$$

Moreover, we have the Spitzer identities

$$E\left[e^{i\xi \bar{X}_T}\right] = \exp\left[\sum_1^\infty \frac{z^k}{k} \int_0^\infty (e^{ix\xi} - 1)d_x P(X_k < x)\right], \tag{13.17}$$

and

$$E\left[e^{i\xi \underline{X}_T}\right] = \exp\left[\sum_1^\infty \frac{z^k}{k} \int_{-\infty}^0 (e^{ix\xi} - 1)d_x P(X_k < x)\right]. \qquad (13.18)$$

Set

$$\phi_+(\xi) = E\left[e^{i\xi \bar{X}_T}\right], \qquad (13.19)$$

$$\phi_-(\xi) = E\left[e^{i\xi \underline{X}_T}\right], \qquad (13.20)$$

and write Eq. (13.15)-Eq. (13.16) as

$$(1 - z)/[1 - z\hat{p}(-\xi)] = \phi_+(\xi)\phi_-(\xi). \qquad (13.21)$$

Lemma 13.2 *a) ϕ_+ (resp., ϕ_-) is the Fourier transform of a distribution $P_+(dx)$ supported on $(-\infty, 0]$ (resp., $P_-(dx)$ supported on $[0, +\infty)$).*

b) $\phi_+(\xi)$ (resp., $\phi_-(\xi)$) is holomorphic in the half-plane $\Im\xi > 0$ (resp., $\Im\xi < 0$) and continuous up to the boundary of the half-plane.

Proof. We have

$$\begin{aligned}
\phi_+(\xi) &= E\left[e^{i\xi \bar{X}_T}\right] \\
&= \sum_n (1 - z)z^n \int_0^{+\infty} e^{ix\xi} dP(\bar{X}_n < x) \\
&= \int_0^{+\infty} e^{ix\xi} d\left(\sum_n (1 - z)z^n P(\bar{X}_n < x)\right) \\
&= \int_{-\infty}^0 e^{-ix\xi} P_+(dx),
\end{aligned}$$

where

$$P_+(dx) = d\left(\sum_n (1 - z)z^n(-P(\bar{X}_n < -x))\right).$$

This proves a) for the sign "+"; the proof for the sign "-" is similar, and b) follows from a). $\qquad \square$

The Spitzer identities Eq. (13.17)-Eq. (13.18) are by no means computationally effective. More convenient formulas can be obtained under additional conditions on p.

Lemma 13.3   *Let Eq. (13.4) hold. Then*
  a) there exist $-\epsilon_0 \leq \sigma_- < 0 < \sigma_+ \leq \epsilon_0$ such that

$$\Re[1 - e^{-r}\hat{p}(-\xi)] > 0, \quad \Im\xi \in (\sigma_-, \sigma_+); \tag{13.22}$$

b) $\phi_+(\xi)$ is holomorphic in the half-plane $\Im\xi > \sigma_-$, and can be defined, for any $\omega_- > \sigma_-$ and $\Im\xi > \omega_-$, by

$$\phi_+(\xi) \;=\; \exp\left[\frac{1}{2\pi i}\int_{-\infty+i\omega_-}^{+\infty+i\omega_-} \frac{e^{-r}\hat{p}'(-\eta)}{1 - e^{-r}\hat{p}(-\eta)} \ln\frac{\eta-\xi}{\eta} d\eta\right] \tag{13.23}$$

$$=\; \exp\left[\frac{1}{2\pi i}\int_{-\infty+i\omega_-}^{+\infty+i\omega_-} \frac{\xi\ln[1 - e^{-r}\hat{p}(-\eta)]}{\eta(\xi-\eta)} d\eta\right] \tag{13.24}$$

$$=\; \frac{a_+(0)}{a_+(\xi)}, \tag{13.25}$$

where

$$a_+(\xi) = \exp\left[\frac{1}{2\pi i}\int_{-\infty+i\omega_-}^{+\infty+i\omega_-} \frac{\ln[1 - e^{-r}\hat{p}(-\eta)]}{\eta-\xi} d\eta\right]; \tag{13.26}$$

c) $\phi_-(\xi)$ is holomorphic in the half-plane $\Im\xi < \sigma_+$, and can be defined, for any $\omega_+ < \sigma_+$ and $\Im\xi < \omega_+$, by

$$\phi_-(\xi) \;=\; \exp\left[-\frac{1}{2\pi i}\int_{-\infty+i\omega_+}^{+\infty+i\omega_+} \frac{e^{-r}\hat{p}'(-\eta)}{1 - e^{-r}\hat{p}(-\eta)} \ln\frac{\eta-\xi}{\eta} d\eta\right] \tag{13.27}$$

$$=\; \exp\left[-\frac{1}{2\pi i}\int_{-\infty+i\omega_+}^{+\infty+i\omega_+} \frac{\xi\ln[1 - e^{-r}\hat{p}(-\eta)]}{\eta(\xi-\eta)} d\eta\right] \tag{13.28}$$

$$=\; \frac{a_-(0)}{a_-(\xi)}, \tag{13.29}$$

where

$$a_-(\xi) = \exp\left[-\frac{1}{2\pi i}\int_{-\infty+i\omega_+}^{+\infty+i\omega_+} \frac{\ln[1 - e^{-r}\hat{p}(-\eta)]}{\eta-\xi} d\eta\right]. \tag{13.30}$$

Proof.   a) For real σ, and η on the line $\Im\eta = \sigma$, we have

$$\Re\hat{p}(-\eta) \leq M(\sigma) := \int_{-\infty}^{+\infty} e^{-\sigma x} p(x)dx.$$

Clearly, $M(0) = 1$, and by continuity of M, there exists a neighbourhood of zero, denote it (σ_-, σ_+) such that for all $\sigma \in (\sigma_-, \sigma_+)$, $e^{-r}M(\sigma) < 1$ and Eq. (13.22) holds.

b) Set $z = e^{-r}$. Since the Fourier transform of a sum of independent random variables is the product of the Fourier transforms of summands, and $Y_1, Y_2, \ldots$ are independent identically distributed random variables, we have for $\xi \in \mathbf{R}$:

$$\sum_1^\infty \frac{z^k}{k} \int_0^\infty (e^{ix\xi} - 1) d_x P(X_k < x)$$

$$= \sum_1^\infty \frac{z^k}{k} \int_0^\infty (e^{ix\xi} - 1)(2\pi)^{-1} \int_{-\infty}^{+\infty} e^{-ix\eta} \hat{p}(-\eta)^k d\eta dx$$

Take $\omega_- \in (\sigma_-, 0)$, and shift the line of integration:

$$= \sum_1^\infty \frac{z^k}{k} \int_0^\infty (e^{ix\xi} - 1)(2\pi)^{-1} \int_{-\infty+i\omega_-}^{+\infty+i\omega_-} e^{-ix\eta} \hat{p}(-\eta)^k d\eta dx$$

Assume that Eq. (13.4) holds with $\rho > 1$. Then the integrand admits a bound via the integrable function $Ce^{\omega - x}(1 + |\eta|)^{-\rho}$. Hence, we may apply the Fubini theorem and integrate w.r.t. x first:

$$= \sum_1^\infty \frac{z^k}{k}(2\pi i)^{-1} \int_{-\infty+i\omega_-}^{+\infty+i\omega_-} \hat{p}(-\eta)^k [(\eta - \xi)^{-1} - \eta^{-1}] d\eta$$

(In the case $\rho \in (0, 1]$, we have to resort to the theory of oscillatory integrals in order to justify the change of order of the integration). As $\omega_- \to 0$,

$$C(\omega_-) := \sup_{\Im\eta=\omega_-} |\hat{p}(-\eta)| \to 1;$$

hence, for any $z \in (0, 1)$, there exists $\omega_- \in (\sigma_-, 0)$ such that $zC(\omega_-) < 1$. This implies that $\sum \int$ converges absolutely, and for such an ω_-, we can apply the Fubini theorem and change the order of the integration and summation:

$$= -(2\pi i)^{-1} \int_{-\infty+i\omega_-}^{+\infty+i\omega_-} \ln[1 - z\hat{p}(-\eta)][(\eta - \xi)^{-1} - \eta^{-1}] d\eta.$$

This proves Eq. (13.24)-Eq. (13.25), and Eq. (13.23) is deduced from Eq. (13.24) by integration by part.

c) is proved as b).   □

13.3.2 *Some useful properties of the factors $a_\pm$*

Lemma 13.4   *a) We have*

$$a(\xi) = a_+(\xi)a_-(\xi) \qquad (13.31)$$

b)For any $\omega \in (\sigma_-, 0)$, there exist $C, \rho_1 > 0$ such that for all ξ in the half-plane $\Im\xi \geq \omega$,

$$|a_+(\xi)^{\pm 1} - 1| \leq C(1 + |\xi|)^{-\rho_1}; \qquad (13.32)$$

c) For any $\omega \in (0, \sigma_+)$, there exist $C, \rho_1 > 0$ such that for all ξ in the half-plane $\Im\xi \leq \omega$,

$$|a_-(\xi)^{\pm 1} - 1| \leq C(1 + |\xi|)^{-\rho_1}. \qquad (13.33)$$

Proof.   a) follows from Eq. (13.21), Eq. (13.25), Eq. (13.29) and the equality $a(0) = 1 - e^r$.

b) It suffices to show that the integral in Eq. (13.26) admits an estimate via $C(1 + |\xi|)^{-\rho_1}$ for ξ in the half-plane $\Im\xi \geq \omega$. Take $\omega_- \in (\sigma_-, \omega)$. From Eq. (13.4), it follows that the integrand in Eq. (13.26) admits an upper bound via

$$C_1(1 + |\eta|)^{-\rho}|\eta - \xi|^{-1},$$

where C_1 and $\rho > 0$ are constants. By considering separately cases $|\eta| \leq |\xi|/2$, $|\eta| \geq 2|\xi|$ and $|\xi|/2 \leq |\eta| \leq 2|\xi|$, and using the triangle inequality, it is easy to prove that there exists C_2 such that for all η on the line $\Im\eta = \omega_-$ and all ξ in the half-plane $\Im\xi \geq \omega$,

$$C_1(1+|\eta|)^{-\rho}|\eta-\xi|^{-1} \leq C_2(1+|\xi|)^{-\rho/2}[(1+|\eta-\xi|)^{-1-\rho/2}+(1+|\eta|)^{-1-\rho/2}].$$

The RHS is integrable over the line $\Im\eta = \omega_-$, and the result is $C(1 + |\xi|)^{-\rho/2}$, with some constant C; Eq. (13.32) follows.

c) Eq. (13.33) is derived in the same fashion.   □

13.3.3 *The case of exponential polynomials*

The discrete time model is more flexible than the continuous time model since an empirical probability density can easily be approximated by an appropriate model one so that the factors in the Wiener-Hopf factorization formula are computed (relatively) easily. Here we consider the simplest approximation by exponential polynomials.[1] Set $p \equiv p_- + p_+$, where $p_\pm = 1_{\mathbf{R}_\pm} p$. If p_- is an exponential polynomial:

$$p_-(x) = \sum_{j=1}^{m^+} c_j^+ e^{\lambda_+ x} |x|^j 1_{\mathbf{R}_-}(x), \qquad (13.34)$$

where m^+ is a non-negative integer, $\lambda_+ > 0$, and c_j^+ are real.

Similarly, if p_+ is an exponential polynomial:

$$p_+(x) = \sum_{j=1}^{m^-} c_j^- e^{\lambda_- x} x^j 1_{\mathbf{R}_+}(x), \qquad (13.35)$$

where m^- is a non-negative integer, $\lambda_- < 0$, and c_j^- are real. We are going to show that if both $p_\pm$ are exponential polynomials then $\hat{p}$, ϕ_- and ϕ_+ are rational functions. For η in the half-plane $\Im \eta < \lambda_+$,

$$
\begin{aligned}
\hat{p}_-(-\eta) &= \int_{-\infty}^0 e^{ix\eta} p_-(x) dx \\
&= \int_{-\infty}^0 \sum_{j=1}^{m^+} c_j^+ e^{ix\eta + \lambda_+ x} (-x)^j dx \\
&= \sum_{j=1}^{m^+} c_j^+ \Gamma(j+1)(\lambda_+ + i\eta)^{-j-1},
\end{aligned}
$$

and for η in the half-plane $\Im \eta > \lambda_-$,

$$\hat{p}_+(-\eta) = \sum_{j=1}^{m^-} c_j^- \Gamma(j+1)(-\lambda_- - i\eta)^{-j-1}.$$

Whence we see that

$$a(\xi) = 1 - e^{-r} \hat{p}(-\xi). \qquad (13.36)$$

is a rational function, i.e., function:

$$a(\eta) = \frac{P(\eta)}{Q(\eta)}, \qquad (13.37)$$

---

[1] More elaborate approximations are possible as well, see for example, Boyarchenko and Levendorskiĭ, (2001b).

where P and Q are polynomials, and therefore, the factor

$$\frac{e^{-r}\hat{p}'(-\eta)}{1 - e^{-r}\hat{p}(-\eta)}$$

in Eq. (13.27) is the rational function of the form $R(\eta)/(P(\eta)Q(\eta))$, where $R = P'Q - PQ'$ is a polynomial of degree $\deg R = \deg P + \deg Q - 1$. Since for a fixed ξ,

$$\ln\frac{\eta - \xi}{\eta} = \ln(1 - \xi/\eta) = O(|\eta|^{-1})$$

as $\eta \to \infty$, we conclude that on any line $\Im\eta = \omega$, which does not pass through a root of PQ, the integrand in Eq. (13.27) admits an estimate via $C(1 + |\eta|)^{-2}$, and the same holds in the half-plane $\Im\eta \geq \omega$, if there are no roots of PQ in this half-plane. Therefore, we can apply the residue theorem and shift the line of the integration: $\omega_+ \to +\infty$. Each zero of PQ contributes to the resulting formula, and in the result, we obtain that ϕ_- is a rational function. Similarly, ϕ_+ is, and since ϕ_- (resp., ϕ_+) is bounded and does not vanish in the half-plane $\Im\xi < 0$ (resp., $\Im\xi > 0$), we conclude that

$$\phi_-(\xi) = \prod_j \frac{-\beta_j}{-\beta_j + i\xi} \prod_l \frac{-\gamma_l + i\xi}{-\gamma_l}, \tag{13.38}$$

where $\{-i\beta_j\}$ (resp., $\{-i\gamma_j\}$) are all the zeroes of P (resp., Q) in the upper half-plane. Similarly, $\phi_+(\xi)$ is defined by zeroes in the lower half-plane.

13.4 Optimal exercise boundary and rational price of the option

In this Section, we present the analytical formulas for the optimal exercise price and the rational price of the perpetual American put option in discrete time.

The former can be derived as

$$h_* = \ln(K\phi_-(-i)), \tag{13.39}$$

where $\phi_-(-i)$ is given by analytical expression Eq. (13.28). Given the optimal h_*, we calculate the rational put price as

$$V_*(x) = \frac{K}{2\pi} \int_{-\infty+i\omega_+}^{+\infty+i\omega_+} \frac{e^{i(x-h_*)\xi}\phi_-(\xi)}{(-i\xi)(1-i\xi)}d\xi, \tag{13.40}$$

where $\omega_+ \in (0,\sigma_+)$ is arbitrary.

Notice, that to derive the solution in the class of hitting times $\mathcal{M}_0$, we used the following properties of the payoff function g:

(i) g is continuous on $\mathbf{R}$;
(ii) g is bounded and positive in some neighbourhood of $-\infty$;
(iii) there exists h_* such that
for all $x < h_*$, $(\phi_-(D)^{-1}g)(x) > 0$, and
for all $x > h_*$, $(\phi_-(D)^{-1}g)(x) < 0$.

Hence the result can be generalized for any payoff functions satisfying the properties above. These properties are most easily verified for the payoffs given by Eq. (5.81). It is also possible to impose additional conditions on the parameters γ_j in Eq. (5.81) to obtain the optimal solution in the class $\mathcal{M}$; the conditions and proof (based on the reduction to the case of the put) are essentially the same as in Chapter 5, where the continuous time model is studied.

Below we give the simplest example, when a discrete time process is not supposed to correspond to the observation of a Lévy process (in continuous time).

Example 13.1 Let

$$p_\pm(x) = \frac{\mp\lambda_\mp}{2}\mathbf{1}_{\mathbf{R}_\pm}(x)e^{\lambda_\mp x},$$

where $\lambda_- < -1 < 0 < \lambda_+$. Then

$$\hat{p}_-(-\eta) = \frac{1}{2}\lambda_+ \int_{-\infty}^0 e^{ix\eta+\lambda_+ x}dx = \frac{\lambda_+}{2(\lambda_+ + i\eta)},$$

$$\hat{p}_+(-\eta) = \frac{1}{2}\lambda_+ \int_0^{+\infty} e^{ix\eta+\lambda_- x}dx = \frac{-\lambda_-}{2(-\lambda_- - i\eta)},$$

and

$$a(\eta) = 1 - e^{-r}\hat{p}(-\eta)$$

$$= 1 - \frac{1}{2e^r}\left[\frac{-\lambda_-}{-\lambda_- - i\eta} + \frac{\lambda_+}{\lambda_+ + i\eta}\right]$$

$$= \frac{2(1-e^r)\lambda_-\lambda_+ + (1-2e^r)(\lambda_+ + \lambda_-)i\eta + 2e^r\eta^2}{2e^r(\lambda_+ + i\eta)(-\lambda_- - i\eta)}.$$

Denote by $-i\beta_-$ (resp., $-i\beta_+$) the root of the numerator in the upper half-plane (resp., lower half-plane); then

$$-i\beta_\mp = \frac{i(2e^r - 1)(\lambda_+ + \lambda_-) \pm i\sqrt{D}}{4e^r};$$

$$D := (2e^r - 1)^2(\lambda_+ + \lambda_-)^2 - 16e^r(e^r - 1)\lambda_+\lambda_-,$$

and we have

$$a(\eta) = -\frac{(\eta + i\beta_-)(\eta + i\beta_+)}{2e^r(\eta - i\lambda_+)(\eta - i\lambda_-)}.$$

By using Eq. (13.38), we obtain

$$\phi_-(\xi) = \frac{(\lambda_+ + i\xi)(-\beta_-)}{\lambda_+(-\beta_- + i\xi)}.$$

Insert into the formula for the optimal exercise price:

$$H_* = e^{h_*} = K\frac{(\lambda_+ + 1)(-\beta_-)}{\lambda_+(-\beta_- + 1)},$$

and then into the formula for the price of the perpetual American put: for $x > h_*$,

$$V_*(x) = \frac{K}{2\pi}\int_{-\infty + i\omega_+}^{+\infty + i\omega_+}\frac{e^{i(x - h_*)\xi}(\lambda_+ + i\xi)(-\beta_-)}{\lambda_+(-\beta_- + i\xi)(-i\xi)(1 - i\xi)}d\xi.$$

Under condition Eq. (13.22), $i\sigma_+$ lies below $-i\beta_-$, hence $i\omega_+$ does as well, and when we push the line of the integration up, it crosses the pole $-i\beta_-$. By the residue theorem, we obtain

$$V_*(x) = \frac{K(\lambda_+ + \beta_-)e^{\beta_-(x - h_*)}}{\lambda_+(1 - \beta_-)}.$$

Chapter 14

Feller processes of normal inverse Gaussian type

In this Chapter, we describe main results of the paper Barndorff-Nielsen and Levendorskiĭ (2001). We consider and analyse natural generalisations of constructions of NIG processes and some related processes. The resulting Feller processes are somewhat similar to the NIG Lévy process but may, for instance, possess mean-reverting features. In contrast to the RLPE case, the infinitesimal generators are no longer PDO with constant symbols, and hence simple explicit pricing formulas are not available. Nevertheless, effective approximations to solutions of the corresponding generalization of the Black-Scholes equation can be derived. This generalization is an analogue of the Black-Scholes equation with variable coefficients in the Gaussian modelling, which is used by some practitioners to reduce the smile.

14.1 Introduction

We construct a class of Feller processes with generators possessing the most nice properties from the point of view of the theory of pseudodifferential operators; this class naturally generalizes the class of NIG processes. Similarly, generalizations of other classes of RLPE can be constructed, and they enjoy similar nice properties. Namely, the corresponding PDO belong to the class of *classical PDO* (see Hörmander (1985) and the definition in Chapter 16). Notice that in the monograph of Jacob (1996), where a pseudo-differential approach to the study of stochastic processes is strongly advocated, a class of PDO with non-smooth symbols (model examples being generators of Lévy stable processes) is considered; this leads to more difficult situations having much less relevance to applications in Financial

Mathematics and Physics.[1]

The aim of the Chapter is to consider generalizations of the construction of NIG Lévy processes described in Chapter 3. In the probabilistic language, we want to consider Feller processes such that for any fixed x, the exponent ψ in the equality $E^x[e^{i\xi(X_t-x)}] = e^{-t\psi(x,\xi)}$ is a characteristic exponent of NIG Lévy type, but with one or more of the parameters depending on x; in the language of the theory of PDO, we want to consider processes whose generators are PDO with "non-constant" symbols, i.e., symbols depending not only on the dual variable ξ but on x as well. A natural way from the probabilistic viewpoint is to consider processes obtained by subordination from general diffusion processes; this leads to the necessity of calculation of the symbol of the generator. Another, simpler, variant is to consider processes whose generators are PDO's with symbols $-a(x,\xi)$ given by the same formula as the characteristic exponent of a NIG process, with μ, δ, α and β depending on x:

$$a(x,\xi) = -i\mu(x)\xi + \delta(x)[(\alpha(x)^2 - (\beta(x) + i\xi)^2)^{1/2} - (\alpha(x)^2 - \beta(x)^2)^{1/2}].$$
$$(14.1)$$

We consider and compare these constructions. One can try various types of x-dependence, including fairly weird ones; we consider relatively simple versions which may have useful applications.

Recall the roles played by the steepness parameter, α, and the asymmetry parameter, β: $\alpha - \beta$ describes the rate of exponential decay of the right tail of the density function, and $\alpha + \beta$ describes the decay of the left tail. The scale parameter, δ, plays essentially the same role as the variance in Gaussian models. In other words, the larger the value of $\alpha - \beta$ the smaller the probability of large positive jumps, and the larger the value of $\alpha+\beta$ the smaller the probability of large negative jumps. If we want to reproduce a mean-reverting effect then at high levels of x, we should have probability of large positive jumps smaller than that of negative jumps; at small levels of x the probability of large positive jumps should be larger than that of negative jumps. Thus, $(\alpha(x) - \beta(x))/(\alpha(x) + \beta(x))$ must be increasing. If we want to have a less volatile behaviour for small levels of x, then we

---

[1]There is one useful property which generators of NIG and other $RLPE$ processes fail to have: the transmission property, Boutet de Monvel (1971), or a weaker smoothness-in-a-half-space property, Eskin (1973), which simplifies the treatment of boundary value problems. This property ensures that a solution to a "sufficiently good" boundary value problem, e.g., the Dirichlet problem, with smooth data is smooth up to the boundary.

may either decrease the scale parameter δ (which is in direct analogy with a standard device in Gaussian modelling) or increase α. For instance, one may expect that if for some $c > 0, \rho > 1$,

$$\alpha(x) + \beta(x) \geq cx^{-\rho}, \quad x > 0,$$

then the trajectories of the process never reach 0 from above. Processes of this type are suitable for interest rate modelling purposes. To treat such processes, the calculus of PDO with degenerate symbols is needed; for such a calculus, see Levendorskiĭ (1993) and Levendorskiĭ and Paneah (1994).

In this book, we consider the simpler case of bounded α, β, δ, μ, assuming that δ and $\alpha \pm \beta$ are bounded away from 0. In addition, we assume that these parameters are smooth and their derivatives are small. The simplest example which we have in mind, and which is capable of reproducing the mean-reverting effect, is the case of constant δ and α, and β given by

$$\beta(x) = -\frac{2\chi}{\pi} \arctan(\epsilon(x - x_0)) + \beta_0, \tag{14.2}$$

where $\epsilon > 0, \chi > 0$, and $|\beta_0 \pm \chi| < \alpha$. The derivatives of β admit estimates

$$|\beta^{(s)}(x)| \leq C_s \epsilon^s, \quad s = 0, 1, \ldots, \tag{14.3}$$

where the C_s are independent of ϵ, and if we assume that ϵ is small, we can obtain asymptotic solutions in terms (roughly speaking) of a power series in ϵ.

Another example obtains when ϵ in Eq. (14.2) is not small but $\epsilon_1 = \chi/\alpha$ is small; in this case, ϵ_1 plays the part of ϵ above, and if both ϵ and ϵ_1 are small then an asymptotic solution in terms of a series in the still smaller parameter $\epsilon\epsilon_1$ is obtained.

By using a characterization theorem for certain operators satisfying the positive maximum principle (Courrége (1966b)) and the pseudodifferential operators technique, one can show that a general theorem due to Hille-Yosida-Ray (see Courrége (1966a), Ethier and Kurtz (1986), Jacob (1996)) is applicable to PDO with the symbol Eq. (14.1) and α, β, δ specified as above (see Subsection 14.2.1 for details), and therefore the PDO $-a(x, D)$ is the infinitesimal generator of a Feller semigroup on C_0, the space of continuous functions vanishing at infinity.

If a small parameter is present then, as we will show, the two constructions of NIG-like Feller processes give processes with approximately equal generators.

14.2 Constructions of *NIG*-like Feller process via pseudod- ifferential operators

14.2.1 *Naive construction: NIG-like generators with state- dependent parameters*

Definition 14.1   Let $U \in \mathbf{R}^n$ be an open domain whose closure contains the origin, and let $m \in \mathbf{R}$.

We write $a \in S^m(\mathbf{R}^n \times (\mathbf{R}^n + i\bar{U}))$ if the following two conditions are satisfied[2]

(i) $a \in C^\infty(\mathbf{R}^n_x \times \mathbf{R}^n_\xi)$, together with all its derivatives, admits an ana- lytic continuation w.r.t. ξ into a tube domain $\Im\xi \in U$

(ii) for any multi-indices α, β, the derivative $a^{(\alpha)}_{(\beta)}$ admits a continuous extension up to the boundary of U, and satisfies an estimate

$$|a^{(\alpha)}_{(\beta)}(x,\xi)| \le C_{\alpha\beta}\langle\xi\rangle^{m-|\alpha|}, \tag{14.4}$$

where the constants $C_{\alpha\beta}$ are independent of $(x,\xi) \in \mathbf{R}^n \times (\mathbf{R}^n + i\bar{U})$.

Since in many cases the holomorphicity of a is not required, we will use this definition with $U = \emptyset$ by letting $\bar{U} = \{0\}$. For this U, we recover the standard Hörmander class $S^m_{1,0}(\mathbf{R}^n \times \mathbf{R}^n)$.

Definition 14.2   Let $m \in (0,2]$, $a \in S^m(\mathbf{R}^n \times (\mathbf{R}^n + i\bar{U}))$ and, for each fixed $x \in \mathbf{R}^n$, suppose $a(x,\xi)$ is the characteristic exponent of a Lévy process. Then we write $a \in FLS^m(\mathbf{R}^n \times (\mathbf{R}^n + i\bar{U}))$.

Let Eq. (14.4) be valid on $\mathbf{R}^n \times \mathbf{R}^n$, i.e., $a \in S^m(\mathbf{R}^n \times (\mathbf{R}^n + i\{0\}))$. Then a PDO $a(x,D)$ maps $\mathcal{S}(\mathbf{R}^n)$ into itself, continuously (see Theorem 16.2).

The next fact is a variation of many similar statements in the theory of PDO; for the proof, see Chapter 16.

Theorem 14.1   *Let Eq. (14.4) be valid on* $\mathbf{R}^n \times \mathbf{R}^n$, *and let there exist* $c > 0$ *such that on* $\mathbf{R}^n \times \mathbf{R}^n$

$$\Re a(x,\xi) + 1 \ge c\langle\xi\rangle^m. \tag{14.5}$$

Then there exists $\lambda > 0$ *such that* $a(x,D) + \lambda : \mathcal{S}(\mathbf{R}^n) \to \mathcal{S}(\mathbf{R}^n)$ *is invert- ible.*

---

[2]The more standard notation would be $S^m_{1,0}(\mathbf{R}^n \times (\mathbf{R}^n + i\bar{U}))$; we have omitted the lower indices to simplify the notation.

Theorem 14.2   *Let $m \in (0,2]$ and $a \in FLS^m(\mathbf{R}^n \times (\mathbf{R}^n + i\bar{U}))$. Then a PDO $a(x,D)$ has a closed extension $(A, D(A)), D(A) \subset C_0(\mathbf{R}^n)$, such that $-A$ is the generator of a Feller semigroup on $C_0(\mathbf{R}^n)$.*

Proof.   By the theorem due to Hille-Yosida-Ray (see, e.g., Courrége (1966a), Ethier and Kurtz (1986), Jacob (1996)) it is necessary and sufficient to verify the following three conditions:

(i) $\mathcal{D}(a(x,D)) := \mathcal{S}(\mathbf{R}^n)$ is dense in C_0;
(ii) $a(x,D)$ satisfies the positive maximum principle on $\mathcal{D}(a(x,D))$;
(iii) for some $\lambda > 0$, the range of $a(x,D) + \lambda$ is dense in $C_0(\mathbf{R}^n)$.

Since $\mathcal{S}(\mathbf{R}^n)$ is dense in $C_0(\mathbf{R}^n)$, (i) is fulfilled, and if we take Theorem 14.1 into account, we obtain (iii). Finally, (ii) is a special case of a theorem due to Courrége (1966b); for a pseudo-differential version of this result, see Jacob (1996).   □

Notice that in Courrége (1966b) the smoothness of the symbol was not required, and an analogue of Theorem 14.2 can be established for much nastier symbols than here (see Jacob (1996)). We use the simplest conditions suitable for our purposes.

Definition 14.3   Let the conditions of Theorem 14.2 hold.

Then we call a Feller process X with generator $-A$ a *Feller-Lévy process* (on $\mathbf{R}^n$) of order m and *exponential type* $\bar{U}$ and write $X \in FLP^m(\mathbf{R}^n; \bar{U})$. If we do not want to specify the order m and/or U, we say that X is a regular Feller-Lévy process of exponential type.

If the symbol a of A is independent of x, we call the process X a Lévy process (on $\mathbf{R}^n$) of *order m* and exponential type $\bar{U}$; if we do not specify the order m and/or the exponential type $\bar{U}$, we say that X is a regular Lévy process of exponential type.

In the sequel, we identify $a(x,D)$ with its extension, A.

By choosing a particular Lévy process as a starting point, we can obtain special classes. In the following definition, we use NIG Lévy as a model, and we consider the simplest case possible; more involved versions can also be considered.

Definition 14.4   (*NIG-like Feller processes in 1D*) Let $\mu, \delta, \alpha, \beta \in C_b^\infty(\mathbf{R})$, δ and α be positive, μ and β real-valued, and let there exist $C, c > 0$ such that for all x,

$$\delta(x) > c, \quad \alpha(x) - |\beta(x)| > c, \quad |\mu(x)| \le C. \tag{14.6}$$

Let a be defined by Eq. (14.1).

Then we call a Feller process X with the generator $-a(x, D)$ a *NIG-like Feller process*.

Notice that it is a process of order 1 and exponential type $[\lambda_-, \lambda_+]$ for any $\lambda_- < \lambda_+$ satisfying

$$\sup_x \{-\alpha(x) + \beta(x)\} < \lambda_- < 0 < \lambda_+ < \inf_x \{\alpha(x) + \beta(x)\}. \qquad (14.7)$$

Condition Eq. (14.7) can be satisfied due to Eq. (14.6).

Definition 14.5   (Multi-dimensional *NIG*-like Feller processes) Let $\mu, \alpha,$ $\beta \in C_b^\infty(\mathbf{R}^n; \mathbf{R}^n)$, $\delta \in C^\infty(\mathbf{R}^n; \mathbf{R}_{++})$, and let there exist $c > 0$ and open sets $U, V \subset \mathbf{R}^n$ such that $\{0\} \subset \bar{U} \subset V$; for all x, $\delta(x) > c$; and

$$(\alpha(x) - \beta(x) + i\xi, \alpha(x) + \beta(x) - i\xi) \notin \bar{\mathbf{R}}_-, \quad \forall\ (x, \xi) \in \mathbf{R}^n \times (\mathbf{R}^n + iV).$$

Here $(\cdot, \cdot)$ is a bilinear form in $\mathbf{C}^n$, which extends the standard scalar product in $\mathbf{R}^n$.

Let a be defined by

$$\begin{aligned} a(x, \xi) \ &= \ -i\mu(x)\xi + \delta(x)[(\alpha(x) - \beta(x) + i\xi, \alpha(x) + \beta(x) - i\xi)^{1/2} \\ &\quad -(\alpha(x) - \beta(x), \alpha(x) - \beta(x))^{1/2}]. \end{aligned}$$

Then we call a Feller process X with the generator $-a(x, D)$ a *NIG*-like Feller process.

This is a process of order 1 and exponential type $\bar{U}$.

14.2.2   *Constructions via infinitesimal generators: subordination of semigroups of operators*

We will use the following theorem due to Phillips (see Theorem 32.1 in Sato (1999)).

Theorem 14.3   *Let $\{Z_t : t \geq 0\}$ be a subordinator with Lévy measure ρ and drift β_0, and let λ^t denote the law of Z_t. Let $\{P_t : t \geq 0\}$ be a strongly continuous semigroup of linear operators on a Banach space B with infinitesimal generator L. Define*

$$Q_t f = \int_{[0,\infty)} P_s f \lambda^t(ds), \quad f \in B. \qquad (14.8)$$

Then $\{Q_t : t \geq 0\}$ is a strongly continuous contraction semigroup of linear operators on B. Denote its infinitesimal generator by $-A$. Then $\mathcal{D}(L)$ is the core of A, and

$$-Af = \beta_0 Lf + \int_{(0,\infty)} (P_s f - f)\rho(ds). \qquad (14.9)$$

We apply Theorem 14.3 with P_t being the transition semigroup of a diffusion process with the infinitesimal operator L,

$$Lf(x) = \frac{1}{2}(\sigma^2(x)\partial, \partial)f(x) + (b(x), \partial)f(x) + c(x)f(x), \qquad (14.10)$$

where $\sigma^2 \in C_b^\infty(\mathbf{R}^n; \mathrm{End}\mathbf{R}^n)$ is a positive definite (uniformly in x) symmetric matrix, $b \in C_b^\infty(\mathbf{R}^n; \mathbf{R}^n)$, $c \in C_b^\infty(\mathbf{R}^n)$, c non-positive; and with the subordinator having Laplace exponent $\kappa(u) = (d^2 + u)^{\nu/2} - d^\nu$, where $\nu \in (0,2)$, and $d > 0$. This means, in particular, that $\beta_0 = 0$, and the Laplace exponent and the Lévy measure, ρ, are related by

$$\kappa(w) = \int_0^\infty (1 - e^{-ws})\rho(ds). \qquad (14.11)$$

To show that A is a PDO and calculate its symbol, we notice that Eq. (14.9) can be written as

$$-Af = \int_0^\infty (\exp(sL) - 1)\rho(ds)$$

$$= \kappa(-L) = (d^2 - L)^{\nu/2} - d^\nu. \qquad (14.12)$$

Since $d > 0$ and $\Re L$ is a non-positive elliptic operator, $d^2 - \Re L$ is a positive-definite elliptic operator, and, therefore, fractional powers of $d^2 - L$ are well-defined. Moreover, in the theory of PDO there is a well-known result about complex powers of an elliptic PDO, which states that these powers are in turn PDO's; and an asymptotic expansion of the symbol is provided. For PDO on compact manifolds, the result is due to Seeley (1967); an analogue for rather general classes of PDO on $\mathbf{R}^n$ was obtained in Hyakawa and Kumano-go (1971) (see also the monograph Grubb (1996)); and in the case $\bar{U} = \{0\}$, the result in Grubb (1996) suffices for our simple class; in the case of a general U, a straightforward modification of constructions in Grubb (1996) is needed.

Notice, however, that the "*NIG*-generating" Laplace exponent (the case $\nu = 1$) is so simple that no general result on the asymptotic expansion of

the symbol is required: one can easily calculate an asymptotic expansion of
the symbol, $b = b(x, \xi)$, of the square root of an elliptic PDO $d^2 - L(x, D)$
with positive-definite real part, by using the Ansatz

$$b(x, \xi) \sim b_1(x, \xi) + b_0(x, \xi) + b_{-1}(x, \xi) + \cdots, \qquad (14.13)$$

where $b_j \in S^j(\mathbf{R}^n \times (\mathbf{R}^n + i\bar{U}))$, and the composition theorem, one of the
basic tools of the theory of PDO. As the result, we obtain the following
theorem.

Theorem 14.4   *Let $U \subset \mathbf{R}^n$ be an open set whose closure contains 0 and
such that*

$$d^2 - \Re L(x, \xi) > 0 \quad \forall\ (x, \xi) \in \mathbf{R}^n \times (\mathbf{R}^n + i\bar{U}). \qquad (14.14)$$

Then

*a) $\kappa(-L) + d$ is a PDO with the symbol of the class $S^1(\mathbf{R}^n \times (\mathbf{R}^n + i\bar{U}))$,
and the symbol admits an asymptotic expansion Eq. (14.13) in the sense
that for any $N > 0$,*

$$r_N = b - \sum_{j=0}^{N-1} b_{1-j} \in S^{1-N}(\mathbf{R}^n \times (\mathbf{R}^n + i\bar{U})), \qquad (14.15)$$

where

$$b_1(x, \xi) = (d^2 - L(x, \xi))^{1/2}; \qquad (14.16)$$

$$b_0(x, \xi) = -\frac{1}{2} b_1(x, \xi)^{-1} \sum_{|\alpha|=1} b_1^{(\alpha)}(x, \xi) b_{1(\alpha)}(x, \xi); \qquad (14.17)$$

*b) if the coefficients of L depend on a small parameter $\epsilon > 0$ and for any
s derivatives of order s admit an estimate via $C_s \epsilon^s$, where C_s is independent
of ϵ, then uniformly in $\epsilon > 0$,*

$$\epsilon^{j-1} b_j \in S^j(\mathbf{R}^n \times (\mathbf{R}^n + i\bar{U})), \quad \epsilon^{-N} r_N \in S^{1-N}(\mathbf{R}^n \times (\mathbf{R}^n + i\bar{U})); \quad (14.18)$$

*c) let the coefficients of L be of the class $C_b^\infty(\mathbf{R}^n)$ and $d > 0$ be large;
then Eq. (14.15)–Eq. (14.18) are valid with a small parameter d^{-1} instead
of ϵ;*

*d) if the coefficients satisfy the condition in b) and d is a large parameter,
then Eq. (14.15)–Eq. (14.18) are valid with a small parameter ϵ/d instead
of ϵ.*

For the proof and inductive formulae for $b_j, j < 0$, see Chapter 16.

Theorem 14.4 means, in particular, that NIG-like Feller processes constructed by subordination from diffusions with the uniformly elliptic $-L$, where L is the generator of the diffusion, are NIG-like processes in the sense of the "naive" definition. Moreover, if we use the symbol $a(x, \xi) = (d^2 - L(x, \xi))^{1/2} - d$ to construct a NIG-like process, and if the coefficients of L are slowly varying and/or d is large, we obtain a process whose generator differs insignificantly from $-\kappa(-L)$, the generator of the process obtained via subordination.

14.3 Applications for financial mathematics

14.3.1 *Generalised Black-Scholes equation for contingent claims under NIG-like Feller processes*

Let $r > 0$ be the riskless rate, let $S_t = \exp X_t$ be the price process of a stock, where X_t is a NIG-like Feller process with the generator $-a(x, D)$, and let $f(t, X_t)$ be the price of a contingent claim. In Chapter 2, it is explained how to reduce the problem of the calculation of $f(t, X_t)$ to the corresponding boundary problem for a generalised Black-Scholes equation

$$(\partial_t + L - r))f(t, x) = 0,$$

where L is the infinitesimal generator of a Lévy process. It was mentioned that the reduction is valid for any Markov process having absolutely continuous potential kernels.

Lemma 14.1 *For any $t > 0$, $\exp[-ta(x, D)]$ is an integral operator with the kernel of the class C^∞.*

The proof will be given in Chapter 16. Lemma 14.1 implies that we can apply the reduction of Chapter 2 to NIG-like Feller processes, and deduce the generalised Black-Scholes equation

$$(\partial_t - (r + a(x, D_x)))f(t, x) = 0. \tag{14.19}$$

14.3.2 *Pricing of European options under NIG-like Feller processes obtained via subordination*

Let T be the expiry date and $g(X_T)$ the terminal payoff. Let Q_t be a strongly continuous semigroup constructed as in Theorem 14.3. Then by solving equation Eq. (14.19) subject to the terminal condition $f(T, x) = g(x)$, we obtain

$$f(t, x) = e^{-\tau r}(Q_\tau g)(x),$$

for $\tau = T - t > 0$. By applying Eq. (14.8), we find

$$f(t, x) = e^{-\tau r} \int_{[0,\infty)} P_s g(x) \lambda^\tau(ds). \tag{14.20}$$

Thus, if P_s is the generator of a diffusion, we can obtain a pricing formula for the contingent claim by finding first $P_s g$, all $s > 0$, which differs by a factor e^{sr} from the price $\phi(T - s, x)$ of the contingent claim with the expiry date T and the same payoff g:

$$P_s g(x) = e^{sr}\phi(T - s, x),$$

under a diffusion process, and then integrating $e^{-\tau r} P_s g(x)$ w.r.t. the measure $\lambda^\tau(ds)$ to obtain

$$f(t, x) = \int_{[0,\infty)} e^{(s-\tau)r}\phi(T - s, x)\lambda^\tau(ds).$$

Recall that one should choose the parameters of the model so that the EMM-requirement

$$e^x = e^{-\tau r} \int_{[0,\infty)} P_s e^x \lambda^\tau(ds), \quad \forall \tau > 0 \tag{14.21}$$

be met.

14.3.3 *Pricing of European options under NIG-like Feller processes obtained by the naive approach*

The pricing formula is evident

$$f(t, x) = e^{-\tau r} Q_\tau g(x), \tag{14.22}$$

where Q_τ is the transition semigroup of a NIG-like Feller process with the generator $-a(x, D)$; but in order to apply it, we need to obtain an explicit formula for Q_τ. That can be derived from the representation theorem for analytic semigroups Theorem 15.18 similarly to Chapter 8, where the transition semigroup was computed for the case of an operator of a boundary problem for a generator of NIG and some other Lévy processes, in order to compute the rational prices of barrier options.

In order that the RHS in Eq. (14.20) and Eq. (14.22) be finite, some regularity conditions on g are needed, and these conditions are related to the domain U in the definition of the generator of a NIG-like Feller process; for instance, in 1D when U is an interval (λ_-, λ_+), it suffices to assume that g is piecewise continuous and satisfies estimates

$$g(x) \le Ce^{-\omega_\mp x}, \quad \forall \pm x > 0, \tag{14.23}$$

with $\lambda_- < \omega_- < \omega_+ < \lambda_+$. In the case of European puts and calls, it amounts to the restriction on λ_-, λ_+: $\lambda_- < -1 < 0 < \lambda_+$. Due to the put-call parity, it suffices to calculate the price of the European put, for which $g(x) = (K - e^x)_+$, where K is the strike price. Thus, below, we discuss the pricing of the European put.

We consider a NIG-like Feller process in 1D with the generator $-a(x, D)$, where a is defined by Eq. (14.1), and $\mu, \delta, \alpha, \beta$ satisfy Eq. (14.6) and Eq. (14.7). The EMM-requirement reduces to

$$r + a(x, -i) = 0. \tag{14.24}$$

If δ, α, β are already chosen, one can use Eq. (14.24) and Eq. (14.1) to find the drift μ.

The construction of the transition semigroup starts with

Lemma 14.2 *Let $\mathcal{B}$ be either the Sobolev space $H^s(\mathbf{R})$, where $s \in \mathbf{R}$, or the Hölder space $C^s(\mathbf{R})$, where s is a positive non-integer.*

Then there exist $C_0 > 0$ and $\theta \in (\pi/2, \pi)$ such that if $\arg\lambda \in [-\theta, \theta]$, then

$$\| \lambda(\lambda + r + a(x, D))^{-1} \|_{\mathcal{B} \to \mathcal{B}} \le C_0. \tag{14.25}$$

Proof. Fix large C and consider first the region $\Sigma_{C,\theta} = \{\lambda \mid |\lambda| \ge C, \arg\lambda \in [-\theta, \theta]\}$. Since

$$a(x, \xi) \sim -i\mu\xi + \delta|\xi|, \quad \text{as } \xi \to \pm\infty,$$

for C fixed, we can easily find $\theta \in (\pi/2, \pi)$ and C_1 such that for all $\lambda \in \Sigma_{C,\theta}$ and all $(x, \xi) \in \mathbf{R} \times (\mathbf{R} + i\{0\})$,

$$|\lambda(\lambda + r + a(x, \xi))^{-1}| \leq C_1. \tag{14.26}$$

By using Eq. (14.26), and arguing as in the proof of Theorem 14.1 (cf. also Theorem 16.12), we obtain that Eq. (14.25) holds for $\lambda \in \Sigma_{C,\theta}$, with some C_0 independent of these λ.

To prove that for C fixed, there exists $\theta \in (\pi/2, \pi)$ such that Eq. (14.25) holds for λ satisfying $|\lambda| \leq C$ and $\arg \lambda \in [-\theta, \theta]$ it suffices to notice that since $-a(x, D)$ is a generator of the Feller process, $r + \Re a(x, D)$ is positive-definite.

Remark 14.1. Since the boundedness theorem is valid for much more general spaces, the estimate Eq. (14.25) and the formulas and estimates below are also valid in these spaces.

The estimate Eq. (14.25) means that the representation theorem for the semigroup with the generator $-r - a(x, D)$ is applicable, and the following formula is valid:

$$\exp[-\tau(r + a(x, D))]g = e^{-r\tau}Q_\tau g$$

$$= (2\pi i)^{-1} \int_{\mathcal{L}_\theta} e^{\lambda\tau}(\lambda + r + a(x, D))^{-1}g d\lambda. \tag{14.27}$$

Here $\mathcal{L}_\theta$ is the contour $\lambda = \lambda(\sigma)$, $-\infty < \sigma < +\infty$, where $\arg \lambda(\sigma) = -\theta, \sigma < 0$, $\arg \lambda(\sigma) = \theta, \sigma > 0$.

By using an asymptotic expansion of the symbol $R_\lambda(x, \xi)$ of the resolvent $(\lambda + r + a(x, D))^{-1}$:

$$R_\lambda(x, \xi) \sim (\lambda + r + a(x, \xi))^{-1} + \cdots \tag{14.28}$$

(for the proof and the full asymptotic expansion, see Chapter 16), we can compute the RHS in Eq. (14.27) in the form of a series. Since

$$(2\pi i)^{-1} \int_{\mathcal{L}_\theta} e^{\lambda\tau}(\lambda + r + a(x, \xi))^{-1}d\lambda = \exp[-\tau(r + a(x, \xi))],$$

the leading term in the asymptotic expansion of the RHS in Eq. (14.27) is

$$(2\pi)^{-1} \int_{-\infty+i\sigma}^{+\infty+i\sigma} \exp[ix\xi - \tau(r + a(x, \xi))]\hat{g}(\xi)d\xi,$$

where $\sigma \in (\lambda_-, \lambda_+)$ is chosen so that $\hat{g}$ is well-defined on the line $\Im\xi = \sigma$.

Consider the put with the strike price normalized to 1: $K = 1$. We must take $\sigma \in (0, \lambda_+)$, and compute

$$\hat{g}(\xi) = -\frac{1}{\xi(\xi + i)}.$$

To sum up: a formula for the leading term for the price of the European put with the strike price normalized to 1 is

$$f(t, x) = -\frac{1}{2\pi} \int_{-\infty+i\sigma}^{+\infty+i\sigma} \frac{\exp[ix\xi - \tau(r + a(x, \xi))]}{\xi(\xi + i)} d\xi + \cdots. \tag{14.29}$$

In Chapter 16, we give formulas for the next terms of the asymptotic expansion Eq. (14.29), and show that the first omitted term is already fairly small: if the symbol $a(x, \xi)$ depends on parameters (ϵ, d) and satisfies estimates

$$|a_{(\beta)}^{(\alpha)}(x, \xi)| \leq C_{\alpha\beta}\epsilon^{|\beta|}d^{1-|\alpha|-\min\{1,|\beta|\}} \tag{14.30}$$

for any α, β, where $C_{\alpha\beta}$ is independent of (ϵ, d), then the first omitted term in Eq. (14.29) admits an estimate via $C\tau^2\epsilon$, where C is independent of (τ, ϵ, d), and the next term is less still: of order $\tau^2\epsilon^2/d$.

Notice that the leading term looks exactly as in the case of the option pricing under Lévy processes, only when we calculate $f(t, x)$, we use the characteristic exponent depending on x. Thus, the leading term can be calculated as easily as in the case of Lévy processes.

Remark 14.2. Consider the NIG-like Feller process defined by the symbol Eq. (14.1) with constant δ, parameters μ, α, β being bounded and having bounded derivatives, and satisfying

$$\alpha_0 := \min \alpha(x) >> \beta^0 := \max |\beta(x)|. \tag{14.31}$$

Then we have Eq. (14.30) with $\epsilon = 1$ and $d = \alpha_0$.

If the parameters α, β and μ depend on a small parameter $\epsilon > 0$ in such a way that any of their derivatives of order s admits an estimate via $C_s\epsilon^s$, where C_s is independent of ϵ, then we have Eq. (14.30), and the effective small parameter is ϵ/d, i.e., the second omitted term in Eq. (14.29) is very small. The first omitted term in Eq. (14.29) (see Eq. (16.40)) is more involved than the leading term but since it is small – near expiry, very small indeed – it can be calculated with relatively large error, which simplifies the task of the development of appropriate computational procedures.

14.4 Discussion and conclusions

We have used two approaches for construction of a class of Feller processes, generalizing the class of Lévy processes, in particular the Normal Inverse Gaussian Lévy processes: via subordination, and by describing a class of PDO to which the generators belong; the processes themselves have been constructed by using the representation theorem for analytic semigroups. We have shown that the class of NIG-like Feller processes obtained by the first approach is a subclass of the NIG-like Feller processes obtained by the second approach, and have discussed applicability of both types of processes to option pricing.

A model for shocks based on the subordination approach may seem more natural from the probabilistic viewpoint, but it may be not so easy to fit it to the data so that the EMM-requirement Eq. (14.21) is met. So, our observation that symbols of generators obtained under the two approaches differ little if the derivatives of the coefficients of a subordinated diffusion are small can be used to justify the usage of the naive approach. The EMM-requirement for the latter approach is easy to satisfy, and one can obtain approximate analytic pricing formulae, which are computationally as easy (or difficult) as the pricing formulae for the corresponding Lévy process.

The symbols and the pricing formulae differ little even if derivatives are not small but Eq. (14.31) holds. Notice that empirical studies in, inter alia, Barndorff-Nielsen and Jiang (1998) allow one to expect that Eq. (14.31) usually holds, and hence the pricing formula Eq. (14.29) can be used.

One may use another construction of NIG-like processes: suppose, that there is a coordinate system in which the process under consideration is a NIG Lévy. In this case, the natural question is what the properties of the generator written in an initial coordinate system are, in particular, what its symbol looks like; this question can easily be answered by applying the change-of-variables formula in the theory of PDO.

Finally, we note that results, similar to the ones in Section 14.2-Section 14.3, can be obtained for other Lévy-like Feller processes obtained as modifications of other RLPE.

Chapter 15

Pseudo-differential operators with constant symbols

This Chapter aims at the systematic development of basics of the PDO-machinery and the theory of function spaces in the simplest situation, when symbols are independent of the state variable. Together with the Calculus of PDO with variable symbols, which is constructed in Chapter 16, this Chapter can be used to obtain analogues of results of Chapters 7 and 8 for barrier and touch-and-out options under Lévy-like Feller processes constructed in Chapter 14, the multi-dimensional case including. The exposition is deliberately purely analytical; we aim to show what is the natural order for the things to appear, from the point of view of Analysis, and how one arrives at general formulas, which can be used in various applications, without using the notion of stochastic integrals.

We also demonstrate how the Wiener-Hopf factorization method works in more general situations than in the main text, for option pricing under more general classes of processes in particular.

15.1 Introduction

A specialist with the PDE-background tends to regard the Black-Scholes equation as a primitive object of Mathematical Finance, and the exposition in Wilmott *et al.* (1993) is a model example of this approach. The price of a contingent claim *is defined as* a solution to the Black-Scholes equation, which is specified by appropriate boundary and regularity conditions; among those, is the specification of the behaviour at infinity. Since the courses in ODE and PDE are standard, many specialists know the technique quite well, but the knowledge of PDO seems to be not wide-spread.

The aim of the Chapter is to give a systematic exposition of basic facts of the theory of PDO, which are needed for the generalization of the PDE-approach to Gaussian Mathematical Finance to the case of non-Gaussian Mathematical Finance. The basic theory presented below allows one to calculate prices of contingent claims formally, without mentioning stochastic integrals.

Local regularity properties are naturally formulated in terms of appropriate spaces, like C^m and the Sobolev spaces H^m. In Gaussian theory, the spaces C^m of non-negative integer indexes m arise, and in the case of processes without the diffusion component, the generic case is non-integer m. The corresponding spaces are called Hölder spaces. The spaces C^m are more natural from the point of view of applications to Mathematical Finance (one prefers to know the price at each point, not in the sense of generalized functions) but the study in the scale $\{H^m\}$ is more simple since the Fourier transform can be applied much easier. After the regularity of the solution in terms of the scale $\{H^m\}$ is established, the regularity in the scale $\{C^m\}$ can be deduced by using the Sobolev embedding theorem. It is possible to work with the scale $\{C^m\}$ from the beginning till the end but this requires additional conditions on symbols of PDO.

When the region is unbounded, the behaviour of the solution at the infinity must be specified, and the standard (very convenient) device is to consider the Generalized Black-Scholes equation in spaces with appropriate weights, which capture the behaviour of the data and solutions. In the variable $x = \ln S$, the solution may grow exponentially, the main example being the European call option with the payoff $(e^x - K)_+$, therefore the natural weights are exponential.

The theory of PDO and action of PDO in function spaces is a complicated construction, and when one tries to learn how to handle it, one feels that there are must be easier ways. In simplest situations, like in Chapters 7 and 8, this is really so. It is possible to avoid the usage of the systematic theory of function spaces and action of PDO in these spaces, when the results are obtained in the explicit form, and hence the verification of necessary regularity conditions is straightforward. Usually, this is possible only in the case of PDO with constant symbols and domains with flat boundaries, when the usage of the Fourier transform greatly simplifies the study of boundary value problems.

As we saw in Chapter 14, in the case of PDO with variable symbols, the explicit solutions are not available, and this is a situation, where a general theory can establish the existence and uniqueness of the solution in an appropriate function class, prove the regularity of the solution, and obtain effective approximate formulas for the solution. In Chapter 8, we demonstrated a realization of this programme for pricing of barrier options in the simple case of RLPE; this Chapter contains additional potentially useful constructions and treats more general classes of symbols and spaces. If one repeats the same constructions in the case of Lévy-like Feller processes and boundary value problems for contingent claims (and uses necessary results of Chapter 16 on PDO with variable symbols, like in Chapter 14), one obtains approximate pricing formulas.

We give a collection of main definitions and results of the theory of PDO with constant symbols, without the connection to Probability, since this connection was illustrated in many places in the main text. The exposition is essentially self-contained; of the reader, only the knowledge of basic Functional Analysis and Complex Analysis is required. All necessary results from the theory of generalized functions and function spaces are listed; in many cases, proofs of the results of the theory of generalized functions are given. We omit some long proofs if the technical tricks in the proofs are not used later, and the proof can easily be found in many monographs. We basically follow the exposition in the monograph Eskin (1973), with some modifications.

15.2 Classes of functions

15.2.1 *General notation and remarks*

We will work with spaces of functions on a finite-dimensional space V, which we identify with $\mathbf{R}^n$ by fixing a basis, or on a subset of $\mathbf{R}^n$. Elements of $V = \mathbf{R}^n$ are denoted by $x, y, z, \ldots$; elements of the dual space V' are denoted by $\xi, \eta, \zeta, \ldots$. The standard scalar product in $\mathbf{R}^n$ will be usually denoted by xy. By using the scalar product, we can identify V and V' and denote the pairing $\langle x, \xi \rangle$ by $x\xi$. When we wish to distinguish $\mathbf{R}^n = V$ from $\mathbf{R}^n = V'$, we write $\mathbf{R}^n{}_x$ and $\mathbf{R}^n{}_\xi$, respectively. $\int_{\mathbf{R}^n} f(x)dx$ denotes the Lebesgue integral.

For $x \in \mathbf{R}^n$, set $\langle x \rangle = (1 + |x|^2)^{1/2}$, and for multi-indices α, β and a function a on $\mathbf{R}^n{}_x \times \mathbf{R}^n{}_\xi$, set $a_{(\beta)}^{(\alpha)}(x, \xi) = \partial_\xi^\alpha D_x^\beta a(x, \xi)$.

Estimates will be uniform on certain sets, usually on the domain of a function; constants in these estimates will be denoted by C, c, C_1, c_1 etc. We adopt the following policy on constants: unless otherwise stated, they can be chosen the same for all values of parameters they can depend on, and they are positive.

$C_b^m(U)$ is a subspace of $C^m(U)$, consisting of functions uniformly bounded on U, together with all derivatives; $C_0^m(U)$ is the subspace of bounded functions vanishing at the infinity with all the derivatives up to the order m.

Sometimes we will use spaces of vector-functions assuming values in normed spaces. For instance, if $\mathcal{B}$ is a normed space and $K \subset \mathbf{R}^n$, then $C_b^m(K; \mathcal{B})$ is the space of functions with the finite norm

$$||f||_{C^m(K;\mathcal{B})} = \sum_{|\alpha| \leq m} \sup_{x \in \mathbf{R}^n} ||f^{(\alpha)}(x)||_{\mathcal{B}}.$$

This is a natural generalization of the definition of the space $C_b^m(K)$. Similarly, one modifies the definitions of other spaces.

15.2.2   The space $\mathcal{S}(\mathbf{R}^n)$

The starting point of the theory of PDO is the definition of the action of PDO in an appropriate space of sufficiently regular functions (*test functions*), and the choice depends on properties of a class of PDO one works with. First of all, it is advisable that the space of test functions be invariant under the action of PDO from a given class. For differential operators on $\mathbf{R}^n$, the natural choice is $C_0^\infty(\mathbf{R}^n)$, since for $u \in C_0^\infty(U)$ and A, a differential operator with smooth coefficients, $Au \in C_0^\infty(\mathbf{R}^n)$. Pseudo-differential operators being non-local, $C_0^\infty(\mathbf{R}^n)$ is not a good candidate, and for many classes of PDO, the best choice is $\mathcal{S}(\mathbf{R}^n)$, the space of infinitely differentiable functions vanishing at the infinity faster any negative power of $\langle x \rangle$, together with all derivatives. The topology in $\mathcal{S}(\mathbf{R}^n)$ is defined by a system of seminorms

$$||u||_{\mathcal{S};\alpha,\beta} = \sup_{x \in \mathbf{R}} |x^\beta u^{(\alpha)}(x)|, \qquad (15.1)$$

where α, β are multi-indices. $\mathcal{S}(\mathbf{R}^n)$ is the Frechet space. For $k, v \in \mathcal{S}(\mathbf{R}^n)$, define the *convolution* $k * v$ by

$$(k * v)(x) = \int_{-\infty}^{+\infty} k(x - y)v(y)dy.$$

By using the Leibnitz rule and the triangle inequality, it is easy to show that $k * v \in \mathcal{S}(\mathbf{R}^n)$, and that a fixed $k \in \mathcal{S}(\mathbf{R}^n)$ defines a continuous operator

$$K : \mathcal{S}(\mathbf{R}^n) \ni v \mapsto k * v \in \mathcal{S}(\mathbf{R}^n).$$

K is called the convolution operator with the kernel k. In many applications, this definition is used for wider spaces and classes of kernels, for instance, with $L_1(\mathbf{R}^n)$ instead of $\mathcal{S}(\mathbf{R}^n)$.

15.2.3 The Fourier transform

For $u \in \mathcal{S}(\mathbf{R}^n)$, define the *Fourier transform* $\mathcal{F}u = \hat{u}$ by

$$\hat{u}(\xi) = \int_{\mathbf{R}^n} e^{-ix\xi} u(x)dx; \tag{15.2}$$

then the inverse Fourier transform $\mathcal{F}^{-1}$ is defined by

$$u(x) = (2\pi)^{-n} \int_{\mathbf{R}^n} e^{ix\xi} \hat{u}(\xi)d\xi. \tag{15.3}$$

In the literature, one can find many versions of the definition of the Fourier transform. For instance, Eskin (1973) uses Eq. (15.2) with $ix\xi$ in the exponent (hence, Eq. (15.3) with $-ix\xi$), and the factor $(2\pi)^{-n}$ can be shared between $\mathcal{F}$ and $\mathcal{F}^{-1}$ differently; but in all cases, if dx and $d\xi$ are the Lebesgue measures in $\mathbf{R}^n{}_x$ and $\mathbf{R}^n{}_\xi$, respectively, the product of the factors in front of the integral signs in Eq. (15.2) and Eq. (15.3) must be $(2\pi)^{-n}$.

The following properties of the Fourier transform are well-known.

Theorem 15.1   *a)* $\mathcal{F}$ *is a topological isomorphism of* $S(\mathbf{R}^n)$, *and* $\mathcal{F}^{-1}$ *is its inverse;*
b) $\mathcal{F}(D_x^\alpha f)(\xi) = \xi^\alpha \hat{f}(\xi)$, *and* $\mathcal{F}(x^\alpha f)(\xi) = (-1)^{|\alpha|} D_\xi^\alpha \hat{f}(\xi)$;
c) $\mathcal{F}(u * v)(\xi) = \hat{u}(\xi)\hat{v}(\xi)$;
d) the Parceval indentity holds:

$$(\hat{u}, \hat{v})_{L_2(\mathbf{R}^n)} = (2\pi)^n (u, v)_{L_2(\mathbf{R}^n)}; \tag{15.4}$$

in particular,

$$\|\hat{u}\|^2_{L_2(\mathbf{R}^n)} = (2\pi)^n \|u\|^2_{L_2(\mathbf{R}^n)}.$$

The Fourier transform Eq. (15.2) is well-defined on a wider space $L_1(\mathbf{R}^n)$, and by using the Parceval identity Eq. (15.4), $\mathcal{F}$ can be extended from a dense subset $\mathcal{S}(\mathbf{R}^n) \subset L_2(\mathbf{R}^n)$ to a topological isomorphism of $L_2(\mathbf{R}^n)$. In the next subsection, a natural generalization of Eq. (15.4) is used to define the Fourier transform in the space of generalized functions. This construction has a disadvantage of being indirect; in some important cases, one can obtain analogues of the direct formulas Eq. (15.2)–Eq. (15.3); the corresponding procedures are considered in Subsection 15.3.3-Subsection 15.3.4.

15.3   Space $\mathcal{S}'(\mathbf{R}^n)$ of generalized functions on $\mathbf{R}^n$

15.3.1   *Generalized functions (distributions)*

A functional ϕ on $\mathcal{S}(\mathbf{R}^n)$ is called linear if for any $\alpha_1, \alpha_2 \in \mathbf{C}$ and $f_1, f_2 \in \mathcal{S}(\mathbf{R}^n)$,

$$(\phi, \alpha_1 f_1 + \alpha_2 f_2) = \overline{\alpha_1}(\phi, f_1) + \overline{\alpha_2}(\phi, f_2).$$

The space of continuous linear functionals on $\mathcal{S}(\mathbf{R}^n)$ is denoted by $\mathcal{S}'(\mathbf{R}^n)$. Its elements are called distributions or generalized functions. The topology in $\mathcal{S}'(\mathbf{R}^n)$ is defined by

$$f_n \to f \quad \Longleftrightarrow \quad (f_n, u) \to (f, u) \,\, \forall \, u \in \mathcal{S}(\mathbf{R}^n).$$

Example 15.1   Let f be a locally integrable function, which admits a bound

$$\int_{\mathbf{R}^n} |f(x)| \langle x \rangle^{-N} dx < +\infty. \tag{15.5}$$

Then we can define a functional ϕ on $\mathcal{S}(\mathbf{R}^n)$ by

$$(\phi, u) = \int_{-\infty}^{+\infty} f(x)\bar{u}(x)dx, \quad u \in \mathcal{S}(\mathbf{R}^n).$$

Clearly, $\phi \in \mathcal{S}'(\mathbf{R}^n)$. Functionals of this form are called *regular*. In the sequel, the regular functional defined by the function f will be denoted by the same letter, f.

The following statement easily follows from the definition.

Lemma 15.1

  (i) If two functions, f and f_1, define the same regular functional and are continuous on an open set Ω, then $f(x) = f_1(x)$, $\forall\, x \in \Omega$.

  (ii) If f and $f_n, n = 1, 2, \ldots$ are measurable, $f_n(x) \to f(x)$ a.e., f satisfies Eq. (15.5), and $|f_n(x)| \le f(x)$, $\forall n, x$, then $f_n \to f$ in $\mathcal{S}'(\mathbf{R}^n)$.

Example 15.2 For $\gamma \in \mathbf{R}^n$, the *Dirac delta-function* δ_γ defined by $(\delta_\gamma, u) = \overline{u(\gamma)}$ belongs to $\mathcal{S}'(\mathbf{R}^n)$. When $\gamma = 0$, the index 0 is usually omitted: $\delta = \delta_0$.

15.3.2   *Operations in $\mathcal{S}'(\mathbf{R}^n)$*

The derivative $D^\alpha f$ of a distribution f is defined by

$$(D^\alpha f, u) = (f, D^\alpha u), \quad \forall\, u \in \mathcal{S}(\mathbf{R}^n).$$

Clearly, it is a linear functional, and since D^α is a continuous operator in $\mathcal{S}(\mathbf{R}^n)$, $D^\alpha f$ is continuous. Hence, $D^\alpha f \in \mathcal{S}'(\mathbf{R}^n)$, and we conclude that generalized functions have derivatives of any order.

Example 15.3 Let $\theta_+ = 1_{(0,+\infty)}$ be the indicator function of $\mathbf{R}_+$: $\theta_+(x) = 1, x > 0$, $\theta_+(x) = 0, x \le 0$. Then

$$(D\theta_+, u) = (\theta_+, Du) = \int_0^{+\infty} \overline{Du(x)}dx = -i\overline{u(0)},$$

i.e., $d\theta_+/dx = \delta$. Similarly, $(D^k\delta, u) = (-1)^k \overline{D^k u(0)}, k \ge 1$.

Example 15.4 If f and its derivatives up to order $m = |\alpha|$ are continuous functions growing not faster than a polynomial at the infinity, then the functional $D^\alpha f$ is a regular functional defined by a function $D^\alpha f$.

Let $a \in C^\infty(\mathbf{R}^n)$ satisfy, for any α:

$$|a^{(\alpha)}(x)| \le C_\alpha \langle x \rangle^{m_\alpha}, \tag{15.6}$$

where C_α and m_α are independent of x. For $f \in \mathcal{S}'(\mathbf{R}^n)$, define the functional af by

$$(af, u) = (f, \bar{a}u), \quad \forall\, u \in \mathcal{S}(\mathbf{R}^n).$$

Clearly, $af \in \mathcal{S}'(\mathbf{R}^n)$, and the-multiplication-by-a operator, with a satisfying Eq. (15.6), is a continuous operator in $\mathcal{S}'(\mathbf{R}^n)$. We conclude that

$$A(x, D) = \sum_{|\alpha| \le m} a_\alpha(x) D^\alpha,$$

differential operators with $C^\infty(\mathbf{R}^n)$-coefficients satisfying Eq. (15.6), are continuous in $\mathcal{S}'(\mathbf{R}^n)$.

15.3.3   *The Fourier transform of generalized functions*

Motivated by Eq. (15.4), one defines the Fourier transform $\hat{f} = \mathcal{F}f$ of a generalized function $f \in \mathcal{S}'(\mathbf{R}^n)$ by duality:

$$(\mathcal{F}f, \mathcal{F}u) = (2\pi)^n(f, u), \quad \forall\, u \in \mathcal{S}(\mathbf{R}^n). \tag{15.7}$$

Example 15.5   The Fourier transform of the delta-function $\delta = \delta_0$ is equal to 1 since with $f = \delta$, the RHS in Eq. (15.7) equals $(2\pi)^n \overline{u(0)}$, and from Eq. (15.3), with $\mathcal{F}f = 1$, the LHS is equal to

$$\int_{\mathbf{R}^n} \overline{\mathcal{F}u(\xi)}d\xi = (2\pi)^n\overline{(F^{-1}\hat{u})(0)} = (2\pi)^n\overline{u(0)}.$$

Theorem 15.2   *a) $\mathcal{F}$ is a topological isomorphism of $\mathcal{S}'(\mathbf{R}^n)$;*
b) $\mathcal{F}(D_x^\alpha f)(\xi) = \xi^\alpha \hat{f}(\xi)$, and $\mathcal{F}(x^\alpha f)(\xi) = (-1)^{|\alpha|} D_\xi^\alpha \hat{f}(\xi)$;

Proof.   a) The continuity of $\mathcal{F}$ in $\mathcal{S}'(\mathbf{R}^n)$ is straightforward from Eq. (15.7). Define the action of $\mathcal{F}^{-1}$ in $\mathcal{S}'(\mathbf{R}^n)$ by

$$(\mathcal{F}^{-1}f, \mathcal{F}^{-1}u) = (2\pi)^{-n}(f, u), \quad \forall\, u \in \mathcal{S}(\mathbf{R}^n);$$

then it is a continuous operator in $\mathcal{S}'(\mathbf{R}^n)$, and $\mathcal{F}^{-1}\mathcal{F}f = f$ for any f.

   b) is immediate from the property b) of the Fourier transform in Theorem 15.1. $\qquad\square$

Thus, we have analogues of the statements a) and b) of Theorem 15.1 but not of part c), where the convolution is treated, and the reason is that the convolution $f * g$ is not defined for arbitrary pair of generalized functions. However, if the Fourier transform $\hat{f} \in C^\infty(\mathbf{R}^n)$ satisfies Eq. (15.6), we may *define* the convolution $f * g$ by

$$f * g = \mathcal{F}^{-1}(\hat{f}\hat{g}),$$

and then

$$\mathcal{F}(f * g) = \hat{f}\hat{g}.$$

15.3.4   The regularization of oscillatory integrals

Suppose that $\hat{u}$, the Fourier transform of a function u, is found, but the integral in Eq. (15.3) does not converge absolutely. If the limit

$$(\mathcal{F}^{-1}\hat{u})(x) = (2\pi)^{-1} \lim_{A,B \to +\infty} \int_{-B}^{A} e^{ix\xi}\hat{u}(\xi)d\xi. \tag{15.8}$$

exists, we can regard Eq. (15.8) as a regularization of the integral Eq. (15.3), and use Eq. (15.8) to calculate $u = \mathcal{F}^{-1}f$ (similar procedure can be applied to the Fourier transform Eq. (15.2), of course). This regularization is still within the scope of the basic Calculus. The next two regularizations of the integrals Eq. (15.2) and Eq. (15.3) (understood as the mere notation for the Fourier transform and the inverse Fourier transform, respectively) use the technique of the theory of generalized functions. In both cases, we assume that $\hat{u}$ is measurable and satisfies an estimate

$$|\hat{u}(\xi)| \le C\langle\xi\rangle^s, \tag{15.9}$$

where C, s are independent of ξ. This is exactly the situation, which we encounter in the next Section, where the solutions to pseudo-differential equations will be found by means of the Fourier transform and its inverse.

Regularization 1. The generalized function u, the inverse Fourier transform of $\hat{u}$, can be defined by

$$\begin{aligned}
(u, v) &= (2\pi)^{-n}(\hat{u}, \hat{v}) \\
&= (2\pi)^{-n} \int_{\mathbf{R}^n} \hat{u}(\xi)\overline{\hat{v}(\xi)}d\xi \\
&= (2\pi)^{-n} \int_{\mathbf{R}^n} d\xi \hat{u}(\xi) \int_{\mathbf{R}^n} dx \overline{e^{ix\xi}v(x)} \\
&= (2\pi)^{-n} \int_{\mathbf{R}^n} d\xi \int_{\mathbf{R}^n} dx e^{-ix\xi}\hat{u}(\xi)\overline{v(x)},
\end{aligned}$$

where the integral is understood as the iterated one. Take a positive integer N, notice that

$$\langle\xi\rangle^{-2N}(1 - \Delta_x)^N e^{-ix\xi} = e^{-ix\xi},$$

where Δ is the Laplacian: $-\Delta = \sum_{j=1}^{n} D_j^n$, and integrate by part. The result is

$$(u,v) = (2\pi)^{-n} \int_{\mathbf{R}^n} d\xi \int_{\mathbf{R}^n} dx e^{-ix\xi} \hat{u}(\xi) \langle\xi\rangle^{-2N} (1-\Delta_x)^N \overline{v(x)}.$$

If $2N > s+n$, the last integral converges absolutely, and we may write

$$(u,v) = (2\pi)^{-n} \int_{\mathbf{R}^n} \int_{\mathbf{R}^n} e^{-ix\xi} \hat{u}(\xi) \langle\xi\rangle^{-2N} (1-\Delta_x)^N \overline{v(x)} d\xi dx. \quad (15.10)$$

The formula Eq. (15.10) allows one to explicitly calculate the pairing of the generalized function u, given by Eq. (15.3), and any test function $v \in \mathcal{S}(\mathbf{R}^n)$. This defines u. It is easy to see that Eq. (15.10) with $2N > s+n$ defines a continuous linear functional over $\mathcal{S}(\mathbf{R}^n)$.

Regularization 2. Take a sequence of uniformly bounded measurable functions ψ_n, converging pointwise to 1. Then consider integrals

$$I_n = (2\pi)^{-n} \int_{\mathbf{R}^n} \int_{\mathbf{R}^n} e^{-ix\xi} \psi_n(\xi) \hat{u}(\xi) \overline{v(x)} d\xi dx.$$

They converge absolutely, and by integrating by parts, we obtain

$$I_n = (2\pi)^{-n} \int_{\mathbf{R}^n} \int_{\mathbf{R}^n} e^{-ix\xi} \psi_n(\xi) \hat{u}(\xi) \langle\xi\rangle^{-2N} (1-\Delta_x)^N \overline{v(x)} d\xi dx.$$

Take $2N > s+n$; then from Eq. (15.9) we conclude that the integrand is bounded by the same integrable function for all n, and by construction, it converges pointwise. By applying the Lebesgue theorem, we conclude that the limit $\lim_{n\to\infty} I_n$ exists and is equal to the RHS in Eq. (15.10). Notice that the RHS in Eq. (15.10) is independent of the choice $2N > s+n$.

15.3.5 *Tensor product of generalized functions*

Set $x' = (x_1, \ldots, x_{n-1})$ and $x = (x', x_n)$. Denote by $\mathcal{S}(\mathbf{R}_{x'}^{n-1}) \otimes \mathcal{S}(\mathbf{R}_{x_n})$ a linear span of functions $u = u_1 \otimes u_2$ of the form $u(x', x_n) = u_1(x') u_2(x_n)$, where $u_1 \in \mathcal{S}(\mathbf{R}^{n-1})$ and $u_2 \in \mathcal{S}(\mathbf{R})$. Clearly, $\mathcal{S}(\mathbf{R}_{x'}^{n-1}) \otimes \mathcal{S}(\mathbf{R}_{x_n})$ is a subset of $\mathcal{S}(\mathbf{R}^n)$.

For $f_1 \in \mathcal{S}'(\mathbf{R}^{n-1})$ and $f_2 \in \mathcal{S}'(\mathbf{R})$, the *tensor product* $f_1 \otimes f_2$ is defined on monomials $u = u_1 \otimes u_2$ by

$$(f_1 \otimes f_2, u) = (f_1, u_1)(f_2, u_2),$$

and extended by linearity to $\mathcal{S}(\mathbf{R}_{x'}^{n-1}) \otimes \mathcal{S}(\mathbf{R}_{x_n})$.

It can be shown that $\mathcal{S}(\mathbf{R}_{x'}^{n-1}) \otimes \mathcal{S}(\mathbf{R}_{x_n})$ is a dense subset in $\mathcal{S}(\mathbf{R}^n)$, and $f_1 \otimes f_2$ admits a unique extension to a continuous linear functional $f \in \mathcal{S}'(\mathbf{R}^n)$. We will denote it by the same symbol $f_1 \otimes f_2$.

Let $v \in \mathcal{S}'(\mathbf{R}^{n-1})$ and $\hat{v}$ be a regular functional. Then the Fourier transform of $w = v \otimes \delta$ is equal to $\hat{w}(\xi) = \hat{v}(\xi')$.

15.3.6   Generalized functions on an open set. The support of a generalized function

If f is a regular functional defined by a locally integrable function $f(x)$, then the *support* of f (denoted by supp f) is the complement to the maximal open set on which $f(x) = 0$ a. e. Let $U \subset \mathbf{R}^n$ be an open set. $\mathcal{S}(U)$ denotes the closure of $C_0^\infty(U)$ in $\mathcal{S}(\mathbf{R}^n)$. The space of continuous linear functionals on $\mathcal{S}(U)$ is denoted by $\mathcal{S}'(U)$. Let $f \in \mathcal{S}'(U)$. The functional $f_U \in \mathcal{S}'(U)$ is called the *restriction* of f on U if $(f, u) = (f_U, u)$ for all $u \in \mathcal{S}(U)$. The restriction operator will be denoted p_U, hence, $f_U = p_U f$. Since $\mathcal{S}(U)$ is a closed subspace of $\mathcal{S}(\mathbf{R}^n)$, any $f \in \mathcal{S}'(U)$ admits an *extension* $lf \in \mathcal{S}'(\mathbf{R}^n)$, by the Hahn-Banach theorem (clearly, an extension is non-unique).

We say that f equals zero on U, if $f_U = 0$. Since $C_0^\infty(U)$ is dense in $\mathcal{S}(U)$, $f_U = 0$ iff $(f, u) = 0$ for all $u \in C_0^\infty(U)$. Let U be the maximal open set on which $f = 0$. Then the complement to U is denoted by supp f and called the support of f. If f is a regular functional, this definition coincides with the one given earlier.

15.4   Pseudo-differential operators with constant symbols on $\mathbf{R}^n$

15.4.1   Definition of PDO with constant symbols

Let a be a measurable function satisfying

$$|a(\xi)| \le C\langle\xi\rangle^m, \tag{15.11}$$

where C, m are independent of ξ. Then we write $a \in S^m(\mathbf{R}^n)$. The-multiplication-by-a operator is continuous in $\mathcal{S}'(\mathbf{R}^n)$, therefore the composition $\mathcal{F}^{-1}a\mathcal{F}$ is a continuous operator in $\mathcal{S}'(\mathbf{R}^n)$. It is denoted by $a(D)$, and $A = a(D) := \mathcal{F}^{-1}a\mathcal{F}$ is called a *pseudodifferential operator* (PDO) with the *symbol* a, of *order* m. The action of $A = a(D)$ on $\mathcal{S}(\mathbf{R}^n)$ can be defined by

$$Au(x) = (2\pi)^{-n} \int_{\mathbf{R}^n} e^{ix\xi} a(\xi)\hat{u}(\xi)d\xi, \qquad (15.12)$$

or equivalently,

$$Au(x) = (2\pi)^{-n} \int_{\mathbf{R}^n} d\xi \int_{\mathbf{R}^n} dy e^{i(x-y)\xi} a(\xi)u(y), \qquad (15.13)$$

where the integral is understood as the iterated one.

Lemma 15.2   *A is a PDO with the symbol $a \in S^m$ iff A is a continuous operator in $S'(\mathbf{R}^n)$, which acts on the oscillating exponents as follows:*

$$Ae^{ix\gamma} = a(\gamma)e^{ix\gamma}. \qquad (15.14)$$

Proof.   Since the Fourier transform of $e^{ix\gamma}$ is equal to $(2\pi)^n \delta_\gamma$, and $a\delta_\gamma = a(\gamma)\delta_\gamma$, we have

$$
\begin{aligned}
\mathcal{F}^{-1}a\mathcal{F}e^{ix\gamma} &= \mathcal{F}^{-1}a(\gamma)(2\pi)^n \delta_\gamma \\
&= a(\gamma)\mathcal{F}^{-1}(2\pi)^n \delta_\gamma \\
&= a(\gamma)e^{ix\gamma}.
\end{aligned}
$$

This proves that $A = a(D)$ acts on oscillating exponents by Eq. (15.14).

Now suppose that A is a continuous operator in $S'(\mathbf{R}^n)$, which acts on oscillating exponents $e_\gamma(x) = e^{ix\gamma}$ by formula Eq. (15.14), where $a(\gamma)$ are some constants. The integral Eq. (15.3):

$$u(x) = (2\pi)^{-n} \int_{\mathbf{R}^n} e_\xi(x)\hat{u}(\xi)d\xi$$

converges in the topology of $S(\mathbf{R}^n)$, therefore

$$Au(x) = (2\pi)^{-n} \int_{\mathbf{R}^n} Ae_\xi(x)\hat{u}(\xi)d\xi,$$

and applying Eq. (15.14), we obtain Eq. (15.12). $\square$

By using Eq. (15.14), it is straightforward to show that

a) Let $A = \sum_{|\alpha|\leq m} a_\alpha D^\alpha, a_\alpha \in \mathbf{C}$, be a differential operator. Then A is a PDO with the symbol $a(\xi) = \sum_{|\alpha|\leq m} a_\alpha \xi^\alpha$.

b) Let the Fourier transform of $k \in \mathcal{S}'(\mathbf{R}^n)$ satisfy Eq. (15.11). Then the *convolution operator* K with the *generalized kernel* k is a PDO with the symbol $\hat{k}$.

15.4.2   The Sobolev spaces $H^s(\mathbf{R}^n)$

For $s \in \mathbf{R}$, denote by $H^s(\mathbf{R}^n)$ the space of distributions $f \in \mathcal{S}'(\mathbf{R}^n)$ with the finite norm $\|f\|_s$ defined by

$$\|f\|_s^2 = \int_{\mathbf{R}^n} |\hat{f}(\xi)|^2 \langle \xi \rangle^{2s} d\xi. \tag{15.15}$$

This definition implies that $\hat{f}$ is locally integrable.

Example 15.6   Since the Fourier transform of the delta-function is 1, $\delta \in H^s(\mathbf{R}^n)$ iff $s < -n/2$.

For $s \in \mathbf{R}$, introduce the symbol $\Lambda^s(\xi) = \langle \xi \rangle^s$.

Lemma 15.3   *For $m, s \in \mathbf{R}$, $\Lambda^s(D) : \mathcal{S}(\mathbf{R}^n) \to \mathcal{S}(\mathbf{R}^n)$, and $\Lambda^s(D) : \mathcal{S}'(\mathbf{R}^n) \to \mathcal{S}'(\mathbf{R}^n)$ are topological automorphisms, and $\Lambda^s(D) : H^m(\mathbf{R}^n) \to H^{m-s}(\mathbf{R}^n)$ is an isometry, with inverses defined by $\Lambda^{-s}(D)$.*

Proof.   Evident.   □

In the following theorem, the main properties of the scale of the *Sobolev spaces* are collected; the proofs can be found in, e.g., Triebel (1978).

Theorem 15.3   *Let $s < s'$. Then*
a) $H^0(\mathbf{R}^n) = L_2(\mathbf{R}^n)$;
b) $H^s(\mathbf{R}^n)$ *has the topology of the Hilbert space, with the scalar product*

$$(u, v)_s = (2\pi)^{-n} \int_{\mathbf{R}^n} \langle \xi \rangle^{2s} \hat{u}(\xi) \overline{\hat{v}(\xi)} d\xi; \tag{15.16}$$

c) $C_0^\infty(\mathbf{R}^n) \subset \mathcal{S}(\mathbf{R}^n) \subset H^s(\mathbf{R}^n) \subset \mathcal{S}'(\mathbf{R}^n)$ *densely, and these embeddings are continuous;*
d) $H^{s'}(\mathbf{R}^n) \subset H^s(\mathbf{R}^n)$, *densely and continuously;*
e) $H^{-s}(\mathbf{R}^n)$ *can be naturally identified with the dual space* $(H^s(\mathbf{R}^n))^*$, *by*

$$(u, v) = (2\pi)^{-n} \int_{\mathbf{R}^n} \hat{u}(\xi) \overline{\hat{v}(\xi)} d\xi. \tag{15.17}$$

Lemma 15.4   *Let $m > 0$ be an integer. Then $u \in H^m(\mathbf{R}^n)$ iff $D^\alpha u \in L_2(\mathbf{R}^n)$, for all $|\alpha| \leq m$, and the norm $\| \cdot \|'_s$, defined by*

$$(\|u\|'_s)^2 = \sum_{|\alpha| \leq m} \|D^\alpha u\|^2_{L_2(\mathbf{R}^n)}, \tag{15.18}$$

is equivalent to the norm Eq. (15.15).

Proof.   Clearly, there exist $C, c > 0$ such that for all $\xi \in \mathbf{R}^n$,

$$c\langle \xi \rangle^{2m} \leq \sum_{|\alpha| \leq m} |\xi^\alpha|^2 \leq C\langle \xi \rangle^{2m},$$

and by multiplying by $|\hat{u}(\xi)|^2$ and integrating over $\mathbf{R}^n$, we obtain

$$c\|u\|^2_s \leq \sum_{|\alpha| \leq m} \|D^\alpha u\|^2_{L_2(\mathbf{R}^n)} \leq C\|u\|^2_s. \tag{15.19}$$

Since all the terms are non-negative, we conclude that $\|u\|_s < \infty$ iff $\|D^\alpha u\|^2_{L_2(\mathbf{R}^n)} < \infty, |\alpha| \leq m$, i.e., the first statement of Lemma holds. The second statement is immediate from Eq. (15.19).   □

15.4.3   *Action of PDO in the scale $H^s(\mathbf{R}^n)$*

Theorem 15.4   *Let $m, s \in \mathbf{R}$ and $a \in S^m(\mathbf{R}^n)$. Then*

$$A = a(D) : H^s(\mathbf{R}^n) \to H^{s-m}(\mathbf{R}^n) \tag{15.20}$$

is bounded.

Proof.   By using Eq. (15.12), Eq. (15.11) and Eq. (15.14),

$$
\begin{aligned}
\|Au\|^2_{s-m} &= \int_{\mathbf{R}^n} \langle \xi \rangle^{2(s-m)} |a(\xi)|^2 |\hat{u}(\xi)|^2 d\xi \\
&\leq C^2 \int_{\mathbf{R}^n} \langle \xi \rangle^{2(s-m)} \langle \xi \rangle^{2m} \hat{u}(\xi)|^2 d\xi \\
&= C^2 \|u\|^2_s.
\end{aligned}
$$

□

Theorem 15.5   *Let $m, s \in \mathbf{R}$, and let $a \in S^m(\mathbf{R}^n)$ satisfy*

$$|a(\xi)^{-1}| \leq C\langle \xi \rangle^{-m}, \tag{15.21}$$

where C is independent of $\xi \in \mathbf{R}^n$. Then the operator Eq. (15.20), and the operator

$$A : \mathcal{S}'(\mathbf{R}^n) \to \mathcal{S}'(\mathbf{R}^n) \tag{15.22}$$

are invertible, the inverse A^{-1} *being a PDO with the symbol* $a(\xi)^{-1}$.

Proof. By construction, AA^{-1} and $A^{-1}A$ act as the identity, and from Eq. (15.21) and Theorem 15.4, $A^{-1} : H^{s-m}(\mathbf{R}^n) \to H^s(\mathbf{R}^n)$ is bounded. Hence, it is the bounded inverse of the operator Eq. (15.20). Since both A, A^{-1} are continuous in $\mathcal{S}'(\mathbf{R}^n)$, the operator Eq. (15.22) is invertible as well. $\qquad \square$

A symbol $a \in S^m(\mathbf{R}^n)$ satisfying Eq. (15.21) and the operator $A = a(D)$ will be called *elliptic*. Usually one calls a and $A = a(D)$ elliptic if Eq. (15.21) is satisfied outside some compact.

15.4.4 Elliptic equations

Consider an equation

$$Au = f,$$

where $A = a(D)$ is a PDO with the elliptic symbol $a \in S^m(\mathbf{R}^n)$, and $f \in H^{s-m}(\mathbf{R}^n)$. By applying A^{-1}, we obtain a unique solution in $H^s(\mathbf{R}^n)$:

$$u = a(D)^{-1}f,$$

or

$$u(x) = (2\pi)^{-n} \int_{\mathbf{R}^n} e^{ix\xi} a(\xi)^{-1} \hat{f}(\xi) d\xi.$$

If the integral does not converge absolutely, it needs to be regularized, e.g., as it was explained in Subsection 15.3.4.

15.4.5 Restriction to a hyperplane

Theorem 15.6 *Let* $s > 1/2$ *and* $n = 1$. *Then the restriction-to-$\{0\}$-operator*

$$p' : C_0^\infty(\mathbf{R}) \ni u \mapsto u(0) \in \mathbf{C}$$

admits a unique bounded extension $p' : H^s(\mathbf{R}) \to \mathbf{C}$.

The proof is essentially the same as the proof of the following theorem in Eskin (1973), Theorem 4.2.

Theorem 15.7 *Let $s > 1/2$ and $n > 1$. Then the restriction-to-the hyperplane* $-x_n = 0$-*operator*

$$p' : C_0^\infty(\mathbf{R}^n) \ni u \mapsto u(\cdot, 0) \in C_0^\infty(\mathbf{R}^{n-1})$$

admits a unique bounded extension $p' : H^s(\mathbf{R}) \to H^{s-1/2}(\mathbf{R}^{n-1})$.

15.4.6 *The Sobolev embedding theorem*

Theorem 15.8 *(Eskin (1973), Theorem 4.3) Let $s > r + n/2$, where $r \geq 0$ is an integer. Then $H^s(\mathbf{R}^n) \subset C_0^r(\mathbf{R}^n)$, densely and continuously.*

15.4.7 *Action in the Hölder spaces*

For a positive non-integer s, denote by $C^s(\mathbf{R}^n)$ the closure of $\mathcal{S}(\mathbf{R}^n)$ in $\mathcal{S}'(\mathbf{R}^n)$, in the norm defined by
for $s \in (0,1)$:

$$\|u\|_{C^s} = \|u\|_{L_\infty} + \sup_{x\in\mathbf{R}^n} \sup_{|h|\leq 1} |h|^{-s}|u(x+h) - u(x)|;$$

for $s = m + s'$, where $m > 0$ is an integer and $s' \in (0,1)$,

$$\|u\|_{C^s} = \sum_{|\alpha|\leq m} \|D^\alpha u\|_{C^{s'}}.$$

These spaces are called *Hölder spaces*. The Hölder spaces constitute a part of the scale of the *Hölder-Zygmund spaces* $\{C^s(\mathbf{R}^n)\}_{s\in\mathbf{R}}$ (for the definition, see, e.g., Triebel (1978)), namely, for non-integer positive s, $C^s(\mathbf{R}^n) = C^s(\mathbf{R}^n)^1$. The scale of the Hölder-Zygmund spaces enjoys the standard property $C^s(\mathbf{R}^n) \subset C^r(\mathbf{R}^n)$, if $s > r$, and the *Sobolev embedding theorem* is valid for the Hölder-Zygmund spaces (see, e.g., Triebel (1978)):

Theorem 15.9 *Let $s > n/2$. Then for any $s' < s - n/2$, $H^s(\mathbf{R}^n) \subset C^{s'}(\mathbf{R}^n)$, densely and continuously.*

---

[1]Note that for integer $s \geq 0$, neither $C^s(\mathbf{R}^n)$ nor $C_0^s(\mathbf{R}^n)$ coincide with $C^s(\mathbf{R}^n)$

To prove the boundedness of a PDO in the scale of the Hölder-Zygmund spaces, one has to impose additional conditions on the symbol. We formulate the boundedness theorem for the Hölder-Zygmund spaces, under the following fairly restrictive condition, which holds in many cases of interest.

Theorem 15.10   *Let* $s, m \in \mathbf{R}$, *and let* $a \in C^\infty(\mathbf{R}^n)$ *satisfy, for any multi-index* α,

$$|a^{(\alpha)}(\xi)| \leq C_\alpha \langle \xi \rangle^{m-|\alpha|}, \tag{15.23}$$

where C_α *is independent of* ξ.
     Then $A = a(D) : C^s(\mathbf{R}^n) \to C^{s-m}(\mathbf{R}^n)$ *is bounded, with the norm admitting an estimate*

$$\|a(D)\| \leq C \sum_{|\alpha| \leq N} \sup_{\xi \in \mathbf{R}^n} \langle \xi \rangle^{-m+|\alpha|} |a^{(\alpha)}(\xi)|, \tag{15.24}$$

where C *and* N *depend on* n, s, m *but not on* a.

Proof.   This is a special case of Theorem 16.7.   □

Theorem 15.11   *Let* $s, m \in \mathbf{R}$, *and let* a *satisfy Eq. (15.21) and Eq. (15.23).*
     Then $A = a(D) : C^s(\mathbf{R}^n) \to C^{s-m}(\mathbf{R}^n)$ *is invertible.*

Proof.   By Theorem 15.5, A is invertible in $\mathcal{S}'(\mathbf{R}^n)$, with the inverse given by $A^{-1} = a(D)^{-1}$. From the Leibnitz rule, and Eq. (15.23) and Eq. (15.21), it follows that $a(\xi)^{-1}$ satisfies Eq. (15.23) with $-m$ instead of m. By Theorem 15.10, $A : C^s(\mathbf{R}^n) \to C^{s-m}(\mathbf{R}^n)$ and $A^{-1} : C^{s-m}(\mathbf{R}^n) \to C^s(\mathbf{R}^n)$ are bounded, hence, they are mutual bounded inverses.   □

It is straightforward to show That if Eq. (15.23) holds then $a(D)$ maps $\mathcal{S}(\mathbf{R}^n)$ into itself, continuously, and this is a topological automorphism, if both Eq. (15.23) and Eq. (15.21) hold.
Remark 15.1 a) Since Theorem 15.10 and Theorem 16.7 are valid for PDO in the Besov spaces, Theorem 15.11 is valid for PDO in the Besov spaces as well, and the same holds for theorems of Section 15.6 on PDO acting in the scale of the Hölder-Zygmund spaces.
     b) To obtain the corresponding statements for PDO acting in the Hölder spaces, one must impose an additional condition: $s, s - m > 0$.

15.5   The action of PDO in the Sobolev spaces on $\mathbf{R}^n{}_\pm$

15.5.1   Spaces $\overset{o\ s}{H}(\mathbf{R}^n{}_\pm)$ and PDO in a half-space

Denote by $\overset{o}{H}{}^s(\mathbf{R}^n{}_\pm)$ a subspace of $H^s(\mathbf{R}^n)$ consisting of distributions f with supp $f \subset \overline{\mathbf{R}^n{}_\pm}$.

Lemma 15.5   *(Eskin (1973), Lemmas 4.2 and 4.3).* $\overset{o\ s}{H}(\mathbf{R}^n{}_\pm)$ *is equal to the closure of* $C_0^\infty(\mathbf{R}^n{}_\pm)$ *in* $H^s(\mathbf{R}^n)$.

Theorem 15.12   *Let* $a \in S^m(\mathbf{R}^n)$ *admit the analytic continuation w.r.t.* ξ_n *into the lower half-plane* $\tau = \Im\xi_n < 0$ *(resp.* $\tau > 0$*) and satisfy an estimate*

$$|a(\xi', \xi_n + i\tau)| \le C(1 + |\xi| + |\tau|)^m \tag{15.25}$$

for all $\xi \in \mathbf{R}^n$, *and* $\tau \le 0$ *(resp.,* $\tau \ge 0$*).*
    Then $a(D) : \overset{o\ s}{H}(\mathbf{R}^n{}_+) \to \overset{o\ s-m}{H}(\mathbf{R}^n{}_+)$ *(resp.,* $a(D) : \overset{o\ s}{H}(\mathbf{R}^n{}_-) \to \overset{o\ s-m}{H}(\mathbf{R}^n{}_-)$*) is bounded.*

Proof.   Consider the case "+". By Theorem 15.4, $a(D) : H^s(\mathbf{R}^n) \to H^{s-m}(\mathbf{R}^n)$ is bounded. By using Eq. (15.25) and the Cauchy Theorem, one shows that for $u \in C_0^\infty(\mathbf{R}^n{}_+)$, and $v \in C_0^\infty(\mathbf{R}^n{}_-)$, $(a(D)u, v) = 0$. Hence, supp $a(D)u \subset \overline{\mathbf{R}^n{}_+}$, and it remains to apply Lemma 15.5.   □

For $m \in \mathbf{R}$, set

$$\Lambda_\pm^m(\xi) = \begin{cases} (1 \mp i\xi)^m, & \text{if } n = 1 \\ (\langle\xi'\rangle \mp i\xi_n)^m, & \text{if } n > 1. \end{cases}$$

Clearly, $\Lambda_\pm^m$ is holomorphic w.r.t. $\xi_n + i\tau$ in the half-space $\pm\tau > 0$, and satisfies Eq. (15.25), hence

$$\Lambda_\pm^m(D) : \overset{o\ s}{H}(\mathbf{R}^n{}_\mp) \to \overset{o\ s-m}{H}(\mathbf{R}^n{}_\mp)$$

is bounded. The same holds with $-m$ instead of m, and $\Lambda_\pm^m\Lambda_\pm^{-m} = 1$; therefore, it is an isomorphism.

15.5.2   Spaces $H^s(\mathbf{R}^n{}_\pm)$

Let $U \subset \mathbf{R}^n$ be an open set. One writes $f \in H^s(U)$ if f is a distribution on U, which admits an extension $lf \in H^s(\mathbf{R}^n)$. The norm in $H^s(U)$ is defined by

$$||f||_{U;s} = \inf ||lf||_s,$$

where infimum is taken over all extensions $lf \in H^s(\mathbf{R}^n)$. Set $p_\pm = p_{\mathbf{R}^n{}_\pm}$. It maps $H^s(\mathbf{R}^n)$ onto $H^s(\mathbf{R}^n{}_\pm)$.

Theorem 15.13 *Let* $a \in S^m(\mathbf{R}^n)$ *admit the analytic continuation w.r.t.* ξ_n *into the upper half-plane* $\tau = \Im\xi_n > 0$ *(resp.* $\tau < 0$*) and satisfy an estimate Eq. (15.25) for all* $\xi \in \mathbf{R}^n$, *and* $\tau \geq 0$ *(resp.,* $\tau \leq 0$*).*
  Then the operator

$$H^s(\mathbf{R}^n{}_+) \ni u \mapsto p_+a(D)lu \in H^{s-m}(\mathbf{R}^n{}_+) \tag{15.26}$$

(resp., the operator

$$H^s(\mathbf{R}^n{}_-) \ni u \mapsto p_-a(D)lu \in H^{s-m}(\mathbf{R}^n{}_-))$$

is well-defined and bounded.

Proof. Consider the case "+". Let $l'u \in H^s(\mathbf{R}^n)$ be another extension of u. Then supp $(lu - l'u) \subset \overline{\mathbf{R}^n{}_-}$, hence $lu - l'u \in \overset{o}{H}{}^s(\mathbf{R}^n{}_-)$, and $a(D)(lu - l'u) \in \overset{o}{H}{}^{s-m}(\mathbf{R}^n{}_-)$, by Theorem 15.12. Hence, $p_+a(D)(lu - l'u) = 0$, and the operator Eq. (15.26) is well-defined. To show the boundedness, take lu with the norm $||lu||_s \leq 2||u||_{\mathbf{R}^n{}_+;s}$; then from Theorem 15.4,

$$||p_+a(D)lu||_{\mathbf{R}^n{}_+;s-m} \leq ||a(D)lu||_{s-m} \leq C||lu||_s \leq 2C||u||_{\mathbf{R}^n{}_+;s}. \qquad \square$$

Denote by $\mathcal{S}(\overline{\mathbf{R}^n{}_\pm})$ the space of restrictions on $\overline{\mathbf{R}^n{}_\pm}$ of functions from $\mathcal{S}(\mathbf{R}^n)$. For any extension $lf \in \mathcal{S}'(\mathbf{R}^n)$ of $f \in \mathcal{S}(\overline{\mathbf{R}^n{}_\pm})$, $p_+D^\alpha lf$ can be identified with the classical derivative $D^\alpha f \in \mathcal{S}(\overline{\mathbf{R}^n{}_\pm})$. This justifies the usage of the notation $D^\alpha f$ instead of $p_+D^\alpha lf$, for $f \in H^s(\mathbf{R}^n{}_+)$. Similarly, for $f \in H^s(\mathbf{R}^n{}_-)$, $D^\alpha f$ is used instead of $p_-D^\alpha lf$.

Lemma 15.6 *Let* $s \geq 0$ *be an integer. Then an equivalent norm in* $H^s(\mathbf{R}^n{}_\pm)$ *can be defined by*

$$||u||'^2_{\mathbf{R}^n{}_\pm,s} = \sum_{|\alpha| \leq s} ||D^\alpha u||^2_{L_2(\mathbf{R}^n{}_\pm)}. \tag{15.27}$$

Proof. For any integer s, there exists an explicit construction of a linear continuous extension operator $l^s : H^s(\mathbf{R}^n{}_+) \to H^s(\mathbf{R}^n)$ satisfying

$$||l^s u||'_s \leq C||u||'_{\mathbf{R}^n{}_\pm,s}$$

(see, e.g., Subsection 2.9.3 in Triebel (1978) or Lemma 4.5 in Eskin (1973)). Hence,

$$\|u\|_{\mathbf{R}^n{}_\pm,s} \leq \|l^s u\|'_s \leq C\|u\|'_{\mathbf{R}^n{}_\pm,s}.$$

The opposite inequality is valid for any extension operator: by Lemma 15.4, the norms $\|\cdot\|_s$ and $\|\cdot\|'_s$ in $H^s(\mathbf{R}^n)$ are equivalent, therefore

$$\|u\|'_{\mathbf{R}_\pm,s} \leq \|l^s u\|'_s \leq C_1\|l^s u\|_s \leq C_2\|u\|_{\mathbf{R}_\pm,s}. \qquad \square$$

Denote by p_a the-restriction-to-hyperplane-$\{x \mid x_n = a\}$ operator, and by using the Lebesgue Theorem, one shows that if $s > 1/2$ and $f \in H^s(\mathbf{R}^n)$, then $p_a f$ is a continuous vector-function of a taking values in $H^{s-1/2}(\mathbf{R}^{n-1})$. It follows that the operator p', defined on $\mathcal{S}(\overline{\mathbf{R}^n}_\pm)$ by $p'f(x') = \lim_{a\downarrow 0} p_a f(x')$, admits a unique bounded extension $p' : H^s(\mathbf{R}^n{}_+) \to H^{s-1/2}(\mathbf{R}^{n-1})$.

15.5.3   *The Cauchy-type integral and its decomposition*

Denote by θ_+ (resp., θ_-) the-multiplication-by-$\mathbf{1}_{(0,+\infty)}(x)$ (resp., $\mathbf{1}_{(-\infty,0)}(x)$) operator. Clearly, $\theta_\pm : L_2(\mathbf{R}^n) \to L_2(\mathbf{R}^n{}_\pm)$ is bounded.

Take $\tau > 0$; then

$$\mathcal{F}(\theta_+(x_n)e^{-\tau x_n})(\xi_n) = 1/(\tau + i\xi_n),$$

and since $\mathcal{F}(uv) = (2\pi)^{-n}\hat{u} * \hat{v}$, we obtain for $f \in \mathcal{S}(\mathbf{R}^n)$,

$$\mathcal{F}(\theta_+(x_n)e^{-\tau x_n}f)(\xi',\xi_n) = (2\pi i)^{-1} \int_{-\infty}^{+\infty} \frac{\hat{f}(\xi',\eta_n)}{\xi_n - i\tau - \eta_n} d\eta_n. \qquad (15.28)$$

By using the Lebesgue theorem, we see that the limit of the LHS in Eq. (15.28) is the Fourier transform of $\theta_+ f$, and therefore,

$$F(\theta_+ f) = \Pi^+ \hat{f}, \qquad (15.29)$$

where

$$\Pi^+ \hat{f}(\xi) := (2\pi i)^{-1} \int_{-\infty}^{+\infty} \frac{\hat{f}(\xi',\eta_n)}{\xi_n - i0 - \eta_n} d\eta_n.$$

Similarly,

$$F(\theta_- f) = \Pi^- \hat{f}, \qquad (15.30)$$

where

$$\Pi^- \hat{f}(\xi) := -(2\pi i)^{-1} \int_{-\infty}^{+\infty} \frac{\hat{f}(\xi', \eta_n)}{\xi_n + i0 - \eta_n} d\eta_n.$$

By using Eq. (15.29) and Eq. (15.30), and a series of rather technical estimates, Eskin (1973) deduces a series of important results.

Theorem 15.14 *(Eskin (1973), Theorem 5.1) For* $|s| < 1/2$, $\theta_\pm$ *admits a unique continuous extension* $\theta_\pm : H^s(\mathbf{R}^n) \to \overset{o\ s}{H}(\mathbf{R}^n{}_\pm)$.

Lemma 15.7 *(Eskin (1973), Lemma 5.4) For* $|s| < 1/2$, *any function* $f \in H^s(\mathbf{R}^n)$ *admits a unique representation* $f = f_+ + f_-$, *where* $f_\pm \in \overset{o\ s}{H}(\mathbf{R}^n{}_\pm)$, *and* $f_\pm = \theta_\pm f$.

Define the extension-by-zero operator $e_\pm : \mathcal{S}(\overline{\mathbf{R}^n{}_\pm}) \to L_2(\mathbf{R}^n)$ by

$$e_\pm f(x) = \begin{cases} f(x), & \pm x_n > 0 \\ 0, & \pm x_n \le 0. \end{cases}$$

From Theorem 15.14 and Lemma 15.7, we deduce

Lemma 15.8 *Let* $|s| < 1/2$. *Then* $e_\pm$ *admits a unique bounded extension* $e_\pm : H^s(\mathbf{R}^n{}_\pm) \to H^s(\mathbf{R}^n)$, *and* $H^s(\mathbf{R}^n{}_\pm)$ *can be identified with* $\overset{o\ s}{H}(\mathbf{R}^n{}_\pm)$.

Theorem 15.15 *(Eskin (1973), Lemma 5.5) Let* $f \in H^{m+s}(\mathbf{R}^n)$, $m > 0$ *integer,* $|s| < 1/2$. *Then*

$$\theta_+ f = \sum_{k=1}^{m} \Lambda_-^{-k}(D) \left[(p'\Lambda_-^{k-1}(D)f) \otimes \delta_0 \right] + \Lambda_-^{-m}(D)\theta_+\Lambda_-^m(D)f, \quad (15.31)$$

and

$$\theta_- f = \sum_{k=1}^{m} \Lambda_+^{-k}(D) \left[(p'\Lambda_+^{k-1}(D)f) \otimes \delta_0 \right] + \Lambda_+^{-m}(D)\theta_-\Lambda_+^m(D)f, \quad (15.32)$$

where p' is the-restriction-to-the hyperplane $x_n = 0$ operator.

Theorem 15.16 *(Eskin (1973), Theorem 5.2). Let* $s = -m + s'$, *where* $m > 0$ *is an integer and* $|s'| < 1/2$.
Then any $f \in \overset{o\ s}{H}(\mathbf{R}^n{}_+) \cap \overset{o\ s}{H}(\mathbf{R}^n{}_-)$ *admits a decomposition*

$$f = \sum_{k=1}^{m} f_k \otimes D^{k-1}\delta_0, \quad (15.33)$$

where $f_k \in H^{s+k-1/2}(\mathbf{R}^{n-1})$.

15.6   Parabolic equations

15.6.1   *The Cauchy problem for the parabolic equation*

We call a symbol a of order $m > 0$ *strongly elliptic*, if a is measurable and satisfies the following two conditions:

$$|a(\xi)| \ \le\ C\langle\xi\rangle^m, \qquad\qquad \xi \in \mathbf{R}^n; \qquad\qquad (15.34)$$

$$\Re a(\xi) \ \ge\ c_0\langle\xi\rangle^m - \sigma_0, \quad \xi \in \mathbf{R}^n; \qquad\qquad (15.35)$$

where $C, c_0 > 0, \sigma_0$ are independent of ξ.

Consider an equation

$$(\partial_t + a(D_x))f(x,t) = g(x,t), \quad t > 0, \qquad\qquad (15.36)$$

subject to the initial condition

$$f(x, +0) = g_0(x). \qquad\qquad (15.37)$$

The (initial) boundary problem Eq. (15.36)–Eq. (15.37) can be solved by various methods. For essentially each of these methods, it is convenient (and for some constructions and/or steps of the proofs, even crucial) to work with a satisfying Eq. (15.35) with non-negative σ_0. So the first natural step is reduction to the case $\sigma_0 = 0$, that is, to the case when a satisfies Eq. (15.34), and a condition

$$\Re a(\xi) \ge c_0\langle\xi\rangle^m, \qquad\qquad (15.38)$$

where $c_0 > 0$ is independent of $\xi \in \mathbf{R}^n$. The reduction is as follows: change the unknown

$$f(x,t) = e^{\sigma_0 t} f^{\sigma_0}(x,t)$$

and the RHS in Eq. (15.36)

$$g(x,t) = e^{\sigma_0 t} g^{\sigma_0}(x,t)$$

Then from Eq. (15.36)-Eq. (15.37), f^{σ_0} is a solution to the problem

$$(\partial_t + a_{\sigma_0}(D_x))f^{\sigma_0}(x,t) \ =\ g^{\sigma_0}(x,t), \quad t > 0;$$
$$f_{\sigma_0}(x, +0) \ =\ g_0(x),$$

where $a_{\sigma_0}(\xi) := a(\xi) + \sigma_0$ satisfies Eq. (15.34) and Eq. (15.38). Having in mind the possibility of such a change of the unknown and the data, we assume in the sequel that a satisfies Eq. (15.34) and Eq. (15.38).

15.6.2 *Reduction to a family of ODE on* $\mathbf{R}_+$

By making the Fourier transform w.r.t. x, we obtain a family of the Cauchy problems on the half-line for ordinary differential equations on $\mathbf{R}_+$, parameterised by $\xi \in \mathbf{R}^n$:

$$(\partial_t + a(\xi))\tilde{f}(\xi, t) = \tilde{g}(\xi, t), \quad t > 0, \tag{15.39}$$

$$\tilde{f}(\xi, 0) = \tilde{g}_0(\xi), \tag{15.40}$$

(here $\tilde{f}$ denoted the "partial" Fourier transform w.r.t x). By solving the Cauchy problem Eq. (15.39)–Eq. (15.40):

$$\tilde{f}(\xi, t) = \int_0^t \exp[(s - t)a(\xi)]\tilde{g}(\xi, s)ds + \exp[-ta(\xi)]\tilde{g}_0(\xi), \tag{15.41}$$

and making the inverse Fourier transform, we obtain the solution to the initial problem Eq. (15.36)–Eq. (15.37)

$$f(x, t) = \int_0^t \exp[(s - t)a(D_x)]g(x, s)ds + \exp[-ta(D_x)]g_0(x). \tag{15.42}$$

Due to Eq. (15.35), for any $t > 0$,

$$p_t(x) = (2\pi)^{-1} \int_{\mathbf{R}^n} \exp[ix\xi - ta(\xi)]d\xi$$

is a continuous uniformly bounded function in x (in fact, $p_t \in C^\infty(\mathbf{R}^n)$), and hence, we deduce from Eq. (15.42)

$$f(t, x) = \int_0^t \int_{\mathbf{R}^n} p_{t-s}(x - y)g(y, s)dyds + \int_{\mathbf{R}^n} p_t(x - y)g_0(y)dy.$$

In the case $g = 0$, which we mainly consider in applications to Financial Mathematics, the last equation reduces to

$$f(t, x) = \int_{\mathbf{R}^n} p_t(x - y)g_0(y)dy. \tag{15.43}$$

In order that the RHS in Eq. (15.41)–Eq. (15.43) be well-defined, g and g_0 must satisfy certain conditions, and one should specify in which sense the limit in Eq. (15.37) is understood.

If $g_0 \in L_1(\mathbf{R}^n)$ then Eq. (15.43) defines a continuous function on $\mathbf{R}^n \times \mathbf{R}_+$. Notice that so far we have the definition of the Fourier transform for generalized functions from $\mathcal{S}'$ only, and hence we cannot allow for exponentially growing data. This is a serious drawback since in some important applications, $g_0(x)$ does grow exponentially as $x \to \infty$; this forces us to introduce spaces with exponential weights in Section 15.9. Below, we restrict ourselves to the case of $g_0 \in H^{s'}(\mathbf{R}^n)$ and $g \in L_2(\mathbf{R}^n \times \mathbf{R}_+)$.

Extend both f and g by zero for $t < 0$, and make the Fourier transform w.r.t. t:

$$\hat{f}(\xi, \eta) = (i\eta + a(\xi))^{-1}(\hat{g}(\xi, \eta) + \hat{g}_0(\xi)).$$

Due to Eq. (15.34) and Eq. (15.38), $\tilde{a}(\xi, \eta) = i\eta + a(\xi)$ satisfies an estimate

$$c(1 + |\xi|^m + |\eta|) \le |\tilde{a}(\xi, \eta)| \le C(1 + |\xi|^m + |\eta|), \tag{15.44}$$

where $C, c > 0$ are independent of $\xi \in \mathbf{R}^n$ and η in the lower half-plane $\Im \eta \le 0$. If $m = 1$, the estimate Eq. (15.44) suggests that we can consider the operator of the problem Eq. (15.36)–Eq. (15.37) in the scale of Sobolev spaces; in the general case, the natural scale is the scale of anisotropic Sobolev spaces.

For $s, r \in \mathbf{R}$, define $H_{m,1}^{(s,r)}(\mathbf{R}^n \times \mathbf{R})$ to be the space of generalized functions with the finite norm

$$\|u\|_{m,1;(s,r)}^2 = \int_{\mathbf{R}^n} \int_{\mathbf{R}} (|\eta| + \langle\xi\rangle^m)^{2s} \langle\xi\rangle^{2r} |\hat{u}(\xi, \eta)|^2 \, d\xi d\eta.$$

Spaces $\overset{o}{H}_{m,1}^{(s,r)}(\mathbf{R}^n \times \mathbf{R}_+)$ are defined by the analogy with $\overset{o}{H}^s(\mathbf{R}^n \times \mathbf{R}_+)$, and similarly to Theorem 15.12, we deduce from Eq. (15.44), that for any s, r,

$$\tilde{a}(D_x, D_t)^{-1} : \overset{o}{H}_{m,1}^{(s-1,r)}(\mathbf{R}^n \times \mathbf{R}_+) \to \overset{o}{H}_{m,1}^{(s,r)}(\mathbf{R}^n \times \mathbf{R}_+) \tag{15.45}$$

is bounded. By making the change of variable $\eta = \eta'\langle\xi\rangle^m$, is easy to verify that for any $\epsilon > 0$,

$$\int_{\mathbf{R}} (|\eta| + \langle\xi\rangle^m)^{-1-\epsilon} |\hat{g}_0(\xi)|^2 d\eta \le C\langle\xi\rangle^{-m\epsilon} |\hat{g}_0(\xi)|^2,$$

therefore if $g_0 \in H^{s'}(\mathbf{R}^n)$, where $s' \geq 0$, then for any $\epsilon > 0$, $\delta_{t=0} \otimes g_0 \in H_{m,1}^{(-1/2-\epsilon,s')}(\mathbf{R}^n \times \mathbf{R})$, and since supp $g_0 \otimes \delta_0 \subset \mathbf{R}^n \times \overline{\mathbf{R}_+}$, we have, for any $\epsilon > 0$,

$$g_0 \otimes \delta_0 \in \overset{o}{H}_{m,1}^{(-1/2-\epsilon,s')}(\mathbf{R}^n \times \mathbf{R}_+). \tag{15.46}$$

If we assume for simplicity that $g \in L_2(\mathbf{R}^n \times \mathbf{R}_+)$, then from Eq. (15.46) and Eq. (15.45) we conclude that

$$f(x,t) = (2\pi)^{-1} \int_{\mathbf{R}} \int_{\mathbf{R}^n} e^{i(x\xi+t\eta)}(i\eta + a(\xi))^{-1}(\hat{g}(\xi,\eta) + \hat{g}_0(\xi))d\xi d\eta$$

belongs to $\overset{o}{H}_{m,1}^{(1/2-\epsilon,0)}(\mathbf{R}^n \times \mathbf{R}_+)$. This statement can be made more exact, but even this form suffices to prove that f is well-defined as a generalized function. The initial condition can also be understood in the sense of generalized functions: take any $v \in \mathcal{S}(\mathbf{R}^n)$, multiply Eq. (15.41) by $\overline{\hat{v}(\xi)}$, and integrate w.r.t. ξ over $\mathbf{R}^n$. By using Eq. (15.34)–Eq. (15.38) and the Lebesgue theorem, it is not difficult to show that

$$\lim_{t \to +0}(f(t,\cdot),v) = (2\pi)^n \int_{\mathbf{R}^n} \hat{g}_0(\xi)\overline{\hat{v}(\xi)}d\xi$$
$$= (g_0, v).$$

Under additional conditions on the data, it is possible to show that $f(t,x) \to g_0(x)$ as $t \to +0$, a. e.

To prove that Eq. (15.37) holds in even stronger sense, and make more exact statements on the regularity of f, the following method is more convenient.

15.6.3 *Parabolic equation as ODE with the operator-valued coefficient*

Let $g_0 \in H^s(\mathbf{R}^n)$. Denote by A^s the unbounded operator in $H^s(\mathbf{R}^n)$ with the domain $H^{s+1}(\mathbf{R}^n)$; the action of A^s is defined by

$$A^s u = a(D_x)u.$$

We can interpret the problem Eq. (15.36)–Eq. (15.37) as the Cauchy problem for the ordinary differential equation on $\mathbf{R}_+$ with the operator-valued coefficient. For the sake of brevity, we consider and solve it in the case $g = 0$:

$$f'(t) + A^s f(t) = 0, \quad t > 0, \tag{15.47}$$

$$f(+0) = g_0. \tag{15.48}$$

Theorem 15.17 *For any $s \in \mathbf{R}$ and $g_0 \in H^s(\mathbf{R}^n)$, the problem Eq. (15.47)– Eq. (15.48) has a solution $f \in C^0([0, +\infty); H^s(\mathbf{R}_+))$.*

The solution is unique, and for any $t_0 > 0, r \in \mathbf{R}, j \in \mathbf{Z}_+$, and $\gamma < c_0$, where $c_0 > 0$ is the constant in Eq. (15.38), it satisfies the following estimate:

$$\sup_{t \geq t_0} ||e^{\gamma t} f^{(j)}(t)||_r < +\infty. \tag{15.49}$$

The proof is based on the following definitions and theorem.

For $\theta \in (0, \pi)$ and $C \geq 0$, set $\Sigma_{\theta, C} = \{\lambda \in \mathbf{C} \mid |\lambda| \geq C, \ \arg \lambda \in [-\theta, \theta]\}$. Set $\Sigma_\theta = \Sigma_{\theta, 0}$.

Definition 15.1 Let A be an operator in the Banach space $\mathcal{B}$, and let there exist $\theta \in (0, \pi)$, $C \geq 0$, and C_1 such that for $\lambda \in \Sigma_{\theta, C}$, $\lambda + A$ is invertible, and the resolvent satisfies the estimate

$$||(\lambda + A)^{-1}|| \leq C_1 (1 + |\lambda|)^{-1}. \tag{15.50}$$

Then A is called a *weakly θ-positive operator*. If $C = 0$, A is called θ-positive.

Let $\mathcal{L}_{\theta, C} = \partial \Sigma_{\theta, C}$ be a regular contour, with a parameterisation $\lambda = \lambda(\sigma)$ satisfying $\arg \lambda(\sigma) = \pm \theta$ for σ in a neighbourhood of $\pm \infty$. Set $\mathcal{L}_\theta = \mathcal{L}_{\theta, 0}$.

The following theorem is a special form of the representation theorem for the analytic semigroups (see Section IX.10 in Yosida (1964)).

Theorem 15.18 *Let A be an unbounded operator in the Banach space $\mathcal{B}$, and let there exist $\theta \in (\pi/2, \pi)$ and C such that A is weakly θ-positive. Then*

a) for any $g_0 \in \mathcal{B}$, and any $t > 0$, the following integral is well-defined

$$\exp(-tA)g_0 = (2\pi i)^{-1} \int_{\mathcal{L}_{\theta, C}} e^{t\lambda} (\lambda + A)^{-1} g_0 d\lambda; \tag{15.51}$$

b) Eq. (15.51) defines a strongly continuous semigroup $\{T_t\}_{t \geq 0}$ in $\mathcal{B}$, i.e.,

- $T_0 = I$;

- $T_t = \exp(-tA)$, $t > 0$;
- $T_{t+\tau} = T_t T_\tau$ for $t, \tau \geq 0$;
- for any $t \geq 0$ and $g_0 \in \mathcal{B}$, $\lim_{\tau \to t} T_\tau g_0 = T_t g_0$ in the topology of $\mathcal{B}$;

c) $f(t) = \exp(-tA)g_0$ is a solution to the problem Eq. (15.47)–Eq. (15.48) with the initial datum $g_0 \in \mathcal{B}$.

To deduce Theorem 15.17 from Theorem 15.18, we need two auxiliary results.

Lemma 15.9 *There exist $C_0 > 0$ and $\theta \in (\pi/2, \pi)$ such that if $(\lambda, \xi) \in \Sigma_\theta \times \mathbf{R}$, then*

$$|(\lambda + a(\xi))^{-1}| \leq C_0(|\lambda| + \langle \xi \rangle^m)^{-1}. \tag{15.52}$$

Proof. If $c > 0$ is sufficiently small and $\langle \xi \rangle^m < c|\lambda|$, then from Eq. (15.34) and the triangle inequality we deduce

$$|\lambda + a(\xi)| \geq (|\lambda| + \langle \xi \rangle^m)/2,$$

and Eq. (15.52) holds for these (ξ, λ). Fix $c > 0$; then from Eq. (15.38), there exists $\theta \in (\pi/2, \pi)$ such that if $|\lambda| \leq c^{-1}\langle \xi \rangle^m$ and $\lambda \in \Sigma_\theta$, then $\Re\lambda \geq -\Re a(\xi)/2$, and hence for some $c_1, c_2 > 0$,

$$|\lambda + a(\xi)| \geq c_1 \langle \xi \rangle^m \geq c_2(|\lambda| + \langle \xi \rangle^m).$$

Thus, Eq. (15.52) holds in this case as well. $\qquad\square$

From Theorem 15.4 and Lemma 15.9, we conclude that there exist $C_1 > 0$ and $\theta \in (\pi/2, \pi)$ such that if $\lambda \in \Sigma_\theta$, then Eq. (15.50) hold. Hence, Theorem 15.18 is applicable, and the solution to the problem Eq. (15.47)–Eq. (15.48) is given by Eq. (15.51) with $A = A^s$.

By making the Fourier transform w.r.t. x, then changing the variable $\lambda = i\eta$, and deforming the contour $\{\eta \in \mathbf{C} \mid i\eta \in \mathcal{L}_\theta\}$ into the real line $\Im\eta = 0$, we obtain that Eq. (15.51) gives the solution Eq. (15.43) to the problem Eq. (15.36)–Eq. (15.37) with $g = 0$. In particular, for any $g_0 \in H^s(\mathbf{R}^n)$, $f(t) = \exp[-tA^s]g_0$ is of the class $C^0([0, +\infty); H^s(\mathbf{R}^n))$, and f satisfies the initial condition Eq. (15.48), where the limit is understood in the sense of the topology of $H^s(\mathbf{R}^n)$.

It remains to prove the estimate Eq. (15.49). First, notice that if we make the change of the unknown $f(t) = e^{-\gamma t}f_\gamma(t)$ in Eq. (15.47)–

Eq. (15.48), we obtain

$$f'_\gamma(t) + (A^s - \gamma)f_\gamma(t) = 0, \qquad (15.53)$$
$$f_\gamma(0) = g_0. \qquad (15.54)$$

Due to Eq. (15.38) and the condition $\gamma < c_0$, the problem Eq. (15.53)–Eq. (15.54) enjoys the same properties as the problem Eq. (15.47)–Eq. (15.48), and estimates Eq. (15.49) for f are equivalent to estimates Eq. (15.49) with $\gamma = 0$ for f_γ. Hence, it suffices to prove Eq. (15.49) with $\gamma = 0$.

By differentiating under the integral sign in Eq. (15.51) and using Eq. (15.52), we obtain

$$\|f^{(j)}(t)\|_s \le C \int_{-\infty}^{+\infty} (1 + |\sigma|)^j e^{t\sigma \cos\theta} d\sigma \|g_0\|_s.$$

For any $t_0 > 0$, the integral converges uniformly in $t \ge t_0$, since $\theta > \pi/2$, and we deduce that Eq. (15.49) holds with $r = s$. By applying to Eq. (15.47) $a(D)^{-1}$, which maps $H^s(\mathbf{R}^n)$ to $H^{s+m}(\mathbf{R}^n)$ due to Eq. (15.42) and Theorem 15.4, we find that

$$f(t) = -a(D)^{-1}f'(t)$$

satisfies Eq. (15.49) with $r = s+m$. By induction, we obtain that Eq. (15.49) holds with any r, and Theorem 15.17 is proved.

15.6.4 *Parabolic equations and the Hölder-Zygmund spaces*

The method in Subsection 15.6.2 uses the Fourier transform, and hence it is difficult to use it in other scales of spaces, e.g., the Hölder-Zygmund spaces, whereas the method in Subsection 15.6.3 based on the general representation theorem for analytic semigroups can be modified quite easily. In fact, we only need to know that $a(D)$ acts in a given scale of spaces, and its resolvent enjoys the estimate Eq. (15.51).

Lemma 15.10   *Let a satisfy the estimates Eq. (15.23) and Eq. (15.38). Then there exist $\theta \in (\pi/2, \pi)$ and $C_j, j \ge 0$, such that for all $\lambda \in \Sigma_\theta$, and $\xi \in \mathbf{R}^n$*

$$\sum_{|\alpha|=j} |D_\xi^\alpha((\lambda + a(\xi))^{-1})|\langle\xi\rangle^j \le C_j(1 + |\lambda|)^{-1}, \quad j = 0, 1, \dots. \qquad (15.55)$$

Proof. For $j = 0$, this is Lemma 15.9, and Eq. (15.55) for $j \geq 1$ can be easily proved by induction, the Leibnitz rule, Eq. (15.50) and Eq. (15.23) being used. □

For $s \in \mathbf{R}$, denote by A^s an unbounded operator in $\mathcal{C}^s(\mathbf{R}^n)$, with the domain

$$\mathcal{D}(A^s) = \{u \in \mathcal{C}^s(\mathbf{R}^n) \mid A^s u := a(D)u \in \mathcal{C}^s(\mathbf{R}^n)\}.$$

It is possible to show that $\mathcal{D}(A^s) = \mathcal{C}^{s+m}(\mathbf{R}^n)$.

From Lemma 15.10 and Theorem 15.10, we obtain

Lemma 15.11 *Let $s, m \in \mathbf{R}$, and let a satisfy the estimates Eq. (15.23) and Eq. (15.38). Then there exist $\theta \in (\pi/2, \pi)$ and C such that for all $\lambda \in \Sigma_\theta$,*

$$\|(\lambda + A^s)^{-1}\|_{\mathcal{C}^s \to \mathcal{C}^s} \leq C(1 + |\lambda|)^{-1}, \tag{15.56}$$

and by replacing in the proof of Theorem 15.17 the scale of the Sobolev spaces with that of the Hölder-Zygmund spaces, we obtain the Hölder-Zygmund analogue of Theorem 15.17.

Theorem 15.19 *Let a satisfy the estimates Eq. (15.23) and Eq. (15.38). Then for any $s \in \mathbf{R}$ and $g_0 \in \mathcal{C}^s(\mathbf{R}^n)$, the problem Eq. (15.47)–Eq. (15.48) has a solution $f \in C^0([0, +\infty); \mathcal{C}^s(\mathbf{R}^n))$.*

The solution is unique. It is given by the RHS of Eq. (15.51), and for any $t_0 > 0$, r, $j \in \mathbf{Z}_+$, and $\gamma < c_0$, where $c_0 > 0$ is the constant in Eq. (15.38), the solution satisfies the following estimate:

$$\sup_{t \geq t_0} \|e^{\gamma t} f^{(j)}(t)\|_{C^r} < +\infty. \tag{15.57}$$

Notice that due to the remark after Theorem 15.10, the results of this subsection are valid for any other scale of Besov spaces.

15.6.5 *The inhomogeneous parabolic equation and the asymptotics of the solution as $t \to +\infty$*

Consider the inhomogeneous variant of the problem Eq. (15.47)–Eq. (15.48):

$$f'(t) + A^s f(t) = g(t), \quad t > 0, \tag{15.58}$$

$$f(0) = g_0. \tag{15.59}$$

Theorem 15.20   *Let a satisfy the estimates Eq. (15.23) and Eq. (15.38).*
Then for any $s \in \mathbf{R}$, and functions $g \in C^0([0, +\infty); C^s(\mathbf{R}^n))$ and $g_0 \in C^s(\mathbf{R}^n)$, the following statements hold:

a) *the problem Eq. (15.58)–Eq. (15.59) has a unique solution of the class $C^0([0, +\infty); C^s(\mathbf{R}^n))$, which is given by*

$$f(t) = \int_0^t T_{t-\tau} g(\tau) d\tau + T_t g_0; \tag{15.60}$$

b) $f \in C^1((0, +\infty); C^s(\mathbf{R}^n)) \cap C^0((0, +\infty); C^{s+m}(\mathbf{R}^n));$
c) *if $g(t) = g$ is independent of t, then f admits the representation*

$$f(t) = f_1 + f_2, \tag{15.61}$$

where

$$
\begin{aligned}
f_1 &= a(D)^{-1} g \in C^s(\mathbf{R}^n), \\
f_2 &= \exp[-tA^s](g_0 - f_1);
\end{aligned}
$$

d) *for any $t_0 > 0$, positive non-integer r, $j \in \mathbf{Z}_+$, and $\gamma < c_0$, where $c_0 > 0$ is the constant in Eq. (15.38), f_2 satisfies the estimate Eq. (15.57).*

Proof.   a)-b) Direct verification; the details are left to the reader as an exercise.

     c) Set $f_2(t) = f(t) - f_1$. The problem Eq. (15.58)–Eq. (15.59) becomes the problem Eq. (15.47)–Eq. (15.48) for f_2 with $g_0 - f_1 \in C^s(\mathbf{R}^n)$ on the RHS of Eq. (15.48). After solving this problem and applying Eq. (15.57), we obtain c).   □

15.7   The Wiener-Hopf equation on a half-line I

15.7.1   *Statement of the problem*

Let $m \geq 0$ and $a \in S^m(\mathbf{R})$. Given (generalized) functions g on $\mathbf{R}_+$ and g^r on $\overline{\mathbf{R}_-}$, consider a problem: find u satisfying

$$
\begin{aligned}
a(D)u(x) &= g^0(x), & x > 0, & \tag{15.62} \\
u(x) &= g^r(x), & x \leq 0. & \tag{15.63}
\end{aligned}
$$

Take any extension lg^r of g^r on $\mathbf{R}$, and introduce $f = u - lg^r$, $g = g^0 - p_+a(D)lg^r$. In terms of f and g, Eq. (15.62) and Eq. (15.63) become

$$a(D)f(x) = g(x), \quad x > 0, \tag{15.64}$$
$$f(x) = 0, \quad x \leq 0. \tag{15.65}$$

Assume that $g \in H^{s-m}(\mathbf{R}_+)$, and interpret the problem Eq. (15.64)–Eq. (15.65) as follows: find $u \in \overset{o}{H}{}^{s}(\mathbf{R}_+)$ satisfying

$$p_+a(D)u = g. \tag{15.66}$$

This is the Wiener-Hopf equation. In order that the problem Eq. (15.66) be well-posed, the symbol a must satisfy some regularity conditions.

Definition 15.2 We say that $a \in S^m_{\text{reg}}(\mathbf{R})$ and call it a *regular symbol* of order m, if the following conditions hold:

(i) $a \in S^m(\mathbf{R})$;
(ii) there exists $C > 0$ such that

$$a(\xi) \neq 0, \quad \forall\, \xi \in \mathbf{R}; \tag{15.67}$$

(iii) there exist non-zero complex constants $d_\pm$ and $\rho_1 \in (0,1]$ such that as $\xi \to \pm\infty$,

$$a(\xi) = d_\pm|\xi|^m + O(|\xi|^{m-\rho_1}); \tag{15.68}$$

(iv) there exist $C > 0$ and $\rho_2 \in (0,1]$ such that for all $\xi \in \mathbf{R}$,

$$|a'(\xi)| \leq C\langle\xi\rangle^{m-\rho_2}. \tag{15.69}$$

Notice that Eq. (15.67)-Eq. (15.68) imply that a is elliptic, i.e., Eq. (15.21) holds.

15.7.2 *The Wiener-Hopf factorization*

The Wiener-Hopf method starts with the construction of functions $a_+(\xi)$ and $a_-(\xi)$, which admit the analytic continuation into the upper half-plane $\Im\xi > 0$ and the lower half-plane $\Im\xi < 0$, respectively, and satisfy

$$a(\xi) = a_-(\xi)a_+(\xi), \quad \xi \in \mathbf{R}. \tag{15.70}$$

Example 15.7   Let

$$a(\xi) = \sum_{j=0}^{m} a_j \xi^j$$

be a polynomial of degree m, with no real zeroes. Clearly, conditions Eq. (15.67)–Eq. (15.69) are satisfied, and if $\{\xi_j\}_{1\leq j\leq m}$ is the set of zeroes of a, then we may set

$$a_+(\xi) = a_m \prod_{\Im\xi_j<0} (\xi - \xi_j),$$

$$a_-(\xi) = \prod_{\Im\xi_j>0} (\xi - \xi_j).$$

In the general case, the construction is rather lengthy, so the reader must be patient.

Choose $d \in \mathbf{C} \setminus \{0\}$ and $\kappa_0 \in \mathbf{C}$ so that the function

$$B_0(\xi) := d^{-1}(1 + i\xi)^{\kappa_0}(1 - i\xi)^{-\kappa_0}a(\xi)(1 + \xi^2)^{-m/2}$$

satisfies

$$\lim_{\xi\to\pm\infty} B_0(\xi) = 1. \tag{15.71}$$

By taking the logarithm of $B_0(\xi)$ and using Eq. (15.68) and Eq. (15.71), we obtain that d and κ_0 solve the system

$$\ln(d_\pm/d) \pm i\pi\kappa_0 = 0.$$

(We have chosen the branch of the logarithm so that $\ln a \in \mathbf{R}$ for a positive a.) We see that d must be equal to

$$d = (d_+d_-)^{1/2} = \exp[\ln(d_+d_-)/2], \tag{15.72}$$

and therefore

$$\kappa_0 = i\ln(d_+/d_-)/2\pi. \tag{15.73}$$

Due to Eq. (15.67) and Eq. (15.69), B_0 is a continuous function, which does not vanish on $\mathbf{R}$, hence from Eq. (15.71), we conclude that the winding number of the curve $\{B_0(\xi) \mid \xi \in (-\infty, +\infty)\}$ around zero

$$l = (2\pi)^{-1} \int_{-\infty}^{+\infty} d\arg B_0(\xi) \tag{15.74}$$

is an integer. Set

$$\kappa_- = m/2 - \kappa_0 - l, \quad \kappa_+ = m/2 + \kappa_0 + l, \qquad (15.75)$$

call κ_- the *index of the factorization* of the symbol a, and introduce

$$B(\xi) = (\xi - i)^l (\xi + i)^{-l} B_0(\xi);$$

then

$$\begin{aligned} B(\xi) &= (-1)^l (1 + i\xi)^l (1 - i\xi)^{-1} B_0(\xi) && (15.76) \\ &= (-1)^l d^{-1} (1 + i\xi)^{-\kappa_-} (1 - i\xi)^{-\kappa_+} a(\xi), && (15.77) \end{aligned}$$

and from Eq. (15.74),

$$(2\pi)^{-1} \int_{-\infty}^{+\infty} d\arg B(\xi) = 0. \qquad (15.78)$$

Due to Eq. (15.78), $b = \ln B$ is well-defined on $\mathbf{R}$, and by using Eq. (15.68), we conclude that

$$B(\xi) = 1 + O(|\xi|^{-\rho_1}), \quad \text{as } \xi \to \pm\infty; \qquad (15.79)$$

hence

$$b(\xi) = O(|\xi|^{-\rho_1}), \quad \text{as } \xi \to \pm\infty. \qquad (15.80)$$

For $\xi \in \mathbf{R}$ and $\sigma > 0$, set

$$\begin{aligned} b_+(\xi + i\sigma) &= -(2\pi i)^{-1} \int_{-\infty}^{+\infty} \frac{b(\eta)}{\xi + i\sigma - \eta} d\eta, && (15.81) \\ b_-(\xi - i\sigma) &= (2\pi i)^{-1} \int_{-\infty}^{+\infty} \frac{b(\eta)}{\xi - i\sigma - \eta} d\eta. && (15.82) \end{aligned}$$

Due to Eq. (15.80), the integrals in Eq. (15.81)–Eq. (15.82) converge. Set

$$\begin{aligned} a_+(\xi) &= d(-1)^l (1 - i\xi)^{\kappa_+} \exp[b_+(\xi)], && \Im\xi > 0, && (15.83) \\ a_-(\xi) &= (1 + i\xi)^{\kappa_-} \exp[b_-(\xi)], && \Im\xi < 0. && (15.84) \end{aligned}$$

Theorem 15.21   *Functions $a_\pm$ enjoy the following properties:*

(a_+) $a_+(\xi)$ *is holomorphic in the upper half-plane $\Im\xi > 0$, and admits the continuous extension up to the boundary $\Im\xi = 0$;*

(b_+) *in the closed half-plane, $a_+(\xi)$ admits an estimate*

$$c(1 + |\xi|)^{\Re\kappa_+} \leq |a_+(\xi)| \leq C(1 + |\xi|)^{\Re\kappa_+}, \qquad (15.85)$$

where $C, c > 0$ are independent of ξ in the half-plane $\Im \xi \geq 0$;

(c_+) *for any $\tau > 0$, $\epsilon > 0$ and $j = 1, 2, \ldots$, there exists $C_{\tau, \epsilon, j}$ such that for all ξ in the half-plane $\Im \xi \geq \tau$,*

$$|a_+^{(j)}(\xi)| \leq C_{\tau, \epsilon, j}(1 + |\xi|)^{\Re \kappa_+ - \rho_1 + \epsilon}; \tag{15.86}$$

(d_+) $a_+^{\pm 1}$ *admits a representation*

$$a_+(\xi)^{\pm 1} = d^{\pm 1}(-1)^l(1 - i\xi)^{\pm \kappa_+} + t_+^{\pm}(\xi), \tag{15.87}$$

where $t_+^{\pm}$ admits the following estimate: for any $\epsilon > 0$, there exists $C_\epsilon > 0$ such that for all ξ in the half-plane $\Im \xi \geq 0$,

$$|t_+^{\pm}(\xi)| \leq C_\epsilon(1 + |\xi|)^{\pm \Re \kappa_+ - \rho + \epsilon}, \tag{15.88}$$

where $\rho = \min\{\rho_1, \rho_2\} \in (0, 1]$;

(a_-) $a_-(\xi)$ *is holomorphic in the lower half-plane $\Im \xi < 0$, and admits the continuous extension up to the boundary $\Im \xi = 0$;*

(b_-) *in the closed half-plane, $a_-(\xi)$ admits an estimate*

$$c(1 + |\xi|)^{\Re \kappa_-} \leq |a_-(\xi)| \leq C(1 + |\xi|)^{\Re \kappa_-}, \tag{15.89}$$

where $C, c > 0$ are independent of ξ in the half-plane $\Im \xi \leq 0$;

(c_-) *for any $\tau > 0$, $\epsilon > 0$ and $j = 1, 2, \ldots$, there exists $C_{\tau, \epsilon, j}$ such that for all ξ in the half-plane $\Im \xi \leq -\tau$,*

$$|a_-^{(j)}(\xi)| \leq C_{\tau, \epsilon, j}(1 + |\xi|)^{\Re \kappa_- - \rho_1 + \epsilon}; \tag{15.90}$$

(d_-) $a_-^{\pm 1}$ *admits a representation*

$$a_-(\xi)^{\pm 1} = (1 + i\xi)^{\pm \kappa_-} + t_-^{\pm}(\xi), \tag{15.91}$$

where $t_-^{\pm}$ admits the following estimate: for any $\epsilon > 0$, there exists $C_\epsilon > 0$ such that for all ξ in the half-plane $\Im \xi \leq 0$,

$$|t_-^{\pm}(\xi)| \leq C_\epsilon(1 + |\xi|)^{\pm \Re \kappa_- - \rho + \epsilon}; \tag{15.92}$$

(e) on the real axis, Eq. (15.70) holds;

(f) conditions $(a_\pm) - (b_\pm)$ define factors in Eq. (15.70) uniquely, up to scalar multiples, i.e., if $a'_\pm$ satisfy $(a_\pm) - (b_\pm)$ and Eq. (15.70), then there exists a constant c such that

$$a'_+ = ca_+, \quad a'_- = c^{-1}a_-. \tag{15.93}$$

Proof.   First, we prove $(a_+) - (d_+)$; $(a_-) - (d_-)$ are proved similarly. Since the function $d(-1)^l(1 - i\xi)^{\kappa_+}$ satisfies $(a_+) - (d_+)$, it follows from Eq. (15.83), that it suffices to prove the corresponding properties of b_+, namely

$b_+(\xi)$ is holomorphic in the upper half-plane $\Im\xi > 0$, admits the continuous extension into the closed half-plane and satisfies estimates Eq. (15.87) and Eq. (15.88) with $\kappa_+ = 0$.

By differentiating under the integral sign in Eq. (15.81) and using Eq. (15.80), we obtain, for ξ in the half-plane $\Im\xi \geq \tau > 0$ and $j = 1, 2, \ldots$:

$$|(b_+)^{(j)}(\xi)| \leq C_\tau \int_{-\infty}^{+\infty} (1 + |\eta|)^{-\rho_1}|\xi - \eta|^{-1-j}d\eta. \tag{15.94}$$

From the triangle inequality, for $\eta \in \mathbf{R}$ and the same ξ,

$$(1 + |\eta|)^{-1} \leq C_{1,\tau}|\xi|^{-1}|\xi - \eta|, \tag{15.95}$$

therefore for any $\omega \in [0, \rho_2]$, the RHS in Eq. (15.94) admits an estimate via

$$C_{2,\tau}|\xi|^{-\omega} \int_{-\infty}^{+\infty} |\xi - \eta|^{-1-j+\omega}d\eta. \tag{15.96}$$

We may take any $\omega < 1$, $\omega \in [0, \rho_1]$; with this choice, for $j \geq 1$, the integral in Eq. (15.96) converges, and we obtain that $b_+(\xi)$ satisfies Eq. (15.87) with $\kappa_+ = 0$.

Now we prove Eq. (15.88) for b_+ with $\kappa_+ = 0$, in the half-plane $\Im\xi > 0$. Fix such ξ, and introduce the following subsets of $\mathbf{R}$:

$$
\begin{aligned}
J_1(\xi) &= \{\eta \in \mathbf{R} \mid |\xi - \eta| \geq 1, \ |\xi| \leq |\eta|/2\}, \\
J_2(\xi) &= \{\eta \in \mathbf{R} \mid |\xi - \eta| \geq 1, \ |\xi| \geq 2|\eta|\}, \\
J_3(\xi) &= \{\eta \in \mathbf{R} \mid |\xi - \eta| \geq 1, \ |\eta|/2 \leq |\xi| \leq 2|\eta|\}, \\
J_4(\xi) &= \{\eta \in \mathbf{R} \mid |\xi - \eta| \leq 1\}.
\end{aligned}
$$

Then for $j = 1, 2, 3, 4$ and $\Im\xi > 0$, define $b_{+,j}(\xi)$ by Eq. (15.81) with the integration over $J_j(\xi)$. Clearly,

$$b_+(\xi) = \sum_{j=1}^{4} b_{+,j}(\xi).$$

Similarly to Eq. (15.94), we obtain for $j = 1, 2, 3$

$$|b_{+,j}(\xi)| \leq C \int_{J_j(\xi)} (1 + |\eta|)^{-\rho_1} |\xi - \eta|^{-1} d\eta. \tag{15.97}$$

For any $\alpha \in [0, 1]$, there exists C_α such that for any $\eta \in J_1(\xi)$,

$$|\xi - \eta|^{-1} \leq C_\alpha (1 + |\xi|)^{-\alpha} (1 + |\eta|)^{-1+\alpha}, \tag{15.98}$$

and from Eq. (15.97) and Eq. (15.98), we deduce for $j = 1$, with arbitrary $\epsilon > 0$,

$$\begin{aligned} |b_{+,j}(\xi)| &\leq C_\epsilon (1 + |\xi|)^{-\rho_1+\epsilon} \int_{J_j(\xi)} (1 + |\eta|)^{-1-\epsilon} d\eta \tag{15.99} \\ &\leq C_{1,\epsilon} (1 + |\xi|)^{-\rho_1+\epsilon}. \end{aligned}$$

Further, there exist $C, C_1 > 0$ such that for any $\epsilon \in (0, \rho_1)$ and all $\eta \in J_2(\xi)$,

$$\begin{aligned} (1 + |\eta|)^{-\rho_1} |\xi - \eta|^{-1} &\leq C(1 + |\eta|)^{-\rho_1}(1 + |\xi|)^{-1} \tag{15.100} \\ &\leq C_1(1 + |\eta|)^{-1-\epsilon}(1 + |\xi|)^{-\rho_1+\epsilon}, \end{aligned}$$

and from Eq. (15.97) and Eq. (15.100) we deduce Eq. (15.99) with $j = 2$. In the case $j = 3$, the proof of Eq. (15.99) is different:

$$\begin{aligned} |(b_{+,3}(\xi)| &\leq C(1 + |\xi|)^{-\rho_1} \int_{1 \leq |\xi-\eta| \leq 3|\xi|} (1 + |\xi - \eta|)^{-1} d\eta \\ &\leq C(1 + |\xi|)^{-\rho_1}(1 + \ln(1 + |\xi|)) \\ &\leq C_\epsilon (1 + |\xi|)^{-\rho_1+\epsilon}. \tag{15.101} \end{aligned}$$

Now we consider $b_{+,4}(\xi)$. Notice that $b_{+,4}(\xi) = 0$ unless $\xi = \zeta + i\sigma$, where $\zeta \in \mathbf{R}$ and $0 < \sigma < 1$, and use the Lagrange formula and Eq. (15.67), Eq. (15.69); we obtain for $\eta \in J_4(\xi)$,

$$b(\eta) = b(\zeta) + b_1(\zeta, \eta)(\eta - \zeta), \tag{15.102}$$

where $b_1(\zeta, \eta)$ admits an estimate

$$|b_1(\zeta, \eta)| \leq C(1 + |\xi|)^{-\rho_2}. \tag{15.103}$$

By substituting Eq. (15.102) in Eq. (15.81) with the integration over $J_4(\xi)$, and using the estimate

$$|b_1(\zeta, \eta)(\eta - \zeta)/(\zeta - \eta + i\sigma)| \leq C(1 + |\xi|)^{-\rho_2} \tag{15.104}$$

which follows from Eq. (15.103), and the limit

$$\lim_{\sigma \to +0} \int_{|\xi - \eta| \leq 1} (\xi - \eta)^{-1} d\eta = \lim_{\sigma \to +0} \int_{|zeta+i| \leq \sigma^{-1}} (\zeta + i)^{-1} d\zeta$$

$$= \lim_{\sigma \to +0} \ln \frac{(\sigma^{-2} + 1)^{1/2} + i}{-(\sigma^{-2} + 1)^{1/2} + i}$$

$$= i\pi, \tag{15.105}$$

we conclude that $b_{+,4}(\xi)$ satisfies the estimate Eq. (15.99) with $\rho = \min\{\rho_1, \rho_2\}$ instead of ρ_1.

We have shown that $b_{+,j}(\xi), j = 1, 2, 3, 4$, satisfy the estimate Eq. (15.99) with ρ instead of ρ_1, hence $b_+(\xi)$ also does, and to finish the proof of $(a_+) - (d_+)$, it remains to show that b_+ admits the continuous extension up to the boundary $\Im \xi = 0$. We have proved the uniform boundedness of $b_{+,j}(\xi)$, as $\Im \xi \to +0$, $b_{+,4}(\xi)$ being represented as a sum of two terms. Of those, the first one has the limit

$$-(2\pi i)^{-1} b(\zeta) i\pi = b(\zeta)/2$$

as $\sigma \to +0$; by the inspection of the proof, it is seen that the integrands in the integrals defining the second term and $b_{+,j}(\xi)$ for $j = 1, 2, 3$ have limits as $\sigma \to +0$ and ζ remains fixed. From the Lebesgue theorem, all these integrals also have limits as $\sigma \to +0$. This finishes the proof of $(a_+) - (d_+)$.

We see that Eq. (15.70) follows from Eq. (15.76) and the following equality:

$$b_+(\xi) + b_-(\xi) = b(\xi)(= \ln B(\xi)), \quad \xi \in \mathbf{R}. \tag{15.106}$$

From the proof of $(a_+) - (d_+)$ above and from its implied counterpart for $(a_-) - (d_-)$, we infer that as $\sigma \to +0$,

$$b_{\pm}(\zeta \pm i\sigma) \to b(\zeta)/2 \pm \tilde{b}(\zeta),$$

where $\tilde{b}$ is the same for both signs $\pm$, and Eq. (15.106) is proved.

It remains to prove part (f). Suppose, there exists another pair $a'_{\pm}$ satisfying $(a_{\pm}) - (b_{\pm})$ and Eq. (15.70). Then on the real axis

$$a'_+(\xi)/a_+(\xi) = a_-(\xi)/a'_-(\xi),$$

and the LHS (resp., the RHS) admits a bounded holomorphic extension into the upper (resp., lower) half-plane. Thus, we have a bounded holo-

morphic function in the whole complex plane. By the Liouville theorem, it
is constant, and Eq. (15.93) is proved.   □

15.7.3   Main Theorems

Take any extension $lg \in H^{s-m}(\mathbf{R})$ and write Eq. (15.66) as

$$a(D)u = lg + g_-, \qquad (15.107)$$

where $g_- \in \overset{o}{H}{}^{s-m}(\mathbf{R}_-)$. On the strength of Eq. (15.85), we can multiply
Eq. (15.107) by $a_+(D)^{-1}$; from Eq. (15.70), the LHS becomes $a_-(D)u$, and
we obtain

$$a_-(D)u = a_+(D)^{-1}lg + g_{1,-}, \qquad (15.108)$$

where on the strength of Theorem 15.12, $g_{1,-} \in \overset{o}{H}{}^{s-\Re\kappa_-}(\mathbf{R}_-)$, $a_-(D)u \in \overset{o}{H}{}^{s-\Re\kappa_-}(\mathbf{R}_+)$, and by Theorem 15.4, $a_+(D)^{-1}lg \in H^{s-\Re\kappa_-}(\mathbf{R})$.

Consider the following 3 cases.

Case I. $s - \Re\kappa_- \in (-1/2, 1/2)$. In this case, we apply Lemma 15.7 and
deduce from Eq. (15.108)

$$a_-(D)u = \theta_+ a_+(D)^{-1}lg \in \overset{o}{H}{}^{s-\Re\kappa_-}(\mathbf{R}_+).$$

By applying $a_-(D)^{-1}$ and using Eq. (15.89) and Theorem 15.12, we obtain

$$u = a_-(D)^{-1}\theta_+ a_+(D)^{-1}lg \in \overset{o}{H}{}^{s}(\mathbf{R}_+). \qquad (15.109)$$

Theorem 15.22   *Let $s - \Re\kappa_- \in (-1/2, 1/2)$. Then the operator*

$$p_+ a(D) : \overset{o}{H}{}^{s}(\mathbf{R}_+) \to H^{s-m}(\mathbf{R}_+)$$

is invertible, with the inverse

$$H^{s-m}(\mathbf{R}_+) \ni g \mapsto u \in H^{s-m}(\mathbf{R}_+),$$

where u is given by Eq. (15.109).

Proof.   We have already shown that Eq. (15.109) defines a bounded
left inverse. By applying to the RHS of Eq. (15.109) $p_+a(D)$ and using
Eq. (15.93), we obtain $p_+a_+(D)\theta_+a_+(D)^{-1}lg$. On the strength of Lemma
15.7, this expression can be represented as

$$p_+a_+(D)a_+(D)^{-1}lg - p_+a_+(D)\theta_-a_+(D)^{-1}lg = g.$$

The second term on the LHS is equal to zero since $\theta_- a_+(D)^{-1} lg \in \overset{o}{H}{}^{s-\Re\kappa_-}$ $(\mathbf{R}_-)$, and hence, from Theorem 15.12, $a_+(D)\theta_- a_+(D)^{-1} lg \in \overset{o}{H}{}^{s-m}(\mathbf{R}_-)$. Hence, the map defined by

$$g \mapsto a_-(D)^{-1}\theta_+ a_+(D)^{-1} lg$$

is the right inverse. □

Corollary 15.1 *Let $s - \Re\kappa_- \in (-1/2, 1/2)$, and let g in Eq. (15.66) belong to $H^r(\mathbf{R}_+)$, where $r + \kappa_+ = q + s'$, q is a positive integer and $s' \in (-1/2, 1/2)$.*

Then $u \in \overset{o}{H}{}^{s}(\mathbf{R}_+)$, the solution to Eq. (15.66), admits a representation

$$u = \sum_{j=1}^{q} c_j(lg)\Lambda_-^{-j}(D)a_-(D)^{-1}\delta_0 + \Lambda_-^{-q}a_-(D)^{-1}\theta_+ \Lambda_-^{q}(D)a_+(D)^{-1} lg,$$

$$(15.110)$$

where

$$c_j(lg) = (\Lambda_-^{j-1}(D)a_+(D)^{-1} lg)(0). \qquad (15.111)$$

Proof. Apply Eq. (15.31) to Eq. (15.109). □

Case II. $s - \Re\kappa_- > 1/2$.

In this case, we may regard f as an element of a wider space $H^{s'-m}(\mathbf{R}_+)$, where $|s' - \Re\kappa_-| < 1/2$, find a unique solution in $\overset{o}{H}{}^{s'}(\mathbf{R}_+) \supset \overset{o}{H}{}^{s}(\mathbf{R}_+)$, and after that check whether the solution defined by Eq. (15.109) belongs to $\overset{o}{H}{}^{s}(\mathbf{R}_+)$. If it does, we have a unique solution of the Wiener-Hopf equation Eq. (15.66), of the class $\overset{o}{H}{}^{s}(\mathbf{R}_+)$, and if it does not, Eq. (15.66) has no solutions of this class. In the latter case, one may introduce into Eq. (15.66) potential operators in order to obtain a solvable problem (see, e.g., Eskin (1973), Section 8), but we will not need this construction here.

Case III. $s - \Re\kappa_- = -q + s'$, where q is a positive integer and $|s'| < 1/2$.

Due to Theorem 15.4, $\Lambda_-(D)^{-q}a_+(D)^{-1} lg \in H^{s'}(\mathbf{R})$, hence we can apply Lemma 15.7:

$$\Lambda_-(D)^{-q}a_+(D)^{-1} lg = \theta_+ \Lambda_-(D)^{-q}a_+(D)^{-1} lg + \theta_- \Lambda_-(D)^{-q}a_+(D)^{-1} lg.$$

$$(15.112)$$

Multiply Eq. (15.112) by $\Lambda_-(D)^q$:

$$
\begin{aligned}
a_+(D)^{-1}lg &= \Lambda_-(D)^q\theta_+\Lambda_-(D)^{-q}a_+(D)^{-1}lg \qquad (15.113)\\
&+ \Lambda_-(D)^q\theta_-\Lambda_-(D)^{-q}a_+(D)^{-1}lg.
\end{aligned}
$$

By inserting Eq. (15.113) into Eq. (15.108) and rearranging terms, we obtain

$$
\begin{aligned}
a_-(D)u - \Lambda_-(D)^q\theta_+\Lambda_-(D)^{-q}a_+(D)^{-1}lg \qquad (15.114)\\
= \Lambda_-(D)^q\theta_-\Lambda_-(D)^{-q}a_+(D)^{-1}lg + g_{1,-}.
\end{aligned}
$$

By Theorem 15.12, the LHS in Eq. (15.114) belongs to $\overset{o}{H}{}^{\,s-\Re\kappa_-}(\mathbf{R}_+)$, and the RHS belongs to $\overset{o}{H}{}^{\,s-\Re\kappa_-}(\mathbf{R}_-)$, hence by Theorem 15.16, there exist constants $c_j, 1 \le j \le q$, such that

$$
a_-(D)u - \Lambda_-(D)^q\theta_+\Lambda_-(D)^{-q}a_+(D)^{-1}lg = \sum_{j=1}^{q} c_j D^{j-1}\delta_0.
$$

By multiplying with $a_-(D)^{-1}$ and leaving u alone on the left, we obtain

Theorem 15.23 *Let $s - \Re\kappa_- = -q + s'$, where q is a positive integer and $|s'| < 1/2$.*

Then for any $g \in H^{s-m}(\mathbf{R}_+)$, a solution to the Wiener-Hopf equation Eq. (15.66) exists but it is non-unique, and the general solution is given by

$$
u = a_-(D)^{-1}\Lambda_-(D)^q\theta_+\Lambda_-(D)^{-q}a_+(D)^{-1}lg + a_-(D)^{-1}\sum_{j=1}^{q} c_j D^{j-1}\delta_0.
$$
$$(15.115)$$

One of standard ways to obtain a well-posed problem is to add to Eq. (15.66) appropriate boundary conditions (see, e.g., Eskin (1973), Section 8); for our purposes, a more appropriate way to choose a unique solution is a specification of the behaviour of the solutions to the Wiener-Hopf equation Eq. (15.66), near the boundary. Possible types of the behaviour are studied in the next Subsection.

15.7.4 *The asymptotics of the solution near the boundary*

To simplify the exposition, we restrict ourselves to a subclass of $S^m_{\mathrm{reg}}(\mathbf{R})$, which will arise in our applications to Financial Mathematics, though the general case can be treated in the same manner.

Let $m \in (0, 2]$, $a \in S_{\text{reg}}^m(\mathbf{R})$, and let $\kappa_\pm$ defined from Eq. (15.75), Eq. (15.73) and Eq. (15.68) satisfy: satisfy

$$\kappa_- \in (-1/2, 3/2); \quad \rho_j + \kappa_- > 1. \tag{15.116}$$

Let g, the RHS in Eq. (15.66), be sufficiently smooth; for simplicity, $g \in H^r(\mathbf{R}_+)$, where $r > 1/2 - \kappa_+$, though smaller r (depending on m and $\kappa_\pm$) may suffice. We look for a solution to Eq. (15.66) in $\overset{o}{H}{}^s(\mathbf{R}_+)$, where $s = 0$; when convenient, we may (and will) take smaller s.

Theorem 15.24 *Let $m \in (0, 2)$, $a \in S_{\text{reg}}^m(\mathbf{R})$, Eq. (15.116) hold, $g \in H^r(\mathbf{R}_+)$, where $r > 1/2 - \kappa_+$, and consider a solution u to the Wiener-Hopf equation Eq. (15.66), of the class $L_2(\mathbf{R}_+)$.*

Then

I. In the case $\Re\kappa_- \in (1/2, 3/2)$, the following three statements hold:

a) for any $c \in \mathbf{C} \setminus \{0\}$, there exists the unique u, which admits the following representation, as $x \to +0$:

$$u(x) = cx_+^{\kappa_- - 1} + O(x_+^{\Re\kappa_- + \rho - 1 - \epsilon}), \tag{15.117}$$

where $x_+ = \max\{x, 0\}$, $\rho = \min\{\rho_1, \rho_2\}$, and $\epsilon > 0$ is arbitrary;

b) there exists the unique u, which admits the following representation, as $x \to +0$:

$$u(x) = \Gamma(\kappa_- + 1)^{-1} c_1(lg) x_+^{\kappa_-} + O(x_+^{\Re\kappa_- + \rho - \epsilon}), \tag{15.118}$$

where $\rho = \min\{\rho_1, \rho_2\}$, $\epsilon > 0$ is arbitrary, and

$$c_1(lg) = (a_+(D)^{-1}lg)(0); \tag{15.119}$$

c) any solution to the Wiener-Hopf equation Eq. (15.66) of the class $L_2(\mathbf{R}_+)$ admits either the representation Eq. (15.117) or Eq. (15.118).

II. In the case $\Re\kappa_- \in (-1/2, 1/2]$, the solution $u \in L_2(\mathbf{R}_+)$ exists; it is unique and admits the representation Eq. (15.118).

Proof. I. From Eq. (15.115),

$$u = \Lambda_-(D)a_-(D)^{-1}\theta_+ \Lambda_-^{-1}(D)a_+(D)^{-1}lg + ca_-(D)^{-1}\delta_0, \tag{15.120}$$

where c is an arbitrary constant. By choosing $lg \in H^r(\mathbf{R})$ and using the assumption $r + \kappa_+ > 1/2$, we see that the equation Eq. (15.31) (with $m = 1$)

is applicable to $f = \Lambda_-^{-1}(D)a_+(D)^{-1}lg \in H^{r+\kappa++1}(\mathbf{R})$, and hence we can rewrite Eq. (15.120) as

$$
\begin{aligned}
u \;=\;& ca_-(D)^{-1}\delta_0 + c_1 a_-(D)^{-1}\Lambda_-^{-1}(D)\delta_0 \\
& + a_-(D)^{-1}\Lambda_-^{-1}(D)\theta_+\Lambda_-(D)a_+(D)^{-1}lg,
\end{aligned}
\tag{15.121}
$$

where c is an arbitrary constant, and $c_1 = (a_+(D)^{-1}lg)(0)$. Suppose, $c \neq 0$. By using Eq. (15.91) and taking into account that $\delta_0 \in \overset{o}{H}{}^{-1/2-\epsilon}(\mathbf{R}_+)$, $\forall\, \epsilon > 0$, we deduce from Eq. (15.121)

$$
u = c(1+iD)^{-\kappa_-}\delta_0 + v_1 + v_2 + v_3,
\tag{15.122}
$$

where

$$
\begin{aligned}
v_1 \;&=\; ct_-^-(D)\delta_0 \in \overset{o}{H}{}^{\Re\kappa_-+\rho-1/2-\epsilon}(\mathbf{R}_+),\ \forall\, \epsilon > 0; \\
v_2 \;&=\; c_1 a_-(D)^{-1}\Lambda_-^{-1}(D)\delta_0 \in \overset{o}{H}{}^{\Re\kappa_-+1/2-\epsilon}(\mathbf{R}_+),\ \forall\, \epsilon > 0; \\
v_3 \;&=\; a_-(D)^{-1}\Lambda_-^{-1}(D)\theta_+\Lambda_-(D)a_+(D)^{-1}lg \in \overset{o}{H}{}^{\Re\kappa_-+1/2}(\mathbf{R}_+).
\end{aligned}
$$

If $\Re\nu > 0$, we have

$$
\mathcal{F}(x_+^{\nu-1}e^{-x})(\xi) = \int_0^{+\infty} e^{-ix\xi - x}x^{\nu-1}dx = \Gamma(\nu)(1+i\xi)^{-\nu},
\tag{15.123}
$$

therefore

$$
(1+iD)^{-\nu}\delta_0 = \Gamma(\nu)^{-1}x_+^{\nu-1}e^{-x}.
\tag{15.124}
$$

By using Theorem 15.9 and Eq. (15.116), we conclude that for any $\epsilon > 0$, $v_1 \in C^{\Re\kappa_-+\rho-1-\epsilon}(\mathbf{R})$, and $v_2, v_3 \in C^{\Re\kappa_--\epsilon}(\mathbf{R})$. Since they are supported on $[0,+\infty)$ and $\rho \leq 1$, we conclude that $v_j(x) = O(x^{\Re\kappa_-+\rho-1-\epsilon})$, for any $\epsilon > 0$. By applying Eq. (15.124) with $\nu = \kappa_-$ to the first term in Eq. (15.122), we obtain Eq. (15.117).

This proves a), and to prove b), we set $c = 0$ in Eq. (15.121), and apply Eq. (15.91) to the first remaining term on the RHS:

$$
u = c_1(lg)(1+iD)^{-\kappa_-+1}\delta_0 + v_{11} + v_3,
\tag{15.125}
$$

where

$$
v_{11} = c_1(lg)t_-^-(D)\Lambda_-^{-1}(D)\delta_0 \in \overset{o}{H}{}^{\kappa_-+\rho+1/2-\epsilon}(\mathbf{R}_+),\ \forall\, \epsilon > 0,
$$

and v_3 is the same as in the proof of a). The same argument as above shows that

$$v_{11}(x) + v_3(x) = O(x^{\Re\kappa_- + \rho - \epsilon}), \quad x \to +0,$$

and by applying Eq. (15.124) with $\nu = \kappa_- + 1$ to the first term in Eq. (15.125), we obtain Eq. (15.118).

II. If $\Re\kappa_- = 1/2$, take $s < 0$ such that $s - \kappa_- \in (-3/2, -1/2)$; then the same argument as in the part I shows that the solution $u \in \overset{o}{H}\!^s(\mathbf{R}_+)$ admits either the representation Eq. (15.117) or Eq. (15.118). Since $x_+^{-1/2}$ is not square integrable in the neighbourhood of zero, Eq. (15.117) is impossible.

It remains to consider the case $\Re\kappa_- \in (-1/2, 1/2)$, when the solution is unique and given by Eq. (15.109). By applying Eq. (15.31) to Eq. (15.109) and arguing as in the part I, we arrive at Eq. (15.118). $\qquad\square$

In the following corollary of Theorem 15.24, we list cases when the bounded and continuous solution exists and it is unique.

Theorem 15.25 *Let assumptions of Theorem 15.24 hold, and let $u \in L_2(\mathbf{R}_+)$ be a solution to the Wiener-Hopf equation Eq. (15.66).*

Then a) if $\kappa_- \in (-1/2, 0)$, and $c_1(lg) \neq 0$, then any solution u is unbounded as $x \to +0$;

b) if $\kappa_- = 0$, then a bounded solution u exists and it is unique. The u is continuous outside the origin, and if $c_1(lg) \neq 0$, it is discontinuous at 0; if $c_1(lg) = 0$, $u \in C_0(\mathbf{R})$;

c) if $\kappa_- \in (0, 1)$, then a bounded u exists; it is unique and belongs to $C_0(\mathbf{R})$;

d) if $\kappa_- = 1$, then a continuous bounded u exists; it is unique and belongs to $C_0(\mathbf{R})$;

e) if $\kappa_- \in (1, 3/2)$, then all u form a 1-dimensional lineal in $C_0(\mathbf{R})$.

In the next theorem, we consider cases when $u \in C_0(\mathbf{R})$, and study the properties of the derivative u' near 0.

Theorem 15.26 *Let assumptions of Theorem 15.24 hold, and let $u \in L_2(\mathbf{R}_+)$ be a solution to the Wiener-Hopf equation Eq. (15.66).*

Then

a) if $0 \leq \kappa_- < 1$, and $c_1(lg) \neq 0$, then $u'(x)$ is unbounded as $x \to +0$;

b) if $\kappa_- = 1$, then $u'(+0) = c_1(lg)$ exists;

c) if $0 < \kappa_- \leq 1$ and $c_1(lg) = 0$, then $u'(+0) = 0$ exists, and $u \in C^1(\mathbf{R})$;

*d) if $1 < \kappa_- < 3/2$, there exists a unique u with bounded u'; it is given
by Eq. (15.118) and belongs to $C^1(\mathbf{R})$.*

Proof.   Note that the behaviour of u' near the origin is the same as the
behaviour of $(1+iD)u = u + u'$, apply $(1+iD)$ to Eq. (15.121) and argue
exactly as in the proofs of Theorem 15.24 and Theorem 15.25.   □

15.8   Parabolic equations on $[0,T] \times \mathbf{R}_+$

15.8.1   *The statement of the boundary problem*

Let $m > 0$, and let $a \in S^m(\mathbf{R})$ satisfy Eq. (15.68) with $\Re d_+ > 0$. Then a is
strongly elliptic, that is, Eq. (15.35) holds. Consider the following problem:

$$(\partial_t + a(D_x))u(x,t) = g(t,x), \quad x > 0,\ t > 0; \qquad (15.126)$$
$$u(0,x) = g_0(x), \quad x > 0; \qquad (15.127)$$
$$u(t,x) = g^r(t,x), \quad x \le 0,\ t \le 0. \qquad (15.128)$$

By changing the unknown

$$u(x,t) = e^{\sigma_0 t} u^{\sigma_0}(x,t),$$

and similarly changing the data, we obtain the problem

$$(\partial_t + a_{\sigma_0}(D_x))u^{\sigma_0}(x,t) = g^{\sigma_0}(t,x), \quad x > 0,\ t > 0; \quad (15.129)$$
$$u^{\sigma_0}(0,x) = g_0(x), \quad x > 0; \qquad (15.130)$$
$$u^{\sigma_0}(t,x) = g^{r,\sigma_0}(t,x), \quad x \le 0,\ t \le 0, \quad (15.131)$$

where $a_{\sigma_0}(\xi) := a(\xi) + \sigma_0$ satisfies Eq. (15.38). In particular, a_{σ_0} satisfies
Eq. (15.67), and if we assume that a satisfies Eq. (15.69), we can conclude
that a_{σ_0} belongs to $S^m_{\text{reg}}(\mathbf{R})$ and satisfies Eq. (15.38). Having in mind
this possibility of changing the unknown and data, we assume that a itself
belongs to $S^m_{\text{reg}}(\mathbf{R})$ and satisfies Eq. (15.38).

Suppose that g^r is sufficiently regular, say, $g^r \in C^1([0,+\infty); H^r(\mathbf{R}_-))$,
where $r \ge m$ (smaller r are also admissible), take any extension $lg^r \in
C^0([0,+\infty); H^r(\mathbf{R}))$, and define

$$f(t,x) = u(t,x) - lg^r(t,x), \qquad x \in \mathbf{R},\ t \ge 0;$$
$$G(t,x) = g(t,x) + (lg^r)'_t(x,t) + a(D_x)lg^r(t,x), \quad x > 0,\ t > 0;$$
$$G_0(x) = g_0(x) - lg^r(x), \qquad x > 0.$$

In terms of f, the problem Eq. (15.126)–Eq. (15.128) becomes

$$(\partial_t + a(D_x))f(x, t) = G(t, x), \quad x > 0, \ t > 0; \qquad (15.132)$$

$$f(0, x) = G_0(x), \quad x > 0; \qquad (15.133)$$

$$f(t, x) = 0, \quad x \leq 0, \ t \leq 0. \qquad (15.134)$$

As in Subsection 15.6.3, we consider the problem Eq. (15.132)–Eq. (15.134) as ODE with the operator coefficient. This time, the latter is not an operator in the whole space but the operator of the Wiener-Hopf equation, and hence the resolvent must be studied by using the technique of Section 15.7. The technique needs some modification in order to obtain the uniform estimate Eq. (15.50) for the resolvent.

15.8.2 *The Wiener-Hopf factorization with a parameter*

Let θ be the same as in Lemma 15.9. We define d, l, κ_0, and κ_- as in Subsection 15.7.2, but change the definitions of $B_0, B, b = \ln B, b_\pm$ and $a_\pm$ in order to be able to obtain estimates uniform in $\lambda \in \Sigma_\theta$. We set

$$\Lambda^s_\mp(\lambda, \xi) = (1 + |\lambda|^{1/m} \pm i\xi)^s, \qquad (15.135)$$

$$B(\lambda, \xi) := (-1)^l d^{-1} \Lambda_-^{-\kappa_-}(\lambda, \xi) \Lambda_+^{-\kappa_+}(\lambda, \xi)(\lambda + a(\xi)). \qquad (15.136)$$

Due to Eq. (15.52),

$$B(\lambda, \xi) \neq 0, \quad \forall \ (\lambda, \xi) \in \Sigma_\theta \times \mathbf{R}, \qquad (15.137)$$

and clearly, for any $\lambda \in \Sigma_\theta$,

$$\lim_{\xi \to \pm\infty} B(\lambda, \xi) = \lim_{\xi \to \pm\infty} B(0, \xi) = 1, \qquad (15.138)$$

since $B(0, \xi) = B(\xi)$ satisfies Eq. (15.79). Therefore, the winding number around zero of the curve $\{B(\lambda, \xi) \mid -\infty < \xi < +\infty\}$ is independent of $\lambda \in \Sigma_\theta$; on the strength of Eq. (15.78),

$$(2\pi)^{-1} \int_{-\infty}^{+\infty} d \arg B(\lambda, \xi) = 0. \qquad (15.139)$$

By using Eq. (15.137) and Eq. (15.139), we conclude that $b = \ln B$ is well-defined on $\Sigma_\theta \times \mathbf{R}$.

It follows from Eq. (15.68), that uniformly in $(\lambda, \xi) \in \Sigma_\theta \times \mathbf{R}$,

$$|B(\lambda, \xi)| \le C(1 + |\lambda| + |\xi|^{m-\rho_1})/(1 + |\lambda| + |\xi|^m), \qquad (15.140)$$

and as $\xi \to \pm\infty$,

$$B(\lambda, \xi) = 1 + O(\langle\xi\rangle^{-\rho_1}), \qquad (15.141)$$

with the constant in the O-term depending on λ.

Set $b = \ln B$, and for $(\lambda, \xi) \in \Sigma_\theta \times \mathbf{R}$ and $\sigma > 0$, set

$$b_+(\lambda, \xi + i\sigma) = -(2\pi i)^{-1} \int_{-\infty}^{+\infty} \frac{b(\lambda, \eta)}{\xi + i\sigma - \eta} d\eta, \qquad (15.142)$$

$$b_-(\lambda, \xi - i\sigma) = (2\pi i)^{-1} \int_{-\infty}^{+\infty} \frac{b(\lambda, \eta)}{\xi - i\sigma - \eta} d\eta. \qquad (15.143)$$

Due to Eq. (15.141), the integrals in Eq. (15.142)–Eq. (15.143) converge. Set

$$\begin{aligned}
a_+(\lambda, \xi) &= d(-1)^l \Lambda_+^{\kappa_+}(\lambda, \xi) \exp[b_+(\lambda, \xi)], & \Im\xi > 0, & \quad (15.144) \\
a_-(\lambda, \xi) &= \Lambda_-^{\kappa_-}(\lambda, \xi) \exp[b_-(\lambda, \xi)], & \Im\xi < 0. & \quad (15.145)
\end{aligned}$$

The following theorem is an analogue of Theorem 15.21; we omit parts $(c_\pm) - (d_\pm)$ since estimates in $(d_\pm)$, uniform in λ, do not hold in general, and we will not need the parameter-depending analogues of $(c_\pm)$ (and the proof requires additional conditions on a).

Theorem 15.27　*Functions $a_\pm$ enjoy the following properties:*

(a_+) $\forall \lambda \in \Sigma_\theta$, $a_+(\lambda, \xi)$ is holomorphic in the upper half-plane $\Im\xi > 0$, and admits the continuous extension up to the boundary $\Im\xi = 0$;

(b_+) there exist $C, c > 0$ such that for all $\lambda \in \Sigma_\theta$ and all ξ in the upper half-plane $\Im\xi \ge 0$,

$$c(\langle\xi\rangle + |\lambda|^{1/m})^{\Re\kappa_+} \le |a_+(\lambda, \xi)| \le C(\langle\xi\rangle + |\lambda|^{1/m})^{\Re\kappa_+}; \qquad (15.146)$$

(a_-) $\forall \lambda \in \Sigma_\theta$, $a_-(\lambda, \xi)$ is holomorphic in the lower half-plane $\Im\xi < 0$, and admits the continuous extension up to the boundary $\Im\xi = 0$;

(b_-) there exist $C, c > 0$ such that for all $\lambda \in \Sigma_\theta$ and all ξ in the lower half-plane $\Im\xi \le 0$,

$$c(\langle\xi\rangle + |\lambda|^{1/m})^{\Re\kappa_-} \le |a_-(\lambda, \xi)| \le C(\langle\xi\rangle + |\lambda|^{1/m})^{\Re\kappa_-}; \qquad (15.147)$$

(c) *for all* $(\lambda, \xi) \in \Sigma_\theta \times \mathbf{R}$,

$$\lambda + a(\xi) = a_+(\lambda, \xi)a_-(\lambda, \xi); \tag{15.148}$$

(d) *for any* $\lambda \in \Sigma_\theta$, *conditions* $(a_\pm), (b_\pm), (c)$ *define* $a_\pm(\lambda, \cdot)$ *uniquely, up to scalar multiples.*

Proof. Parts $(a_\pm)$, (c) and (d) are immediate from parts $(a_\pm), (e)$ and (f) of Theorem 15.21, and the proof of $(b_\pm)$ is a modification of the proof of the same parts of Theorem 15.21. As in the proof of Theorem 15.21, it suffices to show that $b_\pm$ are uniformly bounded: there exists C such that for all $\lambda \in \Sigma_\theta$ and all ξ in an open half-plane $\pm \Im \xi > 0$,

$$|b_\pm(\lambda, \xi)| \leq C. \tag{15.149}$$

We prove Eq. (15.149) for the sign "+"; the proof for the sign "-" is essentially the same. Let $\lambda \in \Sigma_\theta$ and $\Im \xi > 0$. Set $K(\lambda) = (1 + |\lambda|)^{1/m}$, and introduce the following subsets of $\mathbf{R}$:

$$
\begin{aligned}
J_1(\lambda, \xi) &= \{\eta \in \mathbf{R} \mid |\xi - \eta| \geq K(\lambda), \ |\xi| \leq |\eta|/2\}, \\
J_2(\lambda, \xi) &= \{\eta \in \mathbf{R} \mid |\xi - \eta| \geq K(\lambda), \ |\xi| \geq 2|\eta|\}, \\
J_3(\lambda, \xi) &= \{\eta \in \mathbf{R} \mid |\xi - \eta| \geq K(\lambda), \ |\eta|/2 \leq |\xi| \leq 2|\eta|\}, \\
J_4(\lambda, \xi) &= \{\eta \in \mathbf{R} \mid |\xi - \eta| \leq K(\lambda)\}.
\end{aligned}
$$

Then for $j = 1, 2, 3, 4$ and $\Im \xi > 0$, define $b_{+,j}(\lambda, \xi)$ by Eq. (15.142) with the integration over $J_j(\lambda, \xi)$. From Eq. (15.34), and Eq. (15.69) and Eq. (15.38), we conclude that $B(\lambda, \xi)$ is uniformly bounded and bounded away from zero on $\Sigma_\theta \times \mathbf{R}$:

$$C^{-1} \leq |B(\lambda, \xi)| \leq C, \tag{15.150}$$

and $\partial_\eta b(\lambda, \eta) = \partial_\eta B(\lambda, \eta)/B(\lambda, \eta)$ admits an estimate

$$|\partial_\eta b(\lambda, \eta)| \leq C(\langle\xi\rangle + |\lambda|^{1/m})^{-\rho_2}, \tag{15.151}$$

where C is independent of $(\lambda, \xi) \in \Sigma_\theta \times \mathbf{R}$. By using Eq. (15.140), Eq. (15.150) Eq. (15.151) and repeating the proof of the boundedness of b_+ in the proof of Theorem 15.21, we obtain that $b_{j,+}$ are uniformly bounded, and Eq. (15.149) follows.

15.8.3 Reduction to ODE with the operator-valued coefficient and the solution

We have not developed a theory of the Wiener-Hopf equation in the Hölder spaces, and the construction of such a theory is much more involved than the construction of the theory for the Sobolev spaces. Besides, this construction needs additional conditions even in the case of operators in the whole space –see Eq. (15.23). This explains why here (unlike Subsection 15.6.3) we work in the scale of Sobolev spaces. Notice however that after the solution is found, and an explicit formula based on Eq. (15.51) is written, it is possible to describe the properties of the solution in terms of the Hölder estimates like we did in Subsection 15.7.4.

Similarly to Eq. (15.58)–Eq. (15.59), we want to interpret the problem Eq. (15.132)–Eq. (15.135) as

$$f'(t) + A^s f(t) = G(t), \quad t > 0, \tag{15.152}$$

$$f(0) = G_0, \tag{15.153}$$

where A^s is an unbounded operator in $H^{s-m}(\mathbf{R}_+)$; the data $G_0 \in H^{s-m}(\mathbf{R}_+)$ and $G \in C^0([0, +\infty); H^{s-m}(\mathbf{R}_+))$, and the solution f is sought in the space $C^0([0, +\infty); H^{s-m}(\mathbf{R}_+))$. An appropriate s can be chosen and A^s can be relatively easily defined if

$$\Re \kappa_\pm \in [0, m]. \tag{15.154}$$

In applications to Financial Mathematics, which we consider, this condition is satisfied.

Take any s satisfying

$$s - m \in (-1/2, 1/2), \tag{15.155}$$

and for $g \in H^{s-m}(R_+)$, set

$$(A^s)^{-1} g = a_-(0, D)^{-1} \theta_+ a_+(0, D)^{-1} lg, \tag{15.156}$$

where $lg \in H^{s-m}(\mathbf{R})$ is an arbitrary extension of g. From Eq. (15.146)–Eq. (15.147), and the assumption $\Re \kappa_\pm \geq 0$, it follows that $a_+(0, D)^{-1}$ is bounded in $H^{s-m}(\mathbf{R})$, and $a_-(0, D)^{-1}$ is bounded in $\overset{o}{H}^{s-m}(\mathbf{R}_+)$; the latter space can be identified with $H^{s-m}(\mathbf{R}_+)$ in view of Eq. (15.155) and on the strength of Lemma 15.8. Finally, θ_+ can be regarded as a bounded operator from $H^{s-m}(\mathbf{R})$ to $H^{s-m}(\mathbf{R}_+)$, and therefore $(A^s)^{-1}$ can be regarded as a bounded operator in $H^{s-m}(\mathbf{R}_+)$. By applying $p_+a_+(D)e_+$ to $(A^s)^{-1}g$, we obtain

$$p_+a_+(D)\theta_+a_+(D)^{-1}lg = p_+lg = g$$

(for more details, see the proof of Theorem 15.22), hence the kernel of $(A^s)^{-1}$ is trivial, and we can introduce A^s as the left inverse to $(A^s)^{-1}$. Thus, A^s is the operator in $H^{s-m}(\mathbf{R}_+)$ with the domain

$$\mathcal{D}(A^s) = \{(A^s)^{-1}u \mid u \in H^{s-m}(\mathbf{R}_+)\},$$

the action being defined by $p_+a(D)e_+$.

Lemma 15.12 *There exists C such that for all $\lambda \in \Sigma_\theta$,*

$$||(\lambda + A^s)^{-1}||_{H^{s-m}(\mathbf{R}_+) \to H^{s-m}(\mathbf{R}_+)} \leq C(1 + |\lambda|)^{-1}. \tag{15.157}$$

Proof. The same argument as above shows that

$$(\lambda + A^s)^{-1}g = a_-(\lambda, D)^{-1}\theta_+a_+(\lambda, D)^{-1}lg, \tag{15.158}$$

where $lg \in H^{s-m}(\mathbf{R})$ is arbitrary extension of $g \in H^{s-m}(\mathbf{R}_+)$. From Eq. (15.146)–Eq. (15.147) and Eq. (15.154) it follows that there exists $C > 0$ such that

$$|(1 + |\lambda|)^{\Re\kappa_+/m}a_+(\lambda, \xi)^{-1}| \leq C, \quad \forall \lambda \in \Sigma_\theta, \Im\xi \geq 0,$$

and

$$|(1 + |\lambda|)^{\Re\kappa_-/m}a_-(\lambda, \xi)^{-1}| \leq C, \quad \forall \lambda \in \Sigma_\theta, \Im\xi \leq 0,$$

and we conclude that

$$(1 + |\lambda|)^{\Re\kappa_+/m}a_+(\lambda, D)^{-1} : H^{s-m}(\mathbf{R}) \to H^{s-m}(\mathbf{R}) \tag{15.159}$$

and

$$(1 + |\lambda|)^{\Re\kappa_-/m}a_-(\lambda, D)^{-1} : \overset{o}{H}{}^{s-m}(\mathbf{R}_+) \to \overset{o}{H}{}^{s-m}(\mathbf{R}_+) \tag{15.160}$$

are bounded uniformly in $\lambda \in \Sigma_\theta$. Using the identification of spaces $\overset{o}{H}{}^{s-m}(\mathbf{R}_+)$ and $H^{s-m}(\mathbf{R}_+)$, the equality $\kappa_+ + \kappa_- = m$ and Eq. (15.158)–Eq. (15.160), we obtain Eq. (15.157). $\square$

With the estimate Eq. (15.157) at hand, we can use Theorem 15.18 with $\mathcal{B} = H^{s-m}(\mathbf{R}_+)$, define $T_t = \exp[-tA^s]$ by Eq. (15.51) and obtain analogues of Theorem 15.19 and Theorem 15.20. We state the inhomogeneous version.

Theorem 15.28 *Let a satisfy conditions Eq. (15.34)–Eq. (15.38), Eq. (15.67)–Eq. (15.69) and Eq. (15.154), and let s satisfy condition Eq. (15.155).*

Then for any $G \in C^0([0, +\infty); H^{s-m}(\mathbf{R}_+))$ and $G_0 \in H^{s-m}(\mathbf{R}_+)$, the following statements hold:

a) the problem Eq. (15.152)–Eq. (15.153) has a unique solution $f \in C^0([0, +\infty); H^{s-m}(\mathbf{R}_+))$, which is given by

$$f(t) = \int_0^t T_{t-\tau} G(\tau) d\tau + T_t G_0; \tag{15.161}$$

b) if $s - \Re\kappa_- < 1/2$, then

$$f \in C^1((0, +\infty); H^{s-m}(\mathbf{R}_+)) \cap C^0((0, +\infty); \overset{o}{H}{}^s(\mathbf{R}_+));$$

c) if $s - \Re\kappa_- \geq 1/2$, then for any $\epsilon > 0$,

$$f \in C^1((0, +\infty); H^{s-m}(\mathbf{R}_+)) \cap C^0([0, +\infty); H^{1/2+\Re\kappa_- -\epsilon}(\mathbf{R}_+));$$

d) for any $t_0 > 0$, $j \in \mathbf{Z}_+$, and $\gamma < c_0$, where $c_0 > 0$ is the constant in Eq. (15.38), f_2 satisfies the estimate

$$\sup_{t \geq t_0} \|e^{\gamma t} f^{(j)}(t)\|_{H^{s-m}(\mathbf{R}_+)} < +\infty. \tag{15.162}$$

15.9 PDO in the Sobolev spaces with exponential weights, in 1D

In this Section, real $\lambda_\pm$ and $\omega_\pm$ are assumed to satisfy $\lambda_- \leq 0 \leq \lambda_+$ and $\omega_- \leq 0 \leq \omega_+$.

15.9.1 *Generalized functions*

Definition 15.3 $\mathcal{S}(\mathbf{R}; [\lambda_-, \lambda_+])$ denotes the space of C^∞-functions such that for any $\gamma \in [\lambda_-, \lambda_+]$, $e^{\gamma x} u \in \mathcal{S}(\mathbf{R})$. The topology in $\mathcal{S}(\mathbf{R}; [\lambda_-, \lambda_+])$ is defined by a system of seminorms

$$\|u\|_{\mathcal{S};[\lambda_-,\lambda_+];s,N} = \sup_{x \in \mathbf{R}} |x^s D^N (e^{\lambda_+ + x} + e^{\lambda_- - x}) u(x)|,$$

where $N, s \geq 0$ are integers.

$\mathcal{S}'(\mathbf{R}; [-\lambda_+, -\lambda_-])$ denotes the space of continuous linear functionals in $\mathcal{S}(\mathbf{R}; [\lambda_-, \lambda_+])$. Its elements are called distributions or generalized functions.

Definition 15.4 For $\gamma \in \mathbf{R}$ and a regular function u, u_γ is defined by $u_\gamma(x) = e^{\gamma x} u(x)$. For $\gamma \in [-\lambda_+, -\lambda_-]$ and $u \in \mathcal{S}'(\mathbf{R}; [-\lambda_+, -\lambda_-])$, define $u_\gamma \in \mathcal{S}'(\mathbf{R}; [-\lambda_+ - \gamma, -\lambda_- - \gamma])$ by

$$(u_\gamma, v) = (u, v_\gamma), \quad \forall\, v \in \mathcal{S}(\mathbf{R}; [\lambda_- + \gamma, \lambda_+ + \gamma]),$$

and $(e^{\lambda_- - x} + e^{\lambda_+ + x})^{-1} u \in \mathcal{S}'(\mathbf{R})$ is defined by

$$\left((e^{\lambda_- - x} + e^{\lambda_+ + x})^{-1} u, v\right) = \left(u, (e^{\lambda_- - x} + e^{\lambda_+ + x})^{-1} v\right), \quad \forall\, v \in \mathcal{S}(\mathbf{R}).$$

Lemma 15.13 *a) If $\lambda_- = 0 = \lambda_+$, then $\mathcal{S}(\mathbf{R}; [\lambda_-, \lambda_+]) = \mathcal{S}(\mathbf{R})$.*

b) The-multiplication-by- $(e^{\lambda_+ + x} + e^{\lambda_- - x})$ operator establishes a topological isomorphism between $\mathcal{S}(\mathbf{R}; [\lambda_-, \lambda_+])$ and $\mathcal{S}(\mathbf{R})$ (and a topological automorphism of $C_0^\infty(\mathbf{R})$);

c) The-multiplication-by-$(e^{\lambda_+ + x} + e^{\lambda_- - x})^{-1}$ operator establishes a topological isomorphism between $\mathcal{S}'(\mathbf{R}; [-\lambda_+, -\lambda_-])$ and $\mathcal{S}'(\mathbf{R})$;

d) For $\gamma \in [\lambda_-, \lambda_+]$, the map

$$\mathcal{S}(\mathbf{R}; [\lambda_-, \lambda_+]) \ni u \mapsto u_\gamma \in \mathcal{S}(\mathbf{R}; [\lambda_- - \gamma, \lambda_+ - \gamma])$$

and for any $\gamma \in \mathbf{R}$, the map

$$C_0^\infty(\mathbf{R}) \ni u \mapsto u_\gamma \in C_0^\infty(\mathbf{R})$$

are topological isomorphisms;

e) For $\gamma \in [-\lambda_+, -\lambda_-]$, the map

$$\mathcal{S}'(\mathbf{R}; [-\lambda_+, -\lambda_-]) \ni u \mapsto u_\gamma \in \mathcal{S}'(\mathbf{R}; [-\lambda_+ - \gamma, -\lambda_- - \gamma])$$

is a topological isomorphism;

f) $C_0^\infty(\mathbf{R})$ is embedded into $\mathcal{S}(\mathbf{R}; [\lambda_-, \lambda_+])$, densely and continuously.

g) If $\lambda'_- \leq \lambda_- \leq \lambda_+ \leq \lambda'_+$, then $\mathcal{S}(\mathbf{R}; [\lambda'_-, \lambda'_+]) \subset \mathcal{S}(\mathbf{R}; [\lambda_-, \lambda_+])$, densely and continuously; in particular, $\mathcal{S}(\mathbf{R}; [\lambda'_-, \lambda'_+]) \subset \mathcal{S}(\mathbf{R})$, densely and continuously;

h) If $\lambda'_- \le \lambda_- \le \lambda_+ \le \lambda'_+$, *then* $\mathcal{S}'(\mathbf{R}; [-\lambda_+, -\lambda_-]) \subset \mathcal{S}'(\mathbf{R}; [-\lambda'_+, -\lambda'_-])$, *densely and continuously.*

Proof.   a), b) and d) are immediate from the definition, and c) and e) follow from b) and d), respectively, by duality.

f) follows from b) and Theorem 15.3, part c).

g) Observe that

$$e^{\lambda_+ x} + e^{\lambda_- x} \le e^{\lambda'_+ x} + e^{\lambda'_- x},$$

and use the definition of $\mathcal{S}(\mathbf{R}; [\lambda'_-, \lambda'_+])$.

h) The embedding follows from g), by duality, and the denseness follows from f). $\square$

From g), the Fourier transform $\hat{u}$ of $u \in \mathcal{S}(\mathbf{R}; [\lambda_-, \lambda_+]) \subset \mathcal{S}(\mathbf{R})$ is well-defined, and it is straightforward to show that

a) $\hat{u}(\xi)$ admits the analytic continuation into the strip $\Im \xi \in [\lambda_-, \lambda_+]$, and the continuous extension up to the boundary;

b)   for each $\tau \in [\lambda_-, \lambda_+]$, $\hat{u}(\cdot + i\tau) \in \mathcal{S}(\mathbf{R})$, and $\hat{u} \in C^\infty([\lambda_-, \lambda_+]; \mathcal{S}(\mathbf{R}))$.

Definition 15.5   For $u \in \mathcal{S}'(\mathbf{R}; [-\lambda_+, -\lambda_-])$ and $\gamma \in [-\lambda_+, -\lambda_-]$, define $\hat{u}(\cdot + i\gamma) \in \mathcal{S}'(\mathbf{R})$ by

$$(\hat{u}(\cdot + i\gamma), \hat{v}(\cdot - i\gamma)) = 2\pi(u, v), \quad \forall\, v \in \mathcal{S}(\mathbf{R}; [\lambda_-, \lambda_+]).$$

15.9.2   *The Sobolev spaces* $H^{s,\gamma}(\mathbf{R})$

Definition 15.6   Let s and $\gamma \in \mathbf{R}$. We say that a distribution $u \in \mathcal{S}'(\mathbf{R}; [-|\gamma|, |\gamma|])$ belongs to $H^{s,\gamma}(\mathbf{R})$ if and only if $u_\gamma \in H^s(\mathbf{R})$. The norm in $H^{s,\gamma}(\mathbf{R})$ is defined by

$$||u||_{s,\gamma} = ||u_\gamma||_s,$$

where $||\cdot||_s$ is the norm in the Sobolev space $H^s(\mathbf{R})$.

Clearly, $\hat{u}(\cdot + i\gamma) = \widehat{u_\gamma}$, therefore $u \in H^{s,\gamma}(\mathbf{R})$ if and only if the norm

$$||u||_{s,\gamma} = \left(\int_{-\infty + i\gamma}^{+\infty + i\gamma} (1 + |\xi|^2)^s |\hat{u}(\xi)|^2 d\xi \right)^{1/2} \tag{15.163}$$

is finite.

If $u_\gamma \in L_1(\mathbf{R})$, one can calculate $\hat{u}(\xi)$ on the line $\Im\xi = \gamma$ explicitly: for $\xi = \eta + i\gamma$,

$$
\begin{aligned}
\hat{u}(\xi) &= \int_{-\infty}^{+\infty} e^{-ix\eta} u_\gamma(x) dx \\
&= \int_{-\infty}^{+\infty} e^{-ix\eta} e^{\gamma x} u(x) dx \\
&= \int_{-\infty}^{+\infty} e^{-ix\xi} u(x) dx,
\end{aligned}
$$

which is Eq. (15.2), the only difference being that in Section 15.2, ξ is assumed real.

Example 15.8 Let $u(x) = \theta_+(x)e^{\beta x}$. Then the Fourier transform $\hat{u}(\xi)$ is well-defined for $\Im\xi < -\Re\beta$:

$$
\hat{u}(\xi) = \int_0^{+\infty} e^{-ix\xi} e^{\beta x} dx = -(\beta - i\xi)^{-1},
$$

and it follows that $u \in H^{s,\gamma}(\mathbf{R})$, if and only if $s < 1/2$ and $\gamma < -\Re\beta$.

For $s \in \mathbf{R}$, and $\lambda \geq 0$, define $\Lambda_\lambda^s(D)$ as the PDO with the symbol $(1 + \lambda^2 + \xi^2)^{s/2}$.

Lemma 15.14 *Let* $m, s \in \mathbf{R}$, $\rho \in \mathbf{R}$, $\gamma \in [\lambda_-, \lambda_+]$ *and* $\lambda \geq \max\{|\lambda_- - \rho|, \lambda_+ - \rho\}$.
Then

$$
\Lambda_\lambda^s(D)e^{\rho x} : \mathcal{S}(\mathbf{R}; [\lambda_-, \lambda_+]) \to \mathcal{S}(\mathbf{R}; [\lambda_- - \rho, \lambda_+ - \rho]), \qquad (15.164)
$$

is a topological isomorphism.

Proof. On the strength of Lemma 15.13 d), it suffices to consider the case $\rho = 0$; since $\Lambda_\lambda^s(D)$ and $\Lambda_\lambda^{-s}(D)$ are mutual inverses as operators in $\mathcal{S}(\mathbf{R}) \supset \mathcal{S}(\mathbf{R}; [\lambda_-, \lambda_+])$, it remains to show that for any s, and any integers $k, N \geq 0$,

$$
M_{\lambda_\pm; k, N; s} := \sup_{x \in \mathbf{R}} |x^k D^N e^{\lambda_\pm x} \Lambda_\lambda^s(D) u(x)|
$$

admits a bound via a linear combination of terms of the form $M_{\lambda_\pm; k', N'; 0}$. Since $\lambda \geq \max\{\lambda_+, -\lambda_-\}$, and $\Lambda_\lambda^s(\xi)$ is holomorphic in a strip $\Im\xi \in$

$[\lambda_-, \lambda_+]$, we have

$$e^{\gamma x} \Lambda_\lambda^s(D) = \Lambda_\lambda^s(D + i\gamma) e^{\gamma x},$$

for any $\gamma \in [\lambda_-, \lambda_+]$. Hence,

$$M_{\lambda_\pm; k, N; s} = \sup_{x \in \mathbf{R}} |x^k D^N \Lambda_\lambda^s(D + i\lambda_\pm) e^{\lambda_\pm x} u(x)|. \tag{15.165}$$

By Lemma 15.3, $\Lambda_\lambda^s(D + i\lambda_\pm)$ is continuous in $\mathcal{S}(\mathbf{R})$, which implies that the RHS in Eq. (15.165) admits an estimate via a linear combination of terms of the form $M_{\lambda_\pm; k', N'; 0}$.   □

Corollary 15.2   *Let conditions of Lemma 15.14 hold, and let*

$$e^{\rho x} \Lambda_\lambda^s(D) : \mathcal{S}'(\mathbf{R}; [-\lambda_+ + \rho, -\lambda_- + \rho]) \to \mathcal{S}'(\mathbf{R}; [-\lambda_+, -\lambda_-]) \tag{15.166}$$

be defined by duality: for $u \in \mathcal{S}'(\mathbf{R}; [-\lambda_+ + \rho, -\lambda_- + \rho])$ and $v \in \mathcal{S}(\mathbf{R}; [\lambda_-, \lambda_+])$,

$$(e^{\rho x} \Lambda_\lambda^s(D) u, v) = (u, \Lambda_\lambda^s(D) e^{\rho x} v).$$

Then the operator Eq. (15.166) is a topological isomorphism.

Lemma 15.15   *Let $m, s \in \mathbf{R}$, $\gamma, \gamma - \rho \in [\lambda_-, \lambda_+]$ and $\lambda \geq |\gamma - \rho|$. Then*

$$\Lambda_\lambda^s(D) e^{\rho x} : H^{m, \gamma}(\mathbf{R}) \to H^{m-s, \gamma - \rho}(\mathbf{R})$$

is a topological isomorphism, with the inverse defined by $e^{-\rho x} \Lambda_\lambda^{-s}(D)$.

Proof.   By definition,

$$H^{m, \gamma}(\mathbf{R}) \ni u \mapsto u_\gamma \in H^s(\mathbf{R})$$

is an isometry, hence it suffices to prove that

$$e^{(\gamma - \rho) x} \Lambda_\lambda^s(D) e^{(\rho - \gamma) x} = \Lambda_\lambda^s(D + i(\gamma - \rho)) : H^m(\mathbf{R}) \to H^{m-s}(\mathbf{R}) \tag{15.167}$$

is a topological isomorphism. Notice that the equality in Eq. (15.167) holds since $\lambda \geq |\gamma - \rho|$, and on the strength of the same condition, there exist $C, c > 0$ such that

$$c\langle \xi \rangle^s \leq |\Lambda_\lambda^s(\xi + i(\gamma - \rho))| \leq C\langle \xi \rangle^s, \quad \forall \xi \in \mathbf{R},$$

and by applying Theorem 15.5, we conclude that the operator Eq. (15.167) is a topological isomorphism.   □

Theorem 15.29   *Let $s < s'$, and $\lambda_- \leq \gamma \leq \lambda_+$. Then*
a) $H^{0,\gamma}(\mathbf{R}) = L_2(\mathbf{R}; e^{2\gamma}dx)$, *and* $H^{s,0}(\mathbf{R}) = H^s(\mathbf{R})$;
b) $H^{s,\gamma}(\mathbf{R})$ *has the topology of the Hilbert space, with the scalar product*

$$(u,v)_{s,\gamma} = (2\pi)^{-1} \int_{-\infty}^{+\infty} \langle \eta \rangle^{2s} \hat{u}(\eta + i\gamma) \overline{\hat{v}(\eta + i\gamma)} d\eta; \qquad (15.168)$$

c) $C_0^\infty(\mathbf{R}) \subset \mathcal{S}(\mathbf{R}; [\lambda_-, \lambda_+]) \subset H^s(\mathbf{R}) \subset \mathcal{S}'(\mathbf{R}; [-\lambda_+, -\lambda_-])$ *densely, and these embeddings are continuous;*
d) $H^{s',\gamma}(\mathbf{R}) \subset H^{s,\gamma}(\mathbf{R})$, *densely and continuously;*
e) $H^{-s,-\gamma}(\mathbf{R})$ *can be naturally identified with the dual space* $(H^{s,\gamma}(\mathbf{R}))^*$, *by*

$$(w,v) = (2\pi)^{-1} \int_{-\infty+i\gamma}^{+\infty+i\gamma} \hat{w}(\bar\xi)\overline{\hat{v}(\xi)} d\xi. \qquad (15.169)$$

Proof.   a) Evident.
   b) We can define $(u,v)_{s,\gamma} = (u_\gamma, v_\gamma)_s$, and then

$$\begin{aligned}
(u,v)_{s,\gamma} &= (2\pi)^{-1} \int_{-\infty}^{+\infty} \langle \eta \rangle^{2s} \widehat{u_\gamma}(\eta) \overline{\widehat{v_\gamma}(\eta)} d\eta \\
&= (2\pi)^{-1} \int_{-\infty}^{+\infty} \langle \eta \rangle^{2s} \hat{u}(\eta + i\gamma) \overline{\hat{v}(\eta + i\gamma)} d\eta.
\end{aligned}$$

   c) By using topological isomorphisms defined by the multiplication-by-$e^{\gamma x}$ operator, we reduce to the case $s = 0$. After that we apply part c) of Theorem 15.3 and parts f)–h) of Lemma 15.13.
   d) Lemma 15.15 with $s = 0$ and part d) of Lemma 15.13 reduce to the part d) of Theorem 15.3.
   e) Set $\lambda = |\gamma|$, and introduce an equivalent norm in $H^s(\mathbf{R})$ by

$$\|u\|_s' = \|\Lambda_\lambda^s(D)u\|_0.$$

The corresponding norm in $H^{s,\gamma}(\mathbf{R})$ is

$$\|u\|_{s,\gamma}' = \|\Lambda_\lambda^s(D)u_\gamma\|_0,$$

and the scalar product is

$$(u,v)_{s,\gamma}' = (\Lambda_\lambda^{2s}(D)u_\gamma, v_\gamma)_0.$$

Since $H^{s,\gamma}(\mathbf{R})$ is the Hilbert space, any $\phi \in (H^{s,\gamma}(\mathbf{R}))^*$ can be defined by some $u \in H^{s,\gamma}(\mathbf{R})$:

$$
\begin{aligned}
(\phi, v) &= (u, v)_{s,\gamma} \\
&= (\Lambda_\lambda^{2s}(D)u_\gamma, v_\gamma)_0 \\
&= (e^{\gamma x}\Lambda_\lambda^{2s}(D)e^{\gamma x}u, v) \\
&= (\Lambda_\lambda^{2s}(D + i\gamma)e^{2\gamma x}u, v),
\end{aligned}
$$

and by the same calculation, for a fixed $u \in H^{s,\gamma}(\mathbf{R})$, the RHS defines a continuous linear functional in $H^{s,\gamma}(\mathbf{R})$.

Hence,

$$\Lambda_\lambda^{2s}(D + i\gamma)e^{2\gamma x} : H^{s,\gamma}(\mathbf{R}) \to (H^{s,\gamma}(\mathbf{R}))^*$$

is an isomorphism, and the same argument as in the proof Lemma 15.15 shows that

$$\Lambda_\lambda^{2s}(D + i\gamma)e^{2\gamma x} : H^{s,\gamma}(\mathbf{R}) \to H^{-s,-\gamma}(\mathbf{R})$$

is a topological isomorphism. This proves that $(H^{s,\gamma}(\mathbf{R}))^*$ is isomorphic to $H^{-s,-\gamma}(\mathbf{R})$. To finish the proof of e), take $w \in H^{-s,-\gamma}(\mathbf{R})$ and $v \in H^{s,\gamma}(\mathbf{R})$, and consider

$$
\begin{aligned}
(w, v) &= (w_{-\gamma}, v_\gamma) \\
&= (2\pi)^{-1} \int_{-\infty}^{+\infty} \widehat{w_{-\gamma}}(\eta)\overline{\widehat{v_\gamma}(\eta)}d\eta \\
&= (2\pi)^{-1} \int_{-\infty+i\gamma}^{+\infty+i\gamma} \hat{w}(\xi)\overline{\hat{v}(\xi)}d\xi.
\end{aligned}
$$

$\square$

The following lemma and theorem are evident corollaries of Lemma 15.4 and Theorem 15.6, respectively.

Lemma 15.16   *Let $s \geq 0$ be an integer, and $\gamma \in \mathbf{R}$. Then an equivalent norm in $H^{s,\gamma}(\mathbf{R})$ can be defined by*

$$\|u\|_{s,\gamma}^{\prime 2} = \sum_{|\alpha| \leq s} \|e^{\gamma x}D^\alpha u\|_{L_2(\mathbf{R})}^2.$$

Theorem 15.30   *Let $s > 1/2$ and $\gamma \in \mathbf{R}$. Then the restriction-to-$\{0\}$-operator*

$$p' : C_0^\infty(\mathbf{R}) \ni u \mapsto u(0) \in \mathbf{C}$$

admits a unique bounded extension $p' : H^{s,\gamma}(\mathbf{R}) \to \mathbf{C}$.

15.9.3   PDO with the symbols holomorphic in a strip, and their action in the scale $H^{s,\gamma}(\mathbf{R})$

Definition 15.7   Let m and $\omega_- < \omega_+$ be real, and $0 \in [\omega_-, \omega_+]$. We write $a \in S^m(\mathbf{R} + i[\omega_-, \omega_+])$ if the following conditions hold:

(i) $a(\xi)$ is holomorphic in the strip $\Im\xi \in (\omega_-, \omega_+)$;

(ii) a is continuous up to the boundary of the strip;

(iii) there exist $C > 0$ such that for all ξ in the strip $\Im\xi \in [\omega_-, \omega_+]$,

$$|a(\xi)| \leq C\langle\xi\rangle^m. \tag{15.170}$$

If Eq. (15.170) holds for ξ in the half-plane $\Im\xi \leq \omega_+$ (resp., $\Im\xi \geq \omega_-$), we write $a \in S^m(\mathbf{R} + i(-\infty, \omega_+])$ (resp., $a \in S^m(\mathbf{R} + i[\omega_-, +\infty)))$.

For $m, s \in \mathbf{R}$, $\gamma \in [\omega_-, \omega_+]$, and $a \in S^m(\mathbf{R} + i[\omega_-, \omega_+])$, define

$$a(D) : H^{s,\gamma}(\mathbf{R}) \to H^{s-m,\gamma}(\mathbf{R})$$

by

$$\widehat{a(D)u}(\xi) = a(\xi)\hat{u}(\xi), \quad \Im\xi = \gamma;$$

if $a(\cdot + i\gamma)\hat{u}(\cdot + i\gamma) \in L_1(\mathbf{R})$, we can use the explicit formula

$$a(D)u(x) = (2\pi)^{-1} \int_{-\infty+i\gamma}^{+\infty+i\gamma} e^{ix\xi}a(\xi)\hat{u}(\xi)dx. \tag{15.171}$$

Theorem 15.31   *Let $m, s \in \mathbf{R}$ and $\gamma \in [\omega_-, \omega_+]$, and let $a \in S^m(\mathbf{R} + i[\omega_-, \omega_+])$. Then the operator*

$$a(D) : H^{s,\gamma}(\mathbf{R}) \to H^{s-m,\gamma}(\mathbf{R}) \tag{15.172}$$

is continuous, with the norm bounded by the constant C in Eq. (15.170).

Proof.   Since $H^{s,\gamma}(\mathbf{R}) \ni u \mapsto u_\gamma \in H^s(\mathbf{R})$ is a topological isomorphism, it suffices to prove that

$$e^{\gamma x}a(D)e^{-\gamma x} = a(D + i\gamma) : H^s(\mathbf{R}) \to H^{s-m}(\mathbf{R})$$

is continuous, with the norm bounded by the constant C in Eq. (15.170). But this is immediate from Theorem 15.4.   □

Theorem 15.32   *Let $m, s \in \mathbf{R}$, and $\gamma \in [\omega_-, \omega_+]$, and let $a \in S^m(\mathbf{R} + i[\omega_-, \omega_+])$ satisfy*

$$|a(\xi)^{-1}| \leq C\langle\xi\rangle^{-m}, \quad \Im\xi = \gamma, \qquad (15.173)$$

where C is independent of ξ on the line $\Im\xi = \gamma$.
    Then the operator Eq. (15.172) is invertible.

Proof.   By definition, AA^{-1} and $A^{-1}A$ act as the identity, and from Eq. (15.173) and Theorem 15.31, $A^{-1} : H^{s-m,\gamma}(\mathbf{R}) \to H^{s,\gamma}(\mathbf{R})$ is bounded. Thus, it is the bounded inverse to the operator Eq. (15.172). $\qquad\square$

Lemma 15.17   *Let the following conditions hold*
    a) $a \in S^m(\mathbf{R} + i[\omega_-, \omega_+])$;
    b) there exist non-zero limits

$$d_\pm = \lim a(\xi)|\xi|^{-m}, \qquad (15.174)$$

as $\Re\xi \to \pm\infty$, with ξ remaining in the strip $\Im\xi \in [\omega_-, \omega_+]$;
    Then
    (i) The set of zeroes of a in the strip $\Im\xi \in (\omega_-, \omega_+)$ is either empty or a bounded discrete set, the accumulation points being possible on the lines $\Im\xi = \lambda_\pm$ only;
    (ii) There exists a discrete set $\mathcal{Z}(a) \in (\lambda_-, \lambda_+)$ with $\lambda_\pm$ as the only possible accumulation points, such that for any $\gamma \in (\lambda_-, \lambda_+)\backslash\mathcal{Z}(a)$, Eq. (15.173) holds.

Proof.   (i) Condition a) implies that a is holomorphic in the strip (ω_-, ω_+) and continuous up to the boundary of the strip. From the condition b), it follows that there exists an open bounded subset U of the strip $\Im\xi \in (\omega_-, \omega_+)$ such that a has no zeroes in the strip outside U. Since a is holomorphic in U, its zeroes in U form a discrete set with possible accumulation points at the boundary of the strip only.
    (ii) Follows from (i) and Eq. (15.174). $\qquad\square$

Corollary 15.3   *Let a satisfy conditions of Lemma 15.17, and let $\mathcal{Z}(a)$ be the set defined in Lemma 15.17.*
    Then for any $\gamma \in (\omega_-, \omega_+)\backslash\mathcal{Z}(a)$, the operator Eq. (15.172) is invertible.

15.9.4 Action of PDO in the Hölder-Zygmund spaces with exponential weights

Definition 15.8 Let $s, \gamma \in \mathbf{R}$. We write $u \in \mathcal{C}^{s,\gamma}(\mathbf{R})$ if and only if $u_\gamma \in \mathcal{C}^s(\mathbf{R})$.

For integer $r \geq 0$ and $\gamma \in \mathbf{R}$, we write $u \in C_0^{r,\gamma}(\mathbf{R})$ if and only if $u_\gamma \in C_0^r(\mathbf{R})$.

The reader can easily deduce from Theorem 15.8-Theorem 15.11 their weighted analogues:

Theorem 15.33 *Let $s > r + 1/2$, where $r \geq 0$ is an integer, and $\gamma \in \mathbf{R}$. Then $H^{s,\gamma}(\mathbf{R}) \subset C_0^{r,\gamma}(\mathbf{R})$, densely and continuously.*

Theorem 15.34 *Let $s > 1/2$, and $\gamma \in \mathbf{R}$. Then for any $s' < s - 1/2$, $H^{s,\gamma}(\mathbf{R}) \subset \mathcal{C}^{s',\gamma}(\mathbf{R})$, densely and continuously.*

Theorem 15.35 *Let $m \in \mathbf{R}$, and let $a \in C^\infty(\mathbf{R} + i[\omega_-, \omega_+])$ satisfy, for any multi-index α,*

$$|a^{(\alpha)}(\xi)| \leq C_\alpha \langle \xi \rangle^{m-|\alpha|}, \tag{15.175}$$

where C_α is independent of $\xi \in \mathbf{R} + i[\omega_-, \omega_+]$.

Then for any $s \in \mathbf{R}$ and $\gamma \in [\omega_-, \omega_+]$, $A = a(D) : \mathcal{C}^{s,\gamma}(\mathbf{R}) \to \mathcal{C}^{s-m,\gamma}(\mathbf{R})$ is bounded, with the norm admitting an estimate

$$\|a(D)\| \leq C \sum_{|\alpha| \leq N} \sup_{\xi \in \mathbf{R}+i\gamma} \langle \xi \rangle^{-m+|\alpha|} |a^{(\alpha)}(\xi)|, \tag{15.176}$$

where C and N depend on n, s, m but not on a.

Theorem 15.36 *Let $m \in \mathbf{R}$, and let a satisfy Eq. (15.173) and Eq. (15.176). Then for any $s, \gamma \in \mathbf{R}$, $a(D) : \mathcal{C}^{s,\gamma}(\mathbf{R}) \to \mathcal{C}^{s-m,\gamma}(\mathbf{R})$ is invertible.*

The following theorem is an evident analogue of Corollary 15.3 for the Hölder-Zygmund spaces.

Theorem 15.37 *Let a satisfy Eq. (15.176) and conditions of Lemma 15.17, and let $\mathcal{Z}(a)$ be the set defined in Lemma 15.17.*

Then for any $\gamma \in (\omega_-, \omega_+) \setminus \mathcal{Z}(a)$, an operator $a(D) : \mathcal{C}^{s,\gamma}(\mathbf{R}) \to \mathcal{C}^{s-m,\gamma}(\mathbf{R})$ is invertible.

15.10 The Sobolev spaces with exponential weights and PDO on a half-line

Essentially, here we reformulate definitions and main results of Section 15.5. As in Subsection 15.9.2, all the proofs are reduced to the case of the Sobolev spaces without the weight but one additional feature emerges: the embedding of the Sobolev spaces with different weights. This feature makes it possible to write down the asymptotics of solutions at the infinity.

15.10.1 Spaces $\overset{o}{H}{}^{s,\gamma}(\mathbf{R}_\pm)$

Definition 15.9 Let $s,\gamma \in \mathbf{R}$. We write $u \in \overset{o}{H}{}^{s,\gamma}(\mathbf{R}_\pm)$ iff $u_\gamma \in \overset{o}{H}{}^{s}(\mathbf{R}_\pm)$.

Lemma 15.18 $\overset{o}{H}{}^{s,\gamma}(\mathbf{R}_\pm)$ *is the closure of* $C_0^\infty(\mathbf{R}_\pm)$ *in* $H^{s,\gamma}(\mathbf{R})$.

Proof. The map $u \mapsto u_\gamma$ defines an automorphism of $C_0^\infty(\mathbf{R}_\pm)$ and a topological isomorphism between $\overset{o}{H}{}^{s,\gamma}(\mathbf{R}_\pm)$ and $\overset{o}{H}{}^{s}(\mathbf{R}_\pm)$, hence it remains to apply Lemma 15.5. □

Evidently, $u \in H^{0,\gamma}(\mathbf{R}_\pm)$ can be identified with a function from $L_2(\mathbf{R}_\pm; e^{2\gamma x}dx)$, extended by 0 on $\mathbf{R}_\mp$.

Theorem 15.38 *Let a be holomorphic in the half-plane $\Im\xi < \gamma$ (resp., $\Im\xi > \gamma$), continuous up to the boundary $\Im\xi = \gamma$, and satisfy an estimate*

$$|a(\xi)| \le C\langle\xi\rangle^m \tag{15.177}$$

in the closed half-plane.
Then $a(D) : \overset{o}{H}{}^{s,\gamma}(\mathbf{R}_+) \to \overset{o}{H}{}^{s-m,\gamma}(\mathbf{R}_+)$ (resp., $a(D) : \overset{o}{H}{}^{s,\gamma}(\mathbf{R}_-) \to \overset{o}{H}{}^{s-m,\gamma}(\mathbf{R}_-)$) is bounded.

Proof. Use the isomorphism

$$\overset{o}{H}{}^{r,\gamma}(\mathbf{R}_\pm) \ni u \mapsto u_\gamma \in \overset{o}{H}{}^{r}(\mathbf{R}_\pm) \tag{15.178}$$

with $r = s$ and $r = s - m$, and Theorem 15.12. □

For $\lambda \ge 0$ and $m \in \mathbf{R}$, define

$$\Lambda^m_{\lambda,\pm}(\xi) = (1+\lambda \mp i\xi)^m (= \exp[m\ln(1+\lambda \mp i\xi)]).$$

Lemma 15.19   *Let $\lambda > |\gamma| - 1$. Then for any $s \in \mathbf{R}$,*

$$\Lambda^m_{\lambda,\pm}(D) : \overset{o}{H}{}^{s,\gamma}(\mathbf{R}_{\mp}) \to \overset{o}{H}{}^{s-m,\gamma}(\mathbf{R}_{\mp}) \tag{15.179}$$

is a topological isomorphism.

Proof.   Clearly, $\Lambda^m_{\lambda,\pm}$ satisfies the condition of Theorem 15.38, for any m, hence the operator Eq. (15.179) and its counterpart with $-m$ instead of m are continuous. Since $\Lambda^m_{\lambda,\pm}(D)\Lambda^{-m}_{\lambda,\pm}(D) = I$ and the same holds for the product in the reverse order, Eq. (15.179) is the topological isomorphism☐

Theorem 15.39   *Let $s' \leq s$ and $\gamma' \leq \gamma$. Then*

$$\overset{o}{H}{}^{s,\gamma}(\mathbf{R}_+) \subset \overset{o}{H}{}^{s',\gamma'}(\mathbf{R}_+) \quad \text{and} \quad \overset{o}{H}{}^{s,\gamma}(\mathbf{R}_-) \subset \overset{o}{H}{}^{s',\gamma}(\mathbf{R}_-),$$

densely and continuously.

Proof.   With $\gamma = \gamma'$, this is an evident corollary of Eq. (15.29) d), therefore it suffices to consider the case $s = s'$. Take $\lambda > |\gamma|$, and use Lemma 15.19 to reduce to the case $s = 0$, i.e., to the statements:

$$L_2(\mathbf{R}_+; e^{2\gamma x} dx) \subset L_2(\mathbf{R}_+; e^{2\gamma' x} dx), \quad L_2(\mathbf{R}_-; e^{2\gamma' x} dx) \subset L_2(\mathbf{R}_-; e^{2\gamma x} dx),$$

densely and continuously, which are evident for $\gamma' \leq \gamma$.   □

15.10.2   Spaces $H^{s,\gamma}(\mathbf{R}_\pm)$

Definition 15.10   Let $s, \gamma \in \mathbf{R}$. We write $u \in H^{s,\gamma}(\mathbf{R}_\pm)$ iff $u_\gamma \in H^s(\mathbf{R}_\pm)$. The norm in $H^{s,\gamma}(\mathbf{R}_\pm)$ is denoted by $\|\cdot\|_{\mathbf{R}_\pm;s,\gamma}$.

Clearly, $p_\pm$, the-restriction-to-$\mathbf{R}_\pm$-operator, maps $H^{s,\gamma}(\mathbf{R}^n)$ onto $H^{s,\gamma}(\mathbf{R}^n_\pm)$. The following lemma is a straightforward generalization (and corollary) of Lemma 15.6.

Lemma 15.20   *Let $s \geq 0$ be an integer, and $\gamma \in \mathbf{R}$. Then an equivalent norm in $H^{s,\gamma}(\mathbf{R}_\pm)$ can be defined by*

$$\|u\|'^2_{\mathbf{R}_\pm;s,\gamma} = \sum_{|\alpha| \leq s} \|e^{\gamma x} D^\alpha u\|^2_{L_2(\mathbf{R}_\pm)}. \tag{15.180}$$

Theorem 15.40   *Let a be holomorphic in the half-plane $\Im\xi > \gamma$ (resp., $\Im\xi < \gamma$), continuous up to the boundary $\Im\xi = \gamma$, and satisfy an estimate Eq. (15.177) for all $\Im\xi \geq \gamma$ (resp., $\Im\xi \leq \gamma$).*

Then the operator

$$H^{s,\gamma}(\mathbf{R}_+) \ni u \mapsto p_+ a(D) l u \in H^{s-m,\gamma}(\mathbf{R}_+)$$

(resp., the operator

$$H^{s,\gamma}(\mathbf{R}_-) \ni u \mapsto p_- a(D) l u \in H^{s-m,\gamma}(\mathbf{R}_-))$$

is well-defined and bounded.

Proof. Use the isomorphism

$$\overset{o}{H}{}^{r,\gamma}(\mathbf{R}_\pm) \ni u \mapsto u_\gamma \in \overset{o}{H}{}^r(\mathbf{R}_\pm) \tag{15.181}$$

with $r = s$ and $r = s - m$, and Theorem 15.13. □

Lemma 15.21 *Let $\lambda > |\gamma| - 1$. Then for any $s \in \mathbf{R}$,*

$$p_\pm \Lambda^m_{\lambda,\pm}(D) l : H^{s,\gamma}(\mathbf{R}_\pm) \to H^{s-m,\gamma}(\mathbf{R}_\pm) \tag{15.182}$$

are topological isomorphisms.

Proof. Clearly, $\Lambda^m_{\lambda,\pm}$ satisfies the condition of Theorem 15.40, for any m, hence the operator Eq. (15.182) and its counterpart with $-m$ instead of m are continuous. Since for any $u \in H^{s-m,\gamma}(\mathbf{R}_\pm)$, and an extension operator l, we have

$$p_\pm \Lambda^m_{\lambda,\pm}(D) l\, p_\pm \Lambda^{-m}_{\lambda,\pm}(D) l u = p_\pm \Lambda^m_{\lambda,\pm}(D) \Lambda^{-m}_{\lambda,\pm}(D) l u = u$$

(cf. the proof of Theorem 15.13), and the same holds for the product in the reverse order, with $u \in H^{s,\gamma}(\mathbf{R}_\pm)$, the operators in Eq. (15.182) are topological isomorphisms. □

Theorem 15.41 *Let $s' \le s$ and $\gamma' \le \gamma$. Then*

$$H^{s,\gamma}(\mathbf{R}_+) \subset H^{s',\gamma'}(\mathbf{R}_+) \quad \text{and} \quad H^{s,\gamma'}(\mathbf{R}_-) \subset H^{s',\gamma}(\mathbf{R}_-),$$

densely and continuously.

Proof. With $\gamma = \gamma'$, this is an evident corollary of Eq. (15.29) d), therefore it suffices to consider the case $s = s'$. Take $\lambda > |\gamma|$, and use Lemma 15.21 to reduce to the case $s = 0$, i.e., to the statements:

$$L_2(\mathbf{R}_+; e^{2\gamma x} dx) \subset L_2(\mathbf{R}_+; e^{2\gamma' x} dx), \quad L_2(\mathbf{R}_-; e^{2\gamma' x} dx) \subset L_2(\mathbf{R}_-; e^{2\gamma x} dx),$$

densely and continuously, which are evident for $\gamma' \le \gamma$. □

15.10.3 *The Cauchy-type integral and its decomposition*

The results of this subsection are generalizations (and immediate corollaries) of results in Subsection 15.5.3.

First, notice that operators $\theta_\pm$ are well-defined on $C_0^\infty(\mathbf{R})$, and are bounded operators from $L_2(\mathbf{R})$ to $L_2(\mathbf{R}_\pm)$.

Theorem 15.42   *(cf. Theorem 15.14) For $\gamma \in \mathbf{R}$ and $|s| < 1/2$, $\theta_\pm$ admits a unique continuous extension $\theta_\pm : H^{s,\gamma}(\mathbf{R}) \to \overset{o}{H}{}^{s,\gamma}(\mathbf{R}_\pm)$.*

Lemma 15.22   *(cf. Lemma 15.7) Let $\gamma \in \mathbf{R}$ and $|s| < 1/2$. Then any function $f \in H^{s,\gamma}(\mathbf{R})$ admits a unique representation $f = f_+ + f_-$, where $f_\pm \in \overset{o}{H}{}^{s,\gamma}(\mathbf{R}_\pm)$, and $f_\pm = \theta_\pm f$.*

Define the extension-by-zero operator $e_\pm : p_\pm (C_0^\infty(\mathbf{R})) \to L_2(\mathbf{R})$ by

$$e_\pm f(x) = \begin{cases} f(x), & \pm x > 0 \\ 0, & \pm x \le 0. \end{cases}$$

Lemma 15.23   *(cf. Lemma 15.8) Let $\gamma \in \mathbf{R}$ and $|s| < 1/2$. Then $e_\pm$ admits a unique bounded extension $e_\pm : H^{s,\gamma}(\mathbf{R}_\pm) \to H^{s,\gamma}(\mathbf{R})$, and $H^{s,\gamma}(\mathbf{R}_\pm)$ can be identified with $\overset{o}{H}{}^{s,\gamma}(\mathbf{R}_\pm)$.*

Theorem 15.43   *(cf. Theorem 15.15) Let $f \in H^{m+s,\gamma}(\mathbf{R})$, $m > 0$ integer, $|s| < 1/2$, and $\gamma \in \mathbf{R}$. Then for $\lambda > |\gamma| - 1$,*

$$\theta_+ f = \sum_{k=1}^{m} f_{j,-}\Lambda_{\lambda,-}^{-k}(D)\delta_0 + \Lambda_{\lambda,-}^{-m}(D)\theta_+\Lambda_{\lambda,-}^m(D)f, \tag{15.183}$$

where $f_{j,-} := p'\Lambda_{\lambda,-}^{k-1}(D)f \in \mathbf{C}$, and

$$\theta_- f = \sum_{k=1}^{m} f_{j,+}\Lambda_{\lambda,+}^{-k}(D)\delta_0 + \Lambda_{\lambda,+}^{-m}(D)\theta_-\Lambda_{\lambda,+}^m(D)f, \tag{15.184}$$

where $f_{j,+} := p'\Lambda_{\lambda,+}^{k-1}(D)f \in \mathbf{C}$.

Theorem 15.44   *(cf. Theorem 15.16) Let $\gamma \in \mathbf{R}$ and $s = -m+s'$, where $m > 0$ is an integer and $|s'| < 1/2$. Then any $f \in \overset{o}{H}{}^{s,\gamma}(\mathbf{R}_+) \cap \overset{o}{H}{}^{s,\gamma}(\mathbf{R}_-)$ admits a decomposition*

$$f = \sum_{k=1}^{m} f_k D^{k-1}\delta_0, \tag{15.185}$$

where $f_k \in \mathbf{C}$.

15.11   Parabolic equations in spaces with exponential weights

The results on parabolic equations in $\mathbf{R} \times [0, +\infty)$, in weighted spaces, can be easily obtained from results of Section 15.6 by adding the index γ in the notation of spaces, and assuming that γ is chosen so that Eq. (15.34) and Eq. (15.35) hold on the line $\Im \xi = \gamma$. Details are left to the reader.

15.12   The Wiener-Hopf equation on a half-line II

15.12.1   *Statement of the problem*

Let $m \geq 0$, $\lambda_- \leq 0 \leq \lambda_+$, $\lambda_- < \lambda_+$ and $a \in S^m(\mathbf{R}; [\lambda_-, \lambda_+])$. Given (generalized) functions g on $\mathbf{R}_+$ and g^r on $\overline{\mathbf{R}_-}$, consider a problem: find u satisfying

$$a(D)u(x) \ = \ g^0(x), \quad x > 0, \tag{15.186}$$
$$u(x) \ = \ g^r(x), \quad x \leq 0. \tag{15.187}$$

Take any extension lg^r of g^r on $\mathbf{R}$, and introduce $f = u - lg^r$, $g = g^0 - p_+ a(D)lg^r$. In terms of f and g, Eq. (15.186) and Eq. (15.187) become

$$a(D)f(x) \ = \ g(x), \quad x > 0, \tag{15.188}$$
$$f(x) \ = \ 0, \quad x \leq 0. \tag{15.189}$$

Assume that $g \in H^{s-m,\gamma}(\mathbf{R}_+)$, where $\gamma \in [\lambda_-, \lambda_+]$, and interpret the problem Eq. (15.188)–Eq. (15.189) as follows: find $u \in \overset{o}{H}{}^{s,\gamma}(\mathbf{R}_+)$ satisfying

$$p_+ a(D)u = g. \tag{15.190}$$

This is the Wiener-Hopf equation. In order that the problem Eq. (15.190) be well-posed, the symbol a must satisfy some regularity conditions.

Definition 15.11   We say that $a \in S^m_{\text{reg}}(\mathbf{R} + i[\lambda_-, \lambda_+])$ and call it a *regular symbol* of order m, if the following conditions hold:

(i) $a \in S^m(\mathbf{R} + i[\lambda_-, \lambda_+])$;
(ii) there exist non-zero complex constants $d_\pm$ and $\rho_1 \in (0, 1]$ such that

$$a(\xi) = d_\pm |\xi|^m + O(|\xi|^{m-\rho_1}), \tag{15.191}$$

as $\Re\xi \to \pm\infty$, with ξ remaining in the strip $\Im\xi \in [\lambda_-, \lambda_+]$;

(iii) there exist $C > 0$ and $\rho_2 \in (0,1]$ such that for all $\xi \in \mathbf{R} + i[\lambda_-, \lambda_+]$,

$$|a'(\xi)| \le C\langle\xi\rangle^{m-\rho_2}. \tag{15.192}$$

Notice that $a \in S_{\text{reg}}^m(\mathbf{R} + i[\lambda_-, \lambda_+])$ satisfy conditions of Lemma 15.17, hence there exists a discrete set $\mathcal{Z}(a) \in (\lambda_-, \lambda_+)$ with $\lambda_\pm$ as the only possible accumulation points, such that for any $\gamma \in (\lambda_-, \lambda_+) \setminus \mathcal{Z}(a)$

$$|a(\xi)^{-1}| \le C_\gamma \langle\xi\rangle^{-m}, \quad \forall\, \xi \in \mathbf{R} + i\gamma, \tag{15.193}$$

where C_γ depends on γ but not on $\xi \in \mathbf{R} + i\gamma$.

15.12.2   The Wiener-Hopf factorization of symbols holomorphic in a strip

Fix $\gamma \in (\lambda_-, \lambda_+) \setminus \mathcal{Z}(a)$. Exactly as in Section 15.7, we can construct the factors $a_\pm = a_{\gamma,\pm}$ in the Wiener-Hopf factorization formula

$$a(\xi) = a_{\gamma,-}(\xi)a_{\gamma,+}(\xi), \tag{15.194}$$

on the line $\Im\xi = \gamma$ instead of the real line in Section 15.7. Clearly, they enjoy all the properties listed in Theorem 15.21, with the half-plane $\Im\xi < \gamma$ (resp., $\Im\xi > \gamma$) in the part of the lower half-plane $\Im\xi < 0$ (resp., $\Im\xi > 0$); the orders $\kappa_\pm = \kappa_\pm(\gamma)$ depend on $\gamma \in (\lambda_-, \lambda_+)\setminus\mathcal{Z}(a)$, too. However, $\kappa_\pm(\gamma)$ are constant on each connected component of $(\lambda_-, \lambda_+) \setminus \mathcal{Z}(a)$: to see this, notice that $\kappa_\pm(\gamma)$ depend continuously on γ, and since the limits $d_\pm$ are independent of γ, the analysis of the calculation of $\kappa_\pm(\gamma)$ shows that for any $\gamma',\gamma'' \in (\lambda_-, \lambda_+) \setminus \mathcal{Z}(a)$, the difference $\kappa_+(\gamma') - \kappa_+(\gamma'')$ is an integer (and the same holds for κ_-'s).

Since a is holomorphic in the strip $\Im\xi \in (\lambda_-, \lambda_+)$, and $a_{\gamma,+}(\xi)^{-1}$ (resp., $a_{\gamma,-}(\xi)^{-1}$) is holomorphic in the half-plane $\Im\xi > \gamma$ (resp., $\Im\xi < \gamma$), and each of these functions is continuous up to the boundary of the corresponding domain, we can analytically extend $a_{\gamma,\pm}$ on wider half-planes by

$$a_{\gamma,-}(\xi) = a(\xi)/a_{\gamma,+}(\xi), \quad \Im\xi \in [\gamma, \lambda_+], \tag{15.195}$$

$$a_{\gamma,+}(\xi) = a(\xi)/a_{\gamma,-}(\xi), \quad \Im\xi \in [\lambda_-, \gamma]. \tag{15.196}$$

Note that $a_{\gamma,-}$ (resp., $a_{\gamma,-}$) may have zeroes in the strip $\Im\xi \in (\gamma, \lambda_+]$ (resp., $\Im\xi \in [\lambda_-, \gamma)$).

By using properties of $a \in S^m_{reg}(\mathbf{R} + i[\lambda_-, \lambda_+])$ and Eq. (15.195)–Eq. (15.196), we deduce from Theorem 15.21 the following theorem.

Theorem 15.45   *Let* $a \in S^m_{reg}(\mathbf{R}; [\lambda_-, \lambda_+])$. *Then for any* $\gamma \in (\lambda_-, \lambda_+) \setminus \mathcal{Z}(a)$, *there exist functions* $a_{\gamma,\pm}$ *and constants* $\kappa_\pm(\gamma) \in \mathbf{C}$, *with the following properties:*

(a_+) $a_{\gamma,+}(\xi)$ *is holomorphic in the half-plane* $\Im \xi > \lambda_-$, *admits the continuous extension up to the boundary* $\Im \xi = \lambda_-$, *and satisfies an estimate*

$$|a_{\gamma,+}(\xi)| \le C(1 + |\xi|)^{\Re \kappa_+(\gamma)}, \tag{15.197}$$

where C *is independent of* $\Im \xi \ge \lambda_-$;

(b_+) *in the half-plane* $\Im \xi \ge \gamma$, $a_{\gamma,+}(\xi)$ *admits an estimate*

$$c(1 + |\xi|)^{\Re \kappa_+(\gamma)} \le |a_{\gamma,+}(\xi)|, \tag{15.198}$$

where $c > 0$ *is independent of* ξ, $\Im \xi \ge \gamma$;

(c_+) *for any* $\tau > \lambda_-$, $\epsilon > 0$ *and* $j = 1, 2, \ldots$, *there exists* $C_{\tau,\epsilon,j}$ *such that for all* ξ *in the half-plane* $\Im \xi \ge \tau$,

$$|a^{(j)}_{\gamma,+}(\xi)| \le C_{\tau,\epsilon,j}(1 + |\xi|)^{\Re \kappa_+(\gamma) - \rho + \epsilon}, \tag{15.199}$$

where $\rho = \min\{\rho_1, \rho_2\} \in (0, 1]$;

(d_+) $a^{\pm 1}_{\gamma,+}$ *admits a representation*

$$a_{\gamma,+}(\xi)^{\pm 1} = d^{\pm 1}(-1)^l(1 + \lambda - i\xi)^{\pm \kappa_+(\gamma)} + t^{\pm}_{\gamma,\lambda;+}(\xi), \tag{15.200}$$

where d *is defined by Eq. (15.72)*, $\lambda = \max\{-\lambda_-, \lambda_+\}$, *and* $t^{\pm}_{\gamma,\lambda,+}$ *admits the following estimate: for any* $\epsilon > 0$, *there exists* $C_\epsilon > 0$ *such that for all* ξ *in the half-plane* $\Im \xi \ge \gamma$,

$$|t^{\pm}_{\gamma,\lambda;+}(\xi)| \le C_\epsilon(1 + |\xi|)^{\pm \Re \kappa_+(\gamma) - \rho + \epsilon}; \tag{15.201}$$

(a_-) $a_{\gamma,-}(\xi)$ *is holomorphic in the half-plane* $\Im \xi < \lambda_+$, *admits the continuous extension up to the boundary* $\Im \xi = \lambda_+$, *and satisfies an estimate*

$$|a_{\gamma,-}(\xi)| \le C(1 + |\xi|)^{\Re \kappa_-(\gamma)}, \tag{15.202}$$

where C *is independent of* $\Im \xi \le \lambda_+$;

(b_-) *in the half-plane* $\Im \xi \le \gamma$, $a_{\gamma,-}(\xi)$ *admits an estimate*

$$c(1 + |\xi|)^{\Re \kappa_-(\gamma)} \le |a_{\gamma,-}(\xi)|, \tag{15.203}$$

where $c > 0$ *is independent of* ξ, $\Im \xi \le \gamma$;

(c_-) *for any* $\tau < \lambda_+$, $\epsilon > 0$ *and* $j = 1, 2, \ldots$, *there exists* $C_{\tau, \epsilon, j}$ *such that for all* ξ *in the half-plane* $\Im \xi \leq \tau$,

$$|a_{\gamma,-}^{(j)}(\xi)| \leq C_{\tau,\epsilon,j}(1 + |\xi|)^{\Re \kappa_-(\gamma) - \rho + \epsilon}, \qquad (15.204)$$

where $\rho = \min\{\rho_1, \rho_2\} \in (0, 1]$;
(d_-) $a_{\gamma,-}^{\pm 1}$ *admits a representation*

$$a_{\gamma,-}(\xi)^{\pm 1} = (1 + \lambda + i\xi)^{\pm \kappa_-(\gamma)} + t_{\gamma,\lambda;-}^{\pm}(\xi), \qquad (15.205)$$

where $\lambda = \max\{-\lambda_-, \lambda_+\}$, *and* $t_{\gamma,\lambda,-}^{\pm}$ *admits the following estimate: for any* $\epsilon > 0$, *there exists* $C_\epsilon > 0$ *such that for all* ξ *in the half-plane* $\Im \xi \leq \gamma$,

$$|t_{\gamma,\lambda;-}^{\pm}(\xi)| \leq C_\epsilon(1 + |\xi|)^{\pm \Re \kappa_-(\gamma) - \rho + \epsilon}; \qquad (15.206)$$

(e) Eq. (15.194) holds in the strip $\Im \xi \in [\lambda_-, \lambda_+]$;
(f) conditions $(a_\pm) - (b_\pm)$ *define factors in Eq. (15.194) uniquely, up to scalar multiples.*

15.12.3   *Main Theorems*

The results below can be deduced from Theorem 15.45 exactly as their analogues in Subsection 15.7.3 are deduced from Theorem 15.21.

We assume that $a \in S_{\text{reg}}^m(\mathbf{R} + i[\lambda_-, \lambda_+])$, and we fix $\gamma \in (\lambda_-, \lambda_+) \setminus \mathcal{Z}(a)$.

Theorem 15.46   *Let* $s - \Re \kappa_-(\gamma) \in (-1/2, 1/2)$.
   Then the operator

$$p_+a(D) : \overset{o}{H}{}^{s,\gamma}(\mathbf{R}_+) \to H^{s-m,\gamma}(\mathbf{R}_+)$$

is invertible, with the inverse given by

$$H^{s-m,\gamma}(\mathbf{R}_+) \ni g \mapsto u \in \overset{o}{H}{}^{s,\gamma}(\mathbf{R}_+),$$

where

$$u = a_{\gamma,-}(D)^{-1}\theta_+ a_{\gamma,+}(D)^{-1}lg \in \overset{o}{H}{}^{s,\gamma}(\mathbf{R}_+), \qquad (15.207)$$

and $lg \in H^{s-m,\gamma}(\mathbf{R})$ *is an arbitrary extension of* g.

Corollary 15.4   *Let* $s - \Re \kappa_-(\gamma) \in (-1/2, 1/2)$, *and let* g *in Eq. (15.190) belong to* $H^{r,\gamma}(\mathbf{R}_+)$, *where* $r + \kappa_+(\gamma) = q + s'$, q *is a positive integer and* $s' \in (-1/2, 1/2)$.

Then $u \in \overset{o}{H}{}^{s,\gamma}(\mathbf{R}_+)$, the solution to Eq. (15.190), admits a representation

$$u = \sum_{j=1}^{q} c_j(lg)\Lambda_{\lambda,-}^{-j}(D)a_{\gamma,-}(D)^{-1}\delta_0 + \Lambda_{\lambda,-}^{-q}a_{\gamma,-}(D)^{-1}\theta + \Lambda_{\lambda,-}^{q}(D)a_{\gamma,+}(D)^{-1}lg,$$

(15.208)

where $\lambda = \max\{-\lambda_-, \lambda_+\}$, and

$$c_j(lg) = (\Lambda_{\lambda,-}^{j-1}a_{\gamma,+}(D)^{-1}lg)(0).$$

(15.209)

Theorem 15.47 *Let $s - \Re\kappa_-(\gamma) = -q + s'$, where q is a positive integer and $|s'| < 1/2$.*

Then for any $g \in H^{s-m,\gamma}(\mathbf{R}_+)$, a solution to the Wiener-Hopf equation Eq. (15.190) exists but it is non-unique, and the general solution is given by

$$u = a_{\gamma,-}(D)^{-1}\Lambda_{\lambda,-}(D)^{q}\theta + \Lambda_{\lambda,-}(D)^{-q}a_{\gamma,+}(D)^{-1}lg + a_{\gamma,-}(D)^{-1}\sum_{j=1}^{q}c_j D^{j-1}\delta_0.$$

(15.210)

15.12.4 The asymptotics of solutions near the boundary and the free boundary problems

We leave to the reader the straightforward reformulations of all the results of Subsections 6.4 and 6.5.

15.12.5 The asymptotics of solutions at the infinity

We assume that $a \in S_{\text{reg}}^{m}(\mathbf{R}+i[\lambda_-, \lambda_+])$, and we fix $\gamma_1, \gamma_2 \in (\lambda_-, \lambda_+)\backslash\mathcal{Z}(a)$, $\gamma_1 < \gamma_2$. In the strip $\Im\xi \in (\gamma_1, \gamma_2)$, there may exist finitely many zeroes $\xi_1, \ldots, \xi_q$ of the symbol a. Let k_j be the multiplicity of a zero ξ_j.

Theorem 15.48 *Let $u \in \overset{o}{H}{}^{s,\gamma_1}(\mathbf{R}_+)$ be a solution to Eq. (15.190).*

Then there exist $u_1 \in H^{s,\gamma_2}(\mathbf{R}_+)$ and constants $c_{jl}, j = 1, \ldots, q, l = 1, \ldots, k_j$, such that $u(x)$ has the following asymptotics, as $x \to +\infty$:

$$u(x) = \sum_{j=1}^{q}\sum_{l=1}^{k_j} c_{jl}x^{l-1}\exp[i\xi_j x] + u_1(x).$$

(15.211)

growing data]

15.13   Parabolic equations on R × R₊ with exponentially growing data

Assume that $m > 0$, $a \in S^m_{\mathrm{reg}}(\mathbf{R} + i[\lambda_-, \lambda_+])$, and Eq. (15.191) holds with $\Re d_\pm > 0$, and consider the problem

$$(\partial_t + a(D_x))f(x,t) \; = \; g(x,t), \quad t > 0, x > 0; \qquad (15.212)$$
$$f(x,t) \; = \; 0, \qquad x \leq 0, t \geq 0; \qquad (15.213)$$
$$f(x, +0) \; = \; g_0(x), \qquad x \geq 0. \qquad (15.214)$$

(For simplicity, we impose the homogeneous boundary condition Eq. (15.213), which corresponds to the case of barrier options without a rebate; the general case can easily be reduced to this one by the appropriate change of the unknown function). Assume that the data grow exponentially, for instance, $g_0 \in H^{s,\gamma}(\mathbf{R}_+)$, and $g \in C([0,+\infty); H^{s-m,\gamma}(\mathbf{R}_+))$, where $\gamma \in (\lambda_-, \lambda_+) \setminus \mathcal{Z}(a)$. From Eq. (15.191) and Eq. (15.193), we conclude that Eq. (15.35) holds on the line $\Im \xi = \gamma$: there exist $c_0 > 0$ and $\sigma_0 \in \mathbf{R}$ such that

$$\Re a(\xi) \geq c_0 \langle \xi \rangle^m - \sigma_0, \quad \Im \xi = \gamma. \qquad (15.215)$$

Change the unknown

$$f(x,t) = e^{\sigma_0 t - \gamma x} f_{\sigma_0,\gamma}(x,t)$$

and the RHS in Eq. (15.212) and Eq. (15.214):

$$g(x,t) \; = \; e^{\sigma_0 t - \gamma x} g_{\sigma_0,\gamma}(x,t),$$
$$g_0(x) \; = \; e^{-\gamma x} g_{0,\gamma}(x).$$

In terms of $f_{\sigma_0,\gamma}$ and $g_{\sigma_0,\gamma}$, the problem Eq. (15.212)-Eq. (15.37) becomes

$$(\partial_t + a_{\sigma_0,\gamma}(D_x))f_{\sigma_0,\gamma}(x,t) \; = \; g_{\sigma_0,\gamma}(x,t), \quad t > 0, x > 0; \; (15.216)$$
$$f_{\sigma_0,\gamma}(x,t) \; = \; 0, \qquad x \leq 0, t \geq 0; \; (15.217)$$
$$f_{\sigma_0,\gamma}(x, +0) \; = \; g_{0,\gamma}(x), \qquad x \geq 0, \qquad (15.218)$$

where $a_{\sigma_0,\gamma}(\xi) := a(\xi + i\gamma) + \sigma_0$ satisfies Eq. (15.38):

$$\Re a_{\sigma_0,\gamma}(\xi) \geq c_0 \langle \xi \rangle^m, \quad \xi \in \mathbf{R}, \qquad (15.219)$$

and the data do not exhibit the exponential growth: $g_{0,\gamma} \in H^s(\mathbf{R}_+)$, and $g_{\sigma_0,\gamma} \in C([0,+\infty); H^{s-m}(\mathbf{R}_+))$. By using Eq. (15.219) and taking into account that $a_{\sigma_0,\gamma} \in S^m_{\mathbf{R}^n reg}(\mathbf{R})$, we can use the results of Section 15.8 to solve the problem Eq. (15.216)-Eq. (15.218), and then obtain the solution to the problem Eq. (15.212)-Eq. (15.214). The details are left to the reader.

Chapter 16

Elements of calculus of pseudodifferential operators

In this Chapter, we list basic definitions and facts for simple classes of PDO in $\mathbf{R}^n$, which are necessary for the proofs of the results on NIG-like Feller processes in Chapter 14, and calculation of approximate prices of European options in Chapter 14 and basket options and exchange options in Chapter 9. The results of this Chapter can be used to calculate prices of barrier options under Lévy-like Feller processes.

In contrast to the case of PDO with constant symbols, where the Fourier transform establishes the equivalence of the action of PDO and the multiplication operator, and so rather weak regularity conditions on symbols suffice, here appropriate estimates on the derivatives of symbols must be imposed. For simplicity, one usually assumes that symbols are infinitely smooth, and imposes conditions on all derivatives, though weaker conditions suffice to obtain the main results. In Section 16.1, we explain the main ingredients and structure of the general theory of PDO for the simplest class. We omit the most technical proofs like the composition theorem and the theorem on the boundedness in appropriate scales of Banach spaces but we include several proofs, which demonstrate how the theory of PDO works in relatively simple situations.

In Section 16.2, PDO depending on a parameter are considered; this variant of the theory of PDO is needed in order to obtain approximate solutions to pseudo-differential equations, when the exact analytical formulas are non-available, and in Section 16.3, we consider PDO with symbols holomorphic in a tube domain; this variant of the theory of PDO is necessary to treat problems with exponentially growing data. In Section 16.4, the proofs of the technical results of Chapter 14 are presented. The transformation of the symbol of a PDO under a change of variables is considered in the last section.

16.1 Basics of the theory of PDO with symbols of the class $S^m_{1,0}(\mathbf{R}^n \times \mathbf{R}^n)$

Definition 16.1 Let $m \in \mathbf{R}$. We write $a \in S^m_{1,0}(\mathbf{R}^n \times \mathbf{R}^n)$, if a is infinitely smooth, and for all multi-indices α, β the derivative $a^{(\alpha)}_{(\beta)} := \partial^\alpha_\xi D^\beta_x a$ satisfies the following estimate

$$|a^{(\alpha)}_{(\beta)}(x,\xi)| \le C_{\alpha,\beta}\langle\xi\rangle^{m-|\alpha|}, \tag{16.1}$$

where constant $C_{\alpha,\beta}$ is independent of (x,ξ).

We set $S^{-\infty}(\mathbf{R}^n \times \mathbf{R}^n) := \cap_m S^m_{1,0}(\mathbf{R}^n \times \mathbf{R}^n)$.

We start with this by now quite classical case since results for PDO with symbols of the class $S^m(\mathbf{R}^n \times (\mathbf{R}^n + i\bar{U}))$ can be deduced quite easily from the results for $S^m_{1,0}(\mathbf{R}^n \times \mathbf{R}^n)$. Most of the results below, with the exception of the boundedness theorem for the Hölder spaces, can be found Grubb (1996) and Hörmander (1985) (and local versions in Shubin (1978)); however, the form and proofs of some results, which we give below, do not necessarily coincide with the proofs in these monographs.

16.1.1 *Asymptotic summation and the composition theorem*

The following notation and theorem simplify many formulations in the theory of PDO.

Definition 16.2 We say that $a \in S^m_{1,0}(\mathbf{R}^n \times \mathbf{R}^n)$ admits an *asymptotic expansion*

$$a \sim \sum_{j=0}^{+\infty} a_j, \tag{16.2}$$

if for any N

$$r_N := a - \sum_{j=0}^{N-1} a_j \in S^{m-N}_{1,0}(\mathbf{R}^n \times \mathbf{R}^n). \tag{16.3}$$

The celebrated subclass of $S_{1,0}^m(\mathbf{R}^n \times \mathbf{R}^n)$ (historically, the first class of PDO) is the class S^m of *classical PDO* of order m, with symbols admitting the asymptotic expansion Eq. (16.2) having the following property: $a_j(x,\xi)$ are positively homogeneous w.r.t. ξ, of order $m - j$, outside a unit ball:

$$a_j(x, t\xi) = t^{m-j} a_j(x, \xi),$$

for all $|\xi| \geq 1$ and $t > 0$.

Remark 16.1. In the theory of PDO, it is often convenient to use a weaker form of Eq. (16.3): $r_N \in S_{1,0}^{m-M}(\mathbf{R}^n \times \mathbf{R}^n)$, where $M \to +\infty$ as $N \to +\infty$, but we will not need this form here.

For large $|\xi|$, the error term $r_N(x, \xi)$ is relatively small, and in the case of symbols depending on a parameter, it is relatively small uniformly in (x, ξ), so one can regard Eq. (16.2) as an approximate equality.

Theorem 16.1   *(Asymptotic summation; Shubin (1978), Proposition 3.5).*
Let $a_j \in S_{1,0}^{m-j}(\mathbf{R}^n \times \mathbf{R}^n), j = 0, 1, \ldots.$
    Then

(i) *there exists* $a \in S_{1,0}^m(\mathbf{R}^n \times \mathbf{R}^n)$ *such that Eq. (16.2) holds, and*
(ii) *if* $a^1 \in S_{1,0}^m(\mathbf{R}^n \times \mathbf{R}^n)$ *is another symbol satisfying Eq. (16.2), then* $a^1 - a \in S^{-\infty}(\mathbf{R}^n \times \mathbf{R}^n).$

On the space $\mathcal{S}(\mathbf{R}^n)$, the action of a PDO $a(x, D)$ with *symbol* $a \in S_{1,0}^m(\mathbf{R}^n \times \mathbf{R}^n)$ is defined by

$$a(x, D)u(x) = (2\pi)^{-n} \int_{\mathbf{R}^n} e^{ix\xi} a(x, \xi) \hat{u}(\xi) d\xi. \tag{16.4}$$

Theorem 16.2   *Let* $a \in S_{1,0}^m(\mathbf{R}^n \times \mathbf{R}^n).$
    Then a PDO $a(x, D)$ *maps* $\mathcal{S}(\mathbf{R}^n)$ *into itself, continuously.*

The proof is a straightforward exercise.
    If a is a polynomial in ξ:

$$a(x, \xi) = \sum_{|\alpha| \leq m} a_\alpha(x) \xi^\alpha,$$

then Eq. (16.4) gives the definition of a differential operator

$$a(x, D)u(x) = \sum_{|\alpha| \leq m} a_\alpha(x)(D^\alpha u)(x).$$

If we write the coefficients on the right, we obtain another operator, denote it a_r:

$$a_r(x, D)u = \sum_{|\alpha|\leq m} (D^\alpha(a_\alpha u))(x).$$

The corresponding general definition of a PDO $a_r(x, D)$ with the *right symbol*[1] a for $a \in S_{1,0}^m(\mathbf{R}^n \times \mathbf{R}^n)$ is

$$a_r(x, D) = (2\pi)^{-n} \int_{-\infty}^{+\infty} \int_{-\infty}^{+\infty} e^{i(x-y)\xi} a(y, \xi)u(y)dyd\xi,$$

where the integral is understood as the iterated one. PDO with the right symbols naturally arise when one considers the adjoint operators. The following theorem ensures that the *adjoint operator* belongs to the same class of PDO, and gives the formula for its symbol. Its proof and the proof of the *Composition Theorem* are rather technical, and we refer the reader to Shubin (1978), Hörmander (1985) and Grubb (1996).

Theorem 16.3   *Let $a \in S_{1,0}^m(\mathbf{R}^n \times \mathbf{R}^n)$.*
Then the (complex) adjoint $a(x, D)^*$ defined by

$$(a(x, D)u, v) = (u, a(x, D)^*v)$$

is a PDO whose (left) symbol a^* belongs to $S_{1,0}^m(\mathbf{R}^n \times \mathbf{R}^n)$ and admits an asymptotic expansion

$$a^*(x, \xi) \sim \sum_{|\alpha|\geq 0} (\alpha!)^{-1}\bar{a}_{(\alpha)}^{(\alpha)}(x, \xi).$$

Theorem 16.3 and Theorem 16.2 allow one to define the action of $a(x, D)$ on $\mathcal{S}'(\mathbf{R}^n)$ by duality:

$$\langle a(x, D)\phi, f\rangle = \langle \phi, a(x, D)^*f\rangle, \quad \forall f \in \mathcal{S}(\mathbf{R}^n).$$

Clearly, if $\phi \in \mathcal{S}(\mathbf{R}^n)$ then the new definition of $a(x, D)\phi$ coincides with the old one. Further, $a(x, D)$ is a continuous map from $\mathcal{S}'(\mathbf{R}^n)$ into itself. This map can be defined as a unique continuous extension of the map defined by Eq. (16.4) on $\mathcal{S}(\mathbf{R}^n)$, and the standard agreement in the theory of PDO is to denote this map by the same symbol $a(x, D)$; the restriction of $a(x, D)$ on any subspace $L \subset \mathcal{S}'(\mathbf{R}^n)$ is also denoted by the same symbol.

[1]In this context, Eq. (16.4) is the definition of the PDO $a(x, D)$ with the *left symbol a*.

The next basic fact and the most important tool in the theory is the Composition Theorem.

Theorem 16.4   *Let $a \in S_{1,0}^m(\mathbf{R}^n \times \mathbf{R}^n)$ and $b \in S_{1,0}^{m'}(\mathbf{R}^n \times \mathbf{R}^n)$. Then $C = a(x, D)b(x, D)$ is a PDO with the symbol $c \in S_{1,0}^{m+m'}(\mathbf{R}^n \times \mathbf{R}^n)$, which admits an asymptotic expansion*

$$c(x, \xi) \sim \sum_{|\alpha| \geq 0} (\alpha!)^{-1} a^{(\alpha)}(x, \xi) b_{(\alpha)}(x, \xi), \tag{16.5}$$

in the sense that for any integer $N > 0$,

$$r_N = c - \sum_{0 \leq |\alpha| \leq N-1} (\alpha!)^{-1} a^{(\alpha)} b_{(\alpha)} \in S_{1,0}^{m+m'-N}(\mathbf{R}^n \times \mathbf{R}^n). \tag{16.6}$$

16.1.2   Parametrix and approximate square root

Definition 16.3   We write $a \in IS_{1,0}^m(\mathbf{R}^n \times \mathbf{R}^n)$ iff $a \in S_{1,0}^m(\mathbf{R}^n \times \mathbf{R}^n)$ is invertible and admits a bound

$$|a(x, \xi)^{-1}| \leq C\langle \xi \rangle^{-m}, \tag{16.7}$$

where C is independent of (x, ξ).

We call a an *elliptic symbol*, and $A = a(x, D)$ an *elliptic operator*.

Remark 16.2.   The standard definition of an elliptic symbol requires Eq. (16.7) outside a compact set in ξ-space. We use Eq. (16.7), since it suffices for our purposes and admits a trivial generalization for the case of operators depending on a parameter.

The following definition formalizes an intuitive notion of an approximate inverse.

Definition 16.4   We say that $B = b(x, D)$ is a *parametrix* of $A = a(x, D)$ if and only if

$$AB = I + t_1(x, D), \quad BA = I + t_2(x, D), \tag{16.8}$$

where $t_j \in S^{-\infty}(\mathbf{R}^n \times \mathbf{R}^n)$.

Theorem 16.5   *(Parametrix construction) Let $a \in IS_{1,0}^m(\mathbf{R}^n \times \mathbf{R}^n)$. Then $A = a(x, D)$ has a parametrix $B = b(x, D)$, where $b \in S_{1,0}^{-m}(\mathbf{R}^n \times \mathbf{R}^n)$ admits an asymptotic expansion*

$$b \sim b_{-m} + b_{-m-1} + \cdots, \tag{16.9}$$

where

$$b_{-m} = 1/a \in S_{1,0}^{-m}(\mathbf{R}^n \times \mathbf{R}^n), \tag{16.10}$$

and $b_{-m-s} \in S_{1,0}^{-m-s}(\mathbf{R}^n \times \mathbf{R}^n), s = 1, 2, \ldots$ *are defined inductively by*

$$b_{-m-s} = -a^{-1} \sum_{j<s, j+|\alpha|=s} (\alpha!)^{-1} a^{(\alpha)} (b_{-m-j})_{(\alpha)}. \tag{16.11}$$

Proof. Step 1. We construct b such that

$$Ab(x, D) = I + t(x, D), \tag{16.12}$$

and similarly one can construct $b'(x, D)$ such that

$$b'(x, D)A = I + t'(x, D), \tag{16.13}$$

where $t, t' \in S^{-\infty}(\mathbf{R}^n \times \mathbf{R}^n)$. By mimicking the standard argument on the equality of the left and right inverses, one deduces that Eq. (16.13) holds with $b(x, D)$ (and generally, with different $t' \in S^{-\infty}(\mathbf{R}^n \times \mathbf{R}^n)$).

Step 2. From Eq. (16.7), we deduce that $b_{-m} := 1/a \in S_{1,0}^{-m}(\mathbf{R}^n \times \mathbf{R}^n)$, and by substituting the asymptotic expansion Eq. (16.9) with yet unknown $b_{-m-s} \in S_{1,0}^{-m-s}(\mathbf{R}^n \times \mathbf{R}^n), s = 1, 2, \ldots$ (for any sequence of such $b_{-m-s}, s \geq 1$, b is defined by Theorem 16.1), and by using the composition theorem we obtain Eq. (16.12), where $t \in S_{1,0}^{-1}(\mathbf{R}^n \times \mathbf{R}^n)$ admits an asymptotic expansion

$$t \sim \sum_{s \geq 1} t_s, \tag{16.14}$$

with $t_s \in S_{1,0}^{-s}(\mathbf{R}^n \times \mathbf{R}^n), s \geq 1$, given by

$$\begin{aligned} t_s &= \sum_{j+|\alpha|=s} (\alpha!)^{-1} a^{(\alpha)} (b_{-m-j})_{(\alpha)} \\ &= ab_{-m-s} + \sum_{j<s, j+|\alpha|=s} (\alpha!)^{-1} a^{(\alpha)} (b_{-m-j})_{(\alpha)}. \end{aligned} \tag{16.15}$$

Define $b_{-m-s}, s \geq 1$, by Eq. (16.11). Then by induction, we find $b_{-m-s} \in S_{1,0}^{-m-s}(\mathbf{R}^n \times \mathbf{R}^n)$, and the RHS in Eq. (16.15) is zero. Hence, t given by Eq. (16.14) is of the class $S_{1,0}^{-\infty}(\mathbf{R}^n \times \mathbf{R}^n)$, and $b(x, D)$ is a parametrix of $a(x, D)$. $\square$

Theorem 16.6   (*Asymptotic square root*) *Let* $a \in IS_{1,0}^m(\mathbf{R}^n \times \mathbf{R}^n)$ *satisfy*

$$a(x,\xi) \notin \bar{R}_-, \quad \forall\, (x,\xi) \in \mathbf{R}^n \times \mathbf{R}^n. \tag{16.16}$$

Then there exists $b \in S_{1,0}^{m/2}(\mathbf{R}^n \times \mathbf{R}^n)$ *such that*

$$b(x,D)^2 = a(x,D) + t(x,D), \tag{16.17}$$

where $t \in S^{-\infty}(\mathbf{R}^n \times \mathbf{R}^n)$, *and* b *admits an asymptotic expansion*

$$b \sim \sum_{j=0}^{+\infty} b_{m/2-j}, \tag{16.18}$$

where

$$b_{m/2} := a^{1/2} \in S_{1,0}^{m/2}(\mathbf{R}^n \times \mathbf{R}^n), \tag{16.19}$$

and $b_{m/2-s} \in S_{1,0}^{m/2-s}(\mathbf{R}^n \times \mathbf{R}^n), s \geq 1$, *are defined inductively by*

$$b_{m/2-s} = -\frac{1}{2}b_{m/2}^{-1} \sum_{j,k<s,|\alpha|+k+j=s} (\alpha!)^{-1}(b_{m/2-k})^{(\alpha)}(b_{m/2-j})_{(\alpha)}. \tag{16.20}$$

Proof.   Fix a branch of $\ln$ by the requirement $\ln a \in \mathbf{R}$ for $a > 0$, and set

$$b_{m/2}(x,\xi) = a(x,\xi)^{1/2} := \exp[\frac{1}{2}\ln a(x,\xi)].$$

Under assumption Eq. (16.16), the symbol $b_{m/2}$ is well-defined, and by using Eq. (16.7), one can easily check that it belongs to $S_{1,0}^{m/2}(\mathbf{R}^n \times \mathbf{R}^n)$. Fix any sequence of $b_{m/2-s} \in S_{1,0}^{m/2-s}(\mathbf{R}^n \times \mathbf{R}^n), s \geq 1$, define $b \in S_{1,0}^{m/2}(\mathbf{R}^n \times \mathbf{R}^n)$ by Eq. (16.18), by using Theorem 16.1, and calculate the symbol of $b(x,D)^2$ by using the composition theorem. We obtain that it admits an asymptotic expansion

$$b_{m/2}^2 + \sum_{s \geq 1} t^s, \tag{16.21}$$

where

$$\begin{aligned}
t^s &= \sum_{|\alpha|+k+j=s} (\alpha!)^{-1}(b_{m/2-k})^{(\alpha)}(b_{m/2-j})_{(\alpha)} \\
&= 2b_{m/2-s}b_{m/2} \\
&\quad + \sum_{j,k<s,|\alpha|+k+j=s} (\alpha!)^{-1}(b_{m/2-k})^{(\alpha)}(b_{m/2-j})_{(\alpha)}. \tag{16.22}
\end{aligned}$$

If we define $b_{m/2-s}, s \geq 1$, by Eq. (16.20), we obtain that the RHS in Eq. (16.22) vanishes, and Eq. (16.21) gives Eq. (16.17). $\qquad\qquad\qquad$ □

16.1.3   *Boundedness theorem*

One also needs a boundedness result for PDO in Banach spaces embedded in $\mathcal{S}'(\mathbf{R}^n)$. Such most popular and simple spaces are L_2-based Sobolev spaces $H^s(\mathbf{R}^n)$, since in this case estimates for norms can easily be obtained by means of the Fourier transform (see, e.g., Eskin (1973), Taylor (1981), Hórmander (1985) and Grubb (1996)). For the theory of stochastic processes, Hölder spaces $C^s(\mathbf{R}^n)$ are more appropriate. Until relatively recent times, only local Hölder estimates were available (see, e.g., Taylor (1981)); in Yamazaki (1986), global estimates are obtained for Besov spaces $B_{p,q}^s, p, q \in (0, \infty]$, and results, which are necessary for us, follow as special cases, since

for $s \in \mathbf{R}$, $\quad B_{2,2}^s$ is the Sobolev space $H^s(\mathbf{R}^n)$;

for $s > 0$, $B_{\infty,\infty}^s(\mathbf{R}^n)$ is the Hölder-Zygmund space $C^s(\mathbf{R}^n)$,

and finally,

for non-integer $s > 0$, $C^s(\mathbf{R}^n)$ is the Hölder space, with the norm defined by

for $s \in (0, 1)$:

$$||u||_{C^s} = ||u||_{L_\infty} + \sup_{x \in \mathbf{R}^n} \sup_{|h| \leq 1} |h|^{-s} |u(x+h) - u(x)|;$$

for $s = m + s'$, where $m > 0$ is an integer and $s' \in (0, 1)$,

$$||u||_{C^s} = \sum_{|\alpha| \leq m} ||D^\alpha u||_{C^{s'}}.$$

Theorem 16.7   *Let $p, q \in (0, \infty]$, $m, s, \in \mathbf{R}$, and $a \in S_{1,0}^m(\mathbf{R}^n \times \mathbf{R}^n)$. Then $a(x, D) : B_{p,q}^s(\mathbf{R}^n) \to B_{p,q}^{s-m}(\mathbf{R}^n)$ is bounded, and its norm admits an estimate*

$$||a(x, D)|| \leq C \sup_{|\alpha|+|\beta| \leq N} \sup_{(x,\xi) \in \mathbf{R}^n \times \mathbf{R}^n} \langle \xi \rangle^{|\alpha|-m} |a_{(\beta)}^{(\alpha)}(x, \xi)|, \qquad (16.23)$$

where the constants C and N depend on s, m, p, q and n but not on $a \in S_{1,0}^m(\mathbf{R}^n \times \mathbf{R}^n)$.

16.1.4 *The inverse operator and the square root*

The results of this subsection can be found in Grubb (1996).

Theorem 16.8 *Let* $a \in IS_{1,0}^m(\mathbf{R}^n \times \mathbf{R}^n)$, *and let for some* s, $A = a(x, D)$: $H^s(\mathbf{R}^n) \to H^{s-m}(\mathbf{R}^n)$ *be invertible.*

Then the inverse is a PDO of the class $S_{1,0}^{-m}(\mathbf{R}^n \times \mathbf{R}^n)$, *and its symbol admits the same asymptotic expansion Eq. (16.9) as the parametrix.*

Corollary 16.1 *Under the conditions of Theorem 16.8, A is an invertible operator in* $\mathcal{S}(\mathbf{R}^n)$, *and for any r,* $A : H^r(\mathbf{R}^n) \to H^{r-m}(\mathbf{R}^n)$ *is invertible.*

Proof. $\mathcal{S}(\mathbf{R}^n) \subset H^r(\mathbf{R}^n)$, for any r, hence both A and A^{-1} maps $\mathcal{S}(\mathbf{R}^n)$ into itself. Therefore, they are mutual inverses as operators in $\mathcal{S}(\mathbf{R}^n)$. Since $\mathcal{S}(\mathbf{R}^n) \subset H^r(\mathbf{R}^n)$ densely, and $A^{-1} : H^{r-m}(\mathbf{R}^n) \to H^r(\mathbf{R}^n)$ is bounded, we conclude that A^{-1} is the inverse to $A : H^r(\mathbf{R}^n) \to H^{r-m}(\mathbf{R}^n)$. □

Remark 16.3. Corollary 16.1 is valid not for the scale $H^s(\mathbf{R}^n)$ only but for many other scales of spaces as well.

Theorem 16.9 *Let the conditions of Theorem 16.6 hold, and let* $\Re a(x, D)$ *be positive-definite, and* $\Im a(x, D)(\Re a(x, D))^{-1}$ *be bounded.*

Then there exists a PDO $B = b(x, D)$ such that $B^2 = A$, and its symbol $b \in S_{1,0}^{m/2}(\mathbf{R}^n \times \mathbf{R}^n)$ *admits the same asymptotic expansion Eq. (16.18) as an approximate square root.*

16.2 Operators depending on parameters

Consider a PDO with the symbol depending on a parameter (or parameters). If the dependence is nice, one can exploit it and obtain useful results, e.g., prove the invertibility of the operator for large (or small, depending on the situation) values of the parameter(s), and derive approximate formulae for the inverse. As it turns out, the simplest way to realize this possibility is to repeat the whole sequence of definitions and theorems from the very beginning by explicitly specifying the dependence on the parameter(s). The proofs themselves can be repeated word by word, without any change except in the notation. For similar results about operators with a parameter, see, e.g., Shubin (1978) and Grubb (1996).

We consider the case when there are two parameters – one, call it ϵ, describing the possible smallness of the derivatives w.r.t. x, and the other, call it d, which describes the smallness of the derivatives w.r.t. ξ. The case when only derivatives w.r.t. x (respectively ξ) are small obtains by fixing d (respectively ϵ).

So, let $\mathcal{E} \subset (0,1]$ and $\mathcal{D} \subset [1,+\infty)$ be the sets on which ϵ and d live; we assume that the statement $\epsilon/d \to 0$ makes sense on the set $\mathcal{E} \times \mathcal{D}$, and we regard a pair (ϵ, d) as a parameter.

The starting point is a natural generalization of the class $S^m_{1,0}(\mathbf{R}^n \times \mathbf{R}^n)$.

Definition 16.5 Let $m \in \mathbf{R}$. We write $a \in S^m_{1,0}(\mathcal{E} \times \mathcal{D}; \mathbf{R}^n \times \mathbf{R}^n)$ if $a = a(\epsilon, d; x, \xi)$ satisfies estimates

$$|a^{(\alpha)}_{(\beta)}(\epsilon, d; x, \xi)| \le C_{\alpha\beta} \epsilon^{|\beta|} (d + |\xi|)^{m-|\alpha|}, \qquad (16.24)$$

for all multi-indices α, β, where the constants $C_{\alpha\beta}$ are independent of $\epsilon \in \mathcal{E}, d \in \mathcal{D}, (x, \xi) \in \mathbf{R}^n \times \mathbf{R}^n$.

We set

$$S^{-\infty}((\mathcal{E} \times \mathcal{D}); \mathbf{R}^n \times \mathbf{R}^n) := \cap_{m \in \mathbf{R}} S^m_{1,0}((\mathcal{E} \times \mathcal{D}); \mathbf{R}^n \times \mathbf{R}^n).$$

Sometimes we will use these definitions with

$$(\mathcal{E} \times \mathcal{D})_{\epsilon_0} = \{(\epsilon, d) \in \mathcal{E} \times \mathcal{D} \mid \epsilon/d < \epsilon_0\}$$

instead of $\mathcal{E} \times \mathcal{D}$.

Definition 16.6 We say that $a \in S^m_{1,0}(\mathcal{E} \times \mathcal{D}; \mathbf{R}^n \times \mathbf{R}^n)$ admits an asymptotic expansion Eq. (16.2) if for any N

$$r_N := a - \sum_{j=0}^{N-1} a_j \in \epsilon^N S^{m-N}_{1,0}(\mathcal{E} \times \mathcal{D}; \mathbf{R}^n \times \mathbf{R}^n). \qquad (16.25)$$

Theorem 16.10 Let $\epsilon^{-j} a_j \in S^{m-j}_{1,0}(\mathcal{E} \times \mathcal{D}; \mathbf{R}^n \times \mathbf{R}^n), \quad j = 0, 1, \dots$
Then there exists $a \in S^m_{1,0}(\mathcal{E} \times \mathcal{D}; \mathbf{R}^n \times \mathbf{R}^n)$ such that Eq. (16.2) holds in the sense Eq. (16.25).

Theorem 16.11 Let $a \in S^m_{1,0}(\mathcal{E} \times \mathcal{D}; \mathbf{R}^n \times \mathbf{R}^n)$ and $b \in S^{m'}_{1,0}(\mathcal{E} \times \mathcal{D}; \mathbf{R}^n \times \mathbf{R}^n)$.
Then $C = a(x, D)b(x, D)$ is a PDO with the symbol $c \in S^{m+m'}_{1,0}(\mathcal{E} \times \mathcal{D}; \mathbf{R}^n \times \mathbf{R}^n)$, which admits an asymptotic expansion Eq. (16.5) in the sense that for

any integer $N > 0$,

$$r_N = c - \sum_{0 \le |\alpha| \le N-1} (\alpha!)^{-1} a^{(\alpha)} b_{(\alpha)} \in \epsilon^N S_{1,0}^{m+m'-N}(\mathcal{E} \times \mathcal{D}; \mathbf{R}^n \times \mathbf{R}^n).$$

(16.26)

Definition 16.7 We write $a \in IS_{1,0}^m(\mathcal{E} \times \mathcal{D}; \mathbf{R}^n \times \mathbf{R}^n)$ if and only if $a \in S_{1,0}^m(\mathcal{E} \times \mathcal{D}; \mathbf{R}^n \times \mathbf{R}^n)$, and there exists $\epsilon_0 > 0$ such that if $\epsilon/d < \epsilon_0$ then $a(\epsilon, d; x, \xi)$ is invertible and admits a bound

$$|a(\epsilon, d, x, \xi)^{-1}| \le C(d^2 + |\xi|^2)^{-m/2},$$

where C is independent of (ϵ, d, x, ξ) with $\epsilon/d < \epsilon_0$.

We call $A = a(\epsilon, d; x, D)$ an elliptic operator with a parameter.

In the sequel, we omit arguments ϵ, d, and write $a(x, D)$.

Theorem 16.12 *Let $a \in IS_{1,0}^m(\mathcal{E} \times \mathcal{D}; \mathbf{R}^n \times \mathbf{R}^n)$, and $s, s - m > 0$ be positive non-integers.*
There exists $\epsilon_1 > 0$ such that if $\epsilon/d < \epsilon_1$, then $A = a(x, D) : C^s(\mathbf{R}^n) \to C^{s-m}(\mathbf{R}^n)$ is invertible, and its inverse B is a PDO, whose symbol $b \in S_{1,0}^{-m}((\mathcal{E} \times \mathcal{D})_{\epsilon_1}; \mathbf{R}^n \times \mathbf{R}^n)$ admits the asymptotic expansion Eq. (16.9) in the sense of Definition 16.6, where

$$b_{-m} = 1/a \in S_{1,0}^{-m}((\mathcal{E} \times \mathcal{D})_{\epsilon_1}; \mathbf{R}^n \times \mathbf{R}^n),$$

and

$$b_{-m-s} \in \epsilon^s S_{1,0}^{-m-s}((\mathcal{E} \times \mathcal{D})_{\epsilon_1}; \mathbf{R}^n \times \mathbf{R}^n), \quad s \ge 1,$$

are determined by Eq. (16.11).

Proof. Define $b_{-m} = 1/a$, $B^0 = b_{-m}(x, D)$. Since $a \in IS_{1,0}^m(\mathcal{E} \times \mathcal{D}; \mathbf{R}^n \times \mathbf{R}^n)$, there exists $\epsilon_0 > 0$ such that $b_{-m} \in S_{1,0}^{-m}((\mathcal{E} \times \mathcal{D})_{\epsilon_0}; \mathbf{R}^n \times \mathbf{R}^n)$, and by applying Theorem 16.11, we obtain

$$AB^0 = I + t_1(x, D), \quad B^0 A = I + t_2(x, D), \quad (16.27)$$

where $t_j \in \epsilon S_{1,0}^{-1}((\mathcal{E} \times \mathcal{D})_{\epsilon_0}; \mathbf{R}^n \times \mathbf{R}^n)$. Hence, $(d/\epsilon)t_j \in S_{1,0}^0(\mathbf{R}^n \times \mathbf{R}^n)$ uniformly in $(\epsilon, d) \in (\mathcal{E} \times \mathcal{D})_{\epsilon_0}$, and by the boundedness theorem, there exists C such that for all $(\epsilon, d) \in (\mathcal{E} \times \mathcal{D})_{\epsilon_0}$,

$$\|(d/\epsilon)t_1(x, D)\|_{C^{s-m} \to C^{s-m}} \le C, \quad (16.28)$$

and

$$\|(d/\epsilon)t_2(x, D)\|_{C^s \to C^s} \leq C. \tag{16.29}$$

When $\epsilon/d < \epsilon_1 := \min\{\epsilon_0, 1/C\}$, we conclude from Eq. (16.27)–Eq. (16.29) that AB^0 and B^0A are invertible in $C^{s-m}(\mathbf{R}^n)$ and $C^s(\mathbf{R}^n)$, respectively. By the boundedness theorem, $B^0 : C^{s-m}(\mathbf{R}^n) \to C^s(\mathbf{R}^n)$ is bounded, and hence, $B^0(1 + t_1(x, D))^{-1}$ and $(1 + t_2(x, D))^{-1}B^0$ are bounded right and left inverses to $A : C^s(\mathbf{R}^n) \to C^{s-m}(\mathbf{R}^n)$.

An analogue of Theorem 16.8 for operators with parameter(s) is valid: a parametrix B has the symbol $b \in S_{1,0}^{-m}((\mathcal{E} \times \mathcal{D})_{\epsilon_0}; \mathbf{R}^n \times \mathbf{R}^n)$, which can be constructed exactly as in Theorem 16.5, and A^{-1} is a PDO with the symbol of the class $S_{1,0}^{-m}((\mathcal{E} \times \mathcal{D})_{\epsilon_1}; \mathbf{R}^n \times \mathbf{R}^n)$.

They satisfy Eq. (16.8) with $t_j \in S^{-\infty}((\mathcal{E} \times \mathcal{D})_{\epsilon_0}; \mathbf{R}^n \times \mathbf{R}^n)$. By multiplying the left equality in Eq. (16.8) by A^{-1} from the right and using Theorem 16.11, we find $A^{-1} - B = t(x, D)$, where $t \in S^{-\infty}((\mathcal{E} \times \mathcal{D})_{\epsilon_1}; \mathbf{R}^n \times \mathbf{R}^n)$. This proves that the asymptotic expansion for the symbol of the parametrix is the asymptotic expansion for the symbol of the inverse. $\qquad\square$

Remark 16.4. Theorem 16.12 is valid for other spaces as well; for instance, in the scale of Sobolev spaces $H^s(\mathbf{R}^n)$, it is valid without the restrictions on s and m.

Theorem 16.13   *Let $\Re a \in IS_{1,0}^m(\mathcal{E} \times \mathcal{D}; \mathbf{R}^n \times \mathbf{R}^n)$ be positive, and $\Im a \in S_{1,0}^m(\mathcal{E} \times \mathcal{D}; \mathbf{R}^n \times \mathbf{R}^n)$.*
Then there exist $\epsilon_1 > 0$ and $\tilde{b} \in S_{1,0}^{m/2}((\mathcal{E} \times \mathcal{D})_{\epsilon_1}; \mathbf{R}^n \times \mathbf{R}^n)$ such that

$$\tilde{b}(x, D)^2 = a(x, D), \tag{16.30}$$

and $\tilde{b}$ admits the asymptotic expansion Eq. (16.18) in the sense of Definition 16.6, with the terms given by Eq. (16.19)–Eq. (16.20).

Proof.   Exactly the same argument as in the proof of Theorem 16.6 allows us to construct $b \in S_{1,0}^m((\mathcal{E} \times \mathcal{D})_{\epsilon_0}; \mathbf{R}^n \times \mathbf{R}^n)$, which satisfies Eq. (16.17) with $t \in S^{-\infty}((\mathcal{E} \times \mathcal{D})_{\epsilon_0}; \mathbf{R}^n \times \mathbf{R}^n)$; Eq. (16.18) is understood in the sense of Definition 16.6, and all the terms are given by Eq. (16.19)–Eq. (16.20). By using a straightforward modification of the results on fractional powers in Seeley (1967), Shubin (1978) and Grubb (1996), we obtain that if $\epsilon_0 > 0$ is sufficiently small and $(\epsilon, d) \in (\mathcal{E} \times \mathcal{D})_{\epsilon_0}$, then $B = a(x, D)^{1/2}$ is well-defined, its symbol $\tilde{b}$ belongs to $S_{1,0}^{m/2}((\mathcal{E} \times \mathcal{D})_{\epsilon_0}; \mathbf{R}^n \times \mathbf{R}^n)$, and $\tilde{b} - a^{1/2} \in$

$\epsilon S_{1,0}^{m/2-1}((\mathcal{E} \times \mathcal{D})_{\epsilon_0}; \mathbf{R}^n \times \mathbf{R}^n)$. It follows that

$$\tilde{b} = b + k, \tag{16.31}$$

where $k \in \epsilon S_{1,0}^{m/2-1}((\mathcal{E} \times \mathcal{D})_{\epsilon_0}; \mathbf{R}^n \times \mathbf{R}^n)$. Suppose, that for some $j \geq 1$,

$$k \in \epsilon^j S_{1,0}^{m/2-j}((\mathcal{E} \times \mathcal{D})_{\epsilon_0}; \mathbf{R}^n \times \mathbf{R}^n), \tag{16.32}$$

and show that then Eq. (16.32) holds with $j+1$ instead of j; this will finish the proof of the Theorem.

By calculating $\tilde{b}(x, D)^2$ with the help of Theorem 16.11 and taking Eq. (16.30)–Eq. (16.32) and Eq. (16.17) into account, we find that

$$T := b(x, D)k(x, D) + k(x, D)b(x, D)$$

is a PDO with the symbol $t \in \epsilon^{j+1} S_{1,0}^{m-j-1}((\mathcal{E} \times \mathcal{D})_{\epsilon_0}; \mathbf{R}^n \times \mathbf{R}^n)$.

Apply the parametrix of $b(x, D)$ to $T = t(x, D)$, and use Theorem 16.11; the result is that $2k \in \epsilon^{j+1} S_{1,0}^{m/2-j-1}((\mathcal{E} \times \mathcal{D})_{\epsilon_0}; \mathbf{R}^n \times \mathbf{R}^n)$, and the verification is complete. $\square$

16.3 Operators with symbols holomorphic in a tube domain

Let $U \subset \mathbf{R}^n$ be an open set such that its closure contains the origin: $\bar{U} \ni \{0\}$, and consider the classes $S^m(\mathbf{R}^n) \times (\mathbf{R}^n + i\bar{U})) = S_{1,0}^m(\mathbf{R}^n \times (\mathbf{R}^n + i\bar{U}))$ introduced in Definition 14.1. If we work with the same spaces as in Subsection 16.1, we can repeat all the statements there word by word by simply adding $+i\bar{U}$ in the notation of each class of symbols. This means that we make no use of the fact that symbols admit holomorphic continuation into the tube domain, and if we consider European options with bounded payoffs, e.g., European puts, we may do it and lose no essential information.

When the payoff is exponentially growing at infinity, as is the case with European calls, appropriate spaces are spaces with exponential weights, and one can consider the action of PDO in such spaces if and only if their symbols admit analytic continuation into an appropriate tube domain. For PDO of the class $S_{1,0}^m(\mathbf{R}^n \times (\mathbf{R}^n + i\bar{U}))$, the part of $\mathcal{S}(\mathbf{R}^n)$ is played by

$$\mathcal{S}(\mathbf{R}^n; \bar{U}) = \{u \mid e^{\langle x, y \rangle} u \in \mathcal{S}(\mathbf{R}^n), \ \forall \ y \in \bar{U}\},$$

with a natural system of seminorms, and the following theorem can be trivially deduced from Theorem 16.2 by using the equality

$$e^{\langle x,y\rangle}a(x,D)u = \left(e^{\langle x,y\rangle}a(x,D)e^{-\langle x,y\rangle}\right)e^{\langle x,y\rangle}u$$
$$= a(x,D+iy)e^{\langle x,y\rangle}u.$$

Theorem 16.14   *Let $a \in S^m_{1,0}(\mathbf{R}^n \times (\mathbf{R}^n + i\bar{U}))$. Then $a(x,D)$ is a continuous operator in $\mathcal{S}(\mathbf{R}^n;\bar{U})$.*

As in Subsection 16.1, we define by duality the action of $a(x,D)$ in $\mathcal{S}'(\mathbf{R}^n;\bar{U})$, the space of continuous linear functionals over $\mathcal{S}(\mathbf{R}^n;-\bar{U})$. The next step, namely, the action in Banach subspaces of $\mathcal{S}'(\mathbf{R}^n;\bar{U})$, is not very difficult but technically more involved.

To make the main idea clear, we restrict ourselves to the 1D-case, when $U = (\lambda_-,\lambda_+)$ is an interval, and $\lambda_- \leq -1 < 0 \leq \lambda_+$. The multi-dimensional case can be treated similarly.

Definition 16.8   *Let $\omega_- \leq \omega_+$ and $s > 0$ be non-integer. $C^s(\mathbf{R};[\omega_-,\omega_+])$ denotes the space of functions with the finite norm*

$$\|u\|_{C^s(\mathbf{R};[\omega_-,\omega_+])} = \|(e^{\omega_- x} + e^{\omega_+ x})u\|_{C^s(\mathbf{R})}. \tag{16.33}$$

Similarly, one defines Sobolev (and Besov) spaces with weight.

Theorem 16.15   *Let $a \in S^m_{1,0}(\mathbf{R} \times (\mathbf{R}+i[\lambda_-,\lambda_+]))$, $[\omega_-,\omega_+] \subset [\lambda_-,\lambda_+]$, and $s, s-m$ be positive non-integers.*
Then $a(x,D): C^s(\mathbf{R};[\omega_-,\omega_+]) \to C^{s-m}(\mathbf{R};[\omega_-,\omega_+])$ is bounded, and its norm admits an estimate

$$\|a(x,D)\| \leq C \sup_{|\alpha|+|\beta|\leq N} \sup_{(x,\xi)\in\mathbf{R}\times(\mathbf{R}+i[\omega_-,\omega_+])} \langle\xi\rangle^{|\alpha|-m}|a^{(\alpha)}_{(\beta)}(x,\xi)|, \tag{16.34}$$

where constants C and N depend on s,m and ω_-,ω_+ but not on $a \in S^m_{1,0}(\mathbf{R} \times (\mathbf{R}+i[\lambda_-,\lambda_+]))$.

Proof.   For any $u \in C^s(\mathbf{R};[\omega_-,\omega_+])$

$$\|a(x,D)u\|_{C^s(\mathbf{R};[\omega_-,\omega_+])} \leq \|e^{\omega_- x}a(x,D)u\|_{C^s(\mathbf{R})} + \|e^{\omega_+ x}a(x,D)u\|_{C^s(\mathbf{R})}$$
$$= \|(e^{\omega_- x}a(x,D)e^{-\omega_- x})e^{\omega_- x}u\|_{C^s(\mathbf{R})}$$
$$+\|(e^{\omega_+ x}a(x,D)e^{-\omega_+ x})e^{\omega_+ x}u\|_{C^s(\mathbf{R})}$$

By using the equality

$$e^{\omega_\pm x}a(x,D)e^{-\omega_\pm x} = a(x,D+i\omega_\pm),$$

and Theorem 16.7, we continue

$$
\begin{aligned}
&= \quad ||a(x, D + i\omega_-)e^{\omega - x}u||_{C^s(\mathbf{R})} + ||a(x, D + i\omega_+)e^{\omega + x}u||_{C^s(\mathbf{R})} \\
&\le \quad C\left(||e^{\omega - x}u||_{C^s(\mathbf{R})} + ||e^{\omega + x}u||_{C^s(\mathbf{R})}\right),
\end{aligned}
$$

where C can be chosen in the form of the RHS in Eq. (16.34). The sum in the brackets defines the norm equivalent to the norm Eq. (16.33), which finishes the proof of the Theorem. $\qquad\square$

We live to the reader as an exercise the proof for spaces defined by Eq. (16.33) with the weight $(e^{\omega - x} + e^{\omega + x})^{-1}$ instead of $e^{\omega - x} + e^{\omega + x}$.

16.4   Proofs of auxiliary technical results

Proof of Theorem 14.1. If $m \le 0$, then $a(x, D)$ is bounded in $L_2(\mathbf{R}^n)$, therefore for λ large enough, $\lambda + a(x, D)$ is invertible in $L_2(\mathbf{R}^n)$. By Corollary 16.1, it is invertible in $\mathcal{S}(\mathbf{R}^n)$.

Now let $m > 0$. Due to Eq. (14.5), for λ large enough, $b(\lambda; x, \xi) = (\lambda + a(x, \xi))^{-1}$ is well-defined on $\mathbf{R}^n \times \mathbf{R}^n$. By using the composition theorem, it is straightforward to show that

$$
b(\lambda; x, D)(\lambda + a(x, D)) = I + t(\lambda; x, D), \tag{16.35}
$$

where t satisfies: for any pair of multi-indices (α, β),

$$
\lim_{\lambda \to +\infty} \sup_{\mathbf{R}^n \times \mathbf{R}^n} |t^{(\alpha)}_{(\beta)}(\lambda; x, \xi)| \langle \xi \rangle^{|\alpha|} = 0. \tag{16.36}
$$

It follows from the boundedness theorem and Eq. (16.36) that if λ is sufficiently large, the RHS in Eq. (16.35) is an invertible operator in $L_2(\mathbf{R}^n)$. Hence, for these λ, $a(x, D) + \lambda : H^s(\mathbf{R}^n) \to L_2(\mathbf{R}^n)$ has a bounded left inverse $(I + t(\lambda; x, D))^{-1}b(\lambda; x, D)$. Similarly, it has a bounded right inverse, hence it is invertible. By Corollary 6.10, $a(x, D) + \lambda$ is invertible in $\mathcal{S}(\mathbf{R}^n)$. Theorem 14.1 has thus been proved.

Proof of Theorem 14.4. a) We have $a(x, \xi) := d^2 - L(x, \xi) \in S^2_{1,0}(\mathbf{R}^n \times (\mathbf{R}^n + i\bar{U}))$ for any U, and if U satisfies Eq. (14.14), we see that Eq. (16.16) holds for all $(x, \xi) \in \mathbf{R}^n \times (\mathbf{R}^n + i\bar{U})$. Hence, the analogues of Theorem 16.9 and Theorem 16.6 for PDO with symbols holomorphic in a tube domain are valid, which gives not only Eq. (14.15)–Eq. (14.17) but the other terms of the asymptotic expansion of the symbol as well (see Eq. (16.18)–Eq. (16.20)).

b)–d) are special cases of the analogues of Theorems 6.11 and 6.7 for PDO depending on a parameter.

Theorem 14.4 has thus been proved.

Proof of Lemma 14.1. By using Eq. (14.26) and repeating the proof of Theorem 16.8, it is possible to show that the symbol of $(\lambda + r + \psi(x, D))^{-1}$, call it $R(\lambda; x, \xi)$, satisfies estimates

$$|R^{(\alpha)}_{(\beta)}(\lambda; x, \xi)| \leq C_{\alpha\beta}(|\lambda| + |\xi| + 1)^{-1}\langle\xi\rangle^{-|\alpha|}, \qquad (16.37)$$

for all multi-indices α and β, therefore for any $t > 0$, the symbol $q_t(x, \xi)$ of the operator

$$\exp[-t(r + \psi(x, D)] = (2\pi i)^{-1} \int_{L_\theta} e^{\lambda t} R(\lambda; x, D) d\lambda,$$

decays as $\xi \to \infty$ faster than any power of $\langle\xi\rangle$, together with all derivatives. But the kernel $k_t(x, y)$ of a PDO $\exp[-t(r+\psi(x, D)]$ is expressed via symbol as follows:

$$k_t(x, y) = (2\pi)^{-n} \int_{-\infty}^{+\infty} e^{i(x-y)\xi} q_t(x, \xi) d\xi,$$

and by differentiating under the integral sign, we conclude that $k_t \in C^\infty(\mathbf{R}^n \times \mathbf{R}^n)$.

Calculation of the omitted terms of the asymptotic expansion Eq. (14.28)
We use Theorem 16.8 and Theorem 16.5, and Eq. (16.9)–Eq. (16.13) with $\lambda + r + a(x, \xi)$ instead of $a(x, \xi)$. For instance, the RHS of Eq. (14.28) with two terms (the only case which may have some relevance to practice) is

$$(\lambda + r + a(x, \xi))^{-1} + (\lambda + r + a(x, \xi))^{-3} \sum_{|\alpha|=1} a^{(\alpha)}(x, \xi) a_{(\alpha)}(x, \xi) + \cdots \quad (16.38)$$

By substituting Eq. (16.38) into Eq. (14.27) we can obtain the next terms in Eq. (14.29). In particular, the first omitted term is equal to

$$\frac{i}{4\pi^2} \int_{L_\theta} \int_{-\infty+i\sigma}^{+\infty+i\sigma} \frac{\exp[\lambda\tau + ix\xi] \sum_{|\alpha|=1} a^{(\alpha)}(x, \xi) a_{(\alpha)}(x, \xi)}{\xi(\xi + i)(\lambda + r + a(x, \xi))^3} d\xi d\lambda, \quad (16.39)$$

where $\sigma \in (0, \lambda_+)$. The integral converges absolutely, hence we can apply the Fubini theorem and change the order of integration. After that we can transform the contour $\mathcal{L}_\theta$ by pushing it to the left. There is only one pole of order three, and when it is crossed, by the residue theorem the term

$$-\frac{\tau^2}{4\pi}\int_{-\infty+i\sigma}^{+\infty+i\sigma} \frac{\exp[ix\xi - \tau(r + a(x,\xi))]\sum_{|\alpha|=1} a^{(\alpha)}(x,\xi)a_{(\alpha)}(x,\xi)}{\xi(\xi+i)}d\xi$$

(16.40)

appears. After that we can push the contour to infinity. Since the integrand in Eq. (16.39) admits a bound via

$$C(x,\xi)e^{\Re\lambda\tau}|\lambda|^{-1},$$

we obtain 0 in the limit. If the derivatives of the symbol admit estimates Eq. (14.30), the integrand in Eq. (16.40) admits an estimate via

$$C\epsilon\exp(-\tau|\xi|)|\xi|^{-2}.$$

Since for $\sigma \neq 0$ fixed,

$$\int_{-\infty+i\sigma}^{+\infty+i\sigma} \exp(-\tau|\xi|)|\xi|^{-2}d\xi \leq C_1,$$

where C_1 is independent of τ, we conclude that the expression in Eq. (16.40), which is the first omitted term in Eq. (14.29), is of order $\tau^2\epsilon$. Similarly, the next term comes from an expression Eq. (16.40) with $\sum_{|\alpha|=2}$, and hence is of order $\tau^2\epsilon^2/d$, as claimed at the end of Section 14.3. All the next terms can be calculated as well, but they are relatively small w.r.t. the first omitted term, and hence of no practical significance.

16.5 Change of variables and pricing of multi-asset contracts

Let $\kappa : \mathbf{R}^n \to \mathbf{R}^n$ be a diffeomorphism, which coincides with the identity operator outside some compact. It induces the map

$$\kappa^* : \mathcal{S}(\mathbf{R}^n) \ni u \mapsto u \circ \kappa \in \mathcal{S}(\mathbf{R}^n),$$

which is clearly an isomorphism. Let A be a PDO with the symbol $a \in S_{1,0}^m(\mathbf{R}^n \times \mathbf{R}^n)$, and define an operator

$$A_1 : \mathcal{S}(\mathbf{R}^n) \ni u \mapsto [A(u \circ \kappa)] \circ \kappa^{-1} \in \mathcal{S}(\mathbf{R}^n).$$

Then (see, e.g., Theorem 4.2 in Shubin (1978)) the following theorem is valid.

Theorem 16.16 A_1 *is a PDO with the symbol* $a_1 \in S_{1,0}^m(\mathbf{R}^n \times \mathbf{R}^n)$, *which admits an asymptotic expansion*

$$a_1(y,\eta)|_{y=\kappa(x)} \sim \sum_\alpha (\alpha!)^{-1} a^{(\alpha)}(x,{}^t\kappa'(x)\eta) \cdot D_z^\alpha e^{i\kappa_1(x,z)\eta}|_{z=x}, \qquad (16.41)$$

where $a^\alpha(x,\xi) = \partial_\xi^\alpha a(x,\xi)$, *and*

$$\kappa_1(x,z) = \kappa(z) - \kappa(x) - \kappa'(x)(z-x).$$

Notice that Theorem 16.16 is valid for the other classes of symbols, which we consider.

By using Theorem 16.16 and approximate calculations, similar to the ones made in the preceding section, we can obtain approximate formulas for the solution to the problem Eq. (9.25)-Eq. (9.26), and hence, approximations to prices of basket options and exchange options.

16.6   Pricing of barrier options under Lévy-like Feller processes

As we have seen in Chapter 8, the pricing formula is straightforward if an explicit formula for the resolvent $(\lambda + A)^{-1}$ is available, where A is the operator of the appropriate boundary value problem for the stationary Generalized Black-Scholes equation. In Chapter 8, we considered option pricing under RLPE, when the generator was a PDO with constant symbol, and so the explicit construction was possible.

At the end of Chapter 14, we have constructed an approximate resolvent for the Generalized Black-Scholes equation in the case of pricing of European options under NIG-like Feller processes and used it to obtain an approximate pricing formula. The first step of the construction of the approximate resolvent was the inversion of the symbol; the PDO with the symbol $(\lambda + a(x,\xi))^{-1}$ served as an initial approximation, and the corrections could be calculated by means of the calculus of PDO.

The same program, with inevitable complications, can be realized in order to construct an approximate resolvent $(\lambda + A)^{-1}$, where A is an operator of a boundary problem on $\mathbf{R}_+$, say, and acts as $u \mapsto p_+ a(x, D)u$, on functions u, which vanish on $\mathbf{R}_-$. We

i) first, construct the Wiener-Hopf factors of the symbol $\lambda + a(x, \xi)$ for each x (and $\lambda \in \Sigma_{\theta,C}$, for some $\theta \in (\pi/2, \pi)$ and $C \geq 0$):

$$\lambda + a(x, \xi) = a_-(\lambda; x, \xi)a_+(\lambda; x, \xi),$$

ii) then, assuming that a is a symbol from a good class (that is, its derivatives are small in an appropriate sense) and using the explicit formulas for the factors, obtained in Chapter 3, we show that the factors also belong to classes of symbols with sufficiently good properties, uniformly in $\lambda \in \Sigma_{\theta,C}$, for some $\theta \in (\pi/2, \pi)$ and $C \geq 0$;

iii) next, define the initial approximation to the resolvent by

$$R_\lambda^0 u = a_-(\lambda; x, D)\theta_+ a_+(\lambda; x, D)lu,$$

where lu is an extension on $\mathbf{R}$ of a function u defined on $\mathbf{R}_+$ (say, $u \in L_2(\mathbf{R}_+)$, and $l = e_+$), and by using the calculus of PDO and the theory of action of PDO in appropriate function spaces on a half-line (here the generalization of the theory of Chapter 15 for the case of PDO with variable symbols is needed), show that

$$R_\lambda^0(\lambda + A) = I - T_\lambda,$$

where T_λ is an operator with the small norm, uniformly in $\lambda \in \Sigma_{\theta,C}$, for some $\theta \in (\pi/2, \pi)$ and $C \geq 0$;

iv) finally, we can calculate the resolvent with any precision, by summing the following series:

$$(\lambda + A)^{-1} = (I + T_\lambda + T_\lambda^2 + \cdots)R_\lambda^0. \tag{16.42}$$

By using Eq. (16.42) and Theorem 15.18, we can find an approximate price for a barrier option under a Lévy-like Feller process.

Of course, the concrete realization of the program requires long calculations and additional constructions.

Bibliography

Abel, A.B. and Eberly, J.C. (1999) "The effects of irreversibility and uncertainty on capital accumulation", *Journal of Monetary Economics* **44**, 339–377.

Barles, G., Burdeau, J., Romano, M. and Samsoen, N. (1995) "Critical stock price near expiration", *Mathem. Finance* **5**, 77-95.

Barndorff-Nielsen, O.E. (1977) "Exponentially decreasing distributions for the logarithm of particle size", *Proc. Roy. Soc. London. Ser. A* **353**, 401–419.

Barndorff-Nielsen, O.E. (1998) "Processes of normal inverse Gaussian type", *Finance and Stochastics* **2**, 41-68.

Barndorff-Nielsen, O.E. and Jiang, W. (1998) "An initial analysis of some German stock price series", Working Paper Series, 15, Aarhus: CAF Univ. of Aarhus/Aarhus School of Business.

Barndorff-Nielsen, O.E. and Levendorskiĭ, S.Z. (2001) "Feller processes of Normal Inverse Gaussian type", *Quantitative Finance* **1**, 318-331.

Barndorff-Nielsen, O.E., Nicolato, E. and Shephard, N. (2001) "Some recent developments in stochastic volatility modelling", Working paper

Barndorff-Nielsen, O.E. and Prause, K. (2001) "Apparent scaling", *Finance and Stochastics* **5**, 103-113.

Barndorff-Nielsen, O.E. and Shephard, N. (2001a) "Modelling by Lévy processes for financial econometrics", in *Lévy processes: Theory and Applications*, O.E. Barndorff-Nielsen, T. Mikosch and S. Resnik (Eds.), Birkhäuser, 283-318.

Barndorff-Nielsen, O.E. and Shephard, N. (2001b) "Non-Gaussian Ornstein-Uhlenbeck-based models and some of their uses in financial economics (with discussion)", *J. Royal Stat. Soc.* **63**. 167-241.

Barndorff-Nielsen, O.E. and Shephard, N. (2001c) "Normal modified stable processes", Working paper

Barndorff-Nielsen O.E. and Shephard N. (2002) *Lévy based dynamics models for financial economics*, forthcoming.

Bernanke, B.S. (1983) "Irreversibility, uncertainty, and cyclical investment",

Quarterly Journal of Economics **98**, 85-106.

Bertoin, J. (1996) *Lévy processes*, Cambridge University Press, Cambridge.

Bielecki, T.R. and Rutkowski, M. (2001) *Credit risk: modelling, valuation and hedging*, Springer-Verlag, Berlin Heidelberg New York

Black, F. and Cox, J.C. (1976) "Valuing corporate securities: Some effects of bond indenture provisions", *Journal of Finance* **31**, 351-367.

Black, F. and Scholes, M. (1973) "The pricing of options and corporate liabilities", *J. of Political Economy* **81**, 637-659.

Blumenthal, R.M. and Getoor, R.K. (1968) *Markov processes and potential theory*, Academic Press, New York.

Borovkov, A.A. (1972) *Stochastic processes in queuing theory*, Nauka, Moscow, 1972 (Transl. Springer, New York, 1976).

Bouchaud, J.-P. and Potters, M. (2000) *Theory of financial risk*, Cambridge University Press, Cambridge.

Boutet de Monvel, L. (1971) "Boundary problems for pseudo-differential operators", *Acta Math.* **126**, 11-51.

Boyarchenko, S.I. (2001) " Capital accumulation under non-Gaussian processes and the Marshallian law", CARESS Working Paper #01-03, Univ. of Pennsylvania, Philadelphia.

Boyarchenko, S.I. and Levendorskiĭ, S.Z. (1998) "On rational pricing of derivative securities for a family of non-Gaussian processes", Preprint 98/7, Insititut für Mathematik, Universität Potsdam, Potsdam.

Boyarchenko, S.I. and Levendorskiĭ, S.Z. (1999a) "Generalizations of the Black-Scholes equation for truncated Lévy processes", unpublished manuscript

Boyarchenko, S.I. and Levendorskiĭ, S.Z. (1999b) "Option pricing for truncated Lévy processes", In Applications of Physics in Financial Analysis (Europhysics conference abstracts, Dublin, July 15-17 (1999)), P. Alstrom, K.B. Lauritsen (Eds.), European Physical Society, 1999, S5.

Boyarchenko, S.I. and Levendorskiĭ, S.Z. (2000) "Option pricing for truncated Lévy processes", *Intern. Journ. Theor. and Appl. Finance* **3:3**, 549-552.

Boyarchenko, S.I. and Levendorskiĭ, S.Z. (2001a) " Option pricing and hedging under regular Lévy Processes of exponential type", in *Trends in Mathematics. Mathematical Finance*, M. Kohlman and S.'Tang (Eds.), 121-130.

Boyarchenko, S.I. and Levendorskiĭ, S.Z. (2001b) " Pricing of perpetual Bermudan options", submitted to *Quantitative Finance*

Boyarchenko, S.I. and Levendorskiĭ, S.Z. (2002a) "Perpetual American options under Lévy processes", *SIAM Journ. of Control and Optimization*, forthcoming.

Boyarchenko, S.I., and Levendorskiĭ, S.Z. (2002b) "Barrier options and touch-and-out options under regular Lévy processes of exponential type", submitted to *Annals of Applied Probability*

Carr, P. (1998) "Randomization and the American put", *Review of Financial Studies* **11:3**, 597-626.

Carr, P. and Faguet, D. (1994) "Fast accurate valuation of American options",

Working paper, Cornell University.

Carr, P., Geman, H., Madan, D.B. and Yor, M. (2001) "The fine structure of asset returns: An empirical investigation", *Journ. of Business*, forthcoming

Carr, P. and Madan, D.B. (1998) "Option valuation using the fast Fourier transform", *Journal of Computational Finance* **2**, 61-73.

Clark, P.K. (1973) "A subordinated stochastic process model with fixed variance for speculative prices", *Econometrica* **41**, 135-156.

Cont, R. and da Fonséca, J. (2001) "Deformation of implied volatility surfaces: an empirical analysis", R.I. No 466. Centre de Mathematiques Appliques, Ecole Polytechnique, Paris.

Courrége, Ph. (1966a) "Sur la forme intégro-différentielle des opérateurs de C_k^∞ da **C** satisfaisant au principe du maximum", *Sém. Théorie du Potentiel*, 1965/66. Exposé **2**

Courrége, Ph. (1966b) "Sur la forme intégro-différentielle du générateur infinitésimal d'un semi-group de Feller sur une variété", *Sém. Théorie du Potentiel*, 1965/66. Exposé **3**

Darling, D.A., Liggett, T. and Taylor, H.M. (1972) "Optimal stopping for partial sums", *Annals of Mathem. Statistics* **43**, 1363-1368.

Deaton, A. and Laroque, G. (1992): "On the Behavior of Commodity Prices," *Review of Economic Studies*, 59:1, 1–23.

Delbaen, F. and Schachermayer, W. (1994) "A general version of the fundamental theorem of asset pricing", *Math. Ann.* **300**, 463-520.

Delbaen, F. and Schachermayer, W. (1996) "The variance optimal martingale measure for continuous processes", *Bernoulli* **9**, 81-105.

Dixit, A.K. and Pindyck, R.S. (1994) *Investment under uncertainty*, 2d ed., Princeton University Press, Princeton, New Jersey.

Duffie, D. (1996) *Dynamic asset pricing theory.* 2d ed., Princeton University Press, Princeton, New Jersey.

Duffie, D., Pan, J. and Singleton, K. (2000) "Transform analysis and asset pricing for affine jump-diffusions", *Econometrica* **68**, 1343-1376.

Eberlein, E. (2001a) "Application of generalized hyperbolic Lévy motions to Finance", in *Lévy processes: Theory and Applications*, O.E. Barndorff-Nielsen, T. Mikosch and S. Resnik (Eds.), Birkhäuser, 319-337.

Eberlein, E. (2001b) "Recent advances in more realistic risk management: the hyperbolic model", in *Mastering Risk Volume 2: Applications*, Carol Alexander (Ed.), Prentice Hall-Financial Times, 56-72.

Eberlein, E., Breckling, J. and Kokic, P. (2000a) "A new framework for the evaluation of market and credit risk", in *Data mining and Computational Finance*, G. Bol, G. Nakhaezadeh, K.-H. Vollmer (Eds.), Physica-Verlag, Wirtschaftswissenschaftliche Beitrage Bd. **174**, 51-67.

Eberlein, E., Breckling, J. and Kokic, P. (2000b) "A tailored suit for risk management: the hyperbolic model", in *Measuring risk in complex stochastic systems*, J. Franke, W. Härdle and G. Stahl (Eds.), Lecture Notes in Statistics **157**, 189-202.

Eberlein, E. and Jacod, J. (1997) "On the range of options prices", *Finance and Stochastics* **1**, 131-140.

Eberlein, E., Kallsen, J. and Kirsten, J. (2001) "Risk management based on stochastic volatility", FDM Preprint 72, University of Freiburg.

Eberlein, E. and Keller, U. (1995) "Hyperbolic distributions in Finance", *Bernoulli* **1**, 281-299.

Eberlein, E., Keller, U. and Prause, K. (1998) "New insights into smile, mispricing and value at risk: The hyperbolic model", *Journ. of Business* **71**, 371-406.

Eberlein, E. and Özkan, F. (2001) "The defaultible Lévy term structure: ratings and restructuring", FDM Preprint 72, University of Freiburg.

Eberlein, E. and Prause, K. (2001) "The generalized hyperbolic model: financial derivatives and risk measures", in *Mathematical Finance- Bachelier Congress 2000*, H. Geman, D. Madan, S. Pliska, T. Vorst (Eds.), Springer-Verlag

Eberlein, E. and Raible, S. (1999) "Term structure models driven by general Lévy processes", *Math. Finance* **9**, 31-53.

Eberlein, E. and Raible, S. (2001) "Some analytic facts on the generalized hyperbolic model", in *Proceedings of the 3rd European Meetings of Mathematicians*, Birkhäuser

Elliot, D.F. and Rao, K.R. (1982) *Fast transforms: Algorithms, analyses, applications*, Academic Press, New York

Eskin, G.I. (1973) *Boundary problems for elliptic pseudo-differential equations*, Nauka, Moscow (Transl. of Mathematical Monographs, 52, Providence, Rhode Island: Amer. Math. Soc., 1980).

Ethier, St. N. and Kurtz, Th. G. (1986) *Markov processes*, Wiley Series in Probability and Mathematical Statistics, John Wiley & Sons, New York

Fama, E.F. (1965) "The behavior of stock market prices", *Journ. of Business* **38**, 34-105.

Fedoryuk, M.V. (1988) *The saddle point method*, Nauka, Moscow (In Russian)

Föllmer, H. and Leukert, P. (1999) "Quantile hedging", *Finance and Stochastics* **3**, 251-273.

Föllmer, H. and Schweizer, M. (1991) "Hedging of contingent claims under incomplete information", in *Applied Stochastic Analysis*, M.H.A. Davies and R.J .Elliott (Eds.), New York, Gordon and Bleach, 389-414.

Föllmer, H. and Sondermann, D. (1986) "Hedging of non-redundant contingent claims", in *Contributions to Mathematical Economics*, A. Mas-Collel, W. Hildebrand (Eds.), North-Holland, Amsterdam, 205-223.

Fons, J.S. (1994) "Using default rates to model the term structure of credit risk", *Financial Analysts Journal*, September/October, 25-32.

Geman, H. and Yor, M. (1996) "Pricing and hedging double-barrier options: A probabilistic approach", *Mathem. Finance* **6:4**, 365-378.

Gerber, H. and Shiu, E. (1994) "Option pricing by Esscher transforms (with discussion)", *Trans. Soc. Actuaries* **46**, 99-191.

Geske, R. and Johnson, H.E. (1984) "The American put option valued analytically", *Journ. of Finance* **39** 1511-1524.

Goll, T. and Kallsen, J. (2000) "Optimal portfolios for logarithmic utility", *Stochastic Processes and their Applications* **89**, 31-48.

Goll, Th. and Rüschendorf, L. (2001) "Minimax and minimal distance martingale measures and their relationship to portfolio optimization", *Finance and Stochastics* **5:4**, 557-581.

Gouriéroux, C., Laurent, J.P. and Pham, P. "Mean-variance hedging and numéraire", *Mathem. Finance*

Grubb, G. (1996) *Functional calculus of pseudo-differential boundary problems*, Birkhäuser, Boston Basel Berlin

Heston, S.L. (1993) "A closed-form solution for options with stochastic volatility, with applications to bond and currency options", *Rev. Finan. Stud.* **6**, 327-343.

Hörmander, L. (1985) *The analysis of linear partial differential operators III*, Springer-Verlag, Berlin

Hubbard, R.G. (1994) "Investment under uncertainty: keeping one's options open", *Journal of Economic Literature* **32**, 1816–1831.

Hull, J.C. (2000) *Options, futures & other derivatives.* 4th ed., Prentice Hall, New Jersey.

Hyakawa, K. and Kumano-go, H. (1971) "Complex powers of a system of pseudo-differential operators", *Proc. Japan Acad.* **47**, 359-364.

Ingersoll, J.E., Jr. (2000) "Digital contracts: Simple tools for pricing complex derivatives", *Journal of Business* **73:1**, 67-88.

Jacob, N. (1996) *Pseudo-differential operators and Markov processes*, Academie Verlag, Berlin

Jones, E.P., Mason, S.P. and Rosenfeld, E. (1984) "Contingent claims analysis of corporate capital structures: An empirical investigation", *Journal of Finance* **39**, 611–627.

Kallsen, J. (1998) "Semimartingale modelling in Finance. Dissertation", Mathematische Fakultät, Universität Freiburg im Breisgau.

Kallsen, J. (2000) "Optimal portfolios for exponential Lévy processes", *Mathematical Methods of Operations Research* **51:3**, 357-374.

Karatzas, I. and Shreve, S.E. (1998) *Methods of mathematical Finance*, Springer-Verlag, Berlin Heidelberg New York.

Keller, U. (1997) "Realistic modelling of financial derivatives. Dissertation", Mathematische Fakultät, Universität Freiburg im Breisgau.

Koponen, I. (1995) "Analytic approach to the problem of convergence of truncated Lévy flights towards the Gaussian stochastic process", *Physics Review E* **52**, 1197–1199.

Kramkov, D. and Schachermayer, W. (1999) "The asymptotic elasticity of utility functions and optimal investment in incomplete markets", *Ann. Appl. Probab.* **9**, 904-950.

Kwok, Y.-K. (1998) *Mathematical models of financial derivatives*, Springer-

Verlag, Berlin Heidelberg New York.

Lamberton, D. (1995) "Critical price for an American option near maturity", in *Seminar on Stochastic Analysis, Random Fields and Applications*, E. Bolthausen, M. Dozzi, F. Russo (Eds.), Birkhaüser, Boston Basel Berlin, 353-358.

Lander, D.M. and Pinches, G.E. (1998) "Challenges to the practical implementation of modelling and valuing real options", *The Quarterly Review of Economics and Finance* **38, Special Issue**, 537–567.

Leland, H.E. (1994a) "Corporate debt value, bond covenants, and optimal capital structure", *Journal of Finance* **49**, 1213–1252.

Leland, H.E. (1994b) "Bond prices, yield spreads, and optimal capital structure with default risk", Working paper 240, IBER, University of California, Berkeley (1994b).

Leland, H.E. and Toft, K.B. (1996) "Optimal capital structure, endogenous bankruptcy, and the term structure of credit spreads", *Journal of Finance* **51**, 987–1019.

Levendorskiĭ, S.Z. (1993) *Degenerate elliptic equations*, Kluwer Academic Publishers, Dordrecht

Levendorskiĭ, S.Z. and Paneah, B. (1994) "Degenerate elliptic equations and boundary problems", in *Encyclopaedia of Mathematical Sciences* **v.63**, Yu.V. Egorov and M.A. Shubin (Eds.), Springer-Verlag, Berlin Heidelberg New York, p.131-202.

Levendorskiĭ, S.Z. and Zherder, V.M. (2001) "Fast option pricing under regular Lévy processes of exponential type", submitted to *Journal of Computational Finance*.

Longstaff, F.A. and Schwartz, E.S. (1995) "A simple approach to valuing risky and floating rate debt", *Journal of Finance* **50**, 789–819.

Madan, D.B., Carr, P. and Chang, E.C. (1998) "The variance Gamma process and option pricing", *European Finance Review* **2**, 79–105.

Madan, D.B. and Milne, F. (1991) "Option pricing with VG martingale components", *Mathem. Finance* **1**, 39–55.

Madan, D.B. and Seneta, E. (1990) "The VG model for share market returns", *Journ. of Business* **63**, 511-524.

Mandelbrot, B.B. (1963) "The variation of certain speculative prices", *Journ. of Business* **36**, 394-419.

Mandelbrot, B.B. (1997) *Fractals and scaling in Finance: Discontinuity, concentration, risk*, Springer-Verlag, New York.

Mantegna, R.N. and Stanley, H.E. (1994) "Stochastic process with ultraslow convergence to a gaussian: the truncated Lévy flight", *Phys. Rev. Lett.* **73**, 2946–2949.

Mantegna, R.N. and Stanley, H.E. (1997) "Physics investigation of financial markets", *Proceedings of the International School of Physics "Enrico Fermi"*, Course CXXXIV, F. Mallamace and H.E. Stanley (Eds.), IOS Press, Amsterdam, 473–489.

Mantegna, R.N. and Stanley, H.E. (2000) *An introduction to Econophysics. Correlation and complexity in Finance,* Cambridge University Press, Cambridge.

Matacz, A. (2000) "Financial modelling and option theory with the truncated Lévy process", *Intern. Journ. Theor. and Appl. Finance* **3**:1, 143-160.

McKean, H-P. (1965) "A free boundary problem for the heat equation arising from a problem of mathematical economics", *Industrial Management Review* **6**, 32-39.

Merton, R.C. (1973) "Theory of rational option pricing", *Bell Journal of Economics and Management Science #* **4 (Spring)**, 141.

Merton, R.C. (1990) *Continuous time Finance,* Blackwell, Cambridge, MA/Oxford.

Mordecki, E. (2000), "Optimal stopping and perpetual options for Lévy processes", Prepublicaciones de Matemática de la Universidad de la Republica, 2000/35, (2000).

Mordecki, E. (1998) "Optimal stopping for a compound Poisson process with exponential jumps", *Publicaciones Matemáticas del Uruguay* **7**, 55–66.

Mordecki, E. (1999) "Optimal stopping for a diffusion with jumps", *Finance and Stochastics* **3**, 227-236.

Mordecki, E. (2000) "Optimal stopping and perpetual options for Lévy processes", Talk presented at the 1 World Congress of the Bachelier Finance Society, June 2000.

Musiela, M. and Rutkowski, M. (1997) *Martingale methods in financial modelling,* Springer-Verlag, Berlin Heidelberg New York.

Novikov, E.A. (1994) "Infinitely divisible distributions in turbulence", *Physics Review E* **50**, R3303-3305.

Pelsser, A. (2000) "Pricing double barrier options using Laplace transform", *Finance Stochastics* **4:1**, 95-104.

Pham, H. Rheinländer, T. and Schweizer, M. (1998) "Mean-variance hedging for continuous processes: New Proofs and Examples", *Finance and Stochastics* **2**, 173–198.

Prabhu, N.U. (1980) *Stochastic storage processes. Queues, insurance risks and dams,* Springer, New York.

Prause, K. (1998) "The generalized hyperbolic models: estimation, financial derivatives and risk measurement", PhD thesis. Mathematics Faculty, Freiburg

Raible, R. (2000) "Lévy processes in Finance: Theory, Numerics, and Empirical Facts. Dissertation", Mathematische Fakultät, Universität Freiburg im Breisgau.

Revuz, D. (1970) "Mesures associees aux fonctionnelles additives de Markov. I", *Trans. of AMS* **148**, 501-531.

Rogers, L.C.G. and Williams, D. (1994) *Diffusions, Markov processes, and martingales. V.1,* 2d ed., Wiley, New York [1st ed. by D. Williams, 1979].

Rubinstein, M. and Reiner, M. (1991) "Breaking down the barriers", *Risk* **4**, 28-35.

Sarig, O. and A. Warga, A. (1989) "Some empirical estimates of the risk structure of interest rates", *Journal of Finance* **44**, 1351–1360.

Sato, K. (1999) *Lévy processes and infinitely divisible distributions*, Cambridge University Press, Cambridge.

Schweizer, M. (1996) "Approximation pricing and the variance-optimal martingale measure", *Ann. Probab.* 24:1, 206-236.

Schweizer, M. (1999) "A minimality property of the minimal martingale measure", *Stat. Probab. Lett.* **42**, 27-31.

Seeley, R. (1967) "Complex powers of an elliptic operator", *Amer.Math.Soc. Proc. Symp. Pure Math.* **10** 288-307.

Sharpe, M.J. (1989) *General theory of Markov processes*, Academic Press, New York.

Shiryaev, A.N. (1999) *Essentials of stochastic Finance. Facts, models, theory*, World Scientific, Singapore New Jersey London Hong Kong.

Shubin, M.A. (1978) *Spectral theory and pseudo-differential operators*, Nauka, Moskow (Transl. 1980)

Spitzer, F. (1964) *Principles of random walk*, Van Nostrand, Princeton.

Taylor, M. (1981) *Pseudo-differential operators*, Princeton University Press, Princeton NJ

Triebel, H. (1978) *Interpolation theory, function spaces, differential operators.* VEB Deutscher Verlag der Wissenschaften, Berlin.

Wiener, N. and Hopf, E. (1931) "Über eine classe singulärer Integralgleichungen", *Sitzber. Deutsch. Akad. Wiss. Berlin, Kl. Math. Phys. Tech.*, 696-706.

Wilmott P., Dewynne J.N. and Howison S. (1993) *Option pricing: Mathematical models and computation*, Oxford Financial Press, Oxford.

Wilmott, P., Howison, S. and Dewynne, J. (1995) *The mathematics of financial derivatives. A student introduction*, Cambridge University Press, Cambridge.

Yamazaki, M. (1986) "A quasi-homogeneous version of paradifferential operators, I. Boundedness on spaces of Besov type", *J.Fac.Sci.Univ. Tokyo Sect. IA Math.* **33**, 131–174.

Yang, S.R. and Brorsen, B.W. (1992): "Nonlinear Dynamics of Daily Cash Prices," *American Journal of Agricultural Economics*, 74:3, 706–715.

Yosida, K. (1964) *Functional analysis*, Springer-Verlag, Berlin, Heidelberg, New-York

Zhou, C. (1997) "A jump-diffusion approach to modelling credit risk and valuing defaultable securities", Board of Governors of the Federal Reserve System, Finance and Economics Discussion Papers Series: 1997/27.

Zhu, J. (2000) *Modular pricing of options* (Lecture Notes in Economics and Mathematical Systems. Vol. 493), Springer-Verlag, Berlin Heidelberg New York.

Index

OECD REVIEWS
OF FOREIGN
DIRECT INVESTMENT

ORGANISATION FOR ECONOMIC CO-OPERATION AND DEVELOPMENT

ORGANISATION FOR ECONOMIC CO-OPERATION
AND DEVELOPMENT

Pursuant to Article 1 of the Convention signed in Paris on 14th December 1960, and which came into force on 30th September 1961, the Organisation for Economic Co-operation and Development (OECD) shall promote policies designed:

— to achieve the highest sustainable economic growth and employment and a rising standard of living in Member countries, while maintaining financial stability, and thus to contribute to the development of the world economy;

— to contribute to sound economic expansion in Member as well as non-member countries in the process of economic development; and

— to contribute to the expansion of world trade on a multilateral, non-discriminatory basis in accordance with international obligations.

The original Member countries of the OECD are Austria, Belgium, Canada, Denmark, France, Germany, Greece, Iceland, Ireland, Italy, Luxembourg, the Netherlands, Norway, Portugal, Spain, Sweden, Switzerland, Turkey, the United Kingdom and the United States. The following countries became Members subsequently through accession at the dates indicated hereafter: Japan (28th April 1964), Finland (28th January 1969), Australia (7th June 1971), New Zealand (29th May 1973) and Mexico (18th May 1994). The Commission of the European Communities takes part in the work of the OECD (Article 13 of the OECD Convention).

Publié en français sous le titre :
EXAMENS DE L'OCDE SUR L'INVESTISSEMENT DIRECT ÉTRANGER
DANEMARK